THE LETTERS

OF

STEPHEN GARDINER

THE LETTERS

OF

STEPHEN GARDINER

Edited by

JAMES ARTHUR MULLER, PH.D.

PROFESSOR OF MODERN CHURCH HISTORY
EPISCOPAL THEOLOGICAL SCHOOL
CAMBRIDGE, MASSACHUSETTS

GREENWOOD PRESS, PUBLISHERS
WESTPORT, CONNECTICUT

Originally published in 1933
by The University Press, Cambridge, England

First Greenwood Reprinting 1970

Library of Congress Catalogue Card Number 68-19272

SBN 8371-4223-7

Printed in the United States of America

To my Wife

CONTENTS

Note. Letters here marked * have not hitherto been printed in full; those marked †
have not hitherto been printed from the manuscript version here used; those
marked ‡ have not been reprinted since the sixteenth century; those marked § are
not calendared in the *Letters and Papers of the Reign of Henry VIII*. The last sign
is not used with letters written subsequently to that reign. The same signs are used
in the text with other meanings—*see* p. xxxvii.

xi

PREFACE

I AM peculiarly indebted to my friends and former colleagues, Dr L. R. Shero, Professor of Greek in Swarthmore College, Pennsylvania, and Dr Irville F. Davidson, Professor of Latin in St Stephen's College, Columbia University, for assistance in the translation and editing of some of the letters. Nos. 63 and 72, on the pronunciation of Greek, have been translated and edited by Dr Shero, who has also read and corrected the proof of portions of No. 125. The translation of this last is mainly the work of Dr Davidson, who has also assisted me in the translation of five of the shorter letters. Both have helped me identify classical allusions and have given me valuable suggestions as to the editing of the Latin texts.

The transcript of two Italian letters, No. 162 and No. 4 in the Appendix, the manuscript copy of which is in a remarkably difficult hand, was made by Miss Helen M. Briggs of the University of London, whose translation of them I have used as a basis of my own, and who kindly corrected the letters in proof with the manuscript.

I am debtor to librarians and their assistants in many repositories, and especially to the staffs of the British Museum and the Public Record Office for their unfailing helpfulness and efficiency.

Particular courtesies have been shown me or information and expert opinion on special matters given me by the Rev. C. H. Smyth of Corpus Christi College, Cambridge, the Rev. Canon Claude Jenkins of Lambeth, Mr G. C. Crump, formerly of the Public Record Office, Mr A. E. Stamp and Mr A. C. Wood of the same institution, Mr R. Flower of the British Museum, Mr H. I. Pink of the University Library, Cambridge, M. H. Omont of the Bibliothèque Nationale, Mr W. B. Briggs of the Harvard Library, Mr F. J. Snell of the Inner Temple, Mr E. Galen Thompson, Librarian to the Earl of Ellesmere, the Hon. Philip P. Cary, York Herald, of the College of Arms, Mr J. R. H. Weaver of Trinity College, Oxford, Dr W. H. S. Jones of St Catharine's College, Cambridge, Professors W. C. Greene, C. H. Grandgent, and E. A. Whitney of Harvard, and my colleague, the Rev. Professor W. H. P. Hatch of the Episcopal Theological School.

I have received no little help in the solution of knotty problems from the members of the Thursday evening seminar at the Institute of Historical Research, London, especially Miss E. Jeffries Davis, Mr C. H. Williams, and Professor A. F. Pollard. M. Pierre Janelle of Clermont-Ferrand has graciously answered questions on phases of Gardiner's literary activity of which he is making a special study.

Miss Doris Leach has capably assisted me in the transcription of several of the letters and in discovering sources of information on some of the less known persons named in them.

A grant from the Milton Fund by the Corporation of Harvard University enabled me to spend portions of two summers in England collecting material for this volume and to pay for a considerable amount of secretarial aid. A subsequent sabbatical leave of absence with salary, granted by the Trustees of the Episcopal Theological School, made it possible for me to complete the work.

It has been a joy to have such considerate and careful publishers as the Cambridge University Press, and my thanks are due to all by whom the work of the Press is conducted, and especially to Mr S. C. Roberts, Secretary, and Mr C. E. Carrington, Educational Secretary.

Recalling how courteously I was assisted by the attendants at the Bishop of London's Registry when looking up material there, it is with reluctance that I add a word of protest against the practice of that Registry of demanding a fee for every consultation of a register, no matter what the purpose for which the consultation is made. If the presence of scholars or the production of registers for them taxes the capacity of the Registry and the time of the Registrar, it would seem that at least the older documents might be deposited in some library, such as Lambeth or the British Museum, where accredited students could have access to them. It is much to be regretted that the invaluable historical material in English episcopal registers is not in all places as freely accessible as are the Canterbury registers at Lambeth.

J. A. M.

March 1933

INTRODUCTION

As secretary to Cardinal Wolsey, counsellor of Henry VIII, chief minister of that monarch for the last six years of his reign, and Lord Chancellor under Queen Mary, Gardiner had a hand in practically every diplomatic and political manœuvre of his time, and was the friend—or enemy—of every person of prominence. All this is reflected in his letters. He was likewise bishop of one of the most important of English dioceses and leader of conservative churchmen. His letters form a running comment from the conservative or Catholic point of view on the Henrician and Edwardine reformations. They also express the opinion of one who was admitted on all hands to be the ablest English jurist of his day, on such constitutional matters as the relation of the royal supremacy and of the royal power in general to parliamentary enactment and the Common Law; they illustrate the activities and ideas of a University Chancellor who was at once humanist, legist, and theologian; they abound in vivid comment on notable contemporaries, and in illuminating allusions to customs of the day; and they reveal a many-sided personality which attacked life vigorously, alertly, and not without humour.

Moreover, since many of them were written informally and rapidly, and sent without revision, they afford admirable examples of colloquial English as used by a man of culture in the second quarter of the sixteenth century.

The letters fall naturally into groups, *e.g.*, those written while secretary to the Cardinal, or on a particular embassy, or while prisoner in the Fleet. In this edition each group is preceded by an introductory note in explanation of the circumstances in which the letters were written and of the chief matters referred to, with some indication of the letters in the group which are of most interest and importance.

A summary sketch of Gardiner's life is given at p. xxv. Authorities for statements made therein and for many statements concerning his activities, made throughout this collection, as well as fuller references to authorities on most phases of his career, may be found in my *Stephen Gardiner and the Tudor Reaction*, London and New York, 1926.

WHAT IS INCLUDED IN THIS EDITION

This edition includes all the letters written by Gardiner in his own name, known to me, except four letters to John Cheke on the pronunciation of Greek. These four, one of which is virtually a treatise, and Cheke's replies, of even greater length, were published in Cheke's *De Pronuntiatione Graecae*, 1555, and reprinted in Havercamp, *Sylloge Altera*, 1740. They are usually regarded as among Gardiner's published works and would be more fittingly reprinted in an edition of them.

Letters written by Gardiner in his name and that of one or more of his colleagues on diplomatic missions, or on committees of the Privy Council, diplomatic and administrative memoranda in his hand, and letters drafted by him for the Council or the King are not here printed. Their inclusion would more than double the bulk of the collection, and, although they are of Gardiner's composition, they obviously do not afford as intimate an expression of his views as letters written solely in his own name. Moreover, some of them have been printed, with more or less accuracy, in Pocock's *Records of the Reformation*, and many, with entire accuracy, in the *State Papers of the Reign of Henry VIII*.

Considerations of space have also contributed to the exclusion of letters to Gardiner; but when such letters are direct answers to letters from him, or are directly answered by letters from him, reference is made to their location and, where it seemed to be in point, their content is briefly indicated.

Translations of Latin and Italian letters are added, except

in those cases in which translations or English abstracts are printed elsewhere.

Of the one hundred and seventy-three letters here printed, eight are prefatory letters from Gardiner's published works, seven of which have not been reprinted since the sixteenth century. Of the rest, seventy-five have been elsewhere printed in full, with varying degrees of accuracy, and scattered through more than a score of volumes. Ninety have not been hitherto printed in full. Of the five items in the Appendix, one is from a rare sixteenth-century book; four have not been previously printed.

Of the letters written before the death of Henry VIII, all but ten have been calendared in the *Letters and Papers of the Reign of Henry VIII*, the summaries there given varying considerably in fullness and adequacy; of those written during the reigns of Edward VI and Mary, only seven are listed in Lemon's *Calendar of State Papers*, and these with the briefest possible indication of their content. None of the items in the Appendix are mentioned in either of these calendars.

SOURCES

The originals of one hundred and twelve of the letters are extant, as are Gardiner's drafts of large parts of two and of the whole of a third, as well as contemporary copies of two made under his direction and endorsed by him. All the originals, except five in the Parker collection at Corpus Christi College, Cambridge, and one in the Stadt Bibliotek, Breslau, are preserved in the Public Record Office and the British Museum. For the rest, manuscript copies in various collections, chiefly in London, Paris, and Cambridge, or early-printed books have, of necessity, been relied upon. Beside the eight published prefatory letters, early-printed books supply seventeen letters and part of an eighteenth. One is taken from Noailles, *Ambassades*, two from Stow, *Annales*, and fourteen and part of another from

Foxe, *Actes and Monuments*. A manuscript copy, or perhaps Gardiner's draft, of one of those in Stow, was, and presumably still is, among the Egerton Papers, but I have been unable to find it at Bridgewater House.

Since the source from which each letter is printed is indicated immediately after its heading, there is no need for more detailed reference to these sources here. Two of them, however, call for special remark.

B.M., Add. MS. 28,571 supplies manuscript copies of seven hitherto unpublished letters, as well as parts of three printed in Foxe. The history of the volume is obscure. It contains the book plate of John Fuller Russell and was purchased by the British Museum in 1871 from the Rev. J. C. Jackson who, on 23 November, 1870, wrote to the Museum saying that it had been left in his hands by a wealthy gentleman who did not care to possess it, and describing it as a collection of original autographs said to have belonged to Bishop Burnet. There are indeed some autograph letters in the volume, but the letters on ff. 3–21 are clearly copies, of the sixteenth century. They are in two hands, ff. 3–12, 15–20 being in one; ff. 13–14, 21 in another. Nos. 126–7, 140–3, and App. 3, in this edition, two letters to Gardiner mentioned on pp. 285, 431, below, and a note from the royal visitors of 1547 to Gardiner's chancellor are in the first hand, parts of Nos. 120, 133, 135 in the second. The leaves of the manuscript have been bound into the volume of which they now form a part out of their proper sequence, so that, for example, No. 126 begins on f. 16 v., goes through f. 20 v., and ends on f. 6 r. Moreover, the opening leaf of the letter which finishes on ff. 13–4, (No. 135) has found its way into the Bibliothèque Nationale, in Paris, as f. 48 of MS. Latin 6051.

B.N., MS. Latin 6051 is a folio volume of 51 leaves, containing (ff. 30–46 r.) a copy, probably of the sixteenth century, of the longest letter in our collection, No. 125, as well as the two opening pages of No. 130 (ff. 46 v.–47 r.) and those of No. 135, already mentioned (f. 48 r. and v.). Ff. 30–46 r. are in one hand, ff. 46 v.–48 in another, which is the same as that of ff. 13–14, 21 of Add. MS. 28,571. This would seem to indicate that Gardiner's letters in these two manuscripts were originally in one collection. M. H. Omont of the Bibliothèque Nationale tells me that nothing is known of the history of MS. Latin 6051, except that it was acquired by the library in 1732, with Colbert's collection of manuscripts; and he hazards the suggestion that, since it appears to have been at one time completely wet, it may have been rescued from a shipwreck. The tracing of the relation of this to B.M., Add. MS. 28,571 would make a pleasant problem for one interested in the wanderings of manuscripts.

I have searched for reference to Gardiner letters through all the publications of the Historical Manuscripts Commission, all the printed calendars of the period, all the catalogues of manuscript collections of French and English libraries to be found in the British Museum, as well as the catalogues, both printed and in manuscript, of the collections at the British Museum, the libraries at Oxford and Cambridge, and the Vatican. I have also consulted the leading London booksellers who deal in manuscripts for possible record or knowledge of the sale of Gardiner letters. There is record of the sale of some Privy Council letters bearing his signature, but none of letters from him as an individual. M. Janelle tells me that he has hunted in vain for Gardiner material at Strasbourg.

TREATMENT AND ARRANGEMENT OF TEXT

With the exception of two brief notes (Nos. 168, 173), all letters taken from manuscripts in England have been corrected in proof with the manuscripts; all from manuscripts on the Continent have been corrected in proof with photostatic reproductions of the manuscripts; all from early-printed books have been corrected in proof with the printed texts.

In preparing the text for publication and in its arrangement,

I have endeavoured to follow the recommendations of the Committee of the Conference of Anglo-American Historians, embodied in their reports on the editing of historical documents, printed in the *Bulletin of the Institute of Historical Research*, London, June, 1923, and June, 1925.

The original spelling is reproduced as accurately as possible, except that abbreviations are extended (in italics, where there is any uncertainty about them), modern use followed in the cases of *i* and *j*, *u* and *v*, and modern methods of capitalization and punctuation adopted. Since some diversity exists in modern use in the printing of *i*, *j*, *u*, *v* in Latin, it should be noted that in Latin texts *i* is used for both vocal and consonantal *i*, *u* for vocal and *v* for consonantal *u*. A note on Gardiner's English spelling, punctuation, use of capitals, and abbreviation, and the treatment of the last in this edition, is given at p. 520. For a similar note in reference to manuscript copies *see* p. 523.

Footnotes are rsserved for textual matters exclusively. For explanation of signs and abbreviations used in them *see* p. xxxvii.

Identifications of persons and places are given in the index.

Historical or explanatory matter is given either in the introductory notes to groups of letters, or in connection with the introductory résumé preceding each letter; where fuller treatment of specific topics is necessary a note or notes follow the letter. Locations of Scripture quotations are not ordinarily given, since they can be readily found with the help of a concordance. For pages on which they occur *see* Index, 'Scripture'.

In Gardiner holographs all crossings out, interlineations, and other corrections are indicated in the footnotes. In letters printed from manuscript copies no note has been made of what are clearly scribal errors, or of the scribe's correction of his own errors.

The paragraphing in Gardiner holographs is here followed, but letters taken from manuscript copies, several of which are of considerable length and without break, are here divided into paragraphs.

The letters from Foxe, Stow, and Gardiner's printed books have been treated in much the same way as those from manuscripts; that is, the original spelling has been retained, but capitalization, punctuation, and paragraphing have been modernized, and present-day usage in the case of *i* and *j*, *u* and *v* followed. For the usage of the books referred to *see* p. 525.

The first edition, 1563, has been used as the basic text of all letters from Foxe. This has been compared with the other editions issued in Foxe's lifetime; namely, 1570, 1576, 1583. Verbal differences, not mere differences in spelling or those due to printer's errors, are recorded in the footnotes. It should be noted, however, that of the Gardiner letters printed in 1563 only one was reprinted in 1570 and 1576, and five in 1583.

Variants in Foxe's text in editions subsequent to his death are not here noted; but in a few instances I have indicated emendations in the best modern edition of Foxe, that by J. Pratt (in the Church Historians of England Series, 8 vols. in 16, London, 1853–70). I have indicated the location of the letters from Foxe in the Pratt edition, as well as in the editions of 1563–83.

As here printed each letter is preceded by a heading giving the person to whom it was addressed and the place and date of writing. This is followed by an indication of the source from which it is taken. An asterisk (*) following, indicates that the letter is holograph. If it has been calendared in the *Letters and Papers of the Reign of Henry VIII*, the letters *L.P.*, with the appropriate reference numbers, are added; and if it has been printed elsewhere, title and page of the work in which it appears are given. An explanatory list of abbreviations and short titles used in such references may be found at p. 526. No attempt has been made to point out erroneous readings in hitherto printed versions of the letters.

At the end of each letter the address and contemporary

endorsement, if any, are given. Endorsements or notes in later hands are not reproduced. When no address is here printed the address is missing from the manuscript. As was customary in his day, Gardiner's letters were normally written on folio leaves, then folded into four, sealed, and addressed on the back of the outer leaf. In some cases this leaf, when nothing was written on the inside of it, was not preserved; hence the missing address.

As far as the addresses are preserved in the holograph letters, they are in Gardiner's hand, except those to Nos. 78, 85–6, 88, 91, 94, 98, 101–3, 105, 107–9, which are in that of one of his secretaries; the words below the address, however, in Nos. 86, 101–3, 105 are in Gardiner's hand.

Needless to say, endorsements are in the hand of the recipient of the letter or his secretary, not in that of the writer.

When postscripts are here printed before the signature they are so placed in the manuscript. It was customary to sign letters not immediately after the last sentence, but at the bottom of the page, and if some space intervened, as it often did, a postscript could be inserted above the signature.

In headings and notes, dates are given according to modern usage, the first of January, not the twenty-fifth of March, being taken as the beginning of the year; but where year dates occur in the sources, they are printed as there given, with the correction in brackets.

In a few cases where it seemed that an obsolete word would be likely to cause misunderstanding, I have bracketed an explanatory word in the text, but for the most part the meaning of obsolete words is given in the glossary at p. 528.

The bracket [ ] in the text signifies that the words or letters it encloses would, in my judgment, have been in the manuscript had it not been mutilated; the bracket < > indicates material inserted by me to complete the sense or clarify the meaning. In the headings, the bracket [ ] indicates that the name, date, or place enclosed is not found in the letter, its address, or its contemporary endorsement, but is supplied from other evidence.

SOME DATES IN GARDINER'S LIFE

c. 1497	Born at Bury St Edmunds.
1511	As youth, in Paris, meets Erasmus.
1511–24	Student and teacher at Cambridge.
Oct. (?), 1524–July, 1529	Secretary to Wolsey.
1525	Master of Trinity Hall, Cambridge.
July–Sept., 1527	Accompanies Wolsey to France.
Feb.–Sept., 1528	Embassy to Clement VII at Orvieto.
Jan.–June, 1529	Embassy to Clement VII at Rome.
June–July, 1529	Counsel for Henry VIII in divorce trial in Legatine Court.
July, 1529–Apr., 1534	Principal Secretary to Henry VIII.
Sept., 1531	Bishop of Winchester.
Jan.–Mar., 1532	Embassy to France.
Apr., 1532	Defends rights of Convocation.
May, 1533	Counsel for Henry VIII in divorce trial in Archbishop's Court.
Sept.–Nov., 1533	Sent to intimate to Clement VII, at Marseilles, Henry's appeal to a General Council.
Jan.–Mar., 1534	Opposes royal ecclesiastical policy in Parliament.
Sept., 1535	Completes *De Vera Obedientia* and reply to brief of Paul III.
Oct., 1535–Sept., 1538	Resident ambassador in France.
May, 1539	Advocates Act of Six Articles in Parliament.
Feb.–Mar., 1540	Controversy with Robert Barnes.
June, 1540	Fall of Cromwell.
July, 1540	Counsel for Henry VIII in divorce of Anne of Cleves.
July (?), 1540	Chancellor of Cambridge University.
Nov., 1540–Sept., 1541	Embassy to Charles V at Ratisbon.
Lent, 1542	Designated by Henry VIII as his chief minister.
May–Oct., 1542	Controversy with Cheke and Smith on Greek pronunciation.
1542–6	Purveyor to the forces, in wars with Scotland and France.
Apr.–May, 1543	Influential in preparing the *King's Book*.

July–Oct., 1544	With the army and Council at Boulogne.
Oct.–Nov., 1544	Embassy to Charles V at Brussels.
1544–6	Writes against Bucer, Turner, Joye.
Oct., 1545–Mar., 1546	Embassy to Charles V at Bruges and Antwerp.
June, 1546	Mission to Boulogne to confer with Hertford on its defence.
28 Jan., 1547	Death of Henry VIII.
Aug., 1547	Protests against injunctions of Edward VI.
25 Sept., 1547–7 Jan., 1548	Prisoner in the Fleet.
Nov. (?), 1547	Ousted from Chancellorship of Cambridge.
19 Jan.–20 Feb., 1548	Prisoner in his house in Southwark.
May, 1548	Completes third book against Bucer.
29 June, 1548	St Peter's Day sermon at Court.
30 June, 1548–3 Aug., 1553	Prisoner in the Tower; writes against Cranmer and others on the Sacrament.
12 Oct., 1549	Warwick overthrows Somerset.
15 Dec., 1550	Trial begins.
14 Feb., 1551	Deprived of bishopric of Winchester.
1551 (?)	Ousted from Mastership of Trinity Hall.
6 July, 1553	Death of Edward VI.
Aug., 1553	Released from Tower; restored to see of Winchester, Mastership of Trinity Hall, and Chancellorship of Cambridge; made Lord Chancellor of England (23 Aug.).
1 Oct., 1553	Crowns Queen Mary.
Nov., 1553	Secures repeal of Edwardine ecclesiastical legislation.
25 Jan.–7 Feb., 1554	Wyatt's rebellion.
25 July, 1554	Performs wedding of Philip and Mary.
Nov., 1554	Welcomes Cardinal Pole.
Dec., 1554	Secures reenactment of heresy laws.
Jan., 1555	Condemns five reformers to the stake.
May–June, 1555	Mission to mediate peace between France and Empire.
21 Oct., 1555	Last speech in Parliament.
12 Nov., 1555	Dies at Whitehall.
Feb., 1556	His body carried to Winchester.

A SKETCH OF GARDINER'S LIFE

Stephen Gardiner, born about 1497 at Bury St Edmunds, was the son of John Gardiner, a reasonably well-to-do cloth-maker (d. 1507), and Agnes his wife.

In 1511 we find him in Paris in the household of a Mr Eden —doubtless either Thomas or Richard Eden, named in John Gardiner's will as trustees for his children. Erasmus appears to have been an intimate of the Eden household, for Gardiner later recalled how, at that time, he daily prepared for him his favourite salad. Afterwards, at Cambridge, Erasmus offered to take Gardiner into his service, but the offer was declined.

Gardiner entered Trinity Hall, Cambridge, probably in the autumn of 1511, studying chiefly Civil and Canon Law, but at the same time in all likelihood coming under the influence of the humanistic group there. In 1518 he became Bachelor of Civil Law; in 1521, Doctor in that faculty; and, in 1522, Doctor of Canon Law. He lectured at the University in Civil Law, 1521–2; in Canon Law, 1522–3; and in both, 1523–4. He was probably not ordained to the priesthood before 1521.

It was perhaps while on a mission from the University to Wolsey in 1523 that he was first brought to the Cardinal's notice. At any rate we find him, in the autumn of 1524, in Wolsey's service, where he remained till 1529.

In 1525 he was elected Master of Trinity Hall, an office he held, except for a brief period of deprivation under Edward VI, until his death. He is mentioned as Archdeacon of Taunton in 1526, and of Worcester in 1528.

He accompanied the Cardinal on his triumphal journey to France in 1527, by which time he had become thoroughly conversant with 'the King's matter,' as the contemplated divorce of Henry VIII from Catherine of Aragon was called; and in

1528 he was dispatched, in company with Edward Fox, to Pope Clement VII, then at Orvieto, to secure a commission enabling Wolsey and Campeggio to decide the case in England. Early in 1529 he was again sent to the Papal Court, now at Rome, to secure evidence of the falsity of a brief alleged by Catherine to have been issued by Pope Julius II in her behalf. He was recalled in June to take part in the trial of the case before Wolsey and Campeggio, and, immediately after the failure of these judges to give sentence, was made Principal Secretary to the King.

He was believed, by some of his contemporaries, to have plotted with the Boleyn party to undo his old master. The evidence for this is tenuous. The most that can be said with certainty is that, understanding the inevitability of Wolsey's fall if the Pope failed to sanction the annulment of Henry's marriage, he sought to ingratiate himself with both Henry and Anne Boleyn from the moment that he saw clearly that Clement, under pressure of Catherine's nephew, the Emperor Charles V, was unable to grant Henry's desires. Wolsey, after his fall, appears to have continued to regard Gardiner as his friend, and Gardiner did everything in his power to save the Cardinal's colleges from dissolution.

From 1529 to 1532 he was increasingly active in the King's business, and was rewarded with the archdeaconry of Norfolk in 1529, with that of Leicester in March, 1531, and with the bishopric of Winchester in September of the same year. He was consecrated 3 December, 1531. Winchester was the wealthiest see in England and, next to Canterbury, the most important. It included both the present dioceses of Winchester and South-wark, the bishop's chief residence being at Winchester House, Southwark, near the Church of St Mary Overies, now South-wark Cathedral.

When, early in 1532, Gardiner was in France negotiating an alliance against the Emperor, Henry VIII complained that his absence was the lack of his right hand. Thomas Cromwell, who reported this to Gardiner, was himself doing his best to fill the lack. On his return Gardiner had more than an intimation of the direction in which Cromwell was about to lead—or encourage—the King, in the demand made on Convocation, in April, that it surrender its right to legislate on faith and morals. Gardiner led the opposition to this in Convocation and, with Thomas More, in Parliament; which resulted in his loss of the royal favour for a time, and, in all probability, of the see of Canterbury, which became vacant at Warham's death, three months later, and was given to Cranmer in January, 1533. Gardiner's abilities as diplomat and legist were, however, necessary to the King, and he was again at Court in June, 1532. In October he accompanied Henry to Calais for an interview with Francis I, and in May, 1533 acted as chief counsel in Henry's suit, now before Archbishop Cranmer, for the annulment of his marriage with Catherine. In the autumn of the same year he was sent to Marseilles, to intimate to Clement VII, who came thither for an interview with Francis I, Henry's appeal from his judgment to that of a General Council.

On his return he again came in conflict with the policy of the King and Cromwell, in the Parliament of 1534, opposing the anti-clerical and anti-papal measures of its first session. This resulted in his complete loss of the royal favour. Cromwell succeeded him as Principal Secretary in April, when he retired to his diocese, remaining there a year and a half.

Although he had opposed the ecclesiastical measures in Parliament up to the point of their adoption, he acquiesced in them when they became law, declaring that an act of Parliament discharged his conscience. Hence, after the passage of the Supremacy Act in the November session of 1534, he made no difficulty about renouncing the Roman obedience, which he did on 10 February, 1535, and later that year wrote a defence of the royal supremacy (*De Vera Obedientia Oratio*) as well as a reply to the Papal brief denouncing Henry for the execution of Bishop Fisher.

In October, 1535, he was sent as ambassador to the French Court, where he stayed three years. It was rumoured that Cromwell, fearing his opposition at home, saw to it that he was kept there.

For a year and a half after his return he had little opportunity for successful opposition to Cromwell. He was said, with probable truth, to have been the author of the Act of the Six Articles in 1539, but it was not until the beginning of 1540 that events discredited Cromwell's foreign policy, and Robert Barnes, a reforming protégé of Cromwell, involved himself in a controversy with Gardiner and, by his words and actions, gave colour to the charge that Cromwell was supporting heretical preachers and seeking to overthrow the established religion. Both Cromwell and Barnes were attainted by Parliament, Cromwell being executed and Barnes burned in July, 1540.

From this time until the last few months of the reign Gardiner was the most influential member of Henry's Council, and although he by no means wielded the power of Wolsey or even, perhaps, that of Cromwell, there was probably no one who knew so well how to suggest matters to the King as to make him believe they were his own policies, nor how better to play upon Henry's 'virtuous desire' to be the 'stay of Christendom.' On the whole, Gardiner succeeded, during Henry's life, in effecting his aims; namely, the retention in the Church of Catholic theology and episcopal power; the keeping of England from any approach, theological or political, to the German Protestants; and a close alliance with the Empire, thus forestalling a possible combination of Continental powers under Papal leadership against England, yet making for the retention of orthodoxy in England, and ensuring profitable commercial intercourse with the Imperial territory of Flanders. Gardiner's dread of Protestantism was no less political than theological, for he was convinced that it would, as in Germany, bring with it civil war and anarchy.

Immediately after Cromwell's fall, he acted as the King's chief counsel in the divorce of Anne of Cleves; and it was at his house in Southwark that Henry met his next wife, Catherine Howard. He succeeded Cromwell as Chancellor of Cambridge University in 1540, and at the end of that year went on a special embassy to the Imperial Court where he remained, moving with it from Namur to Ratisbon, until July, 1541, paving the way for an English alliance with the Empire.

In the spring of 1542, according to Gardiner's own statement, Henry specifically designated him as his chief minister. In the Convocation of that year he endeavoured to secure a new translation of the Bible, free from what he believed to be the Protestant bias of Tyndale's and Coverdale's work. In the same year he had a lengthy controversy with John Cheke and Thomas Smith on the pronunciation of Greek; and negotiated with Chapuys, Imperial ambassador in England, for the completion of the alliance with Charles V. These negotiations, interrupted by war with Scotland, during which Gardiner, as Purveyor General, had the oversight of provisioning the English forces, were concluded in February, 1543, by a treaty providing for a joint invasion of France within the next two years.

On 12 July, 1543, he performed the wedding ceremony of the King and his sixth and last wife, Catherine Parr. He was, in this year, the dominant member of the committee which prepared the *King's Book*, a revision of the *Bishops' Book* of 1537 in the Catholic direction; he led the Council in the suppression of heretical books, plays, and preachers; and undoubtedly welcomed, though it is not clear that in the first instance he instigated, the collection of evidence against persons in the King's household at Windsor, and among Cranmer's clergy at Canterbury, who were disseminating Protestant opinions. This activity led to a counter-attack. One of his secretaries and probable kinsman, Germain Gardiner, was executed in March, 1544, for denying the royal supremacy, and there is evidence for believing that an attempt was made to persuade the King to commit Gardiner himself to the Tower. But he retained the royal favour and, after again supervising supplies and munitions in the renewed war with Scotland, 1543-4, and for the invasion of France in the summer of 1544, he led the commission which treated with France for peace, and, when satisfactory terms were not reached, he and Hertford went to Brussels to induce Charles V to put pressure on the French. This mission was unsuccessful, but in 1545 Charles offered to mediate, and Gardiner was sent to the Imperial Court to make peace with France, and, at the same time, to revise and cement the Imperial alliance. He failed in the first but was successful in the second, thereby enabling England to exact better terms from France in 1546.

During the last three years of Henry's reign, despite his absorption in affairs of state, his pen was busy refuting Protestant writers. It was probably early in 1544 that he published his pamphlet against William Turner. In the same year appeared his first book against Martin Bucer, with whom he had debated at Ratisbon in 1541; in 1546 his second. In 1546 also were published his refutation of George Joye, and his *Detection of the Devils Sophistrie*.

He maintained his ascendancy in the Council until the latter half of 1546, when, with the increasing illness of the King, Hertford (later Duke of Somerset), uncle of Prince Edward, and Lisle (later Earl of Warwick and Duke of Northumberland) set about to gain control in the coming reign. There were preliminary clashes with Gardiner and his supporters in the Council in October, and before the end of the year the rash words and acts of Surrey, leading to his own execution and the imprisonment of his father, the Duke of Norfolk, Gardiner's chief ally among the nobility, ensured the success of the Hertford-Lisle group, to whom Paget, Gardiner's one-time pupil and recent supporter, went over. Although they succeeded in having Gardiner's name excluded from the list of executors in Henry VIII's will, he acted as chief officiant at Henry's funeral in February, 1547, and attended the Archbishop at Edward VI's coronation. He retired soon after to his diocese, but did not hesitate to advise Hertford, now Duke of Somerset and Protector, on matters of governmental policy, and to protest to him against what he believed to be the subversive tendencies of the reformers encouraged at Court. He declined to assist Cranmer in preparing a book of homilies and urged him to drop the project. But the *First Book of Homilies* was issued 31 July, 1547, accompanied by royal injunctions requiring its use and that of Erasmus' *Paraphrase upon the New Testament*. Gardiner protested to the Council, in Somerset's absence, against the injunctions, not only because they fostered what, in his opinion, was untrue and dangerous doctrine, but also because they were illegal and unconstitutional. He was summoned before the Council and, on his refusal to promise that he would, three weeks hence, when there would be a visitation of his diocese, obey the injunctions unconditionally, he was committed to the Fleet, 25 September, 1547. Here he was kept without indictment, conviction, or any judicial process, till 7 January, 1548. This was an effective way of preventing him from organizing a conservative opposition in the Parliament of 1547.

On his release he again retired to his diocese, where he finished his third book against Bucer (*Exetasis*, not published till 1554), but he was soon again summoned before the Council, where he appeared 26 May, 1548, and, shortly after, was asked to preach on the recent religious changes. This he did on St Peter's Day, 29 June, 1548. The next day he was sent to the Tower because, it was said, he had disobeyed the royal command not to speak of matters in controversy touching the Sacrament. He was again kept in confinement without either indictment or conviction.

Two years had passed when, in June, 1550, Somerset, after his fall and restoration to the Council, went, with some other councillors, to visit Gardiner, and, on the latter's promise of conformity to the Prayer Book (the first book of Edward VI), assured him of his release. This assurance was given while Warwick was absent from London, and was part of Somerset's plan to build up conservative support against him. But Cecil reported the move to Warwick, who not only quashed it, but, with Cecil's assistance, tried to trap Gardiner into statements which would have effected his easy deprivation. When this plan failed, a set of articles on religious changes was presented for his subscription, and on his refusal to accept them unconditionally, the revenues of his bishopric were sequestered, 19 June, 1550. Finally on 15 December, 1550, he was brought to trial for contempt of authority in his St Peter's Day sermon, and for refusal to conform himself to the King's commands. The trial lasted four months, during which he ably defended himself, but the outcome was a foregone conclusion. On 14 February, 1551, sentence of deprivation was given. He was removed to a 'meaner lodging' in the Tower, where he remained till the accession of Queen Mary. During his five years in the Tower he produced six volumes of theological controversy, chiefly on the Sacrament of the Altar.

On Mary's entry into London, 3 August, 1553, he was released. He at once resumed jurisdiction over his bishopric, was admitted to the Privy Council, and restored to the Mastership of Trinity Hall and the Chancellorship of Cambridge University, from both of which he had been ousted in Edward's reign. On 23 August he was made Lord Chancellor of England. It was he who placed the crown upon Mary's head.

Mary's dearest desire was the reunion of England with Rome, and Gardiner as her foremost minister could not have been averse to it, although he averred that in this matter 'the Queen went before him, and that it was her own motion.' The reign of Edward had undoubtedly done much to convince him that the maintenance of Catholicism without either the Pope or a strong and orthodox monarch like Henry VIII was extremely difficult. At the same time he saw clearly that religious changes must have parliamentary sanction and that such sanction could not be gained without definite assurances from the Pope that there would be no attempt to recover former monastic property now in lay hands. In Mary's first Parliament he secured the repeal of all Edwardine ecclesiastical legislation, thus effecting a return to conditions in the latter years of Henry VIII.

Although he continued to favour friendship with the Emperor, he opposed the marriage of the Queen with the Emperor's son, Philip of Spain, fearing that it would cause immediate popular disaffection, and ultimately involve England in Philip's continental wars. He put forward his young friend Edward Courtenay, great-grandson of Edward IV, as candidate for the Queen's hand; but when he had become convinced of Mary's unalterable determination to wed Philip, he came out for the match, did his best to win others to favour it, and saw that the marriage treaty was so drawn up as to prevent the government of England from passing into any but English hands, or England from being drawn into Philip's wars. His worst fears were realized by Wyatt's rebellion, but by his influence over Courtenay who, he learned, had been flirting with Carew and Wyatt, he extracted from that young man the whole of Carew's plot. This precipitated the rising two months before it was planned, a circumstance which did much to save the government.

He shielded Courtenay from the results of his implication in the movement, and was accused of shielding Elizabeth. Although he had no love for her, it is probably true that he realized that her execution would be a political blunder. He hoped to have her excluded from the succession by statute.

He performed the wedding ceremony of Philip and Mary in his cathedral at Winchester 25 July, 1554, and in November, after receiving from Cardinal Pole assurances as to church property in lay possession, secured parliamentary consent to

the reconciliation with Rome. He also secured the re-enactment of the heresy laws which had been repealed under
Edward VI. He appears to have felt that the mere reappearance
of these laws on the statute books would frighten the reformers
into flight or conformity. In his Southwark church, in January,
1555, he presided at the first trial of offenders under these laws,
and condemned five, Hooper, Rogers, Bradford, Saunders, and
Taylor, to the stake. This was the only time in the reign in
which he took part in a heresy trial. When he saw that neither
the re-enactment of the laws, nor the condemnation of some
of the leaders, was sufficient to bring their followers to conformity, he 'gave over the matter,' in the words of John Foxe,
'as utterly discouraged.' Persons of known Protestant lean-
ings, such as Roger Ascham and Sir Thomas Smith, were, if
willing to conform outwardly to the religion established, protected by Gardiner from inquisition into their private views.

His last diplomatic mission was in the spring of 1555, when
he endeavoured, in vain, to mediate peace at a conference between French and Imperial representatives near Calais. In
September he had a severe attack of dropsy and jaundice, and
early in October was forbidden by his physicians to leave his
house. He insisted, however, on delivering the opening speech
in Parliament, 21 October, in an endeavour to win support for
the government in the face of growing discontent. The effort
left him exhausted. He was lodged in the Royal Palace,
Whitehall, where he died, 12 November, 1555. The following
February his body was taken to Winchester and sometime
thereafter laid in the chantry where it still rests.

RECENT GARDINER LITERATURE

Since the publication of my *Stephen Gardiner and the Tudor Reaction*, New York, Macmillan, London, S.P.C.K., 1926, two noteworthy contributions to Gardiner literature have been made. One is the publication of Gardiner's Episcopal Register, edited by Mr Herbert Chitty, with an introduction by Mr Henry Elliott Malden, Canterbury and York Society, Oxford, 1930. The other is M. Pierre Janelle's *Obedience in Church and State, Three Political Tracts by Stephen Gardiner*, Cambridge University Press, 1930. This contains a reprint of Gardiner's *De Vera Obedientia*, in both its Latin and English forms, and gives us for the first time in print two other writings of Gardiner's: his reply to the Papal brief in condemnation of Bishop Fisher's execution, and a short tract against Bucer. A contemporary English translation of the former and a modern translation of the latter are also given. (For certain necessary corrections of statements in M. Janelle's preface about the time of composition and publication of the *De Vera Obedientia*, and the time of composition of the reply to the Papal brief, see Note to No. 51 in this volume.)

M. Janelle has also published a bibliography of the Gardiner-Bucer controversy in *Revue des Sciences Religieuses*, Strasbourg, July, 1927, and has printed in part a contemporary poem on Gardiner by a certain William Palmer, in the *Bulletin of the Institute of Historical Research*, London, June and November, 1928. Though obviously not a trustworthy source of information about Gardiner, this is an illuminating expression of contemporary Protestant feeling concerning him.

Another item which can be called recent in no other sense than that it has but recently come to my attention, is a manuscript volume in the Library at Besançon, which, according to the description given in the printed catalogue of that library, is an account of the Anglo-Saxon and Norman invasions of England, written by Gardiner for Philip II, and translated into Italian by George Rainsford (*Catalogue Général des Manuscrits des Bibliothèques Publiques de France, Départements*, XXXII, *Besançon*, I, ed. A. Castan, Paris, 1897, p. 822). When I wrote my *Stephen Gardiner and the Tudor Reaction* I was wholly unaware, not only of the existence of this volume, but of the fact that Gardiner had ever written anything of the sort. M. Janelle writes me that it had also been unknown to him until I called his attention to it. I came upon the description of it in a search for notices of Gardiner letters in the printed catalogues of the manuscript collections in the French departmental libraries. I have not yet seen the manuscript. M. Janelle promises to look it up, and it is to be hoped that if he finds the volume of interest, he will publish it.

Perhaps it should be added that the unsigned article on Gardiner in the recent, so-called 14th, edition of the *Encyclopaedia Britannica* is inferior to that in the 11th edition, by Mr James Gairdner. It appears to be a not too intelligent condensation of Mr Gairdner's article.

SIGNS AND ABBREVIATIONS USED

SIGNS

The asterisk (*), used in headings, indicates that the manuscript source of the letter referred to is a Gardiner holograph. The sign †, used in the text of holograph letters, indicates that the word it follows or the phrase of two or more words which it precedes and follows are interlined in the manuscript. (When used in the footnotes it stands for the word 'interlined.') The sign ‡, used similarly, but only in No. 125, indicates that the word or phrase so marked does not occur in the Harbin copy of the manuscript. For explanation of the use of brackets *see* p. xxii above.

ABBREVIATIONS USED IN THE FOOTNOTES

abv. for *above*   *w.* for *with*
alt. for *altered*   *writ.* for *written*
c.o. for *crossed out*   The sign † for *interlined*

Words or letters indicated in the footnotes as crossed out (*c.o.*) always *follow* in the manuscript the word in the text to which the note number is appended.

For the meaning of abbreviated references to manuscripts in the footnotes, see the heading of the letter under which they occur.

ABBREVIATIONS USED IN THE HEADINGS

Manuscripts are cited under the designations used in the repositories where they are found, the first number or numbers following such designation being that of the manuscript, the last number (or numbers, when joined by a hyphen) being that of the folio or page. Where folios or pages have been renumbered, it is the new number which is here cited. In each case the citation of a manuscript is preceded by a reference to the repository. Those given in abbreviation are as follows:

B.M., British Museum.
B.N., Bibliothèque Nationale, Paris.

Camb. Univ. Lib., Cambridge University Library.

C.C.C.C., Corpus Christi College, Cambridge.

R.O., Public Record Office, London.

The Calendar of *Letters and Papers, Foreign and Domestic, of the Reign of Henry VIII* (ed. J. S. Brewer, J. Gairdner, R. H. Brodie), London, 1862–1910, is cited as *L.P.*

The *State Papers during the Reign of Henry VIII*, London, 1830–52, is cited as *St. P.*

Well-known histories and printed collections of documents such as those of Burnet, Ellis, Pocock, Wilkins, are cited under the names of author or editor only. Titles and editions used may be found on pp. 526–7.

ERRATUM

p. 148, l. 21. *For* 'the Mayor of Canterbury' *read* 'an Alderman of Canterbury.'

INTRODUCTORY NOTE TO NOS. 1–11

These letters were written while Gardiner was in Wolsey's service. The first, to Erasmus, contains the only autobiographical reference to Gardiner's early youth that we have. Nos. 2 and 3 were written on his first mission to the Pope, in 1528. Eighteen other letters, written by him in the names of himself and one or both of his colleagues (Edward Fox and Sir Gregory Casale) while on this embassy, are not here printed (*see* above, p. xvi). The object of the embassy was to secure a Papal commission enabling Wolsey and Campeggio to examine the validity of the dispensation of Julius II, which had permitted Henry VIII to marry his deceased brother's wife, and to give sentence accordingly on the marriage. It was desired that this commission contain a Papal pronouncement or decretal settling certain questions of law, hence it was called a 'decretal commission.' The commission granted by Clement VII and taken to England by Fox was not in this form, hence Gardiner remained at the Papal Court until he succeeded in persuading the Pope to issue a secret decretal commission which Campeggio was to bring with him. *See* No. 3. This was granted at the moment of some French military successes in Italy, but by the time Campeggio reached England (October, 1528) the power of Charles V, nephew of Catherine of Aragon, was once more in the ascendant, and Campeggio was instructed to delay the trial and give no decision without new orders from the Pope. He refused, moreover, to put the secret decretal in Wolsey's hands.

Further delay resulted from Catherine's production of a copy of what was said to be a brief of Julius II remedying all defects in his bull of dispensation. Gardiner was again dispatched to the Papal Court, in January, 1529, whither Sir Francis Brian and Peter Vannes had been sent shortly before, to secure the Pope's decision that the brief was false. The undated letter, No. 4, a graceful farewell note to a fellow-member of Wolsey's household, is probably to be placed, as in *L.P.*, on the eve of Gardiner's departure. Nos. 5–10 were written while on this mission, No. 11 just after his return. He found Imperial pressure on the Pope stronger now than in the previous year, and although there is some evidence that Clement expressed his private opinion that the brief was a forgery (*L.P.*, IV, 5181, 5733, 5742), he said he could give no decision without hearing both sides (*ib.*, 5474, 21 April, 1529). He acted, thought

Gardiner, as if he did not care how Henry's case was settled, so he did not have to settle it himself, and said he wished Catherine were in her grave (Nos. 9, 10).

For joint letters from Gardiner and his colleagues, and instructions to Gardiner during this mission, *see L.P.*, IV, 5183–5576, *passim*.

Meanwhile Wolsey and the King had decided to begin the trial, and Gardiner was summoned home to assist in it. For his activities at the trial *see* Janelle, *Obedience in Church and State*, pp. xvii–xix. Campeggio succeeded in putting off a decision, and, on 23 July, 1529, prorogued the court for vacation till October. On 28 July Gardiner became Principal Secretary to the King.

The court never sat again, for, although Campeggio was as yet unaware of it, Clement had signed, on 15 July, the advocation of the case to Rome. The French had been thoroughly defeated in Italy, and Clement had gone completely over to the Emperor, sealing this alliance with him by the Treaty of Barcelona, 29 June.

For fuller references to authorities on matters connected with Gardiner's two missions to the Papal Court *see* J. Gairdner, 'New Lights on the Divorce of Henry VIII,' *Eng. Hist. Rev.*, XI, XII.

1. *To* ERASMUS

[London?], 28 February, [1526 or 1527]

Stadtbibliothek, Breslau, Codex Rehdigeranus 254, 177–8.* Enthoven, *Briefe an Eras.*, 73. Allen, *Ep. Eras.*, VI, 265.

Recalls how, when a lad in the Eden household in Paris (in 1511), he daily prepared a salad for Erasmus, and how Erasmus later offered to take him into his service. (If Gardiner be correct in placing the publication of the *Moria* sixteen years before he wrote, and if the *Moria* appeared, as it almost certainly did, in 1511, the year date of this letter would be 1527. But the reply of Erasmus is, in all the authorized editions of his letters, dated 3 September, 1526. Leclerc changed this to 1527, which is followed by Horawitz and Enthoven. Mr P. S. Allen, however, sees no reason for doubting the earlier date, and gives one good reason for retaining it—*Ep. Eras.*, VI, 404. For a free English translation of Gardiner's letter *see* my *Gardiner*, 4; for Erasmus' reply, *ib.*, 5, and Allen, VI, 404.)

S. Gardinerus Erasmo Rhoterodamo S.P.

Quantumcunque reclamet infancia mea, ne ad Erasmum scribam, in omni eruditionis genere principem virum, illud tamen a me impetrare

non potuit, ut sileam omnino; tam potens alioqui ipsa viribusque tam valida, ut modum pro imperio posset adhibere. Nam nec sinit interdum quod sentio exprimere, et tamen surdis nunc canit affectibus meis, ne tibi se prodant quoquo modo, tam commoda presertim occasione oblata tum scribendi tum scripta per tabellarium mittendi ad te. Vel scribentibus certatim ex Anglia reliquis, solus taceret Stephanus ille qui, quoties de Erasmo sermo incidit, se illi coquum aliquando fuisse gloriose satis iactitare solet? hoc modo scilicet eruditionis sue fidem audientibus facturus; non aliter profecto quam qui sanctos eo nomine se volunt haberi, quod Sanctam semel Terram pedibus calcarunt. Scribendum certe fuit, ne vel circa te ingratus amicis tuis videar, qui non illi gracias habeam, in cuius scriptis aliquamdiu versatus nonnihil inde frugis collegerim, vel aliis mentitus, dum me tibi tam notum ubique predicarem olim fuisse et familiarem. Ceterum si fas sit memoriam istam tuam optimis quibusque rebus diligentissime adservandis a te destinatam ob rem quandam nugatoriam ad preterita revocare, annon recordaris sexdecem abhinc annos, cum apud Edenum quendam Anglum, in vico Sancti Ioannis Lutecie tum divertentem, hospes esses, quo tempore primum Moriam edidisti, ni fallor, tuam, et iam magnam librorum vim tibi comparasti tum Grecorum tum Latinorum, fuisse id temporis cum Edeno illo puellum quendam, cui cotidie iubebas ut lactucas pararet tibi cum butiro et omphatio coctas, atque illum tibi cibum ab eodem tam eleganter instructum diceres ut nunquam alias? Ipsus ego sum, Stephanus Gardinerus, tui amantissimus ac tecum absente absens hucusque bona fide versatus, sed aulicis iam tandem negociis a te sic distractus, ut te[†] amare, quod facio, deinceps liceat, frui vero dulcissima illa scriptorum tuorum consuetudine vereor ut liceat aliquando. O me certe infelicem, cui illam conditionem amplecti non contigit, quam tu per Gerardum, bibliopolam Cantabrigensem, mihi obtulisti! si tamen is mihi non est mentitus, nimirum ut tibi inservirem; tum quidem pro mutis illis literis tuis quas utcunque degustavi[1], vivi tui pectoris energian preceptorem habiturus. Sed stultus qui queror que mutari non possunt. Et plura verba facturo manum iam iniicit ipsa quam dixi infancia, nec sinit hoc tempore esse loquatiorem. Itaque vale, doctissime Erasme, et Stephanum ut olim palato tuo in parandis certe[2] lactucis non ineptissimum coquum, sic nunc, si qua te possit fortuna iuvare, amicum non infidelem tibi

---

1 vi *c.o.*
2 certes *w.* s *c.o.*

futurum velis existimare. Iterum vale. Ex edibus Reverendissimi
Cardinalis, ultimo Februarii.

Tibi deditissimus,

STEPHANUS GARDINERUS

2. *To* WOLSEY

Calais, 18 February, 1528

R.O., S.P. 1, 46, 270–1.* *L.P.*, IV, 3938. Pocock, I, 78.

Sir Robert Wingfield has shown him the defenceless condition of Calais.

Pleasith it your Grace to understande that synnes my cumming hither
to Calays, Master Deputie, in whom for your Graces sake I have founde
moch kindnes, hath at lenght declared and shewed unto me the poore
state and condition of this towne, gretly mornyng and lamenting the
same; and, upon such letters as he hath receyved from the capitain of
Boleyn, wherof I suppose he hath advertised your Grace, moch more
perplexed and troubled in mynde howe the necessites of this towne, if
wer shulde nowe ensue, as it is spoken, shalbe releved, oonles your
Grace cause provision to be made in tyme, like as, I doubte not, and
have also said unto him, your Grace hath already doon. Nevertheles,
hering with myn eres complayntes made on every partye, aswel of extreme povertie and det as also want and skarcyte of vytal, I thought I
coulde noo lesse doo but to advertise your Grace therof; whom I wel
knowe to have singuler respecte and consideration to the mayntenaunce
of this towne, which nowe specially requirith your Graces help and
counfort to be adhibite in tyme.

This night arryved here the Popes ambassadour, having very fayre
passage. I harde say by his servauntes that Thadeus was at Dover; but
as yet he camme not here. Tomorowe in the mornyng Master Fox and I
take our journay by post towardes Parys, God willing; Who preserve
your good Grace. At Calays the xviij day of February.

Your Graces most humble
servaunt and dayly bedeman

STEVEN GARDYNER

Addressed: To my Lord Legates good Grace.
Endorsed: Doctor Stevyns, the xviij^th of February, 1527 ⟨28⟩.

4

3. *To* HENRY VIII

Viterbo, 11 June, [1528]

R.O., S.P. 1, 48, 162–3.* *L.P.*, IV, 4355. *St. P.*, VII, 77.

> The Pope is sending the secret decretal commission with Campeggio; thinks
> the Pope has a sincere love for Henry; has been troubled by Henry's displeasure.
> (If word of Henry's displeasure reached Gardiner, as is here suggested, from
> Tuke, the letter is lost, but an extant letter from Edward Fox mentions it—
> *L.P.*, IV, 4290. For the Pope's letter to Henry, mentioned here, *see ib.*, 4348.)

Pleasith yt your Highnes to understande that, endevoring myself as far
as my poore wit, lernyng, industrye, and diligence coulde extende, I
have at the last conduced the setting forwarde of the Cardinal Campegius, as shal appere unto your Majestie by such letters of the said
Campegius as he wrote unto me, and as[†] I sende unto Master Fox to
be declared unto your Highnes at lenght; not doubting but, whenne
your Grace shal have herde the processe of our doinges here, and what
we have doon for the diligent and spedy accomplishement of your Graces
commaundementes, I shal appere unto your Majestie always in good
mynde and wil to have been, and to be, of oon sorte; and in your
Highnes causes soo to have conjoyned faith and diligence, grounded
upon a sincere mynde and intent, as hitherto I have had them in like
consideration, with noo lesse studye and desire of mynde to declare the
oon thenne the other; being to me, in myn opinion, asmoch hevynes to
be accused or suspected in the jugement of your Majestie of my diligence
or sincerite in this matier, as if it wer doubted *de fide*, which offense is
infamis et capitalis. Wherfor most humbly and upon my knees I desire
your Highnes to here my justificacion in that behaulf, accompting al the
poore service I have or maye do to be wel employed and highly rewarded, if it may suffise *ad probandum fidem et diligenciam Maiestati
vestre.*

It may like your Highnes to be also advertised that, after moch difficulte, many altercacions, and other meanes used to compasse and conduce the atteyning of the commission decretal in secrete maner, and
finally moch travayling howe to assure the Popes Holynes that the same
shuld soo be secretly kepte, at the last, upon difficultie founde of the sure
conveying therof to your Highnes, and chaunces which might fortune
in the waye, his Holines coulde oonly satisfie himself in sending it by
the Cardinal Campegius, and soo hath promised us, like as by his letters

your Majestie shal understande. Which, knowing it to be nowe more tyme your Highnes had dedes then promises, and wolde therfor not somoch regarde our relation, we caused, with moch difficultie, his Holynes to wryte; in which letters we wold have had his Holines to expresse the matier in special termes, but for feare *ne litere interciderent*, we coulde not obteyne that of him; but he said your Majestie shal understande his mynde by these wordes: *Inventuri sumus aliquam formam satisfaciendi Maiestati tue etc.*; assuring your Highnes that his Holynes hath, in myn opinion, a fast and sincere love towardes your Grace, not grounded upon his necessites, but upon such devocion as he hath perceyved and doth dayly understande to be in your Majestie towardes this see. In the jugement wherof, like as I maye be deceyved, and with protestacion therof write unto your Highnes, soo I have good matier, outwarde and apparaunt, wherupon to grounde my said opinion, and therfor have thought convenient to signifie the same unto your Grace. Wherin if I sawe otherwise, I wolde likewise soo write; being of this determination evermore, al other respectes set aparte, to saye and write unto your Majestie the truth and lightlywodes of truth as they shal appere unto me, whether the same shal delighte and please for the tyme or otherwise†; knowing wel that to be the oonly thing which shal obteyne *solidam veram et perpetuam gratiam a Maiestate vestra, que templum est fidei et veritatis unicum in orbe relictum, in quo certa harum numina esse creduntur.*

Which thing moved me by myn other letters to expresse such dispayre as I thenne had, being moch more thenne I coulde by wordes in convenient maner expresse; trusting always that in compassing and conducing such thinges as depende upon a nother mannes acte, your Highnes wil not conjoyne *studium et voluntatem meam cum eventu;* but perceyving *fidem, studium, et voluntatem meam* to have effectually concurred, as it hath and shal ever doo, soo to accepte and repute the same accordingly; as my trust is, and ever hath been, your Highnes wil graciously doo, and esteme me a true and faythful subgiet, and for the benevolence which your Majestie hath above my merites shewed unto me, as sincerely, ernestly, and ⟨with⟩ asmoch good wil to the uttermost of my litel power *etiam cum iactura vite*, being in that cace *non iactura sed lucrum*, in the execution of your Highnes commaundementes and accheving of your desires[1], to procede and employe *pro portione facultatum* as any other.

---

1 *alt. from* desirous

Thus your Majestie nowe understandith howmoch the wordes spoken by your Grace to Master Tuke doo prik me; and having, bifore the receipte of those letters, as this berer canne tel, brought al thinges to conclusion, compelle me to trouble and moleste your Highnes with moo wordes thenne wer convenient for me to use unto your Grace, soo[1] rudely cowched and inelegantly writen. Nevertheles, considering they procede *ex iusto dolore meo*, I ha[ve] good hope your Highnes wil soo accepte and take them in good parte accordingly. Thus I praye Almighty God long to preserve your most noble and royal astate. At Viterbe, the xj[th] day of June.

Your Highnes most humble subget,
servaunt, and dayly oratour,

STEVEN GARDYNER

Addressed: To the Kinges Highnes.

Endorsed: Master Gardyner to the Kinges Highnes, from Viterbe.

4. *To* [THOMAS] ARUNDEL

Westminster, [*c.* 18–20 January, 1529]

R.O., S.P. 1, 52, 149.* *L.P.*, IV, 5184.

Bids Arundel good-bye (before starting on his second mission to the Pope).

Gentil Master Arundel: By these letters I shal take youe by the hande and byd youe most hartely fare wel, supplying that which I coulde not yesterday doo; aswel for that ye, wayting upon my Lordes Grace, and I, hasted to[2] repare hither, were sodenly sondred, as also that, in very deade, my stomak wold not suffre me soo to doo. But thowgh I departe from youe in body, I departe not in mynde and sowle; which, considering it may be where I lyst, ye may be wel assured it shalbe ever where youe be during my lif, whersoever this body shal fortune to wandre. As knowith God, Who sende youe most hartely wel to fare. At Westmester, this mornyng.

Entierly your own,

STEVEN GARDYNER

1 ear *c.o.*   2 c *c.o.*

5. *To* WOLSEY

Dover, [22] January, [1529]

R.O., S.P. 1, 52, 161–2.* *L.P.*, IV, 5195.

Has embarked for Calais. (Gardiner's date, 21 January, is an evident slip for 22 January. *See* n. in *L.P.*)

Pleasith your Grace to understande that this Friday in the mornyng, the tyde and wynde being propicious, I entred the ship to passe to Calays, entending from thens to passe with al diligence towardes Parys and there to abyde my letters. Thus Almighty Jesus preserve your good Grace and sende me good passage with like spede in my journey. From Dover, this Fryday, the xxjᵗⁱ day of January.

Your Graces most bounden servaunt
and dayly bedeman,

STEVEN GARDYNER

Addressed: To my Lorde Legates good Grace.
Endorsed: Doctor Stevyns, of the¹ xxijᵗʰ of January.

6. *To* WOLSEY

Lyons, 31 January, [1529]

B.M., Vit. B, XI, 46–7.* Mutilated. *L.P.*, IV, 5237.

The Pope is ill; the effect his death would have on the commission to Wolsey and Campeggio. (For instructions to Brian and Vannes and prophecy concerning Angelus *see L.P.*, IV, 4977, 5014. Wolsey feared that Charles V intended to raise to the Papacy Cardinal Quiñones, whose monastic name was Francis of the Angels.)

Pleasith it your Grace to understande that, arryving here a[t Lyons] this Saterday in the mornyng by vijᵗʰ of the clok, and intendi[ng] this day to my expedition from hens with Master Secretary and Master Doctor Benet, whom I founde here abyding my cummyng, as it was ordred by your Graces letters, I entende, God willing, to morowe to departe hens towardes Rome; from whens, by reaporte of diverse that I have en- countred in the waye, I here confirmation of such tydinges concernyng the Popes extreme sikenes as I wrote unto your Grace from Parys of the relation of Bayly Robe[rtet]. N[evertheles], whether the Pope be re- covered or noo it is [here in doubte], and it is supposed by conjecture

¹ the *repeated*

8

that he is rather amen[ded then] otherwise, for that there cummith noo tydinges to[1] the contrary; w[hich] is to be thought shal soone be spred abrode. Howbeit, forasmoc[h] as your Grace, in instructions nowe geven to Master Brian a[nd] Master Peter, notith the prophicie of[2] Angelus to [be the] pope, there chaunces in this tyme of the worlde soo m[any] thinges *vaticiniis predicta* that these tidinges doo moch a[lter]⟨*i.e.*, disturb⟩ me, considering that of oon writing *de calamitatibus P[ape] subiungitur,* '*Papa cito moritur*,' which if it shulde chaun[ce, as] God forbede it shulde[3], the commission geven to your Grace [and to] my Lorde Campegius *morte pontificis concedentis* wer [wholly] extincte and adnihilate, oonles the same wer *in illius [v]it[a in]cepta exequi et perpetuare*, which may be doon *solo decre[to] citacionis*, as Master Doctor Wolman and Master Doctor Bel can shewe unto your Grace. *Fortasse quod etiam spero frustra timeo ac nimis timeo, nec satis probabitur quare locum aliquem vaticiniis vanis ac stultis predictionibus dem[4]; tamen animo reputans quam egre latura sit regia maiestas que hactenus impetrata sunt sic frustrari* I cannot . . . . am compelled to communicate unto your Grace . . . . *vel stultum vel temerarium* knowing wel that your Grace [hath] soo to harte this thinge[5] *nemo ne quid secus accidat magis timeat. In omnem eventum* these thinges lettith not my journ[ey] ne shal not hindre my diligence, but shal procede in the same accordingly, [6]by the grace of God, Who preserve your good Gr[ace]. From Lyons, the last day of January.

Your Graces most humble ser[vaunt] and bedeman,

STEVEN GARDYN[ER]

Addressed: To my lorde Legates good Grace.

7. *To* HENRY VIII

Rome, 15 February, [1529]

R.O., S.P. 1, 53, 16–17.* *L.P.*, IV, 5294.

Fears his coming will be useless.

Pleasith it your Majestie to understande that, albeit I have noo matier of importaunce to signifie unto the same, yet I have thought good by these my letters to advertise your Highnes of myn arryval here; with this also,

1 †*abv.* th(?) *c.o.*	2 frier *c.o.*	3 y *c.o.*
4 †*abv.* ascultem *c.o.*	5 ut *c.o.*	6 b *writ. over* Al(?)

that oonles I finde the Popes Holynes of other disposition then as yet by conjectures I canne perceyve he shulde be of, I shal not doo that service to your Highnes by my cummyng hither that I wolde have doon; like as your Majestie shal more particularly perceyve by such letters as Master Bryan writeth unto the same at this tyme, the specialtes wherof I am not pryve unto, by reason of my late arryval here, but oonly by hym perceyving. Nevertheles, by such thinges as I have herde bifore my cummyng here, and that which I have seen and herde synnes my cummyng hither, that al thinges be not here in such trayne as I trusted to have founde them, but very far discrepaunt from lightlywode of atteyning your Highnes purpose, nevertheles, these lightlywodes shal in noo parte let me to experiment al wayes and meanes possible for comprobacion of my fidelite and due obsequie in the accomplishement of your Highnes commaundement. In doing wherof my trust and hope is your Highnes wil accepte my true intent and diligent service, which I shal not fayle to employe according to my most bounden dutie during my lif, by the grace of God, Who ever preserve your most noble and royal astate. From Rome, the xv^{th} day of February.

> Your Highnes most humble subget,
> servaunt, and dayly oratour,
>
> STEVEN GARDYNER

Addressed: To the Kinges Highnes.
Endorsed: Doctor Stephens to the Kinges Majestie.

8. *To* HENRY VIII

Rome, 3 March, [1529]

R.O., S.P. 1, 53, 85–6.* *L.P.*, IV, 5348. *St. P.*, VII, 152.

Has little hope of succeeding with the Pope, for the Imperialists now have the upper hand in central Italy; why the Pope's promise (made the previous summer, not to revoke the commission and to confirm the Legates' sentence— see Ehses, *Römische Dokumente*, No. 23) has not been sent. (*See also* No. 9.)

Pleasith it your Majestie to understande that, like as we by our commen letters have signified to my Lorde Legates Grace, to be declared unto your Highnes, we cannot as yet have accesse to the Popes presence, ne, by reason of the variete of his sikenes, canne tel whenne to have. The Bishop of Verone shewed us that, in his opinion, he thought we shulde not speke with the Pope this moneth, which delay is moch to our regret, and soomoch the [m]ore for th[a]t we perceyve [not] such causes of hope here to atteyne any thing at the Poopes hande, as your Highnes trusted of at my departure out of Englande. ThEmperialles have in these parties the superior hande, aswel for that it lieth in them to stop the accesse of vitayl and soo famen this countrie, as also that nowe here is in these quartiers noo strenght for the liege, but they may at ther libertie goo whither they wyl; being nowe the Prince of Orenge within these iij^{xx}⟨60⟩ myles, with xij^M⟨12,000⟩ men, who hath within two dayes past expugned a citie called Matrice, which oonly on this side the realme remayned for the liege. The Seignour Renzius hath but iiij^M⟨4000⟩ men and is ccc ⟨300⟩ myles hens, keping that presidie in the cities of Barlet and of Trane in Apulia, yet in possession †of the liege†; which, as thambassadours of Fraunce and Venise confesse, with whom we have commened, and likewise with other experte in those parties for that purpose, is noo let to thEmperialles, but that they maye goo out of the realme and cumme hither or to Florence, as they shal thinke good. Which thinges be, in our commen letters to my Lord Legat, writen more at large. As touching the promyse made by the Pope and de-lyvered to Master Gregory†, wherof the said Master Gregory at my laste departing hens had writen to my Lord Legate, and your Majestie at my last departing from the same spake unto me, marveling that the said Master Gregory had not sent the same by his kynnesman Vin-centius, I understande by the said Master Gregory, that it is, as your Highnes toke it, that the Pope hath made such a wryting; and bycause it was at Bononye at the depech of the said Master Vincentius, therfor it was not sent, but it is here save, to be sent bifore, or sent by oon of us at our retourne, as sha[l] stond[e w]ith your Highnes pleasour. Praying Almighty God to preserve your most noble and royal person. From Rome, the iij^{de} daye of Marche.

Your Highnes most humble subget,
servaunt, and dayly oratour,

STEVEN GARDYNER

Addressed: To the Kinges Highnes.

Endorsed: Master Gardiner, from Rome, to the Kinges Majestie.

9. *To* HENRY VIII

Rome, 21 April, [1529]

R.O., S.P. 1, 53, 226–8.* *L.P.*, IV, 5476. Burnet, V, 448.

The Pope dare not offend the Emperor; he acts as if he cared not how the King's case were settled, so he did it not himself; Gardiner has something to say about the brief (of Julius II), if Campeggio will promise to give sentence; thinks Clement's promise (*see* No. 8) is as much to Henry's purpose as the decretal kept secret by Campeggio. (The references to the King's bulls, to counsel employed at Rome, and to the Pope's dispensing power are in answer to a letter from the King—*L.P.*, IV, 5427. The mention of the Pope's dispensing power is an indication of the new line of defence soon to be put forward on Henry's behalf, namely, that the bull of Julius II, permitting his marriage with Catherine, was invalid, not because of irregularities, but because no pope had power to dispense with the divine law forbidding marriage with a deceased brother's wife. This letter was obviously endorsed after December, 1531.)

Pleasith it your Majestie to understande that, besides all other meanes used to the Popes Holynes for atteyning and accheving your Highnes purpose and intent, such as in our commen letters to my Lorde Legates Grace and my several letters to the same be conteyned at lenght, I have also aparte shewed unto the Popes Holynes that which your Highnes shewed me in your galery at Hamptoncourt, concernyng the sollicitacion of the princes of Almayn, and such other matier as shuld and ought to feare the Popes said Holynes; adding also those reasons which might induce the same to adhere expressely to your Highnes and the French King, and soo to take the more corage to accomplish your Highnes desires; using al wayes possible to enforce him to doo sumwhat, being a man of such nature as he never resolvith any thing, but by summe violent affection compelled therunto. And considering we canne spede noo better at his hande, it agreeth with that your Majestie, of your high wisedom, bifore perpended: that his Holynes wolde doo nothing which might offende thEmperour, oonles he first determyned himself to adhere to your Highnes and the French King, and soo to declare himself, conteyning himself noo lenger in neutralite; which he wil not doo, ne, the state of the affayres here considered, it wer for his welth soo to doo, oonless the liege otherwise proceded thenne they yet doo, or that his Holynes wold determyne himself to leave thiese parties, and establish his see in some other place; forasmoch as, here being, he is dayly in the daungier of thEmperialles, like as we have signified by our other letters.

12

His Holynes is in a gret perplexite and agonye of mynde, ne canne tel what to doo. He semeth in wordes, facion, and maner of speking, as though he wolde doo sumwhat for your Highnes; and yet, whenne it commith to the point, nothing he doth. I dare not saye certainly whither it be for feare or want of good wil, for I were loth to make a lye of hym[1], or to your Highnes, my prince, souverain lorde, and master. Finally, I perceyve this by the Pope and al other here, that soo your Highnes cause were determyned there by my Lordes Legates, they wolde be glad therof. And, as I thinke, if thEmperour wolde make any sute against that which shalbe doon there, they wolde serve him as they nowe doo your Highnes, and soo dryve of the tyme; for they seme to be soo mynded, as in this cause they wolde suffre moch but doo very litel. Wherfor, if my Lord Campegius wyl set apart al other respectes and frankely promyse your Highnes to geve sentence for youe, there must be your Highnes remedye short and expedite; ne ther shall want wyt, by an other meanes, to mete with such delayes as this false counterfete breve hath caused. For with these men here your Highnes shal by noo sute proufyt; which thing I wryte unto your Highnes as of my most bounden dutie I ought to[2] doo. There shal every day rise newe devices, and noon take effecte, but long delayes and wasted tyme. Wherfor, doing what I canne yet to get the best, althowe we be fully answered therin, I shal doo what I canne to get the commission amplified asmoch as may be, and, at the lest, to extende to the reprobation of the brief— if I canne, for I dare promise noo thing to your Majestie at this mannes hande. And that which shalbe obteyned, if any be obteyned, shalbe, according to your Highnes pleas*our*, sent by Master Bryan.

And where as your Highnes in your gracious letters directed to me and my colleges, marvelith that I have not or this tyme advertised the same of such bulles as your Majestie willed me to impetrate here, I thought veryly that forasmuch as the same[3] be to be impetrate at the Popes hande, and that we signified[4] unto your Majestie, by our letters, of the Popes gret sikenes and howe we coulde not have accesse unto the same, that it had been superfluous for me, in my letters, to make any mention of the said bulles, signifying unto your Highnes nowe that, having those matiers, as it becommith me to have, in good remembraunce, I have not yet broken with the Popes Holynes in them, ne thought good to interrupte the prosecution of your Highnes matier with the pursuite

1 of *c.o.*	2 *alt. from* too
3 *a letter c.o.*	4 b *c.o.*

13

of those; saving that I spake a worde to the Popes Holynes *de ecclesiis cathedralibus*, and his Holynes said nothing coulde be doon tyl the Cardinal Sanctorum Quatuor be recovered. In other thinges I spake not; for our audience with the Popes Holynes hath been soo skarse that we thought it litel ynowe to spende the same in your Highnes principal matier.

And to advertise your Highnes what counsail is here conducted for the defence of your Majesties cause, the same shal understande that this Courte, as it hath suffred in al other thinges, soo it is also moch appeyred in lerned men, and of them that be, we dare not trust every oon, *ne causa Maiestatis vestre illis denudata*, they should *prodere illam adversariis*. Wherfor counseling as yet oonly with two, the oon called Dominus Michael, the other Dominus Sigismundus, we, perceyving nothing to be sollicited openly on the other syed, and that here as yet hath been noo nede to dispute openly, have not communicate your Highnes matier to noo moo. And as for that article, *Quod papa non posset dispensare*, the Pope himself wil here noo disputacions in it; and, soo he might reteyne your Highnes good mynde, he semith not to care for himself whither your Highnes cause be decided by that article or noo, soo he did it not. But surely it apperith, as a man may gather by his facion and maner, that he hath made his accounpte noo further to medle in your Highnes matier, neyther with your Majestie ne against the same, but folowe that shalbe doon by his legates there. Wherfor, if my Lorde Campegius wolde promise your Majestie to geve sentence frankely and apertely, having *propitium iudicem*, I wold trust, being there with such consultacions as I shulde bringe from hense, to saye sumwhat to this breve there, *apud illos et ista est sacra anchora Maiestatis vestre*; for fromhens shal cum nothing but delayes; desiring your Highnes not to shewe this to my Lorde Campegius, ne my Lordes Grace.

Master Gregory sendith presently unto your Highnes the promyse made by the Popes Holynes concernyng your Highnes cause at such tyme as I went to Venise for his cause. Which promyse, in the first thre wordes, viz., *Cum nos iusticiam eius cause perpendentes, etc.* doth make asmoch, and more, for the mayntenaunce of that shalbe doon in your Highnes cause, thenne if the commission[1] decretal, being in Cardinal Campegius handes, shulde be shewed. And this your Highnes shal have at your liberte to shewe to whom of your Counsail it shal please

---

1 dtcl *c.o.*

14

your Grace; thinking, in my poore opinion, that it wer not the best, therfore, to move the Pope in that matier again in this adverse tyme.

I most humbly desire your Majestie that I maye be a suter to the same for the said Master Gregory; soo as, by your most gracious commaundement, payment may be made there to his factours of such diettes as your Highnes allowith him. For omitting to speke of his true, faythful, and diligent service, which I have hertofore and doo nowe perceyve in him here, I assure your Highnes he lyveth here sumptuously and chargeably[1], to your Highnes honnour, and, in this gret skasete, must nedes be dryven to extremite, oonles your Highnes be gratious lord unto him[2] in that behaulf.

Thus having noon other matier wherof privately to wryte unto your Majestie, besides that is conteyned in our commen letters to my Lord Legates Grace, desiring your Highnes that I maye knowe your pleasour what to doo in case noon other thing canne be obteyned here, I shal make an ende of these letters; praying Almighty God to preserve your most noble and royal astate, with a short expedition of this cause, according to your Highnes purpose and desire. From Rome, the xxj[th] day of Apryl.

Your Highnes most humble subge[t],
servaunt, and dayly oratour,

STEVEN GARDYNER

Addressed: To the Kinges Highnes.
Endorsed: The Bishop of Wynchestre to the Kinges Majestie.

10. *To* HENRY VIII

Rome, 4 May, [1529]

R.O., S.P. I, 53, 275–6.* *L.P.*, IV, 5518. Burnet, VI, 23.

Has been unable to accomplish anything; Henry has not been well handled by some; the Pope wishes Catherine were in her grave.

Pleasith it your Majestie to be advertised that endevering ourself to the best of our powers, al joyntely, and I myself aparte applying al my poore wit and learnyng to atteyne at the Popes hande sumparte of the accomplyshement of your Highnes desires, finally have nothing prevayled; but nowe see it called in question whither the auctorite geven to the

<hr>

1 g *in this word writ. over* b   2 unto *c.o.*

legates there shulde be revoked or noo. The circumstaunce wherof [an]d what hath been doon and said therin, your Highnes shal understande by our commen letters which we have writen to my Lorde Legates Grace; but, to saye as I conjecture, I thinke that matier was moved but for a stop of our other sutes[1], and that it is not ernestely ment. And albeit there is mencion of the Quene in that matier as thowe she shuld have a proctor for the same, yet the Pope, two daye⟨s⟩ bifore, in an other communication, said that thEmperour had advertised him howe the Quene wolde doo nothing in this matier, in suyng ne speking to any man[†], for the let, delaye, or hindraunce of this matier, but as your Highnes shal wil and commaunde her to doo; and that thEmperour said he wolde therfore more ernestely loke unto the cause himself. I merveled moch when the Pope said this, and me thought he spake it as thought he wolde we shulde signifie the same unto your Highnes, and I noted it the more for[2] bicause your Highnes had commaunded me to enquire out who shulde be here the Quenes proctour; and it semed spoken for the nones as to put me out of doubte therof. But whither the Pope hath this writen out of Spayne or out of Englande I wot not what to saye. But it semed straunge to us to rede in Cardinal Campegius letters that neyther he ne Campanus made, on the Popes behaulf, any promyse to your Highnes, but oonly in general termes; considering that upon these special termes *de plenitudine potestatis*, and trust that the Pope wolde use that in your Highnes cause, I was sent hither, like as in my instructions [is] c[ont]ayned; which fayling, your Highnes, I doubte not, right well remembrith howe Master Wolman, Master Bel, and I shewed your Highnes such thinges as wer to be required, not to be impetrable. My trust is that your Highnes wil accepte in good parte my true harte and good wil, which according to my most[†] bounden dutie shal never want, but be holly applyed where your Highnes shal commaunde, without respecte or regarde of any other lyving creature; being very sory to see your Highnes cause handled in this sorte. But your Highnes hath soo moch vertue in youe, wherof God is to be thanked, as may suffice to converte other mennes faultes in to goodnes, to your Highnes gret glory, renowne, and immortal fame. Which is al that canne be said after my poore wit herin, considering that your Highnes hath been not wel handled, ne according to your merites, by the Pope or sum other; it becomith not me to arrecte the blame cer-

---

1 ne *c.c.*   2 for *writ. over something else*

taynly to any man. And the Pope showith Cardinal Campegius letters
for his discharge, which thing your Highnes shall moch better judge
and considre by your high wisedom thenne I canne wryte; most humbly
desiring your Highnes that, being in these termes with the Popes Holynes, we may knowe of your Highnes what to doo further.

As touching the bulles to be here impetrate for your Highnes, I have
spoken with the Popes Holynes, and he is content in al poyntes[1] to
graunte as I required him, saving in that matter *de animadversione in
clericos*, to the which he wolde not absolutely assent, but said he wolde
with the Cardinal Sanctorum Quatuor divise that shuld be to your
Highnes satisfaction; wishing therin that he might graunte as easely our
other peticions, which he knowith your Highnes to have more to harte,
as he may these; adding by and by that he wolde, for the welth of
Cristendom, the Quene wer in her grave; and, as he thought, thEmperour would be therof most glad of al; saying also that he thought like
as thEmperour hath destroyed the temperaltes of the Church, soo shal
she[2] be the cause of the destruction of the spiritualties; making exclama-
tion of his misfortune in who⟨se⟩ personne these two adversites should
chaunce, and upon the occasion of that famyle. Whenne we speke with
him we thinke we shulde have al thing, and in the ende his counsail
denyeth al. By reason the Cardinal Sanctorum Quatuor hath been sik,
and is every other day sikely, and for the most parte whenne the
Cardinal is hol the Pope is sik, we have yet noo expedition of the saide
bulles; trusting that your Highnes wil have consideration of these
lettes accordingly. Praying Almighty God to preserve your most noble
and royal astate. From Rome the iiij[th] daye of Maye.

Your Highnes most humble subject,
servaunt, and dayly oratour,

STEVEN GARDYNER

Addressed: To the Kinges Highnes.

1 s *c.o.*   2 *writ. over* be

17

11. *To* Casale *and* Vannes

Westminster, 25 June, [1529]

B.M., Vit. B, xi, 172.* *L.P.*, iv, 5715. *St. P.*, vii, 190. Ellis, ser. 3, ii, 157. A copy in B.M., Arundel 151, 141-2, preserves the address, lacking in the original.

> The advocation of the King's cause to Rome would alienate England and undo Wolsey.

After my most harty commendations, these shalbe to advertise youe that, our Lorde be thanked, I am savely arryved here, and have distinctely and at good lenght declared unto the Kinges Highnes in what astate and condition I left his affayres there, with your diligent and good acquital in his affayres; for the which his Highnes geveth unto youe his most harty thankes. And albeit ye be nowe advertised, aswell by this post as by other letters to youe bifore directed, howe ye shal deameane your self in the letting of the advocation of his Graces cause at thEmperours agentes or the Quenes pursute, yet I thought convenient by these my letters to advertise youe that this advocation of the cause is gretly pondred and considred here, not oonly with the Kinges Grace, but also with al other nobles of the realme; for in cace the Pope, as God forbydde, shulde advocate the said cause, not only therby the Kinges Grace and al his nobles shulde decline from the Pope and See Apostolique, but also the same shulde redounde to my Lorde Cardinalles, our commen masters, utter undoyng. I doubte not therfor ye wil forsee that matier accordingly. And where as by the Kinges letters to youe directed synnes my departing thens, ye wer advised and instructed to make an appellation and protestacion *tanquam a non vicario ad verum vicarium Iesu Christi*, bicause the Kinges Highnes perceyvith by your letters, wryten in cifre to his Grace, that the said appellation might irritate the Popes Holynes, and rather hindre his[1] cause thenne doo good, his plea*sour* therfor is that ye shal forbere to make any such protestacion or appellation, notwithstanding any clause conteyned in his said letters to the contrary, but that ye shal by al dulce and pleasaunte meanes enterteyne the Popes Holynes in good benevolence and favo*ur* towardes the Kinges Highnes, soo that by exasperating him he doo noon acte anewe to the derogacion of his commission and processe to be made therupon here. And as towching the commen affayres of peace

1 it(?) caus *c.o.*

and other the Kinges mynde, I remitte youe to my Lord Legates letters.

Furthermore, I shal desire youe to remembre, and specially youe, Master Peter, that my Lordes Graces bulles for his colleges of Oxforde and Ipswich be expedite with al diligence according to such instructi[ons] as I left with youe; wherof[1] parte[t] be nowe renewed by such minutes as my Lordes Grace sendith unto youe concernyng the same; in al the rest to be sped, to folowe such instructions as I left with youe. Thus most hartely fare ye wel. From [2]Westmester, the xxv day of June.

Yours assuredly to my
litel power,

STEVEN GARDYNER[3]

Address (from Arundel copy): To the Right Honourable Sir Gregorie de Cassalis, Knight, and Master Peter Vannes, the Kinges orator with the Popes Holynes.

---

1 *alt. from* which   2 We *writ. over* Lo
3 *something below signature cut off, leaving the tops of a few letters and, near the end,* ter

INTRODUCTORY NOTE TO NOS. 12–40

These letters were written while Gardiner was Principal Secretary to Henry VIII.

No. 12 fixes the date of his entry upon his new duties, 28 July, 1529. The next eighteen letters (Nos. 13–30) were written to Wolsey between that date and 6 October, 1529. Wolsey, because of the failure of the legatine court to give sentence, was out of favour, but still in office, and Henry had not yet discovered to what extent he could do without him. Gardiner, who was in attendance upon the King, communicated to the Cardinal Henry's wishes and queries, chiefly concerning his possible citation to Rome, as a result of the advocation of his case thither (*see* above, p. 2), and his relations with France arising out of the Treaty of Cambrai of 5 August, 1529. The dates of the undated letters in this group are determined by our knowledge of the King's movements during this period (*cf.* Pollard, *Wolsey*, 237 n.) assisted by the fact that Gardiner, when he does not date the letter, gives the place of writing and the day of the week. The dates assigned to them in *L.P.* appear to be correct in all but two cases (Nos. 13, 25). For Wolsey's replies *see* *L.P.*, IV, 5865–5923, *passim*. Nine more letters from Wolsey to Gardiner, written after his fall, December, 1529–August, 1530, are calendared in *L.P.*, but Gardiner's replies seem no longer to be extant.

Of the rest, No. 36, in which he at once excuses and defends himself for opposing the King's demands in Convocation in 1532, is one of the most revealing of all his letters. No. 37 is significant as showing his appreciation of the place which Cromwell had attained in the counsels of the King. It is likewise distinctly personal, and the allusion near the end reminds one of *Othello*, I, iii, 364: 'There are many events in the womb of time which will be delivered.' The others are short notes, of which two (Nos. 33, 34) are the only extant letters written while on his diplomatic mission to the French Court early in 1532.

12. *To* VANNES

Greenwich, 28 July, [1529]

B.M., Vit. B, xi, 217.* *L.P.*, iv, 5798. Pocock, i, 265. A copy in B.M., Arundel 151, 143 v., preserves the address, lacking in the original. English abstract in *L.P.*

Begins his duties as Principal Secretary to the King to-day.

Mi Petre salutem plurimam. De literis tuis habeo gratias maximas. Utcunque res cesserint, tua opera gratissima est, et Regie Maiestati et Reverendissimo Domino. De hoc te iubeo esse securum. Me habes ex animo amicum, ad omnem† occasionem, in qua res tuas promovere queam. De rebus publicis ex literis Reverendissimi intelliges. Ego aule mancipatus, liber esse non possum, sed melioris conditionis libertinus. Secretarii¹ munus obeo quod ad literas pertinet, et sum a libellis. Quid futurum sit nescio; nam hodie primum aulam ingredior; fortune nostre progressum tu ut² spero brevi videbis. Expecto ut tecum afferas quod bullarum superest expediendum. Commendabis me omnibus amicis meis. Et bene vale. Ex Grenewico, die xxviij Julii.

Totus tuus,

STEPHANUS GARDINERUS

Address (*from Arundel copy*): Reverendo Domino Domino Petro Vannes, Serenissimi Angliae et Franciae Regis etc. Secretario, et eiidem³ apud Sanctissimum Dominum nostrum oratori.

13. *To* WOLSEY

Greenwich, [28 July, 1529]

R.O., S.P. 1, 55, 29–30.* *L.P.*, iv, 5819. Pocock, i, 248.

The King likes Campeggio's promise (*cf.* No. 16); why Gardiner cannot come to Wolsey in person.

Pleasith it your Grace to understande that at my repare unto the Kinges Highnes this mornyng, I shewed unto his Grace the pollicitacion conceyved by my Lord Campegius, which liked his⁴ Highnes very wel; insomoch as he said it coulde not be better devised, ne with more ample wordes. I shulde have cummen unto your Grace, to have declared this

---

1 s *c.o.*   2 sei(?) *c.o.*   3 *MS.*, eiisdem   4 *alt. from* hig

21

by mouth, but that his Highnes, having bifore my cummyng appointed me a chambre and spoken for myn allowaunce, gave me special commaundement not to departe hens, with this addicion, *nescitis neque diem neque horam.* Soo as looking this night that his Highnes wil cal for me *ut experiatur et cognoscat* howe I wil folowe his Graces commaundement in that behaulf, I dare not departe hens; trusting that your Grace wil consider this accordingly. Thus I praye Almighty God to preserve your good Grace. From Grenewich this[1] Wedonsday at afternone.

Your Graces most humble servaunt
and dayly bedeman,

STEVEN GARDYNER

Addressed: To my Lorde Legates good Grace.
Endorsed: Doctor Stevyns letter.

14. *To* WOLSEY

Greenwich, [1 August, 1529]

R.O., S.P. 1, 55, 25–6.* *L.P.*, IV, 5816.

Concerning Viscount Rochford's (Anne Boleyn's father's) claim for a half-year's rent from Durham (Henry VIII had given him the revenues of the vacant see as from Michaelmas, 1528, but Wolsey's officers had retained the money—Pollard, *Wolsey*, 236, 323 n.).

Pleasith it your Grace to understande that yester night I reaported unto the Kinges Highnes your Graces aunswer after the best facion I coulde, and I assure your Grace it was very[2] wel accepted and specially in that point: your Grace said ye wer mynded to have brought al to the Kinges Highnes at the[3] yeres ende, and that as yet ye had receyved nothing, and that, upon declaracion of the Kinges Highnes mynde and entent, your Grace conformed youe therunto and takith that haulf yeres rent to be due unto his Highnes and not unto your Grace. I have spoken with my Lord of Rocheforde and shewed unto him howe your Grace offerith to wryte your letters to such as wer your officers in Durham, to cause them to make payment here, with al diligence, of the haulf yeres rent due at Our Ladyes Dayes last past; for the which he most hertely thankith your Grace and sayth he shal[4] requite it with like kindnes; saying further

1 *alt. from* the 2 veryly *w.* ly *c.o.* 3 ther *w.* r *c.o.* 4 dly *c.o.*

unto me that bicause he wold not be noted to have laboured for the atteyning of that haulf yeres rent[1] from your Grace, and that percace, besides the thing, it shulde be displeasour to your Grace to have it soo[t] noted, he said[2] he coulde be content to receyve the haulf yeres rent for that tyme at your Graces hand, without making buysines therin for the receipt therof at your Graces officers handes. And if your Grace thinke this latter waye good, thenne your pleasour may be to take ordre that tomorowe summe[3] waye be taken with my said Lord of Rocheforde for payment of the said haulf yeres rent, which he rekennith to amounte to the summe of MCC⟨1200⟩. And if that liketh not your Grace,—for to[t] that overture I wolde nayther saye ye nor naye, and sumwhat I doubted whither your Grace wolde like it or noo—but not being content therwith, it maye please youe, according to your first offre, to[4] write the said letters and to delyver them to this bringer, [t]for he[t] is sent for that purpose[5], and the same letters to be writen after such tenour as payment may be made of the money bifore Barthelmewetyde. I promised my said Lord of Rocheforde that he shuld have your Graces letters to morowe in the mornyng; upon trust wherof, he sendith his owne servaunt, this berer.

I sende also unto your Grace the bil, signed with the Kinges hande, desiring the same that it[6] may be sealed and remitted by this messanger. I have noon other matier to wryte unto your Grace, but praye God to preserve youe in god helth. From Grenewich, this Sondaye in the mornyng.

I sende your Grace also the Kinges gistes[7].

Your Graces most humble
and daly bedeman,

S. GARDYNER

Addressed: To my Lorde Legates good Grace.
Endorsed: A letter of Maister Stevyns.

1 inpre(?) *c.o.*	2 to *c.o.*	3 of *c.o.*
4 n(?) *c.o.*	5 as(?) *c.o.*	6 be *c.o.*
7 del *c.o.*		

15. *To* WOLSEY

Greenwich, 1 August, [1529]

R.O., S.P. 1, 55, 27–8.* *L.P.,* IV, 5817.

Sends dispatches from Edward Lee, ambassador in Spain; the King asks favour to John Cooke, and will gladly come to the More.

Pleasith it your Grace to understande that synnes the writing of my last letters, I receyved letters from Master Almoner out of Spayne, directed to the Kinges Highnes and your Grace. I presented al unto his Highnes, but he wold breke up noon of your Graces, but willed me to sende them unto your Grace with that also which is directed unto him, conteyning, as your Grace shal perceyve, noo matier of importaunce.

His Highnes also willed me to signifie unto your Grace that he desireth the same to shewe your favour to John Coke, your Graces registre of Winchestre, in his sutes to your Grace. The Kinges Highnes, put in remembraunce by oon of his chambre, spake unto me after this wise: 'Master Stevens, oon Coke, hath sutes to my Lorde Cardinal[1] concerning his office and other matiers. I have oones spoken unto my Lord in it, to be good unto him, and I praye youe by your letters, which ye shal nowe write unto him, shewe him that I eftsones desire him soo to be.' These wer his Highnes wordes *in forma.*

I have noon other matier to write, but praye God to preserve your good Grace. At Grenewich, this Sonday at night, the first day of August.

Master Treasourer moved the Kinges Highnes howe your Grace[2] is mynded to receyve him and his trayne at the More and defraye his charges, wherwith his Highnes was wel content.

Your Graces most humble
and dayly bedeman,

STEVEN GARDYNE[R]

Addressed: To my Lorde Legates good Grace.
Endorsed: A letter of Maister Stevyns, primo Augusti.

1 *writ. over an erasure*   2 was *c.o.*

16. *To* WOLSEY

Greenwich, [2 August, 1529]

B.M., Vit. B, XII, 163–4.* Mutilated. *L.P.*, IV, 5821. Pocock, I, 266.

Henry agrees with Wolsey's opinion that the advocation of the divorce case
to Rome is the result of the Pope's alliance with the Emperor; Wolsey is to
induce Campeggio to keep the advocation from coming into the Queen's hands,
and to persuade her not to try to have the King's citation to Rome comprised
in it (*cf.* Nos. 25–8); observations on Campeggio's promise (*cf.* No. 13).

Pleasith it your Grace to understande that ha[ving no oppor]tunite
yesternight to shewe such letters as Master B[oner] left with[1] me unto
the Kinges Highness, this morn[yng I shewed] the same unto his
Grace, with the hol circumstaunc[e howe they] came unto your Graces
handes, and also what is y[our Graces] opinion in depeching of the
currour without altera[tion of the] letters devised, and that your Grace
wel perceyveth[2] the [making] of the liege bitwene the Pope and thEmperour to have [been the] cause of graunting forth the advocation, and
that i[t was] likely a special article to be capitulate concernyng [the]
cause, with a general capitulacion *pro defensione* [*pacis*] *et iurium*. Al which
your Graces opinions his Highn[es] alowith, and desirith your Grace
that the post d[eparte] without any innovation. It may please the sa[me
to] speke with my Lord Campegius concerning the t[ermes] of the advocation according to his promyse, a[nd] as nowe it apperith to be graunted
and sent, [so] he wil use all wayes and meanes possible [to get] it in to
his handes or it[3] cumme to the Quenes [handes, if] it be possible; for
his Highnes fearith lest she w[olde not] facylly agre to the alteracion,
but use it as it m[aketh] most to her benefit. Wherfor in case it canno[t
be] but that it shal first cumme unto the Quenes h[andes, the] Kinges
Highnes desirith your Grace to instructe [my Lord] Campegius what
wordes he shal use to the Q[uene], moving and persuading her[t] to be
content to procure [that noo] such thing be comprised in the said advocation a[s shal] irritate the Kinges Highnes and his nobles, and [that]
a king in his owne realme may not be violen[ted; with] such other
reasons and persuasions as your Grace of [your] hight wisedom canne
adde unto the same. This [thing] his Highnes hath gretly to harte, and,
whyles I wrote this letter, sent for me twyes to speke with me ther[e], and

1 you *c.o.*   2 *alt. from* perceyved   3 to *c.o.*

25

at the last tyme asked me for the Cardinal Campegius pollicitacion[1], which I sent yesterdaye unto your Grace. Wherunto his Highnes wolde adde in the first parte, where he saith, *quod nunquam dicet aut aperiet secreta cause*, in the future tense[2], a verbe of the preter tense *quod hactenus non dixit nec aperuit*; for his Highnes said that the said Campegius, having already advertised the Pope *de preterito* may keep his promes, and yet the Kinges Highnes purpose frustrate. I said to that, *quod facta pactis non mutantur*, and if he had already shewed it to the Pope, there is noo remedy by promes; but I thought veryly he had not, and that I have herde him soo said and sworn. Nevertheles I said your Grace might facyly eftsones, for[3] his Highnes satisfaction, knowe that of the said Cardinal Campegius, and be assured of the truth by his oth, *quod hactenus non significavit Pontifici quid illi de causa videatur*, for in the pollicitacion it coulde not be inserted conveniently. Wherunto his Highnes agreed, and desired youer Grace to remembre this in your[4] conference with the said Cardinal Campegius.

Moreover his Highnes willed me to signifie unto your Grace that he hath sent for the ambassadour of Fraunce to be with his Grace here at afternone, entending to shewe unto him these newes of the lege bitwen the Pope and thEmperour, and of thEmperours descent in to Italy; desiring your Grace to speke semblably with thambassadours of Venyse and Ferrare, and to shewe unto them howe this liege is made *in capita ipsorum*, and that it shalbe, therfor, necessary that they [see] unto it ernestly in tyme.

I wolde gladly have commen unto your Grace, b[ut I] ne dare departe hens. Thus I pray Almight[y God] preserve your good Grace. At Grenewich this Mo[nday][5].

Your Graces most humble servaunt
and dayly bedeman,

STEVEN GARDYNER

Addressed: To my Lorde Legates good Grace.
Endorsed: Letters from Master Doctour Stevens.

1 myn *c.o.*	2 his Highnes wold *c.o.*	3 the *c.o.*
4 gr *c.o.*	5 *or* mo[rning](?)	

17. *To* WOLSEY

Waltham, 4 August, [1529]

R.O., S.P. 1, 55, 36–7.* *L.P.*, IV, 5825. Ellis, ser. 3, I, 345.

Henry's fear of the sweating sickness; he will not come to the More but to Tittenhanger.

Pleasith it your Grace to understande that receyving your letters yester night I shewed the continue of them and also red the same unto the Kinges Highnes this mornyng, saving the latter parte concernyng the letters of the King of Denmarke. And where as your Grace in the secounde parte of your letter wrote howe glad ye wolde be to receyve the Kinges Highnes at the More, at that point his Highnes said that, synnes his determination to goo thither, he was advertised howe, at Rikemansworth and other townes aboute the More, certain this yere and of late have had the swet; the oonly name and voyce wherof is soo terrible and fearful in his Highnes eeres that he dare in noowise approch unto the place where it is[t] noysed to have been, and that therfor his Highnes will not goo thither, but in the stede of that goo to Titennehanger[1], and take such chere of your Grace there as he shulde have had at the More; mynding, according to his former gistes, to departe from Barnet upon Saterday cumme sevenightes, and after dyner to goo that night to Titenhanger, and there to be Sondaye al daye, and Monday after brekefast to departe. I said I thought Tytenhanger to lytel to receyve his Highnes[2]. Wherunto his Highnes answerd that your Grace, as he doubted not ye wolde, removing for the tyme with your company to Saint Albons, it shulde serve of the while he wolde tarye there[t]. Which resolution his Grace willed me to signifie unto yours.

Your[3] Graces letters to Master Strangwish wer very wel and thankefully accepted of al parties.

Other letters or newes here be noone, but that the Kinges Highnes is mery, thanked be God; Who preserve your Grace. At Waltham the iiij[th] day of August.

Your Graces most humble
and dayly bedeman,

STEVEN GARDYNER

Addressed: To my Lorde Legates good Grace.
Endorsed: Letters of Maister Stevyns, iiij[to] Augusti.

1 *alt. from* Tikennehanger   2 and *c.o.*   3 *writ.* yours

18. *To* WOLSEY

Hunsdon, 6 August, [1529]

R.O., S.P. 1, 55, 43–4.* *L.P.*, IV, 5831.

Possible amity with Denmark; Henry desires names of the borough towns
(*see* No. 30).

Pleasith it your Grace to understande that this mornyng I shewed unto
the Kinges Highnes your Graces letters of answer to myn, concerning
his Highnes cummyng to Tytenhanger, which liked him very wel, and
upon occasion of the latter clause†, did expedite first my Lord Dacres
byl, which I sende unto your Grace herewith. Secondly, I spake unto
his Grace for the expedition of Doctor Remuchius¹, which in nowise his
Highnes coulde like, that any charge shulde be committed unto him
from his Highnes, saying it was not his hounour to seke for amitie upon
the King of Denmarke. And where I said your Grace wolde soo ordre
it that sute shulde be made from the King of Denmarke unto his Highnes, his Grace said that it coulde never be soo compassed by Remuchius, who, being borne under the King of Denmarkes obeisaunce,
wolde not kepe secrete any thing committed unto him here. In conclusion, his Highnes said that summe wordes might be by your Grace
spoken unto Remuchius, and if he coulde of himself conduce the matier
soo, without any commission or instructions from hens, that the King
of Denmarke shulde make suche sute, it were wel doone. And other
answer thenne this I had not of his Grace concerning that matier;
saving his Highnes signed a letter, which, at my Lord of Norfolkes desire, I made to the King of Denmarke, for spedy delyvery of the ship
of Newcastel.

As towching my Lorde of Worcetour, his Highnes tolde me noo
special matier, but said it wer wel doon your Grace divised sumwhat
for instructions to be sent unto him.

His Highnes is very desirous to have the names of the borough²
townes and desireth your Grace to sende the same unto him. I have writen
to Master Pexsal for them but, as I here saye, he is not with your Grace.

As yet here hath arryved noo letters from any parte, besides those
which I sente unto your Grace out of Spayne, which is to the Kinges
Highnes gret merveyle. These two dayes I have been forth from morne
to night ahunting, by the Kinges Highnes commaundement.

1 *L.P. erroneously reads* Kamuchius; *the first two letters are clearly* Re; *these
are followed by five minims*
2 tymes *c.o.*

28

Thus I praye Almighty God to preserve your good Grace. At Hundesdon, the vj[th] day of August.

Your Graces most humble
and dayly bedeman,

STEVEN GARDYNER

Addressed: To my Lord Legates good Grace.

Endorsed: Master Stevins.

19. *To* WOLSEY

Barnet, [12 August, 1529]

R.O., S.P. 49, 2, 107–8.* *L.P.*, IV, 5844. *St. P.*, IV, 79.

Concerning money for the Earl of Angus and his uncle, Archibald Douglas of Kilspindie.

Pleasith it your Grace to understande that yesternight I shewed unto the Kinges Highnes such resolution as your Grace hath taken with thErle of Anguish, which liked his Grace very wel, and specially in the maner of delyvering them such money as his Highnes geveth them for ther entertenement; that is to say, to be delyvered without mention of yerely entertenement with a certain somme, as your Grace had devised; with that also that your Grace delyver the said money unto them there, bifore ther repare unto his Highnes, to thintent they maye geve thankes unto his Grace therfor. But to augment the portion of Archebolde that it shulde be a hundred powndes, the Kinges Highnes cannot be by me persuaded. His Grace is content to sende a gentilman; and, not resolvyng himself ne directly denying to sende the Capitain of Barwik, thinkith Master Ratclyf a very mete personage. I had noo convenient laysour to speke therof at lenght.

As towching the cummyng of thErle to[1] take his leave at the Kinges Highnes, his Grace wolde that this daye by none the said Erle shulde repare to the towne of Barnet; and there bayting in summe inne, which to be here[2] appointed I[3] have spoken to Master Controller, my Lord of Norfolke shal geve knowlege unto him where he shal repare unto the Kinges Highnes.

I shulde have cumme myself, but the Kinges Highnes specially commaunded me to tary.

1 h c.o.　　2 re writ. over something else　　3 s c.o.

I shewed and communicated al thing to my Lord of Norfolke, who liked al thing very wel.

Thus I pray Almighty God to preserve your good Grace. At Barnet, this Thursday.

Your Graces most humble
and dayly bedeman,

STEVEN GARDYNER

Addressed: To my Lorde Legates good Grace.

Endorsed: Maister Stevyns.

20. *To* WOLSEY

Woodstock, 24 August, [1529]

R.O., S.P. 1, 55, 72–3.* *L.P.*, IV, 5869.

Could not show Wolsey's letters to the King because of moving to-day (to Woodstock); the peace (with Charles V, proclaimed 27 August—*see* Pollard, *Wolsey*, 235) is to be proclaimed.

Pleasith it your Grace to understande that, receyving such letters as your Grace sent unto me by your servaunt, this berer, I wolde have shewed the same unto the Kinges Highnes incontinently, if I coulde have had any opportunite therunto. But, being removing daye, there was noon occasion to shewe the letters and, as for the matier in them conteyned, ⟨it⟩ hath been alredy by the Bishops of London and of Bath reaported unto the same. Nevertheles, I thought convenient to dimisse your Graces servaunt, although as yet, neyther concernyng such pointes as be in your Graces first letters ne yet these last, I knowe nothing of the Kinges pleas*our*, saving that, bifore the arryval of your Graces letters, his[1] Grace willed me to signifie unto yours that his mynde is, proclamation of the peace with such ceremonies and solempnites as have be⟨en⟩ doon in Fraunce, and, according to your Graces discretion, ⟨to⟩ be doon as soone as conveniently may be in London and Calays. The commyng of Langes doth holde in suspense the Kinges Highnes resolution in al other matier, but that his Grace hath shewed me sum-what of his[2] mynde for a letter to be writen to the Bishop of Worcetour, which I have not yet made. Other matier I knowe noon worthy

1 <i>alt. from</i> he   2 l <i>c.o.</i>

advertisement, but praye Almighty God to preserve your Grace. From Wodstok, the xxiiij^ti of August.

Your Graces most humble
and dayly bedeman,

STEVEN GARDYNER

Addressed: To my Lorde Legates good Grace.

Endorsed: Doctor Stevyns, xxiiij Augusti.

21. *To* WOLSEY

Woodstock, 28 August, [1529]

R.O., S.P. 1, 55, 84–5.* *L.P.*, IV, 5875. *St. P.*, I, 337.

The King desires a copy of the Treaty of Madrid, and Wolsey's opinion on present French demands (*cf.* Wolsey's reply, *L.P.*, IV, 5881, and subsequent entries relating to the same subject); he also desires a benefice for Nicholas Delburgo.

Pleasith it your Grace to understande, that forasmoch as Langes is here arryved from the French King, with the qualifications of the treatie of Madrel, the copy wherof the Kinges Highnes supposith to be with youer Grace, his Grace desireth yours to sende the same unto him with your Graces opinion upon such demaundes as the French Kinge¹, by the said Langes, makith at this tyme; the copye wherof, and al other writinges presented unto the Kinges Highnes, I, by his Graces commaundement, sende unto yours herwith; advertising your Grace, that the Kinges Highnes, not as yet openyng any part of his mynde eyther to thambassadours or any other of his Counsail, what answer to make in them, desirith your Grace, with al^t diligence possible, first to shewe your opinion concernyng the same, unto the knowlege wherof he differrith his resolution in that behaulf.

His Highnes willed me also to write unto your Grace in the favour of Frier Nicolas of Oxforde, for his capacite to be sped out of hande, and a benefice to be provyded for him, as sone as any shalbe voyde, according to your Graces promyse, as his Highnes sayth, in that behaulf.

It may please your Grace to remitte, by this berer, the articles of the treaties, forasmoch as here bee noo copies of them, and the Kinges Highnes willed me to sende them with spede. Al other matiers slepe tyl

1 *alt. from* Kinges

31

this be answerd unto. Thus I pray Almighty God to preserve your good Grace. At Wodstok, the xxviij of August.

Your Graces most humble
and dayly bedeman,

STEVEN GARDYNER

Addressed: To my Lord Legates good Grace.
Endorsed: Maister Stevyns, the xxviij of August.

22. *To* WOLSEY

Woodstock, 30 August, [1529]

B.M., Titus B, i, 310–11.* *L.P.*, iv, 5890. *St. P.*, i, 340.

Sends dispatches for Ghinucci, Bishop of Worcester, ambassador in Spain, for Wolsey to read and seal; the King desires Wolsey's opinion on two matters relative to the ratification of the Treaty of Cambrai, and wants copy of Treaty of Amiens, 1527. (*Cf.* Wolsey's reply, *L.P.*, iv, 5893.)

Pleasith it your Grace to understande that nowe at the last the Kinges Highnes is resolved upon the depech of my Lord of Worcetours servaunt, after such forme as your Grace shal perceyve by the Kinges letters directed to the said Bishop; which, according to the Kinges commaundement, I sende open to your Grace to be seen by the same and sealed there. The tenour of them is according to the Kinges instructions in al pointes, not soo wel expressed as your Grace shulde have doon it there, but as in that such was the Kinges pleasour. And glad I am that my said Lorde of Worcetours servaunt is depeched, oon waye[1] or other. The Kinges Highnes hath rewarded the Bishoppes said servaunt with c⟨100⟩ crownes, which Master Tuke hath delyvered unto him. As towching the advertisement of your Grace, sent by Master Tuke, for making the said Bishop ambassadour to thEmperour, I thinke the Kinges Highnes wil otherwise resolve himself; and, at the lest, knowing therof, and differring thexpedition of these letters from yesterday to this daye, as to delyvere and consulte in the meane season therupon, this daye willed me to send forth the same, as they be, unto your Grace, by the said Bishoppes servaunt, as afore; and more I knowe not in that behaulf.

The Kinges Highnes, in goyng forth a huntyng, sodenly called me

1 alt. from wayes

unto him, and willed to write unto your Grace, for knowlege of your advise and opinion, in these pointes folowing:

First, whether thEmperour, not ratifying the peace concluded nowe at Cambraye with the French King, the Kinges Highnes shuld demaunde and take the ratification of the peace concluded with him.

Item, whether, the said ratificacions not yet passed, it wer convenient for the Kinges Highnes to delyver thEmperours bondes, and to geve acquitaunces of the same to the French King, and soo doo an acte in discharge of thEmperour, the peace concluded not yet brought to effecte, ne by delyveraunce of the childern put in execution; which fayling, of necessite the wer shuld retourne.

The Kinges Highnes oonly proponed these questions, without debating or reasonyng the same, and desirith moch to knowe your Graces advise and counsail; and that it may please the same to sende hither such treaties as wer concluded in Fraunce when your Grace was there, with that also which was nowe concluded at Cambray and brought to your Grace by my Lord of London.

This mornyng, upon point of the Kinges going forth, which was very erly and afore he hath at other tymes accustumed, arryved here, from your Grace, Master Doctour Boner, with your Graces mynde and opinion upon such articles as, by the Kinges commaundement, I wrote of unto the same in my last letters; wherin me semith your Grace hath taken very excessive paynes and labours, with gret study and buysnes of mynde, to depech so moch matier by writing and instructions in soo lytel tyme; which I shal extende and set forth to the Kinges Highnes, as my dutie and observaunce towardes your Grace requirith. Nevertheles, for spedy speking with the King, and to speke at laysour, I reckonne gret difficulte; and as for this night, I am ought of hope, by reason the Kinges Highnes is out on hunting, and usith, as your Grace knowith, to cumme in very late; but I shal doo therin the best I can, and sende your Grace answer by the said Master Boner. Unto which tyme I shal noo further molest the same, but pray Almighty God to preserve your good Grace. At Wodstok, the penultime of August.

Your Graces most humble
and dayly bedeman,

STEVEN GARDYNER

Addressed: To my Lord Legates good Grace.
Endorsed: Doctor Stevyns, penultimo Augusti.

33

23. *To* WOLSEY

Woodstock, 31 August, [1529]

R.O., S.P. 1, 55, 100–1.* *L.P.*, IV, 5894. *St. P.*, I, 342.

Does not think Wolsey's suggested qualification of the Treaty of Madrid
serves the King's purpose better than the present treaty. (*Cf.* Pollard, *Wolsey*,
282, on Wolsey's change of attitude to the French alliance at this time.)

Pleasith it your Grace to understande that the Kinges Highnes willed
me, on his behaulf, to geve unto your Grace[1] his most harty thankes for
your gret paynes and labours taken in answeryng, with such diligence,
to the articles proponed by the French oratours, wherin his Highnes
thinkith your Grace hath considered asmoch as coulde be excogitate and
imagined; but what resolution his Grace wil take in the same, I knowe
not as yet, and he hath put it over with thambassadours untyl his
retourne from Langle, whither he goth tomorowe, and retournith not
bifore Saturday ⟨4 Sept.⟩.

As in that parte of your Graces instructions where your Grace semeth
to suspecte sumwhat of the French men, and impute unto them the not
observation of ther convenauntes [2]agred upon at Amyas, towching the
qualification of the treatie of Madryl, the Kinges Highnes, moch moved
therwith, and, adhering to your Graces opinion in that behaulf, was
moch kindled and waxed warme and thought himself not wel handled
by them; in such sorte as, not speking with me, that evenyng willed my
⟨Lorde of⟩ Rocheforde to sende for me and to examine the treatie of
Madryl with your Graces instructions; which we dyd, and this mornyng
had moch reasonyng with his Highnes in that behaulf. Nevertheles, at
the laste it appered unto his Highnes, the treatie of Madryl, without
that qualification divised by your Grace, not to be soo daungerous, as
your Grace had noted it, in al poyntes; as Master Boner shal shewe unto
your Grace; most humbly desiring your Grace to considre it with this
also, *quod preterita[3] dolere magis quam corrigere possumus*, and that, in
very dede, your Graces qualification, to saye truly to your Grace, doth
noo more serve the Kinges purpose thenne as the treatie is nowe
cowched. Thus bolde I am to write unto your Grace thus playnly, desiring the same to take it in good parte. The specialtes of al other pointes

1 on his behaulf *c.o.* 2 g *writ. over* in
3 *first* t *in* preterita *writ. over* e

34

I have shewed[1] to Master Boner. Praying Almighty God to preserve your good Grace. From Wodstok, the last day of August.

Your Graces most humble
and dayly bedeman,

STEVEN GARDYNER

Addressed: To my Lorde Legates good Grace.
Endorsed: Doctor Stevyns, ultimo Augusti.

24. *To* WOLSEY

Woodstock, 3 September, [1529]

R.O., S.P. 1, 55, 120–1.* *L.P.*, IV, 5918.

Defends himself for disagreeing with Wolsey on the Treaty of Madrid.

Pleasith it your Grace to understande that I have receyved of Master Edwardes such treaties as it was the Kinges pleaso*u*r I shuld sende for unto your Grace, which, after the Kinges Highnes hath seen them, I shal not fayle to remitte unto your Grace accordingly.

And as towching your Graces letters which I receyved by the said Master Edwardes, the Kinges Highnes not being here and I by his Graces commaundement now reparing unto the same, canne neyther wryte any resolution to your Grace of the latter parte of your Graces said letters ne, at soo good lenght as I wold, answer to the first parte of the same. Nevertheles my trust is that your Grace, howe soever your Graces opinion in interpretacion of the treatie of Madryl can be defended or otherwise, wil not therin judge otherwise of me, as I perceyve by your Graces letters ye doon not, *quam ut boni viri officio functus videar contradicendo,* and doon therin my dutie both towardes the Kinges Highnes and also your Grace, who I wel knowe moch tendrith the conservation of the amitie of Fraunce *tanquam opus manuum vestrarum multa laude et gloria dignum*; and, if your Grace[2] had been here and seen howe the Kinges Highnes toke it, wold rather have studied howe by summe benigne interpretacion to have made the best of that which is past remedye thenne to have persisted in the blamyng of not observation of convenauntes on the French partie; upon which, if men shulde nowe

1 pl *c.o.*   2 *alt. from* Graces

35

stike and narowly serch, I doubte not but there be many other poyntes wherin it may be objected unto them that they have not clerely folowed there pactes and convenauntes *et hoc quam foret nunc intempestivum,* your Grace of your high wisedom canne wel consider. And they, being of noo moore importaunce thenne is the omission of that qualificacion your Grace had provided for the first article of the treatie of Madryl, shuld not gretly be prejudicial unto the Kinges Highnes. For suerly, Sir, as it is thought here, the clause of *amici amicorum* and *inimici inimicorum* extendith noo further thenne I did write unto your Grace, and soo it was answerd unto Master Chauncelour of the Duchie nowe at Cambraye by the Chauncelour of Fraunce, as he hath here shewed unto the Kinges Counsail.

Thus having noo more laysour to write unto your Grace, I pray God preserve the same. From Wodstok the iij^de day of Septembre.

> Your Graces most humble
> and dayly bedeman,
>
> STEVEN GARDYNER

Addressed: To my Lord Legates good Grace.
Endorsed: Doctor Stevyns, iij Septembris.

25. *To* WOLSEY

Woodstock, 4 [September, 1529]

B.M., Vit. B, XII, 213.* Mutilated. *L.P.*, IV, 5864. *St. P.*, I, 335.

The King desires Wolsey to prevent the execution of the letters citatorial. (*Cf.* Wolsey's reply, *L.P.*, IV, 5923, and other letters from Wolsey to Gardiner, undated, on the same topic, *ib.*, 5865, 5867–8. See also Nos. 16, 26–8. Gardiner's date of this letter, 4 August, is an evident slip, for the King was at Langley 1–4 September.)

Pleasith it your Grace to understande that yesterday[e I was with] the Kinges Highnes at Langley, and very late in the e[vening, ere] I cam hom, I shewed unto his Grace such letters as your G[race had] sent unto me by the messanger and Master Edwardes, [and those] also which your Grace sent with them from my Lord of [Bath] concernyng thexecution of the letters citatorial, not t . . . . . in the Kinges personne, but oonly in vertue of inhibition, t[o be] secretly notified to your Grace and my Lord Campe[gius]. And as towching your Graces letters in the resolution

36

and declaring of your Graces opinion upon such dowtes as [his] Highnes willed me to signifie unto your Grace, they [be] very pleasaunt, agreable, and acceptable unto the s[ame], and gevith unto your Grace for the same your paynes, l[etters], and studye, his most harty thankes.

As concernyng the continue of my Lord of Bathes [letters] and execution of the inhibition, called always by [the] name of letters citatoriall, and that under payne [of] x^M ⟨10,000⟩ ducates, his Highnes is nowe not the best c[ontent], and mervelith moch *de adiectione pene pecuniar[ie, which]* in the copy sent from Rome was not mencioned; a[nd he] desireth your Grace that the copye of the said in[hibition] and letters citatorial may be with al diligence sent [unto] his[1] Highnes. Nevertheles his† Highnes, hav[ing gret] trust and confidence in your Graces dexterite and [wisedom], doubteth not but your Grace, by good handeling [of the] Cardinal Campegius and the Quenes Counsail, w[il† stay] the execution of those letters citatorial, also in your [handes], and to cause them to be content the same inhibition [be] doon and executed by vertue of the Popes brief [un]to your Grace and men-cyonning that matier, which [I] sende unto the same herwith; which brief, forasmoch as it rehersith and testifith unto youe the cause to be adv[oked], the Kinges Highnes supposith that to be sufficient, wherupon ye may grounde the cessacion of your processe, and that it shulde not be nedeful any such letters citatorial, conteyning matier prejudicial to his personne and royal astate, to be shewed to his subget within his own realme. For which considerations, his Highnes wold gladly this breve to be taken in the lieu of the said letters citatorial, if, upon any such reasons as be bifore rehersed, or other as your Grace, of your high wisedom, can divise, it may be compassed to the satisfaction of the Quenes Counsail, without any suspition to arrise therof that any other respect wer coloured therby. And in cace your Grace, *omnibus modis tentatis,* cannot induce the Quenes Counsail to be content, then your Grace, enterteyning there with youe the Cardinal Campegius and them, to advertise the Kinges Highnes therof, to thintent, upon sight of ther letters citatoriall, the Kinges Highnes maye advertise your Grace what is further in that cace to be doon, and howe your Grace shal resolve that matier with them.

I send your Grace two briefs; the oon, as by the copyes apperith, is towching the advocation; and the other, notificacion of the peace taken bitwen the Pope and thEmperour.

1 his *repeated*

In other matiers nothing is yet resolved, but tomorow the Kinges Highnes entendith to commen with his Counsail in them. Thus, having noon other matier to write, I pray Almighty God to preserve your good Grace. At Wodstok, the iiij^th day of August.

Your Graces most humble
and dayly bedeman,

STEVEN GARDYNER

26. *To* WOLSEY

Woodstock, 7 September, [1529]

R.O., S.P. 1, 55, 122–3.* *L.P.*, IV, 5925. *St. P.*, I, 345.

What Wolsey is to say to the French ambassadors; the King wishes to hear further about the letters citatorial, and desires the release of the heretical Prior of Reading. (*Cf. L.P.*, IV, 4004. The Prior was still in jail in October, 1532—*ib.*, V, 1467.)

Pleasith it your Grace to understande that the Kinges Highnes (like as his Grace willed to write unto yours), ensuyng partly such advise as your Grace wrote unto him, and partly his owne opinion, and other of his Counsail, hath geven answer to Monsieur de Langēs upon such articles as wer by him, on the French Kinges behaulf, proponed unto his Highnes; the copy of which answer geven unto him by wryting and, by the Kinges commaundement, subscribed with my hande, I sende unto your Grace, according to the Kinges pleasour, herwith; adding in the margyne tottes, wherby your Grace may perceyve *omne consilium rei geste*, to thintent that the French ambassadour⟨s⟩ resortyng to your Grace, and communicating ther depech unto the same, as the Kinges Highnes hath willed them to doo, your Grace might say to them conformably to that hath been spoken here; like as the Kinges Highnes desirith your Grace to doo. And in cace the said ambassadours shal speke unto your Grace for obteyning of the Kinges Highnes a letter to be writen by his Grace to the French King, of like tenour to that which the French King sent by the Duke of Suffolke, wherin these ambassadours have alredy pressed the Kinges Highnes, and with good wordes be† put over, the Kinges Highnes desirith your Grace soo to answer them with such facion and wordes, as your Graces high wisedom canne wel divise, as may be to ther satisfaction; and over that to saye to them

38

that, considering the Kinges frank liberalite, *ultro et sponte* shewed, it wer not convenient further to presse him.

Yesternight I red unto the Kinges Highnes your Graces letters, in answer to myne, concernyng thexecution of the letters citatorial; who willed me to write unto your Grace that he giveth unto your Grace his most harty thankes for your labours and paynes taken in that behaulf, and desirith moch to knowe the further resolution in that matier. And where your Grace writeth of the delyveraunce of Cardinal Campegius letters, and bryves to him directed, I assure your Grace there camme never noo such to my handes.

Yesterday here arryved letters from Rome, summe directed to the Kinges Highnes, summe to your Grace and to me and other. By alligh⟨t⟩lywode they wer broken up by the[1] waye, out of the pacquettes, but nevertheles the letters wer not opened; but the Kinges Highnes, being desirous to knowe newes, opened al, and bicause they be moch in cifre, his Highnes desirith your Grace that they may be disciphred there and remitted hither again.

The Kinges Highnes willed me also to write unto your Grace that, being sute made unto him in favor of the Prior of Reding, who, for Luthers opinion, is nowe in prison, and hath been a good season, at your Graces commaundement, that oonles the matier be moch notable and very heynos, he desirith your Grace, at his request, to cause the said Priour to be restord[2] to liberte and disharged of that imprisonment.

Other matier I have noon to write unto your Grace at this tyme, but pray Almighty God to preserve your good Grace. At Wodstok, the vij^th day of Septembre.

The ambassadours of Fraunce have taken ther leave of the King, and be on ther waye towardes your Grace.

Your Graces most humble
and dayly bedeman,

STEVEN GARDYNER

Addressed: To my Lord Legates good Grace.
Endorsed: Master Stevyns, the vij^th daie of Septembre.

1 ther *w*. r *c.o.*   2 restorde *w*. *final* e *c.o.*

27. *To* WOLSEY

Woodstock, 8 September, [1529]

B.M., Vit. B, XII, 167.* *L.P.*, IV, 5928. *St. P.*, I, 347.

The King likes Wolsey's device concerning the citation and trusts it will be brought to effect.

Pleasith it your Grace to understande that, according to your Graces letters, delyvered by Master Doctor Boner and Master Doctor Kerne, I have caused them to speke with the Kinges Highnes, who liketh very wel your Graces divise for superseding in the cause, and desireth moch that the same be brought to effecte with al diligence possible, if the Quene canne be induced therunto; wherin his Highnes hath gret confidence in the high wisedom and dexterite of your Grace, soo to worke with her Counsail as nothing further, thenne is alredy by your Grace divised, shalbe¹ by the Quene desired in that behaulf. And in cace, *omnibus tentatis, hoc non successerit,* thenne, *de duobus malis,* his² Highnes wilbe content to admitte the lesse; viz., that rather the inhibition shuld be† prively execute upon your Grace and the Cardinal Campegius, thenne the same with rumour to be divulged in Flaunders; like as his Highnes hath declared at lenght to the said Master Doctor Boner and Doctor Kerne; who forasmoch as they canne reaporte unto your Grace the particularites of al communicacions, I shal omitte further, by wryting, to expresse the same. Praying Almighty God to preserve your good Grace. At Wodstok, the viij day of Septembre.

Your Graces most humble
and dayly bedeman,

STEVEN GARDYNER

28. *To* WOLSEY

Woodstock, 12 September, [1529]

B.M., Vit. B, XII, 165–6.* Mutilated. *L.P.*, IV, 5936. *St. P.*, I, 343.

The King is pleased that Wolsey's device concerning the citation has been effective with the Queen's Council, but is at a loss to know why he desires an interview. (*Cf.* Pollard, *Wolsey,* 237–9.)

Pleasith it your Grace to understande that, incontinently upon the arryval of Master For[est], your Graces servaunt, and delyveraunce of your

---

1 for *c.o.*   2 †*and alt. from* this

Graces [letters], I repared unto the Kinges Highnes and red unto the [same your] Graces letters to me directed; the first parte wherof, [shewing] by what dexteryte your Grace hath conduced th[e Quenes] Counsail to be content with exhibition of the bref [directed] to your Grace, in lieu of the letters citatorial, was [most] acceptable unto the Kinges Highnes; and gevith [unto] your Grace therfor his most harty thankes; trustin[g] that your Grace hath in al circumstaunces soo pr[oceded], as, if the Quene wold herafter resile and goo b[ack from] that she semeth nowe to be contented with, it shuld [not be] in her power soo to doo; but that this acte, doon [before] your Grace and the Cardinal Campegius, ma[y be] prejudicial to her here, at Rome, or elleswhe[re, by] letting and empeching of further prosecutio[n, and of] any citacion or processe impetrate, or to be [impetrate], by her or her proctours, herafter. Wher[in his] Highnes desireth your Grace to have especi[al care] and respecte, as his Grace doutith not [but your Grace] hath, and that it is in al pointes forseen as [apperteyneth].

And where as your Grace, in the ende of [your letter], writeth that ye have certain thinges to shew[e unto] the Kinges Highnes, which your Grace thinki[th not] convenient to be committed to wryting; I as[sure] your Grace, that at the reding therof his H[ighnes] semed to me somwhat altred and moved, after s[uch] sorte as the obscure signifie of newes, appering [to be] of importaunce, doth require. Wherupon his Highne[s w]as, in that desire of further knowlege, troubled, *et frustra tamen coniiciens*[1], what it is that your Grace, the weyes being sure and without feare of interception, shuld, that notwithstanding, not thinke convenient to be put in wryting; knowing also right wel that your Grace is not wont to spare any labo*u*rs or paynes in wryting, whenne the cace soo requiring; musing and merveling, therfore, more and more, what the matier shulde be, willed me, after the minute of these letters conceyved by his Grace, with al diligence to depech his Graces[t] servaunt Curson, this berer, with these my letters unto your Grace, and by them, in his Highnes name, to desire your Grace incontinently, by letters of your Graces owne hande, to be directed unto his Highnes handes, to signifie unto the same oonly *caput rei*, which your Grace meanith; *nam singulas circumstancias enumerare et per literas explicare*, it wer *nimis laboriosum* to your Grace, and such labo*u*r as his Highnes willith your Grace in noowise to take, but oonly, *paucissimis verbis*, to

---

1 *final* s *writ. over* es

41

advertise his Highnes whethe[r] the matier which your Grace meanith be *domesticum* or *externum*; and if it be *externum*, whither from the French King, thEmperour, the Pope, my Lady Margaret, or any other prince; and if it be *domesticum*, and concernith any divise for accheving his Highnes vertuous desires in his gret matier, thenne *brevissime* to note the particularite of the compasse of that divise; or, if it be any other matier in this realme, soo to towche in your said letters [some] parte therof, leaving the circumstances to be [explained] by your Graces mouth (at your cumming[1] hither upo[n] . . . . . . next folowing, at which tyme your Grace shal, [at] your pleasour, repare to his Highnes, as by mou[th I] have shewed unto your Graces servaunt Forest), as his [Highnes] may knowe, by your Graces letters to be sent by this [berer], *summam et effectum* of your Graces mynde; to th[intent] his Highnes maye, in the meane tyme, sumw[hat] quiet his mynde and cogitacion, and muse no [further] thenne nedes, upon occasion of the obscure w[ordes] writen to me in the ende of your Graces said letter.

I shuld have sent these letters by your Gr[aces] servaunt Forest, but that the Kinges Highnes des[ireth] spedy answer, and therfor willed me to dep[ech the] berer[2] Curson. Thus I pray Almig[hty God] to preserve your good Grace. At Wodstok, the [xij] day of Septembre.

Your Graces most humble
and dayly bedeman,

STEVEN GARDYNER

Addressed: To my Lord Legates good Grace.
Endorsed: Doctor Stevyns, xij Septembris.

29. *To* WOLSEY

Woodstock, 13 September, [1529]

R.O., S.P. 1, 55, 127–8.* *L.P.*, IV, 5939.

The King desires Rokwod, under-steward of Calais, to return thither.

Pleasith it your Grace to understande that the Kinges Highnes hath signed a byl in favour of this berer, Master Rokwod, and, forasmoch as his Grace wolde he shulde shortly retourne to Calays to be there present at the hering tyme nowe approching, his Highnes[3] willed me, by

1 *alt. from* cummith   2 berere *with final* e *c.o.*
3 his Hig *writ. over something else*

42

my next letters to your Grace, to make summe mention of him for his spedy expedition at your Graces hande, which I had forgoten to doo in myn other letters, and nowe by these supplye the same. Thus I pray Almighty God to preserve your good Grace. From Wodstok, the xiijth of Septembre.

Your Graces most humble
and dayly bedeman,

STEVEN GARDYNER

Addressed: To my Lorde Legates good Grace.
Endorsed: From Maister Stevyns, the xiijth of September.

30. *To* WOLSEY

Windsor, [6 October, 1529]

R.O., S.P. 1, 55, 188–9.* *L.P.*, IV, 5993.

> The King desires certain writs of Parliament. (According to A. F. Pollard, *Wolsey*, 241–2, the request for a list of parliamentary boroughs in No. 18 meant that Henry had an inkling that Wolsey might turn to Parliament for support, and the removal of the writs from his control was a clear indication that a new Chancellor would preside over the Parliament summoned to meet on 3 November.)

Pleasith it your Grace to understande that, as towching the sending forth of the writtes of Parliament for the shyres of Notingham and Derby, the Kinges plea*sour* is, the same be sent by the handes and advise of my Lord of Norfolkes Grace, and therfor willed me to signifie unto your Grace that ye sende hither the writtes for the said shyres. Thus, having noo further laysour to write of the receipt of your Graces letters by Croke, this berer[1], I pray God to preserve your good Grace. At Windesore, this Wedensday.

> It may please your Grace likewise to sende the writte for the shyres of Bedford and Buckingham; likewise for Hampshire and the towne of Southampton; and likewise the towne of Notingham.

Your Graces most humble
and dayly bedeman,

STEVEN GARDYNER

Addressed: To my Lorde Legates good Grace.
Endorsed: Master Stevens.

1 berere *with final* e *c.o.*

43

31. *To* CROMWELL

Hampton Court, [18 June, 1531]

B.M., Vesp. F, XIII, 257.* Written on same sheet as, and beneath, Cromwell's note of June 18, [1531] (*L.P.*, v, 302, i) to which it is an answer. *L.P.*, v, 302, ii.

Only a few corrections are needed in the minute of instructions sent by Cromwell.

Master Cromwel, after my most harty commendations: Forasmoch as your letters wryten in Laten agreeth with the minute which I, by the Kinges commaundement, conceyved in English, wherwith his Highnes was wel pleased and hath seen the same, it shal[1] not be[2] necessary further to molest his Highnes therin. Wherfor, for the more spedy depech of the same letters, I send them unto youe again, corrected in fewe places wher I thought it requisite. And thus fare ye hartely wel. At Hampton-co*u*rte, this Sonday.

Your⟨s⟩ assuredly,

STEVEN GARDYNER

Master Cromwel, I pray youe be good to John
Godsalve, as I understande ye be alredy.

32. *To* BENET

Greenwich, [22 or 29 December, 1531]

R.O., S.P. 1, 68, 107.* *L.P.*, v, 599. *St. P.*, VII, 331.

Benet is to come to Court at once to receive instructions for his return to Rome. (Benet, who succeeded Gardiner at Rome, had written, 21 October, suggesting that Henry recall him, since there were matters he could only disclose by mouth—*L.P.*, v, 484. He was recalled 4 November, arrived in England before 21 December, and left again for Rome, 1 January—*ib.*, 511, 593, 691; *cf.* 610–11, 614. Gardiner's letter is dated Greenwich, Friday. J. Gairdner dated it 22 December, in *L.P.*, but the remark in it that Benet is to return within four days seems rather to indicate Friday, 29 December. On that day Gardiner started on an embassy to France, riding post through Canterbury to Dover—*ib.*, 614, 620. Hence, if the letter is of 29 December, it must have been written early that day. This is the first extant letter from Gardiner after he became Bishop of Winchester; hence the signature, Ste. Winton, *i.e.*, Stephanus Wintoniensis. He had been consecrated 3 December and installed by proxy 27 December.)

1 shalbe *w*. be *c.o.*   2 f *incomplete follows*

44

Master Docto*ur*, after my most harty commendations: My Lord of
Norfolk and I have spoken with the King, of whom we knowe theffecte
of your charge; and for execution of the matier ye shal reto*ur*ne within
these iiij dayes. Wherfore the Kinges pleas*our* is that ye, leving aparte
al preparation for other apparel, and borowing a gowne of summe of
your frendes, to repare hithre to the Co*ur*te this night in any wise. And
thus most hartely fare ye wel. From Grenewich, this Frydaye.

Your assured frende,

STE. WINTON

Ye¹ may speke to Docto*ur* Wolman
for his lodging here.

Addressed: To my loving frende, Master Docto*ur* Benet.

33. *To* BENET

Rouen, 27 January, [1532]

R.O., S.P. 1, 69, 84–5.* *L.P.*, v, 755.

> Bonner is coming to join Benet and Carne in Rome; Suffolk desires a dis-
> pensation. (*Cf. L.P.*, v, 1025.)

Master Doctor, in my most harty maner I commende me unto youe.
And as concernyng the charge of this bringer, Master Boner, being sent
by the Kinges² Highnes and commaunded to communicate al unto
youe, I shal not nede to wryte any specialte, for I cannot adde or take
away to that I have said and wryten in tymes past†, which ye knowe
welynowe. And yet the Kinges Highnes willed this berer to repaire by
me to be instructe by me howe to use himself there, with whom, I
doubte not, ye and† Master Doctor Kerne canne and wil doo al that
is possible to be doon, and use everything soo as may be most beneficial
to the Kinges purpose, according to such instructions as ye shal have
from the same. My Lord of Suffolk hath³ wryten unto me for his dispensation, whose letters I sende unto youe herwith, and I praye youe,
good Master Doctor, helpe to the ⁴expedition therof, as moch as ye may.

1 *alt. from* I   2 s ma(?) *c.o.*
3 st *c.o.*   4 e *writ. over* x

And thus most hartely fare ye wel. From Roone, the xxvij[th] day of January.

I pray youe recommende me to Master Doctor Kerne.

Your assured frende,

STE. WINTON

Addressed: To the Right Worshipful Master Doctor Benet, the Kinges ambassadour at Rome.

34. *To* BENET

Rouen, 19 February, with postscript, 22 February, [1532]

R.O., S.P. 1, 69, 130–1.* Injured by damp. *L.P.*, v, 816.

Forwards letters from England about 'answering the matter of the Turks' (presumably that Henry would protect the Pope against them if the Pope gave judgment in his favour—*cf. L.P.*, v, 762, 832, 864, and *passim*).

Gentyle Master Doctor, after my most[1] harty commendations: Ye shal receyve herwith a pacquet of letters from the Kinges Highnes addressed to youe and your colleges, the chief point wherof consisteth in answering the matier of the Turkes, which me thinkith is nowe waxed colde and shal waxe colder, if Ferdinand and Vayuoda agree, as it is f[or] trut[h] tolde here howe they both have compromised ther titles in to the arbitrement of the King of Pole, insomoch as Vayuodas facto*ur* hath obteyned of the King our master letters to the[2] King of Poole in that behaulf. If your letters cumme late, ye must considre they cumme from the French Co*ur*te, where the Popes ambassadour hath oones disapointed me, and other say ever they depech currers tomorowe, which summe cal tomowe. Out of England be noo newes. I departe hens tomorowe, soo as I might have taryed at home. Here hath been m*ar*velous gret triumphes in receyving this Q*u*ene. Your letters have been going hens thiese viij[th] dayes, and yet I wryte thiese unassured of a post, otherwise than[3] that he goth tomorowe *i.⟨e.⟩*, *tantost*, and soo I leve my letters open. Wryten the xix day of February.

The⟨?⟩ .... [4] day arryved here Francisco[5], and yet I am not goon, but I goo tomorowe, of the English facion. And, Sir, I thanke youe for

1 *writ*. mast   2 *alt. from* to   3 *writ*. that
4 *the editor of L.P. read or conjectured* xxij *here*   5 Fransco *with* ci†

46

your cassia phistola. And, for the abbey, I shal speke and doo the bes I canne to spede. As I shal spede, ye shalbe advertised from England, with more hast thenne hens. I am sory of your evel jornay and am in any thing holly yours, and soo ye shal finde in dede. I praye youe to recommende me to Master Kerne and shewe him I have sent in to England letters arryved here from him. And thus most hartly fare ye wel. From Roone, the xxij day of February.

Your assured frende,

STE. WINTON

Addressed: To the Right Wurshipfull Master Doctour Benet, the Kinges ambassatour at Rome.

35. *To* BENET

London, 11 May, [1532]

R.O., S.P. 1, 70, 21–2.* *L.P.*, v, 1007. *St. P.*, VII, 369.

Benet is to obtain a dispensation for the marriage of Sussex and Lady Margaret Stanley. (*Cf. L.P.*, v, 1025.)

Master Benet, aftre my moost harty commendacions, thise shalbe moost instantly to desire and pray youe to obteyne with al diligence possible a dispensacion for my Lord of Sussex and the Lady Margaret Stanley[1], according to suche instruction as ye shal receyve in a bill herin enclosed. Wherin also, for thexpedicion of this matier, ye shal receyve a bill of exchaunge of the somme[2] of two hundreth ducattes; hartly eftsones desiring youe with suche diligence to procure thexpedicion of this matier, as the[3] same may be sent by the next currour. And in cace the chargies therof shall excede the said som of cc ⟨200⟩ ducattes, I beseche youe to see it contented, and I shal see youe agayne repaid therof. And thus fare youe aswel as your good harte canne thinke. At London, the xj[th] of May.

I have taken upon me[†] to wryte in this matier, and therfor I hartely praye youe it may be sped and sent with asmoch haste as may

1 *in margin*: They be in secundo et quarto affinitatis
2 *alt. from* sommes   3 m *c.o.*

47

be possible. I have conferred your benefice to your chapelen, and removed al controversy which was moved by gret men.

Your assured frende,

STE. WINTON

Addressed: To my loving frende Master Doctour Benet, the Kinges Highnes ambassadour in the Courte of Rome.

36. *To* HENRY VIII

[Esher, *c.* 15 May, 1532]

B.M., Cleop. E, VI, 203.* Atterbury, 528. Wilkins, III, 752. *L.P.*, V, 1019. Both Atterbury and Wilkins appear to have printed the letter not from the original but from a copy in the records of Convocation. Wilkins, not the original, is calendared in *L.P.*

> Laments the King's displeasure, but defends his support of and his part in the composition of the *Answer of the Ordinaries*, which upheld the right of Convocation to make laws concerning faith and morals (in reply to the *Supplication of the Commons against the Ordinaries. See* my *Gardiner*, Chapter VIII. Parliament, in which Gardiner also opposed the King's wishes on this subject, was prorogued 14 May, and Gardiner seems to have retired at once to his house at Esher—*L.P.*, V, 1013, 1025, 1058. He was, however, again at Court, engaged in diplomatic business, in the second week in June—*ib.*, 1109).

My dutie remembred to your Majestie, with al lowly humilite and reverent honnour: Forasmoch as letted by disease of body I cannot personally repare to your Highnes presens[1], having harde of your Graces Almoner, to my gret discounforte, what opinion your Highnes hath conceyved of me, I am compelled by thiese letters to represent me unto the same; lamenting and wayling my chaunce and fortune to have lost, besides my desertes, asmoch reputacion in your Graces harte as your Highnes, without my merites, hath conferred unto me in estimacion of the worlde. And if I counforted not myself with remembraunce of your Graces goodnes, with whom *veritas semper vincit, et sortis tederet et vite.* I knowe in myself, and canne never forget your Graces benefites, your Highnes notable affection towardes me. I knowe my dutie and bonde to your Highnes. Howmoch I desire to declare in outwarde dedes myn inwarde knowlege, God knoweth, and I trust your

1 *alt. from* present

48

Highnes shal knowe; but in the meane tyme, for want therof, thus I suffer, and knowe noo remedye but your Highnes goodnes to expende what I have doon, what I shulde have doon, and what I maye doo, and not to[t] be miscontent, thowe in correcting of the answer made, I beleved, soo gret a numbre of learned men affirmyng it soo precisely to be true, that was in the answer alleged concerning Goddes lawe; specially considering your Highnes booke against Luther, in myn understanding, most playnly approvith it; the boke wryten in your Graces cause, and[1] translate in to English, semeth to allowe it; and the Counsail of Constance, condempning the articles of Wyclef, manifestly decreeth it. The contrary wherof, if your Grace canne nowe prove, yet I, not lerned in divinite, ne knowing any parte of your Graces proves, am, I trust, without cause of blame in that bihaulf. Whenne I knowe that I knewe not, I shal thenne speke theraftre. It were pitie we lyved if, soo litel expressing our love to God in our deades, we shuld abuse His name and auctorite to your Highnes displeasour, of whom we have receyved soo many benefites. On the other parte, if it be Goddes auctorite to us alotted, thowe we cannot use it condignely, yet we cannot geve it awaye; and it is noo lesse daungier to the receyvour thenne to the gever, as your Highnes of your high wisedom canne consider. I am, for my parte, as I am bounde, most desirous not oonly to doo what maye be doon to your Highnes contentacion, but also applyable to lerne the truth what ought to be doon; trusting your Majestie wyl finally take in good parte that I thinke that truth, for which I have soo good groundes and auctorites, untyl I heve stronger groundes and reasons to the contrary. I shal most gladly conferre with any of your Graces Counsail in this matter, and in the meane tyme I dayly praye to God for knowlege of His truth, and the preservation of your Majestie in moch felicite, alway most redy and desirous to doo as becommith

Your most humble subget, most
bounden chapelen, **and** dayly
bedeman,

STE. WIN[TON]

1 ter (?) *c.o.*

37. *To* CROMWELL

Esher, 30 June, [1532]

B.M., Titus B, i, 378–9.* *L.P.*, v, 1138.

Does not want to pay more than necessary for the temporalities of Winchester diocese. (In 1529 the revenues of the see were £4095, in 1535 and 1536 £3885—*Victoria History of Surrey*, II, 17; *Reg. Gardiner*, 156.)

Master Cromwel, after my most harty commendations: Being advertised by letters from Master Paulet, Controller of the Kinges House, howe it wer expedient for me to be at a point with the Kinges Highnes for my temperaltes, I have thought good by these my letters to remembre youe therof and to desire youe that, considering at my last communicacion[1] with youe in that matier I remitted al to the Kinges pleas*our*, an execut*our* wherof ye be in that behaulf, that ye wil doo for me as ye maye doo for your frende, and procure such an ende as I may be able to perfourme[1]. And other respecte have I not to the quantite of the summe, as I thenne tolde youe; and, though I am of the same molde other be of, a man etc., yet I promyse youe, I use noo colour herin. Truth it[2] is, I wolde be glad to paye nothing, if it were remitted unto me, and the lesse I pay, the better content, soo I pay that the Kinges Highnes is pleased with. But I am in that state by his goodnes[3] and without myn asking or des*er*tes that, as far as my power wyl extend, I shal with noo lesse good wil paye it unto his Highnes thenne I receyve[4] it of other. Wherfor nowe al[5] is in your handes. The delaye of myn ende dependith oonly upon youe; in concluding wherof I praye youe remembre that I receyve lesse of the bishoprich of Winchestre by xiij ͨ ⟨1300⟩ *li.* yerely thenne Bishop Fox did, and owe twyes asmoch as he was worth whenne he dyed, if his inventary wer true, besides thimplementes of the bishoprich, which importith a gret charge, for I finde in noo place a panne. But I praye youe, good Master Cromwel, determyne youe thende for my parte, as shalbe agreable with the Kinges pleas*our*, in such wise as I shulde not seme to hucke of or stike to paye my dutie; for I promyse youe, I meane not soo. I wold I[†] coulde expresse[6] my meanyng always, eyther in wordes or deades or both. Truth is called tymes doughter. Tyme wil have childe at the last, but it[†] is long first. I wold, for my parte, tymes delyveraunce wer as spedy in childing of

1 *alt. from* perfoure   2 I *c.o.*   3 that *c.o.*
4 receyved *w.* d *c.o.*   5 in *c.o.*   6 expresses *w. final* s *c.o.*

truth as conyes be, that bring forth every moneth. God may soo ordre[1] it whenne Him please, Who[2] oonly canne, and, I trust, wyl; without[3] Whom it is but foly to hope of amendement of tymes defaulte. For which I shal praye, and your welfare and prosperyte. From Asher, the last day of June.

Your loving and
assured frende,

STE. WINTON

Addressed: To the Right Worshipful Master Thomas Cromwel, oon of the Kinges most honnorable Counsail.

38. *To* CROMWELL

Langley, [c. 22 August, 1532]

R.O., S.P. 1, 70, 230–1.* *L.P.*, v, 1245.

> Sends treaty with France (sworn to at Windsor, Sunday, 1 September—*L.P.*, v, 1292. The date of the letter is determined by the King's presence at Langley, c. 18–22 August and possibly a day or two longer; he was at Abingdon 25 August—N. H. Nicolas, *Privy Purse of Henry VIII*, London, 1827).

Master Cromwel, after my harty commendations: I sende unto youe herwith by John Godsalve the treaty with Fraunce, and a commission[4] signed, redy to be sealed; to the doing wherof ye must necessaryly helpe or it shal, I fear me, be undoon. I pray youe also to sende to Doctor Olyver or Doctor Lee to be with the King upon Sonday, to be as notaryes at the taking of the oth. Thus fare ye hartely wel. From Langley.

Your assured frend,

STE. WINTON

Addressed: To the Right Wurshipfull Master Thomas Crumwell, oon of the Kinges Pryvay Counsail.

1 ordred *w. final* d *c.o.*	2 Whoo *w. final* o *c.o.*
3 out†	4 red *c.o.*

39. *To* AUDELEY

Greenwich, 1 January, [1533]

R.O., S.P. 1, 74, 5.* *L.P.*, VI, 8. *St. P.*, IV, 631.

Is to issue a commission to Henry Percy to levy men for the Scottish border. (*Cf. L.P.*, VI, 15.)

My Lord: Thise shalbe oonly to advertise the same that the Kinges pleas*our* is, ye cause immediatly a commission to be made under the Kinges Great Seale for my Lord of Northumberland, the Kinges Warden of the Est and Mydle Marches foranempst Scotland, for the levying of asmany of his Highnes subjectes within the Est and West Riding of Yorkshire as he shall think good, for defence or annoyance of Scottes, at any tyme, during the Kinges pleas*our*, at his libertye; which commission ye must send hider by som trusty person in all diligence possible, with your warrant for that purpose, which I woll get you signed, for your discharge in that behalf. From Grenewich, this first day of the newe, and God send you many good newe yeres.

Your loving frende,

STE. WINTON

Addressed: To my singuler good Lord, Sir Thomas Audeley, Knight, Lord Keper of the Kinges Great Seale.

Endorsed: The Bisshop of Wynchester.

40. *To* CROMWELL

Esher, [on or after 13 June, 1533]

R.O., S.P. 1, 76, 224.* *L.P.*, VI, 626.

Concerning the executors of Bishop West. (*Cf. L.P.*, VI, 627. The inventory of West's goods contains the entry, 'cattle remaining, 11 June, 1533'—*ib.*, 625. The first Friday thereafter was 13 June.)

Master Cromwel, after my most harty commendations: Forasmoch as in the communication bitwene youe and me of my Lord of Elys exe-cut*our*s, whose soule God perdonne, ye shewed yourself glad that I shuld be pryve to ther sutes with youe, I have thought good therfor to

recommende them unto youe by my letters, which shal stonde me in as
good stede for bying of such thinges as I desire of them as if I wer
further pryve to ther ende. Wherin they trust somoch in youe as they
be not desirous to have me participaunt unto the same. They shal shewe
youe the inventary and soo use themself as ye shalbe wel contented.
Thus most hartely fare ye wel. From Asher, this Frydaye.

> Your loving and assured
> frende,
>
> STE. WINTON

Addressed: To my loving frende, Master Thomas Crumwell, oon of
the Kinges most honorable Counsail.

INTRODUCTORY NOTE TO NOS. 41-51

These letters were written during the year and a half of Gardiner's retirement to his diocese after his opposition to the ecclesiastical legislation proposed in the first session of the Parliament of 1534. Cromwell had succeeded him in the Principal Secretaryship, and there can be little doubt that he recognized in Cromwell his chief opponent in matters both political and ecclesiastical. Yet such was the influence of the new Secretary that Gardiner found it wise to keep on good terms with him. Of the eleven extant letters of this period, eight are addressed to Cromwell, and in one of the others (No. 44) he mentions his assistance in bringing a suit before the King. The most interesting are Nos. 45 and 49, in the first of which he seeks advice as to how to behave himself so as not further to offend the King on his coming to Guildford, and in the second describes the measures he has taken to see the royal supremacy taught in his diocese. The last letter in the group (No. 51), also addressed to Cromwell, though but a brief note, is important because, with certain other contemporary references, it enables us to fix the date of the composition of Gardiner's celebrated defence of the royal supremacy, *De Vera Obedientia*, and of his answer to the brief of Paul III denouncing Henry VIII for the execution of Bishop Fisher. *See* note on p. 68 below.

Of the three letters not addressed to Cromwell, one (No. 44) is to the Lord High Admiral, Henry's illegitimate son (then 15 years old), in protest against charges, apparently believed by him or his advisers, brought against Gardiner by John Cooke, commissary of the Admiralty in Hampshire, as well as registrar of Gardiner's diocese (Gardiner had inherited him from Wolsey; *cf.* No. 15). The other two are to Gardiner's friends and frequent hosts at Calais, the Lisles. That to Lady Lisle (No. 43) is a peculiarly graceful letter, and the only one of Gardiner's we possess addressed to a woman. It bears no year date, but I see no reason for questioning its assignment to 1534 by the editor of *L.P.*

41. *To* CROMWELL

Farnham, 26 April, [1534]

R.O., S.P. 1, 83, 169–70.* Slightly mutilated. *L.P.*, VII, 542.

Why Canonbie (on the Scottish border) is debatable land.

Master Cromwell, after my most harty commendations: This evenyng at ix of the clok I receyved your letters, and incontinently determyned to make such answer unto the same as wherwith your especial advertisement with your owne hand†, which, as I ought to doo, I take very frendly, might be satisfied, to the contentacion of the Kinges Highnes, our soverain lord; for whose purpose ye labour as becommith youe, and I, for my parte, ought not to be behinde. Wherfor myn answer therin ye shal perceyve by the subscription. As towching Canabe, thus moch I knowe, that it hath been declared to the Kinges Highnes as lande debatable by thre maner of evidences: first, by the depositions of a good nombre of olde men examined by the Lord Dacres and other; secondly, by an old wryting founde among the evidences of the Lord Dacres, declaring the particion of certain baroneyes which wer left debatable; and thirdely, by a plat drawen and made of the situacion of Canabie, wherby it shuld ap[pe]re that it[1] is within the limites of debatable grounde. And this is al that I knowe therin that makith for the Kinges partie; not dowting but the Scottes wyl tel youe asmoch as makith for them and more too. I have caused also my chapelen, Master Runcourne, to subscribe his name to the conclusion, as ye shal perceyve by ⟨t⟩he same. And thus most hartely fare ye wel. From Farneham, the xxvj day of Aprile.

Your owne assured
frende,

[STE. W]INTON

Addressed: To the right worshipful Master Thomas Cromwel, Principal Secretary to the Kinges Highnes.

Endorsed: My Lorde of Winchester.

1 *alt. from* is

42. *To* CROMWELL

Winchester, 5 May, [1534]

B.M., Otho C, x, 171.* Mutilated. *L.P.*, VII, 610. Pocock, II, 536.

Has begun administering the oath to the Act of Succession in his diocese.

Master Cromwel, after my most harty commenda[tions]: Ye shal understand that, receyving the commission¹ ...... from the Kinges Highnes
for taking othes² according to th[e] Acte of his Graces Succession upon
Wedonsday last [past], I used such diligence for thexecution of the said
com[mission] that upon the Monday folowing, which was yesterd[ay],
not oonly assembled here at Winchester my Lord Chamberlain and
asmany of the other commissione[rs] as were within the shire and might
travayle, but [ther] appered bifore us in the gret hal of the caste[l ther]³
my Lord Audeley, a good nombre of ge[ntelmen], al abbottes, pryo*u*rs,
wardens of fryers, and the gov[ernor] of the Fryer Observauntes at
Hampton, nowe in thabse[ns of] the warden, with al the curates of⁴ al
the [other] churches and chapelles within the shire, the [Isle of] Wight
oonly except, which al did take⁵ [the said] oth very obediently, as this
berer canne s[ignifie unto] you. And at the same time the abbo[ttes,
pryo*u*rs], and curates did, according as I had ord[red] them, present
unto us⁶ bylles of al h[ouses] of the religious, and servauntes in ther
hou[ses, and] p*a*rishenes in ther p*a*rishes, menkind only, [above] the
age of xiiij. Soo as having bifor[e divided] the countrye, and distaunce
of oon villag[e from] an other, and made such a limitacion in [the]
townes to sitte as the people shal n[ot nedes] travayle in ther apparaunce
abov[e] .... we know what is to doo by the⁷ .... it
should be execute for the com.......... people, and by all lightlywod
.... wyl be or we canne overcumme it. And in this
latter pointe, if ye have respecte to the⁸ acceleration of the matier, it is
necessary ye knowe our lak here, which is not, I assure, of good wyl in
those that be named commissioners⁹, who have gladly and willingly
taken upon them to doo ther partes allotted unto them; but, of al that
be named, we be but xij that be in the shire present and canne attende it,
and yet of those twelve two be custumers of Hampton and saye they
must attende upon the galyes and spend summe tyme there. For the

---

1 *three minims begin the mutilated word following*   2 *alt. from* other
3 al abbo *c.o.*   4 th *c.o.*   5 taketh *w.* th *c.o.*   6 a *c.o.*
7 *three minims begin the mutilated word following*   8 accle *c.o.*
9 h *c.o.*

remedy hereof, if it be thought requisite to be remedyed, I sende unto
youe the names of such as be thought here mete to be [in] commission
for this purpose. Wherein ye shall percey[ve] a long work, and wil require a long tracte of ty[me], and it be not divided among many com-
missionere[s], considering specially that every mannes name mus[t] be
wryten, as our commission purportith and cert[ifieth]. And yet hitherto
we take men oonly for men a[nd] not women; wherin I praye youe
wryte sumwh[at] again of the Kinges pleas*our*, that we erre not. I [have]
committed theffecte of this matter to be declared un[to] you to this
berer, whom I have likewise desi[red] to sollicite your spedye answer.
And thus m[ost] hartely fare ye wel. From Winchester, vth [of] Maye.

Your assured fre[nde],

STE. WINT[ON]

43. *To* LADY LISLE

London, 20 June, [1534]

R.O., S.P. 3, 14, 50.* *L.P.*, VII, 858.

Commends to her the cause of the bearer, a widow.

Madame, after my most harty commendations: Knowing howe effectually your Ladiship is accustumed to sollicite your frendes cause, and
nothing doubting of your special love and frendship towardes me, I am
soo bold to recommend this wedows cause, berer herof, unto your good
Ladiship, hartely desiring and praying youe to regarde it as it wer myn
owne. I wryte neyther to my good Lord, your husbond, unto whom,
I besech youe, make my most harty commendations, ne to any other
herin, knowing that your Ladiship maye stande in stede sufficient in this
matier, wherin is oonly required justice at the Marshalles hande; which,
by your good meanes, I knowe wel shalbe atteyned. Wherby your
Ladiship shal binde me more and[†] more to doo that shal lye in my litel
power in any such matier of your frendes as shal occurre here. Thus,
my good Lady, most hartely fare ye wel. From London, the xx^{ti} day
of June.

Your Ladishippes to my
litel power,

STE. WINTON

Addressed: To my singuler good Lady, my Lady Lisle.
Endorsed: My Lord of Wynchestre, the xx of Juyn.

44. *To* [*the* DUKE OF RICHMOND]

Winchester, 30 June, [1534]

R.O., S.P. 1, 85, 7–8.* *L.P.*, VII, 905.

John Cooke's complaint against Gardiner is utterly false. (*Cf. L.P.*, VI, 1361.)

After my most humble commendations to your good Grace: Master
Coke hath delyvered unto me your Graces letters wryten in his favo*ur*,
wherin your Grace rehersith at lenght such grieves as Master Cooke
pretendith himself to have susteyned at my hande; which I have considered. And forasmoch I finde that Master Cooke[1] in his long infor-
macion hath not shewed your Grace oon true sentence of my doinges
towardes him, material to be layde to my charge and wherwith he shuld
be nowe greved or have cause to complayne upon me, I have judged in
my mynde that your Grace, for the respecte I knowe your noble harte
hath ever had to truth[2], wold be better pleased with an answer to your
Graces said letters for the tryal of truth thenne that I shuld, folowyng[3]
your Graces request made upon such a grounde, geve courage to Master
Cooke in thexercise of his untrewe reaportes. It is true that the last
yere[4], going beyonde the see, I wylled myn officer to stay the payment
of Master Cookes fee, but it was soo stayed that Master Cooke was
payde, and I forgave Master Cooke, whenne he wept, for kindnesse.
And soo, in that tale of staying, Master Cooke spekith truth, but it is
not, as I have wryten, material. But al his other informations made by
hym to your Grace bee in noo parte concernyng my behavo*ur* trewe,
eyther in answering him or the Kinges letters. The man hath soo spoken
of me there to the Kinges Highnes, your Grace, my Lord Chauncelo*ur*,
Master Secretary, as thought he trusted that I shuld never be harde to
make answer. And nowe it grevith hym that, by Master Secretaryes
meanes, the Kinges Highnes pleaso*ur* is that I shalbe harde, what answer
I canne make[†] to his[5] informations, wherin is my oonly remedye. For
thenne it shal appere that I never did or said in any oon poynte as Master
Cooke hath reaported me. And if your Grace doo not finde myn asseveration herin trewe, let me never be trusted in any other matier. And
most humbly I desire your Grace to consider myn issue herin, which to
your Grace I wold not make soo precisely if I knewe not myself clere,
and that I am desirous your Grace shuld in my matier see Cookes truth

---

1 hath *c.o.*	2 w *c.o.*	3 *alt. from* followe
4 I *c.o.*	5 †*abv.* Master Cookes *c.o.*	

throwly, and the better perceyve hym in thuse of his office of thAdmiralte under your Grace, wherin they talke of his demeanour otherwise here thenne I thinke your Grace hath harde there; but the truth wil shewe itself.

And most humbly I desire your Grace to be soo good and gracious lord unto me that, according to the Kinges pleasour, which Master Secretary hath signified unto me, my declaration maye be harde in such matiers as Master Cooke layth to my charge. I take God to recorde, I neyther bere malice ne grudge to Master Cooke. I moch lamente his foly, that he doth, to his utter undoyng, thus use hymself, and by untrue surmyses to procure[1] such sute and cause of charge. I was never yet occasion wherfor he shuld spend a peny, soo helpe me God. I never mysused hym, neyther in worde ne dede. I never intterrupted hym in the office of my registreship, but have hitherto always and yet doo suffre[2] hym to occupie it that hath hyred it of hym for x $li.$ a yere, of whom he is truely paid[t] his fee, which is x $li.$ by yere[3]. I said I wold staye in payment tyl I knewe the Kinges pleasour, by reason of a[t] faulte which I founde with hym. I denyed not his fee at any tyme; but where as I wold in dede, if there wer noo cause, differre the payment untyl the audite, I doo nowe in that meane while tel hym of his faulte, and that I wyl therin knowe the Kinges pleasour. And to stoppe me therin, Master Cooke sayth I deny his fee, I put him from his office, I regarde not the Kinges letters, I byd fech moo letters. Al which, his sayinges, be of like truth. And nowe he thinkith it good policie that I, agreing with him here, might geve him sum colour to boste and face out for true his former misreaportes, alleging that I was glad to agree with hym rather thenne my deamenour shuld cumme to light, and, to stop his mouth, to kepe in such matier as he hath, and[t] that he hath against me[t]. Wherin I knowe myself soo clere that it might doo me moch hurte to wrappe it up, as Master Cooke requireth. I am sory[4] and loth to troble your Grace with such a rude, longe letter, but I cannot make an ende ne saye ynowe in this matier. And myn opinion of your Graces goodness persuadith me to bileve that your Grace wyl take in good parte my doing in this behaulf, tending to the declaration of my duetie towardes my prince, wherin Master Cooke hath soo towched me, and myn observaunce towardes your Grace, whom I doo esteme and regarde asmoch in harte and as loth wold be to doo that shuld displease youe

---

1 h c.o. 2 writ. suffree
3 s incomplete c.o. 4 to c.o.

59

as any other, my duety to my prince always reserved. As knowith
Almighty God, Who preserve your good Grace. From Winchester,
the last day of June.

Your Graces humble
bedeman,

STE. WINTON

45. *To* CROMWELL

Waltham, 6 July, [1534]

R.O., S.P. 1, 88, 172–3.* *L.P.*, VII, App. 31.

> How shall he conduct himself when the King comes to Guildford? Hopes his
> answer to Cooke's complaint will soon be heard.

Master Secretary, after my most harty commendations: The good successe of my[1] poore affayres hath been, by your frendly handeling, soo
prosperous and pleasaunte unto me, and the continuaunce of your amitie
soo ferme and stable, that in such matiers as bringe me in doubte and
perplexite of mynde, I always thinke ye may best and, as I veryly trust,
wyl redyest procure, as ye have doon in other like cases, my convenient
resolution in the same. I here of certainte that the Kinges Highnes hath
appointed a parte of his Graces progresse to Guyldeford, which is
within my diocese and where I thinke it my dutie, as other ar accustumed
to doo, to wayte and geve attendaunce upon his Majestie for declaration
of my due observaunce towardes the same. I here also, but not soo
certaynly, that the Kinges Highnes entendith incontinently therupon
to passe the sees; which, if it be true, thenne somoch the more wer it my
duetie to present myself, as every good subget shuld, to his Majestie,
with offre of that I have within me or without[2] me, to doo my due service unto his Highnes. Thus I knowe what I shuld doo, which I wold
most gladly doo; but knowing by experience that tyme, opportunite,
and the maner of doing workith asmoch and sumtyme more to the
acceptacion of that is doon, thowe it be w[el doon, then]ne the[†] thing
itself, I am in noo litel perplexite of mynde howe to use myself.

Sumtyme it cummyth in my mynde to make sute that it maye please
the Kinges Highnes to take his pastyme in my poore house[3] at Farneham, in which place I might have good opportunite to[4] doo that I wold

1 myn *w.* n *c.o.*   2 to *c.o.*
3 of *c.o.*   4 be *c.o.*

doo by myn owne mouth. If I camme to Guldeforde not knowing first the Kinges Highnes pleas*our*, for what soever purpose I did it, it¹ might percace not be wel taken, considering the jou*r*ney is appointed for recreation. In effecte, Master Cromwel, I meane that I wold, as I have heretofore wryten unto youe, *abstiner[e] ab omni specie mala*, and in al occasions shew[e] myself soo as I might appere a true subjecte and a faythful servaunt, glad to accomplish my princes pleas*our* and most glad if I wer thought mete to attende upon hym in such cace as his Highne[s] shuld departe his realme. Nevertheles, I maye not be soo delicate as to chose the place of service, but am and shalbe redy to doo service as I shalbe commaunded. This is myn harte, Master Crumwel; for my convenient openyng and declaration wherof, at what tyme, and by what meane, I have nowe recou*r*se unto youe as to myn especial frende, and desire your counsail, what I shal doo: whither to² make request for the Kinges Highnes cummyng to Farneham, myself to cumme to Guldeford, or elles otherwise what to doo and howe to use myself in the premises. Doo herin, good Master Secretary, as ye have doon for me in other caces; for in your resolution shal I acquiete myself, as I have doon in the matier bitwen Master Cooke and me, wherin, like as to my gret counforte, ye³ ⁴have obteyned that, with the Kinges Highnes good contentacion, my declaration shalbe favorably harde; soo nowe myn instaunte sute is that it may be shortly harde⁵, wherby myn⁶ innocentie may shortly and playnly appere in such matiers as Master Coke hath charged me with towardes my prince. Al other matiers I forgeve Cooke, and that alsoo, soo it be first knowen what grounde and truth it hath. Thus amonges other your gret matiers, I trouble youe with myn, but I shal saye to youe as a poore man said oones to my Lord of Norfolk in like cace. 'My smal matier,' quod he, 'is the grettest matier that I have.' I pray youe, good Master Secretary, that I may shortly ⁷here fro youe your answer herunto. And most hartely fare youe wel. From Waltham, the vj^th day of July.

Your assured frende,

STE. WINTON

Addressed: To the Right Wurshipfull Maister Secretary.
Endorsed: From the Bushop of Wynchester, the vj^th day of Julye.

1 *alt. from* is (?)   2 des *c.o.*   3 he *c.o.*
4 h *writ. over* a   5 am *c.o.*   6 *alt. from* my
7 h *writ. over another letter*

61

46. *To* LISLE

Wolvesey (*i.e.*, the bishop's house at Winchester), 19 September, [1534]

R.O., S.P. 3, 8, 69. Letter in clerk's hand, postscript (*i.e.*, paragraph preceding signature), signature, and address in Gardiner's hand. *L.P.*, VII, 1162.

Commends to him a French gentleman who has been in his household.

My veraye good Lorde, after my moost harty commendations: Thise shalbe to desire your Lordship that it woll please the same to shewe unto this gentleman, Loys du Chasteau Neufe, who hathe served me sythe my laste retourne oute of Fraunce and nowe repayreth home to his frendes, asmoche favour in depeching him from thens as your Lord-ship wolde shewe for my sake to any whom I love moost entierly. The gentleman is heyre of a wurshipfull house in Provence and his frendes there entretained me very gentely and hartely; wherfore I am the more desirouse to have him entreated here after the same sorte, as I doubte not but he shalbe of your Lordship, whom Our Lorde preserve. From Wolvesaye, the xixth daye of Septembre.

I thanke youe most hartely, my good Lord, for your kinde letters and pray youe that I may be most hartely commended to my good Lady your wif.

Your Lordshippes assured
frend,

STE. WINTON

Addressed: To my very good Lord, my Lord Lysle, Deputie of Calays.

47. *To* CROMWELL

Wolvesey (at Winchester), 25 March, [1535]

R.O., S.P. 1, 91, 131–2.* Faded, and injured by damp. *L.P.*, VIII, 442.

Concerning the goods of the late parson of Compton.

Master Secretary, after my most harty commend[atio]ns: Having re-ceyved your letters for dely[very] of such [b]ond[es] as wer in my keping of the goo[des] of the late parson of Compton,. unto whom Master [Doctor] Incent is executour, I hartely desire and praye youe to

be content that, being nowe the chief cause of not delyvery at this instaunte tyme, bicause I have not the money soo redy as I might with
myn ease departe therwith, ye wil in the meane tyme of delaye ordre the
matier ther soo as Master Incent, who is executour and to whose use I
have kept it hitherto, may utterly disharge me therof; as I d[oubt]e not
but he wil, and, as he sayth, shewe hymself glad that, the dedes ⟨*i.e.*,
dead's⟩ wyl otherwise fulfilled, such porcion as was appointed to the
Observauntes shalbe disposed [at] the K[inges Majesties] pleasour. In
the meane tyme I shal provide for furnitour of repayment of that[1]
money such† as I toke in to [my handes], partely to kepe [it] sure and
partely to ease myself for the tyme. Thus most hartely fare ye wel.
From Wolsey, upon Our Ladyes Day.

Your assured
frende,

STE. WINTON

Addressed: To the Right Worshipful Master Thomas Cromwel,
Principal Secretary to the Kinges Highnes.

48. *To* CROMWELL

Marwel, 2 May, [1535]

B.M., Cleop. E, IV, 368, with 'Articles' *etc.*, 367.* *L.P.*, VIII, 654;
IX, 1070 (3). Strype, *Mem.*, I, i, 327.

> Problems in the evaluation of ecclesiastical income in Hampshire. (In the
> November session of Parliament, 1534, the firstfruits and tenths of all the sees
> and benefices in England were granted to the King, and on 30 January, 1535,
> commissions were appointed for each county, to ascertain the value of
> ecclesiastical income. For the commission for Hants, headed by Gardiner,
> see *L.P.*, VIII, 149 [77]. For enlightening comment on the distinction made
> by Gardiner between revenues used for the relief of the poor and those for
> education *see* A. F. Leach, *Schools of Medieval England*, London, 1915, 231.)

Master Secretary, after my most harty commendations: Forasmoch as I
send up at this tyme by my servaunt, this berer, the certificat of that hath
been doon by me and other, to whom the Kinges Highnes directed his
Graces letters of commission concernyng the valuation of the spiritualte

1 †*abv.* such *c.o.*

63

in this countie, I have thought good to sende the same first unto youe, and to desire your jugement nowe in the perfection, as I required your advice in myn entre and begynnyng therof. For if any thing be otherwise thenne it shulde be, it maye and shalbe casely amended. I assure youe there hath neyther wanted good wyl ne diligence; and dividing[1] the charge committed unto us in two partes, whereof the oon was, to knowe the true value, the other, to graunte allocations and deductions; as I dare afferme that in the firste parte noo defaulte shalbe founde, but that every promotion is extended to the uttermost, soo have we in the deductions and allocations folowed, in our jugementes, as our dutie is, the wordes of our instructions; not regarding any such reasons as hath been made upon the wordes of the acte, being much more favorable, as they said, thenne we have shewed ourself in that bihaulf. Wherof, by the advice of the rest of my colleges, I have made an entitulacion, which I sende unto youe to be wayed as ye shal thinke good. The title of 'Almes,' althowe in our jugement we understande it, and have made allocations therafter, in the finding and nurishing of[†] old, impotent, and lame men; yet we have not soo demed it in the finding of yong childern to scole; and yet is it soo called alsoo, as the other is, 'almes.' We used herein a distinction of 'fynding'; which in pore and impotent men is without other shift necessary to lyve by, and in childern noo such necessite to finde them to scole. Finally, we satisfied them and ourself also with this resolution: that albeit our certificate in thextentes of ther londes, if we made the summe more thenne[2] we founde, it might greve them—whereof we wold take hede and doo uprightly—yet in the allowaunces we coulde neyther doo good ne harme to them. For if we allowed further thenne we had commission, it wold be controlled there, with our rebuke; and if we allowed to lytel, the[3] remedy laye open to be sued for, if they thought good. We have past over al thing quietly, without any miscontentement shewed by any partie, and without any other sute thenne as shal be thought agreable to the statute made in that bihaulf. Ye shall see in the valuation of my bishoprich a goodly portion; but wherof I shal not receyve nowe very litel above the oon haulf to myne owne[4] use. I am in summe mennes jugementes to strayte in charging myself; but I wyl have myn owne wyl therin, that I may be called self willed for sumwhat. I am bolde to trouble youe with my long letters, in which I talke with youe as I wer present familierly. My ser-

| 1 ond(?) c.o. | 2 f incomplete c.o. |
| 3 l c.o. | 4 h c.o. |

vaunt shal shewe youe the bookes; and further doo as ye shal commande him. And thus most hartly fare ye wel. From[1] Marwel, the ij[de] day of Maye.

Your assured frende,

STE. WINTON

Articles wherein the commissioners have not shewed such favour to the parties in ther allowaunces as they pretended bifore them due by the acte of Parlement in[2] that bihaulf:

First, where as diverse benefices, as apperyth by the particuler bookes, have summe oon, summe two, and summe thre chapelles, besides the parish church; in which chapelles they be bounde to finde prestes; albeit the commissioners in the valuacion have estemed al such proufytes as arryse and growe in any of the said chapelles, yet[3] they have allowed noo deduction of the prestes charge, who is necessary and perpetual, servyng in that chapel.

Item[4], it hath been alleged that such chaunteryes as be not perpetually assigned to any spiritual man, shuld not be charged by this acte of Parlament, specially where there growith noo profyte to the incumbent by any spiritual revenue, and that the incumbent may be removed at pleasour. And this case is alleged in the chapel[5] of the Holy Gost, in the Isle of Wight, and the chauntery of Ticheborn, in the deanry of Alresford.

Item, it hath been alleged, that considering the acte makith mencion of al almesse to be allowed, geven by foundacion, that the fynding of the poore chyldern in the Newe College, besides Winchestre, ought also to be deducted, being ther portion soo litel as it cannot be lesse.

In which matiers, albeit the commissioners have, with the best reasons they coulde, defended ther owne doyng[6] in execution of the Kinges Highnes instructions according to the said acte, yet finally they promysed to make relation of ther sute, to be remedyed by mercy, if it shalbe[7] soo thought convenient.

---

1 Asher *c.o.*	2 †*abv.* of *c.o.*	3 yet *repeated*
4 t *c.o.*	5 *alt. from* chauntrie	6 doynges *c.o.*
7 †*abv.* wer *c.o.*		

49. *To* CROMWELL

Waltham, 10 June, [1535]

R.O., S.P. 1, 93, 45–6.* *L.P.*, VIII, 850. *St. P.*, 1, 430.

How he has fulfilled the command to preach and teach the royal supremacy; has completed the translations of SS. Luke and John.

Master Secretary, after my most harty commendations: Albeit in my last letters to youe, sent with my letters of answer to the Kinges Highnes, I desired of youe to have knowlege thence, howe my Lord of London proceded there in thexecution of the Kinges Highnes commaundement, which was, as I thinke, of oon tenour to us both; yet nowe doubting lest your greate buysines might differre the answer therof lenger thenne I wold it shuld, I have, of myn owne hed, made oute commaundementes thorowe out¹ al my diocesse, of such tenour as my servaunte, this berer, shal shewe youe; in which I thinke I have satisfied theffecte of the Kinges Highnes letters to me directed for somoch. Wherunto if ye thinke any thing to be added in that matier, it may soone be supplied. As touching childern, I have delyvered thiese verses, herin inclosed, to be lerned, to² the scolers of Winchestre; to other pety teachers I geve commaundement in general. This is doon³ onward, and more shalbe, if ye thinke necessary; wherof I praye youe take the payne to advertise⁴ me. And althowe, as I have devised the wordes to be spoken, I preache the matier upon Sonday next in every mannes mouth, yet wyl I prech also, omitting al other respectes of myself, rather thenne I shuld be otherwise taken thenne I am; that is to saye, openly to swere oon thinge and pryvely to worke, saye, or doo otherwise; wherof I was never gylty. Nevertheles, I have as gret cause as any man to desire rest and quiet for the helth of my body; wherunto I thought to have entended, and to absteyne from bookes and wryting, having finished the translation of Saynt Luke and Saynt John, wherin I have spent a gret labour. And nowe restith the levying of the subsidie, and the commissions of sewars, in two places, and the commission⁵ for musters; wherin, upon your advertisement, we have stayed hitherto; abyding nowe whither ye wil commaunde us to doo any thing in it or noo. I seme to be here *in ocio* and I was never more buysied, what with the matiers itself, and what with care lest I doo not well. Finally, as it shal please the Kinges Highnes to ordre expressely, I shal gladly doo⁶; of

1 of *c.o.* (?)   2 †*abv.* by *c.o.*   3 ow *c.o.*
4 y *c.o.*   5 commissioners *w.* ers *c.o.*   6 who *c.o.*

which mynde I have ever constantly been. As knowith God, Who sende youe helth and prosperite. From [1]Waltham, the xth day of June.

Your assured frende,

STE. WINTON

Addressed: To the Right Worshipful Master Thomas Cromwel, Principal Secretary to the Kinges Highnes.
Endorsed: Letters from the Bisshop of Winchester.

50. *To* CROMWELL

Waltham, 26 July, [1535]

R.O., S.P. 1, 88, 174–5.* *L.P.*, VII, App. 32.

Likes not John Hellyer's departure from the realm. (*Cf. L.P.*, IX, p. 493.)

Master Secretary, after my most harty commendations: Forasmoch as this present howre the parish prest of Warblington within my Diocese, whom I have[2] caused to repare unto youe, hath this present houre tolde me of the departure out of the realme of the Vicare of Estmeane, in such facion and maner[3] as I like not, I have therfor sent him unto youe to tel youe the tale himself; wherupon your wisedom shal consider what is to be doon further therin. And thus most hartely fare ye wel. From Waltham, the xxvj[ti] day of Julye.
Your assured frende,

STE. WINTON

Addressed: To the Right Wurshipful Master Thomas Crumwell, [P]rincipall Secretary to the [King]es Hieghnes.
Endorsed: The Busshop of Wynton.

51. *To* CROMWELL

Winchester, [26 September, 1535]

R.O., S.P. 1, 97, 17–18.* *L.P.*, IX, 442. Janelle, *Obedience*, xxi.

Sends his answer to the Papal brief (of 26 July, 1535, denouncing Henry VIII for the execution of Bishop Fisher); has completed his Oration (*i.e.*, *De Vera Obedientia Oratio*).

Master Secretary, after my most harty commendations: I sende unto youe by this berer myn answer to the brief, according to your letters;

---

1 W *writ. over* th   2 w *incomplete c.o.*   3 I *incomplete follows*

which answer, if I might have had[†] with me this night, I had entended to have polyted and clensed it, as I have alredy doon myn oration, which I wyl at London delyver to Bartlet to be prynted. Of this answer I have noon other copye but that I nowe sende, which is soo rude as in many places ye shal rather perceyve what I meane thenne pyke out what I saye. If youe bringe it with youe, I wyl, in a daye and a night, put it *in mundum* and adde a good portion to thende that is not yet wryten, as I divised with my Lord of Cauntourbury to doo. Thus, untyl my meating with youe, most hartely fare ye wel. From Winchestre, this Sonday.

Your loving and
assured frende,

STE. WINTON

Addressed: To the Right Honnorable Master Thomas Crumwel, Principal Secretary to the Kinges Highnes.

Endorsed: The Busshop of Wynton.

NOTE TO NO. 51

The Papal brief here referred to had been addressed to Francis I in the hope that he would execute justice on Henry. Francis had no intention of doing this, but he tried to use the brief to extract from Henry material assistance for his ventures in Italy, sending it to him by a special ambassador, Jean de Dinteville, Bailly of Troyes, who arrived at the English Court on or about 19 September, and was given leave to depart 27 September (*L.P.*, IX, 434, 548, 594 p. 198, 729 [1]). Gardiner's reply to the brief, mentioned in *L.P.*, IX, 213(1)(5), 218, 594, has been recently printed, and the *De Vera Obedientia* reprinted, by M. Pierre Janelle, *Obedience in Church and State*, Cambridge, 1930.

The date, 26 September, assigned to this letter by J. Gairdner in *L.P.*, is apparently correct. Gardiner dates the letter 'Sunday.' 19 and 26 September and 3 October were Sundays. But 19 September is obviously too early, since the brief did not arrive till on or about that day; 3 October is probably too late, for it is reasonably clear that Gardiner, who was commissioned to go to France, on or shortly before 1 October (*ib.*, XIII, ii, 444), to reply to the Bailly of Troyes' communication, would not have been so commissioned had he not already shown his willingness to defend the royal supremacy in his *De Vera*, which, it is clear from this letter, had been completed just before the answer to the brief. Edward Fox, who went in October as ambassador to the German princes, appears to have taken a manuscript copy of the *De Vera* with him (*ib.*, IX, 403). A dozen copies were sent by Cromwell on 19 November to Gardiner, then at the French Court (*ib.*, 848). It is highly probable that these were the first copies off the press, for Chapuys, Imperial ambassador in England, did not, apparently, know of the book or secure a copy till on or shortly before 13 December (*ib.*, 964, 965). These conclusions as to dates differ from those expressed by M. Janelle in his *Obedience in Church and State*, pp. xxi, xxii, xxv, but he tells me that he was not, at the time of writing his book, aware of all the material bearing on the matter, and that he now agrees with these conclusions.

INTRODUCTORY NOTE TO NOS. 52–60

These letters were written during the three years Gardiner spent as ambassador at the French Court, 1535–8. Except for two drafts of joint letters from him and Sir John Wallop (*L.P.*, x, 374–5), not here printed (*see* above, p. xvi), none of his diplomatic dispatches of this period appear to exist. Of the nine letters in this group all but two are brief notes. The two longer letters are of outstanding importance. One (No. 53) contains his opinion of a proposed league between Henry VIII and the German Protestant princes, in which he considers not only the possible doctrinal effects of concord with the Protestants, but also their attitude to the royal supremacy, in the light of the Catholicism of their own head, the Emperor. The other (No. 60) is a resumé of matters in negotiation with France, which he wrote for Bonner, who succeeded him in 1538. This is of interest not only because of its succinct presentation of the diplomatic situation, but also, and perhaps chiefly, because of the advice it contains as to how an ambassador ought to behave and by what methods he can extract information from ambassadors of other nations.

52. *To* CROMWELL

Calais, 24 October, [1535]

R.O., S.P. 1, 98, 65–6.* *L.P.*, ix, 676.

His servant has died of the great sickness; strange watery weather retards his journey.

Master Secretary, after my most harty commendations, with like thankes for your good chere: Thiese shalbe to advertise youe that, after a good passage over the sees, thankes be to God, and the losse here at Calays of my servaunt Wodal, who this daye is departed to God of the gret sikenesse, wherwith, as it maye be conjected, he was infected at his late being at London lenger thenne I wold he shuld, I entende, God[1] willing, tomorowe to take my journey towardes the French Courte. My jornyng is slower thenne I wold it wer, and yet is, I feare me, more spedy thenne my horse, by reason of ther travayle on the sees, wyl mayteyne. The Baly of Troys left me worde by the waye that I shulde make noo hast,

1 Godd *w. final* d *c.o.*

but I wold goo never the slower for that, if my horse wold[1] serve. And if youe shal thinke that any gretter acceleration shalbe requisite, I shal thenne use the remedye of the post, but I trust it shal not nede. Thus moch I have thought good to wryte unto youe, to thintent that if the Kinges Highnes shuld divise[†] upon myn arryval in the French Courte or the delaye in my journey, which in the strange watery wether here and thorowe al Fraunce is moch more cumberous thenne it was wont, ye might advertise his Majestie therof accordingly, as my trust is ye wyl, and I most hartely desire[2] youe soo to doo. And even soo fare ye wel. From Calays, the xxiiij[th] daye of Octobre.

Your loving assured
frende,

STE. WINTON

Addressed: To the Right Honnorable Master Thomas Crumwel, Principal Secretary to the Kinges Highnes.
Endorsed: The Busshop of Wynchester.

53. *To* CROMWELL

[Lyons, *c.* middle of February, 1536]

B.M., Harl. 283, 137–41.* Draft. B.M., Cleop. E, v, 226. Copy (probably seventeenth century). *L.P.*, x, 256. Strype, *Mem.*, I, ii, 236. Collier, *Eccl. Hist.*, Records, No. 34. *L.P.* calendars, and Strype and Collier print the copy, not the original draft here followed.

> Gardiner's opinion on the articles proposed by the Protestant princes at Schmalkald as the basis for a league with England. (These articles were presented to Edward Fox, ambassador to the princes, on Christmas Day, 1535. Cromwell sent them, 4 February, 1536, to Gardiner, saying that the King wanted his opinion on them. See *L.P.*, IX, 1016; x, 255. Gardiner replied in particular to articles 1–4 and 7, which provided that Henry VIII was (1) to promote the Gospel as set forth in the Augsburg Confession, except in so far as he and the princes, by common consent, altered anything therein; (2) to join with the princes to defend this doctrine in a future General Council; (3) not to agree to such a council without their consent, but not to refuse one if it were Christian and free, such as they had demanded in their answer to the Pope's ambassador, Vergerio; (4) to try to hinder it, if he and they did not agree upon it; (7) to be associate to the princes' league with the title of Protector of the League. For Henry's answer to the proposal *see ib.*, IX, 1016 [3].)

1 *alt. from* wyl   2 s *c.o.*

71

[1]The opinion of me, the Bishop of Winchester, concernyng the articles presented to the Kinges Highnes from[2] the princes of Germany[3]:

As touching the first article: If this article be [4]graunted unto[4], thenne shal the Kinges Highnes be bounde to the Church of Germanye, and, without ther consent, maye not doo that the Worde of God shal permitte[5], oonles[6] ther[7] comen consent doth concurre therunto. Wherupon, if this capitulation be lawful and shal bynde, thenne shal the Bishop of Rome drawe it for an argument to his parte, that[8] the Worde of God may be restrayned to a commen assent.

Wherfor a leage or bonde herin in such termes is, in my jugement, incompatible; for, by the Worde of God, both they maye reforme ther opinion without our assent, and we without thers, what soever leage wer made to the contrary.

And[9] for the worlde, inasmoch as the Kinges Highnes, being of thastate of a king, and, in his realme, an emperour[10], and hed of the Church of England; and[11] among[12] the[13] prynces of Germany oonly dukes and lower degrees; such also as knowlege thEmperour for ther supreme lord; by reason wherof, the same reasons[14] wherby we prove by Scriptures the Kinges Majestie hed of the Church of England, we prove also thEmperour hed of ther Churches; howe shal they, without the consent of the hed of ther Church, which is thEmperour, establish[15] with us the agrement upon ther religion? Or howe shal we, without derogating the Kinges cause [16]of his prerogative and supremite[16], convenaunt with them in that behaulf; whom we knowe as[†] noo[17] hedes of ther Church, but inferiour membres, as long as they knowlege a superiour [18]in the same Church; that is to saye[18], themself as subget to thEmperour[19]? For[20] as we must be ordred by o⟨ur⟩ hed, [†]the Kinges Highnes[†], soo [21]serveth thEmperour there, that they shulde be ordred by hym[21],

1 Answer (*to left of heading*) *c.o.* 2 †*abv.* by *c.o.*
3 In this article thexception wel considered it *c.o.* 4–4 †*abv.* allowed *c.o.*
5 oon t *c.o.*   6 the *evidently meant to be c.o.* 7 *in margin*
8 by *c.o.* 9 in what *c.o.*
10 it w there t noon(?) of the pr other princes *c.o.*
11 on *c.o.*   12 *in margin* 13 o *meant to be c.o.*
14 wherof *c.o.*   15 without *c.o.* 16–16 †*abv.* therin *c.o.*
17 as † *and c.o.* 18–18 † *abv.* and *c.o.*
19 I feare thanswering of this reason our Emperour the same reason *c.o.*
20 *in margin*
21–21 † *abv.* must they by thers *c.o.*, al(?) *after* thEmperour *being c.o.*

72

according to the Word of God[1]. If they herin wyl not agre with us, thenne shal we varye in a gret †matier. For† eyther they[2] must denye thEmperour ther superior, wherin they be very scrupulose, and seme to attribute very moch unto hym; or elles, graunting that, they must, according to our opinion, which is truth, graunte hym hed of the Church. [3]And it folowith thenne[3] that without hym they canne establish nothing but such as he alone, by the Worde[4] of God, maye refourme at al tymes.

As touching the second: The Kinges Highnes might make such a promyse unto them [5]as is conteyned in this article[5]; and therby be bounde[6], soo as[7] first by the Worde of God al wer discussed; but on ther parte I see not howe ther promyse canne stande and be sure, bicause they knowelege a subjection to thEmperour.

To the thirde article, as concerning the Counsail to be indicted, as they have answered to the Bishop of Rome: Inasmoch as the Kinges Highnes hath nothing adoo with thEmperour, I see not howe his Grace shuld agree to any Counsail to be indicted by [8]the said Emperour[8]. And yet this article doth import that effecte[9], in that it maketh an exception of such a Counsail as shuld be indicted[10] according to the answer made to Peter Paule ⟨Vergerio⟩.

As touching the fourth article: The Kinges Highnes may accomplish this article †for his part†. But I see not howe they coulde doo anything again† for ther parte, †in letting the Counsail, forasmoch a[s]† in case thEmperour wold, as Emperour, calle the Counsail.

To the vij[th] article: Me semeth the worde 'association' soundith not wel. Ne[11] it were convenient that the Kinges Highnes shuld have any[12] lower place thenne to be chief, principal, and hed of the[13] leage, and the rest not to be associate, but adherent and dependaunt[14] therunto, as contrahentes. And if any were[15], oonly the Duke of Saxe to be associate; whom, for that he is an Electour, the Kinges Highnes hath been accustumed to[16] write[17], 'His Cousin,' etc.

The rest of the articles, concernyng mutual defence and money, be

---

1 ther Emperour *c.o.; abv. which* not the said pri(?) † *and c.o.*
2 *alt. from* thies
3–3 † *abv.* and thenne t graunte *c.o.*
4 d *in* worde *writ. over* l
6 having *c.o.*　　　　　7 the worde of *c.o.*
9 remitt(?) *c.o.*　　　　10 by thEmperour *c.o.*
12 other pl *c.o.*　　　　13 ledge *c.o.*
15 associate † *and c.o.*　16 call *c.o.*

5–5 † *abv.* but *c.o.*
8–8 † *abv.* hym *c.o.*
11 ner *w.* r *c.o.*
14 fo *c.o.*
17 him † *in other hand*

very good for the said princes. For they shalbe sure of a¹ gret prince to ther frende, and therwith a summe of money in hande² wherwith they might be percase releved. But as for a reciproque, I see noon to the Kinges Highnes³ for ther parte again, inasmoch as they be so far of, and calle themself thEmperours subgettes.

Finally⁴, where they desire to have al thing ⁵agreed upon⁵ bifore they sende an.ambassadour⁶ to the Kinges Highnes, they speke therin wisely for ther owne commodite. For so shal they⁷ obteyne the glorye, that they shal thenne send †unto us†, not to⁸ lerne of us, but to instructe and tech us; not to sue to us, but to directe our Church in such ceremonyes as by ther deliberacion shuld be commened of and concluded⁹.

Thus, Master¹⁰ Secretary, according to your letters, I wryte unto youe what I thinke; that is to saye, what doubtes and scrupulosites I finde in this matier; wherin percase I wryte sumwhat amysse, bicause I¹¹ understande not fully howe they take thEmperour in Germanye, ne what wilbe ther opinion in hym. But if ¹²they take hym¹², as I gather by ther other wrytinges they doo, thenne our matiers, by waye of leage, shalbe somoch the more perplexe[d] with them. I wold rather advise the Kinges Highnes to geve them money wherwith to defende truth, thenne to entre any leage with ¹³such men¹³, which, †as I feare†, cannot be fast bounde again†, and also† dwel soo† far of. To here ther ambassadours, to commen also with them, to entertayne them, and¹⁴ with them to discusse the very truth, † wer very good†; but upon the Worde of God, to make a newe knot, wherof the oon ende shalbe in Germany, shal declare rather a chaunge of a bonde †of dependaunce† thenne a rydaunce¹⁵ therof. If the Kinges Highnes canne by any meane induce them holly and uniformely to agree upon the mere truth, it shalbe an honnorable deade¹⁶, bysides the secrete merite therof. But in case a bonde wer made, and thenne any of them shulde swarve from any peace of the capitulation byforce of thEmperour, a greve and displeasour shulde ensue, without any commodite of redressing the same. I wryte the wurst, for that ever nedith remedye; the best nedith noo commenda-

---

1 *blotted;* a † *in other hand* 2 to be h *c.o.*
3 I see *c.o.* 4 to ha *c.o.*   5–5 † *abv.* concluded *c.o.*
6 they *c.o.* 7 shal †, *evidently by mistake*
8 instr *c.o.* 9 *a line is here drawn across page*
10 acco *c.o.* 11 d *c.o.*   12–12 † *abv.* to be *c.o.*
13–13 † *abv.* them *c.o.* 14 staye them *c.o.*
15 a *in* rydaunce *writ. over* d 16 by *c.o.*

cion, and ¹the best¹, I doubte not, shal⁺ be followed ⁺with you⁺. Oon thing I² have thought good to put youe in remembraunce of, that it wer wel doon that they wer moved ⁺there in Germany⁺ to agree upon the Kinges style, bicause of his supremecye; aswel as upon the cause of matrimony, wherin God hath geven sentence for the most parte by the deth of the Douager. ³And this cause ⟨*i.e.*, the supremacy⟩ is nowe soo necessary as the other³. For, synnes my cummyng hither, I have been assayed therin; and oon said he thought they in Germanye wold not agree therunto, for feare of geving unto thEmperour overmoch auctorite⁴ over them. Upon which occasion, I made ⁺in this answer⁺ my first reason unto you: The King our master hath a special case, bicause he is emperour in himself ⁺and hath noo superiour⁺. Other kinges, that knowleage an emperour, had rather suffer any manne elles thenne thEmperour⁵ to be hed of ther Church. This, I doubte not, by your wisedom ye canne consider; and thEmperour, which is to gret already, they wyl in noo wise make him gretter⁶.

54. *To* LISLE

Paris, 14 July, [1536]

R.O., S.P. 3, 8, 66.* *L.P.*, XI, 89.

Francis I is ill; uncertain news of the Turks, and of French success in Piedmont (in war against Charles V).

In my most harty maner I recommende me to your good Lordship. And forasmoch as I knowe wel that in this turne of the worlde the newes of importaunce be more fresh to youe there thenne they be in thiese parties, and more suer and certain also, I therfor have and wyl forbere to wryte any thing in those matiers.

The French King is in his waye towardes this towne, but, letted by sikenesse, he disapointeth his daye. And yet his sikenesse is not daungerous, as every man sayeth.

The Turkes cummyng is uncertain, saving that being the tyme of the yeare soo far past, it is⁷ thought that⁸ rather he shuld not cumme thenne⁹ otherwise.

1–1 † *abv*. it shal *c.o.*   2 had almost *c.o.*
3–3 *at foot of page;* this cause is *being* † *abv*. it is *c.o.*
4 *blotted;* aucthorety † *in other hand*   5 † *abv*. hym *c.o.*
6 And this was a pece of the Gret Masters reason to us, whenne we commened with hym; and therfor I put it in here *c.o. The next page (141 r.) is blank. On its reverse is an endorsement in a later hand and a contemporary pen trial, in which appear the names* Richard, John, Kingston, *and* Germanus.
7 *alt. from* it   8 h *c.o.*   9 *writ. over* to

It is said that the French King hath the better hand in Pyemont; the truth Good ⟨*i.e.*, God⟩ knowith.

Other tydinges I have not to signifie to your Lordship, but praye youe that I may be most hartely recommended to my good Lady your wife and¹ al my good Lordes and Master⟨s⟩ of the Consail there. And soo, my good Lord Master, hartely fare ye wel. At Parys the xiiij^th of Julye.

Your Lordshippes
assuredly,

STE. WINTON

Addressed: To my very good Lord, my Lord Lysle, Lord Deputie of Calays.

55. *To* LISLE

Paris, 10 January, [1537]

R.O., S.P. 3, 8, 65.* *L.P.*, XII, i, 59.

> Expects to be in Calais soon; begs to have ready shipping. (Gardiner evidently expected to be soon recalled, as indeed he was, 29 January; but Henry changed his mind before his return—*L.P.*, XII, i, 274, 626.)

My veray good Lorde, aftre my moost harty commendacions, with like thankes for my greate chere at my late being at Calays: Thise shalbe only to desire and pray your Lordship against my returne to Calays, whiche, God willing, shalbe on Monday cum sevennight or theraboutes, to take ordre that I may have redy shipping for me and my horses. For I entende, God willing, to make asmoche spede in my passage as the wynde and wether wil geve me leave. Thus desiring your good Lordship to have me hartly commended to my Lady, I beseche our Lorde have you in his keping. From Parys the xth of January.

Maister Wallopp hath him hartly commended to your Lordship, Maister Porter, and to al the rest of the Counsail, with al other his frendes there.

Your Lordshippes
assuredly,

STE. WINTON

Addressed: To the Righte Honorable, and my veray good Lorde, the Viscounte Lisle, Deputie of Calays.

Endorsed: My Lord of Winchestre, the xth of Janewary.

1 the *c.o.*

76

56. *To* Norfolk

Villeneuve St Georges, 6 June, [1537]

B.M., Harl. 6989, 74–5.* *L.P.*, xii, ii, 46.

News of the war between Francis I and Charles V; peace, without victory of either, would be to Henry's advantage; other diplomatic rumours.

After my most humble commendations to your good Grace: I trust that such letters as I have at sundry tymes wryten to your Grace be cumme unto your handes, but whither they be or noo I have not harde, for I receyved noo letters from your Grace thiese foure monethes past.

The French King is nowe at Founten de Blewe[1] and ther[2] huntith and makith chere, as though he wer in noo wer. His appointement was to goo to Molyns, but nowe it is doubted of by reason that the Burgoignons be noysed to be assembled[3] in a gret numbre, and entende to take Saincte Pol[4], which the French King hath fortified. This Saincte Pol, as your Grace knowith, was newtral, and therfor hath ever heretofore lyved in peace; and nowe it is brought in to the calamite of[5] werre, aswel as Savoye. And wel it maye be noted that, being a werre begonne betwen thEmperour and the French King for Myllain, al ther countries and Myllain also being in quiet, the miserie of werre troubleth only Savoye and Saincte Pol, countries belonging to neyther of them both.

The Gret Master of Fraunce, with whom I spake yesterdaye, estemeth al that thEmperour canne doo very lytel, and sayth that the Borgoionons be in noo numbre as they be bruted[6] abrode to be. And yet al other besides saye otherwise, insomoch as it is said that the French King himself cannot tel whither he shuld send such lanceknightes as he hath in to Italy, as he was determyned, or kepe them for the defense of his countrie.

The French King is accounpted to be charged monethly with payment of lanceknightes oonly cccᴹ ⟨300,000⟩ frankes, which is xxxᴹ ⟨30,000⟩ *li.* sterling, besides xijᴹ ⟨12,000⟩ Italians, which he[7] hath in Pyemont. And men cannot consider howe he shul employe thiese men, but oonly to defend. And ther parties to be defended lye very wyde. Every man spekith of want of money, and very moch.

---

1 *this and all other names of persons, places, countries, and nationalities, except* Turkes, *are underlined in this letter*

2 there *w. final* e *c.o.*   3 t *c.o.*

4 again *c.o.*   5 *writ. over* as

6 † *in other hand*(?) *abv.* bo(?)uted *c.o.*   7 p *c.o.*

Of thEmperour himself we here nothing, saving that he is in Spayne, and wold have money. Many wyl nedes byleve that thEmperour shal wynne us against[1] the French King. I wyl not byleve it tyl I see it; for it is a good rent that the Kinges Highnes our master hath of Fraunce. And me thinkith it wer better for us to wishe such an agrement bitwen the Emperour and the French King, as neyther shuld yeld to other, thenne to helpe the oon to overcumme the other. And what soever men talke here, I cannot knowe that the King our master is otherwise mynded.

The Turkes cummyng is not moch feared; styl it is spoken of, but bicause he taryeth soo long it is no more regarded.

The Bishop of Rome shuld have made a mariage with thEmperour, bitwen[2] a nephieu of his and the Duches of Florence, with hope, as sum men say, to recover the Duchie of Myllain. And nowe they saye that inasmoch as thEmperour doth soo instantly sue unto us for mariage of my Lady Marye to the Infant of Portugale, in contemplation of which mariage thEmperour wyl geve the state of Myllayn to the said[3] Infant, that therfor the mariage with the Bishop of Rome stayeth; and therfor the Italyans doo accounpte us Imperialles. Thus men talke here, and of more certainte I cannot advertise your Grace.

Chastilion[4] goth nowe in to England to be there ambassadour resident, and the Bishop ⟨of Tarbes⟩ retournith. What I shal doo I cannot tel, but I have within thiese foure dayes bought mules and other[5] necessaryes, as though I shuld not be sent for hom, but tary here styl. For, seing I have taryed soo long, I wyl not, with sute to cumme hom, loose any peace of such thanke as elles percace I might have. I wyl serve[6] diligently and truely, and thinke of nothing elles worldly. Almighty God preserve yo[ur] good Grace in moch felicite. At Ville Nove Saincte Geo[rges], the vj[th] of June.

Your Graces humble
bedeman,

STE. WINT[ON]

Addressed: To my Lorde of Norfolkes good Grace.

1 v c.o. 2 the c.o. 3 E c.o.
4 Chastilions w. s c.o. 5 others w. s c.o.
6 r in serve † abv. a letter c.o.

57. *To* LISLE

Lyons, 19 October, [1537]

R.O., S.P. 3, 8, 68.* *L.P.*, XII, ii, 948.

News of the war.

My very good Lord, after my right harty commendacions: I have noon other newes to send youe but such as al the worlde knowyth[1]—that the French King makith here a mervelous preparation to passe over the mountaynes, but al shal not be in a redynes bifore thend of this moneth.

The Turke[2] retyred himself without doing any notable acte, wherby he hath lost his reputacion.

The Venetians, that we ever noted to faver the Turke, have nowe procured[3] a leage against him.

ThEmperour, as it is said, hath taken, besides Narbonne, a castel to countrevayle the taking of Heding by the French King. And thus the worlde waverith and fortune playne.

I thinke they might leave game whenne they wold, for al the poore folke that looke on be wery, and themself also.

I have nowe[4] noon other matier. Wherefore, desiring your Lordship to make my harty commendations to my good Lady, most hartely fare ye wel. At Lyons the xix of Octobre.

Your Lordshippes
assured frend,

STE. WINTON

Addressed: To my very good Lord, my Lord Deputie of Calays.

58. *To* CROMWELL

Pierrelatte, 23 January, [1538]

R.O., S.P. 1, 128, 148–9.* *L.P.*, XIII, i, 131.

Gardiner's posters; he needs horses and money; is distressed at the diplomatic situation (*i.e.*, the truce between Charles and Francis, of 11 January, 1538, and their refusal to accept Henry as peacemaker).

My very good Lord, after my most harty commendations: I send youe herwith Master Wyattes letters, open, as they wer sent me, enclosed in

1 *alt. from* knowle   2 *writ.* Turked
3 t *incomplete follows*   4 nowe *repeated*

79

this pacquet. I though⟨t⟩ Franciscus wold have been retourned from Spayne or this. Nowe I depech Rede, who canne skyl of runnyng. And my posters be in England: Olyver, Massey, Arture Poley, Saintclere, Henry Fraunces, and Story, and then Barnabe who canne doo wel. I have sued to the Kinges Highnes for a passe porte for vj horse, wherof, I thanke youe[t], youe have geven me two. If the Kinges Highnes graunte my sute, such of my[t] men as wyl cumme, may on those horse repare hither that I nowe provide to be brought hither. I praye youe further my sutes both for horse and money, for I have mervelous gret nede of both.

I nede wryte to youe nothing of the matiers conteyned in my letters to the Kinges Highnes; it wer but superfluous. This troublith me that any man shuld thinke we had nede of ther promyses. Me thinkith it wer possible they shuld depende of us. And thenne the Kinges Highnes, as he is emperour in dede in his realme, soo he shuld in deade *imperare* through and over al[t], and himself no further to care what other men doo, but al they to care what he doth. In that me thinke wer quietnesse. And I am wery of travayl, and specially in wryting such displeasaunte matier. I must ever wryte as truth requireth; and shal, as wel as I canne, releave my werynes with remembraunce of my princes goodnes, in whose service[1] my mynde shal never faynte as long as my body maye endure.

This berer hath desired me to wryte that at your next depech in to Spayne, he may be sent; and soo I praye youe that he may be, for upon[2] counforte therof he hath promysed me to make diligence. And thus most hartely fare ye wel. At Pierelate, the xxiij of January.

Your Lordshippes
assuredly,

STE. WINTON

Addressed: To my very good Lord, the Lord Pryve Seale.
Endorsed: My Lord of Winch., xxiij of January.

1 I *c.o.*   2 prome *c.o.*

59. *To* LISLE

Moulins, 12 February, [1538]

R.O., S.P. 3, 8, 67.* *L.P.*, XIII, i, 265.

Asks him to forward a packet; news of the French Court. (The 'two gentlemen' were the Lords of Veniers and Sarzay—Du Bellay, *Mémoires*, ed. v. 4. Bourrilly and F. Vindry, Paris, 1908–19, III, 442.)

My singuler good Lorde, after my most harty commendations to your Lordship and my good Lady: Thise shalbe onely to desire your Lordship to send this, thEmperours pacquet, into Flaunders, according as I doubte not but Master Wyat in his letters requireth your Lordship to doo, making a newe pacquet ther† of[1] and directing the same to Master Hutton. Newes here bee noon, save that the last Sondaye the Grete Master was made Conestable of Fraunce, and this next Sondaye ij gentlemen shall fight at oultrance before the King. And thus, trusting shortly to see youe, in the meane season I shall bidde your good Lordship, with my Lady, most hartely farewell. From Molines the xij[th] of February.

Your Lordshippes assured
to my litel power,

STE. WINTON

Addressed: To my singuler good Lorde, the Lord Visconte Lisle, Deputy of the Towne and Marchies of Calais.

60. *To* BONNER

Vierzon, 20 August, [1538]

Inner Temple, Pety MS. 538, 47, 353–64. Copy, once belonging to Bonner. *L.P.*, XIII, ii, 143 (1). B.M., Add. 21,564, 1–12. Another copy, by same scribe, also once in Bonner's possession. *L.P.*, XIII, ii, 143 (2). The Temple MS. is here followed. The B.M. copy is less carefully made, phrases being sometimes left out and meaningless words inserted. Since it contributes nothing to the determination of the text, its variations from the Temple copy are not here noted.

---

1 them *c.o.*

Résumé of matters in negotiation with France; French digressions from treaty obligations (the treaty for which Pommeraye was commissioner was that of 23 June, 1532); how to remind the French of the pension due to Henry VIII; foresight and speech fitting an ambassador; Henry's desire to see in person possible French brides, before contracting marriage; how to get information from other ambassadors; how to behave at Court and elsewhere. (The interview mentioned under article v was that between Charles V and Francis I at Nice, where, on 18 June, 1538, a ten years truce was concluded.)

The Bysshopp of Winchestre, for the instruccion of Master Docto*u*r Boner in such tenne articles as he hath put in wryteng, and generally in al other thynges concernyng the Kynges Hieghnes affayres, and the office commytted to the sayd Docto*u*r Boner of legacion and ambassyate in the Co*u*rt of France, sayth as foloweth:

The fyrst artycle is: What affayres and matyers the Kynges Hieghnes hath here dependyng, or to be set forth, and in what termes and state the same dooth consyste?

1. To this article the sayd Bysshopp sayth that the Kynges Hieghnes hath with the French Kyng a lege of perpetual amytye, inviolably observed on the Kynges Hieghnes behalf. By this lege ech prince is bounde to other in mutual defence, at the chardge of the requyrer of ayde, of ther states and possessyons, with such a lymytacion of the quantytye of the ayde as is conteyned in that treatye.

2. By this treatye neyther prynce maye maynteyne others trayto*u*r or rebelle, but uppon request made by letters is bounde to delyver them; wherin, whether the Kynges Hieghnes will chardge the French Kyng for the not delyverance of Poole, uppon request made by the Bysshopp of Winchestre, yt ys to be referred to his Majestieys determynacion, beyng the matyer of so great importaunce.

3. By the treatye of perpetual peace, the French King is bounde to paye yerely, at the fyrst dayes of Maye and Novembre, about iiij^{xx} xv^M ⟨95,000⟩ Crounes of the Sonne and od money, and over that tenne thousand crounes, at the sayd two termes, for recompence of salt due as the treates therof purporteth, wherunto I referre myself.

4. That pentyon hath been unpayed foure yere and more at the lest.

5. Ther hath also passed betwene the Kinges Hieghnes and the

French Kyng an other treatye, wherin one Pomeraye was commyssioner for the French Kyng, toucheng mutual ayde to be geven by see, in cace of any invasion to be made by thEmperour on eyther prince; which treatye conteyneth alsoo, besydes other articles, that neither prince shall contracte any mariage ne make any leage in prejudice of thother. This last yere the French Kyng demaunded thayde conteyned in that treatye; wherunto the Bysshopp of Winchestre, by instructyons from the Kynges Hieghnes, reasoned and aledged to the French Kyng and his Counsail howe the Kynges Majestie was not bounde to geve any such ayde by force of that treatye, inasmuch as the French Kyng had before digressed from that treatye, wherby yt could noo lenger oblige the Kynges Hieghnes to doo any thing by force therof.

Fyrst, the French Kyng digressed from that treaty in making allyance with the Bysshopp of Rome, Clement, in maryeng the Dolphin to his niepce.

Secondly, the French Kyng digressed from that treatye in geveng his doughter to the Kyng of Scottes.

Which two mariages wer booth prejudicial to the Kynges Hieghnes, and therfor therby the treatye on ther parte dissolved.

To thiese two objectyons the French Kynges Counsail answered:

First, with the Bisshopp of Rome, they saye they dyd that they dyd to the Kynges Hieghnes benefyte, to obteyne sentence of Clement, which they had obteyned at Marselles, yf commyssion had been sent thither. And thus they goo about to avoyde that.

As for the mariage with the Kyng of Scottes, they saye they made yt by the Kynges Hieghnes consent, alledgeng the late Lorde Rocheforde to have declared the Kynges pleasour unto them in that bihalf.

They saye further how that mariage is not prejudicial, for the Kynges Hieghnes and the French Kyng beyng perpetually allyed and so good frendes, the Kynges Hieghnes maye not alledge thaugmentacion of the French Kynges freendes to be his prejudice, but rather benefyte; and soo the treatye by that mariage is not offended.

This matyer hath been reasoned in England, and there thambassadour hath ceased in it, as the said Bisshopp hath been advertysed. But here, at such tyme as the Bisshopp reasoned with them at Chompiegne, Master Wallopp beyng there present, the French Kynges Counsail was veary styf in there solucions byfore wryten; wherunto the Bysshopp replyed, but they yelded not. And synnes, the Bysshopp never reasoned with them in the matyer.

The Bisshops replicacions wer thiese:

To ther first solucion, which consisteth in facte, the Bisshopp, in replyeng, denyed thaffyrmacion of obteyneng sentence, for he was at Marselles.

To the seconde the Bisshopp sayd, what the Lord of Rocheford said he cannot tel; but it wer not reason a light worde of an ambassadour shold be alledged for an excuse of vyolatyng of a treatye so solempnely made.

To the third the Bisshopp sayd that ther exposicion of prejudice had only a gaye apparance, but in dede yt must nedes be prejudicial to the Kynges Hieghnes that a kyng of Scottes should with such allyance be encoraged and made of a greater stomake; wherby such redresse of justice, as for attemptates on the borders shold be requyred, shalbe the more untowardly answered and slakked, which is lyghtely to folowe; consyderyng that in ther lesser astate the kynges of Scottes have been veary negligent in that behalf. And this prejudice ys apparant, besydes such other as wisdom, not for feare of danger, but for procuryng of more quyet and avoydeng trouble, ⟨sheweth⟩.

⟨6.⟩ The French Kyng also, furst by mouth and aftre by a letter of his owne hand, promysed the Kynges Hieghnes three articles: In any peace he shold make, to have the Kynges Hieghnes principal contrahent; item, not to consent to any Counsail without the Kinges Hieghnes agreament; thyrdly, to ayde the Kynges Hieghnes with lendyng asmuch money as the Kynges Hieghnes did now forbeare.

Soo the matyers be in nombre six:

The peace,
Tharticle of delyvery of rebellyons,
The pentyon,
Tharrerages,
The treaty of Pomeray,
The French Kynges promesse.

Thiese matyers stand in thiese termes:

1. The peace invyolable on the Kynges Hieghnes bihalf, and not called in questyon with the French Kyng.

2. The article of delyvery of rebellyons: The Kynges Hieghnes hath not alledged yt yet openly for a brech, but keapeth yt in store to doo as his Grace shal thinke good.

3. The pencion is without questyon to be payd.

4. The arrerages therof unpayd do so remayne to be demaunded or not demaunded, as the Kynges Hieghnes shal thinke good.

5. The treatye with Pomeray remayneth thus unspoken of further then is before expressed.

6. The promysse the French Kyng sayth he is not bounde to keape, referryng al his promyses without wryteng to be understanded by the wryteng of his owne hand. And thenne the wryteng of his owne hand, he restrayneth yt by a clause of prayour, added in thende; and thus he and his Counsail wil nedes understand yt. And fynally, by the fayth of a gentleman, he sayth, he ment it soo. And neyther he ne the Conestable wil gladly here of it, as they have hitherto said; but yet the occasion of tyme may serve soo that they wil here of it, and therfore the termes yt standyth in be not to be forgoten.

And this is theffect of al matyers dependyng, with declaracion in what state and termes they stande in.

As for matyers to be set forth, the Kynges Hieghnes hath by his last letters suspended al tyl thiese men here shal make any mocion, or the Kynges Majestie shal thinke good to treate further with them.

And thus the first article is answered.

The seconde artycle: What thing is juged to be a good meane to avance and to wel set forth the same, or any other matyer it shall fortune the Kynges Grace to have here; and what is lyke to hindre or hath been hinderance to the same?

To this article the Bisshopp sayth that thambassadour resydent useth always wyth moderacion, aftre a good facion and with dexteryty, as of himself, to put the French Kynges chief counseilour (as is nowe the Conestable) in rememberaunce before the daye of paiment cummyth, to make provysion for the payment at the tyme; sayng, 'Monsieur Le Conestable, although the Kynges Hieghnes my master wryteth not unto me of this matyer, yet, beyng in this roome here, I knowe yt ys my duetye to sollicite at your hande the provysion of such payment wherunto ye be bounde by treatye. I doubt not you wol see unto yt, but other busines may cause youe percace to forget it, and therfore for the zele I have to the sincere observacion of such covenauntes as hath passed, I cannot lesse doo but speake, which I doubt not youe woll take in good parte.' And yf the money be unpayd at after the daye, then, as of yourself, to speake also in lyke sentence to the French Kyng.

85

Neverthelesse, bycause the rememberance of the pencion maye be sumtyme more displeasant thenne thopportunytye of other of the Kynges Hieghnes affayres shold requyre, youe shal do wel to have consyderacion of tymes, and not to be more busye therin thenne shalbe ordred out of England; from whens youe shal do wisely to desire instructyon in that bihalf.

And this is for avanceng the payment of the pentyon.

As for al other matyers, I, the Bisshopp of Winchestre, judge that for thavancement of al other matyers set forth, or to be set forth, youe cannot use noo better meane thenne wysely, diligently, and cyrcumspectly to folowe and observe such instruccion as shalbe prescribed from the Kynges Hieghnes in any matyer to be commytted unto youe.

And fyrst, with yourself to note and consyder what ye be commaunded to doo and saye; and before youe speake with the Kyng, to devyse what he might objecte, and so to prepare what youe wol replye therunto, to thentent youe maye be furnesshed to mayntene communicacion whensoever audyence shalbe geven unto youe; forseyng alwaye that ye commen no further thenne your commyssion woll beare youe, and not to forget, with your owne wytt and learnyng, to maynteyne that shalbe commaunded and ordeyned to be spoken of youe.

Be neyther in communicacion to sharpe, wherby youe shold exasperate them, ne duller in language thenne the cace shal requyre. Thaffectyon ye be commaunded to endure is ever best; and whenne that is not spoken of, to use the moderacion; and so a mynestre with wysdom and dexterytye maye avance or hindre sumwhat thaffayre. But the chief hinderance consisteth ever in thopynyon of proffyt or dysprofyt, which the French Kyng or his Counsail shal conceyve in the matyer which is in hand. If the matyer be thought profytable, it wil easely be avanced, yf other wyse, yt is not regarded. Every man seaketh his owne; and this hath been and is lyke to be thynderance of many good matyers. And further I cannot speake in that matyer.

The third article is: What hath been desired, on the Kynges Hieghnes behalf, toucheng the General Counsail, and of thanswere made therunto?

To this the Bisshopp sayth that first, in the matyer of the General Counsail, the French Kyng made promesse not to agree to any without the Kynges Hieghnes consent; and that of himself, before any such request was made unto him. Afterward his promesse was requyred and was made, as is before written, and thenne refused, as is before expressed.

The fourth article is: What hath been desired on the Kynges Hieghnes behalf for the principal contrahent, and what hath been answered therunto, and to what purpose it is cum?

To this the Bisshopp answereth that the French Kynges promesse was requyred and made as afore, and yt is cum to this purpose, as is before wryten, that nowe he sayth he is not bounde therunto, bicause he is bounde but by wryteng, and the wryteng is, for not fulfyllyng of the request conteyned in yt, voyde. Thus he answereth nowe, and persisteth styll in yt, as is declared before more at lardge.

The fifte: What hath been moved for mariages, and specyally for mariages toucheng the Kynges Hieghnes personne?

To this the Bysshopp sayth that two yeres past the French Kyng moved of himself a mariage betwene the Duke of Orleance and my Lady Mary, which was much talked of; but thenne the French Kyng wold nedes have her as legitime, and so that brake of.

Nowe of late, a lytle before Ester, the French Kyng moved that mariage agayne, and wold be content to take her not legitime, but soo as thEmperour, in contemplacion of that mariage, shold geve the Duchie of Millan to the Duke of Orleance.

This seconde overture hath not been much commened of, but stayed uppon the maner of declareng and openyng it unto thEmperour. For the Kynges Hieghnes wold never agree yt shold be proponed to thEmperour onles the French Kyng wold first, for a reciproque, bynde himself to fulfil the two articles, which he had before promysed, for not agreyng to the Counsail without the Kynges Hieghnes, and, in peace to be taken with thEmperour, to make the Kynges Hieghnes principal contrahent. In tyme of commenyng wheruppon, this treux hath been concluded and thenterview taken effect.

And as concernyng mariage of the Kinges Hieghnes personne, wher as his Majestie, as reason requyred, wold gladly see the personage with whom he shold contract, before he entred a bonde of soo long contynuance as mariage requyreth, and therfor desired that the Quene of Naverne might repayre to Calays with three or foure of the noble ladyes in Fraunce in her cumpanye, the French Kyng hath refused to agree therunto, but yet hath offred that whatsoever personage his Hieghnes could be content to have and chose within the realme, he wold cause her to be conveyed unto his Majestie accordingly. And thus that matyer stayeth, and the Kynges Hieghnes, yf the French Kyng shal speake of yt, and wylbe content to sende for that purpose commyssyon in to England, wil ther be content to commen further of the matyer, and use more acceleracion and fewer delays thenne hath bene used here. And this is al the Bisshopp of Winchestre knoweth concernyng mariages.

The vjth artycle is: Whether I maye have a copye of the mynutes and letters with other wrytenges sent fromhence to the Kynges Hieghnes and my Lord Privie Seale, or hether from them?

To this article the Bisshopp sayth that he never reteyned with him copye of any thing wryten in to England, neyther to the Kynges Hieghnes ne my Lord Privie Seale, for in thosse matyers he hath wryten of, he for himself hath trusted his owne memorye. And as for such letters as hath been wryten unto him out of England, he shal have the copyes, yf he wol wryte them out, with al his herte.

The vijth article is: Who ar the men that ar rekoned to have the most intelligence of the state of thinges here, and of other countreys; of ther nature and qualytyes; and what shalbe most expedyent for me in atteineng of knoweledge by them and the certeyntye of thinges?

To this artycle the Bysshopp sayth that princes ambassadours be rekoned to have the most intelligence of the state of thinges here and of other countreys, for comenly they be chosen men of experyence. And as for ther nature and qualytyes, wyse they be, and without great famylyarytye they wol goo about to knowe what they can, and saye themself as lytle as they maye, for ech one feareth to be noted auctour of any advertysment. Aftre acquantance they maye percace, with long protestacions and many adjuracions not to name them agayne, shewe sumwhat; but elles they wol not shewe what they knowe. I founde Master Wallopp wel acquanted and, as yt wer, deane and most awncyent of ambassadours. In his tyme I acquanted myself, and after his departure remayned in aucthoritie, and had al thambassadours resort unto me, and one, myn especyal freende, whom, within thiese xv days, God hath called to His mercy. Other have resorted unto me, and with al sortes I have used to commen, and of dyverse tales have picked out that hath been lightely; but among ambassadors a trueth is to be knowen. Not that al that they shal saye is always to be beleved; but, uppon occacion of ther talkeng, to serch further; and as a man by experience hath founde and perceyved oon to speake more playnely and truly then an other,

88

so to geve the more credyte unto him. Wherfor, tatteigne knoweledge at ther hand, yt shalbe moost expedyent for youe, by al ways and means, to insinuate yourself in to ther frendshipp, and by conformytye of maners tatteigne their amytye; not pretendyng to serch tydynges at ther handes, for thenne they wol avoyde youe, but first, acquantance only, and thenne yf, by the waye, they wol talke, to note it, and devyse youe to tel them newes, and by such means to induce them indirectly to that which apertly they wold refuse. For no man wold be noted a reaporter of that he knoweth. Fynally, yt ys a rare matyer to happen uppon a certayntye; and the matyer maye be almost past or youe atteigne that maye be called certentye; for oon thing the world laboureth nowe chiefly in, to make by secrecye all thinges uncerten. And therfore in an uncertentye feare reasonablye the worst. And yf youe shold nedes fayle, ther is lesse danger in fearyng to much the worst thenne in beleving with over much securytye that wer the best. For, as tholde proverbe of England ys, the best wil save ytself, the worst had nede of provysion. And to close upp this artycle, I fynde this by experience, that the know-lege of matyers dependeth more upon a comparacion in judgement, by experience what hath been doon, what is lightely and wer reasonable, thenne uppon any reaport; albeyt reaport confyrmeth yt wel, who can chance uppon oon that wylbe so faytheful as to reaporte trulye. Such I happened onne, which is dede, Jesus pardonne his soule. And other have I founde veary honest, who cannot nowe stande in that steade. And this is al I canne saye therin.

The viijth article is: How I shal behave myself to the French Kyng at my cummeng to his Grace, and in delyverance of my letters to him, sent from the Kynges Hieghnes; lykewise to the Conestable, Cardynal of Lorayne, and the Chancelour?

To this the Bisshopp sayth that he with Master Thyrleby have com-myssion to present youe to the French Kyng; and therfor apparelyng yourself in longe geare or shorte as they shalbe, accordyng as the place appoynted for audience shal requyre, youe, takeng with youe the Kynges Hieghnes letters wrapped upp in a cleane paper, shal goo in cumpanye with them and make reverence as they shal doo. And when the Bysshopp shal have signefyed the cause of your sendyng, youe shal then take out the Kynges Hieghnes letters and, kysseng them furst, shal delyver them to the French Kyng, saying that the Kynges Hieghnes maketh by youe unto him his most herty and effectuous recommendacions; and the Bysshopp shal supplye the rest for the first accesse, onles youe thinke good of yourself to desire the French Kyng of favorable audience when youe shal have occacion to have accesse unto him.

And as for the Kynges Hieghnes letters to the Conestable, Cardynal of Lorayne, and the Chauncelour, youe maye in delyverance of them make the Kynges Hieghnes most herty recommendacions unto them, and suffer them to rede the letters. And when they have red, saye that wheras the Kynges Hieghnes, appointyng youe to be his Graces ambassadour resydent in this Court, hath now recommended youe unto them by his gratioux letters, youe of yourself desire them, in contemplatyon of them, to favour youe soo, as yf nede requyre, youe maye have accesse unto them; ther goodnes wherin youe woll not only signefye to the Kynges Hieghnes, but also, yf by your owne service ye can in any parte deserve it, youe wolbe redy to ymploye yt accordyngly; or with such other courtely wordes as ye can better devyse.

The ix[th] article is: *In publicis conventibus* what is thordre, what place, and of the ceremonys therin?

To this the Bisshopp sayth that *in publicis conventibus*, yf youe be invyted to be present, the maner is to goo, onles it shold be to such an acte as youe thinke the Kynges Hieghnes wold not alowe.

When youe be there, your place is next thEmperours ambassadour, and ever before the Kinges of Portinga[le].

The ceremonyes be, that the French Kyng wol appoinct youe oon to leade youe and keape youe cumpanye. Forsee always that youe lese not your place of honour before the King of Portyngale.

The xth: In the obteyneng of audyence, what is the custome, and what to be observed on my behalf?

To this the Bisshopp answereth that whenne ye wol have audience, youe must sende before to the Conestable, or, the Conestable beyng awaye, to the Cardynal of Lorayne, and, in booth ther absence, to Villandre or to him that shalbe noted to have the mayneng of thaffayres; and, signefyeng your desire to have audience, to requyre them to knowe the Kynges pleasour, and, as you shalbe appoincted, to observe and keape your howre and tyme in any wyse, for comenly they tary for no man.

In this cace youe maye be a lytle troubled yf youe have from the Kynges Hieghnes special commaundement to tell your matyer to the French Kyng only; for beyng soo commaunded from home, youe maye not do otherwise, and yet they that shal mayne the affayres wol not therwith be best content.

I cannot tel what I shold saye further, but in your lodgenges abrode requyre to be lodged where thambassadours of England have been lodged; geve som money to the furrors, but not to often. Take hede of pykeng and steleng with a diligent forsight, and force ⟨*i.e.*, foresee⟩ to remove al matyer of occacion. Accomodate yourself to ther maner. And, observeng the premysses, you shal passe over this your office with satysfaccion of your duetye and contentacion of yourself and them, as farre as the dyversytye of the nacion wil permitte and suffer.

Endorsed by Bonner: The copie of the Byshop of Wynchesters answers made to my requestes, delyvered to me at Vieronne ⟨*i.e.*, Vierzon⟩ xx° Augusti.

INTRODUCTORY NOTE TO NOS. 61–8

Of these letters, written 1542–4, two (Nos. 63–4) have to do with things academic, the others with matters arising out of relations with the Empire, renewed by Gardiner's mission to the Imperial Court in 1540–1.

The chief academic matter which occupied his attention, as Chancellor of Cambridge University, in 1542, was the pronunciation of Greek. John Cheke and Thomas Smith had been endeavouring to introduce at Cambridge what they believed to be the ancient pronunciation. Gardiner favoured the current pronunciation, that of contemporary Greeks, and, after requesting Cheke not to proceed with the introduction of his theories, issued a decree, 15 May, 1542, forbidding such innovation (*see L.P.*, XVII, 327[3]). This was followed by a lengthy epistolary discussion with Cheke. The reason for not reprinting this already twice printed correspondence is given above, p. xvi. Moreover, the hitherto unpublished letter to Smith (No. 63) gives Gardiner's views on the topic in sufficient detail. This and No. 64, reminding the Vice-Chancellor of Cambridge, in 1543, of the decree on Greek, and instructing him to reform the 'dissolute manners' of regents who had eaten flesh in Lent, are highly characteristic expressions of Gardiner's mind and method. In No. 63 we also have an incidental discussion of the nature of justice and of certain legal usages.

As for relations with the Empire, Gardiner's mission of 1540–1 had resulted in an agreement between Charles V and Henry VIII to treat for an alliance sometime before the end of April, 1542. On 2 May, 1542, Charles commissioned Chapuys, his ambassador in England, to do so; but before the commission arrived, Gardiner, evidently growing anxious lest Charles no longer desired the alliance, went, on 11 May, to live in a little house in Stepney, near Chapuys' lodging, ostensibly to escape the sweating sickness, but really to sound Chapuys on the subject. How he did so is entertainingly described in No. 61, and further negotiations, after the arrival of the commission, are reported in No. 62. These were interrupted by the war with Scotland, but concluded by a treaty, 11 February, 1543, providing for mutual aid in case of invasion of either monarch's territory, and for a joint expedition against France within the next two years. Norfolk entered French territory in June, 1544, and in July laid siege to Montreuil. Suffolk crossed to Calais, 3 July, and proceeded to invest Boulogne. Gardiner had crossed, 2 July, in his capacity of Purveyor General, a post he had held in the wars with Scotland, 1542-4, superintending the purchase and distribution of victuals and munitions for army and fleet. Two brief notes (Nos. 65-6) were written before the coming of Henry VIII, who reached Calais on 14 July, at night. On 26 July he and his counsellors encamped at Boulogne (*L.P.*, xix, i, 974; ii, App. 10), and it must have been there that Gardiner wrote the Epistle to the Reader (No. 67) with which he prefaced his first book against Bucer.

Boulogne surrendered on 14 September, 1544. Meanwhile Charles V had advanced toward Paris as far as Château-Thierry, and, receiving no reinforcements from Henry, made an advantageous peace with France at Crespy, 18 September, 1544. In a moment of over-confidence at Boulogne, Henry had told the Imperial envoy, Antoine Perrenot, Bishop of Arras (son of the Sieur de Granvelle, Charles' chief minister), that he had no objection to the Emperor making a separate peace. Henry was already negotiating for peace with France, but, as soon as Charles was out of the war, he was at a disadvantage. The French insisted on the restoration of Boulogne, and negotiations broke off, 25 September. They were resumed and broken off again in October, and Hertford and Gardiner were dispatched to the Imperial Court, then at Brussels, to remind Charles that, according to his treaty obligations, he was bound to declare himself again an enemy of France, since France had continued the war by invading English territory at Guisnes. Charles professed every intention of abiding by his treaty with Henry, but said that if he stayed at peace with Francis I he would be better able to secure advantageous terms from him on Henry's behalf. Finally, on 20 November, he asked that he be not pressed to take any definite action for ten weeks. Thirteen letters written by Gardiner in Hertford's name and his own, describing negotiations on this mission, are not here printed (*see* above, p. xvi). The single letter we have from him as an individual at this time is No. 68.

61. *To* HENRY VIII

Stepney, 12 May, 1542

RO., S.P. 1, 170, 115–17.* *L.P.*, XVII, 319. *St. P.*, IX, 23.

How he has contrived to sound the Imperial ambassador, Chapuys, on a possible alliance. (For the answer to this letter *see L.P.*, XVII, 320. *Cf. ib.*, 325.)

Pleasith it your Majestie to understande that yesternyght, after myn arryval at Stepney, I dyvysed to pyke a quarel to speke with thambassadour, in such wise as it might serve to the purpose of that I shuld speke afterward; and therfor sent unto hym this message, that by chaunce I was his neighbour for a seson, and having been thre yeres in Fraunce, I had there lerned a lesson to be bold to send for wyne wheresoever I thought the best to be, and moch more if my frend[1] had it; whereupon I sente[2] nowe unto hym for summe wyne to my supper; for that maner of Fraunce, I sayde, lyked me, and many of ther other conditions I lyked not very wel, for I was a French man oonly in that poynt. Thambassadour lyked the message very wel, and specyally that I sayde I was a French man oonly in that poynte; and therupon sent his secretary unto me to desire me to dyne with hym the next daye, with offre to cumme to[†] salute me in the mornyng folowyng; which he wold have doon, if I[3] had not prevented hym. And soo we camme togyther rather of his provocacion thenne of myn, as he takith it; and I have soo facioned myself in our communication al this forenone that he sueth unto me to be a meane to your Majestie that he maye repare unto the same and be more graciously harde; for he knowith by his owne wisedom that your Majestie maye be the staye of Christendom, and the amitie bytwen your Majestie and thEmperour to be the very meane to extincte the light enterprises of Fraunce, and to expelle the Turke, and to quiet Germanye; and that without your Majestie there canne be nothing stable. And for that purpose he byganne to divise with me howe he might take occasion to have a newe accesse unto your Majestie, instantly to make sute unto the same, on thEmperours byhaulf, to be content to treate upon sum mater that might be an introduction to amytie, not by way of practise, but ernestly, addyng that there was nothing soo dere unto hym as his owne lyfe, but that he wold aventure upon that he shuld open to be prosecuted and performed by thEmperour. He said he could not facion hymself noon other commission

1 it *c.o.*   2 *alt. from* sende   3 d *c.o.*

thenne he hath, and he wold it wer such as might please your Majestie to accepte. 'But,' quod he, 'I have letters from thEmperour to warrante me to propone that I shal propone, and to conclude that I shal conclude; and, for pledge of thEmperour, letters auctentique under his seale; to conferme al I wyl bynde my body and lyfe, and wyl alsoo wryte dyligently and with spede to atteyne them.' Al that the French men doo, he knowith, and grauntyth, and in his jugement thinketh your Majestie oonly mete[t] to[1] be woed and sued for, which he wyl[2] gladly doo, and hath divised with me howe I coulde helpe hym therin. And, forasmoch as I sawe hym in this good trade, I wold not shewe myself over bold therin, but told hym that in dede I wold fayne it wer wel[t], but I durst not myself medle over ernestly in it; but told hym I wold consulte with my Lord Pryve Seale, as of myself, whither he thought it wer best for thambassadour to sewe for audience agayn or not. And with this resolution I departed from thambassadour[3], as it wer to speke with my Lord Pryve Seale, and soo to retourne this night. And to be sure of me, he hath invited me to dyner tomorowe, and, as I perceyve by hym, wyl doo as I shal avise hym, to sue to your Majestie as ernestly as maye be, and therupon to sende, wryte, treate, here, bynde hymself, and doo al thing that might further this matier of[4] amitie bytwen your Majestie and thEmperour; and I doubte not but he wyl use hymself in such sorte and facion as maye be pleasaunt and acceptable to your Highnes.

In our conference we spake of al such matiers as your Highnes had signified unto me by Master Sadler; and thambassadour considered them wisely, and finally concludeth your Majesties amitie most necessary to thEmperour; and, to atteyn that, wyl doo that in hym lyeth. And upon knowlege of your Majesties pleasour, I shal descend with hym to sum particularites, as[5] the same shalbe signified unto me; most humbly desyring your Majestie that I maye be advertysed whither I shal advyse thambassadour to sue to your Majesties Counsayl for audience or to your personne[6]; and I doubte not to frame hym accordingly, for the man is of hymself moch desirous of sum good effecte bytwen your Majestie and thEmperour in a perfection of amytie. And, as I may knowe your Majesties special pleasour, soo shal I further procede, havyng nowe such opportunite therfor as a better coulde not be wished. And thus I praye Almyghty God to preserve your Most

---

1 w *c.o.*   2 wylbe *w.* be *c.o.*   3 to s *c.o.*
4 a *c.o.*   5 it *c.o.*   6 *alt. from* persome

95

Excellent Majestie in long, prosperous, and contynual felicite. At Stepney, this Fryday the xijth of Maye.

> Your Majesties most humble
> and obedient subject, servaunt,
> and dayly bedeman,
>
> STE. WINTON

Addressed: To the Kinges Most Excellent Majestie.

Endorsed: The B. of Wynchestre to the Kinges Majestie, of the 12 of Maye, anno 1542.

62. *To* RUSSELL, BROWNE, *and* SADLER

Stepney, 17 May, 1542

R.O., S.P. 1, 170, 138–41.* *L.P.*, XVII, 329 (where address is erroneously given).

Chapuys' argument that Henry VIII, being great, rich, and wise, should prevent the destruction of Christendom at the hands of France and the Turk, by an alliance with the Empire, thus meriting the title 'Father of Christendom,' and incidentally collecting from France his unpaid pension.

After my most harty commendations: Thiese shalbe to advertise youe that yesterdaye at afternone¹ I was with thambassadour, and talked with hym from two of the clok at after none ²until viij of the clok at nyght, and I founde hym a wonderful glad man that he hath newe letters wherupon to have accesse to the Kynges Majestie. He shewed me his commission signed and sealed in a solempne forme, with ample power to treate and conclude, and to bynde thEmperour, his heyres, and countries for that shalbe concluded in articles of defension, offension, confirmation of old treaties, amplyfying or addyng unto the same.

And thambassadour told me that he hath such ample instruction that he maye conclude in matiers reasonable, without sendyng unto thEmperour again. I asked hym what he ment by matiers reasonable. He sayde he ment nothing therby but that if they wer not such as he thought he shuld not have here moved unto hym being of gretter weight thenne he coulde thinke³ on as yet. And thenne I laboured with hym to knowe sum specyaltie; and he shewed hymself very desirous to divise with me,

<hr>

1 *alt. from* afternonn   2 u *writ. over* t   3 hym *c.o.*

and thenne told me howe the matier we had talked of, †byfore tharryval of thiese lettres†, was but a cold matier—to have old treaties confyrmed. 'Christendom,' quod he, 'is vexed and troubled with dissension of thEmperour and the¹ French Kyng, and also infested with the Turke², by procurement of the French Kyng. In this tragedy the Kynges Majestie³ hitherto hath not intermedled, but geven the lokyng on. Nowe,' he said, 'it is to be considered that this trouble shal ende eyther by agrement or by force. If it ende by force, thenne, if the Turke prevayleth, he shal confounde al. If the French Kyng prevayle, he cannot cesse, but styl serch a newe troble and be intollerable. And if thEmperour have the upper hande, he shalbe thought to gret. If the trouble shuld ende by agrement, it is comenly seen that those which have been newter be, in such agrementes, not always soo provyded for as otherwise they shuld be. The Kynges Majestie,' he sayde, 'hath his astate soo unite and himself soo established in it, as his Highnes nede⟨s⟩ not, for the conservation therof, eyther the amitie of thEmperour or French Kyng, and therfor, in respecte of that particuler intrest, might remayne newter. But in respecte that God hath ordened his Majestie to be soo gret a prince, soo rich a prince, with such excellent wisedom, his Majestie shuld not let Christendom perish in his tyme, but use his gretnesse, his riches, and his wisedom to the pacification and repose of Christendom; wherby his Majestie shuld obteyne the good wyl, gret renowne, and fame of al the worlde, and also deserve rewarde of God.' And herin, he sayth, he wold wishe it wold please the Kinges Majestie to joyne with thEmperour, who takith the Kynges Highnes as his father. And by this acte the Kynges Highnes shal merite to be and be called Father of Christendom. Many moo wordes he spake, which I omytte, tendyng to persuade the Kynges Highnes againste the French Kyng. I asked hym thenne, whither he ment to have the Kinges Majestie to entre werre against Fraunce. He told me he ment thus, that the Kinges Majestie and thEmperour, being conjoyned, shuld thenne by al wayes and meanes bryng the French Kyng to the termes of reason, or elles werre to ensue. I told hym⁴ the Kynges Highnes had noo cause of werre⁵. He sayde the deteyning of the Kynges Majesties money is a most juste cause of werre, consideryng that they doo not oonly deteyne it contrary to ther pactes, as he thought, but also they use it and occupie⁶ it to the trouble of al Christendom. 'And thenne,' quod he,

1 *alt. from* ther(?)   2 p *c.o.*   3 our(?) *c.o.*
4 your *c.o.*   5 I *c.o.*   6 occupieth *w*. th *c.o.*

'what is it to sollicite a Turke to invade Christendom? Doth he not therin procure the Kynges Majesties our masters daungier? If the Turke have an[1] entre, wyl he not over al, and he canne? But,' quod he, 'if the Kynges Majestie and thEmperour joyne, considering that on ther parte[2] shalbe most stedfastly in the quarel against the Turke al Germany, and Spayne most ernestly, the French[3] King shal not dare continue obstinate against al.' Soo, as he rekennyth, that with thauctorite oonly of the Kynges Majestie al shal be quyeted and reason ministred to al parties. And he wold the matier of the Turke to be the principal matier in open apparaunce, wherby to allure the good wyl of the worlde; and other convenauntes to be bytwen the Kynges Majestie and thEmperour upon what poyntes they shuld procede to an hostilite with Fraunce and, after hostilite, upon what articles to take peace and agrement; with provision[4] to be made if the Scot or Denmarke move against the Kynges Majestie at the French Kinges request. And he added this also, howe for assure payment of the pention of Fraunce, in cace of agrement, the Kynges Majestie shuld have of the French king, Bolen, Ardre, Muttrel, and Turwyn, with the appertenauncces of that countie. And if the Kynges Majestie[5] thus joyne with thEmperour, al Christendom shal fynde themself releved by the Kynges Majesties goodnesse: [6]the Kyng of Romaynes brought[7] out of mysery, the Germanye delyvered from feare of the Turke, the Duke of Savoye restored to his right, al Christendom disbourdened from charges of these werres, and the dreade of England sumwhat quykened in the French mennes hartes, wherby they shal the better knowe themself; and concluded that it lyeth nowe in the Kynges Highnes handes to make the worlde newe again. I told hym he spake of moch honnour, but it was costly. To that he replyed and sayd it shuld be apparaunt in reason that theffect desired should folowe without any cost, if the French Kyng be not over moch blynded; for feare of wurse wold enforce hym to agree. And if he dyd not, the Kynges Majestie shuld not nede spende moch more thenne his Majestie nowe spendith in fortifications. This accounpte he made. I tolde hym the fortifications may not cesse for any thing. He sayde not al but sum myght; and this[8] matier of werre shuld be such as wherunto al men wold glad⟨ly⟩ geve al they had. And, on the other syde, if wer folowe not, the Kynges Highnes shal have for interponing of his auctorite somoch honnour as

1 en(?) c.o.   2 is c.o.   3 sh c.o.
4 with c.o.   5 Majesties w. s c.o.   6 t writ. over Ky
7 of c.o.   8 alt. rom the

never prince had, and therwith recover a raunsom of Fraunce, as he rekonneth, nowe being in ther handes due and[1] unpayde. And thenne he went agayn to the other syde: 'If the worst folowed, which is werre, howe canne worldly honno*ur*,' quod he, 'be encreased but with cost?' and[2] reasoned that newtralite was neyther suer ne proufytable in conclusion. And here he made me a gret discourse of Fraunce, howe they even nowe use the Kynges Majestie, bycause they see his Majestie in a newtralite, aswel[t] in reteyning the pention, as also in setting forth other practises with Scotland, with Denmarke, soo as they might have meanes to annoye the Kinges Majestie, if his Highnes did aske it. I told hym thenne that if the Kynges Highnes did ernestly aske it, they wold not refuse it. And thenne he asked whither Fraunce in my jugement wyl gladly paye money continually to such a realme as England is, which pretendith title unto them, and with ther tribute shal waxe richer and richer to be able therby to subdue them. 'They must,' quod he, 'doo ther duetie for feare, or they wyl never doo it, whatsoever they saye unto youe. And if ye wene,' quod he, 'they meane good fayth with youe, ye[t] be abused.' And thenne he sware unto me that he is advertised howe the French Kyng hath excused hymself at Rome, that he practiseth with the Kynges Majestie oonly to interrupte such practise as was bytwen the Kynges Highnes and thEmperour. 'And yet I am sure,' quod thambassadour, 'they make to youe an other demonstration'—with many other reasons that he used, to long to wryte. But by this the Kynges Majestie may perceyve what thEmperour[3] wolde have, and what this man wyl sue for, with offre to conclude in them without sendyng agayn to thEmperour, with such conditions as shalbe requisite for the same. And[4] whenne he had made this discourse he asked howe I liked it. I told[5] hym I wold wishe the Kynges Majestie and thEmperour to be soo conjoyned as myght be to both ther satisfactions and the benefite of Christendom. He told me God had offred this occasion to the augmentacion of the Kynges Highnes honno*ur*; relief and socour to procede from hens to al the rest of Christendom. He asked me whither in discoursyng with the Kynges Majestie he shuld make mention of my being with hym[6], and I told hym it was best naye, considering I had had noo commission to talke with hym. He noted moch unto me the chaunce of our meting, our communication, his desyre of newe letters, and the arryval of them in this opportunite; for he sayth, he hath

1 up *c.o.* 2 the *c.o.* 3 *alt. from* they
4 for(?) the *c.o.* 5 I *c.o.* 6 it me *c.o.*

been soomoch suspecte of merchaundise that, without newe letters and thEmperours owne commission, he shuld with moch feare have repared to the Kynges Highnes to whom, for the gret wisedom he seth in hym, he bearith as gret a reverence as if he wer his natural souverain lord; and yet howe good and affable the Kinges Majestie is to confere with, if the matier be not over untowarde; and yet in al matiers, of what sorte soever they have been, he hath had noo cause to complayne. I have nowe touched the substancyal poyntes of our conference, brevely in respecte of our communication, but more¹ at lenght thenne nedith to be reaported to the Kinges Majestie, which I referre to your discretions. And soo most hartely fare ye wel. At Stepney, this Wedonsday in the mornyng.

Yours assuredly to my
lytel power,

STE. WINTON

Addressed: To my very good Lord, my Lord Admyral, and the Right Honno*u*rable Sir Antony Browne, Knight, Master of the Horses, and Sir Raulf Sadeler, Knight, oon of the Principal Secretaryes to the Kynges [Maj]estie.

Endorsed: My Lord of Winchestre t⟨o⟩ the Counsail at the [Courte], xvij° Maii, anno xxxiiij[°].

63. To THOMAS SMITH

The Court [at Havering], 18 September, [1542]

B.M., Royal App. 87, 34–8. Sixteenth-century copy. *L.P.*, XVII, 803.

Has read Smith's treatise (published at Paris, 1568, as *De recta & emendata Linguae Graecae Pronunciatione*, and reprinted in Havercamp, *Sylloge Altera*, 1740. *See also L.P.*, XVII, 611); now understands Smith's nature better; friendship for Cheke has apparently led him to tax Gardiner with ignorance; Gardiner's edict on Greek pronunciation was not due to the persuasions of Smith's enemies; true, the ancient pronunciation differed from the modern, but usage has made the latter correct; a legal analogy, which Smith, as a teacher of law, should appreciate (he became Regius Professor of law at Cambridge late in 1541 or early in 1542); nor should he ask Gardiner to encourage licence on the plea of liberty; it is the ancient pronunciation which

1 the c.o.

is corrupt, not the modern, which is universally employed by scholars; the sound of diphthongs is unpleasant; modern pronunciation is easier to learn; it is impossible to discover in detail what the ancient pronunciation was; Erasmus' wise reply to Melanchthon concerning scholastic theology; Smith should not waste his talent for law, which Gardiner recognizes, on such trivial matters. (The place of writing is determined by Gardiner's presence in Privy Council meetings at Havering, 13–20 September—Dasent, I, 32–4.)

Inter gravissimas occupationes, Smethe, libellum tuum libuit perlegere, ut quem hominem ex brevi, in congressu, colloquio penitus intro-spicere et perspectum habere non poteram, in tam longo verborum con-textu et continua orationis serie, certius mihi cognitum et exploratum haberem. Neque enim omnino falsum est illud, 'Qualis est homo, talis oratio.' Nec quid alii mihi de te renuntiarunt, sive illi amici tibi sive inimici fuerint; quicquid[1] moror, non iam illis sed mihi credo. Tantum illud optem, ut se quisque nosceret. Quod ne in tuam omnino contu-meliam dictum arripias et me hominem libenter dicacem iudices, ab ea nota ne me ipsum quidem excipio; quem ab humana conditione non

---

In the midst of the most important engagements it has been my pleasure to read your treatise, Smith, from beginning to end. It was impossible for me, in the course of a brief conversation at a public gathering, to acquire a deep insight into your personality or to feel that I had explored beneath its surface. It was my purpose, therefore, by perusing this lengthy composition, with its uninterrupted flow of argument, to make myself better acquainted with you and to become possessed of a more accurate understanding of your nature. For the famous remark that a man's personality is reflected in his speech ⟨cf. Cicero, *Tusc. Disp.*, v, 47 and Seneca, *Epist. Mor.*, 114, 1⟩ is by no means untrue. I have not received information about you, moreover, from other people, whether friends or enemies of yours. If I feel any hesitation concerning you, it is now based on my own judgment, not on theirs.

I could only wish that everyone possessed self-knowledge. Now, that you may not seize upon this remark as in any way an insult, or regard me as a sarcastic person, let me say that I do not exempt even myself from the criticism implied; I do not claim immunity in the slightest degree from the limitations of human nature, as if I were some rare sort of creature ⟨cf. Juvenal, 13, 141⟩. But whatever kind

[1] *MS.*, quicquam

omnino eximo, quasi sim gallinae filius albae. Sed qualis ego cumque sim, non mea, aut morum aut ingenii aut etiam eruditionis, sed muneris praerogativa vobis praesum, vobis impero, edico, severius fortassis quam res exigeret, ni temporum ratio, ni hominum impotentia et effrenis libido duriora remedia efflagitasset. Tu pro tua cum Chaeco amicitia (quae illam quam Dionisius Tyrannus tantopere admiratus est amicitiam aliqua ex parte refert, quatenus certe Chaecum causae subducere, te autem eius loco substituere contendis, omnino exprimit) omnem ex verbis meis occasionem captas ut tecte[1] tamen, ut reverenter, ut placide, ut in factum concepta exceptione, mihi obiicias modo errorem scilicet, modo lapsum, imperitiam, ignorantiam, atque adeo interim mihi tribuens egregia epitheta et facti mei invidiam in homines maledicos, invidiosos, et qui vobis male volunt, quique bolum e faucibus per vos ereptum dolent, rhetorico consilio derivans. Quae si

---

of person I may be, it is not because of any distinction of my own, whether of character or ability or even of learning, but because of the privileges of my office, that I am in control over you, that I give orders to you and issue edicts—doing so, perhaps, in a more severe fashion than the matter at issue would require, were it not that the tendencies of the age, the lack of discipline and the uncontrolled licence to which people are prone, call for stringent correctives.

Now, your friendship for Cheke—one which recalls in some measure the famous friendship ⟨of Damon and Phintias⟩ so greatly admired by the tyrant Dionysius and which, indeed, exactly reproduces it to the extent that you are displaying eagerness to withdraw Cheke from the case and to take his place yourself—this friendship, I say, has led you to seize every opportunity which my words afford to tax me, now actually with some error, now with some slip, at another time with inexperience or ignorance. You do so, to be sure, guardedly and respectfully and gently and as though taking exception merely to an action; and all the while you employ complimentary terms of address, and by the use of rhetorical devices transfer the odium pertaining to my action to persons spoken of as slanderous and envious and as wishing ill to you and your friends, persons who are distressed at having had a choice bite suddenly snatched from their jaws through your agency ⟨cf. Terence, Heaut., 673, and see Havercamp, 564⟩. But even

1 *MS.*, teste

constitutio coniecturalis esset, me nullo pacto suggillarent. Labi nimirum, errare, et falli in facti questione prudentissimus quisque et eruditissimus poterit. At vero in literaria cognitione que possit acrius ignorantia obiici quam si quis dicat hominem non sua sponte sed aliorum delationibus, aliorum hortatu et suasionibus, aliorum consilio quicquam, non suo, statuisse—praesertim cum toties contra et scriptis et literis praessus sim meum me iudicium sequi, a multis confirmatum et probatum quidem, magnis etiam praeiudiciis corroboratum, sed animi mei sententia et disquisitione apud me excussum et deliberatum ac statutum, tandem et in edictum, quod praetuli doctorum virorum approbatione, expositum. Nemo me fefellit, nec aliquo animi mei errore falsus sum. Vos magnas chartas impletis illo vitiosissimo argumenti genere et doctis fastidioso, dum rem non ambiguam sed concessam pergitis illustrare.

---

if this account of the situation were conceivably correct, those people could in no wise browbeat me.

Any person, certainly, however careful and learned, is liable to make slips and errors and blunders when a question of taking action is involved. On the other hand, in an investigation pertaining to the world of letters, what more serious charge of ignorance could be brought against a person than to claim that he had reached a decision, not of his own accord, but by reason of accusations laid by others, or as a result of the urging and the persuasive promptings of others, or in reliance on the opinions of others instead of on his own? Especially do I resent the imputation, since pressure of the opposite sort, derived from writings and from literary works, was so repeatedly brought to bear upon me to follow my own judgment, a judgment supported and approved indeed by many, and reinforced besides by weighty precedents, but one which I, applying my mind to deliberation and inquiry, had pondered over and reflected about and decided upon by myself and then finally made public in the form of an edict, which I promulgated with the approval of scholars. No outsider has led me astray, nor have I been led astray by any error of my own mind. Yet you and your friends fill page after page with that highly objectionable kind of argument, a kind of argument that is offensive to scholars, while you go on elaborating a point about which there is no controversy but which is freely conceded.

Quis enim neget aliam fuisse antiquis sonorum in literis speciem quam quae hodie obtineat? Ego vero quoties hoc concessi! Plato in 'Cratylo' habet antiquiores dixisse ἱμέραν, alios postea ἐμέραν, quod Plato suo seculo ἡμέραν dicebat. Quid potuit ad distinguendos literarum sonos dici manifestius? Et tamen hodie posteriore litera retenta η, sonus antiquissimus qui in ~ι̑ ι tum erat repetitus videtur. Hoc vos negatis fieri recte. In eo proprie quaestio est. Ego vero non quia rectum est fieri dico, sed ideo quia fit rectum esse ut fiat. Citaveram in hoc Aristotelem, quum diceret quasdam voces esse ad placitum, et vulgatam versionem sequutus sum! Quantum legibus versatus cur improbes non video. In quibus nimirum de pacto placitum praedicitur, sive enim συνθήκην pactum voces sive foedus sive conventum, elegantissime exprimit omnia placitum, verbum Latinum purum putum et rei exprimendae appositissimum. Nam et pactum et foedus et conventum

---

For who would deny that the character of the sounds indicated by the letters of the alphabet was different in antiquity from what it is to-day? How many times, indeed, have I conceded this very thing! Plato, in the *Cratylus* ⟨418 B–D⟩, asserts that the word ἡμέρα, which had eta as its initial vowel in the period in which he lived, had been pronounced with an initial iota by men of an earlier age and with an initial epsilon by other people at some later period. What statement could have been made that would indicate more explicitly that the sounds of the letters were differentiated? Yet to-day, though we retain the later spelling with eta, the most ancient pronunciation of the word, which at that time was represented by the spelling with iota, seems to have been revived. You maintain that this is done incorrectly. It is precisely there that the point at issue lies. My contention, indeed, is not that it is done because it is correct but that because it is done it is the correct thing to do. I quoted in this connection a statement of Aristotle ⟨*De Interpr.*, 16ᵃ 19, 16ᵇ 26⟩, a passage in which he declared that certain expressions were conventional—and, what is more, I followed the commonly accepted rendering. Why you, who are so thoroughly acquainted with the field of law, should disapprove of this I fail to see. In that field the term 'convention' is certainly applied to an agreement; for whether you think of συνθήκη as an 'agreement' or a 'covenant' or a 'compact,' all of these notions can be expressed with the greatest elegance by *placitum* ('convention'), a Latin word pure and simple, and most admirably adapted to expressing the idea. For

placitum continet ut genus species, ut non sit cur displiceat ista versio— nisi forte adverbium non recte appositum sentias, quod magis puto, et tamen 'ad' verbum efferre Latine dicimus, significantes secundum verborum seriem rem efferri, ut nihil prohibeat κατὰ Graecum eo adverbio non inepte exprimi. Quod autem petis, ut addere quaedam liceat, hoc est tanquam principium petere, quod ego non dabo.

Nudum est argumentum quod effers de veste. Iurisconsultus de tenendis certis rerum nominibus non pronuntiat, sed quid fiat, enuntiat, non tamen quasi semper id fiat, sed quia maxima ex parte. Vocabula enim iurisconsultorum ad exactam rationem dialectices si exegeris, multos intellectus absurdos gignes, quos semper vitabis. Rerum vocabula non fere mutantur atque ita dicuntur immutabilia, ut a maiori parte denominata. Id quod in plerisque obtinet alibi contractus innumera-

---

'convention' includes 'agreement' and 'covenant' and 'compact' as genus includes species. So there is no reason why that rendering should fail to meet with your approval, unless, as I am inclined to believe, you happen to feel that the preposition ⟨in the phrase 'ad placitum'⟩ is not correctly employed. Yet we say in Latin that the word 'ad' gives extended application, indicating thereby that a notion is extended in meaning to apply to a whole series of terms. So nothing prevents our using this preposition as a not inappropriate equivalent of the Greek κατά. As for your request that certain expansions of the phrase should be permitted ⟨see Havercamp, 484⟩, I shall not grant it, for the expansions would involve a sort of petitio principii.

The argument which you illustrate by talking about clothing ⟨see Havercamp, 484–5⟩ is itself in need of dressing up. A jurist does not render decisions that are concerned with maintaining fixed names for things, but he states what the practice is, not however as though it were always adhered to, but because it is adhered to for the most part. For if you investigate the language of jurists in accordance with the strict principles of dialectic, you will bring to light many strange inconsistencies—and these you will always thereafter avoid. Words for things as a rule do not change and in consequence are called immutable, as being terms employed by the majority of people. That which holds good in most instances is spoken of by the jurist at times, when his attention is fixed on the numerical predominance rather than on pre-

bilis dicit, ὑπερβολὴν numeri, non ἀκριβίαν spectans, alibi et in numerato esse contractu[1]; et mutari usu rerum vocabula plusquam manifestum est, tum Graeca, tum etiam Latina, praesertim cum in utraque lingua figura valeat quae Abusus dicitur. Secundum quam figuram' piscinam' dicimus, non eam rem significantes cui primus nomen imposuit, in qua sunt pisces, sed quam usus induxit, in qua lavamus. Item εὐήθης Graecum primam significationem amisit et eam solum retinet quam usus ascivit. Age vero, si rerum vocabula non mutantur, unde Abusus celebrata figura? Si mutantur, quo colore defendas iurisconsultum, qui rerum vocabula immutabilia affirmet? Dices Abusu id fieri; fateor, sed quem authoritas defendit et contra usum veterem tuetur. Haec enim vis est propria temporis ut, usu accedente, lente ac placide rerum naturam prope modum immutet, rustica urbana, urbana rustica, obscura clara, consona absona mutua vicissitudine sursum deorsum iactando efficiat.

---

cision of statement, as being of unlimited application, at other times as being limited in its application. Yet it is more than clear that words for things, Greek words and Latin words too, do change as a result of use. This is especially so since in both languages the rhetorical figure called 'misuse' ⟨catachresis⟩ plays an important part. It is in accordance with this figure that we employ the word *piscina*, not to mean the thing to which the name was originally applied (a place where there are fish), but to mean the thing which has been substituted for it by usage (a place where we wash). Likewise, the Greek word εὐήθης has lost its original meaning ⟨'good-natured'⟩ and retains only that meaning which usage has adopted ⟨'foolish'⟩. Now, consider this: if words for things do not change, what has made this figure of 'misuse' so widely prevalent? But if they do change, with what show of reason could you defend the jurist who declares that words for things are immutable? You will say that the change occurs by means of 'misuse.' I grant you that; but it is a 'misuse' which authority supports and upholds in the face of the older usage. The passage of time possesses this characteristic property: working slowly and tranquilly, with the co-operation of usage, it alters, to a considerable extent, the character of things; it changes rude to refined and refined to rude, and makes clear what is obscure and discordant what is harmonious, turning things upside down by a process of reciprocal change.

As for myself, I see what the facts were regarding the sounds of the

1 *MS.*, contractus

Ego in sonis quod fuit video, si non clare, ut quid fuerit audacter profitear, ab eo certe distare quod nunc obtinet clarissime cerno et in meis ad Chaecum literis, cum primum scriberem, non obscure professus sum. Quid autem nunc in sonis usus tradat et servet, quoniam omnibus fere sensibus hausi, intellexi atque adeo percepi et comprehendi. Quod certum est, tuendum esse putavi authoritate publica; quod nondum liquet, quod incertum est, tacitae meditationis tanquam in silentio relinquendum[1]. Vos constanter affirmatis in praesenti pronunciatione (nostra dico, non vestra) errorem esse. Ego vero mutationem a vetere manifestam non nego. Sed sane etiam error, quando ita vultis. At communis est error, publicus est, a reliquis omnibus quotquot vivunt mortalium extra vos duos, ubique receptus, probatus, habitus in honore apud homines doctos, non lusciosos, qui duas in una diphthongo vident vocales. Ego, qui errorem communem ius facere didici et veritati non

---

letters. Even if I do not see what they were clearly enough to make a confident declaration about them, I at any rate recognize very clearly that things were formerly different from what they are now; indeed, in my letter to Cheke, when I first wrote to him, I made this declaration in no uncertain terms. On the other hand, I have apprehended what usage now transmits and upholds regarding the sounds, since I have drunk this in with almost all my senses; this, indeed, I have grasped and come to understand. I have thought, therefore, that what is definitely established should be upheld by public authority. As for what is not yet clear, what is uncertain, this I have thought should be left, as it were, in the silence of unspoken meditation.

You and your friends consistently maintain that there is error in the present pronunciation—ours, I mean, not yours. I do not deny that the change from the old pronunciation is obvious. Indeed, error there truly is, since you will have it so. But it is a collective error, an established error, an error accepted and approved of everywhere, by every single living human being except the two of you, an error held in honour among scholars—and by scholars I do not mean half-blind people who see two separate vowels in a single diphthong. It would be strange indeed for me, who have learned to regard a collective error as justice and on occasion to deal with the truth as a matter of secondary consideration, to come to your support in a case which, if not wholly

1 *MS.*, reliquendo

numquam praeiuditium afferre, mirum ni vobis accederem in causa, si
non mala, certe ambigua et, magistratus publicus cum sim, privatorum
temeritati me adiungerem, publico et spreto et contempto concensu!
Haeccine tu suades, legum professor! Jus est ars boni et aequi, ut
eleganter finiunt iurisconsulti, et tamen iisdem authoribus sententia
iudicis iniqua ius dicitur. Cur tam varie? Equidem dicam, summa sit
semper ratio veri et in id tanquam in scopum dirigantur omnia. Sed
citra subsistitur aliquando tamen ac hominum vitio et in falso heretur et
iniquo. Quod cum accidat, propter finem in quem tenditur eodem id
ipsum quo destinatum nomine afficitur, ut tum ius cum sit iniquum,
verum cum sit falsum appelletur. Quod ni fieret, nihil unquam certi,
nihil definiti in quo acquiescamus, haberemus. At vero (inquies)
utrumque appellatur, revera iniquum sive falsum manet, nec rei naturam
mutat appellatio. Imo propter formam quae accessit rei iudicatae, iam
ius et dicitur et est, ac pro veritate accipi et haberi debeat. Ad quem
usum etiam de usu et placito doctorum hominum in sonis respondebo,

---

bad, is certainly questionable, and, in spite of the fact that I am a public
magistrate, to ally myself with the presumptuous behaviour of private
individuals, rejecting and holding in contempt what is publicly agreed
upon. Is that what you are urging upon me—you, a professor of law?

Justice is the art which deals with what is good and fair, as the jurists
neatly define it, and yet the unfair judgment of a judge is called justice
by the same authorities. Why this inconsistency? I shall state my own
position thus. Let there be always the highest possible valuation of
truth and let everything be directed towards it as towards a goal.
Sometimes we stop short of the mark, however, and through the
weakness of human nature are caught fast in what is false and unfair.
When this happens, on account of the end towards which our aim is
directed, the same designation is applied to what has been achieved as
would be applied to what is aimed at, so that it is actually given the
name of justice when it is unfair and of truth when it is false. If this
were not so, we should never have anything sure, anything fixed upon
which to rely. But, you say, whatever name is given to it, in actual
fact it remains unfair or false, and the name does not change its nature.
On the contrary, by reason of the formal conditions which attach to a
matter when it has been adjudicated, it is now called justice and is
justice, and similarly it ought to be received as truth and regarded as such.

Now, following the analogy of this legal usage, I shall give a

videlicet cum sententiae quandam rationem habeat et pari cum sententia authoritate nitatur, omissa quaestione veri et falsi, quae quodam praeiudicio oppressa iaceat, quod publica conspiratione obtinet et amplectamur omnes et sequamur.

At vero vos omnem movetis lapidem, nihil intentatum relinquitis, in falsa instrumenta, in testes corruptos gravissima oratione invehitis, tanquam veri tuendi acerrimi propugnatores. Si caetera defecerint et nihil ex ordine auxilii supersit, restitutionis certe beneficium imploratis, aut saltem vindicias secundum libertatem. Quem docere non valetis, movere conamini. Excusas in re aggrediunda temeritatem. Retexis ab ovo omnem eius rei historiam, ostendis magnam in initio cunctationem— diligentem cum Chaeco deliberationem, magnam cautionem adhibitam, primum ne quem offenderes. Hactenus prudenter. Tandem simulasti tibi quaedam verba inconsulto excidisse. Hic certe fons est huius mali ! Et utinam in nemore Peleo continuisses te, Smethe, ab actione publica.

---

corresponding reply concerning the usage and conventional practice of scholars in the matter of pronunciation. My reason is, of course, that it has somewhat the character of a legal decision and rests upon an authority no less valid. The reply is this: Let us ignore the question of true and false, for that, disposed of by a sort of previous verdict, may well lie quiescent, and let us all embrace and follow that which is in force by general agreement.

You and your friends, however, leave no stone unturned, you try every possible expedient, declaiming against false records and corrupt witnesses with the most solemn rhetoric, as though you were ardent champions of the truth, fighting with all fervour in its defence. If other efforts fail and no assistance, in turn, is available, you beg the favour of a restoration of your former privileges, or, at the very least, a guaranty of freedom ⟨*see* Havercamp, 570⟩. Him whom you have not the power to instruct you try to move. You excuse your forwardness in setting the thing on foot. You repeat the whole story of this incident from the very beginning. You point to your great circumspection in the initial stages, telling of your diligent consultation with Cheke and the great caution you displayed that you might not, in the first place, offend anybody. Thus far you acted wisely. Finally, however, according to your pretence, certain words slipped from you inadvisedly. Therein, surely, lies the source of this unhappy business. How I wish, Smith,

Vide ut gradibus crescit audatia. Quod tunc proferre verebaris, nunc audes defendere. Nempe ab eo tempore scilicet tres iam in Gallia consuluisti, quorum alius non improbavit quod ageres; alius, qui primi nominis, contempsit; ipse vero Graecus et irrisit et sprevit. Haec non ab amico quodam tuo, ut alia, sed teipso refererente didici. Cui causa nulla est ut in teipsum incutiaris. Verum agedum, Smethe, quod a me tantopere contendis, ut dem vel praecibus vestris, vel regiae liberalitati vel equitati (quanquam hoc sane in loco regiae liberalitatis mentionem intempestive facis, ut quae una causam praecipuam dederat edicto meo), ne illa vestris inutiliter periret—verum agedum (inquam) leges apud tuos profiteris publice, ut turpissimum tibi fuerit a me postulare, quod mihi non fuerit legittimum concedere. Quid ergo petis? Vindiciasne secundum libertatem? Tu ni fieri liberti[1] dicis, si minus per leges quod libet licet? At hac ratione nemo est hodie liber, cui aliquid legibus sit

---

that you had refrained from public activity, that your Argo had never left the forests of Pelion ⟨cf. the frequently quoted verse of Ennius' *Medea Exul* (fr. 246, Vahlen)⟩! See how boldness increases with every step. What you then feared to bring forward, you now dare to defend. Of course, since that time you have consulted three scholars in France. Of the three, one expressed no disapproval of what you were engaged in; the second, a man of the first rank, had only contempt for it; while the third, himself a Greek, both ridiculed and despised it. These facts, mind you, I learned not from a certain friend of yours, as I have learned other things, but from your own actual report. You have no reason, though, for being smitten with vexation against yourself.

But really, Smith, in regard to the request that you are so earnestly making of me, that I grant, as a concession either to your prayers or to the generosity or justice of the throne, that this generosity shall not be withdrawn to the disadvantage of your friends—though your reference to the generosity of the throne in this connection is certainly inopportune, seeing that this by itself furnished the particular occasion for my edict—really, I say, it was highly disgraceful for you, who are a professor of law, holding a position of public responsibility among your students, to request of me what it was not lawful for me to grant.

What is it, then, that you are seeking? A guaranty of freedom? Is

[1] *no plausible emendation of this passage suggests itself*

interdictum. Effrenem illam in actione publica licentiam edictum meum coercet. Modestam[1] libertatem nihil imminuit. Sed sit ista vestra licentia libertas, ut etiam rerum nomina aliquando mutentur. Quid igitur mihi author es ut faciam? Abrogemne edictum? Minuam? Mutem? Et officio functus tanquam ex poenitentia munus repetam? Idne leges permittunt ut tanquam puerili sententia, Aio, Nego, Volo, Nolo, temere proferam! Eodem die circa accessoria aliquae partes sunt iudicis, ut Paulus ait. At vero multi iam menses praeterierunt, et tu non de accessoriis sed de re ipsa agis.

Sed fac licere cognita causa. Quid affers causae quod animum moveat? Non consentit (inquies) praesens pronuntiatio cum ea quae olim fuit apud ipsos Graecos. Hoc (inquam) totum extra controversiam sit, ut est, item a causa alienum. Neque enim quicquid fuit continuo

---

it your contention that you are deprived of freedom if you are not permitted by law to do as you please? According to that reasoning no one to-day is free to whom anything is forbidden by law. It is the unbridled licence displayed in public activity that my edict holds in check. It has not interfered at all with a reasonable freedom. But let us grant for the sake of argument that this licence of yours is not licence but genuine freedom, with the result that even the names of the things will be altered some day. What is it, in that case, that you propose to me that I should do? Revoke the edict? Limit its application? Alter it— and in this way, after performing a public duty, retract it as if in re- pentance? Do the laws permit me to blurt out at random as if with the capriciousness of a child: 'I say yes,' 'I say no,' 'I want it,' 'I don't want it'?

It is part of the function of a judge, as Paulus ⟨Julius Paulus?⟩ says, to deal with the accessory matters pertaining to a case on the same day. But in fact many months have already passed, and you are not dealing with any accessory matters but with the actual case itself.

But suppose that though your case has been investigated you are permitted ⟨to continue it⟩. What additional evidence can you bring that would affect one's attitude? Our present pronunciation is not in agree- ment, you will say, with that which formerly was in use among the Greeks. Let that fact, I shall reply, be considered, as it actually is, entirely outside the controversy and likewise unrelated to the case. For whatever has been will not necessarily, as a consequence, continue to be,

1 *MS.*, Modestiam

esse necesse erit, ut non probet hoc esse debere quod ab hoc contingit abesse. Multa fuere in honore vocabula, quae ut folia etiam nunc stant, casui tamen obnoxia cum volet usus. Sed quae nunc obtinet pronuntiatio (inquies) corrupta est. Ego quid corruptum voces nescio. Veterem cur iam corruptam vocem video, quum illa deleta et extincta generetur nova. Sic enim natura rerum exposcit, ut generatio unius sit corruptio alterius. Hic me verbis gravioribus adorieris et me obtestaberis ne vel in re seria ludere et rhetoricari. Dic ergo aliquid serium. Est (inquis) praesens pronunciatio corrupta, barbara, erronea. Haec te docere oportuit. Docui (inquies). Confer autores. Autores ostendunt aliam esse praesentem pronuntiationem, a vetere diversam esse, et alicubi e regione contrariam esse. At ipsa nomina quae causam urgent tuam sunt non ab autoribus petita. Alia sunt enim nova, alia barbara. Sed non licet cuivis mutare sonos (inquies) iam constitutos et certos. Posse quidem mutari sonos res ipsa ostendit. Cur etiam non sit liberum conaris

---

so that your argument does not prove that what happens to be non-existent in the present circumstances ought to exist. Many words have been held in honour in the past which, like leaves, are still in position, but which are liable to fall to the ground when usage wills it.

But, you will say, the pronunciation which is now in force is corrupt. I for my part do not know what you call corrupt. I see why I should speak of a pronunciation that is ancient as already corrupt, since by its suppression and abolition a new pronunciation is brought into being. For this is what the nature of things requires, that the bringing into being of one thing involves the corruption of another.

At this point you will assail me with words of uncommon solemnity and adjure me not to display levity and indulge in idle rhetoric in what, if you will, is a serious matter. Well then, I reply, say something serious yourself. The present pronunciation, you say, is in fact corrupt, barbarous, misguided. But these are assertions which it was your place to substantiate. I have done so, you will say; compare the authorities. The authorities show that the present pronunciation is different, is distinct from the ancient pronunciation, that in places, indeed, it is directly opposed. Yet the very terms which are employed in pressing your point are not derived from the authorities. For some of these terms are new, some are barbarous.

But, you will say, it is not allowable for any casual person to alter sounds which are already established and definitely fixed. On the

tu quidem ostendere, sed quantum ponderis habeant quae profers, alii
viderint. Mihi certe nondum fecisti planum. Quaedam in speciem
similia profers, sed quae sequentem sua sponte auditorem fallunt et
retinent; non retraherent nuntum ⟨?⟩[1]. Quod autem ex legibus affers.
Census et monumenta potiora sunt testibus. Ita demum verum est, si
res huiusmodi fuerit quae convenienter ex literis possit ostendi. Caetera
vero prout rei qualitas fuerit, testium est potior et certior fides. Itaque
crimen homicidii testibus certius quam instrumentis docetur, cum
scriptis mandari is casus non fere solet. Quod[2] si echo pingi posset[3]
et sonus literis clare exprimi, magnum attulisses ex legibus testimonium.
Quia, ut nunc res sese habet, prorsus extra aleas esse videatur.

Fingis literas tanquam statuas quasdam et illam imaginem multis
verbis persequeris. Sed vide, quaeso, quam sint hae statuae a caeteris

---

contrary, that sounds can be changed is, in truth, shown by the very
facts of the case. You, to be sure, attempt to show why it is not freely
permissible; but how much weight the arguments have which you
bring forward is a question I leave to others to decide. You have
certainly not yet made the matter plain to me.

Certain similar arguments you bring forward for display, but they
are arguments which mislead and delay the hearer who follows of his
own accord...⟨The reading of the MS. is unintelligible at this point.⟩
But this you adduce from the field of law. Records and monuments
are more reliable, you contend, than witnesses ⟨*see* Havercamp, 515⟩.
What you say is precisely true if the matter proves to be of the sort
that can appropriately be demonstrated from written documents. So
far as the affair is of a different nature, however, the testimony of
witnesses is more reliable and definite. So the crime of homicide is
more definitely demonstrated by witnesses than by documents, since
such an occurrence is not commonly entrusted to writing.

Now if the echo of a voice could be reproduced in a painting or a
sound be clearly expressed by letters, you might have adduced important corroboration from the field of law. This I say because, as things
are now, anything of that sort would seem to be utterly beside the
point.

Using figurative language, you speak of the letters metaphorically as
statues of various sorts, and follow out your figure at considerable

---

1 *no plausible emendation of this passage suggests itself*
2 *MS.*, Quid   3 *MS.*, possit

dissimiles. Illae enim eum unum referre consueverunt, cuius causa[1] positae sunt. At hae usu et consuetudine in aequalium et comitum suorum naturas degenerant et fiunt tanquam Hermaphroditae, ut in *i* et *u*[2] Latinis litteris, quae ambae vocales primum constitutae ac positae consonantium deinde naturam participarunt. Graeci, ut Plato refert, exili sono ι olim delectabantur, ut nihil mirum sit η et ι, postquam sedes suas proprias aliquandiu retinuissent, euphoniae tandem causa in sonum Graecis primum iucundum tam facile recidisse. Quod ego dico factum esse constat. At quomodo sit factum, a doctisne an ab indoctis, ab eruditis an barbaris, quaestio esse possit. Etiamsi ab eruditis manasse videri debeat, quod passim ab eruditis frequentatur et a vobis[3] solis ideo repudiatur, quoniam aliter sonuerunt veteres. Quod nemo negat.

Sed perge porro. Dic causam saltem fictam probabilem. Magna suavitas in diphthongis. Suavitas autem? Imo vero vastitas et rusticitas.

---

length. But just see, I beg of you, how different your statues are from other statues. For the latter have regularly had the function of representing the single person for whose sake they were set up; while yours, as a result of usage and custom, lose their individuality, taking on the character of their associates and fellows and sometimes becoming, as it were, hermaphrodites. This is true of the Latin letters *i* and *u*, both of which, though at first established as vowels, later came to partake of the nature of consonants. The Greeks, as Plato records, once took delight in the thin sound of the vowel iota, so that it is no wonder that eta and iota, after holding for a time their own individual places, finally for the sake of euphony slipped so easily into the sound that had long been pleasant to Greek ears. It is a well-established fact, I say, that this happened. But how it happened, whether resulting from the practice of learned men or unlearned, of scholars or of ignorant foreigners, might be a question; though, as a matter of fact, this pronunciation would rightly seem to have emanated from scholars because it is regularly employed by scholars far and wide and is rejected, on the ground that the ancients sounded the vowels differently—a fact which no one denies —by you and your friends alone.

But let us go on. Support your case with arguments which, if fictitious, are at least plausible. There is an extremely pleasant quality in the sound of the diphthongs, you declare. A pleasant quality? No,

1 *MS.*, causae   2 *MS.*, o   3 *MS.*, nobis

De vastitate nemo ambigat. De rusticitate autem dico: amplitudinem
vocalium rusticitatem sapere, id quod Therentius in 'Andria' aperte
indicat, cum Davum ancillae respondentem et eius verba repetentem
facit. Ibi enim cum ancilla Davo respondens dixisset 'vestri,' ille, ut
rusticitatem sono exprimeret, 'Cuius,' inquit, 'vostri[1]?' Quod tamen
non ita intelligo ut ubicumque sit vocalis amplior, continuo verbum
rusticum videatur; sed in loco ubi[2] de industria frequentius additum, ut
vocalium numerus augeatur, rusticitati exprimendae fit convenientius.

Est (inquies) facilior et expeditior et ad docendum et ad discendum
hoc pacto lingua. Id ego fortiter pernego; et hoc a vestris confictum est,
ut aliquem saltem habeat pretextum. Ego saepius feci periculum, et
habeo a me institutos, quorum in literis Graecis progressus istam

---

indeed; rather, on the contrary, a coarseness and lack of refinement.
The coarseness nobody disputes. As to the lack of refinement, however,
I make this assertion, that amplitude in the pronunciation of vowels
smacks of such a lack of refinement. This is plainly indicated by Terence
in a passage in the *Andria* ⟨vs. 765; the argument rests upon a mis-
interpretation of the passage⟩ where he represents Davus as replying
to the slave girl and saying her words over after her. For when the
girl in reply to Davus had said 'vestri,' he, in order that lack of refinement might be brought out in the way the word was pronounced, said
'cuius vostri?' This, however, I do not understand as implying that
wherever there is a vowel of greater amplitude, the word is in consequence seen to be lacking in refinement; it is simply that in a place
where an addition is often purposely made with a view to increasing
the amplitude of the vowels, the situation becomes more suitable for
bringing out the lack of refinement.

But, you will say, the language is in this way (viz., with the use of
the ancient pronunciation) easier and simpler to teach and to learn.
This I vigorously deny; it is a contention which has been invented by
your supporters in order that your case might at least have some
plausibility. I have tested it out over and over again, and I can point
to students I have trained whose rapid advance in the study of Greek
readily proves the idleness of your claims concerning the facility of
your method. In my judgment, if the usage of scholars actually had
permitted separate sounds for separate vowels, considerably greater

1 *modern texts of Terence read* nostri   2 *MS.,* ut

vestram facilitatem facile coarguat vanitatis. Si singulis vocalibus singulos sonos usus doctorum hominum permisisset, in elementis certe tradendis nonnihil maioris molestiae accidisset iudicio meo. Nec temere loquor sed cum ratione saepius experta et confirmata. Ergo affer tandem aliquid: rogas videlicet, oras, obsecras, obtestaris per omnia sacra. Preces (inquam) ne valeant sed causa. Pulchrum est (inquies) collapsa reponere, restituere divulsa, componere disiecta, suum rebus nitorem afferre. Liceat etiam nobis aliquid audere citra invidiam stertentibus aliis, vel quia nolunt vel non possunt vel non valent. Cur prohibemur navare operam quae gloriam nobis, academiae celebritatem pariat nullius cum incommodo et plurimorum bono? Quid autem in alterutram partem interesse queat, certe, ut indocti barbari, ignavi qui nihil innovari patiuntur, moleste tulissent? Non fuerat credibile tamen talem eos patronum habituros Episcopum, Cancellarium bonis litteris, etc. Quod sequitur meas laudes habet ad causam commode additas.

---

inconvenience would have resulted, at least in teaching the rudiments of the language. I am not speaking casually, either, but on the basis of principles repeatedly tested and confirmed.

So I bid you bring forward at last some genuine argument. Of course, you make requests and entreaties, you implore and beseech in the name of everything that is holy. Let not entreaties prevail, I shall reply, but the merits of the case.

But it is a fine thing, you will say, to rebuild what has collapsed, to set up what has been torn down, to put together again what has been pulled apart, to restore to things their own proper splendour. We should be permitted, you will continue, while others snore away because of unwillingness or inability or lack of power to act, to take a bold step without arousing any ill will. Why are we prevented from putting something into effect which will bring glory to us and fame to our University without inconveniencing anybody, something that will be to the advantage of a great number of people? And what difference could it make to one side or the other in the controversy, pray, that untutored barbarians, lazy folk who tolerate no innovations, should have taken offence? It was not to be supposed, however, you declare, that these people would have as their supporter such a man as I am, a bishop and a learned chancellor and all the rest. The passage that follows contains complimentary references to me added in a fashion calculated to further your cause. For in the inscription at the head of

Nam dicor in ⟨in⟩scriptione libelli tui literatissimus, cum vos sitis longe literatiores qui toti in literis estis occupati.

At cum Chaecum urgerem ut sonorum tanquam ad punctum restituendorum faceret periculum, ingenue fassus est se id quidem praestare non posse. Et sane utcumque conveniat aurium vestrarum iudicio αι cum nostro *ay*, an ita tamen sonabant Graeci expediri non potest, si nihil aliud, certe propter locorum et temporum intervalla, ut non verisimile sit sonos quos intra paucos annos tam elegantes habere cepimus, a Graecis accepisse vel a Graecis ad nos deductos esse. Sed est aliquid[1] ⟨quadam⟩ prodire tenus, si non datur ultra. Quod in hiis demum verum est quae necessariam rationem utilitatis habent. In quibus profecto, ut habet Horatius, medium et tollerabile interdum conceditur. At vero quae nullam rei aggrediundae necessitatem habent et, potuerit duci ⟨quia⟩ caena sine istis, tanquam symphonia discors

---

your treatise I am referred to as 'most scholarly,' though men like you who are entirely occupied with scholarly pursuits, are far more scholarly than I.

Yet when I was urging Cheke to attempt a restoration of the sounds in every slightest detail, so to speak, he frankly acknowledged that he could not, in fact, accomplish this. And, to be sure, however closely you, following the verdict of your own ears, may judge the Greek αι to coincide with our *ay*, it cannot be found out with certainty whether the Greeks actually gave it this sound—if for no other reason, surely because of the distance in time and space that separates us from them. It is highly unlikely, therefore, that we received from the Greeks sounds which only within the space of a few years have we come to regard as so elegant, or that these sounds were conveyed from the Greeks to us.

But it is something, you will argue, to make any advance at all, even though we are not permitted to go on further ⟨*cf.* Horace, *Epist.*, I, 1, 32⟩. This is precisely true in regard to those activities which are of such a nature that it is necessarily advantageous to engage in them. In such matters, certainly, as Horace puts it ⟨*Ars Poet.*, 368, 374–6⟩, 'moderate and passable achievement' is occasionally permissible. But, on the other hand, matters which involve no necessity of setting anything on foot and, because the feast might have gone on without them, are very properly hissed like an orchestra out of tune—such are the

1 *MS.*, aliud

exhibilabitur merito, habes irritusque conatus et inconsiderata voluntas stomachum potius quam irrisionem debeat excitare. Erasmus Philippo Melanchtoni homini iuveni et innovandis rebus propenso, cum Philippus apud eum per epistolam ageret de extrudendo et eiiciendo Scoto ac nomine eius ex albo scriptorum expungendo atque adeo tota scolastica theologia delenda, respondit homo prudens tum demum se de mutanda theologia scolastica deliberaturum quum de meliore quae substitueretur statuisset. Quod usum habet certum reiicitis, quia vestro iudicio barbarum. Quod inutile est sequimini, quod vobis arrideat. Et tamen fingitis causas utilitatis miras nugas. Linguam nostram Anglicam tanquam Lesbiam normam fingitis, ad quam Graecas diphthongos expenditis. Ut enim Lesbii fabri normam lapidi, sic vos Anglicam Graecae interdum aptatis et novo scribendi modo *pai* cum *i*, non cum *y*, scribitis. Sed eam literam alio sono donastis, ut si vos sequamur, eatenus orthographiam Anglicam emendemus. Nec amplius *pay*

---

matters that you have in hand; and futile effort and unheeding wilfulness might properly arouse indignation rather than derision.

Consider the reply which Erasmus gave to Philip Melanchthon, a young man addicted to introducing innovations, when Melanchthon was making a proposal to him by letter that Scotus should be cast out and expelled, and his name erased from the list of approved writers, and that the whole scholastic theology should to that extent be overthrown. The wise Erasmus replied that when he had determined upon a better theology to substitute for it, and not till then, would he consult about altering the scholastic theology.

That which has a definite use you reject, because in your judgment it is barbarous. That which is unprofitable you follow, because, as you say, it takes your fancy. Yet you invent evidences of utility which are as surprising as they are trifling. You treat our English tongue as though it were a Lesbian measuring-stick in accordance with which you take the measure of the Greek diphthongs. For just as Lesbian craftsmen adapt their measuring-stick to the marble, so you from time to time adapt English to Greek and, employing a new method of spelling, write our word *pay* with an *i* instead of a *y* (*pai*). But you have conferred upon that letter a different sound, so that if we were to follow your example, we should to that extent transform English orthography. We should write no longer *pay* but *pai*—that is, of course, if we accepted you and your friends as authorities. For you

scribamus sed *pai*, vobis videlicet autoribus, qui sonorum autores haberi postulatis, ut nostri (ut Graeci dicunt) phonasci[1] habeamini. Ego edixi ne id fiat. Poenas addidi ne quis contemnat, ne quis sua libidine ad aliorum pernitiem abutatur.

Non expedit de sonis contendere; est enim inutile et ridiculum. Id quod mihi cum praesens praesenti fassus sis, miror quo consilio tantum temporis contriveris in hiis nugis. Si ut occasionem captes ostentandae eloquentiae et te mihi venditandi, falleris multum opinione tua. Ego enim etsi literis delector et stili tui foecunditatem magnam memorie tuae commendationem habere videam, non pono tamen in verbis eruditionem. Et in studiis fere fit, ut quantum ostentationi accesserit, tantum iudicio soleat decrescere. Provincia quam suscepisti, ut leges interpreteris, totum exigit hominem et in eo iudicium incorruptum, integrum,

---

demand to be regarded as authorities in the matter of sounds, so that you may be assigned the rôle of our *phonasci* ('instructors in speech'), to use the Greek term. It was in order that this might not happen that I issued my edict. I included a specification of penalties in order that no one might treat the edict with contempt or wrongly follow his own inclinations to the disadvantage of other people.

It is inadvisable to dispute about pronunciation; it is in fact useless and absurd. I am filled with wonder at what your purpose can have been in wasting so much time on these trifles, a thing which you yourself acknowledged in my very presence that you had done. If it has been in order that you might find an opportunity of showing off your eloquence and recommending yourself to me, you are much mistaken in your expectation. For even though I take delight in literary studies and though I see that the luxuriance of your style provides a convincing testimonial to your powers of memory, I nevertheless do not regard erudition as a mere matter of words. It generally happens in the field of scholarship, as elsewhere, that to the extent to which increased opportunities for display are sought, there is likely to be a decrease in sound judgment.

The particular province of scholarship which you have taken over, that of expounding the law, calls for the exercise of all a man's powers; and in the man who undertakes it there must exist a sound and incorruptible judgment, which recognizes and distinguishes with unusual acuteness the classes to which things belong and the differences be-

1 *MS.*, phonasti

rerum species et differentias acutissime cernens atque distinguens. Cujusmodi bonam indolem in te video magna etiam promittentem, in nugis huiusmodi impediatur.

Hic mea me negocia avocant et finem scribendi facere rogant, quod mihi in ipso impetu et stili cursu est difficillimum, cum alioqui, quoniam res refrixerit, egerrime adducar ut tantum temporis in hiis nugis consumam quae nihil contineant utilitatis. Itaque vale, et sonorum causam, quam primus (ut ais) turbasti, maturiore iudicio cures ita quiescere ut ego prudenter edixisse, alii utiliter paruisse videantur. Ex Aula, xviij° Septembris.

STEPH. WINTON, Cancellarius.

---

tween them. The admirable talent in this direction which I discern in you, a talent which really promises great things, would be hampered by dealing with such trivialities as these.

At this point my duties call me away and demand that I bring my writing to an end. This is a very difficult thing for me to do when my pen is hurrying on with gathered momentum, though from all other points of view, inasmuch as the interest in the subject has been exhausted, I should with the greatest difficulty be induced to spend so much time over these trifles that have no profit in them. So farewell, and I trust that, attaining to a more mature judgment, you may make it your concern to lay to rest the matter of Greek pronunciation, which, as you yourself say, you were the first to stir up, so that I may appear to have issued my edict wisely and other men may appear to have obeyed it with profit. At Court, the xviij[th] of September.

STEPH. WINTON, Chancellor.

The Court [at Hampton Court], 15 May, [1543]

C.C.C.C., MS. 106, 185–8.* Lamb, 43. Strype, *Mem.*, I, ii, 481. Manuscript copies in Camb. Univ. Registry, Liber Rerum Memorabilium, 107 v. (sixteenth century); Bennet's Register of Emm. Coll. Camb., 244; B.M., Add. 5843, 419 (eighteenth century). Ellis, ser. 2, II, 206. Cooper, *Annals*, I, 405. C.C.C.C. is here followed.

> Regents who have eaten flesh during Lent are to be punished; the edict on Greek pronunciation is to be taken seriously. (The year date is determined by the reference to the edict of 1542 and by Edmunds' Vice-Chancellorship; the place by Gardiner's attendance at the Privy Council.)

Master Vicechaunceler, after my right harty commendations: Ye shal understande I have been advertised howe diverse of the regentes of that Universite, who shuld rule and be good example to other, have, the[1] Lente last past, very dissolutly used themself in eating of flesh; which faulte, howe it hath been punished here I am sure ye have harde; wherin I have been noted a gret avauncer and setter[2] forth of that punishement. Which rum*ou*r, albeit it be[3] not trewe, and that in dede the Kinges Majestie hymself, with thadvise of the rest of his Counsayl, did ernestly prosecute, as theffecte hath shewed in sum, that mysordre, yet neverthelesse, by[4] cause thoffense is gretter in scolers thenne in other, and specially called to the state of regentes, I cannot quyetly passe over and neglecte this enformation, having soo apparant and manifest truth as it hath, being† brought to light sondry wayes, as this berer canne enforme youe; unto whom I praye youe geve credence therin. Wherfor I praye youe† travayle with me for reformation, which I wold have soo used as the matier might be punished without encrease of the[5] slaunder, which might doo hurte to the hol Universite. And therfor I have divised and thought good that ye shuld secretely speke with such as be noted faulty and, enducyng them to confesse ther faulte and paye summe fyne by your discretion to be taxed to the use of the Universite, soo to dismisse them without further publishing of ther names; wherin I wold ye used such temperaunce as the payne wer not contempned ne the partie greved above his astate. But I wyl have it in any wise punished,

---

1 *alt. from* this; last *c.o.*   2 ter †

3 now *c.o.*   4 t *c.o.*   5 sh *c.o.*

for I wyl not suffer the Universite with thiese dissolute maners to be corrupte. Londes have not been geven ne lectures founded for any such evel purpose. If thoffenders wyl have pitie of themself and ther owne fame[1], and soo pryvely and secretly with youe submitte themself to punishement, I[2] wyl gladly bere with them; but otherwise, this charitable waye not regarded, I wyl procede to an open inquisition and note the faulte where I finde it. I am not desirous to knowe ther names, but oonly to understande from youe that, by payment of the taxation, the matier is punished. Wherof I praye youe certifie me as shortly as ye shal have doon any thing in it.

The last yere, by consent of the hol Universite, I made an ordre concernyng pronunciation of the Greke tonge, appoynting paynes to the transgressours and finally to the Vicechaunceler, if he sawe them not executed; wherein I pray youe be persuaded that I wyl not be deluded and contempned. I did it seriously and wyl maynteyne it. If youe see the transgressours punished I have cause to be contented, but otherwise I entende, in your and the proctours persons, to use myn auctorite geven me by the Universite; wherunto I trust ye wyl not enforce me. To be Chaunceler of the Universite is oonly honnour, which by contempt is taken awaye; and I wylbe ware to geve any[3] cause to other[t] to contempne me. What enformation I have I wyl not wryte, but by that I shall see fromhensforth I wyl[4] byleve that is past. Howe necessary it is to[5] brydle the arrogance of yought, the experience of your yeres hath, I doubte not, taught youe; and it wold moch greve me privately to have any varyaunce with youe with whom I have had soo olde acquayntaunce; which cannot be if ye suffre them not by tolleration to hope more of youe thenne ye wold avowe they shulde. The Kinges Majestie hath, by the inspiration of the Holy Goost, componed al matiers of religion; which uniformite I praye God it maye in that and al other thinges extende unto us; and forgetting al that is past goo forth in agrement as though ther had been noo such matier. But I wyl withstand fansyes, even in pronunciation, and fight with thenemye of quiet at the first entree. Wherfor I praye youe, Master Vicechaunceler, loke ernestly on thiese matiers and geve me cause, by your industrie, to rejoyse in the Universite, and oonly to care for acquyeting our matiers with the towne; wherein I trust we[6] shal have good spede by the grace

1 with c.o.
3 man, *evidently meant to be c.o.*
5 bl c.o.

2 g c.o.
4 wylb w. b c.o.
6 hav c.o.

of God, Who sende youe hartely wel to fare. At the¹ Courte, the xvth of Maye.

Your assured loving
frende,

STE. WINTON

Addressed: To Master Doctor Edmundes, Vicechaunceler of Cambredge.

65. *To* HENRY VIII

Calais, 5 July, 1544

R.O., S.P. 1, 189, 200–1.* *L.P.*, XIX, i, 844.

Concerning carriages and mares for the invasion of France.

Pleasith it your Most Excellent Majestie to understande that my Lord of Suffolk at his departure this daye wylled me to open such letters as shuld arryve from Master Hal, and, if the matier required hast, to sende the letters strayte forth and advertise him of the contentes; wherfor being this instaunt the very tyme of passage, and appering by the letters howe the caryages required be prested already by Fraunces Hal against the vjth day, which is tomorowe, I send the said letters unto your Majestie, and doo also incontinently advertise my Lord of Suffolk according to his ordre. I retayne here the passeporte for your Majesties meres to put in execution accordyngly. The letters cam to my handes a lytel perished with water, but they be nevertheles legible for theffecte. Almyghty God preserve your Majesties most noble and royal astate in long and prosperous felicite. At Calays the vth of Julye.

Your Majesties most humble
and obedient subget, servaunt,
chapelen, and dayly bedeman,

STE. WINTON

Addressed: To the Kinges Most Excellent Majesty.

Endorsed: The Bishop of Wynchestre to the Kinges Majestie, v° Julii, 1544.

1 t *c.o.*

66. *To* PAGET

Calais, 14 July, 1544

R.O., S.P. 1, 190, 33–4.* *L.P.*, xix, i, 912.

Sends letters from Vaughan, the King's financial agent at Antwerp; trusts Henry has not tried to cross the channel to-day. (It appears, however, that Henry did cross on 14 July, arriving about 7 p.m.—*L.P.*, xix, ii, App. 10.)

Master Paget, after my most harty commendations: I sende unto youe herwith Steven Vaughans letters, which my Lord Gret Master sent this afternone to my Lord Chamberlain and me. I trusted to have delyvered the⟨m⟩† unto youe myself this evenyng, and we wer al in gret expectacion and trust to[1] have seen here at this tyde the Kinges Majestie; and nowe we truste[2] his Majestie did not assaye it, the wether was soo calme. Thus fare ye [3]hartely wel. At Calayce, this Monday at night, the xiiij^th of July.

Your assured loving
frend,

STE. WINTON

Addressed: To the Right Wourshipful Sir Wyllyam Paget, Knight, oon of the Kinges Majesties Principal Secretaryes.

Below address: Hast, hast
with diligence.

Endorsed: My Lord of Wynchestre to Master Secretary, Master Paget, xiiij° Julii, 1544.

67. *To* THE READER

[Camp before Boulogne], 27 July, 1544

From *Stephani VVinton. Episcopi Angli, ad Martinum Bucerum, De Impudenti eiusdem Pseudologia Conquestio.* Louvain, August, 1544. Dated at end, vi Calen. Augusti ⟨27 July⟩, 1544.

Asks that his book be judged as an ex tempore reply to Bucer's unexpected abuse (*cf.* Nos. 97, 144, App. 2, p. 489. For bibliography of the Gardiner-Bucer controversy *see* P. Janelle in *Revue des Sciences Religieuses*, Strasbourg, July 1927. *See also* Janelle, *Obedience in Church and State*, Cambridge, 1930).

1 sev(?)e *c.o.*   2 trusted *w.* d *c.o.*   3 h *writ. over* w

Ad Lectorem

Aequi bonique[1] consules, Lector, pro tuo candore, si quid hic offenderis inconcinnum aut ipso ordine rerum verborumve confusum atque turbatum. Convitio enim inexpectato, quod dissimulare non licebat, inter tumultuosum belli apparatum, ex tempore responsum est. Librarii vero culpam, si quae inciderit, non deprecor, tantum ut illi uni imputetur, postulo. Vale.

To the Reader

Reader, if you find anything here inelegant, or, in the arrangement of subjects or words, confused and disordered, judge it fairly and kindly, in accord with your impartiality. For I have replied on the spur of the moment, in the midst of turbulent preparation for war, to unexpected abuse which could not be overlooked. But the printer's errors, if there be any, I do not ask you to excuse; I ask merely that they be charged to him. Farewell.

68. *To the* BISHOP OF ARRAS

Brussels, 9 November, 1544

R.O., S.P. 1, 195, 50–1. Contemporary copy, endorsed by Gardiner. *L.P.*, xix, ii, 585. *St. P.*, x, 193. English abstract in *L.P.*

> Is troubled by yesterday's conference (*cf. L.P.*, xix, ii, 583), and concerned that Charles V's honour is endangered; disproves arguments used yesterday by Granvelle.

Reverende Domine, Salutem Plurimam. Etsi invitissimus facio ut de rebus publicis privatim agam, ita tamen perturbavit animum hesternus congressus, ut ad levandam animi egritudinem, episcopus cum episcopo, tecum seorsum per literas agere voluerim, quod tu pro tua prudentia accipies non gravate. Si quisquam est, qui nomini et famae Cesaris studet, ego quod salva fide facere licet in hiis nomen profiteor meum. De te vero ac tua in universum familia, patre dico et fratre, quam laudem virtutis et probitatis opinio merita est, eam ego lubenter ad quamquam occasionem promovere sum conatus. Quod non eo dico tamen ut me efferam aut venditem, nedum exprobrem quod pro officio feci, sed ut

----

1 que *supplied by Cologne ed., 1545*

ostendam me, qua privatum, tranquillo esse animo, et qua publicum, vehementer ingemiscere. Nempe quod ad haec usque tempora tam sedulo curatum est, ut Cesareae Maiestatis fides sarcta tecta fuerit, nescio quo malo fato effectum sit, ut non celi iniuriis, sed hominum calumniis, obnoxia deseratur ab iis qui precipuam eius rei curam habere debeant. Ego vero illam deseri et negligi dico, ut mali rumores perpluant, dum nos Gallo relinquimur, tanquam pro noxa dediti, quos pro communi amicitia defendere debeatis. An speratis eos in re tam aperta occasionem datam neglecturos, qui falsa queque ficta et obscura ementiti omnem in eo eloquentiam consumpserunt, ut dolis et technis religiosam[1] hactenus Cesaris fidem contaminarent? Vide quid ipse habeam de Cesare persuasum, scientem, prudentem nolle, non si mundum universum lucrifaceret, cum animae detrimento fidem datam frustrari. Quoniam autem et prudens est, damna quidem sumptus ac pericula, quae salva fide effugere liceat, haud illibenter vitare, id quod certe nemo non nimis iniquus improbet. Suae enim rei, quod sine alterius iniuria fiat, cuique providere atque prospicere etiam laudi datur. Quatenus ergo deserimur, Caesaris tantum errore factum ego interpretor, quem a te et familia tua profectum, qui rem rescissent, clamitabunt, et fucum indignissime factum dicent, ut solidis federibus inter optimos principes innixa amicitia tua renunciatione convulsa labefactetur. Absit invidia verbis meis, loquor enim quod ceteri vociferabuntur. An ab orbe postulabis, ut tibi credant in re incredibili contra tanti Regis tam certam assertionem? Ea mandata ad nos detulisti, ut intelligeres quid peteremus a Gallis, et exposita a te que tum Cesaris exercitui, ut aiebas, imminebat necessitate, a Regia Maiestate benigne responsum est, videlicet, quae non necesse putavit pro suo iure ex federibus agere, sed ex equo et bono suas conditiones moderari. Recitatis tibi conditionibus, hactenus ut suae Maiestati caveatur dictum est, et ne quid federibus imminuatur, expresse est additum, atque ita dimissus es, ut referres Serenissimam Maiestatem a pace non abhorrere, sed cum hiis cautionibus, ut pax cum Gallo coeat, et intercedat consentire; tu de genere fateris nempe ut prospiciatur federibus; itaque cum habeant federa ut Regiae Maiestati satisfiat, et modum etiam certum secundum quem satisfiat, cui quod a Regia Maiestate detractum fuit in rem erat Cesaris, quo conficiat facilius cum hoste pacis leges, hic a te peto, an qui vult caveri et prospici sibi, ut federa prestentur, id est, ut sibi satisfiat, absolute consentit ut deseratur? Dices te tantum retulisse quod dictum fuit. Cur ergo excerpit pater alteram tuae renunci-

1 *MS.*, relegiosam

ationis partem, que supra fidem est, ut sine omni exceptione Regia Maiestas consensisse putetur, omissa illa altera que sensum verum redderet eius quod renuntiare deberes? qui enim sub conditione consentit, haud consentit ille, ni conditio prestetur. Adeo demiror patrem cum illis sis dotibus ornatus homo in republica Christiana summae spei non vereri tuo nomini labeculam illam aspergere, ut renunciator dicaris regii consensus, quod nemo credet, et tanquam fictum aut ementitum omnes culpabunt; nos vero orbi inclamitare et testatum facere cogemur. Dolet has fabulae partes egisse te, vel communi episcoporum causa, ita me Deus amet, hoc tempore presertim, in quo si quid astute aut callide fiat, in eo primas ad episcopos deferunt. Pater tuus me non fert liberius admonentem, et ad quandam lentitudinem revocat, quam vult haberi huius curiae peculiarem. Ego hactenus ne verbo quidem lesi patrem, nec quicquam dixi commotius quam res ipsa tulit; non affici autem et commoveri iis vestris responsis hominis est aut stulti aut stupidi. Servetur honos auribus, abstineatur a probro ac iurgio, ceterum eadem voce dulcia et amara proferre Stoicae est disciplinae, haud probata professio quam modesta Peripateticorum scola repudiavit. Et tamen hiis, sive increpaciones dicam, sive admonitiones, interrumpitur tractatio eorum, quae rem discuterent necessario explicandam. Si ita videtur commodius auctoritate premere, quam placare racionibus, frustra ad vos a doctis et honoratis itur. Quin verbo prescribite, ne quis sit molestus. Video verum quod Terentius ait, Omnes nos, ut res sese dant, ita magni atque humiles sumus, sed prudentis est meminisse omnium rerum esse vicissitudinem ⟨*Hec.*, 380; *Eun.*, 276⟩. Olim cum usui esse poteramus, alia fuit oratio; nunc, cum res nostrae turbatae sint, vestris quoquo modo compositis morosi videmur et petulantes, vobis indigni omnino quibuscum ratione agatur sed imperio. Nempe Boloniam volumus, O rem indignam, scilicet sanguine quesitam nostro. Vos, quibuscum bellum gessimus, haud fertis equanimiter retineri a nobis, quod eodem bello quesitum est, et hostium causam eatenus probatis. Si non esset, mihi crede, in Cesaris ipsius probitate reposita spes aliqua, presentium rerum statum infeli⟨ci⟩ssimum iudicarem. Reliquias prioris belli vultis esse Gallis iustum initium novi. Nos conquerimur de Gallorum invasione contra federa, et bellum vobis videtur responsum Gallos id facere occasione Boloniae. Nos cum replicamus invasionem, quacumque occasione factam, triplicatis ea verba non contineri federibus, at ego de sensu non de verbis locutus sum, et federa casum tantum exigunt, hoc est factum ipsum, ut sufficiat fuisse invasionem, fuerit enim tantum et federibus est locus, sic enim habent federa, casu quo, et cum alibi cautum sit nihil addendum ad interpretationem, vos excipitis occasionem, atque adeo occasionem Boloniae, quasi Gallorum Regi iniuriam intulerimus in bello a vobis probato Boloniam expugnando. Ista ad te scribere non est, opinor, contra stilum curiae. Non cogitatis quam late pateat ad exemplum causa nostra, nec quid murmuret populus satis tenetis; at haec fortasse contemnitis postquam convenerit cum Gallo. Quod ad me attinet, illud precabor, ut omnia cedant in gloriam Dei et reipublicae Christianae tranquillitatem. Illud autem a te impetratum velim, uti agas cum patre, ut quemadmodum Cesar ipse pro sua humanitate et audivit nos libenter, et ut tanto principe dignum est respondit ingenue, sic pater etiam in secundis respicere nos velit, et racionem nostri quam par est habere. Audiat libenter nostras querelas, nec ferat indigne si doleamus, si lamentemur, si asperius etiam aliquando loquamur, qui vestra causa non minus quam nostra atque adeo publica omnium bellum suscipientes coniunctis viribus, nulla nostra culpa relinquimur soli. Si enim consensimus, ut vos vultis, aliqua fuit in eo nostra benignitas; si non consensimus nisi sub conditione quod est verius etiam atque videndum est vobis, ut publicis rumoribus occurratis. Tu bene vale, et haec ab animo in familiam tuam amico et benevolente profecta existimato. Iterum vale. Ex hospitio nostro, nono Novembris.

Tui nominis studiosus, etc.

Headed: Exemplum Literarum ad Arabatensem Episcopum.

Endorsed by Gardiner: Copie of the letters to the Bishop of Arras.

Endorsed in other hand: Copie of my Lord of Winchesters letters to the Bisshop of Arras, ix° Novembris, 1544.

INTRODUCTORY NOTE TO NOS. 69–73

Of these five letters, written March—July, 1545, four have to do with matters academic, for the most part with a Latin play performed at Christ's College, Cambridge. This was *Pammachius*, by Thomas Kirchmeyer or Naogeorgus, a German Protestant. It had been published, with a dedication to Cranmer, in 1538 (reprinted by J. Bolte and E. Schmidt, Berlin, 1891; *cf.* F. Wiener, *Naogeorgus im England*, Berlin, 1907). In it an imaginary pope called Pammachius becomes the servant of Satan, overthrows the Roman emperor, and finally comes into conflict with St Paul, who revisits the earth. One of the fellows of Christ's, Cuthbert Scott (Bishop of Chester under Queen Mary), reported to Gardiner that the play, in the guise of an attack upon Rome, had slandered many of the practices of the English Church; and Gardiner, after reading a copy, sent him by Matthew Parker, Vice-Chancellor, agreed. The letters are admirable expressions, not only of Gardiner's religious temper, but also of what he conceived to be the function of the universities in respect of religion, as well as his own duty as Chancellor of Cambridge. Two of them (Nos. 71–2) touch on the matter of Greek pronunciation (*see* above, pp. 92, 100, 121).

No. 73 is an illustration of a quite different phase of Gardiner's activity—as Purveyor for the King's forces.

69. *To* THOMAS SMITH *and* MATTHEW PARKER

London, 27 March, [1545]

C.C.C.C., MS. 106, 437–8; fly-leaf with address, detached from letter and bound in volume as pp. 443–4 (on one side of which is Parker's draft of his reply).* Parker, *Corresp.*, 20. B.M., Add. 5843, 419. Eighteenth-century copy. C.C.C.C. is here followed.

> Smith (Parker's predecessor as Vice-Chancellor) is, with Parker, to see to the continuance of provision for 'decayed cooks'; Parker, to send information concerning a tragedy played at Christ's. (Parker replied, 3 April, that he had not seen the play, but on inquiry had learned that the Master of Christ's had permitted it, and that all offensive parts had been deleted—Parker, *Corresp.*, 21.)

After my right harty commendations: I have receyved[1] the letters of youe, Master Smyth, and hard the requeste of this berer concernyng the ordre of such wylful persons as wold frowardly breake and dissolve the charitable purpose of[2] those cookes that have among themselfes agreed by pollice to provide for ther own releafe and the socour of other decayed; wherin as ye, Master Doctour Smyth, have in the tyme of your office taken a good[3] ordre in the matier, soo I nowe desire youe both to take the paynes to travayle to gither as the case shal require for continuaunce of the same. There be smal corrodyes in Cambredge for cookes decayed, and as gret lightlywode of ther decaye as in any other place. They maye in dede endure longer with ther smal labour, but somoch lesse doo they gather for the smallenesse of the wages and gayne; which if they perceyve not presently, it shalbe wel doon to bringe them to conformite, and to interrupte the gredynesse of them that wold abuse thoccasion of such possession as they have, to ther private advauntage, with the detriment of other. Herin I praye youe doo what ye canne, and the auctorite that wantith shalbe supplied herafter.

Master Vicechaunceler, I have been enformed that the yought in Christes College, contrary to[4] the mynde of the Master and President, hath of late playde a tragedie called Pammachius, a parte of which tragedie is soo pestiferous as wer intollerable[5]. I wyl geve noo credyte to thinformation but as I shal here from youe; wherein I praye youe that I maye shortly by youe knowe the truth. If it be not soo I wylbe glad, and if it be soo I entende further to travayle, as my duetye is, for the reformation of it. I knowe myn office there and mynde to doo in it asmoch as I maye; requyring youe therfor that in such matiers of innovation and disordre I maye be[t] diligently advertised from youe from tyme to tyme. And soo fare ye wel. At London the xxvij[th] of Mar[ch].

Your loving frend,

STE. WINTON

Addressed: To my lovinge frendes, Master Vicechauncellour of Cambrige, and to Master Doctour Smyth there, and to either of them.

---

1 *writ. over something else*　　2 suc *c.o.*　　3 m *c.o.*
4 *alt. from* th　　5 *r in this word writ. over* b

70. *To* PARKER

London, 23 April, [1545]

C.C.C.C., MS. 106, 439–42.* Parker, *Corresp.*, 22. Lamb, 51. Cooper, *Annals*, 1, 423.

Parker is to assemble heads and doctors and inquire into what was really said in the play, which Gardiner has heard was a mockery of the religion established by the King; the universities should be examples of obedience. (Parker replied, 8 May, that, upon examination, he found only two persons who were offended by the play, one being Scott of Christ's, who had reported the matter to Gardiner, and whose report had stirred up ill-will against him in the College; Parker sent a copy of the play with the deleted parts marked—Parker, *Corresp.*, 24.)

Master Vicechaunceler, after my harty commendacions: Having commodite to send this berer, my chapelen, to the Universite, I have thought good to signifie further my mynde unto youe concernyng the examynation of the truth of the matier of the tragedie played in Christes College; whereof I have harde more then I harde bifore, and have harde somoch that I thynke it necessarye for my discharge to travayle with youe to atteyne the knowlege of the very truth, and further to doo therin as the case shal requyre. And to thintent it maye appere that, howesoever yought, eyther of fraylte, lightnes, or malyce, wold abuse ther giftes, we that be hedes and rulers over them shuld not be seen eyther by sufferaunce or negligence to be blamewordye of ther faulte, I wyl and require youe that upon receipte of thiese my letters ye assemble the masters and presidentes of the colleges with the doctors of the Universite, and, declaring unto them this matier, to require them to assiste youe in the tryal of the truth concernyng the said tragedye; and that, by due examynation of such as wer there, it may be truely knowen what was uttred, and soo by ther jugement approved for good which by the ordre establyshed by the Kinges Majestie in this Churche is reproved, or by them reproved which by the Kinges Majestie is allowed. I have harde specyalties that they reproved Lent fastinges, al ceremonies, and albeit the wordes of Sacrament and Masse wer not named, yet the rest of the matier wryten in that tragedie in the reprofe of them was[1] expressed. And if, as youe wrote to me, they left out sumwhat unspoken, it shuld appere that the rest, being spoken, was, upon a jugement by

1 *writ. over* wer(?)

131

consideration and deliberation, allowed; which, if it be trewe, is a lamentable case and such as hath not chaunced, that such as[1] by the Kinges Majesties privileges and supportacion be there preserved in quiet to lerne al vertue shuld presumptuously mok and skorne the direction of ther prince in matier of religion. I touche oonly herin the truth of obedience, for I estyme such offenders [2]for unlerned and ignorante, unmete to discerne what is truth in the matier. But if the Kinges Majesties directions be not obeyed there, and by us dissembled[3], howe shal we charge the rudenesse abrode that maye allege ther example for pretense of ther fault? This matier is gretter thenne wer expedient to be trewe, and is more certaynly reaported unto me thenne of lightlywode canne be totally false. It is not the faulte of us that be heedes to have in the numbre sum nought, untyl we passe over ther faulte and suffer it unpunished. If I coulde have leysour to cumme myself, I wold not spare to cumme thether[4] for this purpose, being the specyal pointe of[5] my charge. In myn absence I require the ayde of youe to knowe by your examination the truth of the matier; wherein I praye youe use the assistence of the master⟨s⟩, presidentes, and doctors[6] as afore. And as wylde wanton libertie sumtyme brestith oute in yought to ther reproch, soo let sobrenes and gravitie appere in us requisite for thexecution of our charge. Many hath of late repyned at the Kinges Majesties munificence in our privileges and otherwise, and let not us geve cause that they shuld[7] justely soo doo. Our obedience shuld be example to al other in publique directions without occasion of al slaunder. If lernyng shuld nowe[†] be an instrument to sterre up dissension and trouble the commen quietnesse, ther[8] opinion shuld be confermed which not many yeres past have laboured to prove[9], in bokes prynted in Englyshe, that the universities be the corruption of the realme[10]. Oxford lyveth quietly with fewer privileges thenne we have; ther be that wold we had as fewe as theye. I entreate this offense oonly worldlye, bycause the capacitie of thoffenders seemeth to stretche noo further. And he that regardith not his obedience to his prince regardith not moch his obedience to God and His truth, which he hath offended in the other. Wherfor I praye youe let us by due examination finde the faulte where it is, and soo purge

1 hath c.o.   2 f writ. over b
3 w c.o.   4 writ. thother(?)   5 t c.o.
6 of(?) c.o.   7 worthely soo c.o.
8 r † abv. p(?) c.o. or blotted   9 proved w. d c.o.
10 m in realme written as four minims with one c.o.

132

ourself. And what ye shall finde herin I praye youe advertise me with diligence. And soo fare ye wel. At London, the xxiij^ti of Apryl.

Your loving frend,

STE. WINTON

Addressed: To Master Vicechaunceler of the Universite of Cambredge.

71. *To* PARKER

London, 12 May, [1545]

C.C.C.C., MS. 106, 449–52.* Parker, *Corresp.*, 27. Lamb, 54. Cooper, *Annals*, I, 425.

> On reading the play, finds it full of abominable lies; also hears that his decree on Greek pronunciation is not observed; intends to be obeyed. (This was followed by an order of the Privy Council, 16 May, to Parker and the heads, to admonish those concerned in the play not to meddle with anything which should offend the laws and quiet of the realm—Parker, *Corresp.*, 29; *cf.* *L.P.*, xx, i, 746.)

Master Vicechaunceler, after my harty commendations: I perceyve by your letters, which I have receyved with the boke of the tragedie, that ye have assembled the sage of the Universite to knowe, by ther inquisition severally in ther howses, what was uttred that might and ought to offende godly eares in the playing of the same at Christes Colleage. Wherin, as apperith by your letters, reaporte was made unto youe that noo man is[1] offended. And yet perusyng the booke of the tragedie which ye sent me, I finde moch matier not stryken out, al which by the parties own confession was uttred, very nought, and on the other parte sumthing not wel omitted; where allowing and rejecting shuld procede of jugement, and that to be taken for trewe which was uttred, and that for untrewe which they note as[t] untrewe to be omitted and left unspoken. Soo as this boke declarith the parties to have double offended, both in denying that is trewe and also approving that is false; as in sum parte by ther notes[2] doth appere. And in dede in the tragedye[3] untruth is soo maliciously weved with truth as, making the bishop of Rome with certain his abuses[4] the foundation of the matier, the auctours

---

1 † *abv.* was *c.o.*
3 mal *c.o.*

2 *alt. from* noted
4 *alt. from* abusure(?)

133

reproch wherof is true, soo many abhominable and detestable lyes be added and mingled with the other truth, as noo Christen eares shuld paciently heare; and cannot, in the processe of the matier, be, without a mervelous alteration[1] other thenne was nowe used[2], dissevered a sondre. By meane whereof, where al other proufe fayleth, there the boke maketh an undowted proufe of ther lewdenesse to me here; and that which soo many of the Universite, being present, herde and offended them not soo depely but it is nowe worn out and they be noo lenger offended, the same is by exhibition of the booke soo notified unto me and soo grevith me, being absent, as, howe soone soever I forget theffense upon ther reconciliation, I shal hardly of a gret while forget the matier. And if open and notorious faultes, which thoffenders in pompe and triumphe soo uttre[3] as they wold have men knowe them and[4] marke them, shal fromhensforth without al reformation be neglected and forgoten, or soo by sylence hidden as they shal not appere to be corrected, there is[5] smal hope of conservation of good ordre, and a mervelous boldnesse geven to offenders, the meanes of reformation thus taken awaye. Wise men have noted truely that it is *caput audatie impunitatis spes* ⟨*cf.*, Cicero, *Mil.*, 16, 43⟩, which must nedes growe where open faultes be thus neglected and pretermitted; wherein they be chiefly to be blamed that forbere to make[6] reaporte of that they have harde whenne they be required. I wold not be over[7] curious, oonles the crime wer notable, to bring to light his faulte that himself hath used meanes[8] to hide from the worlde. But if the offender be soo† destitute of al feare and shame as thiese players wer, why shuld any man forbere, whenne they walke in the streate naked, to poynt them[9] with his fynger and saye, 'There [10] they goo [10]!' I here many thinges to be very far out of order both openly in the Universite and severally in the colleges, wherof I am sory; and amonges other, in contempte of me, the determination of the pronunciation of certain Grece[11] letters, agreed unto by thauctorite of the hol Universite, to be violate and broken without any correction therfor. The matier is lowe, and the contempte soomoch the more. I was chosen Chaunceler to be soo honored (although above my desertes) of them, and I have† geven noo cause to be despised. I wil doo that I canne for the mayntenaunce of vertue and good ordre there, and chalenge again,

---

1 alteracions *w.* s *c.o.*   2 be *evidently meant to be c.o.*
3 uttred *w.* d *c.o.*   4 v *c.o.*   5 shal *c.o.*
6 t *c.o.*   7 overy *w.* y *c.o.*   8 th *c.o.*
9 *alt. from* hym   10–10 *alt. from* he goth   11 *alt. from* Geece (?)

of dutie, to be regarded after the proportion, not of my qualites, but myn office; requyring youe, Master Vicechaunceler, to communicate these my letters with the masters, presidentes, and doctours, and on my behaulf to desire them gravely to consider of what moment the good ordre of yough⟨t⟩ is, and to withstand the lewde lic[ence] of such as have neyther shame[1] ne feare of punishe[ment] and correction. The lesson of obedience wold be wel taught and practised, and I wylbe more diligent to knowe howe men proufite in it thenne I have been. I have shewed the hol Counsayl the wordes spoken by Master Scot, from whom ye shal shortly receyve answer in that matier. And as touching those that wer chief players in the tragedie, I here very evel matier, and I pray youe cal them unto youe and knowe whither they wyl acknowlege and confesse ther faulte or noo, and to signifie the same unto me. And soo fare ye wel. At London, the xij[th] of Maye.

Your loving frend,

STE. WINTON

Addressed: To my loving frend, Master Vicechaunceler of Cambredge.

72. *To* Parker and the Regents and Non-Regents at Cambridge

London, 18 May, 1545

C.C.C.C., MS. 119, 29–32. Original letter, probably in clerk's hand, with subscription and signature in Gardiner's hand.

> Youth at Cambridge have no respect for authority, as is shown in connection with Greek pronunciation; this leads to irreverence in weightier matters, as in the play *Pammachius*; is aware of the spirit of faction at Cambridge, which does not exist at Oxford; the affair of the play is left to their decision.

Stephanus Winton, S.P.

Dabitis hoc michi pro equanimitate vestra, doctissimi viri, ut vobiscum liberius atque apertius agam que animus iubet commemorare. Utar

---

Stephen of Winchester sends sincere greetings

With your gracious permission, learned friends, I shall discuss with you rather freely and frankly those matters which my thoughts bid me

1 0 *c.o.*

enim iure dicendi meo vestris racionibus inductus atque impulsus. Audio, sentio inter vos non eam esse animorum consensionem, non illa studia, non illam continentiae et severitatis normam servari quam vestrae reipublicae conservandae ratio poscit hoc tempore atque efflagitat. Horum a me testem nolite exigere; ego vero a vestris conscientiis peto testimonium, atque ita peto, ut ad emendationem valeat, quod unum quero, non vestram infamiam, quam ad me pertinere duco. Liceat enim inter nos (iam enim me vobiscum presentem statuo) quod verum est agnoscere, qui primus est gradus ad sanitatem. Ex iuventute apud vos suam fere quisque libidinem sequitur, et quatenus ipsi[1] commodum est paret; cohertionem vero et imperium detrectant plurimi, et quod ille scripsit, maior pars vincit meliorem. Audet omnia temeritas et sibi nihil agendo cavet qui praeficiuntur. Metu autem sublato, quid potest esse sanctum in summa tenerae aetatis impotentia, presertim cum in ipsis Graecarum literarum rudimentis discant contemnere et nomen

---

speak of. For I am prompted and impelled by your practices to avail myself of my right to speak. I am told, and am myself aware, that there does not exist among you the intellectual accord, nor are the scholarly interests and the standards of sobriety and strict discipline being maintained, which the safeguarding of the welfare of your community calls for and demands at this time. Do not insist that I produce a witness to this. No, I look for the witness of your own consciences, and I do so solely with a view to its effecting a reformation. This is the one thing I seek; I seek not your discredit, for in that, I think, I am myself involved. I place myself now, as it were, in your midst and affirm that we should feel free to recognize among ourselves what the truth is; for this is the first step toward recovery.

As a rule, then, each youth under your care follows his own inclinations, rendering obedience only so far as it suits his fancy; indeed, most of them refuse to submit to restraint or to authority, and, in the words of a famous writer ⟨Livy XXI, 4⟩, 'the larger part dominates the better part.' A reckless disposition dares anything and takes heed of those in authority in naught that it does. Now, if fear is removed, what is there that can command respect among those of less mature years, utterly irresponsible as they are at that period of life? This question is particularly pertinent, when in dealing with the very letters of the Greek alphabet they are learning to contemn and make light of

1 *MS.*, illi

meum cum vestra auctoritate floccifacere? Nugae sunt, fateor, si quis rem spectet, sed quae ducunt seria; et humanae naturae conditionem haud imprudenter notavit, qui scripsit innocentiam per gradus ab homine discedere. Et iam video progressum usque ad sacra.

Que tandem ista est pervicatia duorum aut trium nomini meo, vestrae auctoritati, ac receptae apud orbem reliquum consuetudini in literarum pronuntiatione reluctantium? Si se contendant a vero stare, interim certe dum quod vanissimum est pro vero iactant, verum est eos vestram auctoritatem spernere, verum est eos meo nomini facere contumeliam, verum est eos a reliquis omnibus dissentire ac suam arrogantiam spretis et contemptis ceteris mordicus tueri; quorum omnium, quae verissima sunt et clarissima, maiorem nos rationem habere conveniat quam ficte et ad praetextum obiectae veritatis. Gravis est quacunque in re contemptus, certe in re levissima gravissimus. Enim vero quam ego auctoritatem in syllabis exspectem coniunctis [si] in ipsis literarum

---

my office as well as your authority. It is a trifling matter, I admit, if one considers this point ⟨*i.e.*, Greek pronunciation⟩ only, but it paves the way for more serious things; the writer who declared that innocence deserts a man step by step was not lacking in discernment, taking note as he did of a characteristic of human nature. In fact, I perceive that the attitude of which I complain has already made such headway that it affects even religious practices.

Now, what are we to think of the frowardness of the two or three men who are in rebellion against my office, against your authority, and against the accepted practice of the rest of the world in the pronunciation of the Greek letters? If they were to claim that they are relying on the truth, we should find that, while they are flaunting as the truth something extremely frivolous, the truth actually is that they reject your authority, scorn my office, and disagree with everyone else; in fact, spurning and contemning others, they cling obstinately to their own self-assurance. All of which is supremely true and evident, and it is proper that we should have more regard for it than for a pretended truth, put forward merely as a pretext. Arrogance is objectionable in connection with anything, and certainly most objectionable in connection with what is of exceedingly slight importance.

Indeed, what authority could I expect to exercise in regard to combinations of syllables when, in regard to the individual letters, I am

rudimentis contemnor, non nudus sed vestris suffragiis communitus?
Plane quod isti faciunt inter morbos est animi lenia et inania sectantis,
de quibus Plutarchus eleganter in hunc modum (περὶ τοῦ ακούειν):
ταῦτα (inquit) τὰ νοσήματα πολλὴν μὲν ἐρημίαν νοῦ καὶ φρενῶν
ἀγαθῶν, πολλὴν δὲ καὶ τερθρείαν καὶ στωμυλίαν ἐν ταῖς σχολαῖς
πεποίηκε[1] τῶν μειρακίων. Nihil habet profecto hec res solidi, nihil
certi, nihil veri, sed simile est eius quod de nominibus scripsit Aristo-
teles, esse ad placitum ea ponentis, ut si nihil esset aliud, sufficiat placitum
placito opponere et obtineat potius quod primariae apud nos authoritati
placuit quam quod libuit quorundam temeritati.

Pudet in re tantula tot verba facere, et tamen rei ipsius indignitate
premor cum videam ad exemplum perniciosissimum esse, ut cum tanto
veritatum preiudicio a me, a vobis, a legibus et statutis vestris puerili
stultitiae ferula dignae turpiter concedatur. Ego vestra quoad sciam

---

contemned, even though armed and fortified by your approval?
Obviously, what these men are doing is indicative of the intellectual
maladies of which Plutarch writes so aptly in his essay *On Listening*
⟨42 D, E⟩—maladies to which the mind is subject when bent on the
pursuit of the frivolous and the trivial. 'These maladies,' he says,
'have created in the schools where our youth are taught a dearth of
intelligence and sound judgment with an abundance of sophistry and
loquacity.' This matter ⟨of Greek pronunciation⟩ is neither settled,
certain, nor sure, but there is an analogy here to what Aristotle ⟨*De
Interpretatione* 16ᵃ 19⟩ wrote about nouns, that they are conventional
instruments of the person who assigns to them their meanings. So,
even if we were to take nothing else into account, it would be enough
to set one convention over against another, and that which was approved
by the chief authority among us would prevail, rather than that which
has caught the fancy of a few headstrong persons.

I am ashamed to discourse at such length on so trifling a matter; yet
I am overwhelmed by the outrageousness of the situation, realizing as
I do what a thoroughly vicious precedent would be set if, to the serious
impairment of true principles, we—I myself, you, your regulations and
statutes—disgracefully give in to childish folly of a sort that deserves
the rod.

I for my part shall make every effort to guard your interests so far
as I know what they are and am able to do so, and I ask that you have

1 *MS.*, πεποίηκαι

poteroque tueri contendam, vos meum vicissim honorem comiter con-
servatote. Audaciae puerili viri resistite. An speratis spreto atque
contempto me vestram vobis auctoritatem adversus ceterorum insolen-
tiam retenturos? Res ipsa indicat omnem apud vos periisse reverentiam.
Vestri vestra derident apud vos, quod in tragoedia Pammachii etiam
cum pompa sunt professi, ubi quoniam Romanum pontificem merito
exibilant, eodem iure doctores omnes cum irrisione explodunt, in-
spectantibus vobis et mussitantibus. Non expectatum opinor, ut quae
publice apud vos fiant et ita fiant ut publicentur, intra vestros contin-
eantur parietes nec ad alios manent. Rerum vestrarum statum multi
tenent et has vestras discordias et dissensiones clare intelligunt. Multa
animadvertunt quae non censeatis, et illud inprimis nullum fere esse
sodalitium in quo non diversarum partium studia reperias, preside
alicubi sua promovente, alicubi clavum ventis permittente et sibi potius
consulente quam suis. Et quemadmodum Sophocles scripsit in nihil
sapiendo iucundissimam esse vitam, ita quidam vestratium putant in

---

the courtesy to defend my honour in return. As full grown men, resist
their childish arrogance. Or do you suppose that if I am scorned and
contemned you will retain your authority for yourselves against the
arrogance of others?

An actual occurrence demonstrates that all reverence has ceased to
exist among you. Members of your own group make fun of your doings
in your very midst. This they openly acknowledged, even with a
flourish, in the tragedy *Pammachius*. In this play they hiss the Roman
pontiff, who fully deserves it, and accordingly, by the same token,
indicate their derisive rejection of all men of learning, with you looking
on and not raising your voice. You can scarcely have expected that
what is done publicly among you, and in such a way as to receive
publicity, would remain confined within your own walls and not get
abroad. Many know of the state of your affairs and understand clearly
your discords and dissensions. They notice many things which you
would not suppose they did, and in particular the fact that there is
hardly a college in which one may not find party antagonisms, the head
in some cases promoting the interests of his partisans, in others trusting
his rudder to the winds and consulting his own advantage rather than
that of his faction. Just as Sophocles ⟨*Ajax* 554⟩ wrote that life is most
pleasant when there is no intelligent perception, so some of your group

nihil agendo tutissimam; sed falluntur et illi, et ut interim securi sint, tuti certe non sunt, qui commissum munus non exequuntur, rationem aliquando reddituri preter expectacionem.

Apud Oxonienses nihil est horum, et michi dictum fuit a quodam administracionem apud vos commodiorem futuram, si cancellarii unius suffragio ad illorum exemplum procancellarius designaretur. Sed ego semper abhorrui ab istis mutationibus, nisi ubi res posceret evidentissime. Et iam curavi in negocio tragoediae ut omnia vestris arbitriis permittantur. Itaque vos curate ut digni tanta procuratione vestra merito habeamini; ego autem omni ope et consilio enitar ut vestra vobis integra et illibata conserventur. Valete. Londini, xviij° Maii.

Vester amicus ex animo,

STE. WINTON, Cancellarius

Addressed: Doctissimis viris Vicecancellario, regentium etiam et non regentium coetui universo Academiae Cantabrigiensis.

---

think that life is most secure when there is nothing done; but these too are mistaken and, though free from anxiety for a time, certainly enjoy no lasting safety, for they are failing to perform a task assigned to them, of which some day they will unexpectedly have to render an account.

At Oxford there is none of this, and it has been suggested to me that the administration of your affairs would be more satisfactory if the Chancellor's deputy were appointed, in accordance with the Oxford practice, by the Chancellor alone. But I have always shrunk from a change of this sort, unless the situation clearly demanded it.

I have already arranged that in the affair of the tragedy everything shall be entrusted to your decision. Therefore see to it that your being considered worthy of such a responsibility is deserved; while I for my part shall strive with all my might and mind for the maintenance, secure and unimpaired, of your interests. Farewell. At London, the xviij[th] of May.

Your assured friend,

STE. WINTON, Chancellor

Addressed: To the learned Vice-Chancellor and the whole body of learned Masters, whether regents or non-regents, at Cambridge University.

R.O., S.P. 1, 203, 22–5.* *L.P.*, xx, i, 1082.

An estimate of provisions for 8000 men for four months at Boulogne, with adverse criticism of the account sent from there; comments on the military situation at Boulogne.

July, August,
Septembre, Octobre

conteyne dayes cxx.

viij^M ⟨8000⟩ men spende ech daye xxiij quarters of bred corn, after the ordre taken by Master Rowse, which amonteth, in cxx dayes, } ^1MMvij^c ⟨2700 quarters.

And after the rate of thexpenses at Bolen the last moneth, they spend not xvj quarters a daye, and in the xxx daye have spent oonly cccclviij ⟨458⟩ quarters, after which rate for the foure monethes shal suffice } xviij^cxvj ⟨1816⟩ quarters.

Towardes forniter wherof

They have, by ther confession nowe made, in wheate, rye, and barley } mcclxvj ⟨1266⟩ quarters.

Item, in flowre in Humbre barelles, after ther accounpte that² ccc weight of flowre shuld make a quarter, yet they have therin } vij^ciiiij^xx v ⟨785⟩ quarters.

Item, in floure pacqued in hering barelles, accounpting xliiij barelles to make tenne quarters, j bushel, which is ther accounpte, yet they have soo as they nowe rekonne therin } cc quarters.

Item, they have in bisquet c quarters.

The hol quantite of bred corne, as they now confesse, is, after ther owne accounpte, } mmccclj ⟨2351⟩ quarters.

And soo apperith that they have more bred corne, after the rate of ther expenses the laste moneth of July, } v^cxxxv ⟨535⟩ quarters.

And after the proportion made for the hol numbre of viij^M, they shuld want³ of ther complement } cccxlix ⟨349⟩ quarters.

---

1 x *before* M *c.o.*   2 ccc *c.o. and repeated*   3 for *c.o.*

Which quantite of cccxlix[1] quarters that shuld seme to wante, wanteth not in dede, but they make it want by ther accounpte; for where as in the MCC ⟨1200⟩ barelles Humber, being in dede as fyne flowre as makith manchet, being soo specyally pacqued in Hampshire bicause it shuld last, they wold †at Bolen† of that accounpte CCC weight to[2] a quarter, where as the Kinges Majestie hath not ccl answerd hym; and soo that quantite that oft conteyneth[3] MC ⟨1100⟩ quarters they wold in this accounpte make of it but vij^c [4] iiij^{xx} ⟨780⟩, as bifore. And if the chief rulers at Bolen hath for themself spent the ciiij^{xx} ⟨180⟩ barelles, the Kinges Majesties proufite is not in dede wel used.

And where as they rekonne xliiij barelles of the flowre pacqued in hering barelles to make but x quarters, j busher, the accounpte is at the ye unreasonable, for eyther the matier is in dede nought, and thenne it makith nothing, or elles if the saver of the hering hath teynted the utter carste ⟨cruste?⟩, as by like it doth, they make very thyke parynges to waste xxxiiij quarters, which xliiij barelles dyd conteyne to tenne, j bushel. This flowre cam from Master Stannop out of the north and, I thinke, what soever is wryten from Bolen, he wyl answer it. But they at Bolen, what with leving out that they did oones certifie, and framyng thaccounpte of that they doo certifie, the wast is intollerable. For this accounpte, in demaunding the same† waight of fyne flowre that men have of course, and disalowing Master Stannoppes pacquyng, here is wyped out of our rekonnyng vij^c ⟨700⟩ quarters and above.

And yet, as God wyl, for ther tyme appointed they have sufficient, which I speke not bicause I wold not they shuld have more sent and doo the best therin I coulde, but to rejoyce in that they have. And alredy Master Rowse is determyned to send thither, and I wyl wryte unto him therfor; and necessary it wer to send to them to conforte them continuelly. But I praye youe consider what I wryte, and compare it with that they certifie, for relief of the Kinges Majesties trouble.

And hither as touching bred.

And if ther numbre be but vij^M ⟨7000⟩ they have thenne a gret deale⟨?⟩ inough.

As towching drinke:

They have, as they wryte, vij^M ⟨7000⟩ quarters of muste, with hed courne inough, and lxvij^M ⟨67,000⟩ hoppes, which is soo far tomoch

1 alt. from ccccllix   2 w incomplete follows
3 CC c.o.   4 alt. from viij^c

that I accounpte it[1] not, for it wyl serve them to January be ended.

They have somoch bicause they have dronke English bere hitherto. And over this they have ccccxlj ⟨441⟩ buttes of sackes.

If we goo thither to levye[2] the sege, let[3] men cary bisquet in ther bosom; and there they shal finde drynke inough, and inough for xxx^{M} ⟨30,000⟩ men to tary xx dayes, and yet leave the towne wel furnished.

There is malte, hed corne, and hoppes wherwith to brue v^{M} ⟨5000⟩ tonne of bere, very good; and the proportion for the towne is but vj^{c} ⟨600⟩ a moneth. And soo[4] in July, August, Septembre, Octobre, Novembre, ⟨Decembre⟩, January, they shal spende but mmmm ⟨4000⟩, and soo shal they spare m ⟨1000⟩ tonne, and al ther wyne for good felawes that wyl cumme to releave them.

And thus they be in drynke.

As touching ther meate:

First, I wold they had, in stede of heringes, the best meate we have, wherwith to encourage them, but as they ar,

First, the salte beef, being vj^{c}xxxi ⟨631⟩ pypes, wyl serve after x pypes a daye } lxiij dayes.

The beefes alyve with ther shepe, if they shuld eate noon other meate, wold serve } iij dayes.

Chese, v^{c}xlix ⟨549⟩ waye, whiche remayneth in dede; although as ye maye perceyve, they have forgoten to note it in the last remayne, for ye shal see in the title of chese the⟨y⟩ saye ther remayned, the first of June, v^{c}lx ⟨560⟩ waye, and synnes spent x waye, and thenne they shuld saye, Remayne, the first of Julye, v^{c}xlix ⟨549⟩, but they have left out the v^{c} ⟨500⟩. But this jobbe is worth m ⟨1000⟩ li., and shal not goo soo to the purpose. This quantite, allowing ech man j li. a daye, which oon man cannot eate, as it is hardened nowe, accounpting ech last to waye but ccl ⟨250⟩ li., in al cxl^{M} ⟨140,000⟩ li. weght; which wyl serve, after viij^{M} ⟨8000⟩ a daye, } xvij dayes.

---

1 if c.o.   2 relevye w. re c.o.
3 man c.o.   4 writ. over in

Butre, xxxij barelles, ech barel waying ccxxiiij ⟨224⟩ *li.*,
each man[1] *di. li.* ⟨½ pound⟩ by the daye, which is a good ⎬ ij dayes.
quantite,

Bakon, cccxxxvij ⟨337⟩ flyche, valuing them to way xxx
li. a flych, oon with an other, ech man to have *di.* ⟨½⟩ a ⎬ ij ⟨dayes⟩.
daye,

And soo have they furniter in beef, chese, butter, ⎬ iiij[xx] vii ⟨87⟩
and bakon for ⎱ dayes.

And soo remayne xxxiij[2] dayes to be furnished
with other victualles.

In stokfishe iiij[xx] xvij[M] ⟨97,000⟩, after iiij[M] ⟨4000⟩ the daye,   xxiiij dayes.

White hering, xliiij last, after iiij[3] last *di.*[†] ⟨4½ last⟩ a ⎬ ix dayes.
daye, ech man fyve heringes,

And thus be the hol numbre of dayes furnished.

I[4] rekonne not the red hering bycause they like it not, but as for the
white, themself caused it to be kept for hervest hering.

I reckonne not also xxx barelles of honey which wylbe a good releef.

And as for[5] the clx ⟨160⟩ quarters of peason, beinge meate peason and
very good, may with ther bakon and butter and salte beef make the
proportion moch ⟨t⟩he betre[6]. I wold gladly put them in remembraunce
of beanes also, to helpe to stretche to the satisfaction of nature. But as
for meate, eyther I have been moch abused or elles they have of private
provision a very gret quantite, both of beefes, motons, chiese, and
butter. And to encorage them, I trust there wylbe yet dayly adventures.

And nowe Master Secretarye, I begynne my letter to youe after I have
made an ende with my victualles, and thanke youe for yours, and send
unto youe again al ye sent me. I am sory my Lord Ponynges was
troubled with our[7] last letters and wold be soryer he shuld be trayned
out by the French men, for I wene they begynne to doo as they did last,
bicause they wold have us assaye the same enterprise again. And they
begynne to buylde, they may be loked on at laysour, for we knowe by
experience that buylding askith delaye. I wryte this letter out of my

1 oon(?) *c.o.*   2 *alt. from* xxxij   3 † *abv.* v *c.o.*
4 I *is preceded by* In *c.o.*   5 afor *w.* a *c.o.*
6 *writ. over something else*   7 † *abv.* the *c.o.*

malte loft at Fernham, a place fit for the mater, wherin I shal make youe the best chiere I canne. And thus fare ye hartely wel[1]. This evenyng or nicht[2], I cannot tel howe late.

Your assured loving
frend,

STE. WINTON

Addressed: To my loving frend Sir Wyllyam Paget, Knight, oon of the Kinges Majesties two Principal Secretar⟨yes⟩.

Endorsed: My Lord of Wynchestre to Master Secretary, Master Paget, ⟨*blank*⟩ July, 1545, touching victailes at Boulloyn.

1 At f *c.o.*
2 *not clearly written; it may be* night *with* g *unfinished*

INTRODUCTORY NOTE TO NOS. 74–109

These letters were all written on Gardiner's embassy to the Imperial Court, October, 1545–March, 1546.

When Hertford and Gardiner in 1544 had urged the Emperor to declare war against France (*see* p. 93 above), he asked that he be not pressed to take any action for ten weeks. Although he thereupon sent two ambassadors to explain his position to Henry VIII, not only ten weeks but as many months and more passed, and England remained at war with France and Scotland. In the summer of 1545 Francis I expressed his willingness to treat with Henry through the mediation of the German Protestants; and German envoys came to England, but to no purpose. The Emperor, however, not desiring France, England, and his German subjects to become too friendly, undertook the rôle of mediator. On the promise of Francis I to send d'Annebaut, Admiral of France, to the Imperial Court, Henry appointed Gardiner to go thither as his representative. He was to be assisted by Bishop Thirlby, resident ambassador with the Emperor, and Sir Edward Carne, ambassador to Flanders. He reached Bruges on 31 October, whither Charles V came on 3 November.

Gardiner's mission had three objects in view: the making of peace with France; the renovation of the treaty with the Emperor of 11 February, 1543, for which he himself had been largely responsible; and the relief of three English commissaries who were at the moment being grievously handled by a German captain of mercenaries, a subject of the Emperor, in Henry's employ.

This third matter came up first for consideration. Friedrich von Reiffenberg, vassal of Philip, Landgrave of Hesse, and recommended by him, had been engaged in the summer of 1545 to serve England against France with 8000 foot and 1500 horse. Thomas Chamberlain, Governor of the English merchants at Antwerp, Sir Ralph Fane, and Thomas Avery were the commissaries sent to pay him. They reached Cologne early in September and were thereafter subjected to various extortions, while Reiffenberg did nothing; and, finally, on refusal to give an extra month's pay, were arrested and threatened with irons (*see L.P.*, xx, ii, pp. xv ff., and references there given). Their plight and the

Emperor's efforts to rescue them are referred to in several of these letters. Gardiner sincerely, though it seems mistakenly, believed that Philip of Hesse was at the bottom of the business, and felt it was a warning to England to have nothing more to do with Protestants (No. 79).

Negotiations with the French came to nothing. D'Annebaut was accompanied by the Chancellor, Olivier, and Bayard, Secretary of State. For Bayard, Gardiner had a high regard, but not for the Chancellor (*see* No. 84). The French would consider nothing less than the restitution of Boulogne and the comprehension of the Scots in the peace. The English would hear of neither. Money in compensation for Boulogne was offered, but since France was already in England's debt to the amount of 450,000 crowns, to say nothing of at least a million more claimed as due on arrearages of a pension to Henry VIII, the offer seemed to Gardiner a mockery. He suspected that Francis I had been led to hope for better terms from England by the German Protestants, who had renewed their offer of mediation, and through whom Paget, Tunstall, and Tregonwell began futile negotiations at Calais on 20 November, 1545. The Protestants, thought Gardiner, would do England little service by their meddling (Nos. 79, 86, 93).

The third and main object of Gardiner's mission, namely, the renovation of the Anglo-Imperial alliance, was successful. The English wanted certain provisions of the treaty of 1543 (printed in Rymer and summarized in *L.P.*, XVIII, i, 144) so re-worded as to leave no possible doubt of their meaning. The chief difficulties arose over exactly what made an invasion of one monarch's territory sufficient to require the other to declare himself enemy of the invader (Article vi), and to what extent Henry might hire soldiers and buy munitions in, and pass his troops through, Imperial territory when the Emperor was at peace with Henry's enemy (Article xxiv).

Besides the Emperor and his sister Mary, Queen Dowager of Hungary, Regent of Flanders, the persons with whom Gardiner had most to do in his negotiations were Nicolas Perrenot, Sieur de Granvelle, Charles' chief minister, Cornelius Scepperus, Sieur d'Eecke, one of the Emperor's Council and twice envoy to England in 1545, Dr Louis Schore, President of the Council of Flanders, and Louis, Sieur de Praet, member of the same Council, who had been ambassador to England, 1523–5.

Agreement was reached on 20 December, 1545, but owing to various delays, notably the meeting of the Order of the Golden Fleece at the New Year, the final form of the revised treaty was not settled till

16 January, 1546. Hardly had this result been attained when a new difficulty arose. On New Year's Day Gardiner had reminded the Emperor's ministers of the aid due, it was claimed, to Henry from Charles for the past year, under the unrevised treaty, and Granvelle had promised to bring it to the Emperor's attention; but when, a month later, Gardiner once more spoke of it, Granvelle flatly denied having heard or said anything about it. Gardiner expressed his opinion of this freely (Nos. 104–5). The matter was settled, or rather evaded, by a protestation by Gardiner that the aid was due and a counter-protestation by Scepperus, when they exchanged ratifications of the treaty, 13 February, 1546.

The negotiations were reported to the King at great length in joint letters written by Gardiner in the names of himself and his colleagues. These are not here printed (*see* p. xvi above). They are devoted almost exclusively to the diplomatic business in hand, while Gardiner's reflections upon it and upon the course of events in general are given in his personal letters, chiefly to his friend and one-time pupil, Sir William Paget, since 1543 one of the King's two Principal Secretaries. For a study of Gardiner's character and interests these letters are of the utmost importance.

No. 75 reveals his amusement at the outrageous 'conceits' of a band of soldiers *en route* to Boulogne, who, as the Mayor of Canterbury assured him, were so clever at stealing they must have been 'scholars of Cambridge'!

No. 79, in more serious mood, shows his deep concern at the spread of Protestant doctrines. It was called forth by the receipt of *The Lamentacion of a Christian against the Citie of London, made by Roderigo Mors*. Mors was the pen-name of Henry Brinklow, ex-friar and mercer of London, author of this and another tract impugning the regime of Henry VIII. Both have been summarized in *L.P.*, xx, ii, 733, and reprinted in Early Eng. Text Soc., Extra Series, XXII. It was not the edition there reprinted which came into Gardiner's hands, but the one, a copy of which is in the B.M., purporting, in a colophon, to be 'Prynted at Jericho in the Land of Promes By Thome Trauth.' The date 1542, given as part of the title, not of the colophon, would seem to refer to the time of writing, not of printing. The latter in all likelihood was 1545.

Gardiner mistakenly attributed the book to George Joye, and did not hesitate to express his opinion of Joye, or of the pernicious tendency of such books, or of the evils of Protestant doctrine; all of which led him to recall a remark of Bowser (Sir Henry Bourchier) to the infant Prince

Edward, and to make shrewd comment on Henry VIII's utilitarian attitude toward Protestantism. In the same letter he told Paget that he had finished his reply to Joye, which, it seems, from what he says of being engaged in writing for a month past, must have been written for the most part on his journey to Bruges, which had been a leisurely one, since he had not wished to reach there too long before the French Admiral, whose coming had been delayed.

The book to which Gardiner replied was *George Joye confuteth VVinchesters false Articles*, 1543. In it Joye had charged Gardiner with the death of Robert Barnes (burned at the stake, 1540), and had sought to refute certain doctrinal statements or 'articles' which Gardiner had explained to Barnes when Barnes had submitted to his instruction. Gardiner's book is a defence of these articles, but to it he prefixed a brief letter to the Reader (No. 80), and a long letter to Joye, describing his relations with Barnes and defending himself against Joye's charges (No. 81). The latter is the longest single piece of autobiographical writing by Gardiner which we possess, and is, in the opinion of the editor, the most interesting.

Nos. 86 and 87 reveal another side of Gardiner's character—his dejection in difficulty and his resilience of spirit on the first indication of amendment in the situation of which he had almost despaired. No. 86 also illustrates his tendency to ease his mind by putting his thoughts on paper (*see also* No. 85). It is likewise noteworthy as containing one of the few references to his younger days—his acting, in all probability while still at Cambridge, with Paget and Wriothesley, in Plautus' *Miles Gloriosus*.

Other letters worthy of note are No. 83, on the valour of Englishmen and their inability to 'leave when it is well'; No. 91, in which we have his half-humorous, half-serious observations on the disadvantages of wealth; No. 93 on the tendency of the Protestants to exercise the pope's office upside down; No. 97, his second letter to the Reader in his controversy with Bucer; No. 100, revealing his evident delight in the ceremonies at the meeting of the Order of the Golden Fleece, with his picture of one impressive moment, when departed members were commemorated, anticipating Shakespeare's 'Out, out, brief candle!' No. 101 contains his request for the preservation of the Hospitals of St Cross and Mary Magdalene at Winchester (placed at the disposal of the crown by act of Parliament, 1545); No. 102, his apt characterization of the Imperial ministers.

For joint letters from Gardiner and his colleagues, for letters to them, and other documents and memoranda dealing with negotiations on this mission, *see L.P.*, xx, ii, 604–xxi, i, 217, *passim*. For an account of the negotiations see J. Gairdner's introductions to the same.

74. *To* PAGET

London, 18 October, 1545

R.O., S.P. 1, 209, 56–7.* *L.P.*, xx, ii, 610.

Departs to-day for the Imperial Court; it is important that the greyhounds for Mary, Regent of Flanders, be sent with him; comments on Anthony Aucher's request for a pardon for future negligence at Boulogne.

Master Secretary, after my most harty commendations: Yesterdaye I receyved your letters with letters and instructions for my depeche, and, having depeched myself hens, I departe this daye from hens, and whiles I may knowe whither thAdmyral be arryved or noo, I shal use al the diligence I canne. And as I atteyne knowlege of the Admyralles arryval or otherwise, I shal slak or make more hast according to your advise. I have sent this berer, my servaunt, to youe to receyve such houndes and grewhoundes as it shal please the Kinges Majestie to appointe to be sent to my Lady Regent, wherin, I praye youe, helpe to depech him, for although it be a smal matier here, yet is a gret matier thither as I goo.

I pray youe also, if ye see opportunite, to make myn excuse to the Quenes Grace that I did not myn owne duetie to take my leave of her Grace as I wold have doon, if the confusion of myn owne thinges had suffered me to remembre it, ne also have discharged therin that Skepperus committed on me as a parte of his charge.

I have here commened and divised with Master Ryther for the furniter of Bolen, and in the meane tyme have receyved a letter from Master Ager, who allegith hymself to be sik, as by[1] his letters he apperith to be, and that in his wytte he ⟨is⟩ not sufficient; wherof his letters semeth to geve sum testimonie, for he wyl not serve there to be charged oonles he may have a pardon bifore hand for his negligence and otherwise, like a clause in patentes, *absque compoto inde nobis reddendo* but as the prentes made his master, with thre countres shortely, 'I have nought, I owe nought, ner nothing is owing me.' Calays for somoch excedith Bolen, for in Calays Master Mondey serveth diligently without any such protestacion. Master ⟨Ager⟩ dare not aventure soo far at Bolen. A faulte

1 yo *c.o.*

there is, which I thinke Mastre Southwel wyl and canne disclose. And if we cannot bring to passe[1] that diligence wel rewarded in service shal[2] exclude the request for a pardon for negligence and otherwise, there wylbe, besides the gret losse, a gret disordre. Finally, I wold require youe to wryte to Mastre Ager eyther to serve like a man, manly, with such conditions in service as reason wold he shuld be content with, or elles[3] to make sute, for his inhabilite, to be discharged, if that allegacion[4] be trewe. I wold noo man to be so† burdened in his rome as he shulde † byde the aventure of al losses and decayes in victualles, for that wer to moch; and to be bounde to nothing again but to have pardon for negligence and otherwise, like Master Wingfeldes pardon in Fraunce for them he had kylled and shuld kyl, this is over deyntye. Ye told me oones ye love noo extremites, and the meane is best, as the wife confessed to her husbond who coulde hitte it; and I forgette myself and excede it even nowe in wryting. Master Ryther reparith to the Courte to declare what he hath doon. And thus I bydde youe hartely fare wel. At London the xviij[th] of Octobre, this Sonday in the mornyng.

Your assured loving
frend,

STE. WINTON

Addressed: To the Right Wourshippful Sir Wylliam Paget†, Knight, oon of the Kinges Majesties two Principal Secretaries.

Endorsed: The Bisshopp of Winchestre to Master Secretary, Master Paget, xviij° Octobris, 1545.

75. *To* PAGET

Dover, 21 October, 1545

R.O., S.P. 1, 209, 82–3.* *L.P.*, xx, ii, 627.

The outrageous, though not altogether unamusing, behaviour of a band of soldiers at Canterbury.

Master Secretary, after my most harty commendations: Yesterday the wynde was soo aloft[5] and, by reason of the quarter it stode in, the further shore so fowle, that they wold make noo passage. This daye the whether

1 passed *w.* d *c.o.*   2 not *c.o.*
3 not *c.o.*   4 acion *writ. over something else*
5 that *c.o.*

is fayre, and ⟨I⟩ determyne to goo to the shippe upon thending of this letter. God send me good passage and youe hartely wel to fare.

And yet I cannot thus make an ende of my letter, but signifie unto youe what the Mayre of Cauntourbury and his brethern, the aldermen, shewed me of the mysordre lately there by a bande of souldgers, soo outrageous and abhominable as I wold not have wryten upon any other reaporte; and what they tolde me I badde them take hede what they sayde, for, if nede shulde be, I wold charge them therwith. A fourtenigh⟨t⟩ bypast ther cam to Cantourbury a bande of souldgeors from Portysmouth to goo to Boleyn, and divised by the waye, and at Cantourbury, such a sleight of robbing the poore people, with such a colour to exchue the name of theft, as, oon of the aldermen tolde me, they coulde not have doon and som of them had not been scolers of Cambredge. I smyled with myself at it, howe onawars he touched me that[1] am Chaunceler of that Universite. They told me[2] sum of ther conceytes, wherat they laughed not that suffred, and yet the reaporte hath sum myrth in it, somoch as maye be in a noughty matier. He that had noo money wold borowe a grote of his felawe and goo in to the towne, shewing the grote and saying: 'Canne a man finde noo where foure pens? Wyl noo man geve me foure pens?' And therwith ever shewed his grote. Wherupon sum simple bodye, mynding to change the grote, wold geve him foure pens. Whenne he had receyved the pens, he made coursye, put of his cap with a gret many of thankes, and the⟨n⟩, whenne the poore woman asked the grote, he layde his hande on his brest and swore the grote was noon of his, he had borowed it oonly to get foure pens withal, and must nedes geve it again to his felawe as he had promysed; but he wold remembre her kyndnesse, and she shuld not lose by it; and soo, with good wordes, went his waye and left the woman weping. An other had espied a preste, and him he shewed an angel of gold, and therwith said he had to paye money and wanted wight money, and tolde the prest if he coulde helpe him he did him a gret pleasour. The prest thought to get his favour to change his aungel, and beganne to tel in to his hand grotes, mynding to geve him xxiiij for his angel; and whenne the prest had told to twenty, the souldger clapped his hand fast and told the prest he wold make shift with that for this tyme, and told him therwith that in this harde worlde he thought the prest strayned himself of forbere somoch, and suerly he thanked him with al his harte. Whenne the prest asked the angel, the

1 W c.o.   2 men w. n c.o.

152

souldgier swore that both wold skase serve his purpose. After thys sorte wer meny deceyved with good wordes. Other wer deceyved with knokkes, for when oon had sold his sword or his cloke, an other begynneth with the byer with a blowe on the eare, and askith him what he did with his sword or his cloke, and soo toke it awaye. It wer to long to wryte al ther conceytes. I asked the[1] Mayre why he refourmed not the matier, and he said he was told he might medle with noo souldger. I told him I toke it not soo.

They thenne tolde me that after thiese pagauntes playde, and that they wer soo wel knowen that noo man durst bye of them, noo man medle with them, they beganne them to lowe stowrely and grymly, and beganne to swere they wold make the towne a towne of warre. And thenne xxx of them went with a dromslade in to the cathedral churche and beganne to pyke a quarel to the belringer, but he shranke from them to a place where he might pere at them. And thenne they went to an awter that stode in the body of the churche and there made a resemblaunce to synge a Gospel, with *Dominus vobiscum,* and the rest answering; and beganne the *Boke of Generation of Margery[2] Curson,* 'And she begate such a bawde,' etc. And thenne they went to procession, and toke down an image, very gret, of Saincte John Baptiste; and that image they layde on the grownde, and oon cutte of the fynger, an other the nose, and after by peaces mangled the image with such spyteful wordes as have not been harde. And this doon moo of ther felaws reasorted to them to the number of clx ⟨160⟩, and al went in a raye throwe[3] the[4] towne with ther drumslade, and syngyng like men madde. The Mayre waxed in oon wondrous feere, and spake with the pety captayne, and desired they might be kept within ther houses wer they lodged, who promised it shuld soo be.

The Mayre[5] with his brethern watched, for he feared the town shuld, with the yought of the towne ydel foulkes joyning to them, have been put to sak. The souldgerors that night wer kept in whiles it was tenne of the clok. And thenne cummith abrode a certain of them and pyketh a quarel to the watche, and there begynneth a fraye[6], and therupon the towne in a alarum, diverse wer hurte, and the townes men kept ther howses, for avoyding mo[re] inconvenience. The next daye the[7] souldgers

1 they *w.* y *c.o.* 2 Margerye(?) *w.* e(?) *c.o.*
3 *spelled* fthrowe, f *doubtless meant to be c.o.*
4 th *c.o.* 5 *writ.* mary
6 r *in* fraye *writ. over* a 7 men *c.o.*

wer examyned bifore my Lord of Cauntourburye[1], who by lightlywode durst not punishe them, for thre wer sent two[2] ⟨pryson⟩ about tenne of the clok in the mornyng; and ther was a[3] dissension bytwen the aldermen bycause they wold tel precisely truly [4]whither they cam owte of pryson again at oon of the clok in the afternone that same daye or two. And this doon, they taryed in the town vij or viij dayes after, without paying for that they toke, and soo owe the pore men above xxxv *li.*, and almost xl. Mary, the pety captayne swerith he wyl sel his land but he payeth it, and hath in dede noon; and his preferrement in mariage hath not been gret, for he maryed of my neybour, as it is tolde me. This is, in my jugement, a rude bihavour which I coulde not, having laysour, leve on wryten, herby to provoke youe to wryte at lenght to me. My papour is spent and the maryners tary for me. Wherfor fare ye wel. At Dover, xxj[ti] of[5] Octobre in the mornyng.

Your assured loving frend,

STE. WINTON

Addressed: To the Right Wourshipful Sir William Paget, Knight, oon of the Kinges Majesties two Principal Secretaryes.

Below address, in another hand: Hast, post hast, with all delygence.

Endorsed: The Bisshopp of Winchestre to Master Secretary, Master Paget, xxj° Octobris, 1545.

76. *To* PAGET

Nieuport, 26 October, 1545

R.O., S.P. 1, 209, 135–6.* *L.P.*, xx, ii, 668.

Sends letters written to Thirlby from the English commissaries with Reiffenberg; awaits Paget's reply.

Master Secretary, after my right harty commendac⟨i⟩ons: I have seen thies letters wryten to my Lord of Westmester from the commissaryes with thAlmaynes; and I wold thAdmyral had been cum that I might have

---

1 Cauntourburyes *w.* s *c.o.*   2 ? *misspelling for* to.   3 gret *ċ.o.*
4 w *writ. over* b(?)   5 of *repeated*

told[1] my message to the Emperour in that matier. But here I tarye, abyding answer from youe; whom I praye God send hartely wel to fare. At Newporte, the xxvj[ti] of Octobre.

Your assured loving
frend,

STE. WINTON

Shepperus wylbe here with me[2] this daye in his reto*u*rne to the Kinges Majestie. He that brought me thies[t] letters left him on the waye.

Addressed: To the Right Wo*u*rshipful Sir William Paget[t], Knight, oon of the Kinges Majesties two Principal Secretaryes.

Below address, in another hand: To be returned to the Co*u*rte.

Endorsed: The Bisshoppe of Winchestre to Master Secretary, Master Paget, xxvj° Octobris, 1545.

77. *To* PAGET

Bruges, 4 November, 1545

R.O., S.P. 1, 210, 6–7.* *L.P.*, xx, ii, 725. *St. P.*, x, 650.

Chapuys denies knowledge of any new practice between Charles and Francis, and says he has made Charles' mouth water by his suggestion of a marriage with Princess Mary; news of skirmishes in Germany; if Francis hopes for peace through Protestant mediation, the Admiral's coming to the Imperial Court must be for some other purpose. (For the reference in the postscript *see St. P.*, x, 651 n.)

Master Secretary, after my right harty commendations: Synnes my cummying to Bruges, I have spoken with [3]Chapuis, bifore thEmperours arryval, who, as he sayth himself, was commaunded to folowe the Courte tyl our matiers wer past. He, to this interrogatory, Whither in good fayth[t] he knowith any newe practise bytwen Fraunce and thEmperour? denyeth it utterlye. But yet in communication I noted howe he told me that, when the Prince of Piemont sued to thEmperour of late to desire him to remember his matier for recovery of Piemont,

---

1 t c.o.   2 *writ. over something else*   3 C *writ. over* Sk

thEmperour said he thought on his matier, and wold, at Admyralles cummyng, he trusted, bring it in good termes. Chapuis told me a gret long communication bytwen hym and thEmperour, and noted unto me howe lusty thEmperour is nowe, and soo is he in dede over he hath been. But tellyng me of his lustynes, he said therwith he had gret communication with hym of my Lady Mary, and that he made thEmperours mouth water at it. It wer to long to wryte al his communication, but nedes he wold I shold hope wel of thys my journey, and that I shuld take for most certain that thAdmyral cummyth, and yet this was on Mondaye ⟨2 Nov.⟩, and the Countie de Bure could tel me thAdmyral cummyth. It wer too long to wryte al Chapuis talke, and there was noo more material thenne that I[1] have wryten.

Monsieur de Bure hath told me, in the tyme of his accompanying of me to the Courte, how he receyved this daye advertisement from the[2] campes of the Almaynes of the Lansgrave and Brunswike, where there is yet nothing doon but skyrmyshing. Mary[3], letters of the xxj the last moneth signified of taking of Bruneswike in a parlamentacion, but there is noo such matier. He sayth that Bruneswike hath the better bande of men of warre, and the Lansgrave the moo peasauntes. Thus[4] he sayth of that matier.

I note in your letters that the French Kyng wyl have Bolen spoken of, in the communication at Calays, by the Protestantes meanes; and[5] this I oonly feare, that such communication, as the French King wyl beare in hand he maye have there, he wyl require the same here. There is noo reason in it that it shuld soo bee; but I feare that; bicause of thEmperours tale of the French King, if the French King be soo famyliar to tel thEmperour *consilium suum* soo playnly, and thEmperour pretendith noo discontentement in it. Nowe maye youe there easely fishe out whither the Protestantes geve in dede the French King a more lightlywode of good conditions by ther meanes thenne ye be pryve unto; and to trye them therin, it shalbe good nowe ⟨to⟩ consider this: if the Admyral cumme hither and yet the French King practise with us by the Protestantes, and with thEmperours knowlege and contentment, our cause cannot, in my jugement, be the oonly cause of the Admyralles cummyng; that practise †by the Protestantes† taking effecte, his† to be soo frustrate. Upon our communication with Grandevela we shal see a lytel more light and advertise with diligence.

1 was *c.o.*   2 state of *c.o.*   3 th *c.o.*
4 s *c.o.*   5 such *c.o.*

Thus being late, I bydde youe fare wel with al my harte. At Bruges, the iiij^th of Novembre at night.

Your assured loving
frend,

STE. WINTON

My Lord of Westmester noted
that thEmperour did not calle the
French King brother, and therfor
I put it out of my latter, for in
the doubte I had rather have it soo.

Addressed: To the Right Wourshipful Sir Wylliam Paget, Knight, oon of the Kinges Majesties two Principal Secretaryes.

Endorsed: The Bisshopp of Winchestre to Master Paget, Secretary, iiij° Novembris, 1545.

78. *To* PAGET

Bruges, 5 November, 1545

R.O., S.P. 1, 210, 20–1.* *L.P.*, xx, ii, 731.

> The Emperor's advisers are overjoyed that Gardiner has commission to treat of matters between Charles V and Henry VIII; how does the King want him to conduct himself when certain ambassadors and princes visit him? (For the speech by Chremes concerning his slave Syrus *see* Terence *Heaut.*, 887; for the unsigned letter from Paget, referred to at the end of this, *see L. P.*, xx, ii, 714.)

Master Secretary, after my right harty commendations: In fewe wordes, I must have for the while as good opinion of thies men here as we had of Skepperus and his felawe in England. Oon speketh[1], in the comedye, by ⟨*i.e.*, of⟩ Syrus, *Fingit etiam vultus scelus*, but I promyse youe whenne thiese men[2] sawe I had commission with the rest to speke of those matiers bitwen us and thEmperour, they made ernest countenaunce of rejoyse; and if I shuld not cal it ernest, I shuld speke other wise thenne I thinke for the tyme. Skore and al is[3] ours. Our communication was togither as though we wer al oon again; and nowe Monsieur de Prate commened and had x tymes as many wordes as he had the last yere[4] in al our often meatinges. And whenne I sawe them soo *joieulx*, I entred even the same affection with them, and soo departed with them familierly. This after

---

1 of *c.o.*
3 h *incomplete c.o.*

2 *writ.* man
4 a *incomplete c.o.*

noone[1] I goo ⟨to⟩ the Quene, having here al the Kinges Majesties present[2] of houndes and grewhondes, which shalbe a gorgeous[3] matier whenne ther colours be on, which be very gaye. If any chaunge be, I wyl wryte of that as playnly, and as I see any clowdes, wryte of them; and not doo as Jasper Laet doth, saye this or that shal in dede folowe that. I remitte thither but as I here and see for the tyme; soo wyl I testifie. I spake coldely in the matier they wold faynest have harde on, to see whither ther wer any warmeth in them or not; and nowe they shewe themself warme, God graunte it be a natural heate, as I assure youe I must nedes judge it for the tyme. Sumwhat I shal knowe more by the Quenes facion, which I shal advertise incontinently, and spare noo more the Kinges Majesties purse[4] in postes nowe thenne other doo in ther feate, being everyman disposed to spende with the uttermost, besides them that waste—but I staye[5] here for feare of entryng the matier of victualles, etc.

The Prince of Piemont hath sent worde to sende to visite me this afternone. I praye youe by the next let me knowe the Kinges Majesties pleasour howe to use myself[6] in visitacion of ambassadours and such princes, wherin ther is a certayn cursye of Courte used, and is cause sumtyme of knowlege. I wold doo as I shuld not offende, and therfor I praye youe forget not by the next to advertise me of the Kinges Majesties pleasour[7]. Thus I byd youe [8]fare wel and goo to my dyner. I have depeched [9]Nicolas to the commissaryes, as ye shal perceyve by our letters to the Kinges Majestie. Thus fare ye hartely wel. And whenne I forget to make due commendacions to my good lordes and masters as I shuld, I praye youe remembre it, for I mynde it always and yet maye forget, as ye did in subscribing in your name †to your last letter†. At Bruges the[10] vᵗʰ of Novembre.

Your assured loving frend,

STE. WINTON

Addressed: To the Right Wourshipfull Sir Wyllyam Paget, Knight, one of the Kinges Majesties two Principall Secretaries.

Endorsed: The Bisshopp of Winchestre to Master Paget, Secretary, vᵒ Novembris, 1545.

1 they *c.o.*	2 very *c.o.*	3 *alt. from* ge(?)orgeous	4 purses *w. final* s *c.o.*
5 f *c.o.*	6 t *c.o.*	7 pleasours *w. final* s *c.o.*	8 f *writ. over* 1(?)
9 N *writ. over* th	10 x *c.o.*		

Bruges, 5 November, 1545

R.O., S.P. 1, 210, 22–5.* *L.P.*, xx, ii, 732.

Has received Mors' *Lamentation* (*see* above, p. 148), which he takes to be by George Joye; such malicious books may do little hurt while Henry VIII lives, but what will happen when youth, taught to contemn God, grows up? The example of Germany is not encouraging; Philip of Hesse, who is responsible for Reiffenberg, is a glorious champion of the Gospel! Even the baby Prince Edward cried when the Protestants looked at him; Henry VIII has never had any affection for them. Has finished his answer to Joye (*see* Nos. 80–1), but will not answer Mors; never wrote so much in a month before. (The reference to the letter in which *cronorum* was written, is to one from Philip of Hesse to Henry VIII warning him against persons who would have him no longer employ Reiffenberg—*L.P.*, xx, ii, 207.)

Master Secretary, after my right harty commendations: Synnes the depech yesternight, I have† called to my remembraunce that I wrote unto youe by Francisco from Newporte, and howe nere it turneth to ernest that I wrote there but to expresse thextremite of myn affection. I bad, soo we might have peax, send me to[1] Jherico; which ye have not doon†, but ye have goon somwhat towarde it, for ye have sumwhat eased the journey, but yet not moch; and that I shuld not take the payne to goo to Jherico, ye have, by my servaunt Olyver, sent Jherico to me; which thing, although ye have frendly doon, yet I had almost as leve a goon to Jherico in dede as to have Jherico sent me after that sorte. And howe fondly it cam in to my penne to wryte, 'Send me to Jherico,' and therwith cummyth to passe that ye send Jherico to me, and Jherico after that sorte! I have, in joye[2] myngled with sorowe, considered with myselfe[3] the chaunce. And by thenne ye have redde of my letter thus far, I thinke ye shal† muse sumwhat and be serching in your imagination what Jherico meanyth, wherin I spend with youe thus many wordes in vayne; bycause the grounde of the matier of Jherico which ye sent me is in dede wordes, but wordes so ordred and used as they importe a juste cause of lamentacion and sorowe, and such as wyl engendre dedes as horse heres doo snakes, if they be[4] suffred to putrifie. Of the bookes cast abrode in London, ye have sent me oon; and that is in thende noted to be prynted at Jherico, as he sayth, by Tom Trouth; and

---

1 † *abv.* not *c.o.*   2 might *c.o.*   3 fe *writ. over* h   4 not *c.o.*

he that wold have truth, I feare me†, shuld be fayne to travayle thither to seke hym (out of England).

The auctour of this booke hath *nomen ominosum* and callith himself *Mors*, proponyng and uttering such matier as doth threaten death of body and soule; of the body by dissension, and the soule by damnation. Howmoch is a prince touched to have al such as rulith under hym brought in contempt with the inferiour people! Thaldermen of London, that shuld be in reverence and punishe offenders, they be noted for the lewdest men in the citie. They note the Kinges Majestie not to see the truth. They condempne al the Parlament of ignoraunce, and saye to the people they have commission of God soo to† saye. And I saye, 'theye,' bicause they be above the singuler numbre, although oonly Roderigo Mors writeth this booke, who is in dede a vayneglorious fole[1]; and ever in the booke, whenne he spekith of joye, writeth that worde with a gret letter, wherby[2] his favourers might take counforte to see and rede his name, which is in dede Joye, that workyth sorowe to himself †and other†, and not Mors[3], wherof if he borowed an adjective, it shuld[4] be wel placed. Alas! alas! what meanith this, that a knave lurkyng in a corner, as Joye doth at Antwerpe, shalbe nurished to trouble the realme after this sorte? Al other troubles be trifles in respecte of that. Let men saye of me what they wyl. As he that hath made an ende of his oration may saye, *dixi*, soo, for myn owne pleasour in the worlde, I maye saye, *vixi, fuimus Troes et ingens gloria Dardanidum* ⟨*Aeneid*, II, 325⟩, as he sayde. This oon pleasour is behinde, which in an honest harte is never ended, to see thinges in ther due ordre, soo as our posterite maye saye we cared sumwhat for them. If it wer the truth that is set forth for truthe[5], if those that sette it forth had any qualites wherby a man might gather sum good opinion of the matier, if such as medle with it † waxed sumwhat better with it and not a gret dele the worse, if it wer not throughly knowen and throughly perceyved that thende of the secte is the destruction of Goddes honnour and mannes also, ye might cal me vehement to wryte thus of the matier.

But whenne al this is layde afore our eyes, we suffre an unreasonable trouble with a matier of nought, wherof canne cumme noo good ende. Howe many bookes and skrolles have been cast abrode in London within this yere and the offender never founde owte! Soo

1 *alt. from* foule   2 the *c.o.*   3 s(?) *c.o.*
4 to *c.o.*   5 by *c.o.*

many prestes[1] serched and put from ther goodes for a tyme, soo openly doon, and the offenders never founde owte! Thiese be commen open matiers. As for private attemptates, there have been a gret meany; and such particular tales blowen[2] abrode as cannot be sowen but of the devel. Ye wold have me contemne them, and soo doo I. But I cannot contempne the welth of the realme, wherin I have lyved soo honnourable a lyfe by the Kinges Majesties goodnesse, duryng whose life, which I trust shal be lenger then myne, I feare not thiese fonde malicious folyes. But whenne those that nowe be yonge shal, with the fraylete of yought, wyne a contempte of religion and conceyve an other opinion of God thenne is in dede trewe, what is like to ensue therof? If ⟨in⟩ Germanye such as have been brought up in those opinions had in ther behavour a more perfite reverence and obedience to thEmperour, who, whatsoever he be, he is ther superiour, thenne wold I thinke the lernyng might be good to tech obedience to princes; but I see it is[t] not soo. If I sawe that parte more civile, more honest, more reasonable thenne they wer wont to be, I might thinke[t] the lernyng good for sumwhat in this worlde; for as for the worlde to cumme, I am sure it is nought, for it is newe and agreeth with noo religion that hath been established by God in the Olde Testament or the Newe Testament. A punishement it is, and a terrible punishement—to admonishe an amendment. And howe have we be⟨en⟩ punished with the bestes ⟨i.e., beasts⟩ of that generation! Is not the Lansgrave a goodly champion of Christes Gospel, to worke the feate he hath doon with us, with *Verbum Domini* wryten on his mennes sleves? Maye [3]I not[3] saye thusmoch to youe, who knowith the begynnyng of the matier to have proceded thens and finally maynteyned thens by the letters wherin was wryten *cronorum?* Which worde [4]howe I toke and what I sayde youe canne tel, not by the spirite of prophetie to tel what shuld cumme, but as my mynde gave me *quodam animi presagio.* And I cannot forget the olde Erle of Essex, Bowser, who was with my Lord Prince vij yeres past, whenne the ambassadours of Saxe and Lansgrave wer sent to see my Lord Prince. At which tyme, whenne my Lord Prynce coulde not be brought to frame to loke upon those embassadours and put forth his hand[t], for noo chering, dandelyng, and flatering the nurse and Ladye Mastres coulde use, but my Lord Prince ever[5] cryed and turned awaye his face;

---

1 as *c.o.*

3–3 † *abv.* any *c.o.*

5 every *w.* y *c.o.*

2 ab *blotted and c.o.*

4 h *writ. over* I

and[1] yet at the same tyme†, to accustume him to a sterne countenaunce and rowe gret berd, the said Erle of Essex played with my Lord Prince, toke him by the hand, put his berde nere his face, which my Lord Prince toke pleasour in and was ther with mery. In thende, whenne thambassadours coulde have noon other sight of my Lord Prince, for al the labours taken, my said Lord of Essex cam to my Lord Prince and saide, 'Nowe, ful wel knowist thoue,' quod he, 'that I am thy[2] fathers true manne and thyne, and thiese other be false knaves.' Such spech eskaped him sodenly, for which he might percace have been thenne blamed of sum. But as Pilate said, *Quod scripsi scripsi*. My Lord Prince, God save him, hath asmoch of his father[3], the Kinges Highnes good nature as ever had any[4] childe of his father†; and therupon, a man might saye, was caused in my Lord Prince† an alienation in nature from them. For I never sawe that the Kinges Highnes of himself had any affection to them, but hath ever wisely wayed and considered the natures of them, and understanded them as right as any man coulde describe them. His Highnes, sum tyme of necessite, sum tyme of policie, hath wisely used them, and sumtyme I knowe hath been enformed and told many gretter thinges of them thenne have folowed.

What a god hath the Lansgrave been made, howmoch hath he been extolled! And yet, as ye may here by Monsieur de Prate[5], it is thought abrode, and we have gret lightlywodes to take it for truth, that the Lansgrave hath wrought this matier. And I praye God send us a good ende of our Protestauntes. If they bringe us peace†, I wyl thanke them for so moch, but if they fayne tales and diffame us, as though they sawe apparaunce that we shuld agree with them in opinions, and doo us noo good neyther, thenne they shal serve us in ther feate as evel as Riffenberge doth in his. And suerly Riffenberges noughtynes cummyth the wurst to purpose that might be, wherin the noughtynes is thers; but yet it is noted in us, as the Civil Lawe †callith it†, *quasi delictum quod utamur opera malorum hominum.* The lawe, *si quis commendandi fraudati*[6]⟨?⟩ *mandati*, wold cause the Lansgrave make good al. But what boteth[7] it to speke of lawe where reason faylith? There is a saying that *nimium altercando veritas amittitur.* And soo, with reasonyng, disputing, talking, jangling, warryng, fightyng, and stryvyng, truth, fayth, honestie,

1 y † *and c.o.;* at *c.o.*   2 *alt. from* this(?)
3 fathers *w.* s *c.o.*   4 p *c.o.*
5 b *c.o.*   6 *MS.,* ff   7 *alt. from* both

reason, and al equite is worne and torne, and nedith a very true peace, outwardely and inwardely, to forge them al again and coyne them with the right stampe; for the world is nowe in a wonderful garboyle.

I have finished myn answer to George Joye, and therin, I trust, declare that I have thought on other matiers sumtyme thenne to be such oon as he notith me. And although I goo not aboute to prove myself a saincte, for I have made noo such outwarde visage of hypocrise, yet[1] it shal appere I am not utterly a devel. And if I[t] be a devyl, I am not of that kinde of develles that he notith me of, and such other as have pleasour to have me soo spoken of. And yet that is not the purpose of my[2] answer, but specially to declare certayne thinges that nede declaration not unfrutefully. And that booke I wryte to the worlde. Mary, to the booke of Lamentacion which youe sent me, I wyl oonly answer lamentably to youe, and, lamentyng with youe, counforte myself; digesting in thiese letters so moch displeasour as I receyved in reding of this most abhominable booke. This is the best pastyme I canne have here, whenne I have rydde the buysines, which this matier shal not interrupte in my mynde. This letter hath neyther hast for life nor hast[3] with diligence, but ye maye rede it to yourself at your laysour. And if ye reade it not, it makith noo matier; yet I take not my labour lost; for it is noo payne for me to wright, and I [never] wrote[4] somoch in a moneth as I have doon in th[is], and I loke soo lustely, thankes be to God, that I talke shamfastely of any sikenesse by the waye. God make al[5] that be syk, eyther in body or soule, hol, and send youe hartely[6] wel to fare. At Bruges the vth of Novembre.

Your assured loving
frende,

STE. WINTON

Addressed: To the Right Wourshipful Sir Wylliam Paget, Knight, oon of the Kinges Majesties two Principal Secretaryes.

Below address: At leysour.

Endorsed: The Bisshoppe of Winchestre to Master Paget, Secretary, v^o Novembris, 1545.

1 I *incomplete*	2 p *c.o.*
3 s *incomplete c.o.*	4 *alt. from* wryte
5 ey *c.o.*	6 f *incomplete c.o.*

80. *To the* READER

[Bruges, *c.* 5 November, 1545]

From *A Declaration of such true articles as George Joye hath gone about to confute as false.* London, 1546. 4to edition.

> Has contemned the jolly hunter (*i.e.*, William Turner and his *seconde course of the hunter at the romish fox & hys advocate* ... *steven gardiner—see* p. 478, below) but must answer Joye (*see* above, p. 149); the unlearned may have knowledge enough for right living, but discussion of the Scriptures requires erudition. (For place and date of writing *see* No. 79, p. 163.)

Steven, Bysshoppe of Wynchester, to the Reader

God geve the (Gentle Reader) judgement to discerne truth from untruth. Bytwene whiche two, in the personnes of me and Joye, thou shalte s'e contencion. Wherin I have not such regard to the man, to dispute with him (whom by Saynt Poules counsayll, after so many admonitions, I should exchue), but only to treate the matter, which nedeth true explication. As I have contemned the joyly hunter and other janglers, wisely in my frendes opinions, so should I do Joye, for any thyng he hath said of me. And agaynst Joye I stryve not, who overturneth himselfe, but am enforced to talke with hym, as a medler in the thinge which I can not pretermitte and suffre undeclared. I can not frame my writinges meet for al mennes capacities; eyther lerning fayleth, or the matter wyll not suffre. Good wyll wanteth not, whiche I wolde wisshe were throughly persuaded unto the, with this also, that albeit thartycles of our beleef, with knowledge sufficient for direction of our living to Goddes pleasure, maye be comprehended of rude and unlearned wittes, yet the discussion of the Scriptures requireth Goddes further giftes of erudicion and lernynge.   Farewell.

81. *To* GEORGE JOYE

[Bruges, *c.* 5 November, 1545]

From *A Declaration of such true articles as George Joye hath gone about to confute as false.* London, 1546. 4to edition, ii–x. The emendations

164

listed under 'fautes escaped in the printynge' are here incorporated into the text.

An account of his dealings with Robert Barnes. Barnes railing at Wolsey; his sermon (on Christmas Eve, 1525); how Gardiner persuaded him to recant (February, 1526); their meeting at Hampton Court (1531 or 1532); Gardiner's sermon at Paul's Cross on the first Sunday in Lent (15 February, 1540) answered by Barnes a fortnight later; Henry VIII examines Barnes; Henry's reverence for the Sacrament; Barnes grants himself overcome in argument with Gardiner and asks to be his scholar, but after three days comes no more to school; the recantation sermons of Barnes, Gerard, and Jerome (Easter Week, 1540); Barnes sent to the Tower by the Privy Council when Gardiner was not a member of it; ever 'meant good faith with Barnes.' (*See* above, p. 149; for place and date of writing *see* No. 79, p. 163.)

To George Joye

After your boke hath ben well worne in the handes of youre favourers, it is comme at the laste to myne. If I had soner had it, I wold soner have entered thopenyng of that matter, not to contend with you (whose raylinge I esteme no more then I do the joylye hunters of the foxe, and other of that rable), but to declare the truthe in the matters ye improve ⟨*i.e.*, condemn⟩; therrour wherin is very daungerous and the true understanding very profitable. Ye take upon you to confute Winchesters false articles, as ye terme them; the truth wherof I shall examyne hereafter. In the meane time I mervayle howe such matter as I spake by mouthe, in the instructing and teachinge of Barnes, at suche tyme as by his owne sute to the Kinges Majesty he submitted him selfe to be my scoler, shoulde come to your handes, wrytten or unwritten, and who toulde tales out of scoole. For Barnes had but one scoole felow with him, and betwene us was no wrytinge; but takinge upon me the place of a teacher at Barnes desyre, I uttered some such matters as ye wryte of, but more at large, to Barnes and his scoole felowe by waye of doctrine, with some other explication then ye do set fourthe.

And it shal not be out of purpose to speake somwhat of Barnes, of myne acquaintaunce with hym, and what hath chaunced betwene him and me; whereby may appeare howe truly and charitably you, Maister Joy, and suche as ye be, report of me concerning Barnes, whom I knewe fyrst at Cambridge, a trymme minion frere Augustine, one of a merye skoffynge witte, frerelike, and as a good felowe in company was beloved of many. A doctour of divinitie he was, but never like to have proved to be either martyre or confessor in Christes religion; and yet he began

Luther excedeth in the feate of raylinge, and Joye doth pretely for a scoler; the joyly hunter may compare with eyther.

there to exercise raylinge (which, amonge such as newely professe Christ, is a great pece of connynge, and a great forwardnes to reputacion, speciallye if he rayle of bysshops, as Barnes began, and to please suche of the lower sort as envieth ever auctoritie) cheflye against my Lorde Cardinall, then, under the Kinges Majesty, having the high administracion of the realme.

It chaunced at the same tyme, a frende of Barnes in Cambridge to be sued for juste debte by his neighboure; whiche creditoure, for no intreatie that Barnes could make, wold leave his sute, but have his debte payed him, as the lawe wolde; wherat Barnes waxed angry, and began to preache of it, and, as he warmed in the matter, spake so much the

Barnes beganne at the lewdest opinion of the Anabaptistes, whereby to extinct the ordre of justyce.

more violently and, to shew hym selfe stowte, playnly affirmed in the pulpet that it was not lawful for one Christen man to sue an other, and that he wold stande by and prove by Saynt Paule. Of this preachynge complaynte was made to the Vicechauncelour, and after the matter hard amonge the doctours, and somewhat spoken sharpely by one Doctor Preston (whome Barnes coulde not beare), it was ordered that Barnes should recant that false assertion, which is an article of the Anabaptistes. Upon refusall whereof by Barnes, the matter was brought to my Lorde

A wantonne lyghtnes so to jeste, at those dayes, of one in so high auctoritie, and without all frute of edification.

Cardinalles knowledge, with accumulacion of such raylynges and jestinges as Barnes had made agaynst myters and crosses and all my Lorde Cardinalles havoure, so farre as in his sermons, in place of carnall affections, he termed them cardinall affections, wherin he pleased some at those dayes.

Almost all that have ben notable have ben of my speciall acquayntaunce. I have loved the men and ever hated the noughtie opinion from the begynynge.

At the tyme of this accusacion of Barnes, I was in service with my Lorde Cardinall, of acquayntaunce with Barnes, and not accompted his enemy, and yet, I thanke God, never favoured such straunge opinions as he and some other wantanlie began to set furth. But bycause there was not then in them malyce, and they maynteyned communication havynge some savour of lernynge, I was familiar with such sort of men, and was then sory for Barnes, and glad to helpe him so farre as might stande with my dutie to my Lorde my mayster, agayns whome he rayled. And yet that raylynge, in a frere, had ben easel pardonned, if Barnes had not fondely persisted in the Anabaptiste opinion, denienge sutes to be lawefull amonge Christen men. And laboured with Barnes secretely to bringe that out of his head; wherin h yelded to me, upon the shewinge to hym of a sayenge of Saynt Austen expoundynge the Scripture where Barnes toke his error. So as afterwarde Barnes was content to abjure that opinion, with crosses, staves

nd myters, and all his jestinge matter; and all this tyme toke me for his
rende, as I was in deede, his foly set apart, and had shewed hym, as I
hought, a frendly turne.

When Barnes afterwarde had broken out of the kepynge of the
eres besides Stanforde, and escaped out of the realme, the fyrst
ydynges I hard of hym was in a booke made by hym and prynted,
herin he wrote how Doctor Stevens (by whiche name I was then
alled) had deceyved hym by shewinge him a place of Saynt Austen,
nd thereby had inveygled him to leave his opinion; for I shewed
ym not (he said) the hole sayeng of Saynt Austen, but a pece of the
eginnyng, and if I had redde it him throughly, the latter parte had
ade for confirmation of his opinion. And this rewarde hadde I for the
rst frendly dede I dyd hym. Sins which time, at his repayre into
ngland under saufe conduyte, not to be touched (for such sute he
ade upon pretence that he had matter to shewe worthye to be knowen),
chaunced to meete with him at Hampton Court, where, in the presence
f my Lord of Caunturbury that nowe is, I layed that mysreport of me
 his charge, and there shewed him the boke, to se Saynt Austins
ordes, whiche, in the fyrst parte and also last parte, condemned his
nabaptistical opinion. Whereupon Barnes fyl downe on his knees and
ked me instantlye forgevenes, with promysse to wryte a boke to the
orld, wherin to declare that he had belyed me. Upon which reconcilia-
on I had Barnes home to my house that night and made hym the best
ere I could. And hitherto I trust no man can judge I should persecute
rnes, but Barnes me, bycause I suffred him not to be worthely burnt.
t after he was reconciled I forgate that, and Barnes forgate also to
rge me, and blame him selfe to the worlde of his lye against me. After
is Barnes returned frelie into England, and lyved here triumphantlye,
ll, by his owne pryde and arrogancye, he sought his owne confusion
d persecuted hym selfe; wherein I was onely an occasion as a stumb-
nge stone, but otherwyse no doer, but a sufferer, as, in the truth of the
orye, shall appeare.

In declaration wherof, thinke not amysse of me, Reader, for I
eane onely the reformation of such as, seduced by false prophetes,
 wronge borne in hande, and have fayned lyes tolde them, of suche
 they take for maisters in lerninge, and other, noted to be their
versaries. Among which adversaries I have ben noted, as I have not
 ne am angry at it, but as I have not merited[1], and therfore have

My Lorde Cardinall wold not suffre Barnes raylinge wit ⟨to⟩ be at liberty.

Barnes boke remayneth in print, whereby the truth hereof may appere.

The materiall poyntes of this story be eyther publique within memorie or have suche witnesse as all men wyl (I thinke) beleve, for they be indifferent; and the truth of the matter shulde much declare me, and disprove such as rayle to the contrarye.

1 *misprinted* mented *in 4to;* merited *in 8vo.*

167

taken it for a lesson, what I should have done and ought to do; for elle
I have ben wonderfull negligent to deserve any such brute amonges men
whose helpe I never yet searched to uphold the truth, nether by frend

I deserve no prayse herin, but only by-cause I tell truth.

shyp ne secrete communication. I have not kepte one scoler at Cam
brydge or Oxforde, syns I was bysshop, to be brought up in the Catho
lique opinion, whiche is also myne. I have not gone about to allur
by any worldly entisement any man to it; but have folowed theri
thadmonition of the worde of Scripture I write, *Vana salus hominis*. A
I have ben called, in place, I have used thopportunitie, and as I have be
provoked, I have written and spoken, as I have done to Bucer and a
I do nowe to you, Master Joye; but elles I am persuaded, that being
the truth a matter which God hath to hart, and under him the Kinge
Majestie, I may with untymely busynes in it, and out of my place, rathe
hinder then further.

The Sonday before in the Court at dyner, upon complaynt of the Deane that he was un-provided, the Lorde Great Chamberlain named me, whiche I coulde not refuse.

Accordinge to which determination, when I had preached, th
fyrst Fryday in the beginninge of Lent, Anno MDXXXIX ⟨*i.e.*, 1540⟩
before the Kynges Majesty upon the wordes of the prophet, *Clama, n
cesses*, and had cryed out somewhat that Barnes and some other lyke
not, where I was desyred by a lerned frende to procure that I mygh
preach that day all the Lent, to him I aunswered that I was calle
sodenly to make the sermon I had made, and spake therin that I though
to be spoken, but I wold not medle so farre as to avaunce my se

I take heresies in the Church to be lyke byles in a mans body, whiche, oversone laun-ced, waxe sorer, and in tyme putrifie their matier, and hele of them self with a lytell clensynge playster of the chefe surgeon.

further in the matter, to make my selfe a capitayne against them. Fc
myne opinion was that they shold not dissolve by pollicie against then
but by excesse of their own malyce worke their owne confusion; som
confirmacion wherof incontinentlye folowed, as I shall trulie tel
wherof I have witnes lyving.

I minded some Sonday of that Lent to preache at Paules Cross
as I had ben yeres before accustomed; and upon the fyrst Saturda
in Lente, goinge to Lambehith, there to be occupied all that daye,
devised with my chaplein that he should go that daye and knowe wh
should occupie the crosse that Lent, and to speake for a place for n
on one of the Sondayes, not meaninge the Sondaye that shoulde b
on the morowe, for I had in my mind more reverence to that audienc
then, without some convenient premeditacion, to shewe my self ther
Neverthelesse, my chapleine, repayring to knowe howe the Sonday
were appoynted and understandinge that Barnes shulde preach th
fyrst Sondaye (which was the morowe), thought in his mynde rath
to take that daye for me then any other, specyally because he thoug

wolde speake that was good and Barnes shoulde be disapoynted to
utter that was nought. And so when I had doone my busynes at
Lambehith (whiche ended not afore fyve of the clocke that Saturday),
my chaplein, then wayting for me, told me he had ben so bolde over
me to appoynte me to preach the next daye at Poules Crosse, adding
howe he thoughte better to disapoynte Barnes on the morowe then
some other Catholique man, appointed on other Sondayes.

Wherupon I gathered my wittes to me, called for grace, and determined A part of my sermon at Pouls Crosse the fyrst Sonday of Lent, An. MDxxxix (*i.e.*, 1540).
to declare the Gospell of that Sondaye, conteynynge the devilles thre
emptacions, the matter wherof semed to me very apte to be applyed to
the tyme, and good occasion to note the abuse of Scripture among some,
as the devyll abused it to Christ; which matter in dede I touched somewhat playnly and, in my judgement, truly. And alludinge to the tempta-
on of the devyll to Christ, to cast him selfe downewarde, allegyng
scripture, that he shulde take no hurte, I sayde now a dayes the devill
tempteth the world and byddeth them cast themselfe backeward. There
no forward in the newe teaching, but al backwarde. Now the devill
teacheth, come backe from fastynge, come backe from praying, come
backe from confession, come back from wepinge for thy synnes, and all
backewarde, in so much as he must lerne to say his Pater Noster back-
ward, and where we sayd, 'forgive us our debtes, as we forgyve our
debters,' now it is, 'as thou forgivest our debtes, so I wyll forgyve my
debters,' and so God must forgyve fyrst; and al, I sayd, is turned backewarde. And, amonges other thinges, noted the devilles craft, what shift
he useth to deceyve man whose felicitie he envieth, and therfore
coveteth to have man idle and voyde of good workes, and to be ledde
that idlenes, with a wanne hope to lyve merely ⟨*i.e.*, merrily⟩ and at
his pleasure here, and yet have heaven at the last; and for that purpose
procured out pardons from Rome, wherin heaven was sold for a litle
money, and for to retayle that marchaundise the devyll used freres for
his ministers. Nowe they be gone with all their tromperye, but the
devyll is not yet gonne. And nowe he perceyveth it can no lenger be
borne to buy and sell heaven (both the marchaundyse is abhorred, and
the ministers also—we can not away with freres, ne can abyde the name),
the devyll hath excogitate to offre heaven without workes for it, so
slye that men shall not nede for heaven to worke at all, what soever
oportunite they have to worke. Mary, if they wyll have an higher
place in heaven, God wyll leave no worke unrewarded; but as to be in
heaven, ⟨it⟩ nedes no workes at al, but onely belefe, onely, onely, nothinge

els. And to set forth this the devils craft, there were (I sayde) mynisters but no mo fryers. Fye on the name and the garment! But nowe they be called by an Englyshe name, bretherne, and go apparelled like othe: men, amonges which be some of those that were freres, and served the devyll in retaylinge of heaven in pardons, for they can skyll of the devyls servyce. But if the Kynges Majestie, as he hath banyshed frere: by the Frenche name, wolde also banyshe these that call them self brethren in Englyshe, the devyll shulde be greatly discomforted in hi enterprise, and idlenes therby banyshed, whiche the devyll wyll elle perswade by mysunderstandinge of Scriptures, as he did in thadvaunce ment of pardons.

This my sermon was thought to some very plaine, and Barnes (a he confessed after, and as appeared by that he dyd) coulde not dige: it, but was perswaded and comforted to handle me somewhat rudely whiche he dydde the Sondaye fourtnyght after, in the same place

Barnes preachinge at Pauls Crosse the thyrde Sonday in Lent, An. MDXXXIX (i.e., 1540).

where he toke to intreat the same text of the Gospel that I ha. declared, and lefte the Scripture of the Sonday he preched on; whic had not ben sene in that place before. There he beganne to call for m to comme forth to aunswer him; he termed me to be a fightynge cock and he was another, and one of the game; he sayde I had no spoore:

This glorye endured but tyl the Friday after, by whiche tyme he hadde forgotten al; on the Saturday chase his scolemaister; and the Monday came to scoole lyke a good chylde.

and that he wold shewe. And after he had pleased himselfe in thallegori of a cockefight, then, upon a foolysh conclusion, he cast me openly h: glove; and, not content therwith, he called me forthe by my nam. Gardener, and opposed me in my grammer rules, and sayde if I ha aunswered him in the scoole as I had there preached at the Crosse, l: wolde have given me syxe strypes; and raged after such a sorte as th lyke hath not ben herde doone in a pulpete (ordered to declare th Worde of God in, and not to touche any perticuler man), as he rayled me by name, alludynge to my name, Gardener, what evell herbes sette in the garden of Scripture, so farre beyonde the termes of honest as all men wondered at it, to here a bysshop of the realme as I was, : reviled, and by such one, openly. So as my frendes enforced me to con playne unto the Kinges Majestie, and, for mayntenaunce of comm order, not to passe it over unspoken of. Whereupon I complayne caringe more for the perverse doctryne he wente about to establisshe depraving of me, then for any displeasure could come unto me by h raylynge.

Howe graciouselye the Kinges Majestie herde the complayn and howe indifferentlye his Majestie, after his accustomed goodn

ordered thexamination of it, all good men myghte have cause to re-
oyse, and Barnes no cause of greef, but cause of comforte in the Kinges
Majesties mercye, if he wold have ernestly enbraced it. For what so ever
olowed worthely by justice, the Kinges Majesty offred Barnes asmoch
nercy as ever did prynce any offendour, declarynge howe his Highnes
vas desyrouse of concorde in the truth, rather than the punysshement
f any man that wolde from erroure be reduced to the truth. And one
otable thinge was done, in the hearinge of that matter, by the Kynges
Majestie, when Barnes offered to yelde to his Highnes in his opinion.
he Kynges Grace, syttinge secretely in his closet, and havinge with him
e late Erle of Southampton (whose soule God pardon), the Mayster
f the Horse that nowe is, me, Barnes, Mayster Doctour Cockes, and
octour Robinson, the Kinges Hyghnes, at that offre of Barnes, sayd,
am' (quod his Majestie) 'a mortall man,' and therwith rysynge and
rninge to the Sacrament and puttinge of his bonet, sayde: 'Yonder
the maister of us al, authour of truth, yelde in truth to hym, and I
all' (sayeth the Kinges Majestie) 'defende the truthe. And otherwise
rnes' (quod the Kinges Majestie) 'yelde not to me.' Much more there
as notably spoken by the Kynges Hyghnes to refourme Barnes foly,
his maner, and also lernynge, whiche I touche not, because I shulde
ther empayre and diminishe that was in dede sayde then tell it fullye.
But to the purpose I tell this storye for: I desired the Kynges Majestie
at Barnes and I myght commen to gyther of the matter, oute of his
yghnes presence, in the hearynge of certayne to be appoynted by his
ighnes, as indifferent, to make report of oure dispitions[1], and then
rnes shoulde have no cause to excuse him selfe, if he coulde not con-
nce me, as he dyd in the pulpete, onely touchynge the trueth of hys
ctryne disprovynge myne. For as for his rebukes, I clearlye remytted
d forgave them, and wolde commen as quyetlye wyth hym as yf he
dde used no suche language of me; whiche my petition the Kynges
jestye graunted, and appoynted Mayster Doctour Cockes and Mayster
octour Robynson, with two other, to be indifferent hearers bytwene
rnes and me, and onelye to heare us talke togyther and make reporte
his Hyghnes.
Whereupon that nyght (which was the Fryday after Barnes had
ached so outragiouslye of me) Barnes, I, and the hearers were
rte, where none other might heare us. And for entry of disputation
wene Barnes and me, I told hym I began with forgyving all was

If Barnes had not extremely abused the Kynges Majesties goodnes for a little vaine glory among such as magnified hym for their owne purpose, he had escaped all punishment.

A behaviour and speache of the Kinges Majestie, secretly done, and worthye an open knowledge and eternall memorye.

1 ? *a misprint for* disputations

past that myght touche me. I beganne in frendshyp with him, onel[
intendinge to trye the truthe of the doctrine in controversie betwen
hym and me, and therein I offered hym choyse, whether he wolde hav
me aunswere hym or he to aunswer me. He chase to aunswere me
Whereupon I prepared my self to fashion certayne argumentes to hyn

I reherse this not for
my praise, but to de-
clare Barnes unlerned
arrogancie.

of the Scriptures; and to my fyrst argument he coulde make no aunswere
I made him an other, and thereunto he could say nothing; but the
desyred me that I wolde spare him for aunswer to them that nighte, an
we shulde come togyther agayne erely the nexte morninge, and so g
through. I tolde hym I was content, and yet if I shulde strive with hy[
for glorye, after a childysshe fasshion and lyke a grammariane, suche on
as he fasshioned me in the pulpete, all the tyme he studied for his aunsw[
I shuld decline *Nominativo, convictus, genitivo, convicti &c.*; but that wel

Mayster Doctor Cocks
and Mayster Doctor
Robynson were pre-
sent and knowe this to
be true.

boyeshnesse in dede. And therefore he shoulde have all the night to stud
on to make aunswer, with all my harte; and I wolde also do so mocl
for hym as to tell hym a thyrde of myne argumentes, and badde hy[
thynke upon that agaynste the mornynge also, and so departed for th
nyghte.

In the mornynge, we assembled be tymes, accordynge to the ap
poyntemente. At whyche tyme Barnes wente aboute to assoyle my[
argumentes; I replyed to hys solutyons; and so spente two houres ver[
quyetlye and pacyentlye. And sodaynelye, beyonde all oure expect
tions, when it was Barnes parte to have spoken, he fell on bothe l

I durste never write
forth this, and I had
not the foresaide wit-
nes yet livinge.

knees and desyred me to have pytye upon hym, good Bysshoppe, ar
spake so many wordes to my glory and in prayse of my lerning, as I w
ashamed to heare them, and dare not for vaineglory reherse now. A[
I dyd no more acknowledge his prayse there, to gyve to me that I h
not, then his dispraise in the pulpet, to take from me that I hadde; f
I hadde neyther more or lesse for eyther of both. But such was Barr
havour then, so farre discrepante from that in the pulpet; and theref[
I tell this matter. In that submission Barnes graunted him self overcon
and desyred he myghte be my scoler, to be instructed of me, and :
quired all them presente to be meanes to the Kinges Highnes tha
myght so take hym, and desyred me to forget all, and, he trusted, yf
were with me, his wytte shulde not myslyke me. This chaunge in Bar[
was so farre from that I loked for, that I used it in an other extremi[

It is harde medelynge
with suche maner of
men. Yf a man procure
theyr punishmente as

I toke him up from knelinge, I remembred olde familier knowled
assured hym of me, I refused to be his scolemayster, but beinge, a
perceaved, he was mynded to fall from errour, I wolde communic

172

into hym some honest portion of my lyvynge, and named xl *li.* a yeare, and he to lyve felowelyke with me in my house. And this I reherse because it was tolde abrode afterward how I offered him xl *li.* a yere to leave his opinion but he wold not.

But to Barnes agayne; he wolde nedes be my scoler for ought I coulde do, and sayde God had gyven a gyfte to me wherewith to do muche good; and then, goynge a parte with me from the rest, began familierlye to devyse which scolefelowes it were expediente to have to scoole with hym, and there devised me a great meany of scolers besydes hym selfe, who, refourmed, all shuld be wel (he sayd); and, in speaking of scolers, tolde me many thynges that I knewe not before. But I concluded with him that he myght bringe one to scoole with him and he wolde, but I wolde no moo at ones. Whereupon the Kynges Highnes, advertised of the conclusion of the matter betwene Barnes and me, was content that Barnes shuld repayre to my house at London the Monday folowinge; whiche he dyd with a scolefelowe with him, neither Jerarde nor Jherome, but an other yet a live. And at that time, teaching Barnes, I uttered such articles as ye, Maister Joye, have putte forth in printe, but not all togyther so as ye reherse them, for they have a marke that they have passed your handes; that is to say, be a lyttle corrupte and falsified, as I shewe afterwardes. When Mayster Barnes had gone to scoole two dayes he waxed wery of that humilitye, and came the thyrde day and signified to me that yf I wolde take him one that came to conferre, he wolde come styll, but els he wold no more come. I perceyved from whense the chaunge came, and told him, seinge he had ones yelded him selfe to me as a scoler, I wolde so use him tyll I sawe hym better lerned, able to be my felowe, which he had not yet attayned syns Satterday, at which tyme he made the submission. Hereupon they began to spread abrode an envious rumour of me, that I wold be scoolemaister to all the realme, and many good growes. And so was I rydde of my wayward scoler, and never medled with hym after.

Barnes in dede troubled me yet ones agayn at my beyng at Saynt Mary Spittel by commaundement, and sitting there by the Mayer to here him preache and recante in writinge; to the conceyvinge wherof I was not pryvie. But when Barnes right solemplie and formally had made his recantacion in the formour part of his sermon, at thende of it he cryed out to me and asked me forgivenes with a marvelous circumstance, as though the world shuld think I had had nede of

173

Barnes was not appoynted thus to do, nor it was not nedeful, for I was in no auctoritie wherefore to fere me, nor I medled not further with hym, and had forgiven him before.

There is no thinge more true then this; ne more detestable in a subject, so openly to delude his prince and soverayne lorde, besides the injury to the truth.

This necligence was notable in the late Lorde Crumwell, who, not markynge throughlye what was written in them, caused him self those letters to be redde to other, and so called Barnes and his felowes knaves.

When Barnes was sent to the Towre I was not in the Privye Counsayle.

The numbre of thre signifieth infinite, and so often did I forgive Barnes; and therefore am called his persecutour and was, as Davyd dyd persecute Saul.

suche a publique obtestacion, and nedes I must holde up my hand in token of a graunt. And where I, encombred with shamefastnes dyd not by and by as he required, he called for it agayne, and bad m hold up my hand. So it lyked hym with a courage to playe with me, an to blynde the other submission done secretly, as though it had ben c none other sorte, and therwith to boste his owne charitie and bring myne in doubt. And when he had in the pulpete plaied these two parte to recant his opinion, as he was appoynted, and aske me forgivenesse which he did of wantonnes, then after the prayer he begynneth a proc of a matter, and playnlye and directlye preacheth the contrarye of th he had recanted; so evidentlye as the Mayour, of hym self, aske whither he shuld from the pulpete send him to warde, to be fourt commynge to aunswer for his contemptuouse behaviour, to preache i the same place to the same people the contrarye to his recantacion. B Barnes was not stayed ne spoken to whiles Jherome and Jherard hade both preached and folowed the same trade.

The Kinges Majestie had appointed certayne to make reporte of tl sermons, before which report, one that favored them had written to h frende at the Courte howe gayly they had all handled the matter, bo to satisfie the recantacion and also in the same sermons to utter out tl truth, that it myght sprede without let of the worlde. And this letter l negligence came to light, wherupon, and report of the sermons, th were al apprehended, and by the secret Counsayle (to whiche compar I had then none accesse, ne had not almost a yeare before, ne had n after, so longe as Crumwels tyme lasted) sent to the Towre, and the upon ensued further proces by the hole realme, whereunto I was priv but amonge the rest. And otherwyse then I have rehersed I have n persecuted Barnes; and as I have told the storye, so it was done.

And thinke me not, god ⟨*i.e.*, good⟩ Reader, so moche a beast th al such beinge yet alive in whose presence and knowledge these matt have passed betwene Barnes and me, I wolde vaynlye fayne in sucl tale; wherein I accompte not mine estimation to have over co Barnes, for he was not lerned, and shulde much hyndre myne es mation, if any man could, in that I have tolde, reprove me of a l For so moche the tale may be profitable to the ⟨*i.e.*, thee⟩, Reader, considre howe thinges be blowed and blustered abrode with lyes, a how Barnes death is layde to my charge, that have onely suffred Barnes hand, and never dyd any thing to him, but ever forgave h and he ever used forgevenes, never to amende, but to delude and try

nd if any wold note my blyndenes in vayne glorye, that because
ırnes yelded to be my scoler of policie (as Davyd fayned him self mad
:fore Achis) I colde not espie it, but take it in earnest, I wold to such
y that if Barnes counterfaited in that submission, he deceived moo
wel as me; and, in dede, a man in his owne praise may soone be made
·oole. And one of that company tolde me (whom I take for my frende)
at he had not thought to heare so muche divinitie of me, ne se so much
aritie in a bysshop. How this matter shalbe taken I remitte to the
lifferencie of the reader. I ment good fayth with Barnes and symply,
d further medled not with him then I have rehersed; wherin ap-
areth on my behalf no malice, and there appeareth also upon what
casion I have uttered such articles as Joye wyll now confute for false,
iich, howe substancially he doth, by comparynge his and myne to-
ther, I shall entreate hereafter.

<aside>Thus the holy examples of Scripture be applied to cover lewde mens fautes; when they ly in examinacion, that is, as Abraham denyed Sara, yf they counterfet, that is, as Davyd dyd before Achis. *Exemplum placet.*</aside>

NOTES TO NO. 81

Page 166. The Vice-Chancellor was Edmund Natares—Foxe, v, 415.
Page 168. Gardiner's motto, *Vana salus hominis*, is from Pss. lx, 11;
:ii, 12 (Vulgate, lix, 13; cvii, 13); *see also* below, p. 394. The text of
 sermon on the first Friday in Lent, 1540, was from Is. lviii, 1.
Page 168, margin. The Lord Great Chamberlain in February, 1540,
·s John De Vere, Earl of Oxford, who died 20 March of that year.
·rdiner, however, may be referring to the man who held the office
·en he wrote; namely, Edward Seymour, Earl of Hertford.

82. *To* PAGET

Bruges, 6 November, 1545

)., S.P. 1, 210, 39–42.* *L.P.,* xx, ii, 741. *St. P.,* x, 654.

'onjectures what the French intend by treating with England in two places;
·ill conclude nothing without Henry's signed consent, and asks that the utmost
›ncession Henry will make for peace be sent sealed, not to be opened till all
·se fails.

:ter Secretary, after my right harty commendations: Thiese letters
·teyne noo gret matier, but oonly declare our diligence, which, as oon
›, is the grettest matier that I have for myself, and that myself is in
·d reputacion every where with every man. Oon thing I note, that

the Chaunceler and Bayard cummith with thAdmyral, which might make an argument that eyther the French King myndeth not ernestly with youe there, or the Emperour meanith not ernestly with us here. For hither cummith al the reputacion of Fraunce, Madame de Tamps except; and sum of thiese thre bringith a pease of her also. Nowe, oonles sum cardynal be sent, I knowe not who shuld be sent from the French King of any havour meate to be[†] mached with my Lordes of Norfolk or Herford; and therfor a suspition there maye be, that they entend not in Fraunce to send any commissaryes to Calays. And on the other parte, being our matiers of the peax noo further squared thenne they be, howe I shuld byleve that the Admyral, the Chaunceler, and Bayard shuld cumme for that oonly purpose, I am moch troubled to acquyet my persuasion in it. And sumwhat I note that thAdmyralles name hath been always in the noyse, and the Chaunceler, being the first commissioner and[1] gretter personage in place, not spoken of tyl nowe. [2]Youe maye there set al thing better to gither thenne I canne here, bicause ye knowe what reaporte the Protestantes make from the French King. ThEmperour here, ne his Counsayl, hath not spoken to us any worde, directly or indirectly, wherby we shuld gather that he wold not we shuld treate by meanes of the Protestantes, or the French King eyther; and yet it is to my conscience evidente that he chiefly myndeth the reformation of those Protestantes and the chastisement of them, soo as I thinke he wold not be glad they had somoch honnour as to brynge such a matier to passe. And howe it shuld stand to gither that Fraunce, sendyng such personages hither, if it be for the peax with us oonly, wold thenne disapoint ther voyage with sending meaner men for the same matier to an other place, or, if Fraunce sendith thiese men for conclusion of sum secrete matier, which they desire, wold thenne at the same tyme honnour them, whom they knowe not to be acceptable to thEmperour, and use ther meanes, rather thenne thEmperours, for conclusion of the peaxe with us. And therfor, remembryng what thEmperor hath said, I thinke thus: that the Protestauntes have in dede put the French King in hoope to compasse sumwhat to his purpose, which he folowith by them, and whatsoever they canne obteyne, or saye they might obteyne, to be alleged here, wherby they might calumniate that we be forwarder to the peax by the Protestantes, thenne here by thEmperours mediation. Herunto I doubte not but ye have regarde, and I remembre[3] ye wryte

1 *alt. from* ang   2 Y *writ. over* I   3 th *c.o.*

unto me howe the Kinges Majestie wyl not send any commissioners upon such a request as they made, to have Bolen talked on, and with that precisenes. As long as ye observe that maner of proceding, there canne cum noo hurte to talke with the French men in both places, and in both places to offre like conditions. Mary, if the French men send noo commissaryes at al, or delaye the sending, and use the Protestantes, being goon from them and remaynyng with us, as[1] a bogge to thEmperour, to avaunce ther owne matiers and hindre ours, I leave that to be considered there.

I praye youe, Master Secretarye, send me the memorial[2] that Skepperus made of the treatye, and procure as ye maye that we maye here often from youe, and have knowlege of the Kinges Majestie pleasour from tyme to tyme, as the cace requireth, as I doubte not but ye wyl; and specially, nowe the entervieu in dede faylith, whither we shalbe soo precise in the treulx to agree to noon, if it be required, and what moderation his Highnes thinketh to make in the conditions of the peax; for the tyme of thEmperours being here cannot be long, and sumtyme the passage is cumbersom and stayeth; and, if that is ernestly ment shuld be delayed, it might fortune not ⟨to⟩ have the good opportunite again. We here maye be trusted with degrees, for we be al scrupulous, and such as wold have England as brode as might be. And oon thing the Kinges Majestie maye be assured of[3], that, and we had[4] the Gret Seale of England lying by us to seale what commission we list, with as large instructions as we coulde divise, we wyl never set our hand here to any minute or wryting, as agreed by us, oonles we have the same wryting in forme first signed with the Kinges Majesties hande, from which our[t] shal not vary a letter. Take that for a principel. And therfor the wurst wer we might talke over largely, wherof we wyl have as good regarde as we canne; but, as for any acte prejudicial or towardes it, by asseveration or wryting, we may be trusted wel inough. I am joyned with noo babes, and I have been myself supersticious therin al my lief. Wherfor I wold wishe that we wer here soo instructed as we knewe thextremite of the Kinges Majesties determination concernyng a peace, to be spoken of by degrees[5], and the latter degree to be sent unto us in a letter sealed, with commaundment not to open the letter[6] but by a commen consent of us al thre, at the tyme of an utter refusal, and elles to kepe the letter close, and soo shal we never knowe what the latter and uttermost condition

---

1 b *c.o.*   2 of *c.o.*   3 thenne had *c.o.*
4 g *c.o.*   5 to *c.o.*   6 by *c.o.*

is. And I[1] wryte not this bicause I thinke the Kinges Majestie doth mistruste us to tel it us[2], but, to saye truth, it is better for us to have it secrete thenne otherwise. And, if I shuld divise myn owne instruction to treate in a matier by degrees, I wold have the last degree secrete, both from me and my felawes, for so we men shuld speke most ernestely, and we shuld be sure ⟨it⟩ coulde not cumme abrode by noo espial upon us, if ther wer any, or elles where. If the sea wer not bytwen us, I wold not wryte thus, but I feare lettes therof, and wold wishe if peax[3] might be havisely[4] had, that it wer embraced. For[5], onles we might have a good companion in warre, it wylbe fromhensforth very fashious; and whose[6] companye wer worth the warre I knowe not. Truste is soore decayed in the worlde.

The Duke of Bruneswike[7] and his sonne be in the Lansgraves handes, and, if Monsieur de Hockstrates tale be trewe, there is in the matier a gret treason. Monsieur de Bure hath promysed me the copye of a letter wryten from the Lansgrave[8], who sayth the Duke of Bruneswike dyd yelde himself; the other saye it was upon a parlamentacion. I shal sende the letter whenne I have it.

The Archiebishop of Magunce is chosen, such oon as thEmperour wold have. I have forgoten his name.

The Archebishoprich of Magdeburgh is bestowed also as thEmperour wold have it. Thus I have of those matiers. And soo bydde youe hartely fare wel. At Bruges, the vj of Novembre at night.

Your assured loving frend,

STE. WINTON

Addressed: To the Right Wourshipful Sir Wyllyam Paget, Knight, oon of the Kinges Majesties two Principal Secretaryes.

Below address: Hast, hast.

Endorsed: The Bisshopp of Winchestre to Master Secretary, Master Paget, vjº Novembris, 1545.

---

1 thinke *c.o.*   2 *writ. over* b   3 *alt. from* peace
4 *this word may be so read (meaning* advisedly*), as in* St. P., *or* hamsely *(meaning?), as in* L.P.
5 elles *c.o.*   6 warre *c.o.*   7 is *c.o.*
8 *alt. from* Langgrave

83. *To* PAGET

Bruges, 7 November, 1545

R.O., S.P. 1, 210, 51–2.* *L.P.*, xx, ii, 749. *St. P.*, x, 664.

They are fêted daily; now is the right moment for peace, even if it means giving up Boulogne, for the English are now looked on as the most valiant people in Europe; what Gardiner once said to Francis I about the delivery of Cardinal Pole (in 1537—*cf. L.P.*, xii, i, 939, 1032).

Master Secretary, after my right harty commendations: By our letters to the Kinges Majestie ye shal perceyve that *hactenus bene se habent principia.* We be fereful as a doo is that stayeth harkenyng to every crashe of a bowe. Yesternight we liked not that we harde not from them, and this mornyng they redubbed it with sending for us. My being here is set forth with a gret demonstracion outwardly, for every daye hath had *suam pompam.* Wedonsday ⟨4 Nov.⟩ we went to thEmperour. Thursdaye Grandvela, Praet, and Scory cam to us, which is notable. Frydaye we[1] went to the Quene. And this daye to Grandvelas howse. And we to gither be *conspicui*, and move with an honest[2] companye. But the French men, they pourpose to outbrage us with numbre; they cumme, as they saye[†], with vj^c ⟨600⟩ horse. A mery felowe was with me and tolde me they had nede soo, for oon Englisheman was worth vj French men, both in warre and peax. They cumme al in blak for duel of the Duke of Orlyaunce, and I thinke Pasquillus, if he be mery, wyl saye they cumme soo prostrate, *pulla veste*, to seke peace. Master Secretarye, if we take peace nowe, we establishe the valyauntenesse of Englond for ever; if we leave game nowe, we be wonderful wynners, we be estemed to have treasure infinite, and to excede al other in valyantnesse. Here was with me to visite me the Marques de Terra Nova, with a good meany Italyans, that had great pleasour to talke with me howe we have skourged the Frenchmen, and howe we paye our men and the Frenchemen doo not. They saye we have doon the French men more hurte in oon yere thenne thEmperour hath doon in al his warres. If we leave nowe, we shal wynne this opinion, that we leave required and desired, and might doo what we lyste, wer it not for respecte the Kinges Majestie hath to Cristendom. And whenne soever the Kinges Majestie shuld thinke good to leave Bolen, it shuld not be thought it wer bycause we coulde not [†]kepe it[†], but bicause his Highnes wold

1 † *twice, at end of one line and beginning of next* 2 complayne *c.o.*

not. In this opinion be we abrode in the worlde nowe, and this opinion may be maynteyned by a peace; and by continuaunce in warre, which is chaungeable, maye be hindred. And the French men, as they hate us naturally, being ther squorge, and as the boye[1] hateth the rodde, soo if we cam by any meanes to an afterdel, they wold handel us strangely.

I esteme nothing Bolen in comparyson of the mastery we have wonne in kepyng of it, and defendyng our realme alone. Bolen in processe may be lost many wayes; the name, fame, honnour, and renowne goten by it canne never decaye, if it be nowe established by a peax. They saye that an Englishe man in al feates excellith, if he coulde leave whenne it is[t] wel, which they cal *tollere manum de tabula*. And if Riffemberges lewdnesse maye be an occasion to accelerate a peax, wherby to[t] eskape the thrawldam to such noughty mennes service, we shal saye, *Diligentibus Deum omnia cooperantur in bonum* ⟨Rom. viii, 28⟩. In the desire I shewe to have to[2] peax I make noo foundacion nowe of our wantes at hom, nor of other inconveniences, but having[3] harde yesterdaye at dyner somoch honnour spoken of us, and also by the Italyans, I am afrayde of further warre, for losing any peace of it. The French King told me oones, whenne I had commission to exhorte hym to doo as he was bounde to do by his treatie, and[4] added that it was honnourable for hym to doo as I required hym, that is to saye, to delyver the traytour Pole, and not to[t] regarde the saufconduyte which he said he had graunted, which he might not graunte by his treatie[5]—to stop my mouth he said I coulde noo skyl of prynces honnours, with such a facion and gesture as I was fayne to hold my peace; and soo dyd, and left that worde, and entred with hym [t]in the matier[t] an other waye; but yet I spake truth.

The Admyral wyl be here this night, and thEmperour goth hens upon Thursdaye to Andwerp, and from thens to Utrek. How thinges wyl prove here ye shal see shortly; and I praye youe[t] remember to procure advertisement to us of the Kinges Majesties pleasure howe to answer the Frenchmen, if they make offre of mediation to thEmperour, wherby to seme to remitte any thing to his arbytrement, and to instructe us soo fully as may be. I wryte long bablyng letters to youe to provoke youe to take the more payne by myn example. Ye have many moo to wryte unto, but I remember not that nowe. Thus I bydde youe[6] hartely fare wel, having not yet dronken this daye[7]; having made profession

1 hath *c.o.*   2 ? *a slip for* the *or* a.   3 had *c.o.*
4 hon *c.o.*   5 d *c.o.*   6 *alt. from* your
7 tha *c.o.*

that I wyl serve the Kinges Majestie bifore I serve myself in this tyme of hast. I pray youe forget not my commendations. And soo again fare ye wel. At Bruges, the vijth of Novembre.

Your assure⟨d⟩ loving frende,

STE. WINTON

Addressed: To the Right Wourshipful Sir William Paget, Knight, oon of the Kinges Majesties two Principal Secretaryes.

Endorsed: My Lord of Winchester to Master Secretary Paget, vij° Novembris, 1545.

84. *To* PAGET

Bruges, 4 p.m., 11 November, 1545

R.O., S.P. 1, 210, 87–8.* *L.P.*, xx, ii, 774.

> How he kept his temper despite Olivier's lie; the wisdom and plain speech of Bayard; has been writing and talking since three o'clock yesterday.

Master Secretary, after my right harty commendations: In our long letter to the Kinges Highnes ye shal perceyve our talke with the French men and howe spedely the Chaunceler coulde forge a lye to tel a tale of lending of money, wherin he tented me wonderfully to answer sumwhat more rowndely thenne I did; but bicause I knewe him sumtyme for a Lutherian, and was wel acquaynted with hym in Fraunce, and nowe and thenne disputed togither, and if I had fallen out with hym nowe he wold have said it had been for that. But howe constantely he affermed a lye for a trewe tale, and howe fayne I wold ⟨have⟩ talked with hym as I have doon, upon like occasion, ¹with² the Cardynal of Bellaye! But I refrayned and ever avoyded the geving† chek, and gave oonly a bare mate without any chek; wherin I pleased myself, and thEmperours Counsayl marveyled, I thinke, for al the protestacions wer made for me in the begynnyng. And whenne the Admyral founde his expectacion deceyved in me, he made moch of me, and hath sent Bayard to me. Which Bayarde, in speking of himself, swore to me he coulde not endure to make a lye, his nature wold not bere to counterfete soo; and yet, at his being with me, in the same communication he bare me wrong in

1 w writ. over b   2 bel c.o.

hand. But he yelded in it; soo as, bylike, he canne make a lye but he wyl not byde by it. In ernest, he is very wise, very sobre, and, as went from him by stertes, by conjecture, seen in good lernyng. He spake sumtyme Laten, for his purpose apte, apposite, *et eleganti pronunciacione*. He is coleryk and, in his angre, with auctorite annexed, very stowte, as they cal hym; but I thinke they have noo man canne speke more ne better in ther affayres thenne he canne. He is an nother manner of man thenne the Chaunceler. We spake of the matiers playnly and rowndely, and he and I be entred sufficiently to continue or renewe this practise of peace.

The Protestantes, as he sayth, warrantith the conclusion of the peax there. If it soo be, it is wel; but otherwise they hindre mervelously our matiers; for these men shewe thEmperour al. And I noted that they made in ther prefaces somoch of thEmperour, and, specially the Chaunceler, calling him the high power; and therfor, to prove *bellum iustum ab auctoritate*[1], I named to him thEmperour to be the high power also[†], as ye may marke in our letters.

The Duke of Ferrares brother, the Cardynal of Ferrare, with whom I had acquayntaunce, being in Fraunce, wylled oon that cummyth hither with the Admyral, called Alexander, to repare to me and to make his commendations to me, and, on his bihaulf, to desire me to make his most humble commendacions to the Kinges Majestie, to whom he berith[2] his service, [†]as he sayth[†], for the honno*u*r it hath[3] pleased his Highnes to doo to his howse of Ferrare in tymes past.

In your last letters ye spake a doubtful worde of my long taryng here, wherof I praye youe [†]send me[†] sum playn further knowledge, that I may use myself therafter, for I have here noo horses, and I wyl accommodate myself oonly to serve and to obey *tanquam lutum in manu figuli* ⟨Jer. xviii, 6⟩. I cannot promyse to bring anything to passe, but to serve as I am bydden. That I canne doo, and therin shal want noo good wyl.

If the treatye of peace[4] with Fraunce shalbe here, I praye youe remembre to sende hither the copye of the French Kinges letter, if ye have it[†], and the copye of the wryting obligatory for repayment of CCCCL⟨M⟩ ⟨450,000⟩ crownes *in*[5] *casu cessationis solutionis pensio*[*num*], and I praye youe[†] sollicite a spedy resolution to us.

Yester night supped with me the Countie de Bures, Monsieur de Hocstrate, and a grete meany; soo as, besides a smal tyme of slepe,

1 auctorite *w*. ta †   2 *alt. from* beare   3 *alt. from* had
4 of *meant to be c.o.*   5 caus *c.o.*

I have not ceased talking and wryting synes yesterdaye thre of the clok, and nowe I make an ende with youe, being yet fasting; and bydde youe hartely fare wel. At Bruges the xj[th] of Novembre, at iiij at afternone.

I send youe the coppye of a letter of the Lansgraves, as it was delyvered me by Monsieur de Burez, and I canne get noo man to tel me what it meanith; ye shal get sumbody there[1].

Your assured loving frend,

STE. WINTON

I sende youe herwith the copye of the French Kinges commission, which we have compared with thoriginal.

Addressed: To the Right Woᴜrshipful Sir William Paget, Knight, oon of the Kinges Majesties two Principal Secretaryes.

Endorsed: The Bisshop of Winches[tre] to Master Secretary, Master Paget, xj° Novembris, 1545.

85. *To* PAGET

Bruges, 8 p.m., 11 November, 1545

R.O., S.P. 1, 210, 89–90.* *L.P.*, xx, ii, 775.

Is convinced that the French will make no peace unless they get Boulogne, but they will give no other land for it, and are too poor to give money; writes 'to relieve the earnest thinking of these matters.' ('The great failing the last year' refers to the conduct of Landenberg, a German captain in Henry VIII's employ, who took his money and did nothing—*see L.P.*, xix, i, pp. xxxviii ff.)

Master Secretary, after my right harty commendations: By our letters to the Kinges Highnes[2] youe shal perceyve howe matiers goo here. I take it for a suer grownde, as I compare Bayardes havoᴜr to us with that thEmperours Counsayl tellith us, that the French King wyl never have peace without he have Bolen. And londe he wyl geve noon in recompense. There is noo reason in it, noo more there is not[3] in many other matiers. Our chaunce is to be in a unreasonable worlde. And our wisedom shal appere to wade out of thiese perplexites with the lest hurte that maye be. The French King hath somoch spoken of Bolen that he wyl have, and it hath been soo noysed in the worlde, that in Bolen

---

1 *writ. over something else*   2 your s *c.o.*   3 *alt. from* in

consistith nowe al his reputacion, as he takith it. Ye sawe[1] never[2] felawe more ardently expresse the desire of anything[3] thenne Bayarde dyd of that. Soo they might have it, they care not whither it wer *vi, clam,* or *precario.* The Chaunceler spake a foule worde, to saye, *Rende₂ Boloigne.* That is abjured; they saye nowe they sue for it, desire, praye to have it. They be soo fonde as they wyl departe with noo other[†] lande, and yet be again soo pore as they ar not able to geve us a convenient summe of money for it, and paye us therwith our det. It is a trobelsom cace to medle with a prowde adversarye and a poore.

If we rekonne al the French[4] owe us, [†]it is[†] above xvj^{c}M ‹1,600,000› crownes[5], besides that they shuld geve for Boleyn, if we wer soo disposed to forbere it. Al the relief and socour of this matier must[6] procede from the Kinges Highnes[†], in whose wisedom consisteth the remedye to con- sider howe noughtely the worlde fayleth hym in al degrees, and, at the poynte, thiese Almaignes, as a yerely rencontre of the gret fayling the last yere, wherof the French men take boldnesse. Bayarde inculced moch to me, 'that ye wyl doo, doo spedely for the peace'; and said ther wer[7] a c‹100› spirites in this towne to persuade the contrary, and that wold have the warre. He verified the matier afterwarde in Italians divisers. Whenne I wryte thus to youe I spende tyme in vayne to your purpose, but not to myn owne, for I have noon other waye to releave the ernest thinking of thiese matiers. If we shuld nowe cumme to peace after the French mennes desyres, we shuld have moch honno*u*r. Mary, as Pety Roy[†], as I have harde told, spake of love to King Henry the vij[th]: it was to moch, [†]he said[†], he wold have haulf in love and haulf in money; and soo the French [†]men offre[†] to much honno*u*r in the matier, for they wold have restitucion [†]of Bolen[†] oonly for honno*u*r.

As for the Scottes, Bayard told me secretly, it is[†] not ment to be enemye for ther sake, and if the French King be wel bounde to paye us, he shal not be able to forbere moch money, and ther men the Scottes like not. Monsieur De Prate, in speking of the French mennes gret debte, he wold gladly doo us understande that in our accounpte we [8]might take[8] the French men paying our dettes, being soo gret a summe, payde it us for Bolen. He spake it not soo directly, but, as ye may perceyve, it tended to that sense. I wold make an ende and cannot—I meane of my letters. God graunte us a good ende of the other matiers, and send

---

1 *alt. from* saye   2 sawe *c.o.*   3 † *abv.* it *c.o.*
4 King† *and c.o.*(?)   5 † *abv.* li *c.o.*   6 *alt. from* most
7 werd *w.* d *c.o.*   8-8 † *abv.* sayde *c.o.*

us hartely wel to fare. At Bruges the xjth of Novembre, at viijth of the clok at night, bifore supper.

Your assured loving frend,

STE. WINTON

Addressed: To the Right Wourshipfull Sir Wyllyam Paget, Knight, one of the Kinges Majesties two Principall Secretaries.

Endorsed: The Bisshop of Winches[tre] to Master Secretary, Master Paget, xj° Novembris, 1545.

86. *To* PAGET

Bruges, 13 November, 1545

R.O., S.P. 1, 210, 127–32.* *L.P.*, xx, ii, 788.

> Is so troubled he must write to quiet his mind; England has no friends, is waging a costly war, and is offered a dishonourable peace; if accepted, obligations under it may be voided by a General Council. Recalls the acting of Paget, Wriothesley, and himself in *Miles Gloriosus*; they cannot solve difficulties so easily now. No help can be expected from the Emperor, and from the Protestants only monstrous opinions which will corrupt the realm; 'they use all things to make money on.' Should we continue war or accept the peace offered? Either is 'terrible to advise in.' (*See* No. 87.)

Master Secretary, after my right harty commendations: I am very moch troubled with the state of our affayres; for albeit whenne I[1] am in England I canne quiet myself with speking of my mynde; whenne I am called and doing faythefully therin, and attending diligently to be redy too doo as I am commaunded, I trouble not myself with other divises; yet whenne I am appointed to this place, I cannot forbere ne hold my penne styl, but, as my mynde is encombred with the matiers, soo to be buysy in wryting and divisyng. I consider that we be in warre with Fraunce[2] and Scotland; we have an enemyte with the Bishop of Rome; we have no frendshippe assured here; we have receyved such displeasour of the Lansgrave, chief captayne of the Protestantes, that he hath cause to thinke we be angrye with hym; our warre is noysom to the welth of our owne realme, and it is[†] soo noysom to al[†] marchauntes that must trafique by us and passe the narowe sees as they crye out here wonderfully. Herwith we see at hom a gret apparaunce of lak of such

1 c(?) *c.o.*   2 with *c.o.*

thinges as the continuaunce of warre necessaryly requireth. And whenne, to put awaye this warre, we shewe ourself content to take a peace, we maye have it, but soo miserable, to saye truth, as the French men offre it, that therby the Kinges Majesties noble courage shuld be soo touched as we ought to feare the daungier of his person, after soo long travayl in honnour, in rule, and governement of the worlde, to syt styl with such a peace as to rendre Bolen and let the Scottes alone, oonly for a lytel money, not payde but promysed. I calle two myllyons a lytel money to us that have spent fyve. And, as the worlde is nowe facioned, I wot not what counforte we shuld take in promyses, be they never soo assured by bandes of marchauntes or hostages, of which two, as we stand, hostages be best, but they be casual and sumtyme not moch regarded, as we have seen experience in our tyme in Fraunce with thEmperour, and in Scotland with us. If the French King shuld have nede of money for a feate, he wold be bold of his hostages. And as for merchauntes bandes, ⟨they⟩ must depende upon thexecution of justice, which may be letted by many pretences, and specially if by a Counsayl, as they wold cal it General, al bandes and obligations might be, in† al courtes of justice, by this exception avoyded, that they adhere not to that Counsayl. And the French men wer very like to procure such a¹ clause in the conclusion of the Counsayl, that al such as dyd not adhere to that Counsayl and communicate with it in religion and opinion, shuld not communicate in administracion of justice with those that adhere to the same.

And albeit in pactions and convenauntes ther shuld be articles divised to the contrary, yet if such a Counsayl cam to passe, it wer to be feared they wold, by a *non obstante*, take that remedye† awaye, alleging that noo princes may particulerly and aparte soo bynde themself as by a General Counsayl maye not be considred and refourmed. And we be nowe in a worlde where reason prevayleth not, lernyng prevaylith not, convenauntes be not soo regarded, but the lest pretense suffiseth to avoyde thobservation of² them. This is an other maner of matier thenne where I played Periplectomenus, youe Miliphidippa³, and my Lord Chaunceler Palestrio, and yet our parties be in this⁴ tragedie that nowe is in hand. If we thre shuld nowe sitte together and take counsayl what wer to be doon, as we did in the comedye, we shuld not be a litel troubled, and Palestrio fayne to muse longer for compassing

1 in (?) c.o.   2 it c.o.
3 *alt. from* Miliphippa   4 *alt. from* the

of this matier and seding of it, as the poete callith it, thenne he did there. For if we shuld conclude to embrace the peace as necessary for itself, upon such reasons as the state of the realme wold ministre, whenne we shuld, according to our dueties, remembre the state of the Kinges Majesties person, whom, if we preserve not asmoch as lyeth in us, with continuaunce and mayntenaunce of his honnour, to the repose of his mynde, for prorogation of his life tyl my Lord Prince may cumme to mannes astate, the decaye of his Majesties person bifore that tyme shuld be more ruine to the realme thenne any warre coulde engendre.

In consideration herof we must saye[t], Fye of such a peace as might be soo displeasaunte. And yet in the warre is miserie. Y[oue] wyl saye percace, the Kinges Majestie, for his gret wisedom, canne digeste the displeasour and content himself with necessite of the matier, and willingly contempne his owne honnour for the wealth and preservation of the realme; or elles, for his gret lernyng, understand that to be most honnorable that is most expedient for the realme. I thinke noo prince in Christendom coulde excede his Highnes in thiese considerations, but thenne sum doubte wyl arrise in expoundyng of 'expedient.' And whenne a prince, that hath been dred and feared of his neighbours, shuld[1] be brought in to such cace as he shal not be feared, but lesse regarded thenne he hath ben, I feare me that shal not be thought expedient. And howe soever it shuld be called, I thinke neyther your harte ne myne could endure to see it. This matier shuld here be releaved in reason, but standing the treating here bytwen them and Fraunce, if that take effecte, as it[2] is to be feared it shal, I thinke it but a vayne hope that thEmperour wyl eclarsye and accomplishe the treatie as we wold have it. If thEmperour agree with Fraunce, he wyl not[3] entre warre for our sake as he ought to doo; he wyl not comprehende Bolen and Bulloignois as we desire; and howe[4] he wyl encrease his bonde to[5] us by obligacion of his townes and othirwise, as is divised, it is to be doubted. With the Protestantes[6] I see not what auctorite [t]or feare[t] canne be encreased to us in the worlde, but oonly corruption of the Kinges Majesties realme with ther most abhominable and monstrose opinions. And whenne we shuld have cause to be wery of them al, as we have nowe cause to deteste the Lansgrave, we coulde not soo shortly wype out ther opinions, which engendre a worse warre in mennes hartes thenne any other warre canne be, and more to be feared thenne any other warre is. And thiese Pro-

1 [t] *abv.* to *c.o.*   2 t *meant to be c.o.*   3 et *c.o.*
4 *alt. from* nowe   5 youe *c.o.*   6 *alt. from* Protestants

testantes be entangled with thre encombres; that is to saye, with povertie, with subjection in duetie to hym they resist, thEmperour, and with want of credite and truste. *Non Appollinis responsum magis est verum* ⟨Terence, *Andria*, 698⟩, as he said; and we have prouf by experience *et crimine ab uno disce omnes* ⟨*Aeneid*, II, 65⟩.

They trouble the worlde as promoters[1] of Goddes quarel, and whenne they have putte in a wrong information, as Weple hath sumtyme doon in thExchequer for the[2] King, thenne they shal, as Weple hath doon†, make an agrement for ther commodite and fal in a non sute of ther information. They cannot continue ne prosper, but wrangle to trouble themself and other. And as in a mach of shoting, of hym that is an evel shote †it is sayd† he is good to pul down a syde, soo be they good to undoo a prince that shuld take† them to his matche and frendship. They use al thinges to make money on. I praye God they have doon noo hurte in treating bytwen the French King and us. Howbeit, howe that matier goth youe canne tel better thenne I, and therat I doo but gesse, but I wold mervel if the French King wold offre us a better bargayn by them thenne by the [3]Admyral, who, Bayard sayde, is the Kinges breste. I told him merely ⟨*i.e.*, merrily⟩ again that he was a breste also[4], as I harde saye. He smyled at it and forsware it not; and in dede I have harde that he is Madame dEstampes breste. I promyse youe Bayarde is a stowte felawe and wold fayne have a peax, to the contentacion of his master; and soo wold we. But howe shal it be, if the French King be thus stobernly set, and carith not to overthrowe al the worlde for to obteyne his fansye? Howe hath he† styrred the worlde for Myllayn! And let us certaynly loke that he wyl move against us asmoch as may be, not with directe force; and yet Bayard said oones that the French King might trouble the yerth over Bolen, as the Turke is wont to wynne townes[5], but he prayed us by and by not to take it as a thretenyng, for the French King wold wynne it nowe of the Kinges Majestie by amytie, if he might, with intercession and request.

But thiese fayre wordes, whenne they† appere frustrate, wyl engendre spyteful dedes, if there maye be opportunite and place. Ye wyl aske me thenne: What shal the Kinges Majestie †doo? Shal he† take these base and unsure[6] conditions of peax? I dare not but saye, Naye; for I feare a myscontentement of [7] the Kinges Majestie† to folowe it. What meane I

---

1 *alt. from* promotes   2 they *w.* y *c.o.*   3 A *writ. over* E
4 I *c.o.*   5 n *in* townes *writ. over something else*
6 † *abv.* unnat am *c.o.*   7 *writ. over* to

thenne? To continue in warre styl? Herin[1] I saye this, that he that wold move the Kinges Majestie to continue in werre alone against Fraunce and Scotland, thEmperour being a doubteful frende, shuld not wel consider the preservation of the Kinges Majesties honnour and astate. And yet, ye wyl saye, eyther we must take such a peace as we canne get or, of necessite, continue in wer; for there is noo thirde waye. Ye saye truth; and the other two wayes, wherof oon must nedes be[†], be soo terrible to advise in as I thinke noo man dare speke on this or that side, if he have noo better stomake thenne I have. I have wryten to youe vehemently for peace, and I have noted the sentence of oon that said the worst[2] peace is better thenne the beste warre; but the peace the French men nowe offre is soo far under foote in the first apparaunce, and hath such a feare of the unsure observation of the conditions, as I have bifore said, that I cannot take any counforte in it.

On the other parte, warre, if thEmperour slyppe from us or be not with us, wherof I feare, and styl to werre alone, cannot like me neyther; and I thinke myslyketh a gret meany[3]—and al (those oonly except[4] that cannot lyve without it). God[5] graunte the Kinges Majestie to chose the best of thiese two extremites; and that shal I further and take for the best, and travayl soo far as I canne and am commaunded. Saincte Pol wisheth to be *anathema pro fratribus*, and I[†], to doo service to the Kinges Majestie, I wold smally regarde myself. I speke not this for flatering, for I am past it, and I never used it, but I knowe my duetie, and I knowe of what importaunce the Kinges Majestie⟨s⟩ person is to the realme; and I feare displeasour of adversite in age (whenne reputacion shuld worthely encrease) to be anything towched. If I feare in vayne, there is noo body hurte but myself; and I shal praye God it maye soo cumme to passe. I am here to get knowlege, and al is here hydden. This derke wurking is sum tyme more terrible thenne nedith. But I remembre Skepperus, [6]who hath told me twyes howe thEmperour wyl nowe[7] *tentare extrema* against the[8] Protestantes; and if the French King fal in with thEmperour, that matier is suerly a parte of ther agrement; in which cace we shalbe coldly harde of thEmperour, oonles the[9] Kinges Majestie shuld joyne that wayes also; and thenne oon parte[10] of ther matier is such as we maye

1 wherin *w*. w *c.o.*   2 b *incomplete follows*   3 bes *c.o.*
4 *Gardiner closes his parenthesis here, but it would seem that the rest of the sentence should be included in it*
5 *alt. from* Gr   6 w *writ. over* to   7 *alt. from* noo
8 Ge *c.o.*   9 they *w*. y *c.o.*   10 † *abv.* peace *c.o.*

not speke in it. And the French King, knowing this affection of thEmperour, hath made[1] thEmperour[†] byleve [2]hymself, the French King [2], may have better conditions of peax [†]of us[†] by the[3] Protestantes[†] meane thenne by his. And thus be thinges entangled. Thus we be in a labyrinth. Every thing that wer good to be doon hath an overthwarte matier annexed unto it. Peace is good, but it hath such basse and[4] unsure conditions for thobservation [5]that they deface it.

To agree with thEmperour for[5] repressing of the Protestantes, upon this occasion geven us by the Lansgrave, wer good to allure thEmperour, if anything wold allure hym; but thenne ther is an other matier sayeth naye. Warre for mayntenaunce of that the Kinges Majestie hath goten wer not evel; but thenne to continue warre[6] alone in soo many places, with such unfaythful souldgiers as we shalbe enforced to[7] use, wyl consume and devour that we wold defende[8], and our own also. *Expedi hec et eris mihi magnus Apollo* ⟨Virgil, *Ecl.*, iii, 104⟩. And thus I bidde youe hartely fare wel. I have[†] wryten youe a long letter of probable reasons; whenne ye have harde al, ye ar never the wiser, but rather brought in a more perplexite[9] thenne ye wer bifore. At Bruges the xiij[th] of Novembre.

Thus I make youe an accounpte of my pastyme, muse in the night, and wryte in the daye, whenne I am at lay*sour* from talking and a lytel reding.

Your assured loving
frend,

STE. WINTON

Addressed: To the Right W*our*shipfull Sir Wyllyam Paget, Knight, one of the Kinges Majesties two Principall Secretaries.

Below address: Rede this at leysour.

Endorsed: My Lord of Winchester to Master Secretary, Master Paget, xiij° Novembris, 1545.

1 thEmperour *c.o.;* us † *and c.o. above it*
2–2 †, hymself *being alt. from* he
3 ther *with* r *c.o.*   4 am *c.o.*   5–5 † *abv.* the *c.o.*
6 *alt. from* wer (?)   7 occup *c.o.*   8 *alt. from* defens
9 *first* e *in this word writ. over something else*

87. *To* Paget

Bruges, 14 November, 1545

R.O., S.P. 1, 210, 140–1.* *L.P.*, xx, ii, 794.

After reading yesterday's letter (No. 86) burn it; things look better to-day; the advantage of Granvelle's offer (*see L.P.*, xx, ii, 793); perhaps the Emperor is not glued so fast to France as it seemed.

Master Secretary, after my most harty commendations: I thanke youe for your gentyl confortable letters, which I receyved yesterdaye, wherin ye make noo mention of our depech on Saturdaye ⟨7 Nov.⟩.

Our letters by[1] Nicolas wer not soo pleasaunt as I wold have wished, and I was yesterdaye al malencoly and had noo remedye but make a purgation in a letter, which I neded not have doon, if I had knowen so-moch as I knowe nowe[†]. I send it youe bycause ye want redyng, and whenne ye have doon I praye youe throwe it in the fyre.

I am wondrous desirous of peace, but I assure youe I cannot awaye with al to leve Bolen as the French men wold have it, as ye shal perceyve by my malencolye letters. And this daye I am wel chered, for Grandvela spekith in special termes; and, on the other side, the Chaunceler of Fraunce, for old special acquayntaunce, desireth to speke with me. And the Quene of Hungarye hath this night invited me to suppe with hir tomorowe at night. The French ambassadours dyne there, and we shal have the supper. And joyning herwith the good contentacion of the Kinges Majestie with our doinges, signified yesternight, I am the meter to make mery tomorowe at night.

I praye youe consider in the reading of the notes upon the vij[th] article[2], that those wordes which they like not here be not for us soo material[3] in my jugement. They wer, and ye remembre, divised by Skepperus; but we have not relented in them, but oonly noted what they saye to that we had noted.

And nowe ye see there wherat they wyl by al lykelehode sumwhat styk here, ye maye waye of what importaunce they be, and consider whither the[4] vj article, obteyned in a good forme wherwith to discorage the French men to styk at Bolen, contrevayleth the rest that they wold styk at here. Me thinketh the vij[th] article is al for our purpose nowe; for

---

1 s *incomplete follows*
3 the *c.o.*

2 articles *w.* s *c.o.*
4 first *c.o.*

the French men shal have a very inequal warre to travayl for Bolen without daring make any enterprise upon our peaces to revenge themself, and to be restrayned from geving money to the Scottes to invade us, for feare of bringing thEmperour in to warre against them. This is not the best; for that is peace; but I shal speke nowe like noo cowarte. I had rather be kylled in warre thenne dye in a languishing displeasour of an evel favored peace. I had moch a doo in this matier yesterdaye, as ye shal see by my letters, which I praye youe burne.

I wyl spare noo postes nor wryting. I wyl make youe wery of redyng. I praye God the Protestantes[1] doo noo hurte; wherin I proteste I speke of noo affection of mynde, but as reason leadith me. In this enterteynement thEmperour seeth his subgettes ministres compared with his person[2], and soo contende with hym, as they have the same matier in hand that he hath, with a noyse and brute that they shal mediate that he cannot. Neyther he nor his Counsayl spake of it tyl nowe; but nowe they did. If peace folowe to our welth and benefite, al is wel; other[3] respectes shal blowe over; but if they doo us noo good therin, they have doon us asmoch hurte in ther feate as the Lansgrave hath in his demeanour in recommending Riffenberge and using him as he hath doon, to doo us noo service and doo us contumelie in mysusing the commissaryes.

ThEmperour goth not hens soo sone as was thought he wolde. Diverse vayne brutes have been here spred abrode of the cummyng hither of the French Quene or sending the French Kinges doughter; but they have noo foundation. The French man that cam to require an howre of meting betwixt the Chaunceler and me spake of them as fond tales, and soo he called them. I shal have a gret gesse, in commenyng with the Chaunceler tomorowe, howe ther thinges goo with thEmperour. I shal advertise incontinently. Here hath been soo buysy working bytwen thEmperours Counsayl and thambassadours of Fraunce, and soo secrete that I fansyed[4], as I wrote in our letters to the Kinges Majestie, that the Protestantes pulled at thEmperour to brynge him neare the French King[5] and we pulled the French King nere thEmperour. And whiles we wer pullyng, thEmperours Counsayl and the French ambassadours wer gluyng of them togither by ther communication. But by like the glewe pot is not[6] throughly hote. I shal knowe more tomorowe and soo

---

1 be *c.o.*   2 *writ. over* pre   3 br *c.o.*
4 we *c.o.*   5 *writ.* Kinges   6 clerely *c.o.*

advertise. And thus I bydde youe fare wel. At Bruges, the xiiij[th] of Novembre, at[1] ix of the clok at night.

Your assured loving
frend,

STE. WINTON

Addressed: To the Right Worshipful Sir Wylliam Paget, Knight, oon of the Kinges Majesties two Principal Secretaryes.

Below address: Hast, hast, hast,
            hast for thy life,
            for thy life.

I praye youe dispache my servaunt again, as ye have doon thother.

Endorsed: My Lord of Winchester to Master Secretary, Master Paget, xiiij° Novembris, 1545.

88. *To* PAGET

Bruges, 15 November, 1545

R.O., S.P. 1, 210, 148–9.* *L.P.*, xx, ii, 799.

Sends his discourse with the Chancellor of France (*L.P.*, xx, ii, 798); desires to know the King's pleasure concerning private conferences with the French; has had no leisure to read articles proposed by the Imperialists concerning English treatment of the Emperor's subjects (*ib.*, 802, [2]).

Master Secretary, after my right harty commendations: I wryte herwith my long discours with the Chaunceler of Fraunce, which I thought expedient to thintent ye might knowe what I have said here in our matiers with them throughly.

The ambassadours of Fraunce serch to speke with me, as ye see. If they doo it to put suspition in thEmperours hed, as though we wold agree without[2] ⟨him⟩, that wer the worst; and[3] yet I wyl ease that matier wel ynough. But I praye youe, to remove al scrupule, let a worde therof be touched of the Kinges Majesties pleasour in that behaulf. Myn instructions doo partely beare my soo doyng, and my commission also, for elles I wold have doon nothing that waye.

---

1 nin *c.o.*   2 they *c.o.*   3 I *c.o.*

193

Consider what the Chaunceler sayth of the Protestantes, and what they tel youe.

I am goyng to the Quene of Hungary to supper, and have been, in the wryting of my letters, moch troubled with talking with oon and other[1], and yet I wold send a waye the post or I went to supper, and therfor doo not send tharticles which Scory hath brought, but shal send them by the next. I had nowe noo leysour to rede them, and I thinke long tyl[2] ye have this post.

We goo nowe to Andwerpe, and ye maye loke for noo moo[3] letters of us hens bifore Thursdaye; for soo many dayes wyl it be or we canne cumme there, being the[4] waye soo letted by the trayne, and bicause we cannot departe tomorowe.

Whiles I am wryting this, Master Kerne hath red over the articles offred by Skore, and they shalbe answered with the resolution taken at[5] the Dyet, and, we truste[6], shal not empech our grete entreprise.

We goo dulcely with thiese men, †thEmperours Counsail† here, who be alredy, in my jugement, goon sumwhat over the barre. Mary, ther conclusion semeth to be, if they coulde bringe Fraunce and us to a peace, they wold the lesse feare the vj[th] article. Score said this evenyng that upon Skepperus cummyng we shal goo throwe apace; as I trust. I am sent for to supper. Fare ye hartely wel. At Bruges, the xv[th] of Novembre, at v[th] of the clok at night.

Your assured loving frend,

STE. WINTON

Addressed: To the Right Wourshipfull Sir Wylliam Paget, Knight, one of the Kinges Majesties two Principall Secretaries.

Endorsed: My Lord of Winchester to Master Secretary, Master Paget, xv° Novembris, 1545.

1 whe *c.o.*	2 h(?) *c.o.*
3 *writ. over* more(?)	4 wett *c.o.*
5 *alt. from* as(?)	6 trusted *w.* d *c.o.*

89. *To* Paget

Bruges, 16 November, 1545

R.O., S.P. 1, 210, 160–1.* *L.P.*, xx, ii, 803.

Is still puzzled by the situation; sends letter from the commissaries with Reiffenberg (*L.P.*, xx, ii, 785); conversation with Scepperus (just returned from England. The letter from Paget referred to is doubtless the same as that mentioned in No. 87. It does not appear to be extant. It is evidently not his letter of 6 November to Gardiner and Thirlby, answered by Thirlby 11 November—*L.P.*, xx, ii, 737, 776).

Master Secretary, after my right harty commendations: In our commen letters to the Kinges Majestie we have touched such thinges as we canne divise of thiese doinges here, which ye canne best resolve there. The Kinges Majestie, of his gracious goodnes, sent me, by my servaunt Olyver, recommendations moch to my counforte, addyng that I shuld have a doo with men of a subtel sorte, and that his Highnes durst let me slyppe; and yet, soo let slyppe, I assure[1] youe I stande amased after which dere to runne. And yet for the tyme nowe me semyth thEmperours Counsayl begynneth to entre sumwhat[2] to the purpose onwarde soo, and the French men be soo ernest to have Bolen as they wyl undowtedly *movere omnem lapidem* and, as he saide, *commovere omnia sacra* ⟨*cf.* Plautus, *Pseud.*, 109⟩. That makith them *supplices* to thEmperour, with this solempne ambassiate to joyne themself nerer to hym.

Yesterdaye arryved here oon called Monsieur Vander, with letters from Master Fane and other; which letters we sende unto youe herwith. We [3]have procured a saufconduyte for Riffenberge, and this gentilman hath it to convey to Riffenberge[4]. Of his cummyng to justification this gentylman doubteth, but yet it is good to sende him the saulfconduite. This gentylman told me howe this matier was mayned by the Lansgrave undowtedly[5], and moch detestith the abhomination. Nowe if the Lansgrave wold aske a campe for his tryal, as Riffenberge doth a sauf-conduyte for his justification, he shal seke his adversary, for I do not diffame hym, and Monsieur de Prate is to olde to fight with hym. Yesternight, being at supper with the Quene, where was Monsieur de Prate, he tolde me for certain howe the Lansgrave hath Bronswicke in

1 *writ.* assured; I *c.o.* 2 what *writ. over something else*
3 h *writ. over* p 4 *writ.* Riffenbredge (?)
5 w *in this word writ. over something else*

195

his handes upon a trust, and lamented unto me *dissolutam fere societatem humanam, violata et contempta fide.* Monsieur de Prate is notably wel lerned and not supersticiously lerned.

Skepperus is arryved and hath sent to cumme speke with me. I tary for hym to knowe what he wyl saye to me, bicause he hath spoken with thEmperour this mornyng. I had finished our letters to the Kinges Highnes bifore, and this makith the xth letter from Brucel ⟨*a slip for Bruges*⟩, and ye have wryten but oon, but it was swete. We kepe here noo copye of our letters, for hast to sende them to youe. I praye youe remembre to obteyne as open and absolute instructions as maye be— as for Bolen and those French matiers, I loke to leve to youe at Calays —but for our other matiers here I meane.

Skepperus hath been with me and sayth he is commaunded by thEmperour to be at Antwerpe. He thinketh our matiers shal doo wel, and that, if we have not a peax, we shal have a treulx. He divised with me oon maner of peax: for the Kinges Majestie to kepe Bolen, and[1] to have the frontier for this tyme ended by the water, and let the French King alone with his newe Bolen and the other syde; and soo we shuld have al the countrie ours from Bolen to Calays. It was, he said, a thing he thought on to avoyde the warre, if any meanes might be. He told me Grandvela asked hym howe the Kinges Majestie spake of hym nowe, and Skepper answerd hym, wel. But this is very secrete, and Skepper wold be loth it cam abrode.

Skepper told me that it is for certain that the Duke of Brunneswike was betrayed.

ThEmperour hath appointed a gentylman of good havour to accompany us to Andwerp, and to see that we want nothing.

I praye youe remembre that thiese two dayes folowing we cannot hav[2] any occasion to write.

And thus I bydde youe hartely fare wel.

Bernardin told my Lord of Westmester even nowe that undowtedly the Cardinal Farnes[e] cummyth to thEmperour throwe Fraunce.

Fare ye wel oones again. At Bruges, the xvj^th of Novembre, at night.

Your assured loving
frend,

STE. WINTON

<hr>

1 the Frenc *c.o.*   2 having *w.* ing *c.o.*

Addressed: To the Right Wourshipful Sir William Paget, Knight, oon of the Kinges Majesties two Principal Secretaryes.

Endorsed: The Bisshop of Winchester to Master Secretary, Master Paget, xvj° Novembris, 1545.

90. *To* Paget

Antwerp, 19 November, 1545

R.O., S.P. 1, 210, 186–7.* *L.P.*, xx, ii, 822.

Has had a bad journey, but is glad to be here as soon as the Emperor; likes not the secret meetings with the French.

Master Secretary, after my most harty commendac⟨i⟩ons: I had never a worse journey thenne I had yesterdaye, but I wold not for nothing but we had been here assone as thEmperour, bicause they shuld not have any delaye by pretense of our absence.

I like not the facion of the French ambassadours that wold have me talke with them alone. These secrecies be ever to be suspected. It hath been told here that ye be cumme to Calays. We have receyved but oon letter[1] for xjth, nowe we have sent this.

Tomorowe upon our communication with Grandvela we wyl depech again.

The French ambassadours told us thEmperour wyl departe a Monday ⟨23 Nov.⟩ and soo wyl they also, and therfor the matier of peax is like to be devolved unto youe.

Skepperus told me the French ambassadours, as he hath lerned, have had communication †with thEmperour† of the restitucion of Piemont; but nothing is doon. 'They wold,' quod he, 'have thEmperour entre warre against the Germaynes, and thenne wyl they use ther commodite.'

Our communication tomorowe shal geve more light, and I shal not fayle to use al diligence in advertisement. Thus fare youe hartely wel. At Antwerpe, the xixth[2] of Novembre.

> Your assured loving
> frend,
>
> STE. WINTON

1 l'res *w.* s c.o.   2 *alt. from* xijth

91. *To* PAGET

Antwerp, 20 November, 1545

R.O., S.P. 1, 210, 200–1.* *L.P.*, xx, ii, 831.

The increase of worldly goods makes a man poor; the retention of Boulogne should be considered in the light of this truth. (For the proposed marriages mentioned *see L.P.*, xx, ii, 830. *See also* No. 95 and p. 268 below.)

Master Secretary, after my most harty commendations: By our commen letters, ye shal perceyve the state of the maryages entended; wherin ye maye considre whither the mariage by them offered wold stand us in as good stede for our purpose as that we desired with thEmperour. Youe canne tel what I meane.

If the Kinges Majestie thinkith Bolen soo necessary, it is a worldly thing, and thenne remember this conclusion, that worldly thinges require other worldly thinges for ther mayntenaunce. This is a truth infallible. The lesse a man hath, the lesse he nedeth other helpe, and, by that proportion, the more, the more helpe. I knowe this truth by lernyng and by experience in myself. I maye wryte, as they doo upon medicines, *probatum est*[†]. Al they that made of me bifore I was bishop, required of me to make of them after I was bishop, as though I beganne thenne to have nede of them. There was a good felawe in Cambredge, wel lerned, that for his pleasour maynteyned in communication this paradoxe, that encrease of worldly thinges make men poore and not riche, bicause every worldly thing hath a nede annexed unto it. If sum in England red this, they wold by and by saye it wer[†] wel doon, if this be trewe, to make bishoppes riche, if worldly thinges make them pore. But yet to the purpose again: of Bolen I dare affirme nothing, but am therin *academicus*. But if we kepe it, we must, besides al other forces, have outwarde reputacion by frendship abrode.

Monsieur Skepperus cam even nowe to us and shewed us howe they have been in Counsayl al this daye for[1] our matiers, and tomorowe in

1 *writ. over* with

198

the mornyng Skepper wyl[1] retourne and shewe us in wryting what they saye in our matiers; which we shal thenne send, and not differre this post, bicause we thinke the significacion of the matier of the mariages not mete to be delayed.

If the Quenes servaunt bring the Kinges Majestie a present of hawkes, I praye youe remembre what[2] rewarde the Quene gave my servauntes for the howndes, wherof I have wryten.

We be in gret expectacion to here sumwhat from youe, at the lest of tharryval of our letters. Thus fare ye hartely wel. At Antwerp, the xxti of Novembre.

Your assured loving
frend,

STE. WINTON

Addressed: To the Right Wourshipfull Sir Wylliam Paget, Knight, one of the Kinges Majesties two principall Secretaries.

Endorsed: The Bisshop of Winchester to Master Secretary, Master Paget, xx° Novembris, 1545.

92. *To* PAGET

Antwerp, 21 November, 1545

R.O., S.P. 1, 211, 16–17.* *L.P.*, xx, ii, 838.

Hears of the arrival of Paget, Tunstall, and Tregonwell at Calais (to treat for peace with France by the mediation of the Protestants); the obligation of 450,000 crowns is one of the clearest matters England has against France.

Master Secretary, after my right harty commendations: I have receyved this daye your letters and have also, by the berer, knowlege of your arryval at Calays and of my Lorde[3] of Duresmes and Master Tregonelles, to whom, I praye youe, make my harty commendations. God send youe good spede there with the French men and us spede with both parties here, to the Kinges Majesties contentacion. Youe ar nowe olde inough and knowe with whom ye shal talke. Oon thing I have thought good to signifie to youe, that the obligacion of cccclM ⟨450,000⟩ crownes which ye thinke wer delyvered and not *in esse*, hath a being in England and is oon of the clerest matiers we have against the French men. I have

---

1 b c.o.
2 pres c.o.
3 alt. from Lordes

layde it to ther charge here, and the Chaunceler hath graunted me the being of it. I delyvered Maryliake a copye of it at his being in England. I founde it not spoken of in my Lord of Westmesters instructions, but I knowe it for truth, and it conteynith a bande of payment of somoch money *ratis manentibus pactis* of the perpetual peace. The Chaunceler in his last communication said he had the copie of it, bifore my Lord of Westmester, and wold have avoyded it by allegation that they have not broken the perpetual peace, bicause the tyme of payment of that pention is not cumme during the Kinges Majesties life; which is nothing to the purpose, for that treatie purportith also the observation of the other. And bicause of this odde ende in a corner I was bold to make the Chauncelour an offre for abatement of som money by them dewe, soo the Kinges Majestie might retayne Boleyn, meanyng that peace, and it wyl gayly serve[1] for such a purpose, and therfor I praye youe leave it not owte; for in dede it is a very good matier and *debitum civile et naturale*, for it is the repayment of L^M ⟨50,000⟩ crownes geven and CCCC^M ⟨400,000⟩ spent for the French King in the warres against thEmperour.

It is uncertain whenne thEmperour removith hens and whither he goth.

I trust to here often from youe where ye be nowe. If I sende my men thus from[2] me with dayly postes, oonles they cumme again, I shal spende them, and I dare not forbere wryting oon daye if any thing[t] be doon worthy[t] to be wryten. And nowe youe be out of England it may fortune ⟨to⟩ be long or we here thens, and it hath been long in the tyme of your being there, and nowe if it be lenger it shal sumwhat purge youe. I wold ye wold wryte hom that if the Kinges Majestie be pleased [3] with the matier, that thenne your consent there with our here might suffise for the maner of the wordes, and soo shuld we communicate with youe and resolve lytel scruples[4], I meane in sum conjunctions and ad-verbes litel matiers. We be nowe six lawers on this side the see, oonles ye abandon the profession bicause it is noo more set by abrode, and therfor that ye wrote to thre of us shalbe nowe communicate to us al[5] six.

Thus I byd youe hartely fare⟨wel⟩. And my Lord of Westmester and Master Carne desired me to make ther commendacions, and to desire

1 *writ.* service, *a probable slip*   2 d *c.o.*
3 w *writ. over* t   4 in *c.o.*
5 also *w.* so *c.o.*

youe to recommende them to my Lord of Duresme and Master Tregonel. At Antwerpe, the xxjth of Novembre.

> Your assured loving
> frend,
>
> STE. WINTON

If youe retou*r*ne my man thens and sende the letters by your post or thordinary post, soo maye I aforde ye the moo letters, and percace two in a daye. I shal trust my manne with the hol post money for this tyme and take the rest of him agayn; and after this tyme[1] doo as ye shal agree with me. If ye have not commission to open the letters addressed to the Kinges Majestie, I shal herafter wryte the more matier to youe. Send me word.

Addressed: To the Right Wou*r*shipful Sir Willyam Paget, Knight, oon of the Kinges Majesties two Principal Secretaryes.

Endorsed: The Bisshop of Winchester to Master Secretary, Master Paget, xxj° Novembris, 1545.

93. *To* PAGET

Antwerp, 25 November, 1545

R.O., S.P. 1, 211, 62–3.* *L.P.*, xx, ii, 871.

Wishes Paget better success than he has had; the Protestants, by becoming mediators between princes, begin to 'play the bishop of Rome's part.'

Master Secretary, after my right harty commendations: As I conjecture by your advertisement of the meating of youe[2] and the Frenchmen there, whenne we have ended ye begynne; for even this daye thAdmyral departeth hens, and this daye ye shuld mete, as I take it. God send youe better spede thenne hath been here, or elles there is a gret deale of labour lost in that mater. The[3] French men have been al wayes assayed here if they wold leave Bolen. They have sum counforte to obteyne it, as ye shal see by Maverlies spech to me. I feare me the Protestantes have been very bold in it, to get themself such auctorite as to noyse abrode that they have such reputacion as they be able to mayne thinges that be desperate at thEmperours hande, and to contende with hym in it. If the Germaynes Protestantes maye establishe that auctorite to be medi-

---

1 dy *c.o.*   2 meting *c.o.*   3 *writ.* they

201

atours bytwen princes, thenne they begynne to joyne worldly auctorite to ther Gospel, and playe the bishop of Romes parte, which if they[1] doo as faythfully as he did, by bearing in hand, thenne hath they his office upsy downe. The French trust that the Protestantes shal doo them good, and it maye percase turne clere contrary, as many worldly practises doo. If they may be occasion to us of peax[2], or pryk thiese men forward, thenne they doo us sum good; if not, they have doon us percace moch hurte, with ther being in hand to compasse matiers *directe vel indirecte*. Ye shal soon see howe thinges wyl goo, and I chalenge of youe to here sumwhat. And soo byd youe hartely fare wel. At Antwerpe, the xxv of Novembre.

Youe must remembre our recommendations to my Lord of Duresme and Master Tregonnel.

Your assured loving
frend,

STE. WINTON

This berer is dispached for noo further thenne Calays, and therfor youe must send the letters in to England.

Addressed: To the Right Wourshipful Sir Wyllyam Paget, Knight, oon of the Kinges Majesties two Principal Secretaryes.

Below address: Master Secretary, I pray youe send hom Monsieur Skepperus letters for the merchauntes matiers. We have joyned complaynte of our in Spayne, and promised to send this. We be not yet answerd in thother, but nowe at dyner we shal speke with Skepperus.

Endorsed: The Bisshop of Winchestre to Master Secretary, Master Paget, xxv° Novembris, 1545.

94. *To* PAGET

Antwerp, 26 November, 1545

R.O., S.P. 1, 211, 69–70.* *L.P.*, xx, ii, 876.

Thinks what is told of the French negotiations here (*L.P.*, xx, ii, 875) is true; what Philip de Croy, Duke of Aerschot, thinks of the 'lower sort'; the costly house of Jasper Duche.

1 *alt. from* ther   2 W(?) *c.o.*

Master Secretary, after my right harty commendations: This daye I re-ceyved your letters, and perceyve ye have not yet met with the French men, who, if they be as obstinate as they wer here, ye are like to spede, as I thinke, noo better thenne we have doon in that matier; wherof I shal be sory.

Ye shal in our letters to the Kinges Highnes see sum[1] cause of the Frenchmens[†] being here besides ours, and I thinke thEmperours Counsayl hath told us the truth of the matier which hath been here treated. But whither the being[2] of Grandvela and Scory with the French ambassadours at the tyme of ther departure wer oonly to require an answer for Heding, that may be doubted; and soo moch the more if thEmperour fortune[3] not to goo to Utrik[4], but take his journey in to[†] Almayne by Brucelles, as youe have harde out of England, [†]and sum-thing hath been spoken here[†]. Al the noble men saye styl thEmperour wyl goo to Utryk. Skepperus told us it is impossible, for the waye. If I may byleve that was told me, howe, whatsoever thEmperour doth with Fraunce, he wyl doo never the lesse with us, al[5] is wel. I see yet noo cause to suspecte it.

Monsieur de Bure sheweth himself a very gentylman, and oon that berith his harte to the Kinges Majestie.

The Duke of Ascot hath shewed me a very gret familiarite and courtesie. The man is wise and of good discourse, as the Italyan sayth. And he shewed me of the behavour of our Almaynes and ther abhomina-tion, notyng the gret presumption in the arrogant horsons that noo more feared soo noble a prince as the Kinges Majestie is, and told me of the losenes of the worlde by thies warres; adding that if the princes of the worlde doo not shortly extincte warre and begynne to lyve in ther reputacion, without necessite of the service of the lewde lower[6] sorte by waye of necessite, it is to be feared lest the lower parte by insolence shal attempte gretter thinges.

I have seen a house this daye[7] buylded by Jasper Duche of such cost and elegancy as, under the Kinges Majestie, noo man hath attempted in England. I dare not saye there is noon able. We had there a very gret fest. Al we recommende us to my Lord of Duresme, Master Tregonnel, and youe, whom God send hartely wel to fare. At Antwerpe, the xxvj[ti]

1 wh c.o.   2 with c.o.
3 to c.o.   4 ac(?) c.o.
5 w incomplete c.o.   6 service c.o.
7 buylded by Jasper c.o. then repeated

of Novembre. I send this berer[1] oonly to Calays and geve him post money ther after.

Your assured loving
frend,

STE. WINTON

Addressed: To the Right Wourshipfull Sir Wyllyam Paget, Knight, one of the Kinges Majesties two Principall Secretaries.

Endorsed: My Lord of Winchester to Master Secretary, Master Paget, xxvj° Novembris, 1545.

95. *To* HENRY VIII

Antwerp, 30 November, 1545

R.O., S.P. 1, 211, 130–1.* Edge torn. *L.P.*, xx, ii, 904. *St. P.*, x, 737.

A confidential letter, telling why Charles V does not want to marry Princess Mary, or have his son wed Elizabeth.

Pleasith it your Most Excellent Majestie to underst[and that], accordyng to your Highnes pleasour, signified by letters fr[om your] Majesties Counsail, I have laboured to atteyne knowlege [why] thEmperour doth, neyther for hymself embrace the mariage [of my Lady] Marye, ne accepte the offre of my Lady Elizabeth for hys s[on the] Prynce of Spayne; wherin I have been advertised how[e it hath] been put in thEmperours hed that your Highnes, mystrusting wh[at he] wold attempte in that realme, if he had my Ladye Marye, wo[ld not] in dede be wylling thEmperour had her, whenne the matier shuld [take] effecte. And as towching my Ladye Elizabeth, oonly *qualitas*, as it was termed to me, is that dissuadith them. Thusmoch h[ath] been told me, with gret adjurations and obtestacions of secrec[ie; for] which purpose I directe thiese letters to your Majesties own [handes]. Whom Almyghty God preserve in long and continual fel[icite]. At Antwerpe, the last of Novembre.

Your Majesties most humble [and]
obedient subget, servaunt, and day[ly]
bedeman,

STE. WIN[TON]

1 und(?) *c.o.*

204

Addressed: To the Kynges Most Excellent Majestie.
Below address: In to his own handes.
Endorsed: The Bisshop of Winchester to the Kinges Majestie, ultimo Novembris, 1545.

96. *To* [LORD COBHAM]

Antwerp, 30 November, [1545]

B.M., Harl. 283, 214-5.* *L.P.*, xx, ii, 905. *Chron. of Calais*, 165.

The Emperor's Council promise that such 'pullery and wylde foule' as Cobham requires may pass Gravelines unhindered.

My Lord, after my right harty commendations: I thanke youe for your sondry gentyl letters, and, partly to recompense them, I have spoken diligently to the Emperours Counsayl that such pullery and wylde foule maye passe by Graveling as ye require, without interruption; which I have had promyse shalbe doon without faulte. I have[1] noo newes to wryte of that ye wold[2] knowe; ye be nerer the market of ⟨them⟩ thenne I am. God send them to be in the conclusion such as al good men desire.

Herewith I send two letters, oon to my Lord of Duresme, and an other to Master Wallop, which I praye youe cause to be sent unto them.

I praye youe I maye be commended to my good Lady, with thankes for my good chere to youe both. And soo I praye God send youe hartely wel to fare. At Antwerp, the last of Novembre.

Your good Lordshippes
assuredly,

STE. WINTON

Addressed: To my very goode Lorde, my Lorde Deputie of Calais.

97. *To* THE READER

Utrecht, 12 December, 1545

From *Stephani VVinton. Episcopi Angli, ad Martinum Bucerum Epistola* ... Louvain, March, 1546. Dated at end, *Traiecti*, 12 December, 1545.

Abandoned men pose as reformers of religion and contemn all who withstand them; Bucer their ringleader; courtesy to them is misinterpreted; their character should be exposed (*cf.* Nos. 67, 144, App. 2, p. 489).

1 not *c.o.*   2 ye *c.o.*

Ad Lectorem

Miseram nostrorum temporum conditionem agnosce, Lector, quisquis ex animo pietatem colis, cum fex hominum perditorum probitatis patrocinio se ingerunt, et adumbrata virtutis effigie, sermone tenus, ac scenica pietatis persona suscepta, pellendis vitiis et instaurandae ac restituendae religioni operam navare videri volunt. Cui indignitati etiam illud accedit, ut omnes contemnere prae se, cubitis, pugnis, pedibus omnes quotquot obstiterint de via deturbare, deiicere, prosternere, ruere, nihil vereantur. Quorum Coryphaeus Bucerus, cum me homuntionem verbo contra mutientem offendisset, quibus me habuit modis, quanto cum fastu et supercilio a se repulit atque abiecit cum contemptu, addito tamen quod hominem proderet, impudentissimo de me mendacio, in eiusdem ad Latomum responsione, licet videre. Ego vero tum pulsus ab illo, in illum resilui, et nunc iterum ab eodem cum fastidio reiectus, etiam recalcitro, quem ea causa pungo acrius, ut desinat maledicere, vel ut alii potius desinant hominis nequam et scelerati applaudere maledictis. Civilis autem et modestae collationis formam,

---

To the Reader

Reader, if you sincerely cherish goodness, consider the wretched condition of our times, when abandoned men, the very dregs of humanity, hurl themselves against the defenses of rectitude, and, putting on the semblance of virtue—as far as talk goes—and a theatrical mask of piety, want to appear to be vigorously banishing vices and renewing and restoring religion. To which baseness this also is added: that they do not hestitate in the least to despise others in comparison with themselves, and to push off the road, strike down, lay low, beat to the ground, with arms, fists, feet, everyone who stands in their way.

Since their ringleader, Bucer, insulted me, the 'mannikin,' to use his term, who was 'muttering' against him, it can readily be seen in what light he held me, with what arrogance and disdain he thrust me from him, with what contempt he brushed me aside, adding, however—and this betrayed the man—a most impudent lie about me, in his reply to Latomus. Struck by him at that time, I sprang at him; now again flung off by him with scorn, I kick back and assail him the more vigorously, for this reason: that he may cease to slander, or rather that others may cease to applaud the slanders of a worthless and vicious man.

Moreover, their pride of empty knowledge, and their boasting of

quam rei quae tractatur natura desideret, scientiae istorum inanis tumor
καὶ ψευδωνύμου γνώσεως ⟨1 Tim. vi, 20⟩ iactantia omnino sus-
tulit—nisi quis forte sit qui sui ipsius quam causae maiorem rationem
habeat, ut quod se dignum sit, non quod causae victoria postulet, habeat
praecipuum. Nempe sic est istorum ingenium, ut lenitatem, mansue-
tudinem, modestiam, suaviloquentiam contra disserentium, timiditatem,
ac causae quae agitur diffidentiam et interpretentur ipsi et suis persua-
deant, ut nihil quo fiat animo accipiant recte, sed ad miseram, quam in
rerum eversione expetunt victoriam, pertrahant omnia. Suam in male-
dicendo licentiam, ex ipsa re natam volunt, non animi libidine. Adver-
sarii vero si quid regerant in ipsos veri, tacti ulceris dolorem callide
notant; sin taceant, iniectum iam conscientiae scrupulum gloriantur
et veritatis mole extinctam vocem iactabundi ostentant. Blandas autem
voces et obtestationes atque obsecrationes, amicas denique appella-
tiones et familiaritates, omnino rident taciti; istis tamen animi causa
interdum sese dant, tanquam sobriam aliquam exoptantes disputationem

---

learning falsely so called, have made altogether impossible a courteous
and temperate controversy with them, such as the nature of the matter
handled demands; unless, perchance, there be someone ⟨to dispute with
them⟩ who has so much more regard for himself than for his cause,
that he thinks of prime importance what is becoming to himself ⟨i.e.,
courtesy and moderation⟩, not what the victory of the cause requires.
Indeed, such is their disposition that they interpret gentleness, mildness,
moderation, courteous speech in their opponents as cowardice and lack
of confidence in the cause debated; and they persuade their followers to
take nothing rightly, in the spirit in which it is done, but to constrain
everything to contribute to a sorry victory, which they seek to effect
by the overthrow of established practices.

Their own licence in slandering they claim springs from the subject
itself, not from wantonness of spirit. If, forsooth, their adversaries retort
by flinging a bit of truth at them, they adroitly remark on the pain that
is felt when a sore spot is touched. But if their adversaries say nothing,
they boast that a scruple has now been cast upon their adversaries' conscience, and vauntingly proclaim that the voice of their adversaries
has been silenced by the weight of truth. Words of courtesy, earnest
adjurations and entreaties, in short, conciliatory appeals and friendly
approaches they do nothing but smile at in silence. Yet occasionally they
surrender themselves to these for the sake of diversion, as if heartily

et aliorum petulantiam incusantes, ista se modestia delectari dicunt, obsequuntur ad tempus nonnihil, et aliquatenus mansuescunt. At cum in spem de se aliquam homines induxerint, ut aves ludibundi iam avolant longissime, expatiantur suo more, et ad ingenium redeunt; id quod Gropperus et Gerardus in Bucero sunt experti. Sic nimirum isti dii ludos faciunt hominibus immenso orbis malo. Itaque mihi, quoniam cum Bucero res est, in ea causa adeo, quae omnes omnium non fortunas modo sed vitas etiam, atque illas non praesentis temporis modicas et momentaneas sed aeternas, contineat, imprimis faciundum duxi, ut quicquid in me desiderent alii, ne causa cui inservio quicquam desideret, neve quantum pudori meo parcens meae modestiae adiecero, tantum causae subtraxero necessarii argumenti, cum expediat interdum ad causam illustrandam personam adversario detrahere et latentes in homine simulationes prodere ac facere conspicuas. Hoc est enim homini secundum suam, quod Scriptura nos admonet, stultitiam respondere. Quibus ego rationibus adductus sum ut Bucerum liberius alloquar, quod ne te offendat, Lector, oratum mihi et obsecratum volo. Vale.

---

desiring some sober discussion; and, complaining of the effrontery of others, say they are delighted with this moderation. For the time being they are, in a measure, complaisant, and, to a certain extent, they become gentle. But when they have led men on to some hope for them, they suddenly fly far off like sportive birds; they wander away, according to their custom; they revert to their natural disposition; which Gropper and Gerard have experienced in the case of Bucer. Thus, verily, these gods make sport for men, to the immeasurable calamity of the world.

Accordingly, since my variance is with Bucer, on a matter, moreover, which touches not only the fortunes of all, but their lives as well, and these not merely their present, limited, transitory lives, but their lives for eternity, it seemed to me that I ought especially so to act that no matter what others find lacking in me, the cause which I serve should lack nothing, and that I ought not, out of regard for my reputation, to increase my credit for moderation at the expense of any consideration necessary to the cause. For it is sometimes needful, in order to set a cause in a clear light, to decry the character of an adversary, and to expose and publish the privy duplicities of a man. For this, as Scripture counsels, is to answer a man according to his folly.

For these reasons I have been led to address Bucer rather freely. That this should not offend you, Reader, I would beg and entreat. Farewell.

NOTES TO NO. 97

Page 206. Bucer's lie to Latomus. Bucer, in his *Scripta duo adversaria*, Strasbourg, 1544, written in controversy with the humanist Latomus, one-time friend of Erasmus, misquoted Gardiner on I Cor. vii, 36–8, on celibacy. *Cf.* App. 2, p. 489.

Page 208. Gropper and Gerard. The liberal German Catholic jurist and theologian, Johann Gropper, at first aided the reform efforts of Archbishop Hermann of Cologne, in whose service he was employed 1526–43, and was a leader in the movement toward reunion with the Protestants. He conferred with Bucer at the colloquies at Hagenau and Worms, 1540, and at the Diet of Regensburg (Ratisbon), Spring, 1541. At Worms he was accompanied, in his conferences with Bucer, by Gerard or Gerhard Veltwick, Imperial Secretary, who was also present at Regensburg, and who, according to Melanchthon, was there associated with Gropper and Bucer in the production of the 'Regensburg Book,' containing a statement of matters on which Catholics and Protestants were in agreement. Gropper seems to have come away from Regensburg with the hope that Bucer could be won over to a moderate Catholic position, and, early in 1542, welcomed him in Cologne, whither he came at the invitation of Archbishop Hermann to aid in the reform of the Church. When, however, it became clear that Bucer would yield in nothing but unessentials, Gropper led the opposition to him, and was in part instrumental in effecting his withdrawal (1543) as well as the deposition of the Archbishop (1546) and the retention of the archdiocese of Cologne within the Roman Church. In 1544–5 Gropper and Bucer attacked each other sharply in a series of publications. *See* W. van Gulik, *Johannes Gropper*, Freiburg-i.-B., 1906, chapters IX–XII; H. Eells, *Martin Bucer*, New Haven, 1931, chapters XXIX–XXXV.

98. *To* Paget

[Utrecht, 21] December, 1545

R.O., S.P. 1, 212, 84–5.* *L.P.*, xx, ii, 1007.

> Has never been troubled so much in a week, but cannot accuse the Imperial
> Councillors of craft; has disputed about words, which is what the world is now
> much troubled with, but has come very near complete agreement. (That this
> letter, calendared in *L.P.* as under 19 December, is of 21 December, is clear
> from its mention of the two packets and the very near agreement with the
> Imperialists, both referred to in the joint letter, from Gardiner, Thirlby, and
> Carne, of the latter date—*L.P.*, xx, ii, 1017.)

Master Secretary, after my most harty commendacions: Synnes I cam
out I have not been troubled in oon weke somoch as in this—I meane
in mynde; for here we wer delayed and durst not wryte hom for making
trouble for nothing, and again if we† shuld have accused thiese men
of craft nowe, or evel mynde in the matier, we shuld have doon them
wrong. For, by the conclusion, it is like that sum tyme they wrangled
with us that they might in the meane tyme send to thEmperour, for of
themself they doo nothing. And it is like that they have this conceyte
in ther head, that we, treating with Fraunce, wold use ther doinges to
shewe to the French men, and soo make our bargain. It troubleth them
moch that we treate by meane of the Protestantes; but that is a smal
matier if it ease us. As we here, there is a treulx concluded; wherof, if it
had been soo, we thinke we shuld have hard sumwhat from youe. If ye
be at hom I praye youe help that we maye have the forme of that shal
passe formally prescribed unto us again, as it was last very well, which
I warrante we wyl folowe with *non aliter nec alio modo*.

We have had here disputacion for wordes, and that is a gret¹ parte of
that the wourlde is nowe troubled with. If your matiers frame not to†
the Kinges Majesties contentacion² there, our here may be of somoch
the more estimation, for we be com very nere togither; but I esteme it
noo better thenne the Kinges Majestie wyl accepte it, and have here
agreed to nothing for our parte, but oonly promysed to sende it hom.

We divide our letters in to two pacquettes; in the oon we declare our
travayl, and in the other thende of it for this tyme. In the diversite of
the minutes and our notes upon thers³ and our also, which we sende
again to be perused there, ye maye see al that we have travayled in. And

1 a gret *repeated*   2 our *c.o.*   3 *alt. from* the

210

herwith bydde youe fare wel, with desire to communicate[1] unto us sum parte of your good tydinges there.

Al we recommende us to my Lord of Duresme and Master Tregonnel.

Your assured loving
frend,

STE. WINTON

Addressed: To the Right W*our*shipfull Sir Wyllyam Paget, Knight, one of the Kinges Majesties two Principall Secretaries.

Endorsed: My Lord of Winchester to Master Secretary, Master Paget, ⟨*blank*⟩ Decembris, 1545.

99. *To* PAGET

Utrecht, 2 January, 1546

R.O., S.P. 1, 213, 16–17.* *L.P.*, XXI, i, 9.

> The Emperor is absorbed in the feast of the Order of the Golden Fleece, 'when the world is far out of order'; commends Henry VIII's speech to Commons (on Christmas Eve, 1545—*see L.P.*, XX, ii, 1031).

Master Secretary, after my most harty commendacions: Synnes the xxiij daye of the last moneth, we have dayly[2] and howrely loked for the passeport for this money that shuld goo to Calays, and therupon delayed to wryte, being the matier not worth the charge of the post. Nowe we have sumwhat better matier and therfore send without[3] any lenger tarying therfor, and yet they promyse it from howre to howre. ThEmperour is al nowe in this present fest of the Ordre, whenne the worlde is soo far out of ordre as ther is smal cause to make any fest of thOrdre. It is said the French King wylbe a Protestant, but he wyl, after his facion, playe with both handes; and therfor it is said to me that he sendith hither the Cardynal of Loreyn. Even nowe cam oon to me to knowe whither we wold be at the solemnite of this fest or noo; wherunto we answered to be as it shuld please thEmperour. I send herwith a letter from my Lord Fitzwater to my Lord Chaunceler in Italian.

I thanke youe hartely for your newes, and specially of the Kinges Majesties oration to the Commens, which must nedes be pleasaunt to ever⟨y⟩ honest harte. And if the peace and unite may be made at hom,

---

1 s *c.o.*   2 lo *c.o.*   3 al *c.o.*

as the Kinges Majestie exhorted, al other outward peaces be the lesse to be cared for; for *hec est victoria que vincit mundum, unitas nostra,* which God graunte, and youe hartely wel to fare. At Utrek, the ij^de of January.

Your assured loving
frend,

STE. WINTON

I praye youe make al our recommendations to my Lord of Duresme and Master Tregonel.

Addressed: To the Right Woÿrshipful Sir William Paget, Knight, oon of the Kinges Majesties two Principal Secretaryes.

Endorsed: My Lord of Winchester to Master Secretary, Master Paget, ij° Januarii, 1545⟨46⟩.

100. *To* PAGET

Utrecht, 11 January, 1546

R.O., S.P. 1, 213, 58–63.* *L.P.,* XXI, i, 51. *St. P.,* XI, 9.

The ceremonies at the feast of the Order of the Golden Fleece (Toison d'Or), 2–5 January; was especially impressed by the commemoration of the departed; 'if ye knowe any that lovith noo ceremonyes, geve hym this letter to rede.'

Master Secretary, after my right harty commendations: Here hath been kept the feaste of thOrdre, with a gret ceremonye throughly in every bihaulf. First, the place was honorably and magnifiquely garnished; that is to saye, the body of the church with a gret quantite of riche arres, ^1as it^1 shuld appere reserved to that use to serve at the fest of the Toyson, for it is of that story, and very sumptuous. On both sydes of the quere of the church wer paynted very fynely al the armes of the knightes and companyons of thOrdre that lyved at the last chapter or wer made^2 of the company synnes, with a difference, to knowe^3 who yet lyved and who at this tyme is ded; for al yet lyving had ther armes paynted with ther crestes, and those departed ther armes oonly, with a worde wryten underneth, '*trepasse.*' The nombre of the companyons be fyfty, and soo ther wer on ech side xxv places, which on both sydes, soo far as extended to the places of kinges, was hanged from the armes down^t

1–1 *writ.* at is   2 kn *c.o.*   3 how *c.o.*

212

with cloth of tissue at the bak, and also cloth of tissue cast over the deske bifore, and[†] that henge down to the grownde. The stalles under the rest of tharmes was, for the reredosse, crymsen tafta; to syt in, crymsen saten; and the deskes caste over with crymsen damaske, that dyd hang down to the grownde, which, being ful and, as we saye, cut owte of the hol cloth, made a very gorgeous shewe to the yee; which we had good tyme to behold, tarying soo long for thEmperour as we did. There was put in ordre a numbre of bishoppes, with ther mytres and coopes to receyve thEmperour, with thassembre of al the clergie of the towne to receyve thEmperour also, which stode in the body of the church. There was also a solemne place prepared for thambassadours, and the place wel kept that noo man pressed bifore us, with a forme bifore us to leane at, covered with cloth of tissue and crymsen velvet. And after al thing thus in ordre, thEmperour with his companyons cummyth to the church, which wer viij besides hymself, al appareled in crymsen velvet[1], both kyrtelles and roobes, with hoodes[2] of the same, as the knightes of the Garter have[3], which they here ware on ther hedes in stede of ther cappes, which becamme them notably wel and had a good grace. There cam also, bifore al, the officers of thOrdre, being[†] foure, the chaunceler, the tresaurer, the register, and the chief herauld, whom they cal Toyson. Al thiese foure wer appereled like the companyons without difference, saving the knightes outward roobes wer garnished with embroydery of gold, and ther oonly playn[4] velvet; and Toyson[5] had upon his robe a coler of thOrdre, with al tharmes of the companyons in gold, graved, added unto the same, which made a[6] brave[7] shewe, and[8] was the[†] token to knowe him for chief herauld. Whenne they wer cumme, and thEmperour placed, ech other companyon entred in to his place where his armes stode, having koshens of newe crymsen velvet layde there redy for them; and soo was the Evensong of Saincte Andrewe song at lenghth, and ended by vij of the clok. And soo ended the ceremonye of that daye, which was Saturdaye.

Upon Sondaye, aboute x of the clok [†]in the mornyng[†], thEmperour with[9] his companyons cam to the church, appereled as they wer in the even[10] bifore, where was song the High Masse, with such ceremonyes as it was past oon of the clok or we departed; for whenne it cam

1 *alt. from* vylvet   2 as *c.o.*   3 † *abv.* hath *c.o.*
4 l *c.o.*   5 w *c.o.*   6 br *c.o.*
7 *in margin*   8 de *c.o.*   9 *alt. from* wh
10 evenyng *w.* yng *c.o.*

213

to the tyme of offeryng, not oonly thEmperour hymself offred, and the compagnions, but also ther offred[1], by proctours and deputies, al that wer absent, yet lyving, which was seriously doon, and with a good circumstaunce, wherin thEmperour did wel refreshe us with his facion and bihavour in that presence, whenne Monsieur de Burez supplied the Kinges Majesties absence, who also in thexecution therof set forth the matier very wel to us. For when thEmperour had himself offred[2], which he[3] did with his officers cummyng bifore him, [4]his herauldes and sergauntes, the rest of the compaygnions kepyng styl ther stalles, and oonly putting of ther hoodes as he passed—whenne thEmperour was retourned, it semed ther was a gret loking and expectation who shuld offre first, the French King or the Kinges Majestie. And therewith arryseth Monsieur de Bure, and[5], after cursies made to the Sacrament and thenne to thEmperour, goth to[6] the Kinges Majesties stal, which was next to thEmperour, and soo nere as it was within his cloth of astate; wherfor Monsieur de Bure sumwhat forbare to entre the very seate and wold have stande a lytel a syde. ThEmperour pulled hym by the roobe in to the very place, and caused him to put on his hode, which he dyd, and kept it on whiles Toyson, after ther custume, had rehersed the Kinges Majesties style, and desired him to cum to the offeryng. After which wordes spoken, Monsieur de Bure put of his hoode for cursy at his departure, and thEmperour likewise put of his hoode holly, soo as he[7] dyd after to[8] noon other that executed for the[9] other kinges; which was noted. And whenne Monsieur de Bures cam towardes thofferyng and from thofferyng, in his passage he signified in his cursies to us howe this he did for the King our master; and when he was retourned to hys own stal agayn, thenne, after a lytel pawse, he went to the French Kinges stal and offred for hym, with a signification to the French ambassadour in passing by hym; but this we marked, that whenne Monsieur de Bure departed from the French Kinges stal with cursy, as he did from the King our masters, thEmperour did oonly move his hoode, as he did accustumably to any of them that made cursy to hym. And this was noted, that to avoyde al argumentes that might be made of the higher place bytwen the Kinges Majestie and the French King in this Ordre, bicause the French King beganne the ranke of the

---

1 pr *c.o.*   2 and *c.o.*
3 d *c.o.*   4 h *writ. over* a   5 go *c.o.*
6 *writ.* the, *an evident slip*   7 d *c.o.*
8 *a letter c.o.*   9 fre *c.o.*

other side of thEmperour, thEmperours badge[1] with two pyllers in a fayre table occupied the first place of the other side of the quere, and thenne the French Kinges place †next that†, soo as thEmperour kepyng both the first places on eyther side, the French King had the second place on the left side, and the Kinges Highnes next on ther right side. After thoffering doon by[2] al the compaignons lyving and for them, the chauncelour of thOrdre made a sermon, declaryng the institution of thOrdre and what† was entended therby, and what al ther apparel signified, wherin he spent an howre; and that doon they proceded in the Masse, and, that finished, retourned to our lodging.

At foure of the clok we assembled again in the church, and founde thEmperour⟨s⟩ stal and al the stalles of the kinges, with deskes bifore them, hanged and covered with blak velvet, and the rest hanged and covered with blak cloth, and the high aulter likewise. And morover in the stal of the King of Scottes departed, hanging from the armes, a pece of cloth of gold of thre yardes long, and[3] at the stal of every other compaignon decessed, a pece of velvet of the same length, which made a representacion as it wer of soo many herses. About fyve of the clok thEmperour cam with his compaignons and officers, al appareled in blak cloth, with ther hoodes in stede[4] of cappes, and the Ordre upon the outward[5] garment; and soo continued there whiles the Dirige was song at very gret lenghth; and, that doon, departed.

Mondaye in the mornyng about x of the clok, thEmperour with his compaignons and officers al in blak repared to the church to here the Dirige Masse, being prepared against that tyme fiftie candelles of virgin wax, ech candel having a skochen with the armes of ech oon of thOrdre, both alyve, and deed synnes the last chaptre. These candelles stode light, upon a beme bifore the high aulter, tyl the tyme of thoffering, at which tyme the candel having thEmperour⟨s⟩ armes was taken downe by a pursuyvant, having thEmperours cote armour on hym, and from hym delyvered to an harrault, and by the harralde delyvered to Toyson, who, with rehersal of thEmperours style, called thEmperour to the offeryng and delyvered hym his candel, which thEmperour caryed to thoffering, and as he had offered it, it was kept light and put again in the place where it stode. And thenne was a candel taken downe for the Kinges Majestie, with his armes[6] at it, and Monsieur de Bure going to the

---

1 *alt. from* bagge
3 and *repeated and c.o.*
5 ch *c.o.*

2 † *abv. for c.o.*
4 stedes *w. final* s *c.o.*
6 v(u) *c.o.*

Kinges Majesties stal was invited to thoffering, and the candel delyvered [1]hym, which he offered with a good grace, as he did the daye bifore, and thEmperour had used him likewise. And soo the stalles[2] wer perused, as they wer in ordre. And[3] in every stal where the compaignon is yet lyving[4] there was oon to supplie his place; but whenne the heralde cam to the stal of him[5] that was dede, there was noo man to supplie, but after the chief[t] haralde[6] Toson had named him by his style, he turned him to thEmperour and with a lowde voyce said, '*Il est morte.*' And thenne Toson toke hymself the candel[7], having tharmes of him that is dede, and caryed it up to the aulter very seriously, and offred it, not to the bishop, but delyvered it to oon of the ministres appointed therfor, and from hym was taken to the pursuyvant, who, with a ceremony, blewe it[8] out. And I may saye a circumstaunce also, for there was experimented the conclusion that want of measure destroyeth theffecte, for whenne he blewe tomoch, the candel went not oute but lighted again. Whenne the candel was put oute[9] it was set again in his place with the other burnyng, and soo appered howe many places wer voyde. The behavo*ur* in this matier was used with good ordre, without any fayling or trouble. Ech man knewe his office and neded noo admonition. The lamentable wordes, '*Il est morte,*' with the putting out of the candel, was a good representacion of our estate, howe weake it is indede. Whenne thoffering was doon, the registre of the Ordre redde openly the statutes of thOrdre, with the names of al those that had been of thOrdre synnes the begynnyng; and therin he spent oon howre, soo as[t] it was two of the clok or we went from the church that daye.

Mondaye at night al the blak was taken awaye, and the stalles agin in ther fresh furniter as bifore; and at fyve of the clok thEmperour cam to church with his companyons[10] and officers, al in white damaske, with ther garmentes gyrte, and ther hodes of crymsen velvet on ther hedes, which was a very good sight. And there was Evensong song of Our Lady, very freshely, to recompense the deul bifore; which ended not bifore vij of the clok.

Tuesdaye in the mornyng thEmperour cam again to the church with his compaignons, in white, and harde Masse of Our Lady, very solemnely doon; at which tyme thEmperour oonly did offre, and at that offryng[11]

1 h *writ. over* w   2 *alt. from* stalled   3 whenne *c.o.*
4 *alt. from* le(?)ving   5 *alt. from* his   6 had *c.o.*
7 appointed *c.o.*   8 it *repeated and c.o.*   9 he *c.o.*
10 al in *c.o.*   11 *alt. from* offre; t *incomplete follows*

al the compaignons did cum out of ther stalles, and wayted on the Emperour to the offering, and brought hym again to his stal, which they did not bifore. I note unto youe the more diligently the offeringes, bicause in them we receyved many curseys of them that offered, aswel thEmperour as other, both[1] in going to the offering and the commyng from it. Synnes thiese ceremonies abrode, thEmperour hath spent moch tyme in the chaptre with his compaignons, who sate in counsayl on ther matiers oon daye from two at after noone tyl eleven at night, and the next daye from oon to seven at night; and yet we here not abrode what is therin doon; but Monsieur de Bures hath been with me and told me he wyl advertise the Kinges Majestie what is doon there. And nowe I thinke, or ye have red thus far, ye wyl mervel what I had a doo to wryte this, even asmoch as I have sumtyme when I wryte John Kingston, wherwith I have spent in an afternone asmoch paper as this. And herby ye maye perceyve I am not yet waxed slowtheful in wryting, althought of late postes have goon slowly from us. If ye knowe any that lovith noo ceremonyes, geve hym this letter to rede for special newes. And soo fare ye hartely wel. At Utrek, the xj[th] of January.

Your assured loving
frend,

STE. WINTON

Addressed: To the Right Worshipful Sir Wylliam Paget, Knight, oon of the Kinges Majesties two Principal Secretaries.

Below address: At laysour.

Endorsed: The Bisshopp of Winchestre to Master Secretary, Master Paget, xj⁰ Januarii, 1545⟨46⟩.

NOTE TO NO. 100

Page 217 (above). John Kingston. The editors of *St. P.* call this a sobriquet used by Gardiner, but, as Mr A. E. Stamp suggests, it reads more like a pet name for a book that he was writing. Other instances of its use are not enlightening. *Johannes Kyngston* is written in a contemporary hand on the back of a letter from Cromwell to Gardiner, 5 July, 1536 (B.M. Add. 25,114, f. 175), but not as a part of or in the hand of address or endorsement. A contemporary pen

---

1 *writ. over something else*

trial, not, it seems to me, in Gardiner's hand, on the back of No. 53 above contains the names *Richard, Kingston, John, Germanus, John.* On the margin of a draft of an unsigned, unaddressed letter of 1535, identified by J. Gairdner as in Wriothesley's hand, is a pen trial, possibly in the same hand, in which, among other scribblings, occur *Johannes, Kingstonne, Kingston, Little, Johannes, Bellawey* (R.O., L.P., IX, 1082).

A John Kyngston appears in a list of persons in arrears to Wolsey, 1530; John Kyngston of Tetney was condemned as a rebel at Lincoln, 1537, but not executed; John Kyngston, canon of Oseney, Oxon, was receiving a pension in 1543; a John Kyngeston held property in Grimsby in 1547 (*L.P.*, IV, iii, p. 3047; XII, i, 581; XVIII, i, p. 549; *Pat. Rolls*, I, 200). Two John Kingstons, with whom perhaps one or more of the foregoing may be identified, were almost certainly known to Gardiner: a fellow-student at Cambridge, B.Can.L. 1518, later Bonner's commissary (Venn, *Alum. Cant.*; Foxe, index), and a London printer who, with Henry Sutton, printed service books in Mary's reign (E. G. Duff, *A Century of the Eng. Book Trade*, 1905, 86). What relation, if any, these men bore to Gardiner's enigmatic phrase, it is impossible to say.

101. *To* PAGET

Utrecht, 17 January, 1546

R.O., S.P. 1, 213, 84–5.* *L.P.*, XXI, i, 74.

Hears that Parliament has put hospitals into the King's hands; sues to have St Cross, which he has lately given to his chaplain (Medowe), and Mary Magdalene in Winchester stand; also sues for his servant Davy, against whom, in his absence, a decree has passed in Wales. (Davy later attended Gardiner in the Fleet and the Tower. For his account of Gardiner's imprisonment *see* Foxe, VI, 194.)

Master Secretary, after my most harty commendacions: I understand it hath pleased the Court of Parliament to geve in to the Kinges Majesties handes[†] the disposition of al hospitalles, chaunteries, and other houses; wherof I am very glad and, thus far, if I might without displeasour, wold[†] be an humble suter, both by myself and my frendes, that it wold please his Majestie to have respecte, as I doubte[1] not but his Highnes wyl, to the Hospitalles[2] of Saincte Crosse besides Winchestre and of Mary Magdalene, wherin poore folkes be releved. And the oon,

1 nto *c.o.*   2 les †

which is Mary Magdalenes, I thinke hath noo land of any value, oonly the bishoppes have been content to geve yerely, without any convenaunt but oonly by this title *pro elemosina episcopi*, xxxvj *li*. As for Saincte Crosses, ⟨it⟩ hath not tenne powndes in temporal landes, and the house hath noo commodite for any mannes dwelling. I gave it of late to my chapelen that is here with me, who standith bounde for the fyrst frutes and hath payde sumwhat alredy. Herin I wold frame my sute soo far as might be graciously harde, which youe canne knowe there better thenne I here, and therfor remitte it[t] unto youe to be tempered as ye shal thinke good. I meane not to have any thing a doo with them myself, but thinke them wel in the Kinges Majesties hand from whens I had them; but this I meane: to have them stande ordred at the Kinges Majesties good pleasour, for the countrie is poore and very poore, and thiese two howses sum what[t] garnishe the town, which, by reason of fryers, monkes, and nunnes, whose howses stand al to torne, with the decaye of the inhabitauntes, is nowe moch defaced. And if the Kinges Majestie wylbe good and gratious Lorde to my chapelen that hath it, it shuld be moch to my counforte; wherin I praye youe doo what ye maye, and advise me whither I shuld make any further sute in it or let it alone; which I wyl folowe. Oon thing I assure youe, there is noo man wold geve more for the Howse of Saincte Crosse to pul it downe or dwel in it thenne I wyl to[1] have it stande in the Kinges Majesties patronage as it nowe is. I praye youe doo herin asmoch as ye maye. And this is my fyrst sute.

My seconde is[t] sute for relief of my servaunt Davye, who doth me in travayl notable good service, such as I cannot have doon of any other for money, in tormoyling from place to place; and nowe in his absence here with me there hath passed a decre against hym in Wales for the possession of certain land, which matier was suspended to be ordred by me and an other, and, that fayling, the parties to appere bytwen Halowmes and Christmesse; and in the meane tyme I was sent awaye, and dyd warraunte my man Davye that he shuld suffre noo prejudice in this absence; and in good fayth it wer requisite to have [our] p[riv]ilege defended that travayle in legations. And if my man might recover the possession upon that benefite, it shuld be to me a singuler pleasour; wherin I praye youe send a lettre to my Lord President or obteyne a wrytte of privilege for restitucion upon this cause, or other-

1 let *c.o.*

wise, as ye thinke good[t], soo it be doon. Master Hare knowith sumwhat of the matier; but the possession to be altred in the tyme of his absence here—we ambassadours (herin be youe comprehended) must hold oon with an other. It is a matier of commen right, and therfor I wryte not to my Lord President; and he wold be loth to retracte[1] his ordre, but yet in this cace yt cannot have place. Ye knowe the sodennesse of my cummyng out, and this man was soo necessary as I coulde not want him. A good felowship helpe herin, and wryte unto me[that ye[2] doo soo, for soo shal I courage my man who is nowe hau005f deed. Thus fare ye hartely wel. At Utrek the xvij[th] of January.

Your assured loving

In noo wise forget this.   frend,

STE. WINTON

Addressed: To the Right Wourshipfull Sir Wyllyam Paget, Knight, one of the Kinges Majesties two Principall Secretaries.

Below address: Hast, hast,
              with al hast.

Endorsed: The Bisshop of Winchestre to Master Secretary, Master Paget, xvij° Janu[arii], 1545⟨46⟩.

102. *To* PAGET

Utrecht, 18 January, with postscript, 19 January, [1546]

R.O., S.P. 1, 213, 99–104.* Slightly mutilated. *L.P.*, XXI, i, 87.

To grant some of the Imperial requests concerning merchants will produce good feeling; Granvelle's and de Praet's jealousy of each other; Schore's opinion of himself; Scepperus' circumspection; the Emperor's indecision; what is done at the chapter of the Order of the Golden Fleece; Reiffenberg has come; Scepperus recommends certain mercenaries; the matter of the merchants and Paget's 'recess'; asks Paget's help in the speedy ratification of the treaty. (Paget's 'recess' was the agreement made at Brussels, 6 April, 1545, between Paget, Wotton, and Imperial deputies to release the persons, ships, and goods of the subjects of Charles V and Henry VIII held under arrest in each other's territories, and to submit all differences concerning the treatment of merchants to a diet of commissioners to meet in May, 1545—*L.P.*, xx, i, 494. The commissioners met May–July, first at Gravelines, then at Bourbourg. *See ib.*, p. xlvi and index, 'Bourbourg.')

1 h to retracte *c.o.*   2 *alt. from* he

Master Secretary, after my most harty commendations: Here hath been a mervelous delaye to doo a thing doon, and a gret perplexitie to¹ us howe to acquiete ourself for discharge of our duetie at hom in not wryting or, in wryting, howe to facion the matier. If we shuld have† continued the assuraunce, we shuld have† been haulf parties to the disapoyntement if it had† folowed. If we shuld have² engreved the suspition, percace h[ave] troubled the Kinges Majestie without cause, and doo therin very evel office. Every daye hath had the next daye linked unto hym with hope of depech, and we perceyve by repeticion of letters †from youe there†, to make an ende, that the conclusion here is nowe moch expedient for our affayres as they stand with Fraunce, and in the matier of merchauntes hath moch encombred us, wherin we feared to make a convenaunt not bifore perused there; and yet, having commission to doo it rather thenne staye, we feared blame at hom to staye for it. Nowe we have put over the matier with promyse to be suters. I pr[ay] your helpe that our sute maye be wel taken. Theffecte of ther sute consistyng in two poyntes; that is to saye, releave of the³ impositions according to the treaties⁴, and justice to be ministred to such as canne prove themself spoyled. We have graunted them by wordes many tymes. Nowe they have desired a tyme for the execution of it and, to avoyde the clamour, a maner of examinati[on], biacause the Diet toke noon effecte. If the King[es] Majestie of his benignite wylbe content to condescende somoch to ther satisfaction, it shalbe to them a gret quiet, for undowtedly they be moch cryed out on; and a special facion of examination used, and, in sum oon or two playn matiers, justice ministred⁵ or benevolence shewed⁶, it shal quench a gret meny doubteful exclamations. But howe soever it shal please the Kinges Majestie in dede to doo, we trust his Majestie wyl take our request in good parte, wherof is our chief care, and thenne for the comen welth. The copie of our promyse to be suters⁷ we sende herwith, wherof the first article was concluded at Burborowe and the second dependith therof also in parte, and the rest be but a fewe matiers wherin they may be with reason easely answered or satisfied. Grandvela hath medled in thiese matiers of merchauntes with diminution of his auctorite, for he coulde not⁸ maynteyne his worde that they shuld not be spoken in, which he had signified by Skepperus. Here be men in this Counsayl,

1 w c.o.	2 † abv. upo c.o.	3 ther w. r c.o.
4 we have man c.o.	5 † abv. used c.o.	6 † abv. used c.o.
7 y c.o.	8 have c.o.	

as I have seen in other places, with such humours as engendre fevers sumtyme. Here is Monsieur de Prate, grettest in aunciente, grettest in experience; Monsieur de Grandvela, grettest in the universal auctorite and mouth of thEmperours Counsayl, with an opinion conceyved to be grettest also in that lernyng that shuld doo service. President Skore takith himself grettest, particulerly in thiese parties, and therfor ye shal see in his st[i]le *Consiliorum Status et privati Presidens in inferioribus ditionibus*[1], which I understode not tyl it was expounded; and as for lernyng, Skore berith the other two on his bak, as they saye, and thin[ke]th himself gret inough soo to doo. Nowe thiese g[ret me]n be like gret men throughly, and in agrement like the grettest; and thEmperour, whiles he is here, snarleth them to gither. And Monsieur de Prate hath the goulte, and being here in the myddes of his governement, wherby he is here grettest under thEmperour, it wold engendre an other gowte to goo to often to Grandvelas. On the other parte, Grandvela hath soo many matiers of letters and advertisementes wherin he wyl shewe him-self to medle alone, whenne the rest be there, that they suffre him to be alone whenne he wold have[2] them. And in our matiers we have felt a pece of ther distempere, and it hath wel exercised Skepperus, who shewith himself the same man we toke him for whenne we commened with him in Windesore College, with a gret circumspection and honestie.

I send herwith a minute of the ratificacion to be made there, which we have shewed them here; if it also like there, ye maye shortly depech it, if it be the Kinges Majesties pleasour, for it is in forme and nedith oonly a commaundement to be truely wryten and wel examyned, which I doubte not but youe wyl consider accordinglye. And therwith helpe that, accordyng to [the] Kinges Majesties pleasour, of my demore or retourne [I maye] have a signification certain, if it be possible; [as] in the last letters it was o[rdr]ed to tar[y if] the French ambassadours re-to[ur]ned to this Courte; wherof sumtyme we here they cum and anoon otherwise they cumme not[t]. And it is constantly affermed that the Cardinal of Lorayn was cummyng and thenne revoked to the French King, soo varyable be the French Kinges determinacions; and he hath good cause to be gretly perplexed. For myself, I care oonly soo to cumme hom as may be to the Kinges Majesties contentacion, without errour on my bihaulf to cumme oversoone or tary to long.

1 and *c.o.*   2 † *in other hand abv.* hath *c.o.*

What thEmperour wyl doo noo man canne tel; and what he hath doon in his chapitre here in chosyng of his compaignons noo man canne tel; and thambassadours saye thEmperour is like ¹hymself throughly, and therfor kepith in suspense his chaptre matiers, which men thought shuld have been ended in a daye.

Monsieur de Bure made us a gret dyner upon Thursdaye last, where were assembled to chere us Monsieur de le Grant and other of thEmperours Chamber. We toke it doon by request to digest our malencolye of the dayes bifore. Monsieur de Bure cam for us to² our lodging, and by the waye told me howe in this chaptre thEmperour† doth not oonly chose newe ⟨compaignons⟩, but also of al other compaig[nons, besi]des strange princes whom they touch [not], but of other, if [they] have hard of [any] mysordre in lyving [or demeanou]r they wryte unto them of it and signifie what they here, and wylleth them to amende it, and, if the facte be notorious, enjoyne them to doo this or that for an amendes. And if it be soo, it is not amysse; and if it be soo, I mervel not though the chaptre be soo long. I have harde, †of an† other ³, that the compaignons have also libertie, and be sworne, to tel thEmperour frankely what they thinke⁴ in hym, and therupon such a tale as I wyl not wryte, but tel youe whenne I cum hom.

I wryte to youe somoch of this Ordre, for it lettith the spedy ordre in our matiers and kept Monsieur de Prate yesterday from sealing our convenauntes, which delaye hath engendred youe so long a letter. And nowe ye shal receyve a perfection of letters in the numbre of thre, wherof oon ⟨No. 101⟩ conteynith two sutes, wherin I praye youe doo what ye canne *bono modo nam de fide non dub[ito]*.

Here be in this Courte noo newes, for as thambassadours that may cumme to us have been with us to make provision of them to send hom, for our conjunction with thEmperour is nowe the newes of the† worlde. [Thus] fare ye hartely [we]l. And yet again. Ye shal receyve the copye of our commission noted in the margynne in what places they founde here a scrupule, which is scrupulous in dede, in oon parte for them and in an other parte for us⁵, as we have noted. Soo as whenne we had skanned al, we wer glad they left out our commission, for it importith in itself a confession on our bihaulf as though they had hitherto doon wel. Thus fare ye wel oones ageyn. At Utrek

---

1 h *writ. over* is   2 h *c.o.*
3 wise *c.o.*   4 thinket *w.* t *c.o.*
5 so *c.o.*

the xviijth of January. I wryte noo recommendations for they be understanded.

Your assured loving
frend,

STE. WINTON

Here is Captayn Ryffenberge against whom Master Chamberlain hath
geven a complaynte, and the mattier is committed to be harde by the
Vicechaunceler of Germany, Doctor Navurs, and Monsieur Skepperus,
who wold speke with us in it, but thexpedition of this matier stayeth that.

Monsieur Skepperus hath declared to me tha[t] if the Ki[nges]
Majestie shal have nede of any men, Italyans or other, his Highnes may
be served of such as of whom punishement may be had if they doo not
ther duetie, and in communication of them he spake of oon of the
how[se] of the . . . . ¹ [w]ho wold [glad]ly serve the
Kinges Majestie . . . . [It]alya[n] . . . .
he sayth the man is to be trusted for due execution of his charge.

He spake to me also of an other, of thiese countries, who hath been
with me and served under Monsieur de Bure, who coulde bringe
M ⟨1000⟩ fotemen, and of whose service the Kinges Majestie might be
assured. He is of Monsieur de Praettes recommendation. I said I wold,
as they wer commended, recommend them; and soo I doo, and with a
trust we shal have noo nede of them. In cace they shuld be nedeful in a
distresse, it wer good to use the counsayl of such here as knowe the
conditions of them, and partely upon ther credite to take them, in my
poore opinion. If ye answer me not herin, I shal saye I have wryten,
and procure answer when I cum hom.

Addressed: To the Right Wourshipfull Sir Wyllyam Paget, [Knight,
one] of the [Kinges Majesties two Principall Secretaries].

Below address: Hast for thy life,
for thy life.

Endorsed: [The Bishop of] Wynchester [to Master] Secretary, Master
Paget, xviij° January.

Post scripta: It was soo late in the evening or we coulde here again
from Monsieur de Eke Skepperus² that, not withstanding the dating of

1 *the editors of L.P. appear to have been able to read* es *as* in the middle of this
lacuna
2 † *abv.* de Eke *as if in explanation of it*

224

our letters yester daye, the curro*ur* was stayed tyl this mornyng for this subscription for the marchauntes, al though it be nothing yet. Bicause we had in the preface put out two or thre wordes that liked us not, Monsieur Skepperus went aboute from oon of the Grandvelas [to a]n other to tel them of it, for he wisely preservith himself from ther quarrelles and sayth he cannot tel what wordes signifie aft[er] sum menns exposition. *I*[*n sum*]*ma*, this matier of the marchauntes that hath troubled us somoch, and wherin they had been soo diligent, as I perceyve nowe and is confessed, did sumwhat perplexe them after they had[t] agreed with us on the gross[e of] our capitulacions in the begynnyng of the newe [yere] . . . . as thopini[on] . . . . [t]of them[t] . . . . by this newe convenaunt, wherin is remitted differences and pretenses, they did geve awaye al the merchauntes complayntes. And bicause I refused soo extremely to speke in the matiers of marchaunt[es t]yl al was past, they [1]thought I had that con[cey]te in my hed; which I toke not in that sorte, nor it cannot have any such construction. Nowe it is resolved to [our] subscription, which we make with a[2] condition, annexed to a promise that we wylbe suters. If the merchauntes have payde any thing for this, me thinketh they have smal penyworthes. I wold wishe it wold please the Kinges Majestie to signifie unto us that we might answer them that our sute is obteyned; for saving it had been[t] moch for us to have promysed on the Kinges Majesties bihaulf, this maner of examination and al shuld have stayed or we wold have doon it, for *nihil malum nisi culpa*, yet *in re nihil est*, and it shalbe a joly general answer to such as crye for relief to tel them, whenne oon[3] commith [t]from thEmperour[t], the Kinges Majestie wyl appointe Counsaillo*ur*s to here it. And the like commodite shal they have here for depech of them that have made sute with hand and fote. As for the article for impositions concluded at Borbrough, they [call i]t a pece of your recesse, for soo they terme the capitulacion ye ma[de with them] for the diet. And that was a gret issue in our communication of the merchauntes, that the recesse of Monsieur Pagetto, they said, was not on our bihaulf accomplished; and we defended your parte. They said al is[t] oon[4], not to doo a thing and to doo it without effecte. But soo it is that your Diet had noo effecte; ergo, it is not doon. To this reason we joyned an other: Whenne soever any thing shuld[5] be doon by me, *si per me non stat quominus fiat*, it is to be taken as doon. But soo

1 t *writ. over* b   2 con(?) *c.o.*   3 t *c.o.*
4 to *c.o.*   5 per *c.o.*

it is, it stode not by us *quominus fiat;* ergo, it is to be taken as doon. Wote ye what Skepperus sayth to thiese[1] reasonynges? '*Ve vobis legis peritis!*' And I had wryten this daye sevenight in the mornyng, I wold have wryten in an other tune, for I wyste not what to saye; and I promyse youe had[2] not slept al night. And this lyngering delayes hath moch troubled me, and caused me to be idel for any other matiers, and, wayting to here from Skepperus this mornyng, wryt[e] this *post scripta* wherin I commen with youe ther[in] for myn owne recreation. I praye youe helpe the ratification may be sent shortly, and[3] [re]membre that our parte to be ratified we send it in paper. I wryte therof somoch bicause I have seen an errour therin heretofore. [I have] lerned so moch sinnes [y]esternight of thEmperou[rs ambassa]dour there [with you that] I [canne] saye he is of an honest affection towardes us. And if ye aske me, whenne I cumme hom, howe I knowe it, I am able to sette it forth as playne as is a demonstracion of geometrie. And this currer wer goon, the Vicechaunceler Navers and Skepperus wold talke with us of Ryffenberge, of whom we have an evident demonstracion what he is. And nowe, as Master Chamberlain sayth, he allegith that the Kinges Majesties commissaryes wold have hyred hym to bryng the armye in to the[4] French Kinges countrie and leve them there to the bocherye[5], and convey awaye[6] hymself and the commissaryes from them. This is a gaye issue for a campe, if he wyl maynteyne it but for that purpose[7].

Monsieur[8] Skepperus hath been with us and sayth they like our forme of ratification; soo as keping those wordes, we shal have here noo moo scrupules.

I trust we shal here from youe shortly. And soo fare ye hartely wel, and I praye youe remembre my sutes. At Utrek, the xix daye of January.

[Your] assured loving
frende,

STE. WINTON

1 two *c.o.*	2 *writ. over* it(?)
3 that *c.o.*	4 *alt. from* themperours
5 ye *writ. over something else*	6 themself *c.o.*
7 purposes *w. final* s *c.o.*	8 de Gra *c.o.*

103. *To* PAGET

Utrecht, 27 January, [1546]

R.O., S.P. 1, 213, 169–73.* Mutilated. *L.P.*, XXI, i, 128.

Has 'fashioned with circumstances' the report of an English victory, and given copies to all the ambassadors at Charles V's Court; hears that Francis I's 'ruptures beneath opened' when he heard of his losses; how the Protestant envoys delivered wrong letters to the French King, and other merry tales. (For the victory here mentioned *see L.P.*, XXI, i, pp. xvii ff.)

Master Secretary, after my most harty commendations: Having the commodite of a messanger to Calays, I coulde not omitte to wryte a worde unto youe of the occurrauntes here, being noo matier of substaunce for a commen letter to the Kinges Majestie.

The French men had raysed here a mervelous brute of an o[verthrow]e geven us by them, [which] was delyvered abrode to ambassadours in [such fourme] as ye shal receyve herwith, by tenour wherof the French King is made authour of the matier as wryten in a letter from hym.

Monsieur Skepperus cam to me to knowe whither I had herde any thing of it; and as I had not in dede, soo tolde hym, and by conjecture concluded with hym it coulde not be soo. I thought it not impossible but we might have dis[comfit]ure, for nothing is throughly of oon sorte in this worlde, and warre hath specially his alteracions and diversite of chaunces, but I coulde not byleve this reaporte. And after communication therof with me a good space, being thenne tyme of supper, he departed to his hous, where he had[1] bydden Monsieur de Praet to supper. And incontinently as he wa[s d]eparted, oon brought me a letter from my Lord Depu[tie of] Calays, signifying th[e summ]e of the matie[r, howe we had los]t ccv ⟨205⟩ [and th]e Frenchmen vj^c ⟨600⟩, the flight [of Monsieu]r de Buyes and [Fr]ench horsmen, with the distresse of the victuales[2], al save fyve cartes; and aparte, with the same letter, the declaration of oon that was there, telling the circumstaunce [o]f the matier and the names of al our captaynes[3] that had mischaunce there, in numbre xiiij, wherof I knewe noon but Sir George Pollard and Master Ponynges, whose soules God pardon. After I red [the said lettr]es I con[cluded] that [I never] had in my lief [in so s]mal a matier soo good a chaunce, and soo sent them strayte by my servaunt Wingfeld to Monsieur de Skepperus, who, although he understandith not Englishe, yet for the

---

1 hadd *w. final* d *c.o.*   2 sa *c.o.*   3 there *c.o.*

nerenes of our tonges, with a lytel admonition of Wingfeld, might perceyve hymself what was wryten. And soo he did, and declared it to Monsieur de Praet, who rejoysed very moch in it, and desired me that the letters might be translate to be shewed abrode. And soo they were, and sent unto him the next mornyng. And bicause he founde not the tale fully told in such circumstaunce as wold[1] make the matier to be playnelye perceyved, he cam to me himself, and he and I spent two howers to set the matier in ordre to be red abrode; and we made the title *Vraye Reaporte etc.* A[nd w]e made our men, retourning to Bolen with myrth a[nd re]joyse, to ha[ve] doon [a feate of war] with soo lytel losse, being noon [of any note slain], but oon by chaunce stryken with a peace of ordenaunce, and a bastard brother of the late Lord Ponynges. Oon thing sumwhat troubled us in the tale sent from my Lord Deputie: howe it shuld cum to passe that our men distressed sum of the cartes overnight and sum in the mornyng. Herin we wer soo bolde of our horsemen as to maké them tary in the felde al the night, partely chacyng Monsieur de Bies, and d[istressing] the cartes and v[ictu]alles, wherof they made an ende in the mornyng. [Herin] we kept the grounde of the truth of that was doon, and facioned it with circumstaunces mete for the same; wherin we gessed very nere, as we coulde gather, of that was signified by my Lord Deputie. And after this sorte it is goon abrode, and by this tyme in Italy, for al thambassadours had the copye and have sent it[2] with the Frenchmens, that the oon maye set out the other.

After this Monsieur Grandvela sent me worde by Skepperus howe in Fraunce the French King had sodenly commaunded fyres to be made for this solem victory, and or the fyres wer burnt out he was advertised of[3] howe he had lost asmoch as [vj^c] and his victualment d[i]sapointed, whic[h] al[tred him soo] that he fel [into a fe]ver and his ruptures beneth opened. Nevertheles he is refaicte and metely wel again. And soo nowe the Frenchmen divide the hurte with us by ther own confession, and the Italyans saye that he oonly hath the hurte that hath his enterprise withstanded. The French King coulde not put in his victualles and was letted therof; what wa[s] spent in the letting they counpte not, soo we let hym. Thus the brute is ours and the Frenchmens . . . . . . not nowe l⟨?⟩. . . . . .t as it hath been continued a . . . . . *et serio.* I like not th[at suc]h [an ide]l, shamefast, braging tale shuld be uttred and blowen abrode as it wer with a Kinges breth, as the letter purportith; but a gret

1 t c.o.   2 † abv. them c.o.   3 the c.o.

parte of the worlde semith nowe to be in this opinion: *si saxum in caput incidat id vere malum est; pudor autem et infamia tantum mali adferunt quantum senciuntur, si non senciuntur sunt ne mala quidem.* And by open use the fealing is taken awaye.

Upon Sonday last arryved here the Counsailles letters confermyng our *Vraye Reaporte,* which we have also spredde abrode. We be desirous to here thens, as we trust to doo or thies cum at youe. ThEmperour is here in very good helth, and whenne he goth [hens]¹ or what he wyl doo, noo man can tel, but [they that] knowe nothing saye thEmperour wyl have werre [with Fra]unce. I wold they had [knowledge] and therin knewe the truth. We [will advertise] that is wryten to us therin.

I have spoken with Gerardus who is nowe cum from the Turke, and have had pleasaunte communication with hym of the state of thinges there, which I wyl not spende herin, but have sumwhat to tel whenne I cumme hom.

Oon thing †the same† Gerard² tolde me out of the King³ of Romaynes Courte, that there it was advertised out of Fraunce howe the French King had used the Protestauntes to practise a peace with us and finally findeth them but bestes ⟨*i.e.,* beasts⟩ in compassing of those matiers, and yet they have† been preferred and singulerly commended unto hym as men of witte and understanding, and that herin they† shulde stande him in gret stede. And whenne it cam to the poynte, they wer soo grosse as they delyvered the byllet they shuld have geven the King our master to the French King, and that they shuld have geven to the French King delyvered it unto us. And what this byllet shuld be, wherin the errour was committed, it was not signified, and whither ther wer any such [errour or] noo, or any such byllet, I cannot imagi[ne, oonles i]t wer that u[nadvis]edly they delyvered the letters at ther first [arr]yval in Fraunce to the French King⁴ which wer endossed to the Kinges Majestie, and, as French men be soden, wer sodenly broken up there, and by reason therof⁵ they wanted letters to present to the Kinges Majestie; as in dede they had noon, as ye knowe, but oonly from ther colleges, wherat the Kinges Majestie thenne marveyled, and I myself thought it over negligently handled thenne, and nowe remembre it again by cause of th[at] errour [made in] delyveryng of the byllet, wherat the French King shuld finde faulte, as was wryten to the King

---

1 an *c.o.* 2 *alt. from* Geradd 3 Kinges *w. es c.o.* (?)
4 and thenne *c.o.* 5 *alt. from* wherof

of Romaynes Courte. I did not open the want of thiese letters, which, me thinketh, shuld have been the error*u*r in the byllet, but Gerarde wold fayne divise what it might be; and of error*u*r in delyvery of letters we had many prety tales which partely have chaunced by barbarye in the partie, partely by negligence, and, as it wer, contempte. Of the oon sorte we had example the Duke of Orlyaunce, who cam to the Emperour and put his hand in his pocket to seke for his letters and said he had lost them[1], which was over moch negligent in respecte to such a prynce as he cam to. Of the other sorte we had a mery tale [of a] Germayn, rude and grosse, who[2], when he shuld have [de]lyv[ered his] letters to the French King, put his hand in his poket to take out his letters and first pulled out, in stede of letters, a pece of chese, and thenne pulled out a pece of bakon, and thenne a lumpe of bred, and finally his letters, and soo delyvered them; wherin was set forth very barbary. And by occasion herof we talked of the barbary of the Turkes; and likewise the qualites of those th[at] wer nowe sent by the Protestantes wer spoken of, as men particulerly knowen to them, [as] Doctor Joannes Sledanus, Joannes Sturmius, and the Lansgraves[3] Marshal, who, for the familier discourses they be accustumed to make of the worlde, with an inclination they have to[4] a popularite, might easely be† made[5] negligent to delyver oon byllet for an other, if any such thing happened. What grounde this tale shuld have of chaunging the byllet, if ther wer any, you canne tel. I canne conjecture[6] noon but as I have wryten. But howsoever it was, thusmoch therof[7] may be noted, that the French King, who bifore praysed them, nowe notith them grosse. Howebeit that is noo mervayl neyther, and percace the French King said not soo of them, and yet it† maye be otherwise . . . . [an]d that is noo mervayl neyther in thiese dayes . . . .
. . . . tolde⟨?⟩ of passe tyme which had as moch myrth in it as if it had been trewe, and sum pleasour I have in the wryting of it. It was said also and wryten to the King of Romaynes Courte that the French King, after he sawe the Protestantes coulde not helpe hym to atteyne his purpose in Boleyn, wherin they had geven hym gret hoope, that he said we had procured them to cumme to his Courte to be as our spies, and therfor gave th. . . . . among them, and quikly dis-

---

1 † *abv.* it *c.o.*   2 shuld *c.o.*
3 *writ.* Lansgrad(?)es   4 h *c.o.*
5 *alt. from* make; them *c.o.*   6 coniiecture *w. second* i *c.o.*
7 made *c.o.*

peched them out of his Courte. And if this be ther rewarde in the latter
ende, they verifie the sentence that wisely admonisheth men to forbere
thoffice of a mediatour, who deriveth in to himself the blame of both
extremites, if the thing take not effecte.

As I had wryten thus far, I hard thEmperour wyl departe hens this
day sevenight and goo toward Germanye, bifore which tyme I trust to
here from England[1] and take my leave here and[2] byd them fare wel here
as I doo youe nowe, and hartely wel to fare. At Utrek the xxvij of
January.

[Your] assured
[loving] frend,

STE. WINTON

Addressed: To the Right Wourshipfull Sir Wyllyam Paget Knight
one of the Kinges Majesties two Principall Secretaryes.

Below address: Hast, hast,

hast,
with diligence.

Endorsed: [The Bishop of Winchester to Master Secretary, Master
Paget], xxvij° Januarii.

104. *To* SCEPPERUS

[Utrecht, 7 February, 1546]

R.O., S.P. 1, 214, 87–8. Contemporary copy, endorsed by Gardiner.
L.P., XXI, i, 216. *St. P.*, XI, 50. Manuscript copies, B.M., Galba B, x,
244, and Lansd. 171, 76–7, also containing Scepperus' protestation, are
incorrectly entered in *L.P.*, XXI, i, 217. English abstract in *L.P.*

> Likes not what Scepperus has written; the revised treaty does not affect the aid
> due to Henry from Charles; said so on New Year's Day, when Granvelle pro-
> mised to lay the matter before the Emperor. (This is an answer to a letter and
> protestation from Scepperus that the aid was not due. *L.P.*, XXI, i, 215. The
> date of Gardiner's letter, as well as the occasion of it, is given in *L.P.*, XXI, i,
> 212; the place is determined by *ib.*, 190; *see also* p. 148 above.)

Magnifice Domine. Legi quod misisti, et quanto attentius considero,
minus minusque placet, nec video quo consilio cupiat Grandvellanus ut
istis protestacionibus rem apertam obscuremus. Ista pacta ad subsidii

1 to ta *c.o.*   2 th *c.o.*

causam pertinere, omnino negamus, utpote quibus non id agebatur, ut subsidii nomine debitum auferatur. Qua in re, ne quid ambigatur, Calendis Ianuariis fecimus apud vos testatum, cum adhuc integrum vobis esset reclamare. Quo tempore Grandvellanus ad Cesaream Maiestatem se id relaturum promisit. Ut acta res est, ita narro. Quod si vel negetur, vel non serio actum dicatur, questio inde nascitur expedienda fide. Quod pacti sumus, curavimus haberi ratum. De eo vero quod pactis excipiebatur, equanimiter ferre debetis, ut convencionibus contineri sine contradictione negemus. Atque huc tantum respicit nostra protestacio, cui si aliam opponitis, quid aliud quam tenebras inducitis recenti et calenti dilucidacioni? Quid autem minus utibile quam inter ipsa initia pugnare protestacionibus, in re tam clara, in qua neque nostra negligentia tanta fuit, ut de quo dubitari posset, pretermitteremus silentio, neque vestra diligentia tam solers, ut verba adhiberetis auferendo quod debebatur efficacia. Subsidium enim a vobis oblatum fuit, ut pretensio dici nequeat, a vobis etiam concessum, ne dicatur differentia.

Debetur autem ex eo capite, in quo nulla est obscuritas, aut unquam fuit, nullave difficultas, que novis istis pactis daret occasionem. Que cum ita sint, certum est, subsidii causam manere integram, nec nostris istis pactionibus quoquo modo sublatam, vel nostra inertia, vel vestra solertia. Ut enim vos id minus cavistis, ita nos ne quid huiusmodi fieret, protestacione prospeximus tempestiva. Secundum quae, si ratificacionem vultis, dabimus. Quod autem nec fecimus nec audeamus, dabitis pro vestra humanitate veniam, si agnoscere detrectemus. Itaque tute tecum cogita oro, si quo modo hec res commode sine vestro magno damno et nulla nostra molestia expediatur. Et vale.

T. D. addictiss.

STE. WINTON

Endorsed by Gardiner: A copie of the letters of me, the Bishop of Winchestre, to Skepperus.

Endorsed in other hand: Copie of the Bisshop of Winchestres letter to Scipperius.

105. *To* PAGET

[Bois le Duc], 1 a.m., 14 [*i.e.*, 15] February, [1546]

R.O., S.P. 1, 214, 80–3.* *L.P.*, XXI, i, 214.

If he were superstitious he would predict good results from the revised treaty, because of the auspicious day on which ratifications were exchanged; the gross lying of Granvelle; none but the King should see this letter, lest it injure Scepperus who is an honest man; is 'clearly out with Granvelle.' (*See* above, p. 148, and *cf.* No. 104 and *L.P.*, XXI, i, 212, which also gives place of writing.)

Master Secretary, after my most harty commendations: I hartely thanke youe for your Parlament answers, which I like very wel, and thinke my-self happy to have sumwhat of pleasour to thinke on there, wherwith to tempre¹ the displeasours that I suffre here; which, although they have not torne me in peces, yet they shaked me for the tyme and caused me ⟨to⟩ lose a gret deale of tyme unfruetefully².

At the last ye shal receyve the Emperours† ratification in forme good ynough, but not passed after the best facion; and yet, if al thinges have ther reciprocation, as fayre wether and fowle have, we shuld thinke that bicause we have had† somoch long fowle wether in the passing of this matier, there shal succede fayre wether in the keping of it. And after the supersticion of the Chaldeyes, that noted dayes, we maye consider that the last treatie beganne in light and was passed in the mornyng upon a Sondaye, the xiiij^th daye of this moneth of February, and by reason of light, whenne men comenly† worke, might be a token of buysines, as ther folowed in dede, I am sory for it; soo this conclusion cummyth to passe³ upon the Saturday the xiij^th of the same moneth, being the Sab-bate, and towardes night and within night, which both signifie rest, which God graunte to folowe of it; wherof I wold be glad. But let supersticion goo; and yet every good token wer for the tyme to be embraced to temper the frowardnes of that hath chaunced. But super-sticion is nought; and soo hath been this handlyng⁴, and alsoo grosse. ThEgiptians wold punishe ther chyldern bicause they coulde not stele craftely and cary clene; and an elegant decyete with sum pretty poynte of wytte is wont to be laughed at, and hath sumtyme commendation as a juguler hath; but a playne rude denyal of that was said and doon by three, and in the presence of other, is soo fatte and grosse as it can saver to noo mannes appetite, but be lothesum to al that here of it. Ye wyl

1 r *in* tempre *writ. over* b(?)   2 t *in this word writ. over* f
3 passeth *w.* th *c.o.*   4 *alt. from* handled

aske why we charged not Skepperus to saye truth indifferently, and Skore also, who wer there. Mary, soo dyd we, but wysedom, as we cal it, a dexterite in sayling over the watier[1] of the[2] worlde, is[3] al oon every where; and they canne use it here, as I have seen elleswhere, not to offende authorite if it may be[4] shifted. Skore must nedes saye he harde it spoken of, for he spake in it, as we wrote, but yet, loo! Skore doth not remembre that Grandvela said he wold speke with thEmperour in it. For Skore[5] thought we wold not persiste in it, bycause it was soo lytel. As for Skepperus, ⟨he⟩ sate lowest at the borde and was otherwise occupied, but yet he † harde it spoken of, but howe, he coulde not tel. And Grandvela[6] spake nowe soo sternely in it and denyed it soo stowtely, that it wold [7]have made† oon that might feare a shrewde turne to have forgoten al, and thowgh he had remembred it but a Pater Noster while afore. Nowe if we had spoken to Grandvela *defunctorie* and for maners sake of it, and touched it *transcursim* and in a worde, it had been an other[8] matier; but we entred in to the matier notably, with shewing him the wordes of the proheme, and told hym that by them he shuld not take awaye the ayde alredy due, and charged hym with his promyse in it. And he said it was condicional in Germany. But I charged hym with his promyse at Bruges and with the matier itself, and wold not leave hym tyl it was ordred thEmperour shuld be spoken with in it; and then Skore said it shuld not extende to moch. And al this denyed, forgoten, and not harde! And whenne men of auctorite entre such errour, thenne it must be† borne out; and specially if Grandvela hath bosted his prohem bifore to thEmperour as a thing of such effecte and soo clerkely conceyved as is able to deceyve thre lawers; wherin I have for my pastyme sumwhat wryten to answer his goodly reasons[9], having noo pyth in them. Monsieur Skepperus had myn answer and red it, but he was afraide it was to sharpe, and soo he sayth he hath not copied it, but that he had it, ye maye see by his hande of the receyte of it.

Master Secretary, I most hartely desire youe[10], assone as thiese letters be red to the Kinges Majestie and as it shal please† his Highnes, to other ordre them soo as noo man see them after. Monsieur Skepperus is to his master as he shuld be, and to us of a good syncere honeste, and the cummyng forth of this thing might hurte hym.

1 *alt. from* matier	2 matier *c.o.*	3 *alt. from* as
4 shipped *c.o*	5 s *incomplete*	6 spoken *c.o.*
7 h *writ. over* a	8 A *c.o.*	9 hath *c.o.*
10 as *c.o.*		

I am clerely out with Grandvele, not that I have spoken anything to hym, for therin I have forborn *a comitiis*, but this is *summa contumelia quam non possum dissimulare*, oonles the Kinges Majestie commaunde me and the affayres soo require. I have told Skepperus at large, which wer expedient he told again, and it maye be that this faulte shal cause them to doo the better, and wyl if the tyme serve, *i.⟨e.⟩*, if eyther the French men be froward or we in sum towardnes of peace with Fraunce. But as we be, they thinke we have always nede. I have had a wonderful conflicte in myself for this matier[1], whither by delaying and sending hom I shuld have disapointed this matier or noo; but rather thenne they shuld have pressed that we had remitted it, al had goon[2] lost, for I[3] wyl not aventure the Kinges Majesties displeasour for any thing[4]. But nowe thiese men saye it was ever answred that the ayde was not due. Helpe us, whose fayth is in stryfe here, with that hath been confessed at hom by thambassadour. If the Kinges Majestie thinkith noo tyme nowe[†] to speke further in it, this buysines maye[5] resolve in sylence, and other thinges due by the freshe eclarishement demaunded, as victualles, etc.

I shal speke for Courtpenyng to the Quene, for to here ⟨*i.e.*, her⟩ it is referred; and Skeppere tellith me there wylbe noo doubte but men may cumme throwe by xl, l, and xxx in a companye.

I sende herwith the discourse of the Duke of Savoys ambassadour, not bicause I thinke any frute in it, but bicause I spake of it to thEmperour, to induce him to the warre, to tel him howmoch the Duke of Savoy longyth[6] for it.

I sende also herwith[7] the name of a captayn, which Bochold delyvered me, who wyl delyver the Kinges Majestie a towne of the frontier of Fraunce, without taking any money tyl he hath doon. I asked what towne [†]it is[†], but eyther he wold not or coulde not tel me.

ThEmperour wyl not tary at[8] Mastryke past fyve or sixe dayes, wherfore I praye youe help for my dispach.

Thiese men *properant in Germaniam*, and the matier of entre into the warre they dissemble tyl they knowe howe they finde thinges there.

The obligacions ye see howe they put them of by delaye.

The ayde hath, without frute, encombred us a good season, and the matier of mariage shalbe sent thither by as good a ministre as canne be.

---

1 eythe *c.o.*
3 av *c.o.*
5 for the tyme *c.o.*
7 with †

2 losse *c.o.*
4 Bu *meant to be c.o.*
6 *alt. from* longe(?)th
8 Utri *c.o.*

Thus desiryng ¹youe to² make my commendacions to al, I bydde youe hartely fare wel⁺. At oon of the clok in the mornyng, the xiiij^th of February.

Your assured loving
frend,

STE. WINTON

Addressed: To the Right W*ou*rshipfull Sir Wyllyam Paget, Knight, one of the Kinges Majesties two Principall Secretaries.

Below address: They seale here ther perpetuites with red waxe *de hoc dubitavimus et ita fuit responsum.*

Endorsed: The Bisshopp of Winch. to Master Secretary, Master Paget, xiiij° Februarii, 1545⟨46⟩.

106. *To* PAGET

[Maastricht, 2] March, 1546

R.O., S.P. 1, 214, 198–9.* *L.P.*, XXI, i, 316.

A trustworthy German of old acquaintance tells him that all the ambassadors from the German states are dissuading the Emperor from attacking the Bishop of Cologne; other news. (For place and date of writing *see L.P.*, XXI, i, 315.)

Master Secretary, after my most harty commendations: I thanke youe fore your diligence in depeching of Francisco ³with such diligence, and yet it toke not that effecte, for it was Saturday after none ⟨27 Feb.⟩ or he cam here. But he is cumme, and, as ye shal perceyve by our comen letters to the Kinges Majestie, al thinges better thenne they were.

ThEmperour this daye departith this towne and we also. Here have been with thEmperour ambassadours from al the states of Germany to desire hym on the bihaulf of the Bishop of Colen not to make warre against hym, but to remitte that matier to the Diet. I was very desirous to knowe sum certain truth of ther commissions, and in the myddes of my desire cam to visite me oon whom of al Germany I wold have, for his knowlege and truth, wished to have spoken with; and yet synne= I was at Ratisbone I owght hym a horse and was nowe even for sham= dryven to paye hym, and soo I dyd; but I had rather have geven hym xx markes; and thus the worlde doth mingle swete and sowre togither.

---

1 y *writ. over* t   2 *writ. over* m   3 w *writ. over* a

But his communication, as I examyned hym of particularites, was more worth to me for my satisfaction thenne my coste. He is lerned and of good reputacion. He told me theffecte of the[t] message of al thies ambassadours, which was oonly for the Bishop of Colen. Other particuler matiers I shal tel youe whenne I[1] cumme hom, which shalbe as shortly as I canne. Mary, [2]bicause I have a pasporte general for myself to cary what I lyst, I have advertised Master Vaugham that I wyl cumme by Antwerpe, and if he wyl send any money by me, to carye it under my passeporte, if the other required shuld have any delaye.

I send youe here such newes as are[t] abrode among the ambassadours of that is said and doon at Trent in ther conciliable, where be gaye wordes.

Thus I bydde youe hartely fare wel.

Captayne Buckholt, with whom I shuld have spoken to knowe further of the townes name shuld be delyvered, is not here. He hath of late buryed his wife and lost the gret parte of his lyving. Whenne he was with me, I pressed hym moch to have knowen that I shuld nowe knowe, but he wold in noo wise tel, bicause it was a gret matier, I wrote, but synnes, I feare it was but a practise to get himself in favour to have such money as he chalengith of Chamberlain; but we cannot tel where to have hym. Thus[3] oones again fare ye wel.

Your assured loving
frend,

STE. WINTON

Addressed: To the Right Worshipfull Sir Wyllyam Paget, Knight, oon of the Kinges Majesties Principal Secretaryes.

Endorsed: The Bishop of Winchester to Master Secretary, Master Paget, Martii, 1545⟨46⟩.

1 co *c.o.*   2 b *writ. over* I
3 *writ. over something else*

Antwerp, 6 March, 1546

R.O., S.P. 1, 215, 3–4.* *L.P.*, XXI, i, 337.

What credit is to be given to one Musica who professes to be in the King's service? Sends report of the chapter of the Order of the Golden Fleece; Schore gives him hope that money and victuals may be had.

Master Secretary, after my most harty commendations: Synnes my departure from my Lord of Westmester, I receyved from him letters, with other letters, from oon Musica to youe, which ye shal[1] receyve herwith, and my Lord of Westmesters to me also; whereby ye maye perceyve that Musica is *musicus*, if, cummyng soo late out of England, his mony is goone alredy. Musica, as he wryteth to youe, sawe not me [†]at Mastryke[†], but I harde there of hym, which thiese letters and his bordyng of my Lord of Westmester doo sumwhat conferme to be trewe. The mannes fawte is not in lak of wytte, but in the using of that he hath. Thusmoch I thinke very necessary to wryte, bicause, under the title of the Kinges Majesties service, he wyl take upon hym, as ye may perceyve, both to speke, wryte, and goo; and that he shal speke without commission shalbe taken as spoken of the Kinges Majesties servaunt with commission. I mervel if he shuld be sent for to Duke Mauryce; for Carolicius, he spekith of, who is Duke Mauryce ambassadoui, was with me and hath[2] with me very familiar[3] acquayntaunce and, among other communications, told me of his legation appointed [4]from the Duke his master to the Kinges Majestie, conteyning oonly pleasaunte wordes, and to renewe the favour the Kinges Majestie hath borne to his predecessours; and by reason this Carolicius fyl syk at Spyre, it was letted, but not revoked; and Carolicius trustith to cumme yet herafter this. Youe[5] knowe Musica better thenne I, and my Lord of Westmester wold fayne knowe howe to use hym without blame at hom, wherin my Lord of Westmester wold have my counsayl, and I, for answer, have allowed *prudenciam*, to geve six crownes rather thenne lose xxx, or lende it to him, which hath noo gret difference, oonles my Lord of Westmester may have a larger letter of commendations from youe. But[6] if Musica writeth[7] and gooth in the Kinges Majesties affayres, as in his letters he

---

1 ree *c.o.*
2 of *c.o.*
3 *writ.* famirial
4 fr *writ. over* t(?)
5 *alt. from* your
6 † *abv.* for *c.o.*
7 in *c.o.*

sayth he doth, my Lord of Westmester shalbe perplexed to refuse hym whenne he askith money, and yet with sum care departe with the money and putte it, as they cal it, in hucsters handeling. If ye wryte herin a worde to my Lord of Westmester, ye shal do hym moch pleasour.

I send also herwith a letter from Monsieur de Bure to the Kinges Majestie, conteyning, as Monsieur de Bure sayth, the certificate of thinges doon in this chaptre of the Ordre. In delyveraunce herof, I praye youe forget not Monsieur de Bures protestacion which he made to me concernyng the superscription[1], unsemely and unmete to be wryten from hym, who professeth[2] al service to the Kinges Majestie and hymself unworthy to use such familiarite, but bicause he was nowe the Kinges Majesties proctour, the letter, forme, and direction is made by the commen officer, the registre, after ther forme, which he most humbly desireth the Kinges Majestie not to impute unto hym.

Synnes the departure of Master Carne †to Brucelles†, I have had a long communication with President Skore, who overtoke me in the waye. I wold have knowen the answer of the Quene, but, for al the answer he made to my servauntes, he durst not tel me it tyl he cam to the Quene; and there it shalbe made to Master Carne, and by hym brought to[3] me; for I told hym I wold not from Antwerpe tyl I had it. He gave me lightlywode to have both money and victualles, and, for hymself, thought it reasonable. He put the most doubte in caryages, bicause we have soo evel entreated them; and what we had talked throughly he[4] protested that I shuld take noo hope of any thing tyl he had spoken with the Quene. But undowtedly, he sayth, al that is con-ven⟨au⟩nted shalbe perfourmed on ther parte, both by cause they have conven⟨au⟩nted it and also bicause ther owne proufite is† in it; for our victorie is thers. I cast out a worde to hym that he shuld not lose his gratuite to the Kinges Majestie. In communication he confesseth this to be thEmperours tyme [to] set in fote with us, and said that they wante victualles for such a purpose, wherby I perceyve they have thought on it. Finally I have left hym aswel affected as canne be, and specially he recommendith hym to youe, and soo doo I also, and bydde youe fare well tyl my cummyng, which shalbe as shortly as I canne. I loke this night for Master Carne; and Master Vaugham sayth he wyl send sum

---

1 us *c.o.*   2 eth *writ. over something else*
3 f(?) *c.o.*   4 w *c.o.*

money by me to Calays. Thus eftsones fare ye wel[1]. At Antwerp, the vj[th] of [2]March.

Your assured loving frend,

STE. WINTON

Addressed: To the Right Wourshipfull Sir Wyllyam Paget, Knight, one of the Kinges Majesties two Principall Secretaries.

Endorsed: The Bishop of Wynchester to Master Secretary, Master Paget, vj° Martii, 1545⟨46⟩.

108. *To* PAGET

Antwerp, 7 March, with postscript, 8 March, 1546

R.O., S.P. 1, 215, 13–14; postscript, *ib.*, 38–9.* *L.P.*, XXI, i, 344, 360.

Now feels free to return; report of the death of the Count of Enghien; sends a French libel on England. *P.S.* Damsel's purchase of grain should be approved.

Master Secretary, after my most harty commendations: Nowe this answer is cumme from the Quene, I accounpte myself at libertie to re-tou*r*ne, which I wyl doo as shortly as I canne. The wether is fayre and al the [way]es more p[lea]saunte[3] thenne they were.

Master Governo*u*r shewed me a letter wryten to hym from a wise felawe—I knowe wel the man—wherin is conteyned that the Dolphyn of Fraunce, castyng a cofer out of a wyndowe, hath slayne Monsie*u*r de Engyne. If it be soo, it is fowle wether there, thowe it be never t[he] worse for us.

Here[4] is[5] a French losel hath wryten forth in fayre langage of Laten most fowle matier mixt with abhominable lyes of our realme. Master Damsel delyvered it unto me and I sende it unto youe. There is oon evident lye to, as there be many more, but this is within memorie and it toucheth knowlege, knowl[e]ge which the man bosteth[6]. He sayth that King Henry the vij[th], being of the House of Yorke, maryed King Edwardes doughter, being of the House of Lancastre. Soo diligently had he serched the storyes and such is his knowlege! And he sayth in his preface that the[7] cause why the French men conquere not us is want

1 *alt. from* wyl
3 I(?) *c.o.*
5 *alt. from* as

2 M *writ. over* f
4 Here *is preceded by* The, *evidently meant to be c.o.*
6 *alt. from* bosted
7 they *w.* y *c.o.*

240

of knowlege. And howmoch trewe knowlege he hath, he declarith pretely, making such a notable error*u*r in tyme of memore. Thus I bydde youe hartely fare wel. At Antwerpe the vijth of Marche.

Your assured loving
frende,

STE. WINTON

Addressed: To the Right Wurshipfull Sir Wyllam Paget, Knight, one of the Kinges Majesties two Principall Secretaries.

Post scripta: Ye shal understand that Master Damsel hath made a bargayn for MMM ⟨3000⟩ quarters rye and M ⟨1000⟩ quarters wheate, to be delyvered at London or Calays for xvj *s*. rye and xxv *s*. wheate, good and swete, without any licence of this countrie. He asked myn advice in[1] the[2] accepting of the bargain and I allowed his doing, and soo did Master Vaugham also, and sayth the Kinges Majestie payd asmoch[3] to other. I praye youe to cause Damesyl to be wryten unto that it is liked there, soo as he maye have of Master Vaughand money for furniter of the same. Thusmoch Master Damsel desired me to wryte, which delayed the departing of this post tyl this mornyng. Thus fare ye eftsones hartely wel[4]. At Antwerp[5], the viijth of March.

Your assured loving
frend,

STE. WINTON

Addressed: To the Right Wo*u*rshipfull Sir Wyllm Paget, Knight, one of the Kinges Majesties two Principall Secretaries.

Endorsed: My Lord of Wynchester to Master Secretary, Master Paget, viij° Martii, 1545⟨46⟩.

109. *To* PAGET

Eccloo, 11 March, 1546

R.O., S.P. 1, 215, 59–60.* *L.P.*, XXI, i, 372.

Will deliver to Sir Edward Wotton, treasurer of Calais, the money he brings with him.

Master Secretary, after my right harty commendations: This daye bytwen Eclo and Stekon, in my waye to Calays, I receyved your letters by

---

1 † *abv.* for *c.o.*   2 t *c.o.*   3 as *c.o.*
4 the *c.o.*   5 *alt. from* Atwerp

Nicolas the currour, and shal, accordyng to the contentes therof, delyver to Master Wotton such summes of money as shalbe conveyed in my cumpayne. Hitherto I have but xx^M ⟨20,000⟩ crownes, but Master Chamberlain taryeth behinde and bringeth more, with appoyntement that I shal tary for hym on the waye. For it was thought not good that I shuld have taryed any lenger at Antwerpe, lest they shuld have suspected I had taryed therfor. Master Vaughan said he did asmoch as he coulde to recover that I have, and wyl send by Master Chamberlain the rest. It shal make the lesse matier, seeing we have licence for cc^M ⟨200,000⟩, which ye knewe not at the wryting of your letters; and I trust ye† knowe it by this tyme. And soo I bydde youe hartely fare wel. At Eclo, the xjth of Marche.

Your assured loving
frend,

STE. WINTON

Addressed: To the Right Wourshipfull Sir Wyllyam Paget, Knight, one of the Kinges Majesties two Principall Secretaries.

Endorsed: My Lord of Winchester to Master Secretary, Master Paget, xj Marcii, 1545⟨46⟩.

INTRODUCTORY NOTE TO NOS. 110–4

These five letters complete the correspondence in the reign of Henry VIII. The first two are replies to questions from Paget about matters diplomatic. The next two (Nos. 112–3) have to do with an exchange of lands, requested by Henry VIII, to which, it appears, Gardiner had made some objection. That he had done so seems to indicate that he felt himself secure in the favour of the King, who was then at Oatlands, Gardiner being engaged in governmental business in London. It was at this time that the Hertford-Lisle group were endeavouring to undermine Gardiner's influence in the government, and there can be little doubt that they did everything possible to magnify the King's irritation at his reluctance to give up the coveted lands. How far Paget had already thrown in his lot with Hertford it is impossible to say. The King's rather tart reply to Gardiner has been preserved in Foxe, VI, 138 (*L.P.*, XXI, ii, 493), but we have no manuscript of it, either in draft or final form, hence there is no way of telling which of the King's two secretaries, Paget or Petre, composed it. It was signed by stamp, not by the King's hand (*L.P.*, XXI, ii, 647 [10]).

110. *To* PAGET

Southwark, [23] July, 1546

R.O., S.P. I, 222, 71–2.* *L.P.*, XXI, i, 1329 (1).

Gives his opinion on the form of the oath to be taken by Henry VIII to the treaty with France (concluded 7 June. *Cf. L.P.*, XXI, i, 1014. The date of this letter, [23], supplied by *L.P.*, is doubtless arrived at from Gardiner's statement that he is about to go to Hampton Court, and his absence from the Privy Council meeting at Westminster, 24 July. No meeting is recorded on the 23rd, and he was present again at Westminster on the 25th. The time for the King's oath to the treaty had been postponed on 17 July—*L.P.*, XXI, i, 1295).

Master Secretary, I have considered both the formes of othes, and in my[1] jugement eyther forme is sufficient. This difference I finde, that the forme sent by youe is more civile, for therin it is expressed, by thexplication of *quatenus etc.*, that neyther prince shalbe bounde to[2] observe

---

1 myn *w*. n *c.o.*   2 b(?) more *c.o.*

any[1] more of the leage thenne touchith his parte; that is to say, asmoch as concernith hymself, his heyres, his realmes, and subgettes; wheras elles, leaving out that *quatenus*, after the forme sent from my Lord Admyral, a lawer that wold be seen to knowe more thenne the rest might geve advise not to swere to kepe the hol treatie, lest therby ech prince shuld be bounde to kepe his felaws parte aswel as his owne; and if that wer so, thenne shuld treaties never be broken. And upon this scrupule, although it be grosse, the general forme sent by them, where your *quatenus* is left out, might percace be mysliked. But elles what might move the French King to styk at the forme sent by youe[2], I cannot imagine, for it is[3] agreable to reason and his ratification also. But which soever of the formes passe, it makith noo matier, for that is opened cively with your *quatenus*, the same must be understanded cively in the generalite.

But nowe bicause I wyl be seen to doo sumwhat, I have wryten the former parte of the othe soo far as your forme and thers agree, wherin I have oonly medled with the French Kinges style and placed the word *Christianissimi* to be an adjective to his state, and soo we ever wryte it. I have also added *consanguinei*. And whither to *confederati* ye wyl put *perpetui*, as I praye God it may be in dede, I remitte to youe to be considered.

And thus entending to goo to Hamptoncourte, according to the Kinges Majesties pleasour, I bydde youe[4] hartely fare wel. At my hous this mornyng.

Your assured loving
frend,

STE. WINTON

Addressed: To my loving frend Sir William Paget, Knight, oon of the Kinges Majesties Principal Secretaryes.

Endorsed: The Bisshoppe of Winchestre to Master Secretary, Master Paget, ⟨*blank*⟩ Iulii, 1546.

1 † *abv.* no *c.o.*	2 *alt. from* your
3 *alt. from* as	4 *alt. from* your

London, 11 October, 1546

R.O., S.P. 1, 225, 181–2.* *L.P.*, XXI, ii, 256. *St. P.*, I, 880.

Describes conference with Philip, Duke of Bavaria, nephew of Frederick the Elector, the Rhinegrave, Philip Francis, and Dr Ouercentanus, in September, when they came to negotiate a marriage between Princess Mary and the Duke and a league between Henry VIII and the Elector. (The Duke had also been in England on a similar mission in March, and Mason had returned with him to Heidelberg to continue negotiations with the Elector—*cf. L.P.*, XXI, index.)

Master Secretary, after my[1] most harty commendacions: As towching the conference with Duke Philip and the other, wherof ye desire to be advertised, ye shal understand that, being my Lord Chaunceler, my Lord Gret Master, my Lord Chamberlain, and myself appointed to here what shuld be said on ther parte, they alleging that ther[2] letters, with ther commission, perished[3] at Gravelyng, said theffecte of ther cummyng was upon an overture mad[e] by[4] Master Mason. Wherupon they wer sent to knowe what the Kinges Majestie wold saye un[to] them, and[5] further to[6] knowe a favorabl[e] resolution in the matier of maryage; wheru[pon], they said, the rest shuld depende and ensue. And for the first tyme, bicause we coulde not induce them to begynne to speke any specialtie, and we had noothing to saye[7] to† them, we said, by waye of communication, that we toke the maryage to be rather thende, wherunto the lightlywode of the other matiers shuld be an inducement; and as those appered faysable, soo to speke of the mary[age], and not otherwise. And for the tyme, we said, we toke not Master Massons commission[8] to have allured them hither, which was playnly, precisely, and peremptoryly denyed and refused. Nevertheles, we said, we wold speke with Master Mason against the next mornyng, and so retourne to speke with them; which was doon. And on the morowe Master Mason went with us and clerely veryfied the maner of the[9] answer to such overture as was made† by hym, and ther called to witnesse Duke Philip, who coulde not denye it, wherby appered that they cam nowe as men repentyng the refusal made, and desirous of communication therin; and

---

1 *alt. from* our
3 prerished *w. first* r *c.o.*
5 t *c.o.*
7 to saye *repeated and c.o.*
9 *alt. from* this

2 *alt. from* wer
4 † *abv.* my *c.o.*
6 † *abv.* med(?) *c.o.*
8 commissions *with* s *c.o.*

therupon beganne to declare the conformite and inclination of the Countie Palantyne[1] to a leage with the Kinges Majestie, wherunto the rest of the princes Protestantes shuld be also induced; and therwith exhibyted a *capita* of articles of a leage, agreying, in effecte, with those conteyned in Master Masons instructions; which *capita* we toke of them, and therwith reapared to the Kinges Majestie[2], whose resolution was, that to wynne tyme, wherby to knowe better the state of the [3]thynges, we shuld retourne to them and allege the gretnes and waight of the matier to require commission bifore any further[4] communication; which they might nowe have good opportunite to sende for at good laysour, with allegacion of the Kinges Majesties removing that daye, and our repare to London. They thought we spake reason, and agreed soo to doo. Nevertheles they made a motion that we shuld have procured the Kinges Majesties letters to the Countie Palantyne, which we soo avoyded as they agreed ther request to be unreasonable. And herwith we bad them fare wel, as I doo nowe to youe, and departed, as I doo nowe to youe in thies letters. From London, the xj[th] of Octobre, at night.

> Your assured loving
> frend,
>
> STE. WINT[ON]

Addressed: To the Right Wourshipful Sir Wyllyam Paget, Knight, oon of the Kinges Majesties two Principal Secretaryes.

Endorsed: The Bishop of Winchestre to Master Paget, Secretary, xj° Octobris, 1546.

112. *To* HENRY VIII

London, 2 December, 1546

R.O., S.P. 1, 226, 219–20.* *L.P.*, XXI, ii, 487. *St. P.*, I, 883. Maitland, *Essays*, 330.

Humbly begs pardon if he has offended by an apparent refusal to exchange certain lands with the King (*see* No. 113).

Pleasith it your Most Excellent Majestie to pardonne me that, having noo such opportunite to make humble sute to your Highnes presence as the trouble of my mynde enforcyth me, I am soo bold to moleste your Majestie with thiese my letters, which be oonly to desyre your

1 *alt. from* Palaytyne   2 † *abv. by* ^.o.
3 th *writ. over* ki   4 whi *c.o.*

Highnes, of your accustumed goodnesse and clemencie, to be my good and gratious lorde, and to continue such opinion of me as I have ever trusted and, by manyfold benefites, certaynly knowen your Majestie to have had of me, and not to empayre it, as I veryly trust your Majestie wyl not, tyl your Highnes knowith, by myself, my dedes and bihavour to deserve the same; which I trus[t] never to see. Your Majestie hath bounde noon other of your subgettes m[ore] thenne me; and I have ever, and doo make thaccounpte of your Ma[jesties] benefites, soo as I esteme them worthely, asmoch as any other hat[h] receyved, wherwith I have and doo rejoyse and counforte myself, with a mynde, desire, and entent in service, which is al of duetie, in sum parte to declare myn inward re- joyse of your Highnes fav[our], and that I wold not wyllingly offende your Majestie for noo wordly ⟨*i.e.*, worldly⟩ thing. This is my harte, afore God, and noo man hath harde me saye to the contrary; and if, for want of circumspection, my doinges or saynges be otherwise taken in this matier of land[es], wherin I was spoken with, I must and wyl lamente myn infelici[te], and most humbly on my knees desire your Majestie to pardon it.

I never said naye to any request made, wherwith to resiste your Highnes pleasour, but oonly, in most humble wise, toke upon me to be a suter to your Highnes goodnes, wherunto I have ben[t] bolded by thaboundaunce of your Majesties favour hertofore shewed unto me. Your Highnes hath made me, without my desertes; and though I de- serve not the continuaunce of that favour, yet I wold gladly, by humble prayour and intercession, supplie my want, if I coulde, to have such help at your Highne[s] handes as I knowe others to have had, to be enter- taigne[d] for reputacion whenne ther service hath fayled; wherin I have had as gratious answer from your Majestie as I coulde wishe, for the which I most humbly thanke your Highnes. And yet, bicause I have noo accesse to your Majestie, ne hearing of late any more of this matier, I cannot forbere to open truly my harte to your Highnes, with most humble request to take the same in most gratious parte; for whose most prosperous felicite I shal, according to my duetie, praye duryng my life. At London, the seconde of Decembre.

> Your Majesties most humble and
> obedient subget, servaunt, and
> dayly bedeman,
>
> STE. WINTON

Addressed: To the Kinges Most Excellent Majestie.

Endorsed: The Bishoppe of Winchestre to the Kinges Majestie, the seconde of December, 1546.

113. *To* PAGET

Southwark, 2 December, 1546

R.O., S.P. 1, 226, 221–2.* *L.P.*, XXI, ii, 488. *St. P.*, 1, 884. Maitland, *Essays*, 332.

> Asks Paget to deliver his letter (No. 112) to the King, and find out if he may come himself; hears that his doings are not well taken. (The King replied to Gardiner that he would not deny him audience at 'any meet time,' but if he were willing to exchange the lands, as he professed, he might do so without further molesting him—*L.P.*, XXI, ii, 493.)

Master Secretary, after my right harty commendacions: I trusted to have seen youe here or this tyme, and to have knowen by youe the Kinges Majesties pleas*our*; but your lettes may be diverse, and therfor, as I thought to have wryten by youe to the Kinges Majestie at your being here, soo, not hearing from youe, I have thought requisite to wryte to his Majestie, to supplie my present sute to his person, which I wold gladly make, if it might stand with his pleas*our*. In the meane tyme, I praye youe delyver my letters, and also knowe whither I maye cumme myself; which I have forborn, bycause I have been here appointed for execution of a commission, wherunto I attende, as the tyme requireth; and of the rest, such as came nowe to the Courte, wer specially sent for.

I here noo specialte of the Kinges Majesties myscontentement[1] in this matier of landes[2], but, confusely, that my doinges shuld not be wel taken; wherof I am sory if it soo be, and, al other cares set aparte, care oonly for this, that it shuid be thought I wanted discretion, to[3] neglecte the Kinges Majesties goodnes towardes me, which, as ye knowe, I have ever estemed oonly, and therupon made my wordly ⟨*i.e.*, worldly⟩ foundation. *Nihil ambio nisi principis gratissimi benevolentiam ne videar ingratus, a quo crimine semper longissime abfuit animus*; wherin, to the rest of the worlde I knowe myself purged *quo nomine me duco infelicis-*

---

1 but *c.o.*   2 an *in* landes *writ. over something else*
3 t *c.o.*

248

simum ut ingratitudinis nomine veniam in suspitionem principi de me optime merito. I praye youe send me sum worde. And so fare ye [1]hartely wel. At Southwark, the ij^de of Decembre.

Your assured loving
frend,
STE. WINTON

Addressed: To the Right Wourshipful Sir[2] Wylliam Paget, Knight, oon of the Kinges Majesties two Principal Secretaryes.

Endorsed: The Bishoppe of Winchestre to Master Secretary, Master Paget, ij° Decembris, 1546.

114. *To the* READER

1546

From *A Detection of the Devils Sophistrie, wherwith he robbeth the unlearned people of the true byleef in the most blessed Sacrament of the aulter.* London, 1546. There are two editions of the same date, place and form. The wording is the same in both, but there are variations in spelling. B.M., c. 53, b. 16 is that here followed.

> Seek truth by the direction of the Church and conform knowledge to obedience.

Steven, Bisshop of Winchester, to the Reader

Consyder, Gentle Reader, how full of iniquite this tyme is, in whiche the hyghe mysterie of our religion is so openly assaulted. Byleve not every spirite, and mystruste thyne owne judgement above the reache of thy capacite. If thou beest hungrye for knowlege, take hede thou fallest not on every careyn. Be desyrouse of the very truth, and seke it as thou art ordered, by the direction of Christes Churche, and not as deceytful teachers wold leade the, by theyr secrete wayes. Folowe God and his mynisters, whome he ordereth to rule, and rather conforme knowlege to agree with obedience, where Goddes truthe repugneth not unto it, then with violation of obedience, which is a displeasaunt fault, to enterprise the subversion of Goddes honour and glorie. Finally, reade, when thou readest, with favour to that truth which the consent of

---

1 h *writ. over* w   2 Sir *repeated, doubtless meant to be c.o.*

Christes Church hath from the beginnyng commended unto us; and reverently at theyr handes receyve the true understandynge of Scriptures, whose true testimonie hath certified us of the selfe same Scriptures. And have alwayes in remembraunce the wordes of Saynt James, how God resisteth the presumptuouse and arrogant and geveth grace to suche as be in spirite meke and lowly; which gyfte God graunte the, and well to fare.

INTRODUCTORY NOTE TO NOS. 115–29

These letters were written during the first eight months of Edward VI's reign, while Gardiner, though out of power, was still at liberty. He did not hesitate to advise his former friend and diplomatic colleague Hertford, now Duke of Somerset and Lord Protector, on matters political and ecclesiastical (*see especially* No. 117), nor freely to express his views on what were as yet, for the most part, anticipatory intimations of changes about to take place.

The first letter in the group is to his former protégé Paget, whom, it seems, he still regarded as his friend, although it was now clear that he had gone over to the Protector's party—was in fact the Protector's right-hand man. The letter, showing the Bishop's concern at the avowed intent of a troop of players to give a play in Southwark before Henry VIII's burial, is in the old friendly manner. Indeed, he seems to have taken the political overturn with good grace, feeling that he was on intimate enough footing with both Somerset and Paget to exert some influence on their policies, even if he were himself excluded from the government. We do not have Paget's reply to this letter, but Gardiner's next—and last—to him indicates that he had begun to be aware of a change in Paget's attitude. He makes some straightforward comment on his behaviour, and incidentally says some interesting things about his own philosophy of life (No. 118).

In Nos. 116 and 117 we have his reflections on the Court sermons of two of the reformers, Ridley and Barlow. Ridley's denunciation of images and holy water called forth a spirited defence of both, containing interesting incidental references to the homely attitude of the people toward images, and the royal custom of blessing cramp rings. The actual destruction of images, the spread of Protestant books and plays, the growing disregard of Lent, all set his pen going (Nos. 119–21), drawing from him a denunciation of John Bale, and a frank avowal that, in his opinion, Anne Askew deserved the death at the stake which she suffered in 1546. When speaking of the value of Lent in restraining the English belly, he aptly characterized the shortcomings of the various nations of Europe (No. 120); and, when he was reminded of Henry VIII by the manner of Somerset's writing, gave a notable description of the late sovereign and of his own relations with him (No. 121).

Early in July, 1547, came Cranmer's revival of a proposal, made in Convocation in 1542, to issue a book of homilies; in the composition of which, surprisingly enough, he appears to have invited Gardiner to take part, or at any rate sought his approval of the scheme. Nos. 122–5 are devoted to a discussion of the project, in which Gardiner quite rightly smelt doctrinal innovation (*cf.* Thomas Watson's testimony concerning Gardiner's letters to Cranmer at this time, in Foxe, VI, 205). He appealed to the *King's Book* as the sufficient and still the legal standard of doctrine, as well as to Cranmer's own sense of consistency, urging him to maintain the doctrine to which he had agreed and publicly adhered for some years past. There are two short letters on this subject to Somerset (Nos. 122–3), and two long ones to Cranmer (Nos. 124–5). There is reference to another to Cranmer, the first of the series, which is lost, as are Cranmer's replies, but the two long letters we have give us a reasonably good idea of what Cranmer had to say on the matter. They are, moreover, of supreme interest, not only for their presentation of Gardiner's views and temper, but also for their reference to recent events, and contemporary customs. There is the account of the composition of the *Bishops' Book* in 1537; of the attempt to issue a new translation of the Bible in 1542; of Gardiner's part in the 'plot' against Cranmer in 1543; of Henry VIII's appointment of Gardiner as his chief minister. There are references to poorly attended lectures at Cambridge, and several enlightening passages on the religious habits of the people. We learn of the (to the modern view) amazing behaviour of worshippers who spent their time at Mass going about collecting debts; of parishioners (in very modern fashion) asking who was going to preach and regulating their attendance at service accordingly, and forgetting immediately thereafter what they had heard the preacher say; of the congregation who walked out of church to drink whenever the vicar ascended the pulpit; of the small respect for parish priests; of Englishmen, almost as nimble-witted as Italians, who disliked long sermons; of friars never preaching where they were known. There is the 'merry tale' of the theological mayor of Cambridge and how he preserved himself from heresy when disputing with the scholars; and another of the elderly divine who tried in vain to discover who was the father of Zebedee's children. Finally, there is the remark of Henry VIII in which he referred to himself as 'the old man'!

Although Gardiner was blamed for fearing innovation where none was meant, the event justified his fears. On 31 July, 1547, the *First Book of Homilies* was issued, and with it royal injunctions providing that every parson in the land read one of them each Sunday to his people. As Gardiner had foreseen, Cranmer's homily on salvation taught the doctrine of justification by faith, which he believed to be contrary at once to Catholic truth and to the *King's Book*. By the time he had procured and read the injunctions and the *Homilies* the Protector had set out on his Scottish campaign, so Gardiner addressed a protest to the Council, pointing out not only what he deemed to be the false teaching of the *Homilies* but also the effect which official sanction of Protestant doctrine would be likely to have on the Emperor and his alliance with England (No. 126). This he followed almost immediately by a second letter on the legal aspect of the matter. According to an act of Parliament of 1543, any departure, said Gardiner, not sanctioned by Parliament, from the doctrine established by Parliament was unlawful (No. 127). This gave rise to some significant discussion of the relation of the royal supremacy to Statute Law, in Nos. 128 and 129, carried still farther in No. 130 in the next group. No. 129 is, by the way, that letter of Gardiner's which has, says Burnet, 'more of a Christian and a bishop in it than anything I ever saw of his.'

115. *To* Paget

Southwark, 5 February, 1547

R.O., S.P. 10, 1, 8–9.* In part in Tytler, 1, 21.

Asks Paget to prevent the Earl of Oxford's (John de Vere's) players from giving a play in Southwark between the death and burial of Henry VIII. (The earls of Oxford appear to have had their players as early as 1492— see J. P. Collier, *History of English Dramatic Poetry*, London, 1879, 1, 50.)

Master Secretary, after my right harty commendations: I sent unto youe my servaunt yesterdaye, wherin by your advise I have had redresse; and nowe I wryte unto youe in an other matier sumwhat gretter, as it were bitwen game and ernest. Tomorowe the parisheners of this parish and I have agreed to have solempne Dirige for our late soverain lorde and master, in ernest, as becommith us; and tomorowe certain players of my Lord of Oxfordes, as they saye, entende on the other syde, within this borough of Southwarke, to have a solempne playe, to trye who shal have most resorte, they in game or I in ernest; which me semeth a mervelous contencion, wherin sum shal professe in the name of the commen welth, myrth, and sum[1] sorowe, at oon tyme.

[1] joye *c.o.*

Herin I folowe the commen determynation to sorowe tyl our late master be buryed. And what the lewd felawes shuld meane in the contrary[1] I canne[2] [not] tel, nor cannot refourme it, and therfor wryte u[nto youe] who, by meanes of my Lord Protectour, maye procu[re] an uniformite in the commen welth: al the body to doo oon thing, and in the[3] entering of our old master to lament to gither, and in the crownyng of our newe master to rejoyse to gither; after which folowith incontinently a tyme of lamentacion for synne ⟨i.e., Lent⟩, which is not to be neglected, and wherin I doubt not ye wyl, without me, consider your charge. I have herin spoken with Master Acton, justice of peax, whom the players smally regarde, and presse hym to a peremptorie answer, whither he dare lette them to playe or not. Wherunto he answerth neyther ye nor naye as to the playing; but as to† the assemble of people in this borough, in this tyme, neyther the buryal finished, ne the coronation doon, he pleadeth to the players for the tyme naye, tyl he have commaundement to the contrary. But his naye is not moch regarded, and myn lesse, as partye to players. And therfor I wryte unto youe, wherin if ye wyl not, *propter invidiam*, medle, sende me soo worde, and I wyl myself sewe to my Lord Protectour. For me thinketh it is *nimis barbarum* to playe *in luctu*, and to moch money lost in blakkes, if we ought rather to playe as thiese playing bestes ⟨i.e., beasts⟩ pretendith. For like as *in rebus prosperis* it hath been accustumed *indicere gaudium publicum*, soo it is likewise honorable *in adversis indicere luctum*; which shal set forth the coronation of our newe master as blakke settith forth white. *Quod de hiis nimium multa vale*, and do as ye shal thinke good. And soo fare ye wel. At my house in Southwarke the vth of February.

Your assured loving
frend,

STE. WINTON

Addressed: To the Right Wourshipful Sir William Paget, Knight[4], oon of the Kinges Majesties Two Principal Secretaryes.

Endorsed: The Bishop of Winchestre to Master Secretary, Master Paget, v° Februarii, 1546⟨47⟩.

1 *a letter after* n *in contrary c.o.*   2 t c.o.
3 b c.o.   4 of(?) c.o.

116. *To* RIDLEY

[Southwark, between 23 and 28 February, 1547]

Foxe, *1563*, 751–4; *1583*, II, 1348; ed. Pratt, VI, 58.

Has heard Ridley's sermon at Court (on Ash Wednesday, 23 February). Agrees with Ridley's confutation of Papal authority and pardons, but not with his denunciation of images and holy water. Images are not idols; Luther retained them; even the Church of Rome forbids idolatry; refers to creeping to the cross on Good Friday, and the English laity's attitude toward the crucifix; the right use of images; why not quote the text against graven images to prohibit the graving of type? The *King's Book* contains the true doctrine of images. Holy water is merely a vehicle of grace, as are the King's cramp rings the vehicle of royal healing; Henry VIII's use of these rings; specific directions in Scripture are not needed to validate ceremonies, continued use in the Church is sufficient.

Master Ridley, after right harty commendations: It chaunced me upon Wednesday last paste to be present at your sermond in the Court, wherin I hard you confirm the doctrine in religion set forth by our late soveraine lorde and master, whose soule God pardon, admonishing your audience that ye wold specially travayle in the confutacion of the bishop of Romes pretended authoritie in government and usurped power in perdons, wherby he hathe abused himselfe, in heaven and earthe. Whiche two matters I note to be playne, and here without controversy. In the other two ye spake of, touching images and ceremonies, and, as ye touched it, specially for holy water to drive away devils, for that ye declared your self allwayes desirous to set forth the mere truth, with great desire of unitie, as ye professed, not extending any your asseveration beyond your knowledge, but alwaies adding suche like words, 'as farre as ye had red,' and, 'if any man could shew you furder, ye woulde here him' (wherein ye wer much to be commended)—upon these considerations, and for the desire I have to unitie, I have thought my self bounde to communicate to you that I have red in the matter of images and holy water; to thintent ye may by yourself consider it, and so way ⟨*i.e.*, weigh⟩, before that ye will speake in those two points, as ye may (reteining your owne principles) affirme still that ye would affirme, and may in dede be affermed and mainteyned; wherin I have sene other forget themself.

First, I send unto you herewith (which I am sure ye have red) that Eusebius writeth of images, wherby appeareth that images have ben of

255

great antiquitie in Christes Church. And to say we may not have images, or to call them ⟨idols⟩ when they represente Christ or his sainctes, be over grosse opinions to enter into your learned head, what soever the unlearned woulde trattle. For yow know the texte of the olde law, *Non facies tibi sculptile*, forbiddeth no more images now, then another text forbiddeth to us puddings. And if *omnia* be *munda mundis* to the belly, there can be no cause why they should be of themselves *impura* to the eye; wherin ye can say much more.

And then, when we have images, to cal them idoles, is a like fault in fond foly as if a man woulde call *regem* a tyrant, and then bring in olde writers to prove that *tyrannus* signified once a king, like as *idolum* signified once an image. But like as *tyrannus* was, by consent of men, appropriate to signifie an usurper of that dignitie and an untrue kinge, so hath *idolum* ben appropriate to signifie a false representacion and a false image; in somuch as there was a solemne anathemization of all those that woulde call an image an idoll; as he were worthye to be hanged that woulde call the King our master (God save him!), our true just King, a tyraunt; and yet in talke he might shew that a tyraunt signified some time a king. But speche is regarded in his present signification, whiche I doubte not ye can consider right well.

I verely thinke that, as for the having of images, ye will say inough; and that also, when we have them, we shoulde not despise them in speche, to cal them idols, ne despise them with deedes, to mangle them or cut them, but at the lest, suffer them to stande untorne. Wherin Luther, that pulled away al other regard to them, strave stoutly and obteined, as I have seene in divers of the churches in Germany of his reformation, that they shuld (as they do) stand stil.

All the matter to be feared is exces in worshipping, wherin the Churche of Rome hath ben verye precise; and specially Gregory, writing *Episcopo Massilien.*, whiche is conteyned, [1]*De Consecratione, Distinctio*[1] 3, as foloweth:

Perlatum ad nos fuerat, quod inconsiderato zelo succensus sanctorum imagines sub hac quasi excusatione, ne adorari debuissent, confregeris. Et quidem eas adorari vetuisse, omnino laudamus, fregisse vero reprehendimus. Dic, frater, a quo factum esse sacerdote aliquando auditum est, quod fecisti? Aliud est enim picturam adorare; aliud per picturam historiam quid sit adorandum addiscere. Nam quod legentibus scriptura, hoc et idiotis prestat pictura cernentibus, quia in ipsa ignorantes vident quid sequi debeant, in ipsa legunt qui literas nesciunt. Unde et praecipue gentibus pro leccione pictura est.

Herein is forbidden adoration, and then, in *Sexta Sinodo*, was declared what maner of adoration is forbidden; that is to say, godly adoration to it being a creature, as is conteyned in the chapter *Venerabiles imagines*, in the same Distinccion, in this wise:

Venerabiles imagines Christiani non deos appellant, neque serviunt eis ut diis, neque spem salutis ponunt in eis, neque ab eis exspectant futurum iudicium; sed ad memoriam et recordationem primitivorum venerantur eas et adorant, sed non serviunt eis cultu divino, nec alicui creaturae.

By whiche doctrine all idolatrie is plainly excluded in evident words; so as we can not say that the worshipping of images had his beginning by popery, for Gregory forbad it; onles we shall call that synode popery, because there were so manye bishops. And yet there is forbidden *cultus divinus*, and agreth with our before said doctrin, by which we may crepe before the cros on Good Fryday; wherin we have the image of the crucifixe in honor, and use it in a worshipfull place, and so ernestly looke on it, and conceyve that it signifieth, as we knele and crepe before it, whiles it lyeth there, and whiles that remembraunce is in exercise. With which crosse, neverthelesse, the sexten, when he goeth for a corse ⟨*i.e.*, corpse⟩, will not be afrayd to be homely, and holde it under his gowne whiles he drincketh a pot of ale—a pointe of homelinesse that mighte be lefte, but yet it declareth that he estemed no divinitie in the image. But ever since I was borne, a poore parishoner, a lay man, durst be so bold at a shift (if he were also churche warden) to sell to the use of the church at length, and his owne in the meane time, the silver crosse on Ester Monday that was creped unto on Good Fryday.

In specialties there have ben special abuses, but generally images have ben taken for images, with an office to signifie an holy remembraunce of Christe and his sainctes. And as the sound of speach uttered by a lively image ⟨*i.e.*, a human being⟩ and representing to thunderstanding, by the sense of hearinge, godly matter, doth stirre up the mind and, ther with, the body to consent in outward gesture of worshipfull regard to that sound; so doth the object of thimage, by the sight, work like effect in man, within and withoute; wherin is verelye worshipped that we understand, and yet reverence and worship also shewd to that wherby we attein that understanding; and is to us in the place of an instrument, so as it hath no worship of itself, but remayneth in his nature, of stone or timber, silver, copper, or golde. But when it is in office, and worketh a godly remembraunce in us, by representacion of the thinge signifyed unto us, then we use it worshipfully and honorably, as many do the priest at Mas, whom they little regarde all the day after.

And me thinketh ever, that like as it is an over grosse errour to take an image for God, or to worship it with godly honor, so, to graunt that we may not have images of Christ, and that we may doo no worship before them, or not use them worshipfully, it is inexplicable. For it is one kind of worship to place them worshipfully, so as if a man place an image in the churche or hang it about his neck, as al use to do thimage of the cross, and the knight of thOrder, S. George, this is som peace of worship. And if we may not contemn thimages of Christ and hys saincts, when we have them (for that wer vilany), nor[1] neglect them (for that wer to have them without use, which wer inconvenient, *quia nec natura nec arte quicquam*[2] *fit frustra*), we muste have them in estimation and reputacion, which is not without some honour and worship; and at the lest in the place where we convenientlie use them, as in the church, as where they serve us, rather then we them. And because their service is worshipfull, they be so regarded accordingly for that time of service, and therfore they be called *venerabiles imagines*, and be worshipfully ordred; before whom we knele and bowe and sence, not at that thimages be, but at that thimages signify, which, in our kneling, bowing, and sensing, we knowledge to understand and read in that fashion of contracte writinge, wherin is wrapped up a greate manye of sentences, sodenlye opened with one soden syghte to him that hathe bene exercised in readinge of them.

And me seemeth, after the fayth of Christ receyved and knowen, and thoroughlye purged from heresyes, if, by case, ther wer offred a chose ether to retein painting and graving and forbear writing, or, chosing writing, to forbear both thother giftes, it wold be a probleam, seing if graving wer taken away we could have no printing. And therfore they that presse so much the wordes of *Non facies tibi sculptile*, ever, me thincketh, they condeme printed bookes, the originall wherof is of graving to make *matrices literarum. Sed hoc est furiosum, et sunt tamen qui putant palmarium.* And therfore now it is Englished, 'Thou shalt

1 *1563, 1583*, not   2 *1563*, quiquam; *1583*, quicquam

make no graven images, leste thou worshipe them'; whiche, I here, is newly written in the newe churche—I knowe not the name, but not farre from thOld Jury.

But to the matter of images, wherin I have discoursed at large: I thinke and ⟨i.e., if⟩ ye consider (as I doubt not but ye will) the doctrine set forth by our late soveraine lord, ye shall in that matter see the truthe set forthe by such as had that committed unto them under his Highnes, emonges whom I was not, nor was not privie unto it till it was don. And yet the clause in the boke, for discussion of 'the Lord' and 'Our Lord' hath made many thinke otherwise; but I take Our Lord to witnes, I was not. And that declaration of 'Our Lord' was his Highnes owne devise, *ex se*. For he sawe the fonde Englishing of 'the Lorde' dissevered in speeche whom Our Lorde had congregate. And this I adde, lest, geving authoritie to the boke, I should seme to avaunte my selfe.

Now will I speake somwhat of holy water, wherin I send unto you the xxxiiij chapter in the ix boke of thistory tripartite, where Marcellus the bishop bad Equitius his deacon to cast abrode water by him first halowed, wherewith to drive away the devill. And it is noted how the devill coulde not abyde the vertue of the water, but vanished awaye. And for my parte, it semeth the history may be true. For we be assured by Scripture that, in the name of God, the Churche is able and strong to caste out devils, accordyng to the Gospell, *In nomine meo daemonia eiicient, etc.*; so as if the water wer away, by only calling of the name of God, that maystry ⟨i.e., mastery⟩ may be wrought. And being the vertue of theffect only attributed to the name of God, the question should be only, whether the creature of water may have thoffice to convey the effect of the holynes of thinvocation of Gods name. And first in Christ, the skirt of his garment had suche an office, to minister healthe to the woman, and spettle and cley, to the blinde, and S. Peters shadow, and S. Pawles handkerchers.

And leaving olde stories, here at home the speciall gifte of curation, ministred by the kings of this realm, not of their owne strength, but by invocation of the name of God, hath ben used to be distributed in ringes of gold and silver. And I think effectually; wherin the metal hathe only an office, and the strength is in the name of God, wherin all is wrought. And Helizeus put his staffe in like office. And why the whole Church might not put water in like office, to convey abrode thinvocation of Goddes name, there is no Scripture to the contrary; but there is Scripture, howe other inferiour creatures have ben promoted to like dignitie;

and muche Scripture, how water hathe ben used in like and greater service. And the story I sende unto you sheweth how water hath ben used in the same service, to drive away devils. In which mattier if any shal say he beleveth not the story—and he is not bounde to beleve it, being no Scripture—that man is not to be reasoned with, for theffecte of the Kinges crampe ringes. And yet for such effect as they have wrought, when I was in Fraunce, I have ben my self moche honoured, and of all sortes entreated to have them, with offre of asmoche for them as they wer dubble worth.

Som wil say, What is rings to holy water? Mary, thus I say, If the metal of golde and silver may doo service to cary abrod thinvocation of the name of God effectually for one purpose, water may also serve to carye abrode thinvocation of the name of God wherwith to drive away devils. Here to wil be said, *Non valet argumentum a posse ad esse.* But the story saith the water did that service, and other straungers say and afferm by experience the Kings Majesties rings have don the service. And our late master continued all his life thexercise of that gift of God, and used silver and golde to do that service, to carye abrode the strength of thinvocation of the name of God by him. And he used it among us that served him in it, when he had thoroughly hard and seen what might be saied in the matter, and yet he had no Scripture specially for it, that spake of ringes of silver or golde, no more then is for thasshes, ministred a litle before ye last preached. And as our young soverain lord hath receyved them reverently, so I trust he shall be advertised, *ne negligat gratiam Dei in dono curationum,* but folow his father therin also, not doubting but God will here him, as he hath hard his father and others his progenitours, kinges of this realme; to whose dignitie God addeth this prerogative, as he doth also to inferiour ministers of his Church, in theffect of their prayer, when it pleaseth him.

A man might find some younglings, percase, that wolde say how worldely, wyly, wittie bishops have enveigled symple kings heretofore, and, to conferm their blessings, have also devised how kings should blesse also, and so ⟨have⟩ authoritie to mainteyne where truth fayled. And I have had it objected to me that I used to prove one peace of mine argument ever by a king, as when I reasoned thus: If ye allow nothing but Scripture, what say you to the Kinges ringes? But they be allowed; ergo, somwhat is to be allowed besides Scripture. And another: If images be forbidden, why doothe the King weare S. Georg on his brest? But he weareth S. Georg on his brest; ergo, images be not forbidden.

If saincts be not to bee worshipped, why kepe we S. Georges feast? But we kepe Saint Georges feast; ergo, etc. And in this matter of holy water, if the strength of thinvocation of the name of God to drive awaye devils can not be distribute by water, why can it be destr⟨i⟩bute in silver to drive away diseases, and the daungerous disease of the falling evil? But the rings halowed by the holye Churche may do so; ergo, the water halowed by the Churche may do like service.

These wer sore arguments in his time, and I trust be also yet; and may be conveniently used, to such as wold never make an end of talk, but rake up everye thing that their dull sight cannot penetrate; wherin me thought ye spake effectually, when ye said men must receyve the determynation of the particular Churche, and obey where Gods law repugneth not expreslye.‹ And in this effecte, to drive away devils, that prayer and invocation of the Churche may doo it, Scripture main-teyneth evidentlye; and the same Scripture doth autorise us so to pray, and encourageth us to it. So as if in discussion of holy water, we attribute all theffect to the holines which procedeth from God, by in-vocation of the Church, and take water for an only servaunt to cary abrode holines, there can be no supersticion, where men regarde only prayer, which Scripture authoriseth. And if we shall say that the water can not doo such service, we shall be convinced, in that it doth a greatter service in our baptisme, by Gods speciall ordinaunce. So as we can not say that water can not, or is not apte to do this service; only the stay is, to have a precise place in the New Testament to saye, Use water thus in this service, as we doo in holy water; which methinketh nedeth not, where all is ordred to be well used by us. And when the hole Church agreed upon such an use, or any perticuler Church, or the commen minister of it, and by the exorcisme ordred for it, the thing to be used, purged, there can be but slender matter to improve ⟨i.e., condemn⟩ that custom, wherin God is onely honoured and the power of his name set forth; wher unto all thing boweth and geveth place, all naturall operation set apart and secluded.

And when any man hath denyed that water may do service, because Scripture appointeth it not, that 'because' driveth away muche of the rest the Churche useth, and specially our cramp rings. For if water may not serve to cary abrode theffect of Goddes grace, obteyned by invoca-tion from God by the commen prayer of the Church, howe can the metall of silver or golde cary abrode theffect of the Kinges invocation in the cramp ringes? Which maner of reasoning *ad hominem* Christ used with the Jewes, when he sayd, *Si ego in Belzebub eiicio daemonia, filii vestri in quo eiiciunt?* And if by oure owne principles we should be enforced to saye that our cramp rings be supersticion, where truth enforceth us not so to do, it wer a mervelous punishment. *Si caeci essemus,* as Christ saith, *peccatum*[1] *non haberemus, sed videmus.* And this realme hathe lerning in it, and you a good portion therof; according wherunto I doubt not but ye will waye this matter *non ad popularem trutinam, sed artificis stateram*—I meane that artificer that teacheth the Church our mother (as ye full well declared it) and ordred our mother to geve nourishment unto us. In which poynt, speakinge of the Church, although ye touched an unknowen Church to us, and knowen to God onely, yet ⟨ye⟩ declared the union of that Churche in the permixt Churche, whiche God ordereth men to complayne unto, and to here agayne; wherin thabsurditie is taken away of them that wold have no Churche knowen, but everye man beleve as he wer inwardly taught himself; wherupon foloweth the olde proverbe, Σοὶ μὲν ταῦτα δοκοῦντ' ἐστι⟨ν⟩, ἐμοὶ δὲ τάδε; whiche is farre from the unitie ye so ernestly wished for, wherof, as methought, ye[2] sayd pride is the let, as it is undoubtedly. Whiche fault God amend, and geve you grace so to facion your words as ye maye agree with them in speche, with whom ye be enclined to agree in opinion. For that is the way to releave the world.

And albeit there hathe bene betwene you and me no familiaritie, but, contrarywise, a litle disagreement (which I did not hide from you), yet, considering the fervent zeale ye professed to teache Peters true doctrine, that is to say, Christes true doctrine, wherunto ye thought the doctrine of images and holy water to put away devils agreed not, I have willingly spent this time, to communicate unto you my foly (if it be foli) plainly as it is; wheruppon ye may have occasion the more substantially, fully, and plainlye to open these matters for the relief of such as be fallen from the truth, and confirmation of those that receive and follow it; wherin it hathe ben ever much commended, to have such regard to histories of credite and the continuall use of the Church, rather to shew how a thing, continued from the beginning, as holy water and images have don, maye be well used, then to folowe the light rashe eloquence, whiche is ever *ad manum,* to mocke and improve ⟨*i.e.*, condemn⟩ that is established.

And yet again I come to Marcellus that made a crosse in the water and bad his deacon caste it abrode *cum fide et zelo*; after which sort, if oure holy water wer used, I doubt not but there be many Marcellus, and

1 *1563,* pecatum; *1583,* peccatum   2 *1563,* he; *1583,* ye

many Elizeus, and many at whose prayer God forgiveth sinne, if such as will enjoye that prayer have faythe and zeale as Equitius, and wer as desirous to dryve the devil out of the temple of their body and soule as Equitius out of the temple of Jupiter. So as yf holy use wer coupled with holy water, there should be more plentie of holines then there is. But as men be prophane in their living, so they can not byde to have any thing effectually holye, not so muche as breade and water, fearing lest they shoulde take awaye sinne from us, whiche we love so well. *Solus Christus peccata diluit,* who sprinckleth his blood by hys mynisters, as he hath taught his spouse the Church, in whyche those ministers be ordered, wherin many wayes maketh not many saviours, as ignorauntes doo jest; whereof I neede not speake further unto you, no more I neded not in the rest in respecte of you; but me thoughte ye conjured all menne in your sermon to saye what they thought to you, *id quod hanc mihi expressit epistolam, quam boni consules, et vale.*

Your loving frende,

¹STEVEN WINCHE¹.

Headed: Here foloweth the copie of the letter of Steven Gardner sent to Master Ridley, in the letters above mentioned ⟨*i.e.*, No. 117 below⟩, conteining matter and objections against a certain sermon of the said Master Ridley made at the Courte.

NOTES TO NO. 116

Page 255. Ridley, at this time Master of Pembroke Hall, Cambridge, and Canon of Canterbury and Westminster, was nominated Bishop of Rochester 4 September of this year.

Page 255. For Eusebius on images, *see* his *Church History*, Book VII, Chapter xviii.

Page 256–7. The quotations from Gregory the Great and the Sixth Synod are both from the *Decretum* of Gratian, *Pars Tertia, De Consecratione, Distinctio* III, cc. xxvii, xxviii. The text as printed in Foxe is that of sixteenth-century editions. It is, *e.g.*, identical with that of *Decretum Divi Gratiani*, Lugduni, 1560. For a critical text see *Corpus Juris Canonici*, ed. A. Friedberg, Leipzig, 1879–81, I, 1360. For Gregory's

1–1 1583, Ste. Winchester

letter in English translation see *Nicene and Post-Nicene Fathers*, ser. 2, XIII, 53.

Page 258. Sed hoc est furiosum etc. *Cf.* Terence, *Eunuchus*, 930.

Page 259. The new church near the Old Jewry is, by the editor of Ridley's *Works*, Parker Soc., 1841, 499, said to be 'probably St Stephen's, Coleman Street'; by the editor of Foxe (VI, 746), St Martin's, Ironmonger Lane. This, because of the Privy Council record of the examination, 10 February, 1547, of the wardens and curate of St Martin's, for removal of images and 'setting uppe in their places and abowte the churche walles certaine textes of Scripture, whereof summe were perversely translated' (Dasent, II, 25).

Page 259. 'The doctrine set forth by our late soveraine lord' is *A Necessary Doctrine and Erudition for Any Christian Man*, commonly called *The King's Book*, published 1543 (more easily available in C. Lloyd, *Formularies of Faith in the Reign of Henry VIII*, Oxford, 1825, and 1856). Images are considered under the second commandment, and the phrase *Our Lord* under the second article of the creed. For Gardiner's part in the composition of the book *see* my *Gardiner*, 106–7, 360. For the significance of *Our Lord* and *the Lord* see *ib.*, 354 n. 15.

Page 259. The History Tripartite or *Historia Tripartita* is a combination, in Latin translation, of the Church Histories of Socrates, Sozomen, and Theodoret (covering the years 306–439), made in the sixth century by Cassiodorus and his assistant, Epiphanius Scholasticus. It was a popular medieval manual, and editions were printed in the fifteenth, sixteenth, and seventeenth centuries. The story of Marcellus and the holy water comes from the *History* of Theodoret, Book v, Chapter xxi (*see Nicene and Post-Nicene Fathers*, ser. 2, III, 147).

Page 262. Non ad popularem etc. *Cf.* Cicero, *De Oratore*, II, 38, 159.

Page 262. The Greek proverb, 'to you things seem so, to me otherwise,' is found in an epigram of Evenus, in F. Jacobs, *Delectus Epigrammatum Graecorum*, Gotha, 1826, c. vii, No. 91, where reference is also made to Euripides, *Suppl.*, 476, σοὶ μὲν δοκείτω ταῦτ', ἐμοὶ δὲ τἀντία.

117. *To* SOMERSET

Southwark, 28 February, [1547]

Foxe, *1563*, 732–3; *1583*, II, 1342; ed. Pratt, VI, 24.

Protests against changes proposed in a sermon by Bishop Barlow of St David's. England's need is quiet and concord; let reformers withhold their plans till the King comes of age; Somerset should eschew religious change, let Scotland alone, replenish the treasury, maintain the Imperial alliance, distrust France; copy of letter to Ridley (No. 116, above) is enclosed; because of Gardiner's checking reform in Henry VIII's time, some have expressed the wish to kill him.

May it please your Grace to understand that I have noted some points in my Lord of S. Davids sermon, which I send unto you herewith, wherby to declare unto you som part what I think, for the whole I cannot expres. Somwhat I shall encomber you with my babling, but he hath encombred some frindes more with his tatling. And alas, my Lord! this is a piteous case, that having so much busynes as ye have, these inwarde disorders should be added unto them, to the corage of such as would this realme any waies evil. For this is the thing they would desire, with hope therby to disorder this realme, being nowe a tyme rather to repare that nedeth reparation, then to make any new bildings, which they pretende. Quyet, tranquilitie, unitie, and concord shal mainteine estimation. The contrari may animate the enemie to attempte that was never thoughte on, which God forbid. There was never attemptate of alteration made in England, but upon comfort of discord at home; and woe be to them that mindeth it!

If my Lorde of S. Davies or suche others have their hed combrid with any new plat form, I would wish they wer commaunded betwene this and the Kinges Majesties ful age to draw the plat diligentlye, to hewe the stones, dig the sand, and chop the chalke in the unseasonable time of bilding; and, when the Kings Majestie cometh to full age, to present their labors to him, and, in the meane time, not to disturbe the state of the realme, wherof your Grace is Protector; but that you may, in every parte of religion, lawes, landes, and decrees (whiche foure conteine the State) deliver the same to our sovereigne lord, according to the trust you be put in; which shalbe much to your honor, and as all honest men wish and desire. To which desired effecte there can be nothing so noysom and contrarious as troble and disquiet. Wherein your Grace shalbe speciallye troubled, as on whose shoulders all the weight lieth; and what so ever shall happen amis by the faultes of other, shalbe imputed to your Grace, as doer therof, or wanting foresighte in time to withstande the same. And albeit that you mind not to be faulty in either, yet if the effect be not to the realm as wer to be wished, the prince, and though he were of age, should be excused, and the governors beare the blame. And this is the infelicytie of preheminence and autoritie, and specially in this realme, as stories make mention; whiche should not discourage you, for you nede feare nothing without, if quiet be reserved ⟨*i.e.*, preserved⟩ at home; and at home, if the beginning be resisted, the intended folly may easely be interrupted. But if my brother of S. Davids maie, like a champion with his sword in his hand, make enter ⟨*i.e.*, entry⟩ for the rest, the doore of licence opened, there shall moe by folly thrust in with him then your Grace would wish.

Thus, as I think, I write homely to your Grace, because you wer content I should write, wherin I consider only to have althings well; and, because your Grace is the Protector and the chief director of the realme, to present unto your wisdom what my folly is. I have ben oftentimes blamed for fearing overmuch, and yet I have had an incling that they that so blamed me feared even as much as I. Being in the state that you be in, it shalbe ever commendable to foresee the worst. In quiet ye be strong, in troble ye be greatly weak, and bring your self in daunger of one parte, when parties be, wherwith[1] one to scourg the other. Wheras in concord they be both yours in an honest, reverent, louely ⟨*i.e.*, lowly⟩ feare to doo their dutie; which I doubt not your wisdom can consider. And consider also how noisom any other outward encomber might be, in the time of the minoritie of our sovereign lord. I told the Emperours Counsail that oure late sovereign lord did much for the Emperour, to enter war with him and put his realm in his old daies in the adventure of fortune, whether he should enjoie it or no; for that is the nature of war. And somtime the contemned and abject have had the upper hand. And when ye administer the realm for another, it wer a marvailous question of him that shal enjoy the realm, to say, What ment you in the time of administration to adventure my realme? Why tooke ye not rather, for the time of my minoritie, any peace, what so ever it wer (which is better then the best war, as som men have written)?

I know you have authoritie sufficient and wisdom plenty, and yet, being entred to write, I forget for the time what ye be, and commen with

1 *1583*, therwith

you as I wer talking at Brussels with you, devising of the world at large. And if I wer sworn to say what I think in the state of the world, I would for a time let Skots be Skotts, with dispaire to have them, unlesse it wer by conquest, which shalbe a godly ⟨*i.e.*, goodly⟩ enterprise for our yong master when he cometh to age. And, in the meane time, prepare him mony for it and set the realm in an order [1]which hath nede of it[1]. And for a stay, if thEmperour would offer the King of Romains daughter, as he did, doo with him in our masters minoritie as he did with us in his; wherby al this hath chanced unto him. And by this alliance your estimation shal encrease, and our sovereign lords surtie not a litle increse and be augmented. For of Fraunce it must be taken for a rule, they be so wanton they cannot do wel lenger then they see how they may be scourged if they do not. Here is all the wit that I have, which I offer unto you upon this occasion of writing, and shall praye God to put in youre mind that shalbe for the best, as I trust he wil; and, in the meane time, to extincte this barbarous contention at home, which can serve only to doo hurte and no good.

I had fasshoned a letter to Master Ridley, which I send unto your Grace, and encomber you with these malencoly writings, engendred of this fondnes, which be not worth the reading. And so it may lyke you to use them, for having harde that ye have said unto me, and otherwise harde and sene what you do, I shall go occupie my wit in other matters. And now such as have fonde enterpryses shall see that I letted not their follies, whiche they called Gods Word, but for his time, the King our sovereign lord that dead is, and after his time you, much to your honor and reputacion, ⟨letted them⟩, howsoever any shalbe here not contented; which miscontentation hath ben so fond in some, as they have brest ⟨*i.e.*, burst⟩ out and wished that they might, without breche of lawes, kil me, which is to me a token of a marvelus fury; which hath ben cause why I am glad both to depart hence and to depart the soner, and pray God to order al things for the best, with preservation of our soveraigne lord, and encrese of your Graces honour. At my house in Sothworke, the last of February.

Your Graces humble beadman,

S. W.

Headed: Winchester to the Lord Protector.

1–1 Pratt amends this to which it hath need of

Page 267. Ferdinand, King of the Romans, Archduke of Austria, brother of Charles V, had fifteen children by his first wife, eleven of whom were daughters. When Gardiner was ambassador with the Emperor in 1545, it was suggested that one of these daughters be given in marriage to Prince Edward (*L.P.*, xx, ii, 830), Charles himself saying that there was 'choyse of oon yere, two yere, thre yere, foure yere, fyve yere, and, or he war aware, rekonned tyl he cam to 15 yere; but thenne he cam to a juster rekonnyng and said his brother hath just nyne doughters to mary' (*St. P.*, x, 742). The ensuing negotiations, chiefly over the size of the dote, did not get so far as a specific selection from this bewildering wealth of possibilities.

118. *To* PAGET

Southwark, 1 March, 1547

R.O., S.P. 10, 1, 103–6.*

Objects to Paget's wording of the royal commission renewing episcopal jurisdiction (commissions issued under Henry VIII had, according to the determination of the Council, lapsed with the death of that monarch); mislikes the word 'delegate' as applied to a bishop, who is an ordinary (*i.e.*, one who has jurisdiction in ecclesiastical cases of his own right and not by delegation); his philosophy; was never a persecutor; writes in behalf of Bonner; hears that some people would have no bishops; his commission ought to enable him to do what, as ordinary, he must do. (The commission was issued 2 March, 1547—*Reg. Gardiner*, 79. For Paget's reply of same date *see* Tytler, 1, 24.)

Master Secretary, after my right harty commendations: Being the matier of thexpedition of our commissions committed unto youe, thiese shalbe to require youe to expedite them favorably, as ye promysed me ye wold. This daye I[1] ha[ve] seen your addition, which I like not; for we be called ordinaries of the realme, and there shuld be a request on[2] our parte to make ourself delegates. And I have been exercised in making of treaties, where wordes, as ye knowe, have been thruste in to signifie sumwhat at lenght, and have thenne such an interpretacion as[3] might serve; and we poore bishoppes bee not such a matche as the[4] parties be in treaties. And whenne the lawers of this realme cum to interpretacions,

1 sa *c.o.*   2 your *c.o.*
3 † *abv.* at *c.o.*   4 they *w.* y *c.o.*

it wel help smally to have red the title *de verborum significacione*, for they have a principyl that *ea interpretacio sequenda sit que pro rege facit*. And thenne there is an other underst[an]ding of *pro rege facit*, as though summe tyme it were [to] the kinges proufite to have his subget founde faulty, wherby to forfaicte his goodes, thenne to understand civilye a mannes doing, and bere with simple meanyng where malice appere not. A playne man of my countrie, fayling his apperaunce in the Sterre Chambre and forfayting his recognisaunce of xx *li.*, whenne it was demaunded of hym, he told my Lord Cardynal, in playne Suffolke spech, it was outtaken to paye xx *li.* for pearying, and yet, he said, he peared to. And soo it wold be a mervelous matier, if, after my long service and the losse of my master, I shuld lose that he [1]gave me by construction of[t] a commission; and that I shuld offende in going aboute to doo wel, to see thinges wel by visitacion, and receyving of convictes to my charge as ordinarye, and am but a delegate. And thenne the cace wold be somoch the more straunge if youe might releave it and did not. Ye must graunte archedecons auctorite to visite or they cannot paye ther tenthes, for therupon ther profite doth arrise. And thenne how shal it stand, the archedecon to have more auctorite thenne the bishop, having in his name to be overseer and yet maye not goo see?

And nowe is the tyme whenne such as have office to ordre the people[2] shuld rather have more committed unto them thenne lesse. And there is noo man I thinke soo mad as wyl aventure[3] furder thenne the evident spech of the commission wyl bere, but wyl kepe hym on this side, bicause it hath been doubted whither a man having *mandatum emere fundum centum aureis*, may goo to[t] the uttermost of the summe. The Civile Lawe resolvith a man maye, but I have gret feare of the Commen Lawe in a doubte. And this youe maye explicate *cum fide et officio*, and whenne[4] ye have soo good plentie of other[5] partes of fortune, travayle to adde unto it *benevolentiam*, which oonly continueth *cum cetera defluunt. Et quia facile cetera defluant*, there nedeth noon other lernyng then *reministentia.* Whiles the King our late master lyved, men bare with many thinges in the wel construyng of them, and thought ye bare in your body affections of diverse soules; and sumtyme ye wer angrye for to expresse oon mans affection, and sumtyme an others[6], partely of policie, partely of tendernes; and seldom, whenne it was not wel, your owne. But nowe, what

1 g *writ. over something else*   2 such *c.o.*
3 soo *c.o.*   4 ha *c.o.*
5 *writ. over something else*   6 an *c.o.*

269

soever ye doo *in hoc optimatum statu* where is *suffragiorum equalitas*, it shalbe called your owne and merely your owne, without mitigacion of any instigation to be made by other, if ther be any other. And ye shal geve me leave to divine with youe of wise mens opinions of your doinges, althogh they saye nothing, that if ye procure yourself evel wyl where it nedeth[1] not, or geve[2] occasion of evel spech without necessite, they wyl thinke ye forget yourself overmoch and hindre yourself where it nedith not. I wold not flater the worlde, for that is vanite, ne yet on the other side[3] nyppe where nedeth not, for that is worse thenne vanite†. And what ar youe the better if ye be† called of sum a pyncher of the bishoppes and amonges them me? It healith noo disease in youe; ye slepe never the better; ye have never the better stomake. Nothing is better and sumwhat is worse. Plutarche sayth he that is lx yere old and puttith forthe his hand to the phisician to aske howe his body is, in temperaunce declarith himself not wise ⟨*De Sanit.*, 136 E⟩. And me thinketh the tyme we have lyved is long inough to lerne men what the state of this worlde is and howe soone it is altred. And happy is he[4] that knowith himself, and canne thinke every daye to be the last daye of his honno*ur*, as it maye be of his life. I thanke God I coulde skyl of this philosophie whenne I was as ye be, and[5] howsoever it served for mens purpose to saye I was a *persecutour*, I was never soo in dede. And me thinketh[6] I have felt the rewarde of it, for noo persecution hath hitherto prevayled against me. I have had cause to be angry, and tyme, with auctorite, whenne I might have shewed myself angrye; at which tyme men made fayre whether with me, and I was glad of it. It is not soo easy a matier to further as to hindre, to[7] doo good as[8] to doo† hurte. And if a commission wer soo strayted as a bishop toke hurte by it, yt[9] wer a harde matier to lauf at it, though ye lyved and sawe it. And who canne tel whither he shal lyve to see it or noo? Al is uncertain, and in the uncertainte to doo a certain displeasour which remayneth in memory when[10] benefites vanyshe awaye, hath in it smal policie and lesse thenne I wold wishe to be in youe; and, therfor, without nede in myn owne cace, wherin I thinke ye wyl make noo difficulte, write generally unto youe for al, and specially for my Lord of London; that like as the

---

1 o *c.o.* 2 given *w.* n *c.o.*
3 † *abv.* wise *c.o.* 4 *a letter c.o.*
5 s *c.o.* 6 if *c.o.*
7 g *c.o.* 8 *MS.*, and, *apparently an error for* as
9 *alt. from* ye 10 † *abv.* and *c.o.*

brethern have made a balet and solace themself †in it†, where Boner lamenteth the fal of Winchester, so for recompense of his lamentacion I speke in his cause, with whom I perceyve ye be offended, justely or noo I wyl not reason, for I knowe not nor have been, on my fidelite, ever spoken unto of hym in it. But howe soever he be, I wold wishe ye did best for yourself, which is to love your enemyes, if ye have any, *et vincere in bono malum*. For youe have passed the state of wranglyng and revenging, and be in the state that shuld desire rest, peace, quiet, love, tranquillite, both for your owne sake and the realmes. Ye nede studye to encrease nothinge but love, for in the plenty therof is al felicite. I speke of plentye that bishoppes might have parte, for in thopinion of sum they shuld be served last[1]. But they be but a smal summe, I truste, or smally consider the state and establishement of the realme which hitherto, synnes Christendom receyved, hath not stande without them†. And howe it wold doo if they wer awaye, it wer a[2] newe experience. There is oon wold make[3] me understande he wold not have me, for he hath bosted that he wold he had geven his landes, soo it wer lawful for hym[4], by the lawes of the realme, to kyl me. For he is soo† wel lerned in the Worde that he thinkith he shuld doo God a gret sacrifice in it, to save soo many sowles as shuld then have at libertie Goddes Worde. A godly enterprise and a devoute! But let hym[5] saye what he wyl, soo our commission be wel wryten, expressing al that we shal doo, and denying that we shal not doo; soo as ye[6] expresse that I[7] maye receyve convictes, for that is the oonly cace in which the judges of the realme wyl have me doo it whither I maye or I maye not. Wherin I had experience, as I beganne to tel youe, at my being at the courte, in the sessions here upon Thursday last past, where, coulde I receyve them or coulde I not receyve them, I must pay M⟨1000⟩*li.* if I re- ceyved them not; which was like the balowing the preste made in the north for bryngyng of dukkes again that wer lost, for, he said, the parisheners must bring them again, see them or see them not. Which tale tempered in[8] me thextremite of handeling. But such is the worlde, which I praye youe tempre, that we maye lyve quietly without snatchyng. I wold we shuld wreke our tene, as they saye, upon Scottyshe men and[9] French men, if men must nedes varye with men; and Englishe men love and agree togither, wherin is our strenght. And nowe I praye youe, let

---

1 for *c.o.*   2 nex *c.o.*   3 l *incomplete follows*
4 *alt. from* it   5 self *c.o.*   6 h *c.o.*
7 † *abv.* we *c.o.* 8 t *c.o.*   9 english *c.o.*

me[1] have my commission frendly, and soo as I may have ful auctorite for that I must necessaryly doo, and more thenne I must necessaryly. I warraunte[2] youe I wyl not doo in worldly matiers, but use this opportunite to doo sumwhat elles. And nowe I see youe wyl staye the fondnesse of the worlde against God and his lawe, and maynteyne[3] Goddes truth against that they cal Goddes Worde, I shal occupie myself a whiles in mannes lawes, such as I studied at the begynnyng, and not be idel though I be not best occupied.

And thus trusting I shal have my commission, I [4]wyl trouble youe noo lenger, but bydde youe hartely fare wel. At my house in Southwarke, this Tuesday in the after none.

Your assured loving
frend,

STE. WINTON

Addressed: To the Right Wourshipful Sir William Paget, Knight, oon of the Kinges Majesties two Principal Secretaryes.

Endorsed: The Bisshoppe of Winchestre to Master Secretary, Master Paget, primo Marcii, 1546⟨47⟩.

119. *To* EDWARD VAUGHAN

Wolvesey (at Winchester), 3 May, 1547

Foxe, *1563*, 728–30; *1570*, II, 1522; *1576*, 1297; *1583*, II, 1340; ed. Pratt, VI, 26.

Has heard of the pulling down of images at Portsmouth; asks the Captain of Portsmouth who did it, and under what circumstances. Would preaching against it do good? Would not cast pearls before swine, for such are those, called Lollards, who destroy images; Luther reproved such people; destruction of images tends to subvert government as well as religion, for the images on the escutcheons of the nobility and the royal seal maintain reverence for civil authority; images are books for the illiterate, not a hundredth part of the realm being able to read; Christ did not condemn Caesar's image; false images only are reproved by Scripture. What should be done about it? There can be no greater enterprise against religion than the destruction of images. (*See* pp. 284–5 on the reply to this letter.)

1 *alt. from* my   2 I *c.o.*
3 *first* n *in* maynteyne *writ. over* t   4 w *writ. over* t

Master Vaughan, after my right hartie commendations: In my last letters to my Lord Protector, signyfying, according to the generall commaundement by letters geven to all justices of peace, the state of this shire, I declared (as I supposed trewe) the shire to be in good order, quiet, and conformitie; for I had not then hard of any alteration in this shire which the said letters of commaundment did forbid. Now of late, within these two dayes, I have hard of a great and detestable (if it be trew that is tolde me) inovation in the towne of Portesmouth, where the images of Christ and his sainctes have ben most contemptuously pulled downe and spitfully handled. Herein I thought good both to write to you and the maior, the Kinges Majesties chefe ministers, as well to know the truth as to consult with you for the reformation of it, to the intente I may be sene to discharge my dewtie, and discharge it in dede bothe to God and the Kinges Majestie, under whom I am here appointed[1] to have cure and care, to relive suche as be by any wayes fallen, and preserve the rest that stande from like daunger.

Ye are a gentelman with whom I have had acquaintance, and whom I know to be wise, and esteme to have more knowledge, wysdom, and discretion then to allow any suche enormities; and therefore do the more willingly consult with you herein, with[2] request frendly to know of you the very truthe in the matter—who be the doers, and the circumstance of it, and whether ye think the matter so farre gon with the multitude, and whether the reprofe and disproving of the dede might, without a further danger, be enterprised in the pulpit or not; minding, if it may so be, to send one thither for that purpose upon Sonday nexte comming.

I woulde use preaching as it should not be occasion of any further folly where a folly is begon; and to a multitude perswaded in that opinion of distruction of images I would never preache; for, as Scripture willeth us, we shoulde cast no precious stones before hogges. Such as be infected with that opinion, they be hogges and wors then hogges, if there be any grosser beastes then hogges be, and have ben ever so taken. And in England they are called Lollards, who, denying images, thought therwithall[3] the crafts of painting and[4] graving to be generally superfluous and naught, and against Gods lawes. In Germany such as

---

1 *1563*, appyinted; *1570–83*, appointed, appoynted
2 *1563*, whiche; *1570–83*, with
3 *1563*, therwith, al; *1570–83*, therwithall, therewithall
4 *1570–83 supply* and

maintayned that opinion of distroying of images were accompted the dreggs cast out by Luther[1], after he had tonned all his brewings in Christs religion, and so taken as hogs meat; for the reprofe of whom Luther wrote a boke specially. And I have with mine eies sene the images standing in al such[2] churches where Luther was had in estimation.

For the destruction of images conteineth an enterprise to subvert religion and the state of the worlde with it; and specially[3] the nobilitie, who, by images, set forth and spread abrode, to be red of all people, their linage ⟨and⟩ parentage, with remembrance of their state and acts. And the pursivant carieth not on his brest the Kinges names written in such letters as a few can spell, but suche as all can reade, be they never so rude, being greate knowen letters in images of three lyons and three floures de luce, and other beastes holding those armes. And he that cannot rede the scripture written about the Kinges great seale, [4]either because he can not rede at al, or because the wax doth not expresse it[4], yet he can rede Sainct Georg on horsback on the one[5] side, and the Kinge sitting in his majestie on the other side; and readeth so much written in those images as, if he be an honest man, he wil put of his cap. And although, if the seale were broken by chaunce, he woulde[6] and might make a candel of it, yet he would not be noted to have broken the seale for that purpose, or to cal it a pece of waxe only whiles it continueth whole.

And if by reviling of stockes and stones, in which matter images be graven, the setting of the truth to be red in them of all men shalbe contemned, how shal such writing continue in honor as is comprised in cloutes and pitch, wherof and wherupon our bokes be made, such as few can skil of, and not the hundreth part of the realme? And if we, a few that can reade, because we can reade in one sorte of letters, so privileaged as they have manye reliefes, shall pull away[7] the bookes of the reste, and woulde have our letters only in estimation and blind al them, shall not they have just cause to mistrust what is ment? And if the crosse be a truthe, and it be true that Christ suffred, why may we not have a writyng therof suche as all can reade; that is to say, an image?

If this opinion should procede, when the Kings Majestie hereafter

---

1 *1563*, Luter (*but* Luther *two lines below*); *1570–83*, Luther
2 *1570–83 omit* such   3 *1570–83*, especially
4–4 *omitted in 1570–83;* wax *is an emendation of* way
5 *1563*, on; *1570–83*, one   6 *1563*, woul; *1570–83*, woulde, would
7 *1570–83 supply* away

should shew his person, his lively image, the honor dew by Gods law emonge such might continue; but as for the Kings standards, his banners, his armes, ⟨they⟩ should hardly continue in theyr dew reverence, for feare of Lollards idolatrie, which they gather upon Scripture beastly—not only untrulye.

The Scripture reproveth fals images made of stockes and stones, and so it doth fals men made of flesh and bones. When the emperours mony was shewed to Christ, wherin was the image of the emperour, Christe contemned not that image, calling it an idol, nor noted not the[1] mony to be against Gods law because it had an image in it, as though it were against the precept of God: 'Thou shalt have no graven image'; but taught them good civilitie in calling it the emperours image, and bad them use the monie as it was ordered to be used in his right use.

There is no Scripture that reproveth truth, and al Scripture reproveth falsehod. False writings, false bokes, false images, and false men—all be naught, to be contemned and despised. As for paper, inke, perchemente, stones, wood, bones, A.B. of the chancery hande, and a.b. of the secretary hand, a letter of Germany fasshion, or of any other forme, ⟨they⟩ be all of one estimation, and may be of man, enclining to the devel, used for falshod, or, applying to Gods gratious calling, used to set forth truth.

It is a terible matter to think that this false opinion conceaved against images should trouble any mans head. And suche as I have knowen vexed with that devill (as I have known som) be nevertheles wonderously obstinate in it. And if they can finde one that can spel Latten to help forth their madnes, they be more obdurate then ever were the Jewes, and slander what so ever is saide to them for their relief. Of this sort I know them to be, and therfore if I wist there wer many of that sort with you, I woulde not irritate them by preaching, without frute, but labour for reformation to my Lord Protector. But if you thought there might be other waies used first to a good effect, I would follow your advice, and, proceding with you and the maior, with bothe your helps, to doo that may lie in me to the redresse of the matter, which I take to be suche an enterprise against Christes religion as there cannot be a greater by man excogitate with the devels instigation, and at this time much hurtfull to the common estate, as ye can of your wisdom consider; whom I hartely desire and pray to send me answere by this

---

1 *1576–83*, that

275

bearer to these my letters, to the intent I may use my self in sending of a preacher thither, or writing to my Lord Protector, as the case shal require accordingly. And thus fare you hartely well. From my house at Wolvesaye, the thirde of Maye, 1547.

[1]ST. W.[1]

Headed: A letter of [2]Steven Gardner to Captaine Vaughin[2].

NOTES TO NO. 119

Page 274. On his return to Wittenberg from the Wartburg in 1522, Luther preached eight sermons (published, 1523) against changes instituted by Carlstadt. A large part of the third and fourth was directed against the destruction of images. He dealt with the same topic in a book, published 1525, entitled *Wider die himmlischen Propheten von den Bilden und Sacrament*. See *Luthers Werke,* ed. J. K. Irmischer, Erlangen, 1830 ff., XXVIII, 225; XXIX, 134.

Page 275. A. B. of the chancery hand *etc.* For description and illustration of the chancery and secretary hands, as well as of other styles of sixteenth-century writing, *see* H. Jenkinson, *The Later Court Hands in England*, Cambridge, 1927. Gardiner himself wrote in more than one style, which makes the identification of his hand no easier for a modern student than for his contemporaries. John Clerk, Bishop of Bath and Wells, writing to Wolsey on 18 June, 1528, about a dispatch which was thought to have gone astray, says, 'The letter... was subscribyd with Master Stephyns hand and Sir Gregories. Of Sir Gregories I am sure. Master Stephyns writith 2 or 3 handes... if it were any of his hands it was his Italyon hand' (*St. P.,* VII, 81).

120. *To* SOMERSET

Winchester, 21 May, [1547]

Foxe, *1563*,733–5; *1583*, II, 1342; ed. Pratt, VI, 30. A sixteenth-century manuscript copy of the last twelve lines is in B.M., Add. 28,571, 21 r.

Complains of the circulation of Bale's books; recalls Somerset's promise to suffer no innovation in religion; certain printers, players, and preachers trouble the realm with false doctrine; the defeat of the Protestant leader John Frederick

1–1 *1576–83*, Steph. Wint.
2–2 *1570–83*, Winchester to M. (Maister, Mayster) Vaughan

of Saxony; no commonwealth without true religion can maintain itself; complains of rhymes depraving Lent; the chief sins of England, Germany, France, and Italy; the advantages of Lent; Henry VIII's manner of keeping it; religion will be Somerset's most troublesome problem. (*See* pp. 284–5 on Somerset's reply.)

After my most[1] humble commendations to your Grace: It may like the same to understande, I have seen of late 2 bokes set forth in Englysh by Bale, very pernicious, sedicious, and slaundrous. And albeit that your Grace nedeth not mine advertisement in that matter, yet I am so bolde to troble your Grace with my leters for mine own commoditie, wherwith to satisfie mine owne conscience to write and say as becometh me in such maters, which I desire your Grace to take in good part. For it greveth me not a litle to se, so sone after my late soveraigne lord and maisters death, a boke spread abrode more to his dishonor (if a princes honor may be by vile inferior subjects impeched) then professed enemies have imagined, to note a woman to have suffred under him as a martyr, and the woman therwith to be, by Bales own elucidacion, as he calleth it, so set forth and painted as she aperith to be, and is boasted to be, a sacramentary, and by the lawes worthy (as she suffred) the paines of death. Such like things have, by stealthe, in our late soveraign lords days gone abrode as they do now; and as I ⟨was[2]⟩ wont in such cases to speak, I kepe my wont to write to your Grace now, in whose hands I know the estate of the realm to be fortime in government, and to whom, for respectes of old acquaintance, I wish al felicitie.

In these matters of religion I have ben long exercised, and have (thankes be to God) lived so long as I have sene them throughly tried. And besides that I have lerned in writen bokes of autoritie, I have perceived by bokes written without autoritie, as by Masters Bale, Joye, and other, and specially as Bale useth it[3] now, that Scripture doth, by abuse, service to the right hand and the left at once; in so muche as at one time Bale prayseth Luther, and setteth his death forth in English, with commendation as of a saint, which Luther (whatsoever he was otherwise) stoutly affirmed the presence really of Christes natural body in the Sacrament of the Altar; and yet Bale, the noble clerke, would have Anne Askew, blasphemously deniyng the presence of Christes natural body, to be taken for a saint also. So as Bales sainctes may vary

---

1 *not in 1583*   2 *no auxiliary verb in 1563; 1583,* am
3 *not in 1583*

in heaven, if they chaunse not ⟨to vary⟩ by the way; which might suffise to disprove the mans credit, if thwarting talke were not more desired of many then the truth in dede; which truth was supposed to have bene, both in writing and exercise, well established longe before our late lords death, and Bale and his adherents in their madnes plainly reproved and condemned.

I can not forget your Grace tolde me you wold suffer no innovacion; and in dede if you deliver this realm to the King at 18[1] yeres of age, as the King his father, whose soule God assoyle, left it, as I trust you shal, the act is so honorable and good as it were pity to troble it with any innovacion; whiche were a charge to your Grace more then neded, being alredy burthened hevely. And albeit in the common wealth every man hath his part, yet, as God hath placed you, the matter is, under the Kinges Majestie, chiefly yours and, as it were, yours alone. Every man hath his eye directed unto you both here and abrode. You shal shadow mens doings, if thei be don, which is one incommoditie of high rule. And for my part, besides my dutie to the Kings Majestie and the realme, I wold that your Grace, in whom, since your government, I have found much gentlenes and humanitie, had much honor with good successe as ever any had; and pray to God that men would let your Grace alone, and suffer the realme in the time of your government in quiet among our selves, wherby to be the more able to resist forren trouble; which your grace doth prudently forse.

Certen printers, players, and prechers[2] make a wonderment, as though we knew not yet how to be justified, nor what sacraments we should have. And if the agrement in religion made in the time of our late soveraign lord be of no force in their judgement, what establishment could any new agrement have? And every incertentie is noisom to any realme. And where every man wilbe maister, there must needes be uncertainty[3]. And one thing is marvelous, that at the same time it[4] is taught that al men be liers, at the selfe same time almost every man would be beleved; and emongest them Bale, when his untruth apereth evidently in setting forth the examination of Anne Askewe, which is utterly misreported.

I besech your Grace to pardone my bablinge with you, but I see my late soveraign lord and maister slandred by such simple persones, religion assalted, the realme troubled, and peasable men disquieted, with

1 *1583*, 8   2 *1563*, prethers; *1583*, preachers
3 *1563*, uncertainly; *1583*, uncertaynty   4 *not in 1583*

278

occasion geven to enemies to poynte and say that after Wicliefes strang teaching in the sacraments of Christs Church hath vexed other, it is finally torned unto us to molest and scorg us; for other fruit cannot Bales teaching have, ne the teaching of such other as go about to troble the agreament established here. In which matter I dare not desire your Grace specially to loke ernestly unto it, least I shuld seme to note in you that becometh me not. And I know that your Grace being otherwise occupied, these thinges may crepe in, as it hath bene heretofore. Sometime it may be hard for your Grace to finde out or pull out the roote of this naughtines; but yet I am so bolde to wryte of these, of myne owne stomake, who have ever used for discharge of my selfe to saye and write in time and place as I thought mighte doo good, for reliefe of the mater, remitting the rest to the disposition of God, who hath wrought wonders in these maters since they wer first moved, and geven me such knowledge and experience in them, as I ought to take them (as they be) for corruption and untruth—I meane knowledge and experience of them that be chief stirrers, so infect with untruth as they cannot speake or report truly in common matters. The pretence is of the spirite, and all is for the flesh, women, and meate, with liberty of hand and tongue, a dissolution and dissipation of all estates, cleane contrarious to the place God hath called your Grace thereunto. For it tendeth all to confusion and disorder, which is theffect of untruth.

Bale hath set fourth a prayer for the Duke J⟨ohn⟩ of Saxe, wherin the Duke remitteth to Gods judgment to be shewed here in this worlde the justnes of his cause concerning religion, and desireth God, if his cause be not good, to order him to be taken and to be spoiled of his honor and possessions, with many such gay words wherby to tempt God. Since which prayer the Duke is in deed taken, as al the world sayeth[1]; and[2] at the time of his taking, as the accompt is made, such strangenes in the son, as we saw it here, as hath not bene sene. They happened both to gether (this we know) and be both marvaillous, but whether the one were a token ordred to concurre with other, God knoweth and man cannot define.

Many common welthes have continued without the bishop of Romes jurisdiction, but without the[3] true religion, and with such opinions as Germany mainteined, no estate hath continued in the circuit of the world to us knowen since Christ came. For the Turks and Tartarres government is, as it were, a continuall war, and they uphold there rule

1 *? scribe's or printer's error for* seeth   2 *not in 1583*
3 *not in 1583*

with subdewing of nobilytie by fyre and sworde. Germany with ther new religion cold never have stand, and thogh the Emperor had let them alone. For if it be perswaded the understanding of Gods law to be at larg in women and children, wherby they may have the rule of that, and then Gods law must be the rule of al, is not hereby the rule of al brought into there hands? These of some wilbe called wittye reasons, but they be in deede truthes chyldren, and so is all the eloquence, which some (to disprayse me) saye I have, what so ever they saye of me. For truthe is of it selfe, in a ryght meanynge mannes mouthe, more eloquent then forged matter[1] can with studie bryng fourth.

What rymes be sette fourth to deprave[2] Lent, and how fonde (savyng your Graces honour) and foolyshe! And yet the people paye mony for them. And they can serve for nothyng but to learne the people to rayle, and to cause such as used to make provision for fish against Lent, fearinge now Lent to be so sick, as the rime purporteth, and like to die in deede, to forbeare to make there accustomed provision for the nexte yeare. And therto shall it come, if the common diet be not certeine. For the fishmonger will never hope to have good sale, when the boucher may with fleshe out face him. And fish is the great treasure of this realm and fode inestimable. And these good words I give, although I love it not my selfe. For such as love not fish should nevertheles commend it to other, to the intent the flesh by them forborn might be to such as love it only the more plenty.

The publike diffamation and trifling with Lent is a merveilous matter to them that would say evil of this realme; for there is nothing more commended unto us Christen men in both the Churches of the Grekes and Lattens then Lent is, if al men be not liers. In the King our late soveraigne lordes daies this mater was not thus spoken of. And I think our enemies wold wish we had no Lent. Every contry hath his peculier inclination to naughtines: England and Germany to the belly, the one in licor, the other in meate; France a little beneath the belly; Italy to vanity and pleasures devised; and let an Englishe belly have a further avancement, and nothing can stay it. When I was purveior for the seas, what an exclamacion was there (as your Grace shewed me) of the bishops fasting day, as they called Wednesday, and 'Winchester, Winchester, grand mercy for your wine; I beshrow your hart for your water!' Was not that song, although it was in sport, a signification how

1 *1583*, matters   2 *1583 adds* the

loth men be to have there licence restreyned or there accustomed fare abated, unles it were in extreame necessity?

I here ⟨*i.e.*, hear⟩ say that Lent is thus spoken of by Josephe and Tongue, with other new ⟨men⟩ whome I know not, as to[1] be one of Christs miracles, which God ordeyned not man to imytate and follow; at which teaching all the world will laugh. For Christen men have Christ for an example in althings, both to use the world as he did, only for necessity, and contemne the world as he did, and in case to refuse it and choose the vile death as he did the death of the crosse; which thinges he did like a mayster most perfectly[2], for he was very good[3]; and we must endevor our selfe, in the use of his giftes, to followe that he did—not to faste fortye days without meat as Christ did, for we be but prentises, and cary about a ruinous carcas that must have some dayly reparation with foode, but yet was there never none that sayd howe therfore we should do nothing because we can not do all, and take Christs fast for a miracle only. And yet all that followe Christe truly, they worke daylye miracles in subdewinge and conforming, by Gods grace, there sensual appetites, and humble ⟨*i.e.*, humbly⟩ obeying to the will of God, which no man can of himself do. And Christ promysed that his true servantes shuld worke the works that he did, and greater workes also. Wherfore it is a slender matter to say Lent was one of Christes miracles, for so was it to love his enemyes, and specially those that scourged and bobbed him, which may not be (if that allegation hath place) taught Christen men to followe, because it was a miracle, as they might say.

It wer more tolerable to forget Lent, as Pogge telleth of a priest in the mountaines that knewe not how the yeare went about, and when the weather opened and he went abroad and perceaved his neighbours were towards Palme Sondaye, he devised an excuse to his parysh and badde them prepare therfore, for in dede the yeare had somwhat slipped him, but he wold fassion the matter so as they should be as sone at Easter as the rest. And thus did he passe over Lent with much lesse slaunder then to teach it for a doctrine that Lent was one of Christs miracles, and therefore not to be imitated for us. For although it was in dede a greate miracle (as al Christs doings wer), yet was it ther not a great miracle, ne more against mans nature, then to love them that labored and were busy to take away the naturall life of his manhoode. For as the nature

1 *not in 1583*   2 *1583*, perfect   3 *1583*, god

of man desireth reliefe, so doth it abhorre distruction or hurt. In will and desire men follow Christ in al things; in execution they cannot. For we have brickell vessels, and God geveth his gifts to men as he seith expedient for his Church; so as men cannot heale the lame when they will, as Christ did when he would, but as God shal thinke profitable for the edefication of the flock assembled.

Gregory Nazienzene speaketh of some that enterprised to imitate Christs fast above there power, whose imoderat zeale he doth not disalow, not requiring of all men so to do, for that is an extremite, ne yet assoyllinge the matter as our new schoole men do, that Christen men shoulde let Christs fast alone as a miracle. Which maner of solucion I hard a good fellow make, when it was told him he might not revenge him selfe, and when he were stroken on the one eare, put fourthe the other. 'I am,' quod[1] he, 'a man; I am not God. If Christ being God did so, he might,' quod he, 'if it had pleased him, have done otherwise.' And so when it hath bene alleaged that Christ fasted forty days, 'He might,' quod he, 'have eaten if he had list.' These triflings in sport might be drawen to grave speach, if Christen men shall refuse to follow Christ in miracles. For all hys life was miracles, and his love, that is our badg, most miraculous of all, to dy for his enemies.

I besech your Grace to pardone me, for I am like one[2] of the Common⟨s⟩ House, that, when I am in my tale, thinke I shoulde have liberty to make an ende; and specially writing to your Grace, with whome I accompt I may be bold, assuring you it procedeth of a zeale towardes you, unto whome I wish well, whose intente, althoughe it be suche as it oughte to be, and as it pleased you to shewe me it was, yet suche thynges spreade abroade wherof the evell willers of the realme will take corage and make accompt (although it be wrong) that all goeth on wheles.

If an man had eyther fondly or undiscretly spoken of Lent to engreve it to be an importable burden, I wold wish his reformation, for I have not lerned that all men be[3] bound to kepe the Lent in the forme receaved. But this I reconne, that no Christen man may contempne the forme receaved, being such a devout and profitable imitation of Christ to celebrate his faste, and, in that time, such as have ben in the rest of the yere wordly[4], to prepare them selfes to come, as they shoulde come, to the feaste of Easter; wherof S. Chrisostome speaketh expresly. And for avoyding contempt, a licence truly obteined of the superior serveth.

1 *1583*, quoth (*here and in following instances*)   2 *1563*, on; *1583*, one
3 *1583*, are   4 *1583*, worldlye

And so I hard the Kings Majesty, our soveraigne lorde, declare, when your Grace was present. And therfore he him self was very scrupulous in graunting of licences. And to declare that him self contemned not the fast, he was at charge to have (as your Grace knoweth) the Lent diet daily prepared, as it had bene for him selfe. And the like herof I here ⟨*i.e.*, hear⟩ say your Grace hath ordered for the Kings Majestie that now is, which agreith not with certeyn preaching in this matter, ne the rimes set abroade.

Lent is among Christen men a godly fast[1] to exercise men to forbeare, and in England both godly and pollitike, such as without confusion we can not forbeare, as thexperience shall shew, if it be ever attempted; which God forbid. And yet Lent is buried in rime, and Steven Stockfish bequeathed, not to me, though my name be noted, wherwith for myne own part I cannot be angry, for that is mitigated by their fondnes. But I wold desire of God to have the strength of this realme encreased with reporte of concorde, whiche doth quenche many vaine devices and imaginacions. And if all men be liers, as it is now to my understanding strangely published, me thinke Bale and suche new men as be new liers should be most abhorred and detested, as[2] so muche the more dangerous as thei be newe. That which in Italy and Fraunce is a matter of combate, is now founde to be appropriate to all men. God graunt the truthe to be desired of al men truly! But as one asked, when he sawe an olde philosopher dispute with an other, what thei talked on; and it was answered how the old man was discussing what was vertue; it was replied, 'If the olde man yet dispute of vertue, when will he use it?' So it may be sayd in our religion, 'If we be yet searching for it, when shall we begin [3]to put it in execution?'

I would make an end of my letters[4] and cannot; wherin I accompte my self faultie. And though I may erre, as every man may, yet I lie not, for I say as I thinke, for as[5] much as I have said, and further thinke your Grace hath no trouble troublesom but this matter of religion, unseasonably brought in to the diffamacion of our late soveraigne lords actes, doings, and lawes. I besech your Grace take my meaning and wordes in good part, and pardon my boldnes which groweth of the[6] familiaritie I have [7]heretofore had[7] with your Grace, whiche I cannot

---

1 *1563, 1583,* feast   2 *1583,* and
3 *fragment in B.M., Add.* 28,571, 21 r., *begins here*
4 *B.M.,* letter   5 *B.M.,* so
6 *not in B.M.*   7–7 *B.M.,* had hertofore

forget. And thus enforcing[1] my self to an end, shal pray to[2] Almighty God to preserve your Grace in much felicitie, with encrease of honor and the atcheving of your hartes desire[3]. At Winchester[4], the 21 of May.

Your Graces humble beadman,

S. W.

Headed: An other letter of S. W.

NOTES TO NO. 120

Page 277. The books by Bale referred to are *The first examinacyon of A. Askewe...with the elucydacyon of J. B.,* 1546; *The lattre Examinacyon of A. Askewe...with the elucydacyon of J. B.,* 1547; *The true hystorie of the Christen departynge of...Martyne Luther...translated...by J. Bale* [1546]; the first two have been reprinted by the Parker Society. Anne Askew was burned 16 July, 1546.

Pages 278, 280, 283. The allusions to the text 'all men are liars' (Ps. cxvi, 11 [Vulgate, cxv, 11]; Rom. iii, 4) are to the recantation sermon of Dr Richard Smith, 15 May, 1547, published in 1547 as *A godly and faythfull retractation. See also* pp. 285, 293–5, below.

Page 279. Duke John. John Frederick, Elector of Saxony, was defeated and captured by Charles V at Mühlberg, 24 April, 1547.

Page 280. On Gardiner as 'purveyor for the seas' *see* above, p. 93.

Page 281. For Poggio's tale *see* his *Facetiae,* No. XI (in Broadway Translations ed., 1928, No. XXIII).

Page 282. For Gregory Nazianzen on the Lenten fast *see* his Oration XL, § XXX (Migne, *P. G.,* XXXVI, 401; *N. and P. N. F.,* ser. 2, VII, 371).

Page 282. For Chrysostom on Lent as a preparation for Easter *see* his *Homilies on the Statues,* XX, § 1 (Migne, *P. G.,* XLIX, 197; *N. and P. N. F.,* ser. 1, IX, 471).

Somerset's reply. On 27 May Somerset sent to Gardiner a long letter, probably composed for him by Cranmer or another reforming prelate, in answer at once to this and to the letter to Captain Vaughan (No. 119), which Vaughan had forwarded to Somerset. Foxe broke the letter in two, printing the appropriate part after each of Gardiner's letters to

1 *B.M.,* enforminge
3 *B.M.,* desires
2 *not in B.M.*
4 *end of B.M.*

which it replied—Foxe, *1563*, 730–1, 735–6; ed. Pratt, VI, 28, 34. That it is indeed one letter, not two, is clear from the following:

1. What Foxe prints as the first letter opens with a reference to the receipt of two letters from Gardiner, but answers only one. The other is answered in Foxe's second letter.

2. In Gardiner's reply of 6 June (No. 121), he refers to Somerset's letter of 27 May and proceeds to answer the matter contained in both of Foxe's letters.

3. What Foxe prints as the first letter ends abruptly and without the customary closing phrases; what he prints as the second letter begins without the customary opening commendations and can easily be read to follow on after the first without break.

4. A sixteenth-century manuscript copy of Foxe's second letter, in B.M., Add. 28,571, 3–4, is headed thus: 'The rest of the letter from the Lord Protector to the Bishop of Winchester, omitted in the Boke of Actes and Monuments. The first part of these letters do answere the Bishops letters directed to Master Edwarde Vaghan of Portesmouth.' Foxe's second letter was not reprinted in his editions of 1570 and 1576, and if the writer of this heading were familiar with one of these editions, his remark that the rest of the letter was omitted by Foxe, is not only true but is an indication that what Foxe had printed as a second letter in 1563 was in reality part of the first.

The Protector, in this letter, suggested that Gardiner was too much concerned at the destruction of images and too little at the burning of Scripture (a reference to the burning of unauthorized translations—*see* proclamation of 8 July, 1546, in Foxe, V, 565), and pointed out that images were so easily misunderstood that even Gardiner himself had misinterpreted the image on the King's seal. He went on to express surprise that Gardiner was so earnest against ballads about Lent, yet unconcerned about Dr Smith's book which favoured the Papacy (*A briefe treatyse settynge forth divers truthes . . . not expressed in the scripture but left to ye church by the apostles tradition*, London, 1547).

The date and postscript to the letter, not printed in Foxe, but preserved in the manuscript copy referred to, are as follows:

From London, the 27 of May, 1547.

Your Lordships loving frend,
E. Somerset

And bicause we have begonne to write to you, we are put in remembrance of a certaine letter or boke which you wrote unto us against the Bishop of St Davids sermon and Doctor Ridleis, to the which an answere, then being immediatlie made, was by negligence of us forgotten to be sent. Now we both send you that and also thanswere which the Bishop of St Davides wrote to the same boke of yours.

121. *To* SOMERSET

Winchester, 6 June, [1547]

Foxe, *1563*, 736–9; *1583*, II, 1345; ed. Pratt, VI, 36.

> The tone of Somerset's letters reminds Gardiner of Henry VIII; Henry's wisdom, his regard for Gardiner, his attitude toward the Earl of Wiltshire (father of Anne Boleyn); likes Somerset's proclamation against rumours of innovation; claims forthrightness of speech as a characteristic; has found images at Portsmouth contemptuously handled; explains his misinterpretation of the royal seal (in No. 119, above); Latin and Greek will outlive English as languages of religion; complains of restraint of episcopal preaching (*see Reg. Gardiner*, 81); comments on the brazen serpent; Henry VIII's discussion of images with Cranmer, and his ordering creeping to the cross; hears that Edward VI favours procession; Edward's probable attitude, on coming of age, toward religious changes in his minority; how frequent change in religion favours Rome; Cranmer and Tunstall have soon forgotten the *King's Book*; why Gardiner hears evil tidings before Somerset; knows little of Dr Richard Smith, but dislikes both his book and his retraction (*see* above, pp. 284–5); commends Somerset's rule; advises adherence to Henry VIII's religious establishment; encloses his discussion (not extant) of Barlow's answer to him (sent by Somerset—*see* pp. 285–6).

After my most humble commendations to your good Grace: Upon the returne of my servant Massy with your Graces letters, aunswering to such my letters wherin I signified the robbing of my secretary, I red the same gladly, as by the contentes of the matter I had cause so to doo; which was such a comfortative as I digested easely the rest of the great packet, having bene accustomed therunto in the Kinges my late soveraigne lordes dayes; which fassion of writing his Highnes (God pardon his soul) called 'whetting,' which was not all the moste pleasant unto me at al times. Yet when I sawe in my doings was no hurt, and sometime by occasion therof the matter amended, I was not so coy as alwayes to revers my argument; nor, so that his affaires went wel, I never trobled my selfe whether he made me a wanton or not. And when such as were privy to his leters directed unto me were afrayed I had bene in high displeasure (for the termes of the letters sounded so), yet I my selfe

286

feared it nothing at al. I estemed him, as he was, a wise prince, and what so ever he wrote or said for the present, he would after consider the matter as wisely as any man, and neither hurt or inwardly disfavor him that had bene bold with him; wherof I serve for a proof, for no man could do me hurt during his life. And when he gave me the bishoprik of Winchester, he sayd he had often squared with me, but he loved me never the worse; and for a token therof gave me the bishoprike. And once when he had bene vehement with me, in the presence of the Earle of Wilteshire, and saw me dismayd wyth it, he toke me a part into hys bedde chamber and comforted me, and sayd that hys dyspleasure was not so much to me, as I dyd take it, but he myslyked the matter, and he durst more boldly direct hys spech to me then to the Erle of Wylteshyre. And from that day forward he could not put me out of corage; but if any displeasant words passed from him, as thei did some time, I folded them up in the matter; which hindred me a little, for I was reported unto him that I stouped not and was stubborne. And he had commended unto me certeine mens gentle natur, as he caled it, that wept at every of his wordes; and my[1] thought that my nature was as gentle as theres, for I was sory that he was moved. But els I know when the displeasure was not justly gronded in me, I had no cause to take thought, nor was not at any time in all my life miscontent or grudging at any thinge done by him, I thank God of it.

And therfore being thus brought up, and having first redde your Graces most gentle leters, signifieng the devise of a proclamation to staye these rumors, and redinge the same proclamation which my servant brought with him, I red the more quiet⟨ly⟩ your Graces grete letters, and would have laid them up with out further aunswere, were it not that, percace, my so doing might be mistaken. For glum silence may have a nother construction then frank speach, where a man may speake, as I reconne I may with your Grace. Upon confidence whereof I am so bould to write thus much for my declaratyon touching your Graces letters of the xxvij of May[2], that howe ernest so ever my letters be taken in fearynge any inovation, I neyther inwardly feare it, neither shew any demonstracion in mine outward deeds to the world here, or in communication, that I doo feare it to be done by authority; but in my selfe resist the rumors and vaine enterprises, with confidence in the truthe and your Graces wisdome, for if I feared that[3] in deede whith[4]

1 *1583*, me   2 *1563*, Maij; *1583*, May
3 *1563*, *1583*, it   4 *1583*, which

perswasion it shuld come to passe, I shuld have smal lust to write in it; but I feare more in deede the trouble that mighte arise by light boldnes of other, and thencombre of such matter whiles other outward affaires occupye your Graces mind, then the effect by your direction that hath bene talked on a broade. And yet in the writing I doo speake as the matter leadeth, continuing mine old manner to be ernest; which as some men have disprayesd, so some have commended it. And therfore in a good honeste mater I folow rather mine owne inclination, then to take the paines to speake as butter woulde not melt in my mouth; wherewith I perceave your Grace is not miscontent, for the which I most humbly thanke you.

And firste, as concerning Portestmouth, I wrote to the captaine and maior in the thing as I had information, and by men of credence. And yet I suspended my credit tyll I had hard from thence, as by my letters appere⟨th⟩; and as I was lothe to have it so, so was I loth to beleve it. And to shewe that I feared no innovation[1] by autority, ne regarded not any such danger, went thether my selfe, and in conclusion was in such familiarity with the captayn that, after he had shewed me al the gentle enterteynement he coulde, he desired me to make an exhortation to his men as they stoode handsomely with ther weapons, wherwith they had shewed warlike feates; which I did, and departed in amity with the captaine and soldiers and al the towne; the captain telling me plainly he was nothing offended with any thinge I had said in my sermon, ne there was cause why he should. But the very act in deede in defacing the images had no such ground as Maister Captaine pretended. For I asked specialy for such as had abused those images, and no such coulde be shewed, for that I enquired for openly. And the image of S. John thEvangelist, standing in the chauncell by the high alter, was pulled down, and a table of alablaster broken. And in it an image of Christ crucified so contemptuously handled as was in my hart terrible—to have the one eie bored out and the side perced! Wherwith men were wonderously offended; for it is a very persecution beyond the sea, used in that fourme where the persone cannot be apprehended. And I take such an act to be very slaunderous and, esteming the opinion of breakinge images as unlawfull to be had very daungerous, voyde of all lerning and truth, wrote after my fassion to the capteine; which letters I perceve be[2] come to[3] your Graces handes.

1 *1563*, invocation; *1583*, innovation   2 *1583*, to
3 *1583*, by

I was not very curious in the wrytyng of them, for with me truth goeth out plainely and roundly; and speaking of the Kings seale, uttered the common language I was brought up in, after the olde sorte, when, as I conject, of a good will the people, taking Saynt George for a patron of the realme under God and having some confidence of succor by Gods strength derived by him, to encrease thestimatyon of there prince and soveraign lord, caled there king on horsbake in the feat of armes, S. George on horsbake. My knowledg was not corrupt. I know it representeth the King. And yet my speach came fourthe after the common language, wherin I trust is none offence. For, besides lerning, I by experyence have knowen the preeminens of a kyng both in war and peace. And yet if I had wist my letter shuld have commen to your Graces handes to be aunswered, then I would have bene more precyse in my spech then to give occasion of so long an argument therin. As for S. George himselfe, I have such opynyon of hym as becommeth me, and have red also of Belerephon in Homere, as they call him the father of tales.

I wil leave that matter. And as for bookes, let Latten and Greke continue as long as it shal please God; I am almost past the use of them. What service those letters have done, experience hath shewed; and religion hath continued in them M.V.C ⟨1500⟩ yeares. But as for the English tonge, it selfe hath not continued in one forme of understanding CC ⟨200⟩ yeares; and without Gods work and speciall miracle it shall hardely conteine religion long, when it cannot last it selfe. And what so ever your Graces minde is now in the matter, I know well that, having the government of the realme, your Grace wil use the gift of policy, which is the gift of God.

And even as now at this time bishops be restrayned by a special pollicy to preach onely in there cathedrall churches (the like wherof hath not bene knowen in my time), so upon an other occasion your Grace may percase think expedient to restrayne (further then the Parliament hath alredy don) the common reding of Scriptur, as is now restreined the bishops liberty of preching.

As for the brasen serpent, ⟨it⟩ did not in all mens languag represent Christ; and if I had written to an other then your Grace, I mighte have had the like matter of argument that was taken against me of Saincte George on horsbacke. For Gregory Nasianzene, chiefe devine in the Greke Church, calleth the serpents death the figure of the death of Christ, but not the serpent to be the figure of Christ. And yet when I had done al min argument, I would resolve as is resolved with me in the speach of Sainte George on horsback, that the common speach is otherwise; and so it is in sayinge the serpent to be a true figure of Christ. And yet Gregory Nasiensen called the serpent it selfe ἀντίτυπον of Christe in these words, Ὁ δὲ *etc.* in his sermon *De Pascate*; and yet in *Alma*[1] *chorus Domini* we red *aries, leo, vermis,* spoken of Christ; and some expound the Scripture, *sicut Moyses etc.*⟨Jn. iii, 14⟩, after that sort.

And as your Grace said when I was last at your house with the Frenche imbassador ⟨de Selve⟩, ye wished him and me together disputing, to se when we would make an ende, even so it is in these matters, when they come in argument. For a bye thing, as Saint George on horsback, when it escapeth me, or speakinge of the brasen serpent, following a spech not throghly discussed, shalbe occasion of a digression al out of purpose. And therfore was it a greate gifte of God that our late sovereigne lorde (God rest his soule) set theyse matters in quiet; who had hard al these resons touching images which be now rehersed in your Graces letters; and havinge once my Lorde of Canterbury and me presente with him alone in his pallace that they call otherwise New Hal, handled that matter at length, and discussed with my Lord of Canterbury the understanding of Godes commaund⟨m⟩ent to the Jewes, so as all the clerkes in Christendome could not amend it. And where as one had denied the image of the Trinity to be had, by reosones as be touched in your Graces letters, I hard his Highnes answere to them at a nother time. And when he had him selfe specially commaunded divers images to be abolished, yet, as your Grace knoweth, he both ordered and him selfe put in execution the kneling and crepinge before the image of the crosse, and established agrement in that truth through all this realme; wherby all argumentes to the contrary be assoyled at once.

I wold wish images used as the boke, by his Highnes set forth, doth prescribe, and no otherwise. I know your grace only tenteth[2] me with such reosones as other make unto you; and I am not fully at liberty, althoughe I am bolde inoughe (and some will thinke[3] to bold) to aunswere some thinges as I would to another man mine equall, being so much inferior to your Grace as I am. But me thinketh S. Paules solucion during the Kings Majesties minority shold serve al: *Nos talem consuetudinem non habemus*—'We have no such custom in the Church.'

When our sovereigne lord commeth to his perfect age (which God

---

1 *1563, 1583*, Alme   2 *1583*, tempteth   3 *1563*, thinge; *1583*, thinke

graunt), I doubt not but God will reveale that shalbe necessary for the governing of his people in religion. And if any thing shalbe done in the meane time (as I think ther shall not) by your Graces direction, he may, when he cometh to age, say in the rest, as I here say he sayd now of late concerning procession, that in his fathers time men were wont to follow procession; upon which the Kings Majesties saying, the procession, as I hard, was well furnished afterwards by your Graces commandment. Which speach hath put me in remembrance that if the bishops and other of the clergy shuld agre to any alteration in religion, to the condemnation of any thing set forth by his father, wherby his father might be noted to have wanted knowledg or favor to the truthe, what he would say I cannot tell, but he might use a mervelous speach, and, for the excellency of his spirite, it were like he would; and having so just a cause against bishops as he might have, it were to be feared he would. And when he had spoken, then he might by his lawes doo more then ¹any would gladly suffer of our sort¹ at these dayes. For as the allegation of his auctority represented by your Grace shalbe then aunswered (as youre Grace nowe wryteth unto mee) that² your Grace only desired truth accordinge to Gods Scripture; and it may be then sayd, we bishops, when we have our soveraigne lorde and hed in minority, we fassion the matter as we lust; and then some yong man that woulde have a peace of the byshoppes landes shal saye: 'The beastly Byshops have alwayes done so, and when they can no lenger mainteyne one of ther pleasures of rule and superiority, then they take a nother way and let that go, and, for the tyme they be here, spend up that they have, with *Eate you and drynk you what ye lyste*, and *We together*, wyth *Edamus et bibamus, cras moriemur.*' And if we shall alleage for our defence the strength of Gods truth and the playnesse of Scripture, with the Word of the Lord, and many gay termes, and saye we were convinced by Scriptures, such an excellent judgment as the Kings Majestie is like to have will never credit us in it, ne be abused by such a vayne aunswere. And thys is a worldlye pollityke consyderation, and at home; for the noyse abrode in the world wilbe more slaunderous then this is daungerous.

And touchinge the bishop of Rome, the doyng in this realme hetherto hath never done him so much dyspleasure as an alteratyon in religion during the Kyngs Majesties minoriti shuld serve for hys purpose. For he wanteth not wits to beate into other prynces eares that where

---

1–1 *Pratt amends this to* any of our sort would gladly suffer
2 *1563, 1583 repeat* that

hys autorytye is abolished, there, at every chaunge of governours, shalbe chang in religion; and that hath bene emongs us by a whole consent established, shall, by pretence of a nother understanding in Scripture, streight be brought in question. For they will geve it no other name but a pretence, how stiffely so ever we will affirme otherwise and call it Gods Word.

And here it should much be noted that my Lord of Caunturbury, being the high bishop of the realme, highly in favour with his late sovereigne lord, and my Lord of Duresme, a man of renoumed fame in lerning and gravytie (both put by him in trust for ther councell in the order of the realme), should so sone forget there olde knowledge in Scripture, set fourth by the Kinges Majestys booke, and advise to envey ⟨*i.e.*, inveigh, bring in⟩ such matter of alteracion. Al which thinges be (I know well) by your Grace and them considered. And therfore it is to me incredible that ever any such thing should be in deed with effecte, what so ever the lightnes of talke shall spred a brode, which your Grace hath by proclamacion well stayed. But and ⟨*i.e.*, if⟩ ye had not, and the world talked so fast as ever they did, I assure your Grace I would never feare it, as men feare thinges they like not, unlesse I sawe it in execution. For of this sorte I am, that in all things I thinke should not be done in reason, I feare them not, wherwith to troble me other wise then to take heede, yf I can, and to the hed governores (as now to your Grace) shew my mynd. And such experience hath every man of me that hath commoned with me in any such matters. And therfore, albeit your Grace wryteth wysely that overmuche feare dothe hurt, and accelerateth somtime that was not intended, yet it nedes not to me; for I have lerned that lesson alredy, and would a great many mo had, which in dede should be a great stay. And thus I taulke with your Grace homely, with multiplycacion of speache not necessary, as though I ment to send you as great a packet as I receaved from you.

One thing necessary to aunswere your Grace in, ⟨is⟩ touching your marvaylle how I know soner thinges from thence then your Grace doth ther; which aryseth not upon any desire of knowledge on my behalfe, for evil thinges be oversone knowen, nor[1] upon any slacknes of your Graces[2] behalfe there, who is and is noted very vigilant, as your Graces charge requireth. But thus it is, even as it was when I was in some litle autority: they that were the evill doers in such matters would

---

1 *1563, 1583,* not   2 *1563,* Grace; *1583,* Graces

hyde them from me; so now they have handeled it other wise. For as for Jack of Lentes Testament, ⟨it⟩ was openly solde in Winchester market before I wrot unto your Grace of it. And as for Bales booke called the Elucidacion of Anne Askewes Marterdome, they were in these partes comon, some with leaves unglewed, where Maister Paget was spoken of, and some with leaves glued. And I call them common because I saw at the least foure of them. As for Bales booke touching the death of Luther, wherin was the Duke of [1] Saxons prayer, wherof I wrote, ⟨it⟩ was brought downe into this country by an honest gentelman to whome it was (as I remember he told me) geven at London for newes, and had it a good while eare I wrot to your Grace. I had not then receaved the inhibition for preching wherof men spake otherwise then they knewe.

And in the meane time Doctor Smith recanted, which[2] a priest of this towne (who to mine owne mouth boasted him selfe to be your Graces chaplaine, but I beleved it not) brought downe with speede, and made by meanes to have it broughte to my knowledge; which I knew besydes, for they had by and by filled all the country here abouts of tales of me. And when I saw Doctor Smithes recantacion begin with *Omnis homo mendax*, so Engleshed and such a new humility as he woulde make all the doctors of the Church liers with him selfe, knowing what oppinions were abrode, it enforced me to write unto your Grace for the ease of my conscience; geving this judgement of Smith, that I nether liked his tractation of unwritten verities, ner[3] yet his retractacion, and was glad of my formar judgement, that I neyver had familiaryty with him. I sawe him not that I wot these iij yeres, ne talked with him these vij yeres, as curious as I am noted in the common welth. And wher as in his unwritten verities he was so mad to say, 'Byshops in this realme may make laws,' I have witnes that I said at that word, we should be then dawes, and was by and by sory that ever he had written of the Sacrament of the Alter; which was not, as it was noysed, untouched with that woord, 'All men be liers,' which is a marvaillous word, as it soundeth in our tong, when we saie a man were better have a thief in his house then a lier. And the depraving of mans nature in that sort is not the setting out of the autoryty of the Scripture. For albeit the autoritie of[4] Scripture

1 *not in 1583*
2 *1563, 1583,* with, *which is followed by Pratt who regards* which, *in other later editions, as a misprint (Pratt,* VI, *addenda, p.* 784); *but meaning and grammar clearly demand* which
3 *1563,* more; *1583,* ner   4 *1583 adds* the

dependeth not upon man, yet the ministracion of the letter, which is writing and speaking, is exercised and hath ben from the beginning delivered throgh mans hand and taught by mans mouth; which men[1] the Scripture calleth holly men, and that is contrary to liers. And therfore Saynt Austine in his booke *De Mendacio* sayeth *omnis homo mendax* signifieth *omnis homo peccans.* If Smith had only written of bishops lawes, and then sayd he had (saving your honour) lyed loudly, or, to mittigate the matter, sayd he had erred by ignoraunce, that had ben don truly and humbly; for he that seketh for much company in lieng as he did, hath smale humilty, for he would hyde him selfe by the nomber. And this much as touching Smith, of whom, nor his booke, till he was in trouble, I never hard talking.

But to the matter I wrote of. I have told your Grace how I cam to knowledg of them, very skarcely in tyme, but in the thinge over quickly; and never had any such thought in my lyfe, as I denied to your Grace to be worthely charged with them, by them, I meane, that may herafter charge; for I know no such yet in this worlde, and I never was in myne opinion so madde as to write to your Grace in that sorte. When althinges be wel, I have many causes to rejoyce; but where thinges were otherwise (as I trust they shal not), I have nothing to do to aske any accompt. I trust I shal never forget my selfe so much. I thank God I am even aswel lerned to live in the place of obedience as I was in the place of direction in our late soveraine lords lyfe. And for my quietnes in this estate, accompt my selfe to have a great treasure of your Graces rule and autoritie; and therfore wil worship and honore it other wise then to use such maner of presumption to aske an[2] accompt.

And I know your Grace cannot staye these matters so sodenly, and I esteme it a great matter that thinges be stauld hetherto thus. But if thinges had encreased as the rumores purported, your Grace might have ben encombred more in the execution of your good determinacion. Now thankes be to God, your Grace goith well about to staye it. As for my selfe, I know myne inward determinacion to do, as I maye, my duty to God and the world, and have no cause to complaine of the unyversale dysposicion of them in my dioces. I know but one[3] way of quiet: to kepe and folow such lawes and orders in religion as our late sovereigne lord left with us; which, by his lyfe, all[4] the bishops and clergy sayd was the very truth. And I never red yet or herd any thing

1 *1563, 1583, add* in   2 *1583,* any
3 *1563,* on; *1583,* one   4 *1583,* as

why to swarve from it, ne thinke it expedient to call any one thinge in doubt during the Kinges Majestyes minority, wherby to empaire the strength of thaccord established. Which I write, not mistrusting your Grace in the contrary, but declaring my selfe, and wishing the same mynde to other about you, as I trust they have; for which I shall pray to God, who prospered our late sovereigne lord in that religion[1], as we have sene experience, and, by your Graces forsighte and pollitike goverment, shall send the like prosperyte to our sovereigne lord that now is; wherin I shall do my parte as a subject moste bounden many waies therunto.

I send unto your Grace herewith my discussion of my Lord of Saint Davies purgacion, wherin I walk somwhat more at liberty then writing to your Grace. And yet I take my selfe liberty ynough, with a reverent mynd, nevertheles, to kepe me within my bonds; whiche if I at anye tyme exceade, I truste your Grace will beare with me after your accustomed goodnes; for whose prosperity I shal continually pray, with encrease of honour. At Winchester, the vj of June.

Headed: An other letter of VV.[2] to the L. Protector.

NOTES TO NO. 121

Pages 287, 292. The proclamation referred to is that of 24 May, 1547, ordering the punishment of talebearers and spreaders of false rumours of innovations in religion—R. Steele, *Tudor and Stuart Proclamations*, Oxford, 1910, I, No. 306; Strype, *Mem.*, II, i, 57. *See also* pp. 298, 366, below.

Page 289. For Gregory Nazianzen on the brazen serpent *see* his Oration XLV, § XXII (Migne, *P. G.*, XXXVI, 653; *N. and P. N. F.*, ser. 2, VII, 431).

Page 290. *Alma chorus Domini* are the opening words of the Sarum Sequence for Thursday and Saturday after Pentecost and for the order for matrimony (J. W. Legg, *Sarum Missal*, Oxford, 1916, 416, 472).

Page 293. For Bale's books *see* above, pp. 277, 284.

Page 293. For Richard Smith's tractation and retractation *see* above, pp. 284–5. His writings on the Sacrament at this time were *The Assertion and defence of the sacramente of the aulter*, London, 1546,

1 *an emendation of* rebellion   2 *1583*, W

and *A Defence of the blessed masse*, London, 1546, reissued, 1547, as *A Defence of the sacrifice of the masse*.

Page 294. For St Augustine on *Omnis homo mendax, see,* not his *De Mendacio*, but his *Contra Mendacium,* § 40 (Migne, *P. L.*, XL, 547; *N. and P. N. F.*, ser. 1, III, 500.

Page 294. The difficult and perhaps corrupt passage, 'never had any such thought... in that sorte,' seems to be a disclaimer by Gardiner that he had ever thought that the spread of irreligious books could be then or later laid to Somerset's account.

122. *To* SOMERSET

Winchester, 10 June, 1547

Foxe, *1563*, 739–40; ed. Pratt, VI, 41.

Cranmer writes concerning homilies proposed in Convocation, 1542; Henry VIII's subsequent determinations (in the *King's Book*) made such homilies superfluous; encloses copy of answer to Cranmer (not extant); urges retention of Henry's religious settlement; refers to Somerset's letter of 16 April (not extant).

After moste humble commendationes to your Grace: I have received this day letters from my Lord of Caunterbury towching certayn homilies which the bisshops in the Convocacion holden[1] Anno[2] M.V.xlij agreed to make for stai of such errours as were then by ygnorant preachers sparkeled among the people. For other agrement ther had not then passed among us. Since that time God gave our late soverayne lorde the gyfte of pacificacion in those matters, which, establyshed by his Hyghnes authoryty in the Convocacion, extynguished our devises, and remayneth of force with your Grace; wherin to avoyd many encombrous argumentes which witt can devise agaynst the truth, I sende to your Grace the copy of myne aunswer to my Lord of Caunturbury, to whome I wryte and offer my selfe more largelye then I ever dyd in any matter of the realme, to any man besydes my soverain lord or the chyefe governore, as your Grace. For I am not factious, and use only to saye as I am bounde to saye, as occasion servith; for that is my duty, having no nother thing purposed but truth and honesty, what soever eny man shall otherwyse say of me.

1 *1563*, holding   2 *1563*, Anne

I am busier with your Grace then nedeth; but such commendacions as it pleased your Grace to send me by Maister Coke (for the which I most humbely thanke your Grace) hath engendred thus much more boldnes, that ever me thinketh I should desyre your Grace not to suffer the Kings Majestye our late soverayne lords determynacion to slyppe thancker holde of authoryty, and come to a lose disputacion; for deciscion wherof afterwarde, the burden must reste on youre Grace, unto whome I desyre all properous successe, and thencrease and continuaunce of such honour as God hath graunted to your vertue, not to fall in encombre of any by matter that nede not be sturred.

Yf your Grace thinke not your selfe encombred with my babling and inculking that nedeth not unto you, I woulde aunswer your Graces letters of xvj of Aprell, so as your Grace will, by other letters, withdrawe your name, that I may be seene to dyspute with one not so far above me in authority as your Grace is; which I have thought requisit to advertyse, leste by my sylence your Grace should deme I thought my selfe overcome in those matters, wher indede I am of a contrary mynde, and can shew wherupon to ground me, why I should so thinke. And thus desiring your Grace to take in good parte my doinges, I shall continually praye for the preservacion of your Grace longe in felicyty. At Winchester, the x of June, 1547.

Headed: S. W. to the L. Protector.

123. *To* SOMERSET

[Winchester, shortly after 12 June, 1547]

Foxe, *1563*, 740; ed. Pratt, VI, 41.

Homilies proposed five years ago cannot legally be issued now without a new grant of royal authority; sends copy of letter to Cranmer (No. 124); Cranmer is beginning something he may not live to finish; can admit no innovations.

After my moste humble commendacions to your Grace: Synce my letters unto your Grace, where with I sente unto you such letters as I had written to my Lord of Caunturbury for aunswer to his letters touching homelies, I have eftsones receved other letters from my sayd Lord of Caunterbury, requiring the sayd homelies by vertue of a Convocacion holden v yeres past, wherin we communed of that which toke none effect than, and much lesse nedeth to be put in execution now, ne in my judgement cannot, with out a new autoryte from the Kinges Majestye that now is, commaunding such a matter to be enterprised.

I wrot at length to my Lord of Caunterbury, and send the copy of those letters to your Grace; not to the intent your Grace should loose so much time to rede them, for they be tedyous in length, but only for my discharge; who never medled yet by private letters with any man in the realme to perswade or disswade matters of religion, but with the prince him selfe, or him that had the maniging of the great matters under him. And, folowing this determinacion, am so bold to send your Grace the copy of such letters as I wryte to my Lord of Caunterbury, whose letters to me I could not of congruence forbeare to aunswer ne, aunswering, forbeare to speke frely as I thinke. And sory I am to here the matter of homelies spoken of in this time.

Your Grace hath don prudently to stop the vaine rumors by proclamacion, and it hath wrought good effect, and me thinketh is not best to enterprise any thing to tempt the people with occasion of tales, wherby to breake the proclamacion and offende. And to this effect I wrot to my Lord of Caunterbury. For like as in a naturall body, rest with out trouble doth confirme and strenthen it, so is it in a common welth, troble traveleth and bringeth the thinges to losenes. And my Lord of Caunterbury is not sure of his lyfe, when the olde order is broken and a new brought in by homelies, that he shall continew to se his new device executed; for it is not don in a daye. I would there were nothing elles to do now. I have knowen busines to occupy such as were put in trust, when religion hath bene untouched. A new order engendreth a new cause of ponishment against them that offende; and ponishmentes be not pleasant to such as have the execucion, and yet they must be; for nothing maye be contemned. And thus I travayle in the matter with my Lord of Caunterbury, because he would I should way ⟨*i.e.*, weigh⟩ things, and so do I, as indiferently as ever did man, for the preservacion of the shippe wherin I saile my selfe, and so many other, whose prosperitye I am bounde to wishe. I can admit no inovacions.

Headed: S. W. to the L. Protector.

124. *To* CRANMER

Winchester, [shortly after 12 June, 1547]

Some pages of Gardiner's draft of this letter (less than one-third of the whole) are preserved in a collection made by John Foxe, B.M., Harl. 417, 79–83. An early eighteenth-century copy of the whole is in a collection made by the Rev. George Harbin, B.M., Add. 29,546, 1–9 (cited as H.). In the text as here printed Gardiner's draft is used as far as it goes (pp. 299–301, 306–10), lacunae due to mutilation being filled in from H., except as otherwise indicated. Verbal variations in H. are given in the footnotes, since it is possible that H. copied from some form of the finished letter, rather than the draft. For the rest H. is used. The extant portion of the draft has been printed with inaccurate conjectural emendations in Strype, *Cranmer*, Appendix xxxv.

> Takes Cranmer to task for saying that Henry VIII was seduced in the *King's Book*; is ready to defend the doctrine of that book, which has removed the need of homilies; excuses himself for not writing homilies proposed in 1542; his activities since then; refers to a sermon by Cranmer's chaplain, John Joseph, on justification; how he deals with preachers accused of heresy; characterizes Bale, Joye, and Joseph; says Zwingli saw that the doctrine of justification leads to denial of the Sacrament; refers to the Colloquy of Ratisbon (1546); complains of the inhibition of bishops' preaching (*cf.* pp. 286, 289, above); refutes the contention of Bucer and Sleidan that Protestantism is justified by its political success; civil wars in Germany are warnings against it; praises Henry VIII's settlement of religion; what sort of a homily he (Gardiner) would write on the perfect life; amusingly appraises the religious habits of Englishmen; has not read the *Liber Festivalis* or the *Legenda Aurea*, but defends the use of saints' legends; the translation of the Bible proposed in 1542; despite the need of a new translation, does not advise it or any religious change during the King's minority, nor without a solemn assembly; comments on the small value of preaching in religious services, the few hearers of the King's lectures at Cambridge, and the preaching methods of the friars; sends a copy of this to Somerset.

[After myne humble commendations] to your Grace: Your letters [of] the xij came to my handes the ⟨*blank*⟩ of the same; and u[pon] the reading and[1] advised consideration of the matier in them[2], have thought requisite[3] to answer unto them, and at length to open my mynde frankly[4] in sum poyntes of them, temperyng my wordes soo as I shal[5]

1 Wel layso *c.o.* 2 H. *adds* I 3 t *c.o.*
4 and yet with such respecte in sum (?)† *and c.o.* 5 shalbe *w.* be *c.o.*

not be seen to have forgoten your place and[1] condition, ne such familiarite as hath been bitwen your Grace and me; the remembraunce [2]of which familiarite[2] makith me speke as frely as, on the other side, your astate[3] brydelith me to[4] be more moderate in spech thenne sum[5] matier I shal herafter[†] speke of wold elles suffre and permitte. It grevith me moch to rede[6] wryten from your Grace[7], in the begynning of your letters[8], howe[†] the King our late souverain was seduced[9], [†]and that he knewe[†] by whom he was compassed[10] in that I cal the Kinges Majesties booke; which[11] is not his booke bicause I cal it soo[12], but bicause it was in dede soo[13] acknowledged by the hol Parliament, and acknowleged soo by your Grace thenne[14] and al his life, which, as youe[15] afterward wryte, ye commaunded to be published and red in your diocese[16] [as] his booke, against which, [his] Graces [booke[17]], ye commaunded Joseph he shuld not prech. Al which I thinke your Grace wold not have doon, if ye had not thought the booke to have conteyned truth. And [18]in the truth canne be no seducyng to it as the Kinges booke conteynith[18], but from it, which, if it had been soo[†], I[19] ought to thinke your Grace wold not, for al the princes christened, being soo high a bishop as ye be, have yelded unto[20], for *obedire* [21]*oportet Deo*[21] *magis quam hominibus.* And therfor[22], after your Grace hath foure yere continually[23] lyved in agrement of that doctrine under our late souverain lord, nowe soo sodenly after his death to wryte to me that[24] his Highnes was seduced, it is, I assure[25] youe, a very straunge spech; which, if your Grace shuld bring in to open contencion, as I knowe your Grace of your wisedom

---

1 *H.,* in

2–2 † *abv.* wherof *c.o.*

3 enforcith me to (a†) convenient moderation *c.o.*

4 place my wordes *c.o.*

5 sum † *abv.* the *c.o.*

6 † *abv.* here that *c.o.*

7 that to here *c.o.*

8 that your Grace (wryteth † *and c.o.*) knowith by whom *c.o.*

9 and *meant to be c.o.*

10 *H.,* encompassed

11 I not *c.o.*

12 by *c.o.*

13 ak *c.o.*

14 as *c.o.*

15 saye h *c.o.*

16 according your Graces expectation L(?) *writ. below and c.o.*

17 *above this mutilation there is writ. in a later hand* Graces speech; *H. reads against which your Grace wryteth* ye

18–18 *H.,* to the truth, as the King's book conteyneth, can be no seducing

19 thinke *c.o.*

20 *H. adds* it

21–21 *H.,* Deo oportet

22 nowe *c.o.*

23 agreed th to *c.o.*

24 your Grace knowith by who *c.o.*

25 assured *w.* d *c.o.*

wyl not, but[1] in that cace wyl I, as[2] an old servaunt of my late[3] sovereign lord's, adventure that I have to prove that he was not seduced. And by this argument; viz.: In the truth is no seducing; the King my late sovereign lord, in his book, taught a true doctrine; ergo, he was not seduced.

And moreover I will defend his wisdome and learnyng in these matters to be greater then it may be seemly said of hym by any man that he was seduced. And as often as your Grace shall say he was seduced, you shall more touch your selfe then him, in that ye told hym not so in his life; to the intent he might have rather followed the trewth, then in religion, with the danger of his own soul and the souls of others, to suffer hym to be seduced. If your Grace will say you durst not say the trewth in suche a case, in a case of religion, that were a marvellous allegation to the condemnation of our late sovereign lord, that in your tyme began to professe the meer trewth. And yf your Grace durst and would not, you touch your selfe more then should beseem any other man, beside your selfe, to note in you. These words, my Lord, to say, 'the King our late sovereign lord was seduced in his book,' be words to be spoken by them that durst not or would not shew the trewth in his tyme, and not of your Grace, which can professe neither the one in respect of your selfe, ne the other in respect of him; who made you as you are, and left you his executour to maintayne his acts and laws and not impugne them.

To say he was seduced—which like words when we rede spoken of Eve, that she was seduced, how crafty soever wee note the serpent, wee call that seducyng her fault and blame. And our late sovereign lord was without blame therein, for he was not seduced in deed, but by God's trewth induced into the right way. And hereof his Highnesse made a solemne profession at Hampton Court, not long before his death, where your Grace was present, and I also, with dyvers others, when hys Highnesse sayd that, where others were in extremities, he had ben directed in the mean way of trewth, and therefore was mete to be arbiter between th' other⟨s⟩ to reduce them to the trewth. At which tyme no man told hym that hymselfe was seduced. And although hys body lyveth no longer amonge us, yet hys memory should in such sort continew in honour and reverence, as your Grace should not impute to hym now that was not told hym in his life, *ne injuria defunctus afficiatur*; which hath ben a marvellous consyderation among such as have ben put in

---

1 *not in H.*   2 serv *c.o.*

3 *First page of Gardiner's draft ends here, the next begins at p. 306 below. The text between is from H.*

trust for the deade, to defend hys name from all spots. And the strength of thys word, 'seducing,' is either to condemne hys wit and learnyng or hys will and intent, rather inclined to be lead by affection then to be directed by trewth, which is matter for enemies slanderously to rayle with, rather then to be professed and confessed of us. And further, yf it may be admitted to say our late sovereign lord was seduced in religion, agreed unto by all the realme, is not thereby a window opened for such as dare speke, to speke the lyke of any thing that may be done now? And so all things shall be set at large without stay. Alas! my Lord, let not us bishops be called the breakers of all authorities, and to regard no more religion but to confesse of our selves that, willing, witting, and waking, we lyved under our late sovereign lord, approving a book of religion, by hym set forth, wherein he was seduced.

When I had written thus far, me thought I should have put it out again, because your Grace seemeth afterwards to allow playnly the King's Majesty's book, in that ye say ye commanded Joseph not to preach against yt. And yet I thought yt not amisse to let this part stand, becawse your Grace should perceive my good will, how loath I would be that any such thing should be noted abroad, that your Grace should dissent from hym who had you in such trust, whereas I, a poor man, but one nevertheless made also by hym, dare and will take upon me to defend that he was not seduced in that book. And am therewith able to prove that the book was concluded without me. So as, if trewth would permit, and defence of my late master's honour, I needed not to say so much; but inforced by both, I must and will maintayne, with God's trewth, my late sovereign lord and master's honour, that he was not seduced, and therewith that his book conteyneth the trewth. Wherein, I trust, I shall have your Grace none adversary, but one that can and will uphold the same, howsoever the word 'seduced' came into your letter.

And thus, this word 'seduced' hath produced many words not necessary for your Grace, but necessary for me, whom your Grace now percase tentith, to witte what I would saye; like as you do in the begynning, when you saye you might be justly offended for want of th' homilyes, which ye looked to have received five years passed. And yet in the same words ye declare my juste answer. For having ben so many times in familiarity with you since five years past as I have ben, and no word made of homilies; and concluding together in our last Convocation that we had nothing to do—which decree of 'nothing to do' we thought then we might by authority make, and were not authorized to meddle any further—how can I be now charged with any former order of 5 years past, made of our own motion without authority and, by our own silence, let slip and vanished? If I had indeed offended therein, it had been remytted by our familiarity in other assemblies afterward, and specyally since our agreement to the King's Majesty's book, which took away the mention of all homilies; and all the realme rejoyced so much therein that we regarded no more homilies. And I remember that speaking to the King's Majesty of homilies by us devised to be made, he sayd that divers homilies, made of divers men, might ingender diversity of understandings; and this uniformity of understandynge set forth in his Majesty's book should be a good staye. And thereupon it was moved of a good zeal that there should be no more English books of religion, but only that and the New Testament; which, upon replication of one that would have all Latin books likewise restreyned, was no more spoken of, but the act of Parliament made after the forme that passed. Whereupon I omytted homilies, although I had indeed done in them somewhat. But then I was appoynted to other matters, which might justly have excused me to your Grace, whom by promise, or devise, or order, not being authorized by the King's Majesty, I could not offend.

For so I understand any thing by us spoken in any Convocation, to engender no bond whereupon any offence to ensewe, unlesse the King's Majesty, being made privy thereunto, do expressly and openly and by record allow yt. And yf we should otherwise take yt, we should indeed practise as far as Dr Smyth of Oxford affirmed fondly in words, that wee might make laws. The Convocation order is no order tyll the King's Majesty hath authorized and approved yt. And where is no bond can ensewe none offense. But yf there had, your Grace had pardoned yt long ago; for unlesse a man by protestation sayth, 'Saving my quarrel,' all such matters be extinct by familiarity following, which synce that time hath ben very much, I thanke you. And although it can-not be still as yt hath ben in execution, becawse tyme hath dissevered us, allotting your Grace to more businesse and me to more leisure, yet I see no cause arisen to alter yt. For my last letter can offend your Grace nothing, ne this nether. And as for the homilies, if all fayle to avoyde your Grace's offence, I shall plead the King's pardon, and thereby plead that th' offence cannot be now just; and fynally that I have ben, synce that tyme 5 years, a continuall purveyour of cheese, butter, herrings, and stockfish, twice ambassadour, once at warfare, once sent over the sea to my Lord Protectour, besydes my travaile in religion, more then some

303

thanked me for; and besydes this, the time spent in mourning for my late sovereign lord, with the disposing of my selfe in the state I am now commen unto. All which excuses your Grace knoweth to be trewe, and ought indeed to be avayleable whereby to avoyde all your Grace's just offence for not writing homilies. And yet in my last letters I would not alledge these, but only the King's Majesty's book, the length whereof did indeed put owte all other devices, and worthily, in my mind. For, although your Grace reckoneth up many titles not spoken of at large in the King's Majesty's book, yet they be all touched there, and better for aedification of the simple in few words then many, to be uttered by another that hath not the grace to set it forth; which gift is very rare.

As for amphibologyes in the King's Majesty's book, I know none; for in the knot of the matter, I would speke as the book speketh, for it conteyneth *sanam formam verborum*, and rejecteth the speech of 'faith only' or 'faith alone'; of which 'fayth only' Joseph spoke at the solemne sermon at the Spittle, of the which all the world useth to speke. And being not much above two furlongs out of my diocese, I account yt at hand with me. For I cannot be so negligent, being here, but I must aske how men do in my diocese, and that is halfe way over London Bridge almost. And then yf I be aunswered that in my diocese there is no savour in preaching, but in other places within a furlong of yt, it may be allowed, without the fault of curiosity, although I ask what that is. Mary, in believing that is told me, I am very slow; and in these matters of religion, yf I did at any tyme give credit to a wrong tale, on the condition I might fynde the matter untrew indeed, and the party, the tale were told of, would stand by me and agree to that I should say of hym, ⟨I were willing⟩ to preach even at Pawles Crosse openly that where men report that such a man or such a man hath preached contrary to the King's Majesty's book, and of 'only fayth,' which that book worthily condemneth, 'I will professe amongst you I was too light of credence to beleve such a wrong tale of hym, for the man here present sayeth he spake no such matter, nor he myndeth not to teach any such doctrine, but will mayntaine the agreement in the King's Majesty's book, which conteyneth the true sense of Scriptures in these matters.' And if I might have had the direction of such matters, after myne own device, if I had ever charged any man with any thing by hym uttered contrary to the trew doctrine, and then he would deny it and forswere it, as I have known them accustomed to do, I would never use pains, ne further trouble hym. But such a crewel mynd have I had, I would go to the place of publick audience myselfe, and shew them how the man had ben sore diffamed to me, and then shew how he denyed such matters stowtly and stifly, and so dismisse hym.

All that I have heard is too much to write. But of Joseph it was told me how he triumphed in 'only fayth,' and therewith the qualities of the man described, how he had ben a Fryar Minor in Cambridge, and so reputed among them as in fresh memory he begged for salt herrings in the town, and now and then preached against those that gave rotten herrings. And when his name came so handsomely to stand on the other syde of Joye, so as Bale, Joye, and Joseph verefyed the common saying of the Devil between two fryars, I omytted other names that had ben recommended unto me, and took Joseph, intending by hym and the other two to represent all that trouble religion. In which three, as they be placed, is another conceyt, for Bale is a sacramentary, and Joseph preached *sola fides*, and Zuinglius in his book against Luther sayth that this doctrine, *Sola fides iustificat*, is a foundation and principle to deny the presence of Christ's natural body really in the Sacrament. And although I have not heard so much of Joseph to be a sacramentary, yet becawse Zuinglius lynketh them together as afore, and I had heard that Joseph preached *sola fides*, in that number three there was for all degrees of untrew doctrine one. In which matter of preaching of *sola fides*, yf Joseph hath been misreported, although he be not greatly slaundered by me, yet I will make hym such amends as your Grace thynketh good, whether he be your Grace's chaplain or no; as that Joseph cannot be in such place of estimation, for he that I mean is accounted to have no learnyng, but a fryar quondam as I have rehersed, and, as fryars were wont, had in hys sermon moche rayling, with pretty conceits of my Lord Bishop[1] in hys visitations—a godly matter and fruitfull for the herers! By which token, onlesse I were light, I should not beleve he were your Grace's chaplayne although yt should be told me of divers. I bare away the name Joseph, and so, becawse he had ben a fryar, joyned hym to another. And this is all I will say to hym.

But how much our late sovereign lord abhorred that opynion of only fayth, there remayneth a book, redy to be shewed as I trust, noted with hys Majesty's own hand, which cannot be counterfeit, and declareth he was nether seduced ne compassed. And yt may worthily be called a weather beaten opinion, wherein the Protestants stumbled in

1 *MS.*, Bishops

their last disputation at Ratisbone, which I delyvered your Grace to rede. And the handling of that matter by the Protestants was a prognostick to that hath followed synce by the sworde. And I pray that, to geve strength and authority to our doings here, we may continue in the agreement conteyned in the King's Majesty's book, and all love together, which, I cannot tell how, is wonderfully impayred by this controversy. And upon controversies in preaching, bishops forbidden to preach in their diocese abrode, and among them I, whose preaching your Grace, I thank you, doth commend. But therein, seing your Grace is archbishop and the inhibition has passed by you, by whose suit the matter for the province might have ben otherwyse ordered, I shall stay without further suit for relaxation thereof tyll I see what is further intended. And in the mean tyme lay the charge upon you and pray that the people may do well a while without preaching; as onlesse there be more constancy in such as preach, ⟨not⟩ to say and unsay so oft as we have seen, I thinke that all is but saying without any deeds, but evyll tales, surmises, and wrong reports, eche man redy to undo another, for that in his lyfe he estemeth nothing.

And this is the calamity of this lyfe, having in [1]itselfe [so]o many calamites besides; wherof I have more laysour to thinke on[t] thenne your Grace hath, as my chaunce is nowe, which I rekonne [t]in this respecte[t] very good, after soo many yeres service and[2] in such trouble[3], without daungier passed over, to arryve in this haven of quyetnes, without losse of any notable[t] takel, as the maryners saye; which is a gret matier[4] as the wyndes hath blowen, and if the present astate [5]in this worlde wer to be considered[5], which I have[t] hearde many tymes alleged for confirmation of thopinion [t]of sum[t] in religion. And the Protestantes toke it for a gret argument to establishe ther procedynges, that thEmperour[6] was ever letted, whenne he went aboute to enterprise any thing [a]gainst them, as Bucer declareth at gret lenght [t]in a boke wryten to the worlde[t]. And whenne Sledanus was here in England, he told me the like at Windesore, and then, *tanquam* [7][au]gur, *predixit*[7] theffecte of certain eclypse[s], adding that I shuld see *magnas mutaciones*. And soo I have seen and har[d] mervelous changes[t] synnes that, but [t]otherwise thenne Slendanus toke it, and[t] to de-

---

1 *Gardiner's draft is resumed here*   2 † *abv.* soo *c.o.*
3 w and *c.o.*   4 matiers *w.* s *c.o.*
5–5 † *abv.* here *c.o.*   6 coulde *c.o.*
7–7 † *abv.* tolde me of *c.o.*

stroye ther fansyes, if that [were] t[o] b[e r]egarded. But, for myself, I have seen my souverain lorde[1], with whom I consented in opinion, make the honnorable conquest of Bolen, and honnorably in[2] hys life maynteyne it; and after an honnorable peace made[t], leave this worlde over soone [for[3]] us, but that[4] was due [t]by hym[t] to be payde to nature, discharged it honnorably, buryed honno*u*rably with sorowe and lamentacion of his servauntes and subgettes, and myself, [5]his poore servant, with a lytel flebyting of this worlde, conveyed[5] to an easye astate, without diminution of my reputacion. And therfor whenne I here[6] fondly alleged, or rede more fondly[7] wryten[8], the favo*u*r[9] to[t] that is by[t][10] [t]Bale, Joye, and Joseph, or such lyke[t], newly called the Worde of God, to[11] be embraced for preservation of the worldly astate, I see the clere contrary in experience, and conclude with myself that it provith nought bifore man[12], and take it bifore God to be[13] abhomination.

Which causeth me to spende sum of my layso*u*r to wryte soo long a letter to your Grace, who hath lesse laysour[14]; wyshing that our layso*u*r, gret or lytel, may be spent otherwise thenne to trouble this realme in the tyme of our souverain lordes minorite [w]ith any novelte in matiers of religion, being soo many other [mat]iers, which[15], for that I was soo late a counsailo*u*r, cannot out of my memorye, requyring the hol endevo*u*r of such as have charg, and sylence in the people, who shuld serve and obeye[16] without q[u]areling among themself for matiers in religion; specially considering it is agreed our late souverain is receyved to Goddes mercy, and though [sum] wold saye [he] had [in knowlege] b[ut oo]n yie and sawe not perfitely Goddes truth, yet for us[17] it wer better to goo to hevean with oon yie after hym thenne to travayle here for an other yie, with daungier to lose both. There was good humanite in hym that said, *Malim errare cum Platone quam cum aliis vera sentire*[18] ⟨*cf*. Cicero, *Tusc. Disp.*, I, 17, 39⟩; which affection wer to the worlde

---

1 wh *c.o.*   2 lyve *c.o.*
3 to *in later hand, beside this mutilation; the lower end of* f *is still visible;* H. *reads* for
4 *not in* H.   5–5 [t] *abv*. easely conveyed *c.o.*
6 m *c.o.*   7 matier(?)[t] *and c.o.;* that *c.o.*
8 *in margin*   9 to [t] *and smudged*
10 Joy [t] *and c.o.*   11 prosper *c.o.*
12 it is worse bifore God of bicause it is er me errou*r c.o.*
13 ah *c.o.*   14 which *c.o.*
15 [t] *abv*. as *c.o.*   16 wherwith *c.o.*
17 here(?) *partly torn, and c.o.*(?)
18 but (if [t] *and c.o.*) we were assured *c.o.*

plausible towching our souverain lorde ¹that made us. But¹ we Christen men maye not teache soo², but esteme God above al and his true divinte.

In which cace nevertheles†, whenne the divinte pretended is ³soo rejected of³ many and utterly reproved, soo doubted of many other, as it is suspected and confessed among us, it [is not] necessary; for⁴ our souverain lord is goon from us† to heve[an without it]. It is a mervelous matier, with a certain losse of [humanite] afore⁵ hand to enterprise⁶ to serch⁷ [that] which among a very† fewe hath the name of divinte, and⁸ of† al the rest is soo named as I wyl not reherse ⟨i.e., heresy⟩. And this I wryte, not bicause your Grace entendith ⁹any such thing soo far⁹, [fo]r I may not nor wyl not soo thinke of† youe; but this ¹⁰I take to be¹⁰ trewe, that if† the [walle of auctorite, which I accompted established in our last agrement, be oones broken, and newe water] lett in [at] a lytel gappe, the vehemence of noveltie wyl¹¹ floo further thenne your Grace wold admitte. And whenne men here of newe gere, every man makith his¹² request, sum newe hose, sum newe ¹³cotes, sum newe cappes¹³, sum newe shirtes; like as in religion we have seen attempted¹⁴ where the people thought they might prevayle; which caused the commotion in Germanye *in bello civili rusticorum*, and hath made the s[ame] styrre †there nowe† *in bello civili nobilium*. It was a notable acte of our late souverain lord to †reforme and thenne† moderate religion as he did, which he did not without al¹⁵ trouble. And we be [in a time] whenne al quietnes is required; [as your Grace o]f your wisedom canne consider. [And] our¹⁶ late souverain lord was wont to saye, †[which I shal] never forget, speking of hymself†, [if the ol]d man had not loked to the pacificacion, he sawe men desirous to set forth ther owne fansyes¹⁷, which [he th]ought to have excluded by his pacification. If your Grace wold saye to me nowe that I wasted moch spech in vayne, and declared therby† I had tomoch laysour to wryte somoch in this matier, as though I feared that

---

1-1 † *abv.* that made us seing we graunte(?) we but yet I wold yet *c.o.*
2 but folowe the true divinte *c.o.*
3-3 † *abv.* slaundred and (with †) with *c.o.*
4 wer to heven *c.o.*   5 said *c.o.*
6 a divinte *c.o.*   7 † *abv.* embrace *c.o.*
8 of *c.o.*
9-9 any such thing (but *c.o.*) soo far † *abv.* this for and the walle *c.o.*
10-10 † *abv.* is *c.o.*   11 overdrownde *c.o.*
12 cha *c.o.*   13-13 *H.*, caps, some new cotes
14 † *abv.* chaunced(?) *c.o.*   15 s *c.o.*
16 lord *c.o.*   17 wherby *c.o.*

nedith not to be feared—for your Grace hath commaunded our late souverain lordes booke to be redde, and myndeth nothing nowe but oonly omylies, wherin your Grace wold I shuld wryte, which to doo wer neyther gret payne ne hardnesse to me, and I might assone wryte an homilie as thiese letters. ¹As for the facil[itie in] the matier of wryting, or wryting the [ma]tie[r, I am] not traverse¹, but thenne I consider what contraversie² may arrise in wryting. As for example (for seing I have laysour to wryte, I wyl forgette what laysour your Grace hath to rede), if I shuld make an homilie *de vita perfecta*, I wold note two partes, oon of life, an other of perfitenes. For the grownde of the oon I wold take Saincte John, *Misit³ Deus filium suum ut vivamus per eum*, and for the other, *Estote perfecti sicut pater vester etc.* In declaration of life, I wold take occasion to speke of fayth the ⁴gift of⁴ entre to life, and of charite the very⁵ gift of⁶ life, which who hath not remayneth in deth; and therfor Saincte James said, *Fides sine operibus mortua est*, not expounding that soo as though fayth without charite wer noo fayth, as we saye a deed man is noo man; for I wold [ad]monishe the people in any wise to beware of that facion of teaching and such a sophistical understanding of Saincte James; and for detection thereof declare that deth conteynith not always a denyal of the thing deed not† to be, but oonly where the⁷ name of the thing noted⁸ nowe ded† conteyned bifore† in it a signification of life, as the worde 'man' signifieth a body lyving, and thenne it is truely⁹ sayd that¹⁰ a ded man is noo man, nomore thenne a paynted man. But fayth¹¹ signifieth not† always a life in it, for develles have fayth without life, and whenne we speke of ded fayth, it is like as whenne we speke of a body in dede without life, but apte and mete to receyve life, as spawne is a¹² body without life and deed, but mete to receyve life with convenient circumstaunce. And thenne we saye not that a ¹³body dede¹³ is noo body. And therfor may we not saye that a deade fayth is noo fayth¹⁴. After which understandyng we shuld make Saincte James to treate whither noo fayth might justifie a man [or] noo; which wer a cold matier. And yet soo must we saye, if we wyl expounde this saying that a ded fayth is noo fayth. And in this poynte I wold¹⁵, in my

1–1 *not in H.; the emendations are conjectural*
2 arriseth *c.o.*
5 life *c.o.*
8 ded *c.o.*
11 is fayth *c.o.*
14 which *c.o.*

3 deum *c.o.*
6 life *c.o. and repeated*
9 *alt. from* true(?)
12 ded *c.o.*
15 be *c.o.*(?)

4–4 † *abv.* only *c.o.*
7 word *c.o.*
10 *alt. from* ther(?)
13–13 *H.*, dead body

homilie *de vita*, be† very ernest to shewe that in charite is¹ life, wherunto fayth is thentre; which fayth without charite is not noo fayth, but
dead, and therfor God², that gevith al life, gevith with fayth, charite;
wherof I wold make the moo wordes in the homilie, bicause the handeling of Saincte James in the other sophisitical interpretacion is an entre
to unholsom doctrine.

And if your Grace wold saye, what of this, or to what purpose
shuld it be wryten to youe that myndeth noo such matier, suerly for
nothing but bicause I have plenty of leasour and wryte as though I
talked with† youe, and not al in vayne, for that I have hertofore harde
of other, whom I have harde moch glorye in that exposition, to saye
Saincte James meanith that deed fayth is noo fayth, even as a deed
man is noo man, which, by my faye³, is over far out of the waye.
And yet myn omylie might, in⁴ such an⁵ homilie and company⁶ of
omylies, encountre with oon of⁷ the trade⁸ I have spoken of, and bringe
forth matier of⁹ contencion and altercacion, without al frute or edification. And thusmoch for example of trouble in homylies, which thiese
fyve yeres have rested without any buysines, and the people wel doon
ther dueties, I trust, to God †in heven†, and knowe¹⁰ wel to ther
souverain lord in yerth. And our souverain lord, that¹¹ governed them
without thiese omylies, goen to heven, whither I trust we and the people
shall goo after, although we trouble¹² them with¹³ noo homilies; which
shal hardly be soo accumulate *ex diversis tractatibus*, with diverse facion
of wryting, diverse ¹⁴phrase of speches, diverse conceytes in teachinges¹⁴,
diverse endes percace entended, as¹⁵ some will construe, one to bring in
papistry, another to bring in that hath an ill name ⟨*i.e.*, heresy⟩, with
such other slaunders, as the flying spirits of the ayr be redy to inspire.
For avoyding wherof I think sylence best, with reverence to th'
authority of owr late sovereyn, whose sowle God pardon, and thereyn
to remayne, tyll owr sovereyn lord that now is, cum to his perfect age,
whom God graunt then to fynd suche people as his father left, not
altered with any innovation.

1 † *abv.* if his *c.o.*   2 gevith *c.o.*   3 *H.*, fayth
4 some in(?) *c.o.*   5 *stroke of a letter c.o.*
6 and company †. *H. reads* in such a company, *omitting* an homilie and
7 an other *c.o.*   8 of *c.o.*   9 condition *c.o.*
10 *not in H.*   11 *H.*, who   12 † *abv.* the *c.o.*
13 *writ. over something else and alt. from* without
4–14 *H.*, phrases of speech, divers conceyts in teaching
   end of Gardiner's draft; H. is followed from here to end of letter

And for as moche as your Grace willeth me gently to take upon me the office of a weigher in this matier of homelies, and therein to consyder the patience of the people that have heard so many foolish lying legends, as your Grace calleth them, of the *Festivalls*, *Legenda Aurea*, and such lyke, I will herein, as I have thorougly thought of all parts of this poinet, so straightly and directly as my conscience shall direct my pen, declare how these thyngs weigh in my consyderation, beyng as upright in myne understanding as ever any weigher was at the King's standard beam, where have been men very indifferent, and yet not more indifferent than I shall shew myselfe in this matier.

In the people, for the more nomber of them, such as be most rude, after a short teachyng of God's commandments, they be after led to good lyfe by imitation rather than hearing. They move in the body of the church with much simplicity. And when they have heard words spoken in the pulpit they report they were good and very good and wondrous good, and they were the better to hear them; but what they were, they use to professe they cannot tell, onlesse the manner of yt be new, and then they marvell, and so talk that spake not before. And these we call good men of the countrey. Another sort of people there be that enterprising a knowledge above their capacity, they will take upon them to travaile in everything they hear, and handle yt as substantially as the mayor of Cambridge did, who told his wife when she feared he would sometyme oversee hymselfe in disputing with the schollars, of the Trinity, in which heat somethyng might escape hym unawares, the mayor bad her not fear hym therein, for he had one thyng for a grownd, which preserved hym from all errour in the Trinity, for as long as (quoth he) I say there be 3 Gods and one Person, I care not for them all. Of this sort of men I have known a great many; I mean for their presumption in knowledge. Another sort of men there be that will not be troubled with hearing tyll lerned men agree better. And in these 3 companies be the multitude; whereof 2 parts, for a good zeal to the realm, will as patiently suffer 8 other years whilst owr sovereyn lord that now is cometh to age, as they have done these 8 years past.

And as for lerned men and other wise men of good understanding, they can consyder that it is unseasonable to make any innovation in religion during our sovereyn lord's minority. And every new order is an innovation, though it were for the better. And thus much may be said of hym that were fully perswaded of the foolishnesse of *Legenda Aurea* and the *Festivall,* as your Grace seemeth to be. Which books, what they conteyn, I cannot tell, for I have not red them. And I thinke not impossible but there may be in them many foolish lying tales; and I would wish Christ's religion cleansed and purged from all tales, but so as Christ said, as with the cockle the wheat were not pulled up by the root also; and in a generall sentence of lyes to cast away truth with them. And this difference I put between doctrine and storys: We have a rule to judge doctrine by, whereby we may say this or that doctrine is false and a lye; but in stories we have not so. And therefore to say in the story of Arthur in straunge matters, such as to our understanding appere fond or vain, it were hard to say they were lyes, although they cannot be affirmed for trew. And therefore in stories there is a mean sentence which is called *non liquet.* And of that sort I take the stories of *Legenda Aurea* and the *Festivall,* onlesse there be any story thoroughly allowed and received, wherein I yeild to the knowledge we owe by charity, each to other, or any story that conteyneth plain impiety, which I abhorre and condemne. As for the rest, owt of these extremities, I will say as when I was opposed once meerly ⟨*i.e.,* merrily⟩ of St George and of hys *legenda,* whether I would affirm and avow it for an undoubted trewth or no. Whereunto I answered that, being a lawyer, I durst not affirm yt becawse I could not prove yt, nor deny it becawse I could not reprove ⟨*i.e.,* disprove⟩ it, and in either case I should make my selfe a party, and needed not, and in either answer bynd my selfe to the proof upon danger of folly to say more then I knew.

I was never very inquisitive to proove or reproove such stories as be received or used to be red in the Church, but of Christen simplicity think well of them tyll I see the high powers reprove them. In these mean things I assent unto the determination of the superiours, of whom I have a good opinion, as dewty, in the highest, and, in others, charity bindeth me. I am Prelate of the Order of St George ⟨*i.e.,* the Garter⟩ and yet dyd I never study to defend hym, seing he is armed hymselfe, and our sovereyn lord with his nobles and all the great princes of Christendome have with us embraced him. And yet, me seemeth, I am able, though not to convince him that would maliciously repine against him, for such a one will not be overcome, yet to withstand such reasons as some would devise against him. And if the King our sovereyn lord being in minority, we bishops should, under pretence of *Legenda Aurea* or the *Festivall Book,* do any thing that may touch St George, wherein were at once touched as many as are companions in that Order, yt might be marvelously taken yf the sovereyn of the Order, our sovereyn lord, list to be angry.

I would wish the Church had never suffered anything to be red in it, as it was once concluded, but Scriptures or stories very authentick, and I abhor foolish lyes as any other man. But I cannot call a lye every thing that I know not or lyke not to believe. And therefore me seemeth yt is a very dangerous enterprise to discusse lyes from the trewth, least there follow (whereof good men would be loath) that trewth taken for a lye may so be rejected in some new matter, and on the other syde lyes advanced by ignorance and put in more reputation. This is a marvellous matter and requireth an Hezekias present. By occasion hereof I remember what pains was taken by our late sovereyn lord's commandment to correct the translation of the Bible sent among the people, and how his Highnesse (God pardon his sowle) at a Shroftyde feasted us all, and after dinner towl'd us how gladly he would have that done, and how he would be at the cost to have yt printed again. Whereupon there was used a marvellous diligence, and at my cost a Bible devided into quieres in the Convocation Howse, by your Grace's direction. The fawtes were fownd in a marvellous number and very daungerous, as cannot be denyed; so as we know certainly what the fawtes be, and yet those labours took none effect, which were fruitfull if they had had their execution.

In this matter if I were now asked whether I would geve advice that, during the King's Majestie's minority, those labours should take effect, I would say nay. And yet the people have born to have God's trewth among them so contaminate, sometyme, a man might say, with the malice of the translatour, as may appere where the words and sense be evidently changed, sometyme by ignorance, and sometyme by negligence. But omytting to enquire how it came to passe, we all of the Convocation confessed it so to be, and agreed to amend it, and yet it is not amended. In which matter if zeal to trewth should move us to any labours—but such a zeal were, in the minority of our sovereyn lord clere owt of season, for such rumours might arise that we bishops went now abowt to fashion God's Word after owr own fancy, whilst we want the presence of owr hed, that durst, could, and would controll us. A king's authority to governe hys realme never wanteth, though he were in hys cradle. Hys place is replenished by hys council, as we have now my Lord Protectour. And yet yt is a difference, in the judgment of the people, to direct and order things established and to make in the highest innovations, although yt be for the best; for every man's

313

capacity extendeth not so far, and the best may have a controversy in divers judgments. And therefore I would not geve advice to execute now owr late sovereyn lord's commandment for correction of the Bible. And yet yt were best, for God's Word would be most pure. And also where the printers have set furth with the Bible, in your Grace's name, a preface in which Gregory Nazianzene is not reported as he writeth, I would that rather continewed in sylence then a wonder to be made in the reformation of yt.

St Austin hath works ascribed unto him which, some say, were not his; and yet in many wise men's judgments Erasmus had done better to let them alone, then with his judgment, by guesse, to bring such in dowbt as were St Austin's workes indeed; which cannot be avoyded in a judgment by conjecture. And other judgment cannot be many tymes had in stories and reports. It is abomination indeed that Christen men should maintayn lyes wittingly. And therefore all men must confesse, where they be plainly they ought to be taken away; but upon a sure, a solemne, approved judgment that they be indeed lyes, and in a tyme where there is opportunity to entreat of such matters; which cannot be in the minority of a prince, nor withowt a solemne assembly to here what every man can say, with a mature discussion of that is said, and, as surgeons doe, a confirming and staying with bands of the whole members, or ye go abowt to saw and cut of that is called rotten. There be alredy that are not content with any saints, which would be wel stayed, or *Legenda* or the *Festivall* were by name medled with; least such as would so ⟨*i.e.*, sow⟩ discord would say there were meant somewhat against all saints. What those fond books of *Legenda* and *Festivall* be, or what is in them in speciality I utterly know not, I take God to record, and think there are not many troubled with them. And for such a matter to trouble the realm I weigh it not expedient.

And as to signify to your Grace what a weigher I am, the bishops, prelates, and excellent lerned men your Grace speketh of, in my judgment, be better occupied to preach them selves, as they may have leisure, to exhort the people to vertue, then to send down homilies, which, being never so well made, shall work small effect when they be not handsomely uttered; as appereth in a parish church at Cambridge, where, I hear say, it is ordinary, when the vicar goeth into the pulpit to read that himselfe hath written, then the multitude of the parish goeth straight owt of the church, home to drink. And in Germany, where they had brought all to preaching, there the sermons were maintained by women. And it is contrary to the inclination of us Englishmen to be long in the state of hearers. The King's Majesty founded lectures at Cambridge and furnished them with great lerned men; at the beginning came many hearers, and within a while so few as were able to discourage any man. And even so it is in preching, and specially where the man is not estemed, as priests be not, and should be lesse, if they fell a talking; for so they would call it, to rehearse an homily made by another. The fryars, when they inhabited the realm, had a good policy to maintayne their autority in preching, to shift howses and preche where they were not best acquainted, and with a grete ceremony in gesture, and ever somewhat barking against the bishop and parish priest, or some pretty conceit to entertayne the audience; which fayling, our people be not inclined to be diligent in hearing, onlesse there be news in hand or somewhat to delight. So as I think if the priests should be universally bownd to rede homelies, they should rede them as bachelours do the *Institutes* at Cambridge for their forme, even to them selves and to the walls.

By my trewth, I say to your Grace in my conscience as I think; and think it further not expedient for your Grace, under pretence of a communication among us in a Convocation so long past, not being owr doing confirmed by publick authority, and in owr late sovereyn lord's days, by passing over the thing in silence remitted and past, to enter any such matter now, and, as it were, to charge me with any such order; which indeed byndeth not, and whereunto, if I favoured the matter as much as your Grace seemeth to doe, I durst not yeild to be seen to consent with your Grace in it; for it is no small matter, yf it lyke the prince so to take it, for bishops, who may not assemble withowt special licence ne treat withowt licence of any publick and common matters, to devise a form of order in religion for the whole realm, onlesse the prince, or hys power as head, specially required them so to do. According whereunto I have heard your Grace wisely say, ye would entreat no matters in the Convocation Howse, even when we had autority to assemble, onlesse ye knew the King's Majesty's pleasure first.

Wherefore to make an end of my long babling to your Grace, I have playnly shewed why I do not in any wise allow the enterprise, which may be cause of evil rumours withowt frute or effect, and not to be moved now, in my judgment; adding also why your Grace cannot be offended for my not writing of homilies, and why I dare not enterprise to geve any authority to owr communication not confirmed in that order; which I do not to avoyd any labours, having leysure and grete delight to pass my tyme so, and having such matter to write on as I would desire; wherein, if my Lord Protectour will command me, I will gladly take payne; unto whom I send the copy of these letters, as I did of the last, for I will confer with no man in these publick matters, but for my discharge will signify the same unto hym who hath the account of this realm in hys hand; unto whom and your Grace I wish all felicity. At Winchester, etc.

Headed (in H.): A letter of Stephen Gardiner's, Bishop of Winchester, to Archbishop Cranmer, written in Edward 6th's time.

NOTES TO NO. 124

Page 303. The act of Parliament mentioned is 34 & 35 H. VIII, c. 1.

Page 304. Gardiner's diocese was half way over London Bridge since the present Diocese of Southwark was then part of it.

Page 305. Zwingli's chief writings against Luther on the Sacrament are (1) *Amica Exegesis,* 1527; (2) *Fründlich verglimpfung,* 1527; (3) *Das dise wort Jesu Christi: 'Das ist min lychnam,'* etc., 1527; (4) *Uiber doctor Martin Luthers buch bekenntnuss genannt,* 1528. They are all found in *Zwinglis Werke,* ed. M. Schuler and J. Schulthess, Zürich, 1828–42. Well-chosen excerpts from (1) and (3) may be found in *Ulrich Zwingli, Eine Auswahl aus seinem Schriften,* ed. G. Finsler, W. Köhler, and A. Rüegg, Zürich, 1918, Nos. 23, 24.

Page 306. Colloquy at Ratisbon. *See* H. Eells, *Bucer,* New Haven, 1931, chapter 36.

125. *To* CRANMER

[Waltham?, shortly after 1 July, 1547]

Two manuscript copies of this letter are extant: (1) probably of the sixteenth century, in Bibliothèque Nationale, Latin 6051, 30–46 (hereafter cited as B.N.); (2) of the early eighteenth century, in the collection of the Rev. George Harbin, B.M., Add. 29,546, 9 v.–24 (hereafter cited as H.). B.N., as the earlier and fuller copy, is here used as the basic text. That H., however, is not a copy of B.N., is evident from the fact that it contains some phrases not in B.N. (*see* p. 343, n. 8–8; p. 353, n. 7–7). Words or phrases omitted in H. are marked ‡ (the sign is placed *after* a

316

single omitted word, *before and after* a phrase of two or more omitted words). Other verbal (but not merely orthographic) variants in H. are given in footnotes or, when they are deemed to be the more likely readings, incorporated into the text, with indication in footnotes of the readings which they replace.

Although his last letter (No. 124) amused Cranmer, it was intended seriously; would prevent Cranmer from impairing the authority of the *King's Book*, and with it the royal authority; the Anabaptists, as Aepinus and John Frederick of Saxony warned us, sought to overthrow the royal authority in England; vigilance is needed, especially against anything tending to overturn the established religion or injure the royal name; to say that Henry VIII was led astray or that he led astray the people is not to be tolerated; it is, moreover, a reflection on the three bishops (Heath, Thirlby, and Day) who prepared the section on justification in the *King's Book*; was not guilty of plots against Cranmer as Wriothesley can testify; disclaims any desire to return evil upon anyone; never sought information against Cranmer, who unjustly suspected Gardiner's friend Theobald of carrying such information; never had familiar dealings with William Gardiner (prebendary of Canterbury); Cranmer's inconstancy in belief has a bad effect on the people; 'only faith' has never been the Catholic doctrine; discusses the proposition 'in the truth is no seducing'; quotes Erasmus against Protestantism; Cranmer cannot really wish to join the company of such scum as Joseph; the doctrine of 'only faith' leads to a denial of the Sacrament; Luther shrank from this, but Zwingli saw it was inevitable; there is no ambiguity in the *King's Book*, which condemns 'only faith' as well as 'faith alone'; when Cranmer tried to make a distinction between these two phrases, Henry VIII convinced him otherwise; the merry tale of one who tried to find out who was the father of the sons of Zebedee; refers to having Barnes to school (*see* No. 81); long argument against justification by faith only, considering words of Scripture and of Gregory Nazianzen; Henry VIII's annotations on the *Bishops' Book*; Cranmer's similitude of light and fire considered; Gardiner's similitude of water and fire; the discussion of justification is not necessary for the people; adjures Cranmer not to cause further disturbance in religion; the difference between Cranmer's opposition to the *King's Book* and Gardiner's to the *Bishops' Book*, which was a compromise between Bishops Stokesley and Fox; refers again to the inhibition of bishops' preaching (*see* Nos. 121, 124), and the Bible translation of 1542; business of state has prevented Gardiner from writing homilies; his appointment as chief minister of Henry VIII; enlarges on what he said (in No. 124) about Englishmen not listening to sermons; their attitude at Matins and Mass; small congregations at Waltham (?) and Canterbury; has always obeyed authority; is determined to serve God while he lives. Postscript on misquotation of Gregory Nazianzen in the preface to Cranmer's Bible.

30₂r. After my humble comendacions to your Grace: I have receaved your letters of the fyrst of July and I am glad to understand by the same that my letters had one of theffectes I wrote them for, to make your Grace mery; for suche one[1] entent had I in them, and, knowyng your Graces nature throughly, dyd temper suche musycke as I have, in that twne[2] ⟨*i.e.,* tune⟩ and armony as yt might make you laughe. And what my Lord of Sarysbury can doo therin, in good fayth I knowe not; but I envye not suche a companyon in that feate[3], nor will not grudge at suche a reward as your Grace speaketh of, when we had made you laughe your belly full, to wyshe us at home againe, so your Grace wold lett us depαrte, or we hadd fylled your belly, or elles, for all your wyshe, we shuld not come home a good while. *Sed nunc omisso queramus seria ludo* ⟨*cf.* Horace, *Satires,* 1, i, 27⟩; a verse mete to staye inordynate laughing, whiche the matter addmytteth not. And those parties of my letters, which your Grace notith as matter to laughe at, contayne in them also matter of further consyderacion, when the laughing is don. For, although I have a mery hedd, as your Grace wryteth, yet my woordes be not placed ydely, where I seme meryest, even when I spake of provicion of butter and chese, etc.

I shall awnswere your Graces letters nowe as the matter requireth, so framed as theis my letters maye dyffer frome the other, to obtayne the other effect by me entended, wherby to extinguyshe or deminishe, yf yt were possible, the travaile your Grace taketh to empaire thauctoritie of the Kinges Majesties booke, with thempayring of his name therwith, as I take yt, and as reason shall induce other to take yt, magno cum applausu inimicorum et eorum presertim qui nomini regio non nimis bene volunt, a quibus cavendum esse nobis[4] et magnopere providendum, non semel nec obscure predictum fuit, non enigmate aliquo quo stulti luduntur, sed indicio claro et aperto, quo moventur prudentes. De quo serio nobiscum egit Hippinus ille, idque multis

---

with great applause of enemies and of those especially who are not too well disposed toward royalty, against whom it has been proclaimed not once only, nor ambiguously, not in some riddle by which fools are deceived, but with clear and evident testimony by which thoughtful men are moved, that we must be on our guard and use great foresight. On which point the well known Hippinus talked seriously with us, and that

1 *H.,* an   2 *H.,* town   3 *H.,* seat   4 *H.,* vobis

presentibus, cum affirmaret se non coniicere sed scire susceptum ab Anabaptistis negotium ut hoc regnum everterent, excussis regibus; quod verbum abhominor. Atque id ipsum postea Dux Saxonum, Ioannes Fredericus, hactenus certe amice, missis, que id testarentur, aut interceptis aut repertis nebulonum litteris, Regie Maiestati significavit, diligenter admonens, ut ab ea peste caveret. Hec possent videri ab illis conficta, quo nos in suam factionem traherent, quod unum moliebantur, ni detectum ac proditum apud nos in quibusdam nostratium simile facinus non fuisse omnino illa vana comprobassett. Et extant libelli de eo Anglice conscripti, haud expectandum, ut suum quod vocant 30 v. Evangelium regia unquam auctoritate reponatur. Eiusmodi conatus nefarios bis repressit regia felicitas, et de auctoribus publice sumptum supplicium. Non fingo, non fabulor, non mentior; ut etiam atque etiam providendum sit, ne quid fiat quod imprudentibus nobis atque adeo invitis aliorum promoveat insaniam et ‡quod unum pretendimus non‡ adiuvet omnino.

Hic, si quis me timidum, si suspiciosum, si secus quam per charitatem

---

in the presence of many, when he asserted that he did not conjecture but knew of the undertaking of the Anabaptists to overthrow this royal power and get rid of kings—a saying I loathe. And later the Duke of Saxony, John Frederick, so far surely acting as a friend, sent letters the scoundrels had written, which he had intercepted or discovered, to serve as evidence, and so made this very thing clear to his Royal Majesty, earnestly warning him to beware of this pest. All this might seem fabricated by them to draw us into their party—the very thing they were attempting to do—had not a like crime, detected and betrayed among us in some of our own countrymen, proved that these warnings were not altogether idle. And there exist documents written in English on this point, that there must be no waiting for what they call their Gospel ever to be established by royal authority. Wicked attempts of this kind the King's good fortune twice crushed and punishment was inflicted by the state on the authors. I am not imagining, I am not merely talking, I am not feigning when I urge that we must again and again take care lest anything happen which, without our knowledge and, furthermore, against our will, should forward the madness of others and should not in every way help the one thing we uphold.

If, at this point, someone should say that I am fearful, suspicious,

liceat, de meis divinantem et male ominantem dicat, contendatque non oportere, non expedire hec commemorare, que si in aliquibus putridis et male sanis membris, cuiusmodi semper aliqua habet cuiusvis republice corpus, eruperunt, haud unquam tamen temere conatus suos ad exitum perduxere, patiar, feram, conscientie testimonio nixus, nec de presenti hominum statu admodum contendam. Illud affirmabo, non in re presenti quid sit spectandum solum esse, sed quid aliquando fuit, quidve esse per rerum naturam possit, prudenti bonorum consilio providendum. In eo enim precipua, tum medici in corpore, tum in republica presidis, cura sit, a preteritis sumpta coniectura, potius que aliquo casu eventura timeantur, precavere ne eveniant, quam turbatis atque affectis[1] corporibus, de medela exhibenda tardius cogitare. Que predicta fuere scio, que postea reperta sunt memini; futura nescio nec laboro scire. Ea me una solicitudo tenet, si quid, ne quid, ut ait comicus. Et nihil video in his minus utibile quam constitutam religionem, etiam

---

prophesying or auguring ill from my own imaginings in a manner not permitted by charity, and should contend that it is not necessary or expedient to talk of these matters, for if, in some corrupt and unhealthy members, of which the body of any commonwealth always has some, they have burst forth, still they have never easily brought their attempts to completion—I shall suffer it, I shall bear it, supported by the testimony of conscience; nor shall I dispute much about the present state of mankind. This I shall assert, that it is not only what must be looked to at the present moment which is to be considered by the wise counsel of good men, but what has been at any time or what can possibly be in the nature of things. For herein it should be the special business of the chief magistrate in the case of the commonwealth, as it is of the physician in the case of the body, by drawing inferences from past experience, to take precautions that those things shall not happen which it is feared may by some accident happen, rather than, when bodies are already sick and disordered, to ponder too late on applying a cure. I know what was predicted, I recall what was afterward discovered; I do not know the future nor do I labour to know it. This one anxiety possesses me, that if something happens, something will follow, as the comic poet says. And I see nothing in these matters less useful than to try to overthrow established religion, and that too with some dishonour

1 *B.N.*, effectis; *H.*, affectis

cum aliqua principis constituentis macula, labefactare conari, principis presertim de nobis optime meriti, in cuius filio spes omnes nostras repossitas habemus. Romanum episcopum invisum nobis reddidit religionis causa, que etiam invidia in omnes fere episcopos derivata est. Seduxit in religione Romanus episcopus; odiosa res est et merito. Idem si attribuimus principi, cum eadem sit odii causa, non etiam in parem invidiam inducemus? Ut quemadmodum ille dixit, 'Civis mihi sit qui feriet hostem'; sic contra, odio mihi sit qui corruperit religionem, quisquis is sit, quocumque titulo censeatur. Si sanctum regium nomen cupimus, quod omnes boni cupiunt, et omnes in regno educati cupere maximopere debent, ne quid ab aliis macule huic nomini aspergatur, procurandum est; nedum ipsi, nulla necessitate adacti, nullo usu impulsi, nullo fructu provocati, minus illud reverenter, et tanquam illotis manibus, attingere debeamus. Quanta cum dilligentia observatum videmus a priscis illis humanitatis consultis, ut cum principes viros, data occasione, nominarent, adiicerent eos abs se honoris causa 31 r. nominatos; tantum, viz., abhorrebant a contumelia. Illa morum civilitas

of the prince establishing it, especially a prince deserving the highest of us, in whose son we have reposed all our hopes. He has made the bishop of Rome, for religion's sake, the object of our hatred, and this hatred has also been turned against well-nigh all bishops. The bishop of Rome seduced others in religion; the matter is odious and deservedly so. If we attribute the same thing to the prince, shall we not arouse a like hatred against him, since the cause of it would be the same? Just as the celebrated ⟨Hannibal⟩ said, 'Let him be my fellow-citizen who shall smite the enemy' ⟨Cicero, *Pro Balbo*, 22, 51⟩, so contrariwise let him be an object of my hatred who has corrupted religion, whoever he be, by whatever title he be known.

If we desire the name of king to be sacred, which all good men desire, and all brought up in the kingdom ought above all things to desire, we must take care lest any stigma be cast upon this name by others. Much less ought we ourselves, forced by no necessity, urged by no advantage, lured by no profit, to touch it with too little reverence and, as it were, with unclean hands. We see with what care the custom was observed by cultivated men of old, that when they had occasion to mention princes by name, they always added that they mentioned them *honoris causa*; so far, that is, did they shrink from insult to them. Such was the customary courtesy of the ancients. And shall we commit the error that a

maiorum. Et nos committemus ut princeps, pater a nobis incommodissime ereptus, sed tamen in filio adhuc spirans, quique sempiternam apud nos cum honore memoriam meritus sit, patiemur, inquam, ut in contencione inutili cum aliqua iniuria nominetur, quasi seductus, seduxerit populum, quorum utrumque infame est nec ferendum nobis?

Accepi cum fide relatum de Richardo Rege, illo nimirum qui nepotes ex fratre summo cum scelere extinxit; post perpetratum facinus immanissimum, is, quum aliquando solus esset cum suis quibusdam, quos habebat coniuratissimos, inter media gaudia subito in hanc vocem erupisse, 'Oh! qualem olim de me' inquit 'texent historiam posteri!' Quod[1] si homini pessimo, in tanta immanitate flagitiorum, aliqua fuit ratio fame posterorum, quid nos[2] tandem facere par est, nihill huiusmodi feritatis ingressis? Nullane eiusmodi cogitacio animos nostros subeat, quid de nobis dicturi, scripturi, existimaturi sint posteri? Crudele nimium est, ut quidam scripsit, negligere famam. Et Paulus precipit[3] ut que sunt bone fame curemus. Nullam unquam causam iustam

---

prince, a father most unfortunately reft from us, yet breathing in his son, and one who has deserved eternal memory among us with honour, shall we endure, I say, that in an unprofitable dispute he should be named with any despite, as if he had been seduced and had seduced his people? Either of which conclusions is disgraceful and not to be tolerated by us.

I have heard and believed the story about King Richard, that man, forsooth, who murdered his brother's offspring in most criminal fashion. After the perpetration of this most monstrous deed, he on one occasion was alone with some of his friends whom he considered his closest confederates, and in the midst of their pleasures he suddenly burst out with these words, 'Oh! what sort of a story,' quoth he, 'will posterity some day tell of me!' Now if a most vile man, guilty of such barbarously disgraceful acts, had some consideration of his repute among posterity, what is the proper thing, pray, for us to do who have entered on no such course of savagery? Should no consideration of this sort enter our minds, as to what posterity will say, will write, will think about us? It is too unfeeling, as someone has written, to be careless of reputation. And Paul teaches that we should be careful about what things are of good report. We shall never be able to give any well-grounded reason

1 *H.*, et   2 *H.*, nobis   3 *H.*, praecepit

probabimus orbi, cur tanto cum studio, tanta cum sedulitate, ungulis et dentibus, quod ad me scribit tua Reverendissima Dominatio, contendamus principem tantum cetera felici⟨ssi⟩mum[1], hac una in parte tam infelicem, ut falleretur semper fere a suis, et in condendis legibus, et in constituenda religione, que prima et precipua capita sunt firmande reipublice, cui presidebat.

Egregiam sane naturam predicas hominum Anglorum, semper ad fallacias intentam scilicet. Nam crimine ab uno estimabunt omnes. Cum essent presertim in illam operam religioni navandam delecti ex omni numero episcopi tres, omnium eruditissimi, et doctores totidem, summa omnes et apud principem gratia, et in populum commendatione, qui, si fidem in re tanta fefellerint, quam de reliquis spem exteri possent tandem concipere? Et huic adeo insigni gentis nostre vitio adiungitur ut minimum infelicitas principis, sic esse frustratum ab intimis, sic illusum, sic destitutum et pro ludibrio habitum, cuius quasi os oblinere auderent, obtrudentes illi pro veris falsa, ut seductus seduceret populum, cum aliqua nominis iniuria et animarum dispendio et detrimento gravissimo.

---

to the world for contending with such great zeal, with such great diligence—tooth and nail, as your Most Reverend Lordship writes to me—that a prince, most fortunate in all other respects, in this one was so unfortunate, that he was wellnigh always deceived by his friends, both in making laws and in establishing religion, which are the first and foremost elements of stability in the commonwealth over which he ruled.

You set forth a truly outstanding characteristic of Englishmen, always, indeed, on the look-out for trickery. For from one fault they will judge everyone ⟨*Aeneid*, II, 65⟩. Above all, when there had been chosen for the performance of that work for religion, out of the whole number of bishops, three, the most learned of them all, each a doctor, and all in the highest favour with the prince and of good report among the people —if these men shall have betrayed their trust in so great a matter, what hope could outsiders, pray, entertain about the rest? And moreover to this conspicuous fault of our nation there is added, as a minor consideration, the ill fortune of our prince so to be mocked by his intimates, so befooled, so forsaken and treated as a subject for sport, since they dared to blindfold him, so to speak, thrusting upon him lies for truths, that seduced, he might seduce the people, with no little injury to his reputation and with the most grievous damage to and loss of souls. Even if these

1 *H.*, felicissimum

Nostrarum partium esset hec celare, non prodere, etiam si essent vera, ut si quid illi secus quam oportuit accidisset, cum illo mortuo pati potius, quam in illum a‡ morte inquirere videamur, et[1], Iosepho nescio quo apud populum delatore, contra Regem potius quam pro Rege pronunciare. Non ego in illis eram qui fefellerunt, id quod proximis litteris non rea conscientia expressit, sed ipsa vis cause protulit in medium, ut non meam causam in Rege defendendo me egisse ostendere⟨m⟩[2] quem nihill attingeret, sed publicam; que si a me deserta non esset, iam homine publicis functo negotiis quique nihill haberem in causa privatum, quanto id studiosius agerent qui tractarunt negotium, vell tua Reverendissima Dominatio potius, cuius fidem princeps mortuus ad gloriam sui nominis defendendam delegerat nominatim? ‡Quod a funere superest apud nos moneo[3] ut humano more causam defuncti estimemus‡. Atque hec sic ago quasi esset in libro quod corrigeretur, et Rex aliquid esset ejusmodi passus, ut videretur seductus; id quod contra se habere non dubito me planum facturum.

31 v.

---

things were true, it would be our part to conceal them, not to publish them; so that if anything should have happened to him otherwise than ought to have happened, we should seem rather to suffer with him dead, than to hold an inquiry over him after death, and, some Joseph or other arising as informer before the people, to give judgment against the King rather than for the King. I was not among those who were deceitful, a thing which in my last letter my conscience, not being on the defensive, did not explicitly indicate, but which the very purport of the cause made clear; so that in defending the King I revealed myself not to have pleaded my own cause (for it in no way concerned me) but the public cause. If this ⟨i.e., the public cause⟩ had not been deserted by me, a man who has by this time performed his public duties and had no private interest in the case, how much more zealously ought they to be acting who have undertaken the direction of affairs, or rather, your Most Reverend Lordship, whose loyalty the dead prince had chosen specifically to defend the honour of his name! I recommend—what remains in our power to do after his death —that we appraise the case of the departed as human beings should. I treat these matters as if there were something in the ⟨King's⟩ book that needed correction, and as if the King had actually suffered something of such a nature that he seemed seduced; but I doubt not that I shall make it clear that the contrary is true.

1 *H. adds* cum   2 *H.*, ostenderem   3 *MS.*, mortuo

And nowe to the word 'seducynge' wherein, to dystroye my dystribu-
cion, your Grace doth *rethorice*[1] deflect to the woord 'deceyving,' which
is a generall woord, and 'seducing' a speciall woord. In which 'seducyng,' besydes a deceipt, is notid a leading of the man seduced owt
of the way. In the[‡] which case, he that so leadeth hath no meane to
lay hold on the man seduced, but eyther upon his understanding,
blynded and perverted, or his affection, perverse and dystemperyd; and
besydes theis parties their is no seducyng. Mary, deceyving may be
otherwise; but that is grosse falsod, when a man is trusted, then to wryte
one thing for another; after which sorte I never knew the Kinges
Majestie deceived of any counsaylour, and after which sorte, as your
Grace wryteth, the wisest and best maye be deceyved. And their were
privie to this acte thre busshoppes and thre doctors, who, yf they had
seduced the Kinges Majestie, were worthie great punyshement, but yf
they have deceyved him after this sorte, by putting in that the Kinges
Majestie redd not, yt is pittie they live.

Quicquid sit (as theyr canbe nothing), est vero verius me[2] illi negotio fuisse prorsus alienum. Nec potest esse quicquam vanius quam
quod mihi obiicitur de insidiis et delationibus tuorum. In ea causa
habebas Wrythesleum, amicum summum et[‡] integerrimum, de quo
homine nihill dico nisi veritatis ergo; me autem non prorsus iniquum, sed   32 r.
illius hortatu nonnihill lentiorem, ut verum fatear, ne quid urgerem eam
causam. Nempe, qualis in me antea fuisses nec ipse Wrythesleus ig-
norabat, et sciebat non latere me, viz.[‡], quid in me egeras de litteris
ex Germania. Verebatur ne ego meditarer ultionem, a qua animus semper

---

Whatever there may be (as there can be nothing), it is truer than
truth that I have been utterly alien to this business. Nor can there be
anything more unfounded than what is charged against me concerning
plots and denunciations of your followers. In this case you had Wriothesley, a very great friend and most upright, of whom I say nothing
except for the sake of truth. I myself, moreover, was assuredly not
hostile, but (to tell the truth) because of his exhortation somewhat more
pliant in not urging that case in any way. Of course Wriothesley himself was not ignorant how you had been disposed to me before, and he
knew that it was not hidden from me, viz., what you had done against
me concerning letters from Germany. He feared lest I meditated re-

1 *H.*, rhetorice   2 *B.N.*, in; *H.*, me

325

abhorruit; senciebat animum Regis exulceratum in te, et me eo fuisse loco, ut, si collibuissett, ut tum res erant, nonnihill potuisse⟨m⟩[1]. Egit multis rationibus ut deterreret a vindicta, et te cupiebat haberi sacrosanctum, cui se multum debere fatebatur. In eam partem propenso facile persuasit, et in suam sententiam perduxit, non repugnantem. Iam reddo rationem [2]interne, si placet[2], machinationis. Cum licuit abstinui ab iniuria referenda, de quo mihi ipsi gratulor, vell Deo potius ago gratias, cuius beneficio hos mihi affectus cohibitos sensi et refrenatos. Cum Rex mihi summam rerum permisisset iam ante annos quatuor, si quid in te animi exacerbati haberem, pertentavit presente Wrythesleo, quo tempore quam frigide Regi responderem ne quid dissidii olfaceret, habeo testem ipsum Wrythesleum, et conscientiam coram Deo. Quod non eo dico ut testimonio me ullo purgem tibi, neque in eo laboro; tantum, data occasione, refero quod res est. Si Domino meo sto, cui olim rationem redditurus sum, cetera securus, fortiter sustineo confictas in me calumnias.

---

venge, from which my mind always shrank; he knew that the mind of the King was inflamed against you, and that I was in such a position that, if it had pleased me, as things were, I could have effected somewhat. He pleaded with many arguments to deter me from revenge, and he desired you to be held sacred, to whom, he confessed, he owed much. He easily persuaded me, already so inclined, and brought me to his opinion not at all resisting. Now I give an account, if you please, of the very depths of the machination. When it was permissible to repay evil with evil, I refrained; on which I congratulate myself, or rather give thanks to God, by whose goodness I perceived my passions were restrained and bridled. When four years ago now, the King had entrusted the most important affairs to me, he inquired, in Wriothesley's presence, if I had any embittered feeling toward you. How coldly I answered the King at that time, lest he smell any dissension, I have Wriothesley himself as witness, and my conscience before God. I do not say this to clear myself in your eyes by any testimony, nor do I take pains to convince you. I merely relate, since the opportunity offers, what is the fact. If I am approved of my Master, to whom I shall hereafter render an account, there is nothing else to cause me anxiety, and I steadfastly endure the calumnies invented against me.

1 *H.*, potuissem   2-2 *H.*, si placet, internae

De me, quo sim animo, longissime aberratum est a multis; certe de referenda in quenquam iniuria nunquam cogitavi. Curiosus autem nunquam fui; cui tamen casu oblata tam multa fuere, ut, quod mihi minime cognoscendi cupido forte est intellectum, videretur quibusdam expiscatum studio, cum res longe secus se haberet. Qui nihil retulerunt scio vobis falso habitos suspectos; qui ultro minime rogati effutierunt omnia, et ad me deferenda oblique egerunt, intellexi nunquam in suspitionem adductos fuisse; homines, viz., [1]mihi haud[1] familiares, et cum quibus nunquam intercesserat consuetudo. Dispeream si quem unquam rogavi ut mihi quicquam ex arcanis referret alienarum rerum. Tibaldum[2] tamen, qui cum consuetudo et familiaritas diutina mihi fuit, eo nomine apud te traductum, et ipse multis modis sensit, et ego quoque alias intellexi. Multa, magna et frequens ea de re Theobaldo apud me privatim conquestio fuit, cum lamentaretur fortune iniquitatem et hominum iudicia in calumnias tam propensa. Qua de re studiosius se purgare, nihill putavit aliud nisi lavare laterem. Itaque abstinuit, et tulit equa-

---

As to myself, of what spirit I am, a great mistake has been made by many; certainly I have never thought of returning evil upon anyone. Moreover I have never been meddlesome; yet to me so many things have been presented by accident, that things which I learned by chance, when I was not in the least desirous of learning them, seemed to some people fished out by zeal, which was far from the fact. Those who reported nothing to me were, I know, falsely suspected by you; those who were asked less than nothing and of their own accord blurted out everything and covertly brought reports to me, I perceived were never suspected; men, that is, not at all friends of mine and with whom I had never been intimate. May I perish if ever I asked anyone to tell me anything of the secrets of other people's affairs. That Tibald, however, with whom my intimacy and friendship were long-standing, was on that account traduced to you, he himself felt in many ways, and I also later perceived. Strong, bitter, and frequent was the complaint of Theobald ⟨i.e., Tibald⟩ on this matter to me in private, when he bewailed the unfairness of fortune and the judgments of men so prone to slanders. To make any greater effort to clear himself on this score was, he thought, as profitable as to wash a brick ⟨i.e., a waste of time⟩. Hence he refrained,

1–1 *H.*, haud mihi   2 *H.*, Theobaldum

nimiter suspitiones iniquas. De quo homine facio mentionem ut intelligas ubique longissime aberratum, et in me et in illo quoque.

Fuit mei cognominis in Ecclesia Cantu⟨a⟩riensi[1] quidam homo, vix de facie notus, cum quo semell, aut ad summum bis, dum illac pertransirem, colloquium fuit. Semell etiam ad me scripserat insinuandi sui causa, ut cognominis titulo mihi commendaretur. Audieram hominem strenue, nec omnino insulse, in doctrinam improbatam e suggestu detonare; quod etsi animo meo non omnino displicuisset, nunquam tamen hominem collaudavi, aut coram aut per epistolam; tantum abest ut cum eo ullam habuerim contractam familiaritatem, [2]quo illo[2] commode pro speculatore abuterer, ut mihi referret quod isthic ageretur, id quod a multis creditum fuisse scio, sed falso. Et cum te scirem eo errore vexari, mea quadam pertinacia effectum est, ne quid facerem quo te liberarem[3]. Commedias et tragicommedias in vita nostra communi vidi plurimas errore refertas maximo. Dein alios ex se metiri reliquos animadverti[4], perpaucos vero Paulinis verbis a iudicando deterritos ne iudicarentur

---

and bore unjust suspicions equably. I mention this man that you may know that great mistakes were everywhere made about both myself and him.

There was a certain fellow of my name ⟨William Gardiner⟩ in the church at Canterbury, whom I scarcely knew by sight, with whom once, or at most twice, while I was passing through there, I had a conversation. Once also he had written to me, that he might find favour with me because of his name. I had heard him thunder from the pulpit vigorously, not altogether without wit, against false doctrine. Although this had not been entirely distasteful to me, yet never did I praise the man either to his face or by letter—so far is it from the truth that I had any familiar dealings with him, that I might use him conveniently as a spy to report to me what was going on there; a thing which I know was believed by many, but falsely. And when I knew that you were plagued by this mistaken belief, it came about, by a certain obstinacy on my part, that I would do nothing to set you right. Comedies and tragicomedies without number in our everyday life I have seen, crammed full of the greatest errors. Further, I have noticed that one measures others by himself, that very few truly are deterred by Paul's words from judging that they be not judged. But on these matters I have said more

1 *H.*, Cantuariensi   2–2 *B.N.*, quo illum; *H.*, qua illo (*alt. from* illum)
3 *B.N.*, liberem; *H.*, liberarem   4 *H.*, animadverto

ipsi. Sed de his plus satis. In quibus id unum etiam atque etiam deprecor, ne contumelie causa factum interpretetur, Reverendissima Dominatio tua, quod tocies compello[1] te sine honoris additamento, quem et debitum intelligo, et presto libenter. Sed stili commoditatem secutus sum, ne titulorum interiectio quoties occurreret[2], tenorem orationis abrumperet et dictionis rotund⟨it⟩atem[3] no⟨n⟩nihil impediret.

I have handled this parte as truly as ever man handled any thing, and yet I would never have spoken so farr, and your Grace had not gyven occasion.

Reverendissime Domine, quod[4] ais te Regi libere et aperte dixisse que sentires, ostendis plane et doces Regem, cum, ut addis, tecum benigne rem componeret ac retineret tamen sententiam suam, Reverendissimam Dominationem tuam in partes suas traxisse, et in eius sentenciam tandem te[4] concessisse, quod ille clementer admisit. Cuius generis clementiam etiam ipse cum magna loquendi atque acerba libertate usus essem non semell sum expertus; et in ea parte adiiciam meum minime necessarium testimonium. Sed non hoc agitur num aliquando dixeris que sentires, sed num etiam cum effectu, ut in veri defensione illi te opponeres, tan-

---

than enough. In what I have said I beg this one thing again and again, that it should not be interpreted as an intentional insult, your Most Reverend Lordship, that I so often address you without the addition of your title, which I both understand is due you and gladly offer it. But I have followed convenience of style lest, every time the insertion of titles occur, the thread of the discourse be broken and the flow of diction somewhat impeded.

Most Reverend Lord, as to your saying that you told the King freely and openly what you feel, you show plainly and make clear that the King drew your Most Reverend Lordship into his party when, as you add, he settled the matter with you in friendly fashion and still held to his own opinion, and that you at length yielded to his opinion, which he graciously permitted. Clemency of this sort I myself also have experienced more than once when I had spoken too freely and sharply, and on that point I will add my by no means necessary testimony. But this is not the question, whether at any time you said what you felt, but whether you did so effectively, so that in defence of the truth you put

1 *B.N.*, tuisso; *H.*, compello   2 *B.N.*, occurrerit; *H.*, occurreret
3 *H.*, rotunditatem   4 *H. supplies* te

quam veritatis Evangelice propugnator, ne in religione doctrine minus
probate, minus vere, minus syncere cessisse videreris. Gravius enim est,
et ad rei confirmationem solidius, repugnasse multos et cessisse tandem,
33 r. quam si semper tacuissent. Hoc est enim, quod iurisconsulti dicunt in
contradictorio iudicio obtinere. Quare non sublevat Reverendissimam
Dominationem tuam hec allegatio quod Regi aliquando quicquam
scripseras aut dixeras, imo vero quoniam[1] deinde cesseras. Quod res
ipsa pre se tulit, magis magisque onerat ut post manus semell datas, post
deditionem factam, iugulata semell et prostrata sententia unquam in tua
Dominatione reviviscat; nisi forte tuo exemplo populus discat nihil esse
aliud religionem nostram, nisi temporis causa consentionem factam, et
ad illius o⟨p⟩portunitatem subinde mutabilem. Itaque quod sub principe
mortuo omnes profitebantur fidem nec solitariam nec solam iustificare,
illius, ut apparet, auctoritatem sequuti, nunc postquam ille obierit, te
preceptore, ut ais, et dediscunt illa et desultoria levitate a negatione in
affirmationem, et a contradictiorio in contradictiorium, nullo negotio
transvolant, et fidem solam, que diu iacuerat oppressa et humilis in

---

yourself in opposition to him as a champion of the truth of the Gospel,
lest in religion you seem to have yielded to a doctrine which is
by no means approved, by no means true, by no means sound. For it
is weightier, and more substantial to the confirmation of the matter, that
many have resisted and at length have yielded, than if they had always
held their peace. For this it is which the lawyers call *in contradictorio
iudicio obtinere.* Wherefore this allegation that you had at some time
written or said something to the King, does not help your Most
Reverend Lordship, least of all since afterward you had yielded. What
the incident itself has made clear is more and more aggravated by the
fact that after the pledge once given, after the surrender made, the opinion,
once silenced and destroyed, should ever come to life again in your Lordship; unless perhaps the people should learn by your example that our
religion is nothing but an agreement made for the time being, and then
changeable as occasion arises. And so, as all under the prince who is
dead, following his authority, as is evident, confessed that faith neither
alone nor only justified, now after he is gone, with you as preceptor, as
you say, they unlearn these things, and with superficial headiness flit
from negation to affirmation and from contradictory to contradictory,
without difficulty, and they restore 'only faith,' which long had lain

1 *H.,* quum

330

gradum reponunt a quo antea esset suo merito deturbata; ut de religione dici illud possit ex Gregorio Nazianzeno, Ἕλκει καθέλκει τῇ κινήσει τὴν στάσιν, quod ille tamen in rerum corruptibilium natura valere vult, non item in his que firma perpetuo et immutabilia perstent; cuius generis sit nostra in Deum religio. And as for only fayth, ⟨it⟩ was never the Catholicke doctrine in Christes Churche. But contrarywise, St James Catholique Epistle in playne, expresse woordes learneth us to deny the speche of fayth only, when he sayth, *Non ex fide tantum,* ‡ 'not of faith only.'‡ And those which went aboute in the beginnyng to mayntaine that untruthe of fayth only, they went a nerer waye to their purpose, to denye St James Epistle to have th‡ auctoritie of Scripture, then to enter any exposition; wherin I see men travaile very fondly, even suche as would be noted to have right judgment and to be indyfferent wayers, whose weights[1] nevertheles be not haberdepoys.

Your Graces letter leadeth me againe to the woord 'seducynge,' wheare yt denyeth myne antecedent, to saye, that in truthe is no seducing, which nedeth no further prooff then a rehersall of the same speche againe; for he caryeth his light[2] with him, and nedeth only an admonition with a poynting fynger. For where the latter parte of a speche is made of the first, which Cicero ⟨*Ac.*, ii, 98, 143⟩ callith *ex se connexam propositionem,* yt declareth a truthe and a necessarye truthe, for *si lucet, lucet, si dies est, dies est;* and this speche, 'good is not evill,' is knytt of yt self lykewise, for in *subiecto* is conteyned *predicatum;* I will *in re aperta* no further *ludere exemplis;* but to the purpose. When I saye, 'In truthe is no seducyng,' this is knytt of yt self, as is this spech also, 'In the right waye is no goyng oute of the waye.' Seducyng is a leadinge oute of the waye, and frome truthe and out of truthe; nowe 'in truthe' and 'oute of truthe' be[3] contradictorie, and a negacion maketh a[4] equipollence. So as 'not in truthe' is of[5] the same effect as is 'oute of truth,'

33 v.

---

prostrate and obscure, to the position from which it formerly had been cast down through its own deserts; so that it can be said of religion, in the words of Gregory Nazianzen, that ⟨like a wheel⟩ it pulls upwards and downwards, shifting its position by its own motion ⟨*Carm.,* i, ii, xix, 7⟩; words which, however, he applies to the nature of things corruptible, not of those which endure eternally strong and immutable; of which kind may our belief in God be.

1 *B.N.,* rightes; *H.,* weights   2 *B.N.,* right; *H.,* light
3 *H.,* are   4 *H.,* an   5 *H. supplies* of

and 'not oute of truth' equipolleth to 'in truth.' Wherby appereth howe, forasmuche as seducyng syignyfieth 'out of truth,' 'in truthe,' which was *subiectum* of my proposition, includeth in it by equipollence *predicatio*. And so it is a proposition necessarie, 'In truth is no seducyng,' and such as nedeth no further then, as often as yt is denyed, to say yt againe, which maye be done without nugation[1], for yt proveth yt self. And therfore yt canot be well and properly sayd that in the truth is seducyng, no more then we maye saye that in the truth be lyes, where the fyrst dystroyeth the second, unlesse we will by the woord 'truth' understand only that which yt was or shuld be, or elles that[2] conteyneth for that is conteyned; after which sorte we may saye that the letters and woordes of the truth of the Byble, when the same Byble is in any tonge not truly translate[3], conteyne lyes, and say ther be in that Byble, so evill translate, many lyes. And because we use to call the Byble truthe, we maye saye sometyme that truth hath many lyes in yt, meanyng a Byble not truly translate. But elles in truth can be no lye, nor in truth any seducyng. Mary, yf we change the proposition and for 'in' say 'with,' I have knowne many goe aboute to seduce with the truth. And in the comedy Syrus professeth, and so doo Pseudolus also, that they will not deceyve their maister after the comon sorte, with telling lyes, but after a speciall new sorte, with telling only truth ⟨Terence, *Heaut.*, IV, i; Plautus, *Pseud.*, I, 5⟩. Which lyke parte the sacramentaries, and many other[4], professe at this daye, to deceave the symple with truth, that is to saye, with plaine Scriptures. And suche simple be seduced with the truth, but not in yt, for they be ledd clere oute of yt. And yet in this speche, 'with the truth,' as I have nowe spoken, the woord 'truth' hath

34 r. not his[5] full signification; but apece for the hole, as woord⟨es⟩[6] be many tymes used. And in the use of woordes is the world muche trobled, and, as St Gregory Nazianzene sayth, Λόγῳ παλαίει πᾶς λόγος[7], βίῳ δὲ τίς; ⟨*i.e.*, Every word wrestles with a word, but with life who wrestles? *Carm.*, I, II, xxxiii, 12.⟩

Of Christes and His appostelles woordes we make a great woonderment, *odio plusquam Vatiniano* ⟨*cf*. Catullus, xiv, 3⟩; and as for His and their lyves, we never stryve for the matter. And[8] a man loked on the manners of the world, he woold saye all were justyfied alyke, yf they mett on the fleshe dayes, and oute of the[t] devine service; wherin I confesse I

1 *H.*, negation   2 *H. adds* which   3 *H.*, translated
4 *H.*, others   5 *H.*, its   6 *H.*, words
7 *H. ends Greek quotation here, adding*, etc.   8 *H.*, if

have bene somewhat curyous to marke what precious fruytes growe[1] out of the justyfyeng fayth, that, they say, necessaryly worketh. And emonges[2] other thinges that I have redd, wrytten in our tyme, I have muche noted an epistell of Erasmus wrytten to Bucer, wherin Erasmus declareth what causes moveth him not to embrace their sect. In which causes, fyrst, he allegeth his owne consyence, which could not be perswaded that their sect came of God, and then yt followeth thus: 'Proximum est, quod videam in isto grege multos alienos ab omni sinceritate evangelica. Mitto rumores et suspiciones, de compertis experimento loquor, atque ade⟨o⟩[3] meo malo compertis, nec in vulgo tantum, verum etiam in his qui videntur esse aliquid, ne dicam proceres. De ignotis non est meum iudicare; mundus late patet. Novi quosdam optimos priusquam huic professioni sese[4] addicerent; quales nunc sint nescio; certe aliquot comperi factos deteriores, nullum meliorem, quantum humano iudicio perspici potest.' And after yt followeth: 'Si maritus comperisset uxorem magis morigeram, si preceptor discipulum magis obsequentem, si magistratus civem magis tractabilem, si conductor operam fideliorem, [5]si emptor venditorem[5] minus subdolem, erat magna evangelii commendatio.' The rest is worthy the reding, which is in the xix[th] booke of his Epistells.

I will[‡] leave of this and come to the contention your Grace speaketh of and notith to be at this daye, wherunto I ame not privie. And God forbyd a fryer quondam, as Josepth is, or all the rablement of them

---

'The next point is that I see in that group many alien to all evangelical sincerity. I pass over rumours and suspicions; I speak of things discovered by experience and, moreover, discovered to my misfortune, not merely in the rank and file, but even in those who seem to be something, not to call them leaders. In regard to the unknown it is not mine to judge; for the world is wide. I knew certain men most excellent before they joined themselves to this sect; what they now are, I know not; assuredly I have found some made worse, none better as far as can be perceived by human judgment.' And after it followeth: 'If a husband had found his wife more obliging, if a teacher a pupil more dutiful, if a magistrate a citizen more law-abiding, if a contractor a workman more faithful, if a buyer a seller less crafty, it would be a recommendation of the Gospel.'

1 *H.*, groweth   2 *H.*, among
3 *H.*, adeo   4 *H.*, se
5–5 *B.N. and H.*, si venditor emptorem; *Erasmus*, si emptor venditorem

should be noted auctors of a contention, both against the truth and against so solempn a determinacion of the matter of 'only faith'; and so plaine and evident in that pointe, as all the wittes of Christendome can not, in my judgement, make it playner, as I will after entreate at length.

Interim vero, appello episcopus episcopum, frater fratrem; ferendum censes ut ineptientis fraterculi latratus nomen obtineat contentionis, ut se opponat Regi, regno, episcopis omnibus? Neque enim mihi persuadere possum Reverendissimam Dominationem tuam, re maturius deliberata, velle a bonis deficere ad istos nebulones, et neglecto fratrum co⟨e⟩tu[1] in istam proluviem se dare cum veritatis iniuria manifesta et fame tue certo dispendio; presertim, cum videas sic obsessam religionem, ut, aperta semel porta, impetum irruentium haud queas sustinere. Auctoritate tua, cum volent, facillime abutentur plurimi; reverebuntur, cum tu voles, paucissimi. In pugna navali, que triremibus fit Turcis non fiditur contra Turcas; nec ego Josepho fiderem contra fraterculum Baal[2] ⟨i.e., Bale⟩, qui omnem movet machinam qua intromittatur, nec commodior est transitus quam ut sola fides predicetur. Neque non dubitat eam plantam, si solo nostro coaluerit, continua tandem irrigatione et

34 v.

Meanwhile truly, I, a bishop, address a bishop, a brother a brother. Do you think it endurable that the barking of a foolish little friar should gain the name of a debate, that he should set himself up against the King, the throne, and all the bishops? For I cannot persuade myself that your Most Reverend Lordship, after considering the affair more maturely, wishes to go over from the good to those good-for-nothings, and, neglecting the assemblage of your brethren, to give yourself to that scum, when the harm to truth is clear and the loss of your reputation certain; especially when you see religion so beset that, once the door is open, you cannot withstand the attack of those bursting in. Many, when they wish, will abuse your authority most readily; few will respect it when you wish it. No faith is placed in Turks in a naval battle in Turkish warships against Turks; nor against the little friar Bale would I trust Joseph, who works every engine of warfare that he may gain admittance ⟨i.e., for Protestant doctrine⟩; nor is there an easier entering passage than by the preaching of 'only faith.' Nor does he doubt that that plant, if it shall have struck root in our soil, at length by continual watering and diligent culture, will some time bring forth those

1 *H.*, coetu   2 *H.*, Bale

cultura dilligenti, acerbos illos fructus producturam aliquando, qui vell
semel gustati omnis relique religionis abortum facile sint effecturi. Nihil
nos movent exempla Germanica? Qui homines, antehac invicti, nunc
inviti et reluctantes ab illa inepta conclusiuncula deturbati sunt, quam
nec calamo nec gladio sustinere potuerunt. A qua in ea opinione stulta
pertinacia si tempestive deficere voluissent, iamdudum res suas com-
possitas habuissent, cum summo Romani episcopi et dedecore et detrimento. Sed illius conclusiuncule vis adegit Lutherum, constancie de-
fendende causa, ut sacramentorum misteria interverteret, et ad insanam
necessitatis assertionem dilaberetur. Qui cum in Sacramento Eucharistie
subsisteret, exorti sunt non pauci, qui hominis timiditatem arguerent,
quod plenam illius propositionis vim non auderet prosequi ad extremum,
viz., ut etiam Eucharistiam prorsus extingueret, que cum illa doctrina
consystere non potest; id quod Swinglius et alii tam clare tractant, ut
cuivis sit perspicuum sic inter se iuncta et ἀκόλουθα esse, ut, qui solius
fidei in iustificationem doctrinam admiserit, Sacramentum Eucharistie
quomodo nos predicamus, cogatur denegare.

But nowe I will come to the dyscussion of the amphibologie, as your
Grace calleth yt, wherof I marvaile. And for the openyng of yt, and to

---

bitter fruits which, tasted but once, will readily effect the miscarriage of
all other religion. Do the German examples move us not at all? Those
men, hitherto unconquered, now, unwilling and reluctant, have been
overthrown by that foolish sophism ⟨i.e., justification by faith alone⟩,
which they could maintain neither by pen nor sword. If they had been
willing to withdraw at the proper season from their fatuous persistence
in this opinion, long since would they have had their affairs settled, to
the greatest disgrace and harm of the bishop of Rome. But the force of
that sophism drove Luther, for the sake of defending his consistency,
to pervert the mysteries of the sacraments and fall away to the insane
assertion of necessity. When he halted at the Sacrament of the Eucharist,
there rose up not a few who assailed the timidity of the man because he
did not dare to follow out the full force of that proposition to the end;
viz., that he utterly abolish the Eucharist also, which cannot stand with
that doctrine; a thing which Zwingli and others so clearly handle, that
it is evident to anyone that these things are so joined and interdepen-
dent that whoever has admitted the doctrine of 'only faith' in justification
is compelled to reject the Sacrament of the Eucharist in the way we
profess it.

335

shew that the matter is playnely sett fourth in the Kinges Majesties booke, I shall use two manner of argumentes; one oute of the woordes of the booke, and another of the sence and meanyng of the same woordes. And the argument of the sence shalbe directed to your Graces person; that is called *argumentum ad hominem*; and the argument of the woordes, to all them that shall read this.

35 r.   Fyrst, yt cannot be oute of memorie yet, howe your Grace in the Convocacion House at the‡ fyrst withstode the condempnacion of this doctrine of 'only fayth,' at suche tyme as the booke was fyrst openly read, and your Grace brought then[1] in this simillitude, that lyke as a man, when he seeth, hath his nose on his face and yet seeth not with his nose, but with his eye only, even so, although fayth hath company of other vertues, yet fayth only justyfieth, as the eye only seeth. And ther your Grace could have bene content to have fayth alone reproved, but not fayth only; wheruppon your Grace sayd you woold sheew your mynde to the King, who, to make the matter clere, would have yt termed[2] so as 'only fayth' were as well denyed as 'fayth alone.' And after muche declaracion of your Graces mynde, your Grace agreed to the booke as yt is nowe penned, and so dyd all the realme lykewise; and preachers sett yt fourth accordingly. So as, of the sence, your Grace cannot pretend any amphibologie, for yt was playnely ment against the[3] opinion of 'only fayth,' as your Grace then tooke yt, and, as you seme to saye, those that make contention would veryfie yt nowe; for, seyng your Grace dyd so openly without ambiguite goo frome yt, ye will not, as‡ I truste, what so ever ye wryte, take *vomitum* uppe againe. And the declaracion of this storye shall goo[4] to purge those that meddled in the booke for this parte; that in this doctrine to condempne 'only fayth' and 'fayth alone' in justyfication, the King our sovereigne lord was neither seduced nor deceyved. For he dyscussed yt thorowly and travailed in yt with you, unto whome fynally your Grace cessyd ⟨*i.e.*, yielded⟩, which he, lyke a prince of muche clemencie, most gently reaceyved, and suche[5] in dede, as your Grace saith, was his nature. And thus I knytt uppe the argument of the sence and meanyng.

    As for the woordes of the booke, they be conceyved in a negative, and have so playne, precise, and stronge a[6] forme of speche, as yt cannot be drawne a sunder to make two partes, which is the proper effect of an

| 1 *H.*, them | 2 *B.N.*, temeed (?); *H.*, termed | 3 *H.*, that |
| 4 *H.*, seem | 5 *H.*, so as | 6 *H. supplies* a |

336

amphibologie. And fyrst, to consyder the woordes by them selves. 'Only' is a very single, indivisible word and without ambiguitie; 'alone' is lykewise of the same nature; 'neyther' is also in significacion a stronge negative; and oone alwais, 'fayth,' is restrayned to a speciall acception, as a vertue seperate, and so canot be multiplied. The word 'justificacion' in this proposition is oute of question, because the negative determineth all the significacions of yt. So as, in the wordes consydered a parte, their is no ambiguitie. And as for the composition, ⟨it⟩ hath noone amphibologe, but one single understandinge in St Paule, when he speaketh of fayth, as the woordes leadeth us directly: that in justificacion is ment neyther fayth only ne fayth alone—so the booke speaketh. Which shall enforce all men to saye that by woordes is marked and notyd unto us in the Kinges booke, that neyther fayth in cumpany justyfyeth only[t], ne out of company alone justyfieth; for fayth may not be alone, but with company, ne any waies only be noted to justyfie. For yf fayth justyfieth, not only nor alone, yf yt justyfieth at all, yt justyfieth with company, seyng yt may not be alone, as the booke sayth. The negatyve determineth all cyrcumstaunce in true speache. And yf thone parte of a contradiction[1], the negative, be by the booke, as yt is in deede, determyned true, then is the other parte of the[2] contradiction, the[3] affyrmative, by the same booke determyned false. So as, being true that only fayth justyfieth not, which the booke avoweth, by the meere nature of the woordes of the booke this proposition, 'only fayth justyfieth,' is clerely made false.

Your Grace, in handelyng this place in your letters, [4]ye reherse[4] the woordes of the Kinges booke trulye, and ye frame very handsomly even the same yssue againe, which your Grace made in the Convocacion Howse, before ye yelded to the Kinges booke. All men graunte, your Grace sayth truly, that the presence of all theis vertues is required, and yet a frere quondam maketh nowe the old doute againe. For I will not understand that your Grace your self will swarve frome your self. And yet your Grace, to sett fourth the amphiblogies, pressyth very sore, *et percontando*, sercheth where the booke takyth awaye this dought. Wherin your Grace askyth the question *tanta confidentia*, that, me semeth, your self useth the lyke poynte of mirth herin that one of myne acquayntaunce dyd in a lyke matter, who moved emonge divines for a solempn doubte a matter that had no doubt at all. But he brought yt

---

1 *B.N. adds* in; *omitted in H.*   2 *H. supplies* the
3 *H. supplies* the   4-4 *H.*, rehearses

in with suche a syrcumstaunce that they were somewhat altred, so as they understode not, in that sodaine doubte, that was evidently layd afore their eyes. For he that moved the question facioned yt thus: howe him self had sundry tymes loked uppon dyvers aucthors to knowe, where the Gospell speaketh *de duobus filiis Zebedei,* who was those childrens father. Wherunto no man would awnswere at that tyme; butt within a moneth, a good old man that had mused abrode and at large of the matter, and wandred wyde to fynde that laye even afore[1] hym, as one dyd his glove whiles[2] he held yt in his hand, this divine, I say, mett him that asked the question a moneth after in Chepe syde, and tould him he had studyed sumwhat in the doubt he moved and had found who was those childrens mother, but of the father he had red no thing. Which sort of mery tales can not but come alwaies to hand uppon suche[3] occasyon when yt is ministred. But to the purpose; as that question was assoyled in the woordes layd afore them and neded no searche in dede, so is your Graces question, which you[4] sett fourth so vehemently, assoyled playnly in the same woordes of the booke by your Grace rehersed, in which it is sayd, we be not justyfied by fayth only nor[5] alone. Which woordes playnly awnswere and ‡at hand roundley‡ the question your Grace moveth; even as the word *Zebedei* dyd the solempn question moved by the other. After which sorte, me thinke, your Grace handelyth me, to shewe your self in theis matters mery againe. For either my witt fayleth me or I [6]sawe never[6] question more directly ne more playnly assoyled and awnswered then the booke awnswereth this question, whether we may saye faith alone justyfieth, or only fayth justyfieth; which is done by the negation, 'neyther,' which is a flatt naye[7] to both. For the booke is thus: 'neyther fayth alone ne fayth only.' So as, if suche as travaile in the doctrine of 'fayth only,' brought their water pott to the Kinges booke, they were lyke to goo thence with out lycquo*u*r.

As for your Graces simillitude of fyre, and your debating with
36 v. other, ⟨it⟩ is as thoughe the determinacion in the Kinges Majesties booke had not bene made, ne your Grace yelded therunto. Howe men confesse to your Grace, I knowe not nor I will not enquir. If he that made me reporte of Josephe should debate with your Grace herin, I would be as frayd of him as Pamphilus was of Cryto, when he sayd, *Metuo ne substet hospes* ⟨Terence, *Andria,* 914⟩, not becawse Crytos tale was not

1 *H.,* before   2 *H.,* whyle   3 *H. adds* an   4 *H.,* ye
5 *H.,* ne   6–6 *H.,* never saw   7 *H.,* way

true, but because Symo was not to be comened with by one not accustomed with[1] such a presence. The Stoikes, by argumentes which they called *brevia consectaria*, brought many to say with them, for the tyme they spake with them, even to graunte that *dolor non est malum*. But when one of that sect was once brought into a great travaile and grief *et dolore premeretur*, he could not in dede practise that he had learned in wordes; and, as Cicero writeth, renounced the sect againe and sayd *dolor* was *malum*, and so forsoke the Stoikes opinion in the rest ⟨*Tusc. Disp.*, II, 25, 60⟩. And how muche so ever any man should[2], by debating with your Grace, assent to 'only fayth,' I would not doubt, with as lyttell tyme of communicacion, ⟨to⟩ perswade him the contrary. But, I thanke God, I never went aboute to convince any man privily in that opinion, saving once I wrote my mynd to your Grace. I would not gladly be ussher in that scoole. I had Barns to scoole, by the Kinges Majesties commaundyment, which proved so fondly that I have given up scoole ever synce, and, in dede, afore medeled not.

Uppon this occasyon I will spend some woordes in the very matter yt self, because your Grace speaketh of suche as contend toth and nayle, that only faith justyfieth. Fyrst, this proposition, 'only fayth justyfieth,' is not in theis woordes founde in any parte of Scripture. To this all men must agree; and yf yt be true, yt is not a wrytten veritie in wordes, but deduced oute of the sence, and for somuche unwrytten. Second[3], theis wordes in the affirmative, 'only fayth justyfieth,' be wordes contradictorie to the Kinges Majesties booke, in which booke the sence of the Scripture is trulye declared, and to this all our realme hath agreed. And according to this ground we must saye that theis wordes, 'only fayth justyfieth,' be neyther wordes of Scripture ne agreable to the sence of Scripture, *per locum ab auctoritate* of the Kinges Majesties booke. And to a Frenche man that thought [4]not him self[4] bound by our determinacion, I would omytt this second parte and prosequute the fyrste. And seing theis woordes be not in Scripture, and yf they have any truthe, they 37 r. muste have yt in the sence of Scrypture, in dyscussyon therof, I would ensearche howe in justyficacion 'only' is joyned to fayth, by what auctoritie warranted, and what should direct the readers understanding, wherby to be bould so to doo. I reade that St Paule speaketh of fayth in justyficacion, and so farr I maye be bould to saye, we be justyfied by fayth. But thaddicion of an exclusive requireth[5] further and perfytt in-

1 *H.*, to   2 *B.N. adds* be; *not in H.*   3 *H.*, 2ly
4-4 *H.*, hymselfe not   5 *H. adds* a

sight, seing ther is a company of other vertues ther with fayth, as all men agree, and requireth a longe pryenge, questionyng, and serching, wherby to be able at the last to saye, only fayth worketh justificacion. And thus I would further debate‡ the matter.

If I should direct my understanding by this generall rule, that where so ever Scrypture speaketh of any thinge 'alone,' I may in understanding put 'only' to yt—this rule, yf I followed, would in many places bring fourth marvelous fond understandinges, which I will not rehearse nowe; and therfore yt is not to be receaved. So as their is none other waye to attayne clere understanding of this matter[1], but to laye open, as they doo in an‡ anathomye, all the inward partes of fayth and, on thother syd, all the bowelles of justyfycation; and as they awnswere one to another so fytly[2] as the corespondence can be in them only, then by that tryall I may be bould to putt 'only,' where that appereth, or, yf yt appere not, to leave yt oute. Which matter I will entre thus: St Paule sayth fayth is the upholding and certayne foundacion, which I call ὑπόστασις, of thinges to be hoped for, and a declaracion and light and proffe, for so I would expresse *argumentum*, ἔλεγχος, of thinges that appere not. Justyficacion is a worke of God in man, wherby cometh to man remission of synnes, new lyf, the working of the workes of justice, and, in fewer woordes, the effecte of oure redemption, and wherby Christ is communicate with[3] us and we cladd with Him. In this declaracion of fayth there be in severaltie two thinges noted, which maye be reduced to one reason, that is to saye, thinges hoped and thinges hydden[4]. The one sorte of thinges fayth susteyneth; the other, ‡and them also‡, fayth sheweth and declareth. So as we know nothing in mystery but by fayth, ne uphold any thing that we loke for but by faythe and uppon fayth. Concernyng justyfycacion, being the worke of God, we see that our parte is only to reaceve, which we cannot doo *sine argumento fidei*, for elles we knowe yt not, ne conteyne yt *absque*

37 v. ὑποστάσει *fidei*, for the frayletie of our nature, not able to mayntayne yt. And so this[5] gyft of fayth, as St Paule declareth yt in that place, can be but a begynnynge, a grounde, a foundacion, a convenyent tempering of our fraile and dysordered vesselles[6] to receave Godes workemanshipe, and, after His will, to worke with Him, in the receyte of His gyftes.

Hetherto in the openyng of this matter appereth nothyng why to put 'only' to 'fayth' in justyfycacion, ‡wherby, in dede, fayth in his proper

1 *B.N.*, manner; *H.*, matter	2 *H.*, featly	3 *H.*, unto
4 *H.* hid	5 *H.*, that	6 *H.*, vessell

descryption hath only τὸ εὔλογον to the worke of God in justyfica-cion[‡]. And in lyke wise doth Gregorie Nazianzein expound Christes wordes, where He sayd He could not worke His miracles for their in-credulytie[1]. Whear God wrought His miracles in healing manns body, Gregory Nazianzene notith two partes concurring in that worke: mannes fayth and Godes powre. And as this texte of Christes worde⟨s⟩[2] sheweth that Godes powre wrought not this worke alone, so another texte of Scripture sheweth playnly that fayth dyd yt not alone. For the woman αἱμορροοῦσα[3] ⟨Mt. ix, 20⟩ professed[4] hir fayth and sayd, 'Yf I touche the skirte of His garment, I shalbe hole.' She beleved in Christ, and was therby apte and mete to reaceave the miracle, and yet she was not hole tyll she touched yt; at which tyme Christ sayd, *Quis me tetigit? Sentio virtutem ex me exire.* And al suche as cryed, *Miserere mei, fili David,* declared their fayth, and yet they were not then whole, but by Godes worke[5] after made hole. So as by theis textes we be forbydden to put 'only' eyther to Godes powre, which is the one parte, for so Christ [‡]declared when He[‡] sayd He could not worke for wante of their fayth, or to fayth eyther, which appered in suche as desyred to be hely⟨d⟩[6] ⟨*i.e.,* healed⟩, afore they weare helyd. [‡]And therfore 'only fayth' healed them not, no more then 'only fayth' justyfieth, for fayth, as it is a vertue seperate, is only τὸ εὔλογον to Godes worke. According[‡] wherunto, St Paule sayth, *Accedentem ad Deum oportet credere,* and St John sayd, *Dedit eis potestatem filios Dei fieri, hiis qui credunt in Nomine Eius; et, sine fide impossibile est placere Deo;* with all suche lyke as speke of fayth. Wherfore, unlesse ther be in man fayth, God worketh not in 38 r. him. And in this place we may use 'unlesse.' But howe to joyn 'only' to 'fayth,' cannot appere of any thing is yet sayd.

Then lett us goo further. *Credidit Abraham Deo et reputatum est ei ad iusticiam,* which is a lyke speche, in the worke of justificacion and healing the sowle, to this, *Fides tua te salvam fecit,* spoken in the [‡]working of miracles and[‡] healing of the bodye. For in theis and other, where we rede that Abraham was justyfied by fayth, and God dyd impute and alowe his fayth for justice, yt[7] is declared unto us Godes goodnes, Who [‡]calleth ⟨us⟩ His eiers and[‡] hath made so favorable

---

1 *there is a space here of about four lines in B.N., which may indicate the omission of a Greek quotation by the copyist, or a space left by Gardiner in which to insert one*
2 *H.,* words   3 *supplied by H. (blank in B.N.)*
4 *H.,* professeth   5 *B.N. adds* then; *omitted in H.*
6 *H.,* heled   7 *H.,* hence

an accompte and shewed Him self so gentill an audytour to our father Abraham as He alowed his fayth for justice. Which we muste utherwise consyder then, forgetting in dede the syrcumstance of all the truth, for our ease and fansy, bring in 'only,' or, when fayth in Abraham was accompanyed with many other vertues, to be so bould to saye that God in His allowaunce regarded fayth only, because He named not the rest, but the begynnyng, fayth, wherby to signyfie in yt the rest of fayths company. When Christ sayd, 'Thy fayth hath saved the,' He dyd not put 'only' to yt, nor yt[1] could not [2]truly stond[2] there, but as in a parte maye be accompted all, by him that is master of thaccompte. God may saye to us, *Euge, serve, bone et fidelis,* Who may esteme our dedes as yt lyketh Him, but in the framyng of‡ our accompt we saye we be *servi inutiles* to Him, *et dimitte nobis debita nostra;* and yet may not leave of to worke, for therunto we be hyred *denario diurno,* for our owne proffytt, and to fulfyll Godes will.

[3]And what can warrante us, in whome God worketh justificacion, to dystincte in that one hole worke of justyficacion, wher fayth accompanyed with other vertues is presente, that fayth only is thaccomplyshement of the worke? For[3] yf we may so frame the spec⟨h⟩e as we may declyne, in speche of justifycacion, frome the doer and worker, which is God, *Qui iustificat,* and attribute yt to the other causes and effectes in justificacion, then we must saye remyssion of synnes[4] justyfieth us; new lyf justyfieth us; the feare of God justyfieth us; the spirite of Christ justyfieth us[5]; the working of Godes commaundymentes justyfieth us; ‡hole Christ justyfieth us, being our justyficacion‡. Unto all which, fayth is ‡τὸ εὔλογον‡ *tanquam substancia rerum sperandarum et argumentum non apparentium.* And therfore we may saye by fayth we be[6] justyfied, and so St Paule writeth and sheweth howe God, in His accompte, hath imputed fayth to be reckened for justice. But Scripture useth not this speche, that fayth is justice, otherwise then by Godes imputacion, Whose benignitie attributeth to[7] the beginnyng the hole; as God accepteth mans good will sometyme for the dede yt self when yt pleaseth Him; and yet may not we gather therof that our good will is allwaies[8] the dede yt self, and take that for a rule, wherof St‡ Gregorie

38 v. *(marginal)*

---

1 *B.N.*, yet; *H.*, it   2–2 *H.*, stand trewly
3–3 *not in H.*, *but* And what…worketh justification *c.o.*
4 *H.*, syn
5 *H. adds* the indewing of Christ justifyeth us
6 *H.*, are   7 *H. supplies* to   8 *H.*, alway

Nazanzene, *De Baptismo*, notyth, that he that desyrith baptisme hath therby attayned ⟨it⟩ in dede. And howe can we sever[1] oute fayth with 'only,' where Scripture in justyficacion speaketh of many?

The hole mystery of our redemption and salvacion is included in this texte, *Verbum caro factum est, et habitavit in nobis. Verbum caro factum est* is Godes worke without us; *habitavit in nobis* is Godes worke with us. We be His temples suche as, with fayth, have ὑπόστασιν rerum sperandarum, and be illuminate with knowledge in fayth, which is *argumentum non apparentium. Verbum caro factum*, by dwelling in us, is our justyficacion, our lyf, our salvacion, and that by Godes moste mercyfull allowance in His accompte, wherwith to dyscharge our imperfection[2] in[3] our parte, in furniture of our temple, whe⟨r⟩in[4] God should dwell with us for thaccomplishement of the worke of our salvacion. For yf God dwell not in us, we cannot bring fourth fruite, and yf we bringe not fourth fruite, we muste be cutte downe. And forasmuche as the love of God is a necessary furnyture for mans soule, to revive[5] yt, so as lyf, in us imperfytt, maye, by[6] a further grace, receave Christe, the very perfytt lyf, God with His gyftes[7] of grace furnisheth man to garnyshe His temple, wherin Christ should dwell, the very perfett justyficacion of all synners, and gyveth the gyftes of feare, of love, of obedyence, wherwith to reaceave Christ *in domum suam*. For where love is [8]there God will come to dwell, and where love is[8] not, their is death; and therfore fayth, in suche as yt is a seperate vertue, yt is a dede fayth, as St James sayth, and in dede in a dead place, where the love of God wanteth. And then yf love be so necessar⟨il⟩y[9] required, as *qui non diligit manet in morte, et qui non diligit non novit Deum, et si quis diligit me sermonem meum servabit et ad eum veni⟨e⟩mus[10] et mansionem apud eum faciemus*; and charitie knytteth us to God and uniteth us to Him and is vinculum perfectionis; and lyke as fayth is †τὸ εὔλογον† to reaceave theis gyftes for such as be mete to reaceave them; so theis gyftes, with fayth, be[11] †τὸ εὔλογον† to reaceave Christ into us. And Christ must *habitare in nobis* for our salvacion, or elles *verbum caro factum est* will prouffytt us nothing. And Christ is also the[12] perfytt justyfycacion. Which being true, why shall we saye any thing of fayth seperatly with

39 r.

1 *B.N.*, serve; *H.*, sever   2 *H.*, imperfections   3 *H.*, on
4 *H.*, wherein   5 *B.N.*, receave; *H.*, revive
6 *B.N.*, be; *H.*, by   7 *H.*, gift   8–8 *supplied by H.*
9 *H.*, necessarily   10 *H.*, veniemus   11 *H. supplies* be
12 *H. adds* very

'only' or 'alone,' but rather, omytting those wordes of[1] dyvision and contention, declare the matter as yt is playnely, without any lye at all; which cannot be avoyded where we affyrme 'only' of fayth, and fondly frame yt on our syde that be so ymperfytt (as we would note our selves at other tymes) to the diminution on[2] this poynte of Godes glory, Who is the worker of justification, Whome we robbe by speche of that acte, and attribute yt to our fayth, dyffering nothing frome those that be dyffamed as justitiaries[3], but that they speake of creping to heaven [4]at leasure with[4] good dedes, and theis would flye to heaven sodenly with their 'only fayth,' for ease of carriage.

The text of St Paule, *Arbitramur hominem iustificari fide, absque operibus legis*—here is Moyses lawe shutt oute, but we all graunte that yet fayth is within, accompanyed with other vertues. And this text, in affyrmyng that by fayth we be justyfied, sheweth fayth to be necessary [†]as τὸ εὔλογον[†], but neyther devideth neyther[5] dystincteth any worke of fayth in justificacion frome the rest. So as, perusyng the hole Scripture, or consydering the meanyng of yt, we shall never fynd cause or warentie why to putt 'only' or 'alone' to fayth, unlesse yt be to exclude Moyses lawe, wherof their is nowe no question. But, contrary wyse, in every parte of Scripture well understanded, shall appere evident cause to be afrayde of yt. For taking yt[6] for a principle, as we muste doo, that fayth, charytie, and hope be thre severall vertues, and that ⟨with⟩ all theis, withoute the communication of Christes justice in suche sorte unto us as yt may be owrs[7], we cannot be accompted justyfied before God to make so the accompte as yt maye be called *summa quadrans*, which is ane even reckenynge, to be able to abyde Godes judgement, we be learned to put all theis together, estemynge eche one in his dygnytie and valew, and be afrayd of all 'onlyes,' to interrupt in speche this company. And certayne Scryptures lyncketh too[8] tog⟨e⟩ther, wherby to exclude 'only' frome fayth, as, *qui crediderit et baptizatus fuerit*, where fayth is not alone, ne worketh only, but justificacion is therin attribute to the sacrament. And, to shewe that in that sacrament is the worke of charitie, baptisme conteyneth two effectes: one is to putt of the old man *per remissionem peccatorum*, another, the renewyng of lyf which is *per charitatem*. And St Paule, in his Epistle to the Romaines, notyth unto

39 v.

1 B.N., to; H., of   2 H., in
3 B.N., justificiaries; H., justitiaries   4–4 H., with leysure by
5 H., ne   6 H. *supplies* yt
7 B.N., owre; H., owrs   8 H. *supplies* too

us for exclusyon of 'onlyes' ever *mortem Christi* and *resurrectionem Christi*, the leavyng of synn and yndument of vertue, the dystruction of death and renuyng of lyf; and presysely admonysheth us that, *qui non habet spiritum Christi, hic non est Eius*; and that we cannot have, but by love; and yf I be not His, I cannot be justyfied.

In all this dyscussyon no man could have cause to saye, 'Alas, good poore people, what meaneth[1] men to teache you justyficacion by workes, to the diminution of Godes glory?' Their is no cause to crye oute so, ne the Kinges booke techeth yt so as that weare to be feared; nor I meane yt so nowe, but only to avoyde so many lyes as 'only' would and hath engendred, evill placed with fayth in justyfycacion, as yt is a severall vertue. Wherof one ⟨*i.e.*, one lie⟩ that is notable the Kinges Majesties booke doth exclude, where men would certeynly beleve them[2] selves predestinates, and call that the justyf⟨y⟩eng fayth, after some mens handlyng; which is a mere dreame. And yf the proposycion of 'only fayth' were reaceaved, yt muste nedes slyppe to that knotte; for their yt should rest, and theirwith abhore to here of a condition in Godes promyse; which our late soveraigne lord could not abide. But wher, in that was cald the byshopps booke, the Crede was so expounded as he that sayd yt wold referr yt[3] absolutely to him self which was in every article, the King our late soveraigne lord, with his owne penn, where the Crede expounded sayd, 'I believe everlasting lyf for me,' totted ever on the head this clause, 'Yf I kepe the condicion.' And that booke have I sene, and so I trowe hath your Grace also; wherby appereth he was not deceyved.

And [4]a pece of the travaile to have 'only' to 'beleve'[4] is to exclude the condycion. For dyffamacion[5] wherof, their have[6] bene many argumentes devysed withoute all purpose, and specially of 'gratis.' God, they say, gyveth yt gratis; and so doth He; yf He gyveth yt, as He doth, ‡⟨He⟩ doth yt gratis. For I never hard of gyft unlesse yt be gratis‡. But whiles they speake so muche of 'gratis,' they forgeat that God gyveth us the hole, and gyveth us the gyftes wherby to be able to fulfyll His condycion to enjoye that gyfte. And then by His gyfte of fayth He causeth yt to be called my fayth, and by His gyft of charitie maketh me have love to God and hable to reaceave further gyftes of Christ. And

---

1 *H. supplies* meaneth
3 ? *scribal error for* that
5 *H.*, confirmation

2 *B.N.*, ther; *H.*, them
4–4 *H.*, to have only faith
6 *H.*, has

¹so alltogether¹, as St Paule declaireth in this poynte, under pretence of preserving Godes grace frome injury of the Pellagians, we hyde and darken the confessyon of this² gyfte and make as thoughe we had reaceaved no suche gyfte, but make our accompte after our former povertie in the old Adam, and, for a cloke for synn, make that so stronge as *reatus*, in the opinion of some, goeth not awaye in baptisme. And where in all other fruites of nature their is opportun⟨it⟩e³ of tyme, the fruites of synn be continuall and excused by some⁴ with the violence of originall synn that bresteth oute att all seasons, and yet is not ymputed, by reason of 'only fayth.' And this is the godly doctrine that ensueth of 'only fayth,' and, *concessis principiis*, cannot be stayed. And therfore, yf a man would trye the doctrine, he maye doo yt by the moste certaine rule of tryall, *ab opposito consequentis*; for, *ex veris verum, ex falsis falsum*; and of the doctrine of *sola fydes* followe so many absurdities as muste nedes declare the anticedent to be false. Which matter hath bene as dilligently dyscussed and tryed as ever was any; and, not without a moste certaine knowledge and understanding, of our late sovereigne abhorred and detested; not instructed therin by me, who never commenyd with him privately of⁵ yt. But yt appered ever, when he commenyd in yt, that he had seene throughly what was ment in yt. And as for Scripture to mayntaine yt, the proposition hath none.

And touching your Graces similitude, it ⁶can serve for no⁶ proffe, but for a declaracion of that is proved and knowne for truthe and yet not fully perceyved; which in this proposition is not so. For yt is denyed to be true that only fayth justifieth, and then the similitude can serve for nothing tyll the other be proved. But and yt were proved, the similitude could not aptly declare howe, being fayth not alone, but accompanyed with many vertues, yet only fayth, as a seperate vertue, justyfieth. For the symilitude in the chefe pointe halteth, in that drynesse and light be so *adiacentia* and *actus* in the fyre, as they be not seperable in *subiecto convenienti*. For drynes and lyght be the lyke operacions of fyre as the burnyng is; for as the fyre burneth, so giveth yt light, and as yt both dryeth and burneth that yt toucheth mete to burne, so dryeth yt also, in a convenyent dystaunce, that yt toucheth not. And fyre, *secundum qualitates subiecti*, dryeth and puryfieth, and burneth not, as appereth *in lino vivo*, wherof Plinius speaketh ⟨*Natural*

1-1 *B.N.*, also to gether; *H.*, so alltogether   2 *H.*, his
3 *H.*, oportunity   4 *B.N.*, synn; *H.*, some
5 *H.*, abowt   6-6 *H.*, cannot serve for any

Hist., xix, § 4⟩. And fyre in water maketh liquid and consumeth not;
et quedam animalcula pascuntur igne. Ἄριστον ὕδωρ, as Pindare sayth
⟨*Olympian Odes*, I, 1⟩, and maketh a fytter similitude to expresse the
truthe of that is by the realme concluded in justyficacion; that lyke a⟨s⟩[1]
water, very hotte, scaldeth, and therfore we maye say water scaldeth,
and yet, bycause the heate of that water procedeth frome the fyre, we
can neyther saye water alone skaldeth, ne only water skaldeth; so,
although charitie, obedyence, and other vertues ⟨be⟩ present, we
may saye faith justyfieth, yet maye we not saye fayth alone justyfieth,
ne only fayth justyfieth, no more then we saye only water scaldeth, or
water alone skaldeth, although yt be true that water scaldeth, which
by fyre is made hott, where the nature of [2] fyre accompanyeth the water
in working, as Plutarche writeth.

And theis vertues that accompany fayth have place in justyficacion
‡κατὰ τὸ εὔλογον‡; for suche a conformitie God requireth in man
and worketh by His grace in him, absque invidia operum, aut iniuria
gracie quia neque est volentis, neque currentis, sed miserentis Dei‡;
and yet, eadem misericordia excitati et volumus et currimus. Sic enim
Deo visum est convenire, ex beneplacito voluntatis Sue, secundum
quam et in bonis operibus creavit nos ut ambularemus in illis, et errantes
oves ad facti sui penitentiam incitat, et quibus redeant modis Ecclesiam
Suam docuit, que est columna veritatis; which, and[3] yt hath no more
staye in administracion, but a continuall movinge, and after contention,
contention uppon every manns dreame, and yt is ever sponyng[4] in the sea
without anchour[5] hold, yt is a hard case[6] *ne quid dicam aliud.*

And one thing I note, how our[7] troble begynneth, yf their be suche
scratchers and byters as your Grace wryteth of in the matter of justy-

---

without casting odium upon works and without injury to grace, because
is it neither of him that willeth nor of him that runneth, but of God that
showeth mercy; and yet by the same mercy inspired, we both will and
run. For so to God it seemed fitting, from the good pleasure of His
will, according to which He both created us in good works that we
might walk in them, and inspires the wandering sheep to repentance of
their deed, and, in what manner they may return, He has taught His
Church, which is the pillar of truth;

1 *H.*, as 2 *H. adds* the 3 *H.*, if
4 *H.*, fluctuating 5 *B.N.*, ancbar; *H.*, anchour
6 *H. supplies* case 7 *B.N.*, your; *H.*, owr

fycacion, which in respect of our state, nedeth not be moved. For we be justyfied in the sacrament of baptisme, and, falling after, retorne by the sacrament of penaunce, where fayth is the grounde, and other meanes of reconsyliacion described, as in the Kinges Majesties booke is conteyned. And seyng we have no[1] Jewes to contend with us for Moyses lawe, a great parte of that dysputacion is for the multitude not necessary. And undoughtedly for edyficacion yt hath not at this tyme the oportunytie, and hath, by suche as seke dyssolucyon and abuse Godes truthe, this use nowe, to dystroye and throwe downe the sacramentes and confound religeon, to the dissipacion of the same. Quare[†] te oro, obsecro, obtestor, Reverendissime Domine, adhibeas in consillium prudentiam et eruditionem tuam. Memineris quam personam in re publica sustineas, quo in statu simus[2]. Regem habemus optime indolis et summe spei, sed iuvenem, que est non modica regni infelicitas. Consiliarii sunt viri boni et prudentes, multis ⟨in⟩dolibus prediti, sed et ipsi mortales. In quibus, si quid humanitus accideret, quem casum[3] nemo prestare potest, O duram et diram illius temporis conditionem, sacris iuxta ac profanis commotis et turbidis! Quid opus est turbare porro in sacris, haud dum pacatis et compositis profanis? Nam hactenus citra offensam de publicis loqui tecum licebit. Quicquid in religione tentabitur, tuo id periculo fiet et omnium, si quid non recte evenerit, malo. Nihil quero, nihil molior, sed

41 r.

Wherefore I pray, I beseech, I implore you, Most Reverend Lord, to apply your wisdom and erudition in counsel. You will remember what part you play in the commonwealth, and in what condition we are. We have a king of the best native ability and of the highest promise, but he is young, which is no small misfortune for a kingdom. The counsellors are good and wise men, endowed with many talents, but they also are mortal. If anything fatal should befall them, and no one is able to guarantee that such an event will not happen—O hard and cruel condition of that time, sacred and profane alike in confusion and turmoil! What is the need of further confusion in sacred matters, when secular affairs have not yet been brought to peace and settlement? For so far will it be allowable to speak with you on public matters without offence. Whatever will be tried in religion, it will be at your peril, and to the misfortune of all, if anything shall turn out unhappily. I seek nothing,

1 *B.N.*, nowe; *H.*, no   2 *H.*, sumus
3 *B.N.*, causam; *H.*, casum

348

datam occasionem amplector, ut que sentio eloquar; hoc enim debeo patri mortuo principi de me optime merito, hoc debeo filio, quem meum principem habeo, hoc debeo patri⟨e⟩[1] et bonis omnibus, quorum salus mihi est communis, qui in eadem nave navigo. Ceterum defunctus mea opera, quemcunque fortuna exitum dederit, feram, et ita feram, ut manum Altissimi agnoscere videar, Qui mortificat et vivificat, deducit ad inferos et reducit, et iratus non obliviscitur misereri, quod Illius est proprium. Interim I speake citra stomachum[2] other then the matter provoketh. And how playnly so ever I speake, yt is without such contention as maye have any reproche. St Augustine[3] and St Jherome wrote not more quietly and soberly one to another then your Grace and I do.

Si fas est conferre exempla, here was an experience of the learned men in the Kinges lawe att this assyse, whiles I was a wryting theis letters, who in the courte, pleading their matters, were very earnest with [4]prety quicke sayenges[4] one to another as the matter served, wisely, wittely, and learnedly; and after, at my boorde merely ⟨*i.e.,* merrily⟩, without private grudge, rehersed some parte of their doing, howe eche had charged other, and travailed one another with this and that feate, and so departed very friendes. As in dede, yf men sue whiles they make the lawyers earnestly fall oute, they maye percase be wery of yt, and yt is not looked for of wise men. Godes cause should be more ernest; and yet when St Paule sayth, *Sit sermo vester sale conditus,* and maketh us, as yt were, cookes for the seasonyng of our speche, I ame the boulder to be mery sometyme, so I avoyde *scurrilitatem, que ad rem non pertinet.* And in my longe talke doo force ⟨*i.e.,* foresee⟩ to place matter that maye

---

I design nothing, but I embrace the opportunity granted, that I may speak out what I feel; for this I owe to the father, the dead prince, to whom I am under the deepest obligations; this I owe to the son, whom I hold as my prince; this I owe to my country and all good men whose safety I share, since I sail in the same ship. Now having performed my task, whatever end fortune shall bestow I will bear, and so bear that I may be seen to recognize therein the hand of the Most High, Who destroys and brings to life, leads down to hell and brings back, and though angry, forgets not to pity—a quality which is peculiarly His own. Meanwhile I speak without anger

1 *H.,* patriae   2 *H. adds* no
3 *H.,* Austin   4-4 *H.,* pratyqwick, saying

serve for one purpose or other, and all to the best end, as I ame perswaded.

But nowe I muste turne backe to a parte of your Graces letters[1] not yet touched, where ye aske me the reason and[2] dyversitie, why any man maye not aswell impugne the Kinges Majesties booke, yf their be cause, as I dyd take uppon me to wryte againste the bysshopps booke, agreed on by the bysshopps, and printed by the Kinges Majestis auctorite.

41 v. Wherunto I saye that, whiles that booke was in divising and framyng, I was in Fraunce, ambassadour, a mere stranger to the matter, without any advertisement of yt or knowledge of any specialitie in yt, till the booke was sent me by the Lord Crumwell into Fraunce, alredy printed, with a speciall rehersall of the bysshopps names notyd to be authors and avowers of yt, with a preface of request to the Kinges Majestie to correct and reforme, as he should thinke good. When I sawe this booke, and *Stephanus Winton* putto yt,[‡] as my speciall supscription, to testyfie my doing in yt[‡], who knew nothing of yt tyll yt was don, and dyslyked many thinges in yt when yt was don, and then the preface tempered the conclusion with the forme of our[‡] supplicacion, I thought expedyent for my dyscharge to frame my supplicacion, for my parte, with a further addition; which in one pece was, that truth might be sett oute truly, and not my name to be putto that was not in dede. For albeyt, lyving in a common welth, men muste conforme them selves to the more parte in auctoritie; and to suche actes of Parlyament as were made, me being absent, or present and denyeng them in particuler suffrage, I muste and will, after they be passed withoute my knowledg or against my mynde, honour and reverence them neverthelesse as lawes of the realme, ne can have any collour to ymprove[3] ⟨*i.e.*, condemn⟩ them, and lykewyse any other common resolucion in the clargie or otherwise; yet yf, before the Kinges royall assent to any[4] acte of Parlyament, the clerke of Parlyament, by oversight, would note to the King that, in passing of this or that acte in the upper howse, I by name sayd, 'Content,' where in dede I was not there—and this I putt by case, for I never knew yt, nor[5], for the honor of the Courte, knowe yt cannot be so—but yf yt chaunsed, I might, withoute reproche, signifie to the Kinges Majestie that, where my name is so reported, in dede I never knew of yt, or lyke yt not, for this or that cause. And so I dyd in that booke, least by sayeng nothing after the booke was comme to my handes, I might a[6] bene sene *ipsa*

1 *H.*, letter   2 *H.*, of   3 *H.*, impugne
4 *H.*, an   5 *H.*, and   6 *H.*, have

taciturnitate negotium meo nomine, quamvis male gestum, probare. Wheruppon yt should afterward be brought in question whether I might *reprobare quod semell probaveram;* which doubt I thought to avoyde with wryting, even the fyrst night that ever I reaceaved the booke, and spent one hole night in that matter at Lyons, because I might signyfie my mynde with the next depeche of letters, as I dyd in dede.

And because your Grace in your letters wryteth the amphibologie of the Kinges Majesties booke to be suche a fountaine as wherat both parties maye fetche water, yt bringeth to my memorie that I have rede of φρέαρ in Greeke, which is a well, and therof deduced, as Aristotle sayth, *phratrie* signifieth[1] suche a company of men as have resorte to[2] one well. And Docter Buttes, whose soule God pardon, was wonte to 42 r. speake of a brotherhood merely ⟨*i.e.*, merrily⟩; and I and other have sometyme spoken yt mixtly, as yt were suger and musterd. But the[3] booke your Grace speaketh of was, in my judgement, suche a well as would have made *phratrias* of us, and had water ynoughe in yt to serve us and Germany also, for both parties, as your Grace speketh, and the thurd parte, for a nede. Yt resembled[4] a common storehouse, where every man layd uppe in store suche ware as he lyked, and could tell wheare to fynde to serve his purpose. In the Civile Lawe we have sometyme Homers verses brought in for proffe of two contrary sentences. After I came into Englonde, I had[5] accompted unto me some parte of the handlyng of yt. And yt was shewed me that Bysshope Stokesley (God have mercy on his soule), after he had styfly withstande[6] many thinges, and muche stoutnes had ben[7] betwene him and the Bysshopp of Herford, whose soule God pardon, then Bysshope Stokesley would somewhat relent in the forme, as Bysshope Foxe dyd the lyke. And then, as yt were in a meane, eche parte, by placynge some wordes by[8] speciall markes, with a certayne understanding protestid, tharticle wente fourth; and so to a new article, and so frome one to another. Their is sometyme as evident contradiction as yf yt had bene saved by a proviso. And their remayneth yet one of theis[9] bookes so noted with the Kinges Majesties‡ owne hand, which is a hand knowne, that yt maye appere his Highnes had read and dilligently studyed over every peece[10] of yt.

1 *B.N.*, signifyeng; *H.*, signifieth	2 *H.*, unto
3 *H.*, that	4 *H.*, resembleth
5 *H.*, heard	6 *H.*, withstood
7 *H. supplies* had ben	8 *H.*, with
9 *H.*, those	10 *B.N.*, place; *H.*, peece

But to the purpose; yf that booke had bene by auctoritie concluded in the realme, and remayned all the Kinges tyme to this daye, I would not have begonne to wryte against yt nowe, the King our sovereigne lord being in minoritie; as who should saye I was affrayd before[1], and nowe I have patyently suffered so longe, ever watching for this daye, nowe he is gone that I feared, now goo to yt frely. As a gentilwoman in London sayd, incontinently uppon hir husbandes death, to hir mayd that hir husband favored: 'Come hether, ye gyll,' sayth she, 'I dare call ye[2] nowe by your name, I thancke God.' ‡Yt was notyd a womans parte to be done so sone, even of them that knew she had juste cause so to doo‡. And therfore, if I could have framed my consyence to agree with suche a boke during the Kinges lyf, I would not have wrytten of yt after his death, nor leape into the pulpett to drawe my sword, which I had, all the Kinges lyf, kept in the shethe. But the booke I wrote againste was never auctorized. And I wrote to the prince, to whome all suche as were privie to yt submytted the matter; and because I was named to be one, and was not ther, ne within [3]the fowr[3] sees (in which case neverthelesse the lawes of the ralme take the husband for father of the child, thoughe he were never privie to yt till yt was christioned),

42 v. therfore I wrote. Which my manner of wryting, with the syrcumstaunce of tyme, place, and the truth of the thing, was such as no man can have the lyke at this daye against the Kinges Majesties booke, that dede is, whiche conteyneth a true, resolute doctrine, passed by mature delyberacion, confyrmed by acceptacion and use, wherof we maye saye the Kinges Majestie dyed seased, and so it[4] descended unto his sonne, who I thinke and truste will alter nothing of yt, and would wyshe he might fynde at[5] his full age *rem ea parte integram*, ‡that he would chose whether he would or no‡.

My Lord Protectour hath herin both sayd to me and wrytten to me very wisely, wherby I ought not to feare any suche mattire. And yet your Grace and I talke as ernestly in yt withoute any facte, as two neghbours dyd in puttyng of a cace in dryvinge of shepe, when their were[6] no shepe their; and in dyscussing what might be percase done, multypled many wordes, as [7]their have bene a great many multypled[7] betwene your Grace and me; wherin I have some pastyme[8], and your

1 *H.*, afore
3–3 *B.N.*, iiij^or; *H.*, the fowr
5 *H. supplies* at
7–7 *H.*, yt hath happened

2 *H.*, you
4 *H. supplies* so it
6 *H. supplies* were
8 *H.*, patience

Grace nedeth not to be encombred with them, seyng ye nede not rede them nor awnswere them, but you lyst. And[1] the lawyers principle is, that free ⟨l⟩ibertie in the beginnyng of thact taketh awaye all allegacion of the tediousnes, grief, and laboure in thexecution, with this reason, *licuit non suscipere*; as nowe to your Grace, when ye see theis letters att the fyrst, *licet non legere*; and a grace in Cambridge was denyed *propter longitudinem*.

As towching my wordes of char⟨g⟩ing your Grace for the inhibicion of preaching, I knowe[2] howe easely your Grace could beare yt, or elles I would not have bene so bould, and theffect of yt maye serve me as yt doth[3] your Grace, for an excuse; even as one purchased a restrainte of his parke for certeyne yeres, to thintente he might, under pretence therof, forbeare to shew suche kindnes to his frendes as, by usyng their parkes familliarly the yere before, he was bound. But to speake to you merely, we bysshoppes maye fortune to[4] here of this matter where we would not, that when we be inhibite[5] to doo our duties[6] [7]we bear it easily and make no suit to the contrary, but if we had ben inhibited to receive owr duty[7] in this or that rent, we would have retayned all the counsayle in Westminster Hall for the realece of yte, with supplicacions, peticions, allegacions, and requestes; and yet we have no better evidence for any rent then we have that we should preache. And then, when your Grace speaketh of intituling[8] of the bysshopp to his cathedrall churche, he is ever intituled to the hole dyocesse, and is called 'ordynary' throughe the dyocesse in the Commen Lawes of the realme. But that shalbe lett alone awhile, and upon knowledge of my Lord Protectors letters. 43 r.

I will nowe enter the devise of the homilies, with suche diligence as the gravitie of the matter doth require. And by a similitude ye put me of corrections of the Byble, me semeth ye partly signyfie that when we have made them, they shall have in execution suche lyke effect as the labors in the correction of the Byble had, which were brought to your Grace—and the Bybles be as they were! And yf the homilies be so sarved, I will not be angry. And when I thinke of them, me thinke yt shalbe a marvelouse pece of woorke to bring them *in unam consonantiam*. ‡But *dissonantia* shall better serve one purpose: uppon a new variaunce in homilies to have the matter putt againe in compromise and brought

---

1 *H. adds* then	2 *H.,* knew	3 *H.,* does
4 *H. supplies* to	5 *H.,* inhibited	6 *H.,* duty
7–7 *supplied by H.*	8 *H.,* inhibiting	

to a new judgement[‡]. But howsoever the homelies shall vary, we muste have the Kinges booke for the standerd measure, or elles their shalbe a greater loosenes then wilbe easely bound agayne. But that tyme is not come, *et nolite* [1]*esse solliciti*[1] *de crastino, quia sufficit diei malicia sua.* In my letters I travayled to exchewe your Graces just offence, wherof ye spake[2], for not wryting homilies, which I dyd many wayes avoyde, and justly. For how so ever any promise by me made might have bound me to God, [3]Who is privie to all convenyent promisses, yet that bond remayning, in some cases the bond of performaunce, wherby any man should be offended[3], may be taken away in the worlde. I alleged many worldly matters to avoyde all worldly offence. And nowe your Grace treatith with me of a promise, as yt should bynd, without manns lawe, in[4] consyence. Which I will awnswere thus[5]: that what so ever promise I or any man maketh, in the fulfylling wherof none other man hath any particuler intrest, ther, yf my superiors pleasure comytteth unto me other greater matters, my consyence is dyscharged in following and executing that my superiour commaundeth me, rather then that I had promised, wheras I cannot convenyently doo both together. And I was in dede strayte after called to other busynes, both for the loane at London, wher I was dayly occupied; and further compelled that somer to lye at Stepney, frome my howse to practyse with thEmperours embassadour upon a league; and after that to prepare for the army that went into Scotland the Michaelmas following; and at Chrismas a devise for a nother matter, with suche a varietie of thinges, as those that knew the particularities marvayled to here me preache once in the Kinges Chappel. And in the same Lent, the Kinges Majestie accepted

43 v.   me to be with him in creditt, as Grandevela was with thEmperour, by the same termes; which was kept secrete, but many their be leving that knew yt to be trew. And in theis thinges rehearsed, I dyd [‡]by the Kinges commaundyment[‡] spend the yere after our communication in the Convocacion; which matter⟨s⟩[6], done by a kinges auctorite, dyschargeth my promise towardes God and towardes your Grace.

I have awnswered before, but your Grace putteth a case in the promise of a benifice, and say that yf I had promised Josephe a benyfice, he might catche a flye in his mouth rather then a benyfice, yf I esteme

1–1 *H.*, solliciti esse   2 *H.*, speke
3–3 *H.*, it may so happen that the obligation of performance
4 *B.N.*, and; *H.*, in   5 *B.N.*, this; *H.*, thus
6 *H.*, matters

promises none otherwise in the Convocation. To that I will say that the fullfylling of suche a promise canbe letted with no busynes. But yf I had made suche a promise to Josephe, not included in bondes of manns lawe, yf that Josephe had afterwardes ([1]being the doctrine as it is[1] reproved) preache⟨d⟩ in suche an audyence of 'only fayth,' I would have judged my fayth dyscharged towardes him that so lyttell regardeth Christian fayth; and flyes [2]in dede should have[2] soner caught him then he should have caught my benyfice.

As for the people, concernyng their hering, I doo not speake yt utterly to their reproche, but contrary wise, in another consyderacion, extolle thexcellencie of their wittes, that cannot abide to be longe a teaching. And we be accompted, next the Itallians, the moste ingeniose people of Christendome; we will take a tale for[3] tould eare yt be half tould, and by a woord understand a sentence. This is comonly trew, and appereth in daylie experience. For wher your Grace would take an[4] argumente to the contrary of[5] hering of Masse and Mattyns, wherin is spent seaven houres of the daye, yt is in speech[6] so called hearing, but in dede nothing so practised, nor never was. For in tymes paste, when men came to churche more diligently then some doo nowe, the people in the churche toke[7] smale hede what the priest[8] and the clerkes dyd in the chauncell, but only to stond upp at the Ghosple and knele at the‡ Sacryng, or elles every man was occupied him self severally in severall praiour[9]. And as for the priestes prayour, they could not all have hard and understanded, although they[10] would, and had given eare therunto. For [11]suche an enterprise to bring that[11] to passe is impossible, withoute the priest should torne his face to the people when he prayeth, and occupie many prayers to them to make them hold their peace. And therfore yt was never ment that the people should in dede here the Mattyns or here‡ the Masse, but be present ther and praye them selves in sylence; with[12] commen credytt to the priestes and clerkes, that althoughe they here not a dystincte sounde to knowe what the⟨y⟩ saye, yet to judge that they for their parte were and be well occupied, and in prayour; and so should they be. And good symple folkes[13] were

44 r.

1–1 *H.*, yt being a doctrine   2–2 *H.*, should indeed   3 *H.*, to be
4 *B.N.*, any; *H.*, an   5 *H.*, from
6 *B.N.*, speake; *H.*, speech   7 *B.N.*, take; *H.*, took
8 *H.*, priests   9 *H.*, prayers
10 *B.N. adds* had   11–11 *H.*, to bring such an enterprise
12 *H. adds* a   13 *H.*, folk

wonte so to be, and other, more dyssolute, used to commen in the tyme of Mattyns and Masse of other matters. And I have knowne that, after their lyttell devosyons sayd, as they called them, some used to gather by the penny or two pence suche money as they had lent in grosse. Butt as fore hering of Masse in dede, some, well occupied, hard not, and some, evill occupied, hard not neyther. And thus yt hath bene practized; so as that can be taken for none[1] argument of hering. And I gather no opinion by divination, but by playn comprobacion of the facte, and after that sorte I speake. And yt is a common fation to aske who preacheth, so as the awdyence encreasyth by the man that preacheth, and not by the matter, unlesse they be admonyshe⟨d⟩[2] of some newe[3] matter in hand, and then they wonder very muche. Of this sorte have I sene our contry men, both learned and unlerned. I speake for the numbre, which they them selves will take for no reproche, for they take yt to procede of lyvely currage, farr discrepante frome those we call good sowles, whome they neglect, and study to be comendable to the world and be caled stoute and corragiouse. And who so ever shall see the dayes that priestes shall reade homilies, he shall have the people here them, yf they be bound to be their, as they nowe here Mattyns, and I thinke none otherwise, and as[4] some other here other sermondes at this daye, which they lyke not.

Their is no cause why I should dyffame our people, but yf a man must speake of them, yt were but a fansy to speake otherwise then yt is. And their is in this churche ⟨at Waltham?⟩ good preaching, and solempn rynging to yt, and yet[5] of all this towne their may be percace sometyme not above xx at a sermon. And I was in your Graces churche at Canterbury, uppon Assention Daye was twelvemoneth, where was a place comodious for the herers to repayre unto, where, I thinke, bysydes the children of the scoole and suche as were of the howse, there were but[6] one hundreth[7] for so great a towne. And yet he that preached pretendyd to preache mere godlynes. And at a nother tyme, when I was there[8] and Master Rydley preached, and I dyned after[9] with your Grace,
44 v. I thanke you, ther were not for all Canterbury many more. Wherof I was not sory, because the cheif porte[10] of the sermon was directed to me to sett fourth[11] bysshoppes fare, with other matter impertinent to the towne.

1 *H.*, no	2 *H.*, admonished	3 *H.*, newer
4 *H. supplies* as	5 *H. supplies* yet	6 *H. supplies* but
7 *H.*, hundred	8 *B.N.*, here; *H.*, there	9 *H.*, afterwards
10 *H.*, part	11 *H. adds* the	

And so I wrote as I had sene experience, withoute entent of reproche. I ame glad alwais to suppose the best; but experience taketh away supposition.

As for your Graces exhortacion to obedyence, I take yt in good parte, and trust ye your self will obey our late sovereigne lord [1]that dedd is, I meane his determinacions[1], and, by example, learne other[2] to obey nowe; for that[3] is a greate matter, to induce the people by example. I was never faulty in theis poyntes of not obeyeng, nor[4] murmering, *non solum propter conscientiam, sed etiam propter iram.* For, synce I was bysshope, savinge[5] a lyttell small tyme, I had ever those[6] that were redy to note those faultes, and[7] they had bene in me, wherin myne innosencie hath delyvered me, and ever shall, by Godes grace. I will saye and wryte my mynd freely, as opertunitie shall serve, to the superiours them selves, and not to the people that cannot amend yt; which hath nevertheless bene some other mennes customes, but never myne. For yf I can doo no good by advertisement in place where I maye doo good, I will not wrangle oute of place and tyme only to doo hurte.

This is my determinacion: to serve God whiles I ame here, with all suche giftes as I have reaceaved of Him; which I doo not so perfectly as I should, but somewhat towardes yt, so as, though I be not perfec⟨t⟩ly good, I will not, by Godes grace, be utterly naught; so to care for this world [8]as if I[8] thought to goo hence, and yet to use yt while I ame here[9], and not to be wery of yt oute of reason, ne dyspayre in yt without cause, as in dede I see no cawse why I should.

And thus I have awnswered your Graces longe letter in some parte more merely ⟨*i.e.,* merrily⟩ then I determyned, for so the matter tempted me, but with an honest harte to have all thing[10] well, for Godes honour, with the welth and preservacion of this realme; wherin I have occupied suche a place as I cannot perswade my self to forgeat all and make mery while I maye, and say nothing as[11] I thincke, for feare yt should not be well taken. For I doo not feare that emonge wise men; and what so ever come of yt, I will never encomber my consyence with remembraunce

---

1–1 *B.N.,* (I meane) that dedd is determinations; *H.,* that dead is; I mean his determination

2 *H.,* others   3 *H.,* yt   4 *H.,* or

5 *B.N.,* havinge; *H.,* saving   6 *H. supplies* those

7 *H.,* yf   8–8 *B.N.,* as I never; *H.,* as if I

9 *H. supplies* here   10 *H.,* things

11 *H.,* that

of this, *ve mihi quia tacui*, where percase yt might doo good to speake.

And thus I tell your Grace all the secrete mistery of my wryting and reasoning, which I esteme not folly but adoyng of some parte of my duty [1]towardes God and[1] the world. And so, I truste, your Grace will take yt, and remember and consyder well this matter, and so to use the determinacions of our late soveraigne in religion as your[2] doing therin may be ensample to other to regard your doinges[3] with lyke reverence; which God graunte to be, and send your Grace hart⟨il⟩ye[4] well to fare.

Having wrytten hetherto, and glad to make an end, I found my self enforsed by your Graces letters to speake of Gregorie Nazanzeine somewhat, who undoubtedly is not reported in the proheme to the Byble[5] that is called your Graces, as he speaketh. Wherof I thought necessary to admonyshe your Grace, who, by your letters, semed to enterprise to purge faultes. And that faulte is *notorium facti permanentis*, and as longe as Gregorie Nazianzenes worke [6]contineweth, ever yt speaketh against the same proheme and sayth still continually[6], 'I say not as I ame reported in that proheme.' And for the setting fourth herof, I will wryte Gregorie Nazianzeines woordes in Greke, the very Englyshe of them without cavillacion, and thEnglyshe of the proheme of those woordes; and that is all I can doo for[7] advertysing of the faultes.

Theis be the woordes in the proheme of the Byble
rehersed and attribute to Gregorie Nazianzeine:

I saye not this to dyswade men frome the knowledge of God and reading and studyeng of the Scripture[8], for I say that it is as necessary for the lyf of mans soule as for the body to breathe, and yf yt were possible so to lyve, I would thinke yt good for a man to spend his lyf in that and do no nother thing.

Gregorie Nazianzenes woordes in Greke:

45 v. Καὶ οὐ λέγω τοῦτο μὴ δεῖν πάντοτε μεμνῆσθαι θεοῦ[9], μὴ πάλιν ἐπιφυέσθωσαν ἡμῖν οἱ πάντα εὔκολοι καὶ ταχεῖς. μνημονευτέον

1–1 *H.*, to God and to   2 *B.N.*, our; *H.*, your
3 *H.*, doing   4 *H.*, heartily
5 *H. supplies* to the Bible
6–6 *H.*, remayneth, yt will continually speke against your proheme, and sayeth still
7 *H. adds* the   8 *H.*, Scriptures
9 *H. ends Greek passage here, adding,* etc.

γὰρ θεοῦ μᾶλλον ἢ ἀναπνευστέον, καὶ, εἰ οἷόν τε τοῦτο εἰπε⟨ῖν⟩,
μηδὲ ἄλλό τι ἢ τοῦτο πρακτέον.

The trew Englyshe of Gregorie
Nazanzenes wordes in Greke:

And I say not this that God should not alwaies be had in memorie, least
suche as be always light and legier should assaulte me againe, for God is
to be had in memorye rather then brethe to be drawne, and, yf yt were
convenyent so to say, nothing but this to be done.

Their be many mo faultes[1] to be accompted in learnyng, faultes[‡]
wher, by translation, the auctor is not properly expressyd as he sayth,
which only learned menn note. But in this place the aucthour alleged is
made to saye that he never sayd, and in suche sorte as, yf he sayd so in
dede here, he should be contrary to him self in the same worke. For he
travaileth against the Eunomians, who semed to be of th[‡]oppinion
that their was but one waye to heaven, by studyeng[2] and knowledge in
Scriptures; against whome he sayth that their be many waies to heaven.
But and[3] he should in this place have sayd that the reading and studyeng
of Scripture had bene as necessary for the lyf of mans soule as breath is
for the body, that sayeng should condempn all his enterprise after, and
him self to doo much a mysse, when he would have men spend their
tyme in the dyscussing of the philosophers, [‡]suche as muste be doing
alwaies and cannot hold their tonges[‡]. And howe could a man spend
any tyme in those thinges, yf yt were true that a man should doo
nothing elles but reade and study Scripturs all his lyf? And what a fury
might this sett poore men in, to leave their labour of the ground, where
groweth fruites only for the body, and prepare them bookes, and fall to
spelling, that they may be able to tyll the Scripture, their to reape fruites
to fede the soule. And as the bodely lyf of offendours is, by priviledge of
the realme, preserved by the booke, so the lyf of the soule ⟨is⟩ to be saved   46 r.
by the booke lykewise, and their must be *legit ut clericus* also, or a man
shall never come to heaven. But Gregorie Nazianzeine never sayd so,
and in this worke sayth, 'Noo'; and in the hole purpose of the worke
entendyth the contrarye.

I would not have wrytten thus much, but because your Grace
chargeth me with cavillation and evill wayeng, wher I spake *fide optima*;
[‡]and your Grace ⟨is⟩ percase deceyved, and so I will take yt[‡]. But

---

1 *H. adds* so   2 *H.*, study   3 *H.*, if

359

surely the errour is great and intollerable, yf faultes should not[t] be examined.

Headed (in B.N.): A nother letter from the B*ysshopp* of Wynchester to thArch*bysshopp* of Canterbury.

(In H.): Another letter from Dr Stephen Gardiner, Bishop of Winchester, to Dr Cranmer, Archbishop of Canterbury, written in Edward 6th's time.

NOTES TO NO. 125

Page 318. The sections of the *King's Book* pertinent to Gardiner's discussion in this letter are those on Faith, Justification, and Good Works (*see* Lloyd's edition, 221–5, 363–75, and n. to p. 336, below).

Page 325. The three bishops referred to are Heath, Thirlby, and Day; the three doctors, Cox, Robinson, and Redman (*see* p. 365).

Pages 325–8. For the 'plot' against Cranmer, with which Gardiner here denies connection, and his dealings with William Gardiner of Canterbury *see* my *Gardiner*, 109–13, and 361 n. 41.

Page 333. In the margin beside the quotation from Erasmus there is a note in B.N. reading, *Erasmi ad Bucerum Epistola 19, libro farraginis.* A similar note, in which the number 29 erroneously replaces 19, is in H., in parenthesis in the text. The letter, of 11 November, 1527 (Allen, *Ep. Eras.*, VII, 229), is not in the *Farrago Nova Ep. D. Eras.* (1519), but first appeared in the 1529 Froben edition of the epistles.

Page 335. On Zwingli *see* p. 316, above.

Page 336. The section of the *King's Book* here appealed to by Gardiner reads, 'the perfect faith of a true Christian man. . .containeth the obedience to the whole doctrine and religion of Christ. And thus is faith taken of St Paul. . .where it is said that we be justified by faith. In which places men may not think that we be justified by faith, as it is a several virtue separated from hope and charity, fear of God and repentance; but by it is meant faith neither only ne alone, but with the aforesaid virtues coupled together. . .' Lloyd's edition, 223.

Page 341. For Gregory Nazianzen on Mt. xiii, 58 (Mk. vi, 5–6) *see* his Oration xxx, § x (Migne, *P. G.*, XXXVI, 116; *N. and P. N. F.*, ser. 2, VII, 313).

Page 343. For Gregory Nazianzen on those who desire baptism *see* his Oration XL, §§ XXII, XXIII (Migne, *P. G.*, XXXVI, 388–9; *N. and P. N. F.*, ser. 2, VII, 367–8).

Pages 345, 350–2. The Institution of a Christian Man, known as the *Bishops' Book,* was published in 1537; reprinted in C. Lloyd, *Formularies of Faith in the Reign of Henry VIII*, Oxford, 1825, and 1856.

Page 351. The derivation of *phratry* is not in Aristotle. It is suggested in Budaeus, *Commentarii Linguae Graecae*, 1529, 670.

Page 354. For negotiations at Stepney *see* Nos. 61–2.

Page 358. 'The Byble that is called your Graces,' was the Great Bible (Coverdale's revision of Matthew's combination of Tyndale and Coverdale, 1539) in the editions of 1540–1, for which Cranmer had written a preface.

Page 358. The quotation from Gregory Nazianzen is from his *Oration* XXVII, § V (Migne, *P. G.*, XXXVI, 16; *N. and P. N. F.*, ser. 2, VII, 286).

Page 359. 'The bodely lyf of offendours is...preserved by the booke' is a reference to Benefit of Clergy.

126. *To the* PRIVY COUNCIL

Waltham, [shortly before 30 August, 1547]

B.M., Add. 28,571, 16 v.–20 v. and 6 r. Sixteenth-century copy.

Since Somerset has departed (for Scotland), protests to the Council against the newly issued *Book of Homilies*; one homily (that on salvation) contradicts the *King's Book*, slanders Henry VIII, and is contrary to Scripture and the Fathers; it may also alienate the Emperor; was not responsible for the definition of justification in the *King's Book*; names those who were; Chrysostom is misquoted in the homily on works; complains of the forbidding of processions by the new injunctions; possible political consequences of the *Homilies*; Henry VIII made no changes in religion without a Convocation; the *Homilies*, by despising ceremonies, contradict the new injunctions.

After my most hartie commendacions to your good Lordships: If my Lord Protectors Grace, whome God prospere in his jorney, had not bene departed, I had directed my letters to hym, to declare suche matter as I can not, eyther with a quiet conscience to God or discharge of my dutie to my soverane lord and this realme, passe over in silence. In my Lord Protectours absence I write unto your Lordships, which I desyre you to take in good parte, with suche consideracion and acceptacion of my doing, as myne entent in the same meriteth and deserveth. Wherof, for thexperience I have of you, I have no mistrust.

So yt is, I have red a boke of homelies, set forth in the Kings Majesties name, to be redde thrugh the realme by all curates and parsons (as the title purporteth), wher in I fynd suche matter as mesemeth very unmete to be strengthed with thauthoritie of the Kings Majestie. And knowing the boldnes of the printers in like cases heretofore, can not persuade myselfe of my Lord Protector and you, being enformed what yt conteyneth, will suffre yt to passe in that sorte.

I fynd in this boke too fawltes; one a generall fawlt, another a speciall fawlte. The generall fawlt is, that where, by auctoritie of our late soveragne lord, whose sowle God pardon, and a boke by that auctoritie set forth, the people of this realme have bene by the curates taught a very trew doctrine, that faith doth nether justifie onelie ne alone, but as it is coupled to gether with other vertues, conteyning the obedience to the hole doctrine and religion of Christ (these be the wurdes of the Kings boke), there is an homelie placed in this boke, latelie come abrode, wherin the people shuld be taght that only faith justifieth; with this addition, how this maner of teaching of 'onelie faith justifieth' is old and ancient, and that who impugneth the doctrine of only faith, as it is in this last boke taught, is not to be reputed a trew Christen man. Which is a terrible speache and a marvalous to be publeshed in this realme, to the condemnacion of our late soveragne lord, the condemnation of our selfe, and the prejudicie of the trewth, to affirme that ancient, which is not ancient, and call that the teaching of holy Scripture, which holy Scripture doth not mainteine.

As for the wurdes of holy Scripture, we have one text of St James that denieth, in plaine wurdes, onelie faith to justifie, and none other text is there where 'onely' is put to 'faith' in justification. As for the sence and meaning of the Scripture, the world hath bene well exercised in yt, and 'onely faith' engendred many arguments; which our late soveragne lord throghly perceyved and resolved, as is conteyned in his boke against the teaching of 'onely fath,' which resolution all the realme receyved and have taught accordinglie, during the Kinges Majesties liff and hitherto. In which resolution was no ambiguitie. For when other vertues be cowpled with faith in thacte of justificacion, in that action the hole can not be attribute to any one vertue onely; as if many men cowpled to gether do this or that, it can not be said that this or that man

362

did it onelie. Where vertues be cowpled to gether there can be no 'onely' have place in eny of them. And therfore the Kings Majesties boke was planelie and clerely penned, and, by occation of somme that wold not have yt so, passed and resolved; and ⟨they⟩ stode against yt so long as they might. It was substantiallie framed to withstand ambiguities, and both planelie and trewlie resolved and plainlie and trewlie written.

And for antiquitie, wherof these new homelies make mention, 'onely fa⟨i⟩th' was never teached as yt is set forth in this homelie in any old author that I have redde. And that I dare affirme unto you, unto whome yt becommeth me to write advisedlie, that nether St Austen, St Hierome, St Ambrose, St Barnard, in the Latin Churche, ne Chrisistome, Basill, Gregory Nazianzene, or Oecumenius taght so in the Greke Churche. In whose wurkes we shall fynd, nevertheles, *sola fides* joyned with *iustificat*, where *sola* doth not dissever faith from charitie and hope, with which three vertues God endeweth man when He justifieth hym. But these auctors before rehersed, in their speache of *sola fides*, exclude the wurkes of the law of Moyses and owtward wurkes of man to man; as Chrisostome taketh yt, *De Lege et Fide*, wher he speaketh of *sola fides*. For these inward wurkes of man towardes God, that is to say, of beleving God, loving God, hoping in God, these wurkes were never so severed in thoffice of justificacion, as the homelie newlie termeth yt, as they be in this boke of homelies, where the homelie teacheth that the wurke of fathe, when charitie and hope be present, onely justifieth, and deviseth a reason, bicause faith directeth us to Christ. And so yt doth in dede. But that is no reason why it shuld onelie justifie, for as we be directed to Christ, so we must go to Christ, and that, St Augustine saeth, is by love, and so called, *credere in Deum, amando in Deum ire*. And by hope we take hold of Christ and joyne to Hym. God onelie justefieth, of whom we receive yt, beleving, loving, and hoping; and the grace to beleve, love, and hope, we receyve also of God. Now if these thre vertues, by Gods grace coupled in us to atteyne justificacion, shuld contend betwene themselfe, how cold eny one vertue chalendge 'onely' where all be to gether? There is a preeminence and degre noted in them; but 'onely' there can not be attribute to eny of them, nor hath not bene by any ancient writer. The most parte of the ancient writers that extolle faith, speake of faith alone by this terme, *sola fides*; that is to say, withowt the companye of owtward wurkes. Which faith in dede sayved the thefe on the crosse, for he had no tyme to have owtwarde wurkes, suche as man, having oportunitie, oweth to man, but he had inward wurkes, suche as be from man to God. Those he had; for he beleved, he repented, he loved, and hoped in that short tyme; and that he did by Gods grace, unto whom God ministred then further mercie. And, as the Kings Majesties boke teacheth, where faith signifieth the hole obedience of a Christean man to God, which the thefe had, this fayth alone justifieth; that is to say, alone with his owne companye of penaunce, charitie, and hope. But to say that in this company of penaunce, charitie, and hope, thus cowpled, faith onely justifieth, is a new imagination not writen in any ancient author that hath yet come abrode to my handes. And a great meny of those alleged in theise new homelies have yt not.

And therfore, my Lords, seing the King our late soveraigne lord hath in his boke determined this mattier, and there reproved the teaching of 'onelie fa⟨i⟩th' or 'faith alone' as a vertue separate, it is soroful to me to se eny homelies made after this sort to be sent furth in the name of oure soveraigne lord that now is, with suche a vehemencie to call hym no trew Christen man that denieth that doctrine.

And this is the generall fawlt, which hath a great consyderacion of policie in yt, in this tyme of trowble with the Scottes, and no assurednes with the Frenche men, to have yt broght to the Emperowrs eares that in this realme ariseth the doctrine of 'onelie faith,' which is so diffamed in the world as it is noted to have many other matters emplied in it, which the Germayns have amonge them uttered to their great trowble and confusion. Which I leave to your wisdomes to be further consydered.

And then to have the curates of the realme to beat in to the peoples heades that he is no trew Christen man that denieth the teaching of 'onely faith,' remaning yet in memory that our late soveraigne lord and master that made us, that left so great a jewell, hys son, among us, did speciallie improve ⟨*i.e.*, condemn⟩ that doctrine—what a sclander shall this be to the realme, and what a rejoyce to our enimies, specially in suche a matter as our late soveraigne lord diffined so solemnely in a Parliament, so trewlie, so plainly, with signification of the same to thEmperour and owtward princes! All Christendome understode no better the matter of justification then our late soveragne lord did, and after he had resolved it, thEmperour diffined it in his countries after the same sorte, and the Frenche Kinge likewise.

And in this, our late soveraigne lordes resolution, I was no doer, but a folower, accepting the treuth concluded, as became me. For the

364

doing therin was committed to three of the notable prelates of this realme, the Bisshops of Worceter, Westminster, and Chichester, with thre great clarkes, Doctor Cockes, Doctor Robinson, and Doctor Redman, whose doings therin be also specially reproved by these homelies, and for their labor be noted no Christen men. And as for my selfe, after the doctrine was receyved and agreed, I saw suche light, suche plainenes and trewthe in it, that I have declared my selfe to this realme and the world abrode in writing to mislike the doctrine of 'onely faith,' as it is sett forth in these homelies. Which my doing, the lawes of God mainteyne, and the lawes of the realme also; wherof thone of his nature is immutable, and thother of your wisdomes ye will, I dowt not, continewe. For justification wherof, I will omitte nothing that shall become a Christen bishop and an humble subject, with declaration unto you that I care more for the trewth (as my duetie is) then for all the rest I have in the world. And suche like opinion I have of my Lord Protector and you, or els I wold not write unto you. For I persuade my selfe, when ye know these faltes in the homelies, ye will not let them passe. The King our late soveraigne lord was a noble prince, whom I know well ye will not suffre thus to be towched in condemnation of his doctrine, by bearing in hand of old authors, which in dede mainteyne our late soveraigne lordes teachinges. And that issue I will take with any lerned man, and the bokes shalbe judge, being the matter so evident as, if the bokes were shewed our soveraigne that now is in this ⟨his⟩ age, he were able to perceyve and judge the trewth of this matter, and to se whether his fathers bokes were not better then this.

A speciall falte in this boke is that St Chrisostome, in the homelie of wurkes, is not rehersed and reported as hym selfe writeth; which is a marvelous matter, and shall give notable occation to suche as willeth us evill, to disprove the procedings of this realme, even at hand by our owne boke. For yt shall appeare that St Chrisostomes saings liked not hym that made thomilie. And therfore he added and changed to make hym speake otherwise; which is the faulte of hym that made thomilie, and shuld be my falte yf ⟨I⟩ did not declare yt unto you when yt cometh to my knowlege.

And now I have for so muche discharged my selfe, to shew this matter unto you; which I have trewlie uttered with suche a zeile as I shuld have, and as becometh me to have, to speake in the trewth as a Christen bishop oght, and one so many waies bound to this realme as I am, mynding to uphold the trewth of myne advertisement in as humble a sorte as any subject doo. I hartelie require you, at the reverence of Christes passion, to give remedie herein. The proclamation was by you most prudentlie devised to forbid rumors of innovations. And this boke of homelies, with certain injunctions, floweth abrode withowt authoritie, with a visitacion to follow, to put them in execution.

And as I had writen thus farre, came advertisment to me from suche as be appointed to viset. In which visitation, if suche injunctions as go abrode shuld be commanded, there wold be noted in owtward partes a marvelous innovation, to forbid processions and folowing the crosse; which is matter the commonaltie deliteth in, and in tyme of warre was wunt to be commanded, and was by our late soverane lord, when he conquired Bollen. And if any thing shuld happe amys, as God forbid, our soveraigne lord that now is may marvaile, when he hath perfyt knowlege, how processions be forbidden in his name, ¹and many good men joyfullye of late talked¹ and fownd falte, that the processions in the Court were not folowed with so many as in his howse when he was Prince, and hath bene and may be well used. Herein, beyng a bishop of the realme, I can not forbeare to shew my mynd to you for my discharge to God and to my soveragne lord, when he cometh to age.

And I have bene so late familier with you, and knowing you so muche my good Lordes, that besyde the matter of relligion, wherin myne office bindeth me to speake and preferre the trewth to all other things, I am so bold to go a little beyond my bondes and commen with you in policie. For this I know, and so doth my Lord of Westminster, that Grandevilla, when I was last with thEmperour, told us how the Kings Majesties, our late soveraigne lordes, resolutions in religion muche moved thEmperour to withstand suche persuations as the Frenche King, by meanes of a fryer, used to persuade hym to slippe from us. And if this boke of sermondes shuld go abrode by authoritie, wherby we shuld breake that resolution, I feare as muche as may be feared of devilles abrode, eyther to alter or empaire thEmperours band to this realme; which, if he kepe as he is bound to do, the Frenche men shall never dare to assalte this realme.

Alas, my Lordes, so many great clerkes as this realme hathe, and to have suche homelies for a doctrine amonge the people as these be! We have the trewthe alreadie in the Kings Majesties boke in the same matters the homelies teache, which the homelies do onelie impugne; which can

1–1 *the meaning here may be* and ⟨with⟩ many good men ⟨he⟩ joyfullye of late talked make no edification in the people, but ministre matter to our adversaries to practize against us, and thinke us devided among our selfe, who they know not so sodenlie altered, to beleve now the contrary we beleved in our soveraigne lordes tyme, and withowt any solemne assemble of us to gether to heare suche speak with us as make these homelies. I have writen to my Lord of Canterbury in yt, and declared my minde in lerning, which I am hable to manteyne. Our late soveraigne lord made no alteration in his tyme withowt a convocation of bishops and open debating of the mattier. And now winter approcheth, a tyme mete for yt, which what so ever be done with that circumstance must nedes have the greater reputacion abrode. And in that assemble I will offre my self to defend that determination of our late soveraigne lord as[1] the very trew⟨th⟩, and agreable with tholde ancient teaching of Christes Churche.

I am over long with your Lordships, being so occupied in other busines as ye be. But I forget my selfe in these mattiers, in which I shuld also spend my self to serve God in this office, and the realme I am borne in, with the honour of our late soveraigne lord, which I dowbt not ye regard as muche as I. But as Gods mercie, so often called on by David, neded not for Gods understanding, but to declare his vehement affection and sorrow, even so these many wurds of me to your Lordships, with so often inculcation of the same thing, nedeth not, as I deme of you, to move or sturre you in this matter, but onely to open my conscience unto you, and somwhat to revele my selfe therwith; and God taught me to be importunate where the request is good. Of Whom yt were happy we might be taght to remaine in agrement, to withstand suche corporall enemies as go abowt to annoye this realme, and, by alteracion in religion or otherwise, to do no thing that any man might interprete otherwise then Christen charitie wold; of which infirmitie St Paule lerneth us to have consyderacion, as I mistrust not but your Lordships will. For which effect I shall pray Almightie God, Who continew you long in prosperitie.

I send to your Lordships the boke of homelies which I write of, noted in some places, speciallie in thomelie of salvacion. I take that matter so far owt of the way that I have not muche travelid in the rest, saving in thomelie of wurkes, where suche laudable ceremonies be by name dispised as our late soveraigne lord in his tyme manteined, and suche as the new injunctions, which the printers have sent abrode afore the coming of visitors, orderith to continew. And so the people shall use

1 MS., is

367

them, whiles the curate shall call them noght; which I thinke ye will not suffre so to pas from you. Whom God directe and ayde with His grace to execute His pleasure. At Waltham.

Headed: A letter sent from the Bishop of Winchester to the Kings Most Honorable Counsell.

NOTES TO NO. 126

Page 362. Certain sermons or homilies appointed by the King's Majesty to be declared and read by all parsons, vicars, or curates every Sunday in their churches, known as the *First Book of Homilies*, was published 31 July, 1547; the second in 1563. The Injunctions of 1547 (in W. H. Frere and W. M. Kennedy, *Visitation Articles and Injunctions*, Alcuin Club, 1910, II, 114), provided that 'because through lack of preachers in many places...the people continue in ignorance and blindness, all parsons, vicars, and curates shall read in the churches every Sunday one of the Homilies which are and shall be set forth' (§ 32).

Page 363. For the spurious sermon of Chrysostom, *De Lege et Fide*, said (pp. 365, 374, 382–3) to be misquoted in the *Homilies*, *see* Migne, *P. G.*, XLVIII, 1081.

Page 363. St Augustine. *See* his Tractatus 29 on St John, § 6.

Page 366. For the proclamation *see* p. 295, above.

Page 366. The Injunctions of 1547, § 23, provided that 'they shall not from henceforth in any parish church at any time, use any procession about the church or churchyard or other place, but immediately before High Mass the priests with other of the choir shall kneel in the midst of the church and sing or say plainly and distinctly the Litany which is set forth in English.' This Litany was, as Gardiner here intimates, that set forth in 1544, and was later, with certain omissions, incorporated into the Book of Common Prayer. It is reprinted in the Appendix to *Private Prayers of Queen Elizabeth*, Parker Soc., 1851.

Page 366. The 'fryer' was Gabriel Guzman—*L.P.*, XX, ii, pp. xlix–vi.

127. *To the* PRIVY COUNCIL

[Waltham, 30 August, 1547]

B.M., Add. 28,571, 6 r.–9 r. Sixteenth-century copy; edges torn.

An act of 1543 (34 & 35 H. VIII, c. 1) condemns all who teach contrary to the *King's Book*; the late Chancellor Audley's opinion on the strength of an act of Parliament; the Common Lawyers' opinion concerning the limitations of the royal supremacy; writes to Mason (No. 128); Henry VIII is slandered by the *Homilies*; warns against them that preach 'only faith'; is not 'wilie Winchester'; is determined to preserve his flock. (For the custom of engraving mottoes in the finger-rings given to dignitaries by the serjeants-at-law *see* A. Pulling, *The Order of the Coif*, London, 1884, 245–6.)

After my most hartie commendacions to your good Lordships: Sithens the writing of my last letters unto you, I have red over suche injunctions as the printers have sent abrode; which conteyne matter against our late soveraigne lordes instructions and determinations in his most Catholique boke. And for as muche as I have ben put in remembrance (which when I wrote my last letters I thoght not on) of an acte of Parliament passed in the xxxiiijth yere of our late soveragne lords reigne for thestablishment of his said determinations and instructions, which I have now seen, redde, and consydered, and fynd in myne opinion our late soveragn lordes honour, wisdome, judgement, and trew knoledge in Christen doctrine by as stronge a knot conserved to continew among us as mans lawe can knyt, I entend to use the benefite of that acte for the defence of the simple clergie of my dioces, and make most humble request unto your good Lordships, first by these my letters, that ye will take in good parte my allegacion of the said acte of Parliament for conservacion in religion of the state yt is in, as ye wold if I alledged any other acte of Parliament for defence of any right in my landes, which were a commen case of the realme, as I reckon this also to be.

And I shall never forget that the Lord Audelay, late Chauncelor, told me at suche tyme as he familiarlie desyred me to be his frend, that when our late soveraigne lord devised with hym how to resist the detestable heresie against the Sacrament of thAlter, he advised the Kings Majestie to make an acte of Parliament of yt, adding, as he told me, that thactes of Parliament passed in his highness tyme conteyned so muche beneficiall matter and to so many men of diverse estates in the realme, that when so ever any one acte were towched, every man wold thinke his matter were in dangier; for if any one acte may be contemned or broken in what matter so ever yt be, the rest be in the same danger when yt liketh hym that for the tyme ruleth; putting further unto yt that he never knew or red of any act of Parliament in this realme broken till the

369

same had ben by like authoritie of Parliament repelled. This told me the Lord Audelay (God pardon his sowle) at Easter was fowre yere.

And this act of Parliament that I allege, made the xxxiiijth, conteyneth that all suche as teache, preache, defend, or manteyne any matter or matters, thing or things contrary to the godly instructions and determinations set f[orth by] his Highnes or to be sett forth shall etc., a[nd] finally, after degrees of punishment, at h[is iij^{de}] offence to be demed an heretique. By [which] his Highnes doctrine remaneth in fo[rce] till yt be repelled likewise by Parliam[ent]. I dowt not ye will take yt a res[onable] request to desyre not to be enjoyned [against] that acte, with the danger of a premunire [to the] deputies in the visitation, and ordinaries [which] shall execute after them, seing they visit [by] special jurisdiction and so procede with us [by] the meane of my Lord of Canterbury [to] inhibite and warne the visitacion. And t[hus I] have hard the lerned men of the Commen [Law] say that if any, althogh he be deputed by th[e] King, do, in execution of spirituall jurisdiction, extend the same contrary to any Commen Law or act of Parliament, it is a premunire both to the judge and the parties, althogh it be done in the Kings Majesties name; bicause they say the Kinges Majesties supremac[ie] in visiting and ordring of the Churche is reserved to spirituall jurisdiction. Which their saing cold not sinke into my understanding, that men executing the Kings commission, and having of hym jurisdiction, cold faull in danger of a premunire. But so the best lerned men of the realme have said, and I wold fayne have persuaded them to the contrary.

And seing the premunire is dangerows to all that be parties in the matter, I trust ye will take in good part that I beware of yt, and allow that I allege thacte of Parliament to avoide suche injunctions as might bring a man in that danger. Wherin I write to Master Mason who by inhibition hath, as it were, begunne visitacion with me, and is therfore one with whome I may speake, advertising hym what I will allege at his cumming hither, if he bringe eyther homelie or injunction contrary to thact of Parliament. And I write to your Lordships to thintent there be found no falt in the maner of my proceding, that if I had any suche matter to shew I wold not first secretlie advertise your Lordships, and so avoid to be occation of rumors in the countrey which I am loth to be, for I thinke all quiet most expedient. And yet if your Lordships do not stay the matter, but suffer the visitors to procede with suche maner of injunctions, I must and will allege herin ⟨in⟩ the most quiet and humble maner I can, the said act of Parliament, and desyre the benefyte of yt for conservacion of religion as thact purporteth; and that good simple sowles be not enjoyned to speke in the pulpitt mattier against thact of Parliament; for doing wher of they were in danger to be punished by thordre of the Kings law. And where the curate had on the one Sunday, by auctoritie of thacte of Parliament, redd the King our late soveragne lordes boke, reproving the doctrine of 'onelie faith justifieth,' and bidding the people reverentlie use the ceremonies—if betwene that and the next Sunday folowing, the injunctions and homilies be delivered, and he delite to reade thomelie of salvacion, first he shall tell them that they be no trew Christen men that reprove the doctrine of onely faith. And then one that list to quarrell with the preist, why he told them otherwise the last Sunday before—if the preist saith King Henry the viij^th bad hym teache so—'And was he,' shall the other replie, 'no trew Christen man?'

My Lordes, I pray you pardone me, that I am so bold with you. We wepte all when we buried our late soveraigne lordes bodye, wherin I wold never have ben minister, if I cold have found as good meanes as Martha dyd to call hym to lyfe againe. There is more cause of weping to se his honour go towardes burying, to be noted no trew Christen man; which wordes serveth for no edification in thomelie, but onely for sclander. [And] my Lord Protector is withowt blame, being l[ong a] noble captayne occupied in the warres. You, [my] noble men, as ye were wunt, entend other[wise]. How it cometh to passe I will not serche, [but] this it is. And it is in your handes to stay [the] matter, to lay the falt in the inferior min[isters], as I recken yt to be, to misuse them selfe [in that] is committed unto them. Suche as were pun[ished] for their evill opinions in our late soveraig[ne lordes] tyme shall hardely be good ministers in religion now.

Beware, my Lordes, of [them] that preache 'onely faith.' In which sentenc[e I] write to my Lord of Canterbury. For [that] opinion, by our Parliament condemned, was the c[urse] of Germany that manteyned yt. It cast[eth] away so many partes of our religion when [it] is thrughlie opined. And all that have of late preached it ought, by thact of Parliament, in any wise recant. This is the law of th[e] realme at this day. And the sergiantes of the Commen Law wrote a trew sentence in the rings, *Conservatio legis praeservatio regis*; whos personage is as wurthy now to be preserved as ever was any. For whose safegard I dowbt not ye be as carefull as ever were subjectes. And yet never shall we rede of any realme to have so many encombres at ones as this realme hath, with Scottes in dede, Frenche men in feare, other men not all owt of dowt

371

with this alteracio[n] in religion at home. Which weare to moche alone to [ask] men ‹to› beleve that all the Parliament within this iiij yeres was deceaved in the knoledge of [the] trew Christendome. The King was decea[ved], if these homilies be trew, both tharcheb[ishops] were deceaved, for they agreed unto it, [and] all the bishops were deceaved, with all the l[ay]men in the Parliament. But all these wer[e not] deceyved, my Lordes. We have the trewt[h pu]blished by Parliament; and so my conscienc[e bin]deth me to tell every man that shuld [ask] me. And I cold never lerne to pull uppe my shulders of the Italian fashion and so cast of the matter in silence, or prively agree with men to passe over for a while, till the Kings Highnes cometh to his age. For I have so good opinion of my Lord Protector and you, that ye will heare the trewth, and suche a determinacion with my selfe to leave this estate when trewth were not hard ‹*i.e.*, heard›, that I am resolvid to be playne, as becometh a trew Christen bishop, and as my conscience and trewth leadeth me to open yt unto you, calling every thing by his right name, that ye may understand me. And what so ever falt I have besydes, to declare that I am not wilie Winchester, but playne, humble, and obedient, with as muche affeccion to the preservacion of the Kings Majestie and this realme, as my dewtie bindeth me, which is a very sore bond.

I will not murmour amonge the lower sort that can not amend yt. But I will to my Lord Protector and you speake frelie, where remedie may be obteyned. Wherin I shall desyre you to thinke that I use not so many wurdes for any mistrust I have of your justice, your equitie, your indifference, and favour also towardes me, but onelie to lay before you even the platforme of myne inward determination, which is to preserve the flocke committed unto me as becometh a trew bisshop, and not to enjoy suche possessions as I have withowt regarde to religion, wherby the world may be slandred in the trewth, and say we bishops care not what we say and unsay so that we may enjoye that we have. Of which minde I thanke God I was never. Yet I mistrust not, ne despare not, what so ever the printers have sent forth. And yet I will leave nothing undone towardes you that might let suche matter, if yt be resolved to be sent forth.

As I have written, I will onely with humble request and sewte to you, humble declaration of my conscience, humble allegacion of thacte of Parliament, for me and my dioces, allege in tyme and place convenient that may be justified by the trewth and lerning, and so abide that authoritie shall decerne and determine. Whereunto, if the case so require, I shall yeild as quietlie as ever did man, to lerne other thexample of obedience, by the grace of Almighty God, Wh[o] preserve your good Lordships.

Headed: An other letter sent from the said Bishop of Winchester to the Lordes of the Kings Most Honorable Counsell.

128. *To* Sir John Mason

Waltham, 30 August, 1547

B.M., Add. 32,091, 142–3.*

The injunctions and *Homilies* conflict with an act of Parliament; will petition not to be compelled to offend that act; it is as much to the interest of the laity as the clergy to uphold an act of Parliament; the *Homilies* slander Henry VIII, a true Christian prince.

Master Mason, after my right harty commendacions: Forasmuche as by suche inhibicion as I receyved from you and your college appoynted to visyte in the Kinges Majesties name, I accompte you allredy to have begoon, and take you, as reason is, for my judge and judge of my dyoces in this matier of visytacion, I have thought convenyent some-what to¹ commen with you whiles ye be there by letters, in suche sorte as I entende to doo at your coming hither, whereby ye maye be† in-struct to passe all thinges the more redelye here. The prynters have uttred forthe a great many of injunctions and homylies, and so by meanes published that is demed to be your chardge at your commynge; which if it be so, then is it lyke other chaunces I have seen in my lief, thin-structions to arryve before thambassadours; but suche chaunces as I never lyked in my lief, and yet suche be prynters. Which injunctions and homilies, that yet have none authorytye till you have ben here and declared the Kinges Majesties pleas*our*, I have redd and consydered, and fynde in them suche matier as is contrary to our late soveraigne lordes instructions and determinacions, confirmed by acte of Parliament. Which acte of Parlyament, bicawse it is not yet repeled, standeth in suche force as it is able to mayntayn myne humble suite and petycion, that I and my clergye maye not, by eny newe injunction, be compelled to offende thacte of Parliament yet standing in suche force. Which peticion and request I will make at everye of your syttinges where I am commaunded to appere. And if the preacher ye bring with you square

¹ come(?) c.o.

373

from our late soveraigne lordes doctryne, being yet in force by acte of Parliament, I will allege the force of thacte of Parlyament to the contrary, to declare I sett as muche by relligion as I doo by any parke or warren I have, for conservacion wherof eche man is admitted to alledge thacte of Parlyament. And suche pleas men make for preservacion of their libertyes. You and your companyons shall, for your personnes, be as wellcoom as any men of your degree in this realme, and all thing you shall doo, not contrary to thacte of Parliament yet standing in force, shall be as gladlye and thankfullye taken and executed; but as for thacte of Parlyament which preserveth our late soveraigne lordes doctryne sett forthe in his booke, I will not relent in any thing contrary to it, but for preservacion of my self and my cure, to mayntayne our late soveraigne lordes doctryne, with all the circumstaunce of humilitye and good manner, requyre everye subgectes commen right in an acte of Parlyament. In which matier I have written to my Lordes of the Counsayle, signefying that I have allso written to you, to thintent ye maye be the more fully instructed there before your commynge hither, remembring allwayes that everye acte of Parlyament is as stronge in one cace as in an other, and that which is to daye a spirituall mannes cace may be to morowe a temporall mans cace; and yet in this cace of religion I thinke temporall men will accompte it as muche theirs as ours. Ye shall red[e] in one of the homylies which the prynters sende forthe as a peace of your chardge, that he is no trewe Christen man that denyeth the teaching of 'onely faithe justefyeth'—the acte of Parlyament yet standing and not repeled, which alloweth our late soveraigne lordes doctryne that reproveth 'onely faithe justefyeth'—where is implyed the King our late soveraigne lorde to be no trewe Christen man; which facion of speche I thinke no man in Christendom, not of those we be in varyaunce with, wolde use to that effecte. ThEmperour estemed him for a trewe Christen[1] prynce when he tawght that onelye faithe justefyeth not, notwithstanding the varyaunce of the matier of Rome. And he that had knowen so muche by our late soveraigne lorde as I did—and yet all the worlde knewe inoughe—wolde saye he were a trewe Christen prynce. And as the teaching of 'onely faithe justefyeth' is as false a teaching as ever was, so is it untrewlye handeled, and, for[2] confirmacion of it, St Chrisostome is, in thomilyes ye shoulde bring, untrewlye alleged, as I have signifyed to the Lordes of the Kinges

1 man *c.o.*   2 con *c.o.*

374

Majesties Counsaile; which I have offred †my self† to prove, and knowe
my self hable so to¹ doo. God graunte us grace to joyne charitye
with faithe, and to love to gither against all those that wolde us and the
realme evyll; and therwith ⟨graunte⟩ you hartely well to fare. At
Waltham, the xxxᵗʰ of August, 1547.

Your loving frende

assuredlye,

STE. WINTON

129. To Sir John Godsalve

[Waltham, between c. 12 and 25 September, 1547]

C.C.C.C., MS. 127, 9–10. Sixteenth-century copy, in Parker Collection.
Burnet, v, 163. Eighteenth-century copies of the Parker MS. in B.M.,
Egerton 2350, 160 v. and Camb. Univ. Lib., Baker, xxxi, 27. C.C.C.C.
is here followed.

> Cannot accept Godsalve's advice to conform to the new injunctions; has kept
> his bishopric sixteen years without offending God's law or the King's, and
> would depart from it without doing so; honesty is dearer to him than pos-
> sessions; will do nothing unworthy a Christian bishop, nor willingly lose the
> inheritance of the laws due to an Englishman; fears no hurt from Protector or
> Council; royal commands do not excuse breach of statute; the case of Anne
> Boleyn; following Godsalve's advice might mean loss of his bishopric by his
> own act. (This was certainly written before Gardiner's committal to the
> Fleet, 25 September, 1547. The statement that he writes exactly sixteen years
> from the day he received his bishopric does not enable us to fix the date precisely.
> Henry VIII appears to have written to the Pope on or about 12 September,
> 1531, requesting Gardiner's promotion to the see, and Chapuys, writing 26
> September, 1531, mentions that Winchester has been given to Gardiner—
> L.P., v, 418–9, 432; St.P., vii, 319–20. Since Godsalve was one of the guests
> Gardiner invited to a dinner in the Tower, in June 1550, to celebrate his
> expected release, he was, presumably, a good friend—see Foxe, vi, 195.)

Master Godsalve, after my right harty comendacions, with lieke thankes
for the declaracion of your good mynde towardes me (as ye meane yt),
allthough yt apperith not with myn accompt, such as I have had
leysour to make in this tyme of libertie, syns the death of my late
sovereigne lorde, whose sowle Jesus pardon: For thus have I
reconned, that I was called to this bysshoppricke without thoffence of

1 do c.o.

375

Godes lawe or the Kynges in thatteyninge of it. I have kept my bysshoppricke theis xvj yerys, accomplisshed this very daie that I write[1] these my letters unto you, without offendinge Godes lawe or the Kynges in the reteyninge of it, howe so ever I have of frailtie otherwyse synned. Nowe yf I may playe the thirde part well, to depart from the bysshoppricke without thoffence of Goddes lawe or the Kinges, I shall thinke the tragedie of my liefe well passed over; and in this part to be well handeled is all my care and studie nowe, how to fynisshe this iij^{de} acte well; for so I offende not Godes lawe nor the Kynges, I will no more care to se my bysshoppricke taken from me, then my selfe to be taken from the bysshoppricke.

I am by nature all redy condempned to dye, whiche sentence no man can pardon, ne assure me of delay in thexecucion of it; and so see that of necessitie I shall leave my bysshoppricke to the disposition of the croune from whense I had it, my housholde allso to breake up, and my brynginge up of youth to cease, the rememberance wherof trowbleth me nothinge.

I made in my howse at London a pleasaunt studie that delited me moche, and yet I was glad to come in to the countrie and leave it; and as I have left the use of sumwhat, so can I leave thuse of all tobteyne a more quiet. It is no losse to change for the better. Honestie and truthe are more leefe to me than all the possessions of the realme, and in theise ij, to saye and do frankelie as I might, I never for bare yet; and in theise two, honestie and truth, I take suche pleasure and comfort as I will never leave theim for no respect; for they will abyde by a man, and so will nothinge elles. No man can take theim awey from me but my selfe; and yf my selfe do them awey from me, then my selfe do ondo my selfe, and make my selfe woorthy to lose my bysshoppricke; whereat, such as gape[2] might take more sport then they ar lieke to have at my handes.

What other men have sayed or done in thomilies I can not tell, and what homilies or injunctions shalbe brought hyther I knowe not. Suche as the printers have sold abrode I have red and consydered, and am therfor the better instruct how to use my selfe to the visitours at their repaire hyther; to whome I will use no maner of protestacion, but a playne allegacion, as the matter servithe, and as honestie and truthe shall bynde me to speake; for I will never yelde to do that shoulde not be-seme a Christen bysshop, ne lose the inherytance of the Kynges lawes

<hr>

1 *MS.*, wrote   2 † *abv.* hape *underlined*

due to every Englisshe man, for want of peticion. I will shewe my selfe a trewe subject, humble and obedient, whiche repugnithe not with the preservacion of my dutie to God, and my right in the realme not to be enjoyned ageynst an acte of Parliament. Whiche myn entent I have signified to the Counsaile, with request of redresse in the matter, and not to compelle me to suche an allegacion, whiche, without I wer a best ⟨i.e., beast⟩, I can not pretermytt, and more then a best, yf after I had signified to the Counsail truth and reason in woordes, I shulde then seme in my dedes not to care for yt.

My Lorde Protector, in one of suche letters as he wrote unto me, willed me not to feare to moche; and in dede I knowe hym so well, and dyvers other of my Lordes of the Counsaill, that I can not feare eny hurte at ther handes in thallegacion of Godes lawe and the Kynges; and I will never defame theim so moche to be seene to feare it.

And of what strenkythe an acte of Parliament is, the realme was taught in the case of her that we called Quene Anne; where all suche as spake ageynst her in the Parliament Howse, all though they ded it by speciall commaundement of the Kynge, and spake that was truth, yet they were fayne to have a pardon, by cause that speakinge was ageynst an acte of Parliament. Ded ye never knowe or here tell of any man, that for doynge that the Kynge our late sovereigne lorde willed, devysed, and requyred to be done, he that tooke paynes and was commaunded to do it, was fayne to sue for his pardon, and suche other allso as were doers in it? And I coulde tell who it were. Sure there hathe bene suche a case; and I have bene present whan it hathe bene reasoned that the doinge ageynst an acte of Parliament excusethe not a man even from the case of treason, all thoughe a man ded it by the Kynges comaundement. Ye can call this to your rememberance, when ye thinke furder of it; and when it comythe to your rememberaunce, ye will not be best content with your selfe, I beleve, to have advysed me to entre the breache of an acte of Parliament, withoute suertie of pardon, all thoughe the Kynge comaunded it, and were suche in dede as it were no matter to do it at all.

And thus I answer your letters with worldly civile reasons, and take your mynde and zeale towardes me to be as tender as may be; and yet ye se that the folowinge of your advice might make me lose my bysshopp-ricke by myn owne acte, whiche I am sure ye wolde I shulde kepe, and so wolde I, as might stonde with my truthe and honestie, and non other-wise; as knowythe God, Who send you hartelie well to fare, etc.

INTRODUCTORY NOTES TO NOS. 130–9

These letters were written in the Fleet, whither Gardiner was sent 25 September, 1547, ostensibly because he refused to pledge himself in advance to observe the new injunctions, really, it seems, to prevent him from organizing a conservative opposition in the coming Parliament. (For his own comments on his exclusion from Parliament, *see* Nos. 132, 137, and for his remarks about Cranmer fearing that he will hinder his enterprises, No. 138.)

In No. 130, to Somerset on his return from the Scottish campaign, he not only describes the interview with the Council which ended in his imprisonment, but defends his attitude at the interview as well as his previous protests against the injunctions (in Nos. 126–9 above). While his attack had then been levied against the *Homilies*, he now adds objections to Erasmus' *Paraphrase upon the New Testament*, the use of which was also required by the injunctions, and he elaborates his point that royal commands contrary to statute are at once unconstitutional and an extremely dangerous precedent. He illustrates his legal contention by the rehearsal of several instances in point, and by the apt story of how Cromwell once attempted to persuade Henry VIII to have his will regarded as law. (*Cf.* No. 136, where he comments on the relative functions of King and Parliament in law making.)

We have part of No. 130 in two forms, one, Gardiner's draft, the other, a revised and expanded version printed by Foxe. Both are given here in parallel columns, and may serve as an illustration of Gardiner's methods of literary composition. Whether the expanded version was that sent to Somerset, or was the product of a later working over by Gardiner during his imprisonment, it is impossible to say.

Erasmus' *Paraphrase*, its dangerous teachings and its faulty translation (for its translators see p. 401), runs as a theme through the rest of this group of letters, with occasional reference to the *Homilies*, and to the question of law raised by the injunctions; but what makes them some of the most interesting, certainly the most human, that Gardiner ever wrote is their revelation of his character in adversity, when, as he said, he was 'as one divided from the world,' 'destitute of all such help as friendship, as service, as familiarity, as gentleness seemed to have gotten' him. Yet there is no hint of regret for the stand he had taken.

He tells Somerset plainly that he ought to be thanked rather than blamed for his protests, and maintains that he has done no more, or less, than his duty to commonwealth and Church. It is in these letters that Gardiner appears in a more appealing light than at any other moment of his career.

130. *To* SOMERSET

The Fleet, 14 October, [1547]

No single text of the whole of this letter appears to be extant, but from the existing texts of parts of it a reasonably complete whole may be put together. We have

(1) B.M., Harl. 417, 84–9, Gardiner's draft of about two-fifths of the letter, in a collection of papers made by John Foxe.

(2) B.M., Vesp. D, XVIII, 138–45, a late sixteenth- or early seventeenth-century manuscript copy of about one-half of the letter, in the collection made by Sir Robert Bruce Cotton (d. 1631).

(3) B. N., Latin 6051, 46 v.–47, a sixteenth-century manuscript copy of a small fraction—about six hundred words.

(4) Foxe, *1563*, 740–3 (ed. Pratt, VI, 42–6). Foxe doubtless had a full text before him, but after printing the opening lines, he added *etc.* and skipped more than a third of the letter.

The catalogue of manuscripts in the Bodleian lists a copy of this letter, MS. Tanner, lxxxvii, 61; but this is merely an eighteenth-century excerpt of a few paragraphs from Foxe. It is of no value in determining the text of the letter.

The parts of the letter given in each of the four sources may be roughly indicated thus:

Whole letter: _____
(1) Gardiner's draft: _____
(2) Vesp. D: _____ _
(3) B. N.:   _
(4) Foxe: _   _____

While (1), (2), and (3) represent one version, namely, Gardiner's draft, (4) represents another, revised and expanded. That Foxe printed from such an expanded version and is not himself responsible for additions to the text, is evidenced by the fact that the additions are not such as he would have had any interest in making, and are, moreover, in entire harmony with the thought and style of the rest of the letter. They undoubtedly represent a revision made by Gardiner himself.

A glance at the diagram above makes clear the impossibility of reconstructing a complete text of either draft or expanded version, and the consequent necessity of using the draft version for part of the text and the expanded version for part. In the following pages Vesp. D, which represents the draft version, is used as the basic text of the first two-fifths of the letter; then Gardiner's draft and the expanded version given in Foxe are printed in parallel columns as far as Gardiner's draft extends; that is, for the next two-fifths of the letter; after that, Foxe becomes the sole text. The point at which each source is taken up is indicated in the notes. Portions of Vesp. D are printed in Strype, *Cranmer*, App. xxxvi, and Burnet, v, 166.

The injunctions order the use of the *Book of Homilies* and Erasmus' *Paraphrase upon the New Testament*; these books contradict each other; the *Homilies* also contradict the doctrine established by Parliament (*i.e.*, the *King's Book*); in them Chrysostom is falsely quoted; Erasmus' later opinions contradict the *Paraphrase*; it teaches disrespect for princes, irreverence for the Sacrament, disregard for clerical celibacy, and condones the keeping of concubines; other faults in it; the translation of it into English is faulty; wrote to the Council (Nos. 126–7) hoping to delay the visitation till Somerset's return; the danger of praemunire in disobeying an act of Parliament even at the King's command; the cases of Wolsey, Lord Tiptoft, the exporters of wheat in Henry VIII's reign, the Act of Proclamations (31 H. VIII, c. 8), and Bishop Voysey of Exeter; Lord Chancellor Audley's opinion; the case of jewels; what was learned when altering Court of Augmentations with Paulet and Wriothesley; Viscount Montague's opinion; Gardiner's motto is *Vana salus hominis*; his interview with the Council; was committed to the Fleet (25 September); was taken (7 October) to a conference with Cranmer, who charged him with liking nothing unless he did it himself; disclaims this; has not advised others to object to the *Homilies* and *Paraphrase*; under Henry VIII men freely spoke their conscience; royal injunctions contrary to an act of Parliament set a dangerous precedent; Henry VIII's Council opposed his acting contrary to law; Cromwell once advised Henry to have his will regarded as law, which Gardiner opposed; Somerset has the opportunity to make a true determination concerning justification.

[1]After my moost humble commendacions to your good Grace, with hartie[2] thankes that it haith pleased yow to be content to heare from me:

1 *Vesp. D is used as the basic text from here to p. 387*
2 *not in Foxe and B.N.*

Wherin [1]now I have from your Grace liberty to write at large[1], I cannot finde the like gentellnes in my bodye to spende so muche tyme as I wolde; and therfore I[2] shall nowe desier your Grace to take in good parte thought ⟨i.e., though⟩ I gether my matter into[3] breafe sentences.

The injunctions in this last[4] visitation conteyne a commaundement to se[5] tawght and lerned two bookes, one of[6] homilies, that must be tawght[7]; another of Erasmus Paraphrasis[8], that the [9]prestes must learne[9].

Theis bokes stryve one against[10] another dyrectlye[11]:

The booke of[12] homilies teacheth faith to exclude charitie in the office of justification. Erasmus Paraphrasis teacheth faith to have charitie joyned with him in justification.

The boke of homilies teacheth how men may swere. [13]The Paraphrasis[13] teacheth the contrarie verye extremlye.

The boke of homilies teacheth howe subjectes owe tribute to theire prince, and obedience, verye well. The booke of Paraphrasis, in a place upon St Poule[14], violentilie, and against all truthe, after it hath spoken of dewtie dewe[15] to heathen princes, knytteth the matter up untrulie, that betwene the Christen men at Rome, to whome he writeth, which is a lesson for all, there shoulde be no debte or ryght, but mutuall charitie; which is a mervelous matter.

The boke of homelies in another place openeth the Gospell one waye. The Paraphrasis openeth it clerelye contrarye. The matter is not greate, but bycause there is contrarietie.

1–1 as in Foxe; Vesp. D (and B.N.), now (nowe) I have libertie to write at large from yow (you)

2 not in Foxe

3 Foxe and B.N., into; Vesp. D, in

4 not in Foxe and B.N.

5 Foxe, be; B.N., see

6 Foxe adds the

7 Foxe adds other by priest

8 Vesp. D in one instance spells this word Paraphrasis, otherwise Paraphrases and Paraphrasies, perhaps mistaking the Latin singular Paraphrasis for an English plural. B.N. and Foxe spell it Paraphrasis, which is probably what Gardiner wrote. This spelling is followed here throughout

9–9 Foxe, priest must larne himselfe

10 Foxe and B.N., with

11 Foxe adds etc. and skips to part of letter beginning p. 387 below

12 Vesp. D adds the, omitted in B.N.

13–13 B.N., Erasmus Paraphrasis

14 Both Vesp. D and B.N. add doth, but to make the sentence grammatical either doth must be deleted or knytteth, below, changed to knytt

15 B.N. supplies dewe

Nowe to consider eche of the foresaied[1] bookes alone[2]:

The booke of homilies in the sermon of salvation teacheth the clere contrar[ye] to the doctrine established by thacte of Parliament; even as contrarye as 'includethe' is contrarie to 'excludethe.' For theis be the wordes of the doctrine established by Parliament; wherin in[3] a certaine place[4] ⟨it saith: 'Not onely fayth . . . is required to our justification, but also the other giftes of the grace of God, with a desire to do good workes . . . . And where as in certain places of Scripture our justification is ascribed to faith, . . . it is . . . faith wherin the feare of God, repentence, hope, and charitie be included and comprysed, all whiche must be joyned together in our justification.'⟩ Faithe doth not exclude ⟨'the feare of God, repentence, hope, and charitie.'⟩ The doctrine of the Parliament speaketh how they be joyned in justification. The homile speaketh the vertues to be present in the manne justified, and howe faithe excludeth theim in thoffice of justifieng; which can never be proved, and is in the meane time contrarye to thacte.

The booke of homyles hath in the homilie of salvation, how remission of sinne is taken, accepted, and allowed of God for our[5] perfitt justificacion. The doctrine of the Parliament teacheth justification, for the fulness and perfection therof, to have more partes then remission of sinne, as in the same appereth. And althowght remission of sinne be a justification, yett it is not a full and a[6] perfite.

The boke of homiles numbreth the hallowing of bread, palmes, and candells among papisticall superstitions and abuses. The doctrine of the Parliament willeth theim to be reverentlye usyd; and so do the injunctions nowe sett fourthe; whiche made me thinke the printer[7] myght thrust in an homilie of his owen devise.

The booke of homyles hath wordes of St Crissostom alledged untrulye, not after suche a sorte as might escape by over sight, but of

1 *B.N.*, aforesaied
2 *B.N. supplies* alone   3 *B.N. supplies* in
4 *Vesp. D runs on* faithe doth not exclude   *This not only makes little sense, but does not give* 'the wordes of the doctrine established by Parliament.' *B.N. puts etc. after* place, *and leaves the rest of the line blank; it begins the next line,* Fayth dothe not exclude *and leaves the rest of that line blank. Hence it would seem that the copyist of B.N. had before him Gardiner's draft, or a careful copy of it, in which a space was left for quotations from the* King's Book. *These are here supplied from* A Necessary Doctrine and Erudition for Any Christen Man, *London, 1543, d iiii*
5 *Vesp. D,* your; *B.N.,* our   6 *B.N. supplies* a
7 *Vesp. D,* printers; *B.N.,* printer

382

purpose: as calling that faithe which Crissostome calleth hoope; and in[1] place of one sentence putteth[2] an other which should better serve the purpose of the maker of the homelie. Nowe if one wold reason with me that Crisostome mente this, I wold denye it him, as I may[3]. But I maye affirme that Chrisostome saith not. It is but a diffamation of the truthe —and under suche a princes name as our[4] soverant lorde ys, whose tonge, in this so pure innocentie, hath not bene defiled with any un- truthe! I assure yow, I thought ther was not so greate hast in homelies, but they might have taried the printing either for that onelye cause. Truth is able to mayntene yt selfe and nedeth no help of untrue alliga- tion. It serveth onelye for enemies to tak avantage; all whiche use to be curyous to know what they may reprove. And now all the eyes and eares of the world be turned towardes us. And as they shall have cause to talke honorablie of your valyantnes in the warres, so shall they talke otherwise of that that is done in your absens, yff any thing be amysse.

Now shall I shewe your Grace what autor Erasmus is, to be, by name and speciall commaundment, had in credit in this realme. Yf he be to be beleved, the doctrine of 'onely faithe justifieth' is a verye poyson. And he writeth by expresse termes, and calleth this an other poyson, to denye punishement in purgatory after this life. And an other poyson, to denye the invocation of sainctes and worshipping of theim. And this he calleth a poyson, to saye we nede no satisfactory workes, for that wer to mistrust Christe.

Erasmus in an other place, conferring ⟨i.e., comparing⟩ the state of the Churche in the beginning and nowe, he concludeth, that if St Paule were alive at this daye, he wold not improve ⟨i.e., censure⟩ the present state of the Churche, but cry out of mens faultes. This is Erasmus judgement in his latter dayes.

His worke, the Paraphrasis, which should be auctorised in the realme, which he wrote above 26 yeres a goo, when his penne was wanton, as the matter is so han⟨d⟩led, as being abrode in this realme, were able to minister occasion to evell men to subverte, with religion, the policie and order of the realme.

Theis be the generall wordes, the uttering whereof to your Grace, in the place yow occupye, wer a great faute, unles I wold shewe ye good ground and true, whye to saye so. And therfor I am glade I do rather writt to yow, then to have come and speake with yow, bycause my

1 *B.N. adds* the   2 *B.N.,* putt
3 *B.N. ends here*   4 *Vesp. D,* your

383

wordes in numbre myght flye away; where as written wordes remayne to be redd agayne and agayne.

First, as concerning the pollicye and state of the realme: Whersoever Erasmus might take an occasion to speake his pleasure of princes, he paieth home as roundlye as busshoppes have ben of late touched in playes. And suche places of Scripture as we have used to alledge for the state of princes, he wresteth and wrydeth theim so, as if the people redde him and beleved him, they wold after smalle regard that allegation of theim. And ¹if Erasmus did it¹ truelye, and that the Scripture bound him so to saye, yt were more tolerable; for truthe must have place. But when it is done in some place untrulye, and in some place wantonlye, to checke that estate, yt can be no good doctrine amonges people that should obey.

And this booke of Paraphrasis is not like the other expositions of Scripture, where the aucter speaketh in his owen persone; for Erasmus taketh upon him the Evangelistes person and Christes persone, and enterpriseth to fill uppe Christes tale and his wordes. As for example where the Gospell rehersith Christes speache, when he said, 'Give to the emperoure that is themperowres,' by which speache we gether and trulye gether that Christ confessed themperoure to have a dewtie, Erasmus writeth it with an 'if,' after this sorte, 'if ther be any thing dewe to them'; which condition Christ put not to it, but spake planely, 'Give to Cesar the thinges which arre Ceasers, and unto God the thinges that are Goddes.' And I write the verie wordes of the Paraphrasis as they be in Englishe, for I have the booke with me; and so shall no manne saie that I mysreporte the boke. The wordes be theis: 'Render therfore unto Ceser, if any thing² appertaine unto Ceaser, but first of all, rendre unto God the thinges that appertain unto God; meaning that ⟨it⟩ is no hurte to godlines, if a man, being dedicate to God, do give tribute to a prophane prince, although he ought it not.' Theis be the wordes in the booke ordered to be sett fourthe; wherin what needeth Erasmus to bring in doubte the dutie, when God putteth no doubte at all? Yt were to longe to write to your Grace everye faulte. This one I put for example, wher Erasmus doth corrupt Christes wordes with a condicion which Christ spake not.

The other places of raylinges wolde encomber your Grace over muche. But as I writt, your Grace shall finde true that what so ever might be spoken to defame princes governement is not left unspoken.

1-1 *MS.*, it if Erasmus did
2 *MS.*, thinges; *Paraphrase, Mt. xxii*, thing

Busshoppes be more gentle handled. Erasmus maketh theim verye kinges of the Gospell, and calleth the true kinges of the world prophane kinges. Busshoppes have the sworde, he saieth, of God geven; that is to saie, the Gospell. Prophane princes, as he calleth theim, have a sworde permitted unto theim, and by Homer, he saith, be called 'pastures ⟨*i.e.*, pastors⟩ of the people' ⟨*Iliad*, II, 243 *et al.*⟩. This matter is within the compasse of the Paraphrasis, if it be not lefte oute; with a comendacion also of Thomas Becket of Caunterburye, in excomunicating the King of the realme, that then was, by implecation, for the manor of Oxforde, which the Kinge, as he reherseth, then withhealde. It maye be the translator woulde have left this owte. But Erasmus penne in those dayes ⟨was⟩ verye light.

Moreover when Erasmus teacheth that betwene Christen menne is no debt or right, but charitie, it is a mervelouse matter to the dissolution of lawes and duties. And therin Erasmus dothe violate Goddes Scripture, and saith not true.

Thus farre is the doctrine pernitious for comen pollicie; wherin, never the lesse, yf he had saied truthe, lett the truthe prevayle. But the truthe is not so.

As touching religion in this worke of Paraphrasis, yt is so wantonlye—I beseche your Grace note my wordes—and ther with untrulye handled, as, if we should use to readd it, ther should ensue a mervelous confusion. Some speciallties I will note, but not all.

The Sacrament of the Aulter is so wantonlye talked of by him that, as the world is nowe, the reading of him were the whole subvertion. Erasmus, in his latter dayes, hath for the Sacrament of the Aultar spoken as reverendlye and said as muche for confirmation of it as maye be, and crieth out of them that would take him otherwayes. But this is in thend, when age had tempered him. In his Paraphrasis, whiche he wrott in his wanton age, the wordes and termes were able to subverte, if it were possible, as Christ saith, thelecte.

If the Paraphrasis goo abrode, people shalbe lerned to call the Sacrament of the Aultar holibred and a symbole; at whiche newe name manye will marvayle. And they be wanton wordes spoken of Erasmus without necessitie.

By the doctrine of the Paraphrasis, who so ever hadd done away his wyfe for advotrie might marrye agayne.

By the Paraphrasis all men maye marrye, busshoppes and prestes; wherin Erasmus toke his pleasure to understand St Poule, as though he should describe of whate qualitie pristes wyves shuld be, wherin he forgatt him selfe. For Saincte Poule knewe that if a bysshopp or prest were once maried, his wife must passe with all her faultes; and it shuld be to late to tell what she should be. For otherwise then she is, she will not be, nether for St Poule nor St Peter. And if bushoppes had that previledge, that they might chaunge while the⟨y⟩ founde suche one as Erasmus saith St Poule wold have theim, their estate wold be wonderfullye envied. But St Poule did not speake ther of busshoppes wyves. And so therin he dothe violence to the Scriptures undowbtedlye. Wherfor I write somwhat merely ⟨*i.e.*, merrily⟩ to shewe the absurditie of the thinge.

By the Paraphrasis the keping of a concubyne ys called but a light fault. And that were good for Lankeshire. And Erasmus bringeth it so pretilye, that a ruler of a countrey, yf he be him selfe the servaunt of avarice or ambicion, should not browke with his brother because, being overcome by weaknesse of fleshe, he useth a concubine. Even thus it is Englished in the booke that should gooe fourthe. And when to have a concubine, yt is called a lyght fault, me thinketh if the mayd can redd, yt maye serve well lightlye to perswade hir. And yet if the man doth it, overcome by the weakenesse of his fleshe, as the booke termeth it, is made matter wherin Erasmus speake over lightlye to call it a light fault. And the translator in Englishe wanted speache, when he turned it thus: that a man overcome with the weakenes of his fleshe shuld desyre a concubyne. I am bould with his Grace, to joyne here Erasmus lightnes with the discretion of the translator. Yf to kepe a concubine shalbe by aucthoritie called a light fault, the multitude of theim maye make the faulte heavye.

By the doctrine of the Paraphrasis, everye man must cum to the high pricke of vertue, or to be extremly nought; which differeth far from the teachinge of the homelies, and from the truthe also.

The Paraphrasis teacheth thus: Trulye more glorious it is to dye for the Gospell sake; which deathe, though yt shalbe violent and sore, yet yt shall not come before the daye; when so ever yt commeth yt shall not come with out the providence of God; and by this it cometh to passe that if ye endevor to avoyd it, ye cannot. This ys the doctrine which, if yt were taken for true, meght engender like obstinacy in mayne ⟨*i.e.*, many⟩, as it hath of late in some. Erasmus teacheth here further then he hath warrante by Scripture.

The Paraphrasis in an other place dothe clerelye violente the texte,

and untrulye handle yt, in a matter of tythes, which your Grace is de-
sierous, as appereth by the injunctions, to have truelye paid. Wherin if
Erasmus had said truth, lett truthe prevaile; but when he handelith yt
untrulye, it is petye it should be suffered.

[1] Thus have I here rekened your Grace some special faultes that be Erasmus owne faultes, with a greate nomber that I have not spoken of.

And further your Grace shall understande that he which hath taken the labours to translate Erasmus in to Englishe, hath offended sumtyme, as appereth playnly, by ignoraunce, and sumtyme of purpose[2], to put in[3], leve out, and chaunge as he thought best; wherwith I wyl not nowe[†] encombre your Grace, but assure youe that it[†] is soo. And herin I wyl graunte to your Grace that for every lye I make[4] unto youe, set c⟨100⟩ li. fyne on my hed, and let me lyve here like a begger whiles my revenues paye it. My wordes remayne in wrytyng[5], and be against me matier of recorde. And soo I yeld to have me charged, as the Bishop of London was with offering of the ferme ⟨i.e., farm⟩ of

Thus I have signifyed to your Grace sume speciall faultes that be Erasmus owne faultes, and in my judgement greate faultes, but I have not written al.

And your Grace shal further under stand that he (who it is I know not) who hath taken the labors to translate Erasmus into Englysh, hath for his parte offended some time, as apereth plainely, by ignoraunce, and somtime evidently of purpose, to put in, leave out, and chaunge as he thought best, never to the better, but to the worse; with the specialties wherof I wil not nowe encomber your Grace, but assure you it is so. And here I will graunt to your Grace that for every lye I make unto you, sett on ⟨i.e., one⟩ c pound fyne upon mine head, and let me live here like a beggar whilest my revenewes paye it. My woords you have in writing, and be agaynst me matter of record.

1 *The matter given here in parallel columns is, on the left, Gardiner's draft, on the right, the expanded version printed in Foxe. The draft does not actually begin till the word* labours *in l. 8, the words preceding it being taken from* Vesp. D, *which follows the draft closely. Variants from the draft in* Vesp. D *are not given, since the draft is clearly primary and the variants almost certainly errors.* Vesp. D *omits a passage given in the draft from* And now I, *p. 388, l. 3, through* speke with youe, *p. 390, l. 1, and extends only as far as* Graces retourne, *p. 393, last l.*

2 † *abv.* malice *c.o.*   3 and *c.o.*

4 *alt. from* maye   5 *alt. from* wryten

his bishoprich; which matier I doo remembre whenne I wryte this.

And now[1] I have rehersed to your Grace upon what foundacion my conscience is grounded, I shal truely open unto youe the maner of my procedinges. I never hard of[2] thexecution of the visitacion tyl the tyme of your Graces departure in this voyage, wherin ye have goten moch honno*u*r, and yet with more daungier thenne ye loked for, which hath set forth your valiauntenes. As soone as I harde of the [3]visitacions and the bookes of homilies and injunctions[3], I wrote to the Counsail, trusting upon such ernest advertisement as I made, they wold incontinently have sent for me and, upon knowlege of soo evident matier† as me thought I had to shewe, have stayed whiles your Graces reto*u*rne. I sawe a determina[cion] to doo al thing sodenly at a oon tyme; wherunto although your Grace agreed, yet of your wisedom I conjected ye had rather had it tary whiles your reto*u*rne, if ye had not been pressed. And that worde 'pressed' I noted in your letters to me, whenne ye wrote ye wer pressed on both sides. Me thought if, by bringing myself in

And so I yeld to have me charged, as the Bishop of London was with offering the ferme of his bishopricke; which matter cam to my remembraunce in the writing here of.

And now I have written unto your Grace upon what foundacion my conscience is grounded, I shall truly declare unto you the manner of my proceding from the beginning. I never hard of the execution of the visitacion till your Grace was departed from London northward, and as the bokes flowed a broad by liberty of the printers, they came to my handes. I never slept while I had perused them. As sone as I had found certaine faultes I wrote to the Counsel, trusting upon such ernest advertismente as I made, they would incontinently have sent for me and, upon knowledge of so evident matter as me thoughte I had to shew, have staied til your Graces retorn. I sawe a determinacion to do al thinges sodenly at one time; wherunto although your Grace agreid, yet of your wisdom I conjected ye had rather have had it tarye whiles your returne, yf you had not bene pressed. And that woord 'pressed' I noted in your Graces letters to me, wherin ye wrote ye wer pressed on both sides. Me thought if, by bringing my selfe to most extreme daunger

1 if *c.o.* 2 any of these bokes *c.o.*
3–3 †*; followed by one or two unintelligible letters* † *and evidently meant to be c.o.; all abv.* matier *c.o.*

to most extreme daungier in your absence, I coulde have stayed this matier, besides my duetie to God and my souverain lord, I had also doon youe pleasour; of whom I have this opinion, that willingly and wittingly your Grace wyl neyther breke thacte of Parlament ne[1] commaunde bokes to be bought with auctorite, that conteyne such doctrine as thiese bookes doo. Thus I adventured in your absence, wherin although I had remembraunce of your Grace, yet I made not your Grace my foundation, but God chiefly (as God knowith), with the preservation of our late souverain lordes honnour, that ded is, and the suertie of our souverain lord that nowe is. Let no man [2] be offended[2] with the vehemencie of my wryting, for I wrote with a hol harte; and if I coulde have wryten it with the blode of my harte, I wold have doon it, to have doon good in staying the thing tyl it had been more maturely digested, and tyl your Graces saulf retourne. I touched thacte of Parlament lyvely[3], but as[4] truely as ever was any thing spoken of. And I[5] never wept more bytterly thenne I did for a conceyte that troubled my mynde, which I never spake nor wrote, ne wyl not. I wyl tel it your Grace †by mouth†, if ever it be

in your absence, I could have stayed thys matter, besides my dewty to God and to my soveraigne lord, I had done also your Grace pleasure; of whome I have this fyrme opinion, that willingly and wittingly your Grace will nether breake the act of Parliament ne commaunde bookes to be bought with autoryty, that conteine such doctrin as these bokes do. Thus I adventured in your Graces absence, wherin although I had remembraunce of your Grace, yet I made not your Grace my foundacion, but God chiefly (as God knoweth), with the preservacion of our late soveraine lordes honour, that dead is, and the suertye of our soverayne lorde that now is.

Let no man be offended with the vehemency of my writing, for I wrote with a whole harte; and if I could have written it with the blood of my hart, I would have done it, to have done good in staieng the thing til it had bene more maturely digested, and til your Graces saulf retourne. I touched the act of Parliament lively, but as truly as ever was any thinge spoken of. And I never wept more bitterly then I did for a conceat that trobled my heade, which never passed my lips, ne shall never come out of my penne.

1 reco c.o.
3 in margin beside truely c.o.
5 w incomplete c.o.

2–2 † abv. finde faulte c.o.
4 lyvely c.o.

my chaunce to speke with youe. Whither the King maye commaunde against a Commen Lawe or an acte of Parlament, there is never a judge or other man in the realme ought to knowe more by experience of that the lawers have said thenne I.

Fyrst, my Lord Cardynal that obteyned[1] his legacie[2] by our late souverain lordes request at Rome, yet bicause it was against the lawes of the realme, the judges concluded thoffense of premenire[3]; which matier I bare awaye, and toke it for a lawe of the realme, bicause the lawers said soo, but my reason digested it not.

The lawers, for[4] confirmation of ther doinges, brought in a cace of the Lord Typtoft[5]. An erle he was, and lerned in the Civile Lawes, who being Chaunceler, bicause, in execution of the Kinges commission, he offended the lawes of the realme, he suffred on Tower Hyl. They brought in examples of many judges that had fynes set on ther hedes in like caces for transgression of lawes by the Kinges

I will tell it your Grace and you require it. Now whether the King may commaund against an act of Parliament, and what daunger they may fall in that breake a law with the Kinges consent, I dare saye no man alive at this daye hath had more experience what the judges and lawyers have sayd then I.

First I had experience in myne old mayster the Lord Cardinall, who obteyned hys legacy by oure late soveraygne lordes request at Rome; and in hys syght and knowledge occupyed the same, wyth hys two crosses and mases borne before hym, many yeres. Yet because it was agaynst the lawes of the realme, the judges concluded the offence of the premunire; whych conclusyon I bare away, and take it for a law of the realme, because the lawyers so sayd, but my resone digested it not.

The lawyers, for confirmation of there doinges, brought in a case of the Lord Tiptoft, as I remember (a jolly cyvylyan he was Chauncelor to the Kynge), who, because, in execution of the Kynges commission, he had offended the lawes of the realme, he suffred on Tower Hill. They brought in examples of many judges that had fines set on their heads in like cases for doing against the lawes

1 † *abv.* occupied *c.o.*
3 wherin *c.o.*
5 a fre *c.o.*

2 in o our *c.o.*
4 t *incomplete follows*

commaundement. And this I lerned in that cace.

Synnes that tyme, being of the Counsayl, whenne many proclamations wer devised against the caryers out of corne[1], whenne it cam to punishe the offendours, the judges wold answer, it might not be by the lawes[2], bicause thacte of Parlament gave libertie, wheate being under a price. Wherupon at the last folowed thActe of Proclamations, in the passing wherof wer many large †wordes spoken†.

Whenne the Bishop of Exeter and his chauncelour wer by oon† Body brought in a premenire, I reasoned with the Lord Audely, thenne Chaunceler, soo far as he bad me hold my pease for feare of entryng a premenire myself. But I concluded that although I must take it[3] as of ther auctorite that it

of the realme by the Kings commaundement. And then was brought in the judges oth, not to staye any proces or judgement for any commaundement from the Kinges Majesty. And one article agaynst my Lord Cardinal was that he had graunted injunctions to stay the Common Lawes. And upon that occasion *Magna Charta* was spoken of, and it was made a great matter, the stay of the Common Lawe. And this I lerned in that case.

Sithens that time, being of the Counsel, when many proclamations were devised against the cariers out of corne, at such thime as the transgressors should be ponished, the judges whould answere, it might not be by the lawes; wherupon ensewed the Act of Proclamations, in the passing of which act many liberall wordes were spoken, and a playne promes that, by autority of the Act for Proclamationes, nothing should be made contrary to an act of Parliament or Common Law.

When the Bishop of Exeter and his chauncellor were by one Bodye broughte in a premunire (whiche matter my Lorde Privy Seale cannot forget), I reasoned with the Lord Awdly, then Chauncelor, so far as he bad me hold my peace for fear of entering into a premunire my selfe. Wherupon I

1 the J *c.o.*   2 whe *c.o.*
3 *writ. over something else;* of *c.o.*

is Commen Lawe, yet I could not see howe a man auctorised by the King, as, synnes the Kinges Majestie hath taken upon hym the supremicie, every bishop is, that a man could fal in a premenire.

I reasoned oones in the Parlement Howse, where was free spech without daungier; and there the †Lord Audeley†, Chaunceler thenne, to satisfie me, bicause I was in sum secrete estimacion, as he knewe—'Thoue arte a good felawe, Bishop,' quod he, 'loke the Acte of Supremicie, and there the Kinges doinges be restrayned to spiritual jurisdiction; and in an other acte noo[1] Spiritual Lawe shal have place contrary to a Commen Lawe or an acte of Parlament. And this wer not,' quod he, 'ye bishoppes wold entre in with the Kyng and, by meanes of his supremicie, ordre the layete as ye listed. But we wyl provide,' quod he, 'that the premenire shal never goo of your hedes.' This I bare awaye there and held my pease.

Synnes that tyme in a cace of juelles, I was fayne, with thEmperours ambassadour, Chapuce, whenne he was here, and in thEmperours †Courte also†, defende and maynteyne by commaunde-

stayd, but concluded it semed to me straung that a man autorised by the King (as, sence the Kings Majesty hath taken upon him the supremacy, every bishop is such one) could fall in a premunire.

After, I had reasoned the matter once in the Parliament House, where was free speche without daunger; and there the Lord Awdlye, then Chauncelor, to satysfy me familierly, becawse I was in some secrete estimacion, as he then knew—'Thou art a good felow, Bishop,' quod he (which was the maner of his familier speach), 'looke the Act of Supremacy, and there the Kings doinges be restrayned to spiritual jurisdiction; and in a nother acte it is provided that no Spirituall Lawe shall have place contrary to a Common Lawe or Acte of Parliament. And this wer not,' quod he, 'you bishops would enter in with the Kinge and, by meanes of his supremacie, order the layty as ye listed. But we wil provide,' quod he, 'that the premunire shall ever hang over your heads, and so we lay men shalbe sure to enjoye our inheritaunce by the Common Lawes and acts of Parliament.'

It is not yet full two yeres ago since, in a case of juells, I was fayne, with thEmprors ambassador, and after in the Emprors Court, defende and mainteine by commaundement that the kinges of

[1] lawe c.o.

ment that the Kinges ⟨Majestie⟩[1] was not above thordre of his lawes. And therfor the jueller, although [2]he had the Kinges byl signed, yet it wold not serve, bicause it was not obteyned after the ordre of the lawe; in which matier I was very moch troubled.

Even[3] this tyme twelvemoneth, whenne I was in commission with my Lord Gret Master and thErle of Southampton for altering the Courte of Augmentacion, there was my Lord Montague and other of the Kinges lerned Counsail, of whom I lerned what the King might doo against an acte of Parlement, and what daungier it was to them that medled. It is fresh within memorie, and they canne tel whither I saye true or noo. And therfor, being lerned[†] in soo notable caces, I wrote in your absence therin, as I had lerned[5] by hering the Commen Lawers speke, whose jugementes rule those matiers, howe soever my reason canne digest them. Whenne I wrote therof, the matier was soo[†] reasonable, as I have been lerned the lawes of the realme, that I trusted my Lordes wold have stayed tyl your[7] Graces retourne.

this realme were not above the order of there lawes. And therfore the jueller, although he had the Kinges bil signed, yet it woulde not be allowed in the Kings court, because it was not obteined according to the lawes; in which matter I was very much trobled.

Even this time twelve moneth, when I was in commission with my Lord Great Master and the Erle of Sowthampton for altering the Court of Augmentacions, there was my Lord Mountagu and other of the Kinges learned Counsel, of whome, by occasion of that matter, I learned what the Kinge mighte do contrary to an acte of Parlament, and what daunger it was to them that medled agaynst the act. It is fresh in memory, and they can tell whether I saye[4] trew or no. And therfore, being lerned in so notable cases, I wrote in your Graces absence to the Counsell therin, as I had learned by hering the Commons[6] speake, whose judgements rule those matters, how so ever my reason can disgest them; and so wrot to the Counsayle; which my writings I fashoned so as I trusted my Lorde⟨s⟩ would have staied til your Graces retourne. And thus I have declared to your Grace the purpose of my writing to the

---

1 *supplied from Vesp. D.*   2 h *writ over* t
3 Evens *w.* s *c.o.*   4 *printed* sayed   5 *in the c.o.*
6 *a probable error for* Common Lawyers; *see Gardiner's draft*
7 *a second* your † *and c.o.* cummyng *c.o.*

Whenne my Lordes sent nowe for me, I cam to them †with as moch spede as I might†, with my trinkettes in† my sleves, and bosom trussed ful of bookes to furnishe my former allegations. I was hard very wel and gentylly, and me thought shewed matier that shuld have moved, for I shewed two contrary bookes, as³ is bifore wryten; wherwith they said they wer not moved, adding howe ther consciences agreed not with myn, using many good wordes to bring me to conformite, †as they wold have had it†. Wherunto, knowing that I knewe, I could not relent. But⁴ after I had been a side from them and was retourned, they entred a precise ordre with me, eyther to receyve precisely the injunctions or to refuse; in which cace they had further to saye to me; addyng that your Grace was pryve to that was doon there that day. Myn answer was, that I wold receyve them as far as Goddes lawe and the Kinges wyl

Counsayle so vehement, while¹, nevertheles, I continued with all humilyty to abide the order of autoryty and learne al other obedience; for therunto I have ever had as great regarde as² any man in this realme. And as my word is *Vana salus hominis*, so I assure your Grace I practice it throughly in my deedes.

When my Lords sent last for me, I came to them with as much sped as I mighte, with my sleves and bosom truste full of bookes to furnysh my former allegacions. I was hard very well and gentillye, and me thought I shewed matter that should have moved, for I shewed the two bookes to be contrary, as I have written before; wher with they said they were not moved, adding how there conscience agreid not with mine, using many good woordes to bring me to such conformity as they would have had me at. Wherupon, knowing that I know, I could not relent. But after I had bene a litle beside from them and was retourned, they entered a precise order with me, either to receave precysly the injuncions or to refuse; in which case they had further to saie to me; adding that your Grace was prive to that was done there that daye. My answere was, that I wold receave the injuncions as farre as Gods lawe and the Kings would

1 *Foxe*, which; *Pratt*, while
3 I, c.o.

2 *Foxe adds* to
4 entred c.o.

bynde me. And bicause I sawe they drewe to such a precisenesse, I wold not leave unspoken that I thought might avoyde that folowed. I told them there was thre wekes of delaye[†] to the cummyng of the visiteurs to me. In the meane tyme I offred to goo to Oxford to abyde the discussion there. That offer[†] was not allowed. I desired to goo to my house at London and have lerned men speke with me there. That was not accepted. I entred thenne thallegacion of the Gospel, of the servaunt that said he wold not doo a thing and yet did it[†]; and soo I said it might be that although I thenne said naye[3], as my conscience served me, yet I might chaunge, and was a man that might be tempted. But, as my conscience was thenne, me thought Goddes lawes and the Kinges letted me. A bye communication there was whither I had spoken to any man of that I founde in the bookes; wherin I answerd truely, and wherfor noo man canne blame me. But thenne[4] I told my Lordes that [†]I thoght it hard[†], oonles ther wer a gretter matier thenne this, to sende me to pryson for declaryng my mynde bifore hand [†]and shewing[†] what I mynded to doo[5], bifore it had[6] been by me doon,

bind me. And because I saw they grewe to such precisenes, and remembring how, after a good sort, they had cawsed me to be accompaned before with Master Wingfielde, makinge insinuacions[1] what wold be the end if I would not yelde, I would not therfore leave unspoken that I thought might avoid that folowed. I told them there were iij wekes of delay to the comming of the visytors to me. In the meane tyme I offered to go to Oxford to abide the discussion there; which offere was not allowed. I desired them[2] to go to my howse at London and to have lerned men speke with me there; which was not accepted. I entred then the allegacion of the Gospell, of the servant that sayd he would not do a thing and yet did it; and so I sayde it might be that although I then sayd nay, as my conscience served me, yet I might percase chaung, and was a man that might be tempted. But, as my conscience was then, me thought Gods law and the Kinges letted me. And upon knowledg of there pleasures, that I muste to the Fleet, I told my Lords I thought it hard, unles there were a greater matter then ⟨this⟩, to send me to prison for declaring before hand what I mynded to do, before any

1 *an emendation of* innouacions
2 *Pratt,* then
4 † *abv.* whenne *c.o.*
6 † (*and c.o. evidently by mistake*)

3 yet *c.o.*
5 it shuld take effecte and *c.o.*

395

who had al the meane tyme to repente myself.

Wherunto the answer was such
as displeased me not inwardly somoch, but I have wel digested it,
and, soo al maye be wel, care not
what becommith of my bodye.
I departed as quietly from them
as ever man did, and have endured with as lytel grudge here.
And I have lerned this lesson in
the worlde, never to loke[1] bak-
ward, as Saincte Pol sayth[†], ne
remembre that is past[2]. I wyl never
grudge or complayne of nothing
for myself. As for the matier to
have such bookes recommended
to the realme in the Kinges name
by your Graces direction, me
seemeth very weighty. Al the
worlde knowith[3] the Kinges Highnes himself knewe[4] nothing of
thiese bookes, [5]and therfor[5] nothing canne be ascribed [†]unto
him[†]. Your Grace hath been
soo occupied, as al men knowe
your [†]Grace had[†] noo laysour
yourself to peruse thiese bookes.
And yet[†] of such sorte be the
bookes as I have writen; and if noo
man hath advertised the Counsayil
as I have, it is bycause they have
not red them as I have doon.

thing had bene by me actually
done to resyste the visitacion, who
had all the meane time to thinke
on the matter and repent me.
Wherunto the aunswere was
such as displeased me not inwardly
somuch, but I have well disgested
it, and, so all maye be well, care
not what becometh of my bodye. I
departed as quietly from them as
ever manne dyd, and have endured
with as litle grudge here; and have
lerned this lession in the world,
never to looke bacward, as Saint
Pawle sayth, ne remember that is
past. I will never grudge or complayne of nothing for my selfe.
As for the matter to have such
books recommended to the realme
in the Kinges name by your
Graces direction, me semeth verye
weighty, and your Grace not to
have bene well handled in it. All
the world knoweth the Kinges
Highnes him selfe knew[6] not
these bookes, and therfore nothing can be ascribed unto hym.
Your Grace hath bene, to your
encrease of honour, so occupied,
as all men know your Grace had
no leasure your selfe to peruse
these books. And yet be the bookes
as I have written. I leave the rest
to your Grace. If I, that tell the
Councell my mind of them[7], have

1 on or c.o.
2 and yet thalteracion of my astate (in such a matier † and c.o.) for this maner of
offense is as gret as hath been seen. If commen policie of an estimacion conceyved,
but c.o.   3 y. c.o   4 † abv. did c.o.
5–5 † abv. he can c.o.   6 printed know   7 Foxe adds that

done so farre amisse, because, when I know so much, I will not yet allow them, I shall from hencefourth the more regard the lesson of an old ambassador that bed me let evil tydinges go home to my master afoote, and send only good tidinges by poste—a shift with the worde which agreith not with my nature, as Maister Wallope sayth.

Upon Frydaye last past, my Lord of Cauntourbury sent for me to[1] the deane of Polles house, whither I went with sum gasing of the worlde. There I founde my Lord of Cauntourbury, accompanyed with the Bishop of Rochestre, Master Doctour Cokkes, and Master Ayre; and I was brought thither by the Bishop of Lincoln. What reaporte my Lord of Cauntourbury †hath made† I cannot tel.

My Lord of Cauntourbury was in hand with his homilie of salvation, but nothing sawe I or harde I wherwith to salve my conscience. I made this offer, to yeld †them for that homilie†, if they coulde thenne tel me of oon old wryter that teachith[3] as thomilie doth. My Lord of Cauntourbury wold fal to arguyng, and overcumme me that am called the sophister, by sophistrie. Wherunto I answerd[4]

Upon Fryday last past, my Lorde of Caunterbury sent for me to the deane of Pawles house, whether I went with some gasing of the world. There I founde my Lord of Caunterbury, accompaned with the Bishop of Rochester, Maister Doctor Cox, and Maiester Aire; and I was brought thether by the Bishop of Lincolne. What report my Lord of Caunterbury hath made therof I cannot tel.

My Lord of Caunterbury was in hand with his homely of salvacion, but nothing harde or sawe I to save my conscience in agreing to him, but harde that[2] shoulde justlye confirme me in mine own conscience. I made offer to yelde to them in that homely, yf they coulde shew me any old writer that wrot how fayth excluded charity in the office of justificacion. It is agaynst Scriptures playne

---

1 Polles c.o.   2 Foxe adds I   3 ith *writ. over something else*
4 *End of draft. At the beginning and twice thereafter there are references in a later hand to Burnet, as well as two or three words interlined, repeating Gardiner's words, with the evident intention of making them more legible. These additions have not been indicated since they have no value in determining Gardiner's text*

woordes; and to swarve from Scripture with out eny one doctor to leane to it, were sore. Where Scripture and doctors want, my Lord of Caunterbury woulde falto arguing, and overcom me that am called the Sophister, by sophistry. When I hard my Lords argument I denied

[1]it, and would enter none other declaracion; for I kepe that aunswere til some other then were ther be present. My solucion wherunto, when I declare it, shal make all the rest of the matter very weake, and my Lord not to like his argument at al. One argument I could not assoylle: to come agayne to the Fleete.

My Lorde of Caunterbury charged me that I like nothing unles I doo it my selfe; whereof I am not gylty. I was never autor of any one thing, other spirituall or temporall, I thanke God of it.

I am also charged that al the realm hath receaved these homelies without contradiction save I; wherunto I aunswere, I think they have not red that I have red in these books. What hath bene done I can not tell, now I am kept as I cannot know though I wold. When I was abrode I never sought to knowe more then was brought by common fame. For this shalbe found true, I never advised any man to object any thing against these bokes, no one man, not my chapleins. A kynsman of myne, benefised in my dioces and not unlerned, cam to me and tolde me how he heard a lewde felowe saye that I would not receave the injunctions. 'And Syr,' quod he[2], 'I rebuked him and reviled him and saide you would as redily receive as any man.' I told him that in so saiyng he did very wel. Upon my comming up, a chapleine of mine, a doctor of devinitye, told me he would receave the injunctions quietly and say nothing. I told him it should be well done. If I had taryed in my dioces, yf any man had spoken but my selfe, I would have lost my lyfe for it, nor I thinke there hath not now. This matter was to trye a bishop, whether he careth more for the truth or hys owne rest.

What examples have I sene in this realme, how frely men have sayd there conscience agaynst our late sovereigne lords determinacion and agaynst the act of Parliament! Doctor Crome, a meane man, preached

---

1 *Foxe is followed from here*   2 *Foxe, I*

agaynst our late sovereigne lordes determinacions, and how deintely was he handled to relive his conscience!

If your Grace wold have this for a president, that what so ever the Kinges Counsel, for the time of a princes minoryty, shall send to be preached, must nedes be receaved without allegacion, of what strength is the act of Parliament against the bishop of Rome? The Kings Majesty, when he commeth to his age, will looke to be bold to do asmuch with his subjects as his Counsel did in his minority; wherof the counsellors may be then wery. Presidents be daungerous; for I have sene it almost for a rule, that whatsoever hath ben once done, may then, without question, be don agayne. In our late soverayne lordes time I have sene the Counsell much astonied when the King would have don somwhat agaynst an act of Parliament. It was made then a great matter.

The Lord Cromwell had once put in the Kinges our late sovereigne lordes head to take upon him to have his will and pleasure regarded for a lawe; for that, he sayd, was to be a very kinge. And therupon I was called for at Hampton Court. And as the Lord Cromwel was very stout, 'Come on my Lord of Winchester,' quod he (for that conceat he had, what so ever he talked with me, he knewe ever as much as I, Greke or Laten and all), 'Aunswer the King here,' quod he, 'but speake plainly and direccly, and shrink not, man! Is not that,' quod he, 'that pleaseth the King, a lawe? Have ye not ther in the Civill Lawe,' quod he, '*quod principi placuit*, and so fourth?' quod he, 'I have somwhat forgotten it now.' I stode still and woundred in my mind to what conclusion this should tend. The King sawe me musing, and with ernest gentelnes sayd, 'Aunswere him whether it be so or no.' I would not aunswere my Lord Cromewell, but delivered my speache to the King, and tolde him I had red in dede of kings that had there will alwayes receaved for a lawe, but, I tolde him, the forme of his reigne, to make the lawes his wil, was more sure and quiet. 'And by thys forme of goverment ye be established,' quod I, 'and it is agreable with the nature of your people. If ye begin a new maner of policye, how it will frame, no man can tell; and how this frameth ye can tell; and ⟨I⟩ would never advise your Grace to leave a certeine for an uncerteine.' The King turned his back and left the matter after, til the Lord Cromwel turned the cat in the panne afore company, when he was angry with me, and charged me as though I had played his parte. This tale is trew, and not without purpose to be remembred, how I have ben tossed to and fro in this kind of matter.

Thus I have shewed your Grace the wole matter, with many mooe wordes then I entended in the entrie of my letter, and make now an ende, enforced by werines of my bodye, fed with close aire rather then meat, which my stomack desireth not.

Yet I must saye somwhat in the matter of 'onely faith,' wherin my Lorde of Caunterbury so much traveleth. First, it is sure he shall never prove that he would saie in that matter. But to make an ende of it, either I am a very foole in myne own conceat, whiche may easely be, or I see an occasion geven to your Grace to make suche a true determinacion in it as may bee honorable to youre Grace, the contentation of all the world, the preservacion of the Kynges honour that dead is, without prejudice of the act of Parliament, without derogation to my Lord of Caunterburies honour, without diminucion of the reputacion of the Counsell, and without any glory to the Bishop of Wynchester; whiche is, in some mennes conceat, the greatest matter of all that be yet rehersed. And in good faythe I would I were not, so al were well. Your Graces doing in Scotland is not, to my judgement, more to your Graces honoure then this would be; whiche God graunte, and your Grace mutche honour and felicitie. At the Fleete, the xiiij of October.

Your Graces humble beadman,

S. W.

Headed (in Foxe): S. VV. to the L. Protector.

    (*in B.N.*): Another letter sent from the saied Byshopp of Winchestre to the Lorde Protector.

NOTES TO NO. 130

Page 381. The earliest English edition of Erasmus' *Paraphrase upon the New Testament* in the B.M., or listed in Pollard and Redgrave, *Catalogue of English Books*, 1926, is that dated (Vol. I) 31 January, 1548 (1549 ?), and (Vol. II) 16 August, 1549. Since Gardiner quotes verbatim from the English version of the *Paraphrase* on Mt. xxii, and says 'I have the booke with me' (p. 384), it would seem that, unless there were an edition of at least a portion of it in 1547, he was using a manuscript copy.

The Injunctions of 1547 provided 'that every parson, vicar, curate, chantry-priest, and stipendiary, being under the degree of a bachelor of divinity, shall provide and have of his own, within three months after this visitation, the New Testament both in Latin and in English, with the Paraphrase upon the same of Erasmus, and diligently study the same, conferring the one with the other' (§ 20). 'Also, that they shall provide... within one twelve months next after the said visitation, the Paraphrasis of Erasmus also in English upon the Gospels, and the same set up in some convenient place within the said church that they have cure of, whereas their parishioners may most commodiously resort unto the same' (§ 7). *Cf.* p. 368 above.

Pages 382–3. Misquotation of Chrysostom. *See* p. 368, above.

Pages 385–7. The translator of the *Paraphrase*. From the prefaces to the first volume of the edition of 1548 (49) and to the books of which it is composed, we learn that Nicholas Udal translated the paraphrase on Luke and Thomas Key that on Mark. Udal says that he made corrections in that on Matthew and Acts but does not say who the translators were; he tells us that Princess Mary began the translation of the paraphrase on John, but that when she fell ill, it was completed by Dr Francis Malet. Miles Coverdale, John Olde, Leonard Coxe, and Edmond Alen appear to have been the translators of the second volume.

Page 388. Somerset's 'voyage' and 'honour' refer to his invasion of Scotland and victory at Pinkie; mentioned again on p. 400.

Page 390. Wolsey's praemunire. According to A. F. Pollard, *Wolsey*, 253 n., Gardiner, writing from recollection eighteen years after the event, mixed up the indictment in the King's Bench with the subsequent charges in Parliament.

Page 391. For proclamations against exporting corn *see* R. Steele, *Tudor and Stuart Proclamations*, Oxford, 1910, 1, Nos. 128, 248, 285. For the Act of Proclamations of 1539 *see ib.*, clxxxii ff.

Page 391. The Bishop of Exeter's praemunire. Thomas Winter, Cardinal Wolsey's son, received the archdeaconry of Cornwall in 1537, and immediately leased it to William Body, a layman in Cromwell's service. In 1541 Bishop Voysey's chancellor, Thomas Brerewood, and his principal registrar, John Croft, deprived Body of the archdeaconry. Body thereupon brought action against the Bishop and his deputies under the statute of praemunire. The deputies were convicted. *See* F. Rose-Troup, *Western Rebellion*, London, 1913, Chapter IV.

Page 392. The 'case of jewels' came up for frequent discussion between English and Imperial ambassadors in 1545–6. Jerome Kreckelman, goldsmith of Antwerp, and Gerard Vecman, having the King's safe-conduct, endeavoured to bring 8000 crowns' worth of jewellery into England, but it was seized at Calais by the King's officers. Suit was brought in the Exchequer, where judgment was given in favour of the seizure in 1544. *See L.P.*, xx, i, 337, 942, 1202, p. 586; ii, 906 (5); xxi, i, 8; and index of xx, xxi, under 'Jewels'.

Page 398. Gardiner's kinsman was probably Thomas Harding.

131. *To* SOMERSET

The Fleet, [27 October, 1547]

Foxe, *1563*, 743–6; ed. Pratt, vi, 46.

Cranmer hinted (on 7 October) that Gardiner would be readmitted to the Council if he conformed, but he cannot be so bribed; daily finds new faults in the *Paraphrase*; Erasmus laid the eggs and Luther hatched them; if he agreed with Cranmer on justification for the sake of preferment, would deserve to be hanged; is driven to do as he does by conscience; it is twenty days since he spoke with Cranmer and the hardships of his imprisonment continue; never gathered a faction; never advised Wriothesley, when Chancellor, on religious affairs; advised Somerset not to take sides in religion; Cranmer is entangling Somerset in religious matters; Henry VIII permitted free speech on any matter before it was made law; suspects many others share his religious views; is ready to answer Cranmer in writing; merry tale of the flea on Our Lady's head; justification should be discussed in the universities, not preached to the people; all are justified in baptism; Cranmer will have to resort to Papal methods to convince men of his views; has been overlong in the Fleet.

After my moste humble commendations to your good Grace: Synce the wryting of my last long letters to your good Grace, which as they weried me in writing, so thei have, I thinke, weried your Grace in reading, I have bene in great expectation to here somewhat from your Grace, of whose gentle and favourable minde towardes me I can not doubt, how so ever the declaration thereof at this tyme be hyndred by other by perswasions; wherwith although your Grace may be somwhat moved, I marvaile not. And therfore, whyles all thyng may be tried, do well satisfie my selfe, not mynding by any sute I have or shal make, otherwyse to presse your Grace then may be conveniently obtained of you in the state you nowe present. And yet sue I must, of congruence, for declaration of my humilitie, and also importunely sue, least I should be sene to contempne and to be entred into a melancoly, proudly to disdaine the world, which I assure your Grace I doo not, nor never hadde any suche fantasie; wherof they can be wytnes that have continually sene my behavour synce the death of our late soueraigne lorde, and since my comming to this pryson.

And yet my Lord of Caunterbury, when he sent for me last out of the Fleet, handled me with fayre wordes, declaring me a man mete in his opinion to be called to the Counsell againe; adding howe we (he sayd) did dayly chose in other that were not appointed by our late soveraigne lorde. They were worldly comfortable wordes, and as farre contrarious on the one syde as the Fleete is on the other syde. But I have not, I thanke God, that disceate whiche my Lord of Caunterbury thought to be in me, or would seme to thinke so, wherby to enduce other to thinke the same; as though I wer not moved to saye as I do for any zeale to the truthe, but of perverse frowardnes, as one that like⟨d⟩ not his estate and therfore cared not what became of him. The truth wherof to be otherwyse God knoweth; and I am hable to make to the worlde sufficient profe and testimonye of the contrary, if it be required.

First, as touching the booke of Paraphrasis, wherof I wrote to your Grace speciall faults, and other I have to shew as great as they, I trust; and doubt not the matter it selfe shall sufficiently declare that I have done well to speake against that booke, assuring your Grace that since my comming to prison, many dayes to gether when I looked on it, I sawe every day som new thing in such sort of fault as ought worthelye to condempne the worke. I have favored Erasmus name as much as any other, but I never studied over this booke til now, and now I aggre with them that said Erasmus laid the eggs and Luther hat⟨c⟩hed them; adding further that, of al the monstrous opinions that have arysen, evil men had a woundrous occasion ministred to them of that booke. And therfore I trust the matter of that booke will purge the evil opinion as might be gathered of me, wherin I offer to prove that I said with any learned man, ⟨under⟩ payne of shame and rebuke and to be taken for a malicolyke beast.

As for the booke of homelies, in that poynte where my Lord of Caunterbury would have taught how fayth excludeth charytye in the office of justyfieng, besides that my conscience is otherwise perswaded, and truly perswaded, it doth so touche me outwardlye in the world as, if I would ⟨agree⟩ for any intercession or request, upon offer to be a counsellore, or have as much more land as all the bishopes maye spend, I were worthy (for so agreing, for mede on the one syde, or dread on the other side) first to be whipped in every market towne in the realme,

403

and than hanged for example, as the veriest varlat that ever was bishop in any realme christned; unles my Lord of Caunterbury coulde shew me either Scripture that so sayd or some aunciente writer; wherin I desyre onlye to see but one, where commonly two be required in every matter. But because it is in a matter of only fayth, I requier but one auncient writer, wherby I cared not for my counscience, as some would have it perswaded, if I might excuse my selfe at least to the world, that I were not worthy to be whipped and hanged in all good mens judgements, and mine owne also.

And thys matter I write unto your Grace to declare unto you in what streyts I am tied inwardlye in my conscience by very truth, so I am tied outwardlye in the world with shame; wherby apereth that I resyst not this matter of a wilfull porpose, or that I like it not because I was not a ⟨*i.e.*, of⟩ Counsaylle—which wordes my Lord of Caunterbury used to me. For I am even driven to do as I do of necessyty, on bothe sides in my conscience, before God and the world abroad; wherof if I shew not your Grace such a profe as cannot be denied, let me be out of all credit in every thyng, and be accompted a lier, which I abhore a bove all faultes. Wherupon me semeth my case is myserable, to be so encombred as I am, and yet to be used as I were without cause obstinate, not withstanding al such circumstances as I have used to humble my selfe to learne and abyde. I yelde⟨d⟩ my selfe to be opposed at Oxford, that I might saie, yf I yelded, learning had overcome me. When that was refused, I offred my selfe to go to schole at home, whith offer to yeld to the truth. And although I have to maintayne me both the playne Scriptures, the doctors plaine, and the plain act of Parliament, yet, for conformitye, offred to my Lorde of Caunterbury to yeld if he could shew me one Scripture affirming fayth to exclude charitye in justification, or, Scripture failing, as it doeth in deade, to shewe me but on⟨e⟩ auncient writer that writeth so, with offer to yelde and geve place; which offer excludeth al stubbornes, and all evill opinion that might be conceaved of willfulnes in me.

It is nowe xx dayes ago sence I spake with my Lorde of Caunterbury, when the strongest arguments he made me were, to agre, with hope to be a counsalor agayne, or go to the Fleete from whence I came; for when I made requeste to the contrary, he sayd he had no such commission from the Counsaille. And so here I remayne, without baille or maineprise, wythout comforte of any of my frendes or servauntes, as one devided from the world, no chapleyne to accompany me in prayer, no barbere nor taylor for bodely necessyties, nor liberty to use phisytion for reliefe of dysease, wherof I have nede. And your Grace, who I thinke would shewe me reliefe (for I will never thinke want of good wil in you), is percase perswaded, by means, that I resiste the truth willfully, and that your Grace maye not in any wise shew me the leaste comforte in the world; for then no man shall rule me. And then your Grace that shewed so much favour to the Erle of Southhampton, late Chauncelor, wherin all the world commended your gentlenes—yf your Grace should now any wayes comfort me in prison with the least token of gentilnes, ye might be noted to favour Winchesters faction[1], as som terme it; wheras, I take God to record, I never joined my selfe with any man, nor have secretly encoraged any man to be of my opinion; and yet I have none other opinion but such as the Parliament hath established.

The Earle of Southampton did many thinges whiles he was Chauncelor touching religion, which mislyked me not, but yet did I never advise him so to do; ne made on him the more for it, when he had done. He was one of whome, by reson, I might have bene bolde, but I left him to his conscience. Therin I never said so much secretly to any noble man of the realme as I have to your Grace, at which time I advysed your Grace to be noted nether on the one syde ne the other. And your Grace hath for your selfe as good a name as can be. And I shall saye this without flattery, that like as chaunce very notablye hath advaunced your estate many degrees sence the time of my first acquaintaunce with you, so have you had occasion to shew your vertue, wherby to be thought worthy your estate; by meane wherof you cannot wish a more felicyty then ye have, to be the beginning of such an estate as ye shal leave, by Gods grace, to your posterytye. This is not altogether of mimater out ⟨i.e., out of my matter⟩, for what so ever becom of me, I woulde your Grace did wel.

Men be mortal, and dedes remaine, and me think my Lord of Caunterbury doth not wel to entaungle this ⟨i.e., thus⟩ your Grace with this matter of religion, and to borow of your autoryty the Fleet, the Marshalsea, and the Kinges Bench, with prisonment in his house, wherwith to cause men to agre to that it pleaseth him to call truth in religion, [2] leaving that he setteth furth, not[2] stablished by any lawe in the realme, but contrary to a law in the realme. At the least a law it is not yet; and before a lawe made, I have not sene suche a kinde of imprisonment as I sustain, humbly offering my self redy to lern. Our late soveraigne

1 *1563*, factions   2–2 ? *misprint for* seeing that he setteth furth is not

lord, whose soule God pardon, suffred every man to say his mynd without imprisonment, til the matter were established by lawe.

If my Lord of Canterbury hath the strength of Gods spirit, wyth such a learning in His lawes as he be able to overthrowe with that breath all untruthes and establish truthes, I wolde not desire the let of it by your Grace, ne the worke of Gods truth any way hindred. In which case, if al the realm be perswaded besides my self in this matter, it shal be easy for to reprove me in the face of al the worlde, and drive me to the ground with the sword of Godds Scrypture; which he shuld rather desire to doo, then to borowe the sword your Grace hath the rule of, wherewith to fear men; which is a meane to slaunder al that is don or shal be done, if men be prisoned before a law made. And I cannot beleve but there be more then I, or els I should not be kept so seacreat. For and ⟨*i.e.*, if⟩ all my folkes resorted to me and told me there were no reason to stand alone against all men, to undo them and my self also in this worlde, it were a greater temptation then my Lord of Canterbury made to put me in hope to be a counsailor againe.

Be your Grace assured, the foundation of my ground is a zele to the truth, although I have many worldy considerations to alledge for me, which serve to purge me of wilfulnes, whiche, I assure your Grace, is not my faulte. I will not trouble your Grace with all I coulde saye of my knowledge. What so ever my woordes be of my Lorde of Caunterbury, which the matter enforceth me to speke, I am in none enmity with his person, and that I am able to prove. But my Lord hath, in the homely of salvation, taken suche a matter in hande and so handled it as, if I were his extreame ennemy, I would have wished him to have taken that pece in hand and so handled it as he hath done. For that asseveration, how faithe excluded charity, can nether be proved by Scripture, ne confirmed by any aunciente wryter, or perswaded by any effectuall argument. And one argument my Lorde hathe devysed which he frameth thus: We be justified by faithe wythout all workes of the law. Charitye is a woorke of the law; ergo, we are justified without charitye. The aunswearing of which argument (which I can doo plainlye by autoritye) shall declare that ether my Lorde is deceyved him self, if he take it for a strong argument, when the opinion of his learning shalbe hindred, or if he use it willingly, knowing the fault in it, the lacke is greater a nother way. But the answer to that argumente dissolveth all the matter, wherunto I have an answer made xij. c ⟨1200⟩ yeres bypast, which I wil of my pearil shewe, if my Lord wil avow it for his argument. And if my

Lord wil send me the argument of his hand, I wil send him thanswer of my hand, wherby shal shortly appeare whether I trifle or no.

In the latter end of my last letter to your Grace I spake of a determination, wherof I wished your Grace were author. For wearines of wryting I did not open what I ment in specialty; entendinge now to beginne in the middle of this sorow with a merye tale, but a verye true tale, and not unmete to be rehearsed. Thus it hapned: Certain doctors of devinity at Paris, mindyng with utteraunce of some learning, wher of the⟨y⟩ had store, to requite a gentleman that hadd bidden them to dinner—using a preface, that as he had fed them with bodely meat they wold fede him with spiritual foode—proponed thys question to be disputed amongst them: Whether the asse that caried Our Lady and Christ, when Josephe fledde with them into Egipt, when it caried Our Ladye onlye with Christ in her lappe, caried then as perfecte a burthen as when it caried Our Lady with Christe on her lappe and a flee sittinge on her head. Herein the doctors were in great earnest, and many hote argumentes were betwene them in the matter, with muche spence of language, whether Oure Ladye alone with Christe in her lappe were as perfecte a burthen as Oure Ladye and Christe with a flee upon Our Ladies head. The audyence, which was learned, was wel cheared with laughinge, but other edification the matter hadde not. And it maye be laughed at, whenso ever it is told, to see in what trifles many menne spend their time.

And nowe I shall saye that whiche is straunge at the fyrste readinge, but it is true. The matter of justificatyon, wyth 'onlye faythe justifieth,' and whether faith excludeth charitye in justification, perteineth no more to the use and practise of oure Churche of Englande, althoughe in knowledge it be a grave matter, then the triflinge question I rehearsed perteined to the hearers edification in good livinge. I besche your Grace to know howe I put a difference betwene use and knowledge. The knowledge of justification, as I have said, is, in learninge, of more waighte, and such as, for the entreating of it, manye have wepte even here at home, besides those that have wepte in Germanye; but the use and practise of it is no more necessary in the state of the Church of England then is the handlinge of the other question. And for anye use in the Churche, the one may be forborne as well as the other, considerynge the baptisme of infantes is so duely observed; in which sacrament of baptisme all we be justified before we can talke of this justification we strive for. And unlesse the Church leave the use to christen infantes, which shal not be, there cannot be a time in which the knowledge of the justification we strive for can be practised. But all men shall, as we all readye have, receive their justification in baptisme in their infancy. So as the doctrin of 'only faith justifieth,' if it were true, as the homely declareth, it is no more necessary for the present state of the Church then to know whether the burthen of Our Lady and Christ only were as perfect as the burthen of Our Lady and Christe with a flee sittinge upon Our Ladies heade, whyche the solempne doctors of Paris so earnestlye entreated.

Some wil say I am waxed madde in pryson to compare these two together. But as I compare them for use and practise, the one is as necessarye as the other. And[1] I was bolde to use the mearye example to imprynte the matter the better in your Graces memory. For it is as I saye, when we have all talked; for we all are justified in baptisme ⟨as⟩ yonglinges, and, fallinge after baptisme, we muste arise by the sacrament of penaunce; which must be confessed of all men, unles they be suche as denye all sacraments, as some have done in deede, wadynge so farre in the siftinge of 'onlye faythe' that they have lefte nothinge but faythe alone, and yet spente a greate deale of their faith in the handling of it, or rather all. And that is a generall faulte I fynde, that suche as wryte in that matter doo not handle it faithfullye in alledging the doctors and Scryptures ryghte as they be. Nowe if thys be true that I have wrytten (whyche is true in dede), were it not an honorable[2] part of you to say, 'Whye trouble ye the worlde for a thing not necessarye?' And so put it from the countrye, and make it, as it were, a Checker Chamber case; and so to be sente to the universityes, for whome it is meete soberlye to talke, and not for homelies, where in the people shall here that they shall never practyse because they learne it to late, beinge justifyed before in their infancye in baptisme.

My Lorde of Caunterburye tolde me his intent is onlye to sette out the fredome of Goddes mercye, whiche maye be doone muche more plainlye with puttinge the people in remembraunce of the constante receyved faithe of the Churche in the baptisme of infantes; whereby suche as be justified and saved in the vertue of Christes Passion, as after baptisme by malyce fall not to synne[3], those must retourn to Christe by penaunce, but suche as die before that actual sinne hathe defyled theyr soule agayn, if they die in the innocencye received in baptisme, be salved. And yet those children, when they were christened, did

---

1 *1563 adds* as   2 *an emendation of* horrible
3 *1563 adds* and

nothinge but crye for colde, or when they were over harde griped for feare of fallynge. And when this is beleved, is not Goddes mercye beleved to be ministred after a mooste free liberall sorte, if my Lorde of Caunterburye mynde onlye that the matter shall appear with oute argument, as we practise justification in receiving the sacrament of baptisme? And as for justification by only faith, ⟨it⟩ is al out of use, how so ever we expounde it, as the state of the Church is now.

And it is a terrible matter to thinke on, to see suche a contentyon to ryse uppon a matter not necessarye to be spoken of; wherin if my Lorde of Caunterbury wyl neades travayle, my judgement is that he shall never perswade that faithe excludeth charity in justifycation, unlesse he borowe, of your Graces autoritye, prysonnes; and then he shall percase have some agree unto it, as poore men kneale at Rome when the byshop there goeth by; that is to saye, knocketh on the heade with a halbarde, if he knele not; for that is one pece of thoffice of the byshop of Romes gard.

Finally, there hath bene nothing don but your Grace may use it to thaugmentation of your honor. I have things mo to say, but this matter is over long alredy, and me thinkes I have bene overlong here; and, shewing myself so humble a scoller as I have done, it is much to be beaten because I do not lern wher no man teacheth me; and so willing to learn as I ask but one Scripture, or, Scripture failing, as it dothe for my Lord of Canterburies purpose, I ask but one auncient doctor.

This is my case; for as touching any act of disobedience, my Lords of the Counsel did forsee that I shuld not fall in that danger, and therfore wold not trust my frailty to be in the country when the visitors shuld be there, but made me sure here, least I might have offended, if I had bene there; though I had but a few words to speak, that is to say, 'Saving Gods lawes and the Kinges'; yet they might have ben misreported, and so engendred me more trouble. And this good I have of my being here. Which I suffer paciently, and make it so serve for my purpose in my conceat, as I thanke God I have no displeasure of mind, and only fele such as the body engendreth for want of som necessaries; wherof if I may have relief at your Graces hand, I wil accept it as thankfully as any man hath any benefit at your hand, and as instantly require it of you. And yet, if I have no other comfort from your Grace then I have hetherto had, I wil think nevertheles as wel of your Grace as ever I did, and be only sory that, in the state you be in, the liberty of doing that your hart wold perswade you, should be as straitly enclosed with respects as my body is with walles[1]. Thus desiringe your Grace to take in good part mi bold wryting to you, I shal make ⟨an end⟩, and pray Almighty God for the preservation of your person, with encrease of honor and felicity. At the Flete, or rather in the Flete.

Your Graces humble beadman,

S. W.

Headed: To the Lorde Protector.

132. *To* SOMERSET

[The Fleet, shortly after 4 November, 1547]

Foxe, *1563*, 748; ed. Pratt, VI, 53.

Is imprisoned without cause; sues to be permitted to attend Parliament (which opened 4 November).

After my moost humble commendations to your good Grace: I am verye lothe, knowing your Graces businesse, to trouble you wyth manye letters. And yet, not hearynge from youre Grace anye thyng for aunswere to mine other letters before wrytten, I am so bold to wryte these, wherwith to put your Grace in remembraunce of mine estate in prison, as one dissevered from the use of his servauntes and frendes, and, as it were, buryed quicke; without knowledge of anye just cause wherfore, and with knowledge, by course of time, that nowe the Parliamente is be- gonne, wherof I am a member, unles my fault had cut me of; and wher- unto I was called by wrytte, which I received before my comming hether; where I would also gladly do my duetye, as I am bounden, if I were not deteined and bounden in prison from my liberty that I might so doo. Whiche allegacion I make the rather to your Grace, to the in- tent, with the opening of a necessary sute worthy to be regarded, I myght minister occasion to your Grace, wherupon to shew such gentle- nes to me as, of your own gentle hart, I am perswaded, your Grace

1 *an emendation of* wakes

410

gladly would; for whose preservation with encrease of honor, I shal praye to Almightye God; Who have your Grace in his tuition.

Your Graces humble beadman,

S. W.

Headed: To the Lord Protector.

133. To SOMERSET

[The Fleet, 12 November, 1547]

Foxe, *1563*, 748–9; ed. Pratt, VI, 54. A sixteenth-century manuscript copy of the first twelve lines is in B.M., Add. 28,571, 14 v.

> Has asked for a physician in vain; has been seven weeks saving one day in jail; his stomach nippeth him; deserves thanks for pointing out the faults in the *Paraphrase*; what it will cost the realm; knows of no better method of making the faults of *Paraphrase* and *Homilies* known than that which he used.

After my moost humble commendations to your good Grace: In my thirde letters I signified unto[1] your Grace my neade of the counsaile of a phisition, as the state of my body then required; wherunto because I had no answer, I have[2] used al other meanes of reliefe that I could, to avoide that neade, as one lothe to trouble your Grace with requests not necessary. Master Warden [3]of the Flete[3] and my servaunts know that I faine not, and I [4]have cause to[4] feare[5] the effect wil shewe[6] I fayne not in dede. In this[7] case I may not desperatly forbeare to wryte to your Grace, and thinke that because I have[8] had no[9] aunswer to all mine other letters, among[10] which I made mention of this necessity, that I shuld likewise have[11] none answer to this. As I have determined my self to a truthe in the chefe matters[12], so I eschue to use simulation in bimatters. My mynde, I thanke God, was never so quiet as ⟨it⟩ hathe bene sence my comming hether, which hath relieved my body much, but the bodye hathe nead of other relief, which cannot be had, as I am kept by commaundement.

These vij wekes, saving one daye, I have bene here under suche

1 *B.M.*, to   2 *not in B.M.*   3–3 *not in B.M.*

4–4 *not in B.M.*   5 *B.M. adds* that   6 *B.M. adds* that

7 *B.M.*, which   8 *not in B.M.*   9 *B.M.*, none

10 *B.M.*, amongest   11 *B.M. adds* nowe   12 *end of B.M.*

straite kepinge as I have spoken with no man. And thus me seemeth I se my matter perplexed: your Grace wil meddle with nothing done before your comminge home; and those of the Counsaile that sent me hether canne by them selves doo nothing, nowe your Grace is commen home. Uppon whiche consideration I sue to non of them, and perceave that your Grace, to whome I sue, for some respecte forbeareth to make me aunswer. For suche a paraphrasis I make of your Graces silence, wherin I go nea⟨r⟩ ⟨*i.e.*, nearer⟩, as I thinke, the truthe then Erasmus in hys Paraphrasis sometime, wherin he taketh upon him to gesse the causes of Christes doings.

I thancke God my minde can take no hurte, how vehement so ever these temptations be. But when a certen secte of philosophers, called Stoikes, contemned in their learning stoutly the grefe and disease of the body, they were faine a litle to shrinke when the goute or any disease nipped them. And now my stomak nippeth me, which I have favored as muche as any man in England, and have laden it as light, eyther with meate or drincke, of many yeres, and specially since my comming hether, as any other. And after I sawe I coulde get no aunswere from your Grace for a phisicion, I have lefte of suche studye as I used, and geven my selfe to continuall walkinge for exercise; and, with hope of relief, have delaide anye farther sute in that matter til now. And now I sue enforced, which I do most humbly, with request that imprison-ment—being to me, that was never in prison before, of it self tedious—be not with special commaundement made more grevous, onlesse I were charged with other offence then I am yet charged with, or in my con-science can be.

For me semeth I have deserved thanckes of your Grace and the realm for the disclosinge of the faultes of the Paraphrasis, wherin I have wrytten some specialties, but not al; and have such to shew as I may terme that boke at one woord, 'abhomination,' bothe for the malice and untruthe of muche matter out of Erasmus penne, and also the arrogant ignorancy of the translator into English, considering the booke shoulde be authorised by a king, and, by the injunctions, charge the realme for bying rather above xx.m ⟨20,000⟩ pound then under; wherof I have made accompte by estimate of the nomber of biers and the price of the whole bokes. The translator sheweth him self ignoraunt in Latten and Englishe, a manne farre unmete to meddle with such a matter, and not without malice on his part; wherby your Grace maye take an argumente, what moved them that counselled your Grace to authorise suche a booke in the realme. As for my Lorde of Caunterburies homelye of saluatyon, ⟨it⟩ hath as manye faultes as I have beene weekes in pryson, whyche be vij, besides the generall, that the matter maketh a troble without necessity, and is handled contrary to the teaching of the Parliament.

Finally, in the ij bokes the matter I have to shew is some part so dangerus, as, after I knew it as I know it, the concealment therof wer a greate faulte, if I did not utter it. As for the maner of mine enterprise to utter it, I know not howe to have fashioned it better then to wryte to the Counsell in your absence, and on my knees to declare some parte of it, when I came to them. Receiving their determination of imprisonment, I humbly departed from them hether without grudge, and remain here wythout grudge to any one of them, for they shewed no fashion of any evil minde towardes me. And I have learned in the Civil Lawe that the dede of a nomber is no one mans act, with this also, the autority is to be honored; which rule I observe in thought, woord, and deede. After which sort I remain, with such sutes as I have made to your Grace hetherto, and with this also that I adde, enforced for the relief of my body how litle so ever I do and have cause to set by it; which I most humblye desire your Grace to consider, and to sende me some aunswer by this bearer. And I shal praye Almightye God for the preservation of your Graces felicitye.   Your Graces humble beadman,

⟨S. W.⟩

Headed (*in Foxe*): To the Lord Protector.
(*in B.M.*): A letter to the Lorde Protector owt of the Fleet.

134. *To* Somerset

[The Fleet, between 12 and 20 November, 1547]

Foxe, *1563*, 747; ed. Pratt, VI, 53.

Asks that his chaplain be permitted to visit him. (Since this volume has been set up the editor has concluded that No. 134 was written after No. 135.)

After my most humble commendations to youre good Grace: Whatsoever your Graces considerations be, not to hear me yet nor answer me, and howe so ever I determine and do beare pacientlye the state I am nowe in, reason, neverthelesse, bindeth me to continue my sute, that if your Grace seeth at any time occasion to chaunge your determination, there shall nothing want on my behalf to provoke your Grace so to do. He that is refused at one time may be hard at another, and importunity spedeth when none other mean can prevail; being also a fault in the inferior to dispaier of the superior in so reasonable a request as mine is, which I cannot doo of your Grace for other respectes. I have remained here longe unharde of your Grace, enclosed up more closely, nowe close religions[1] be begon, then ever were anye whiles they were here. No straunger maye speake with me. I cannot have the companye of my chaplaine, whych is necessary for me after so long time. And if your Grace hath no leasure to hear me shortlye, I trust you wil, without delay, suffer my chaplayn to resort unto me, aswell as of your gentlenes ye have suffred the phisition for my body to come to me; for the whyche I most humblye thanke your Grace. Here in I desire your Grace to aunswer me by this bearer, that I maye have some comfort from you; for whose preservation I shall pray to Almighty god.

Your Graces humble beadman,

S. W.

Headed: To the Lord Protector.

135. *To* SOMERSET

The Fleet, [between 12 and 20 November, 1547]

The first third of a sixteenth-century manuscript copy of this letter is in B.N., Latin 6051, 48 r. and v., the remainder of the same copy in B.M., Add. 28,571, 13 r.–14 v. Foxe, *1563*, 803–4; ed. Pratt, VI, 140. The manuscript copy is here used as the basic text. Foxe is cited in the footnotes as F.

Has received Somerset's letter; blames not the Council for his imprisonment, but pleads not guilty; knows that Somerset is not the author of everything in his letter; if not a good Christian, Gardiner is at least a good Englishman; never knew of anyone imprisoned for disagreeing with a doctrine not established by law; has learned that the world is vanity; explains his reference to Somerset's advancement as 'chance' (p. 405); would give his life to prevent the *Paraphrase* from coming into use; desires to be heard.

After my most humble commendations to your good Grace: This day I received your Graces letteres with many sentences in them, wherof in

1 *1563*, religious

414

some I take muche comforte, and [1]specially for the[1] sendinge of a phisition; and for the rest that myght greve me[2], doe so understand them as they greve me not at all. If I have donne amisse, the fault is mine; and I perceve your Grace would not be greved with me onlesse I had offended.

As for the Counsell, I contend not with ther doinnges, no more then he that pleadethe 'not giltie' dothe blame the judge and queste that hathe endyted him and enquirethe[3] on hym. I knowledge authoritie; I honour them and speke reverently of them; and yet, yf my conscience so tellethe me, I must plead 'not giltie,' as I am not giltie of this impresonment. And so must I say, onelesse I would accuse my selfe wrongfully. For I entended ever well; and[4] howe soever I have writen or spoken, I have spoken as I thought. And I have spoken it where I shuld speake it in place; at which time I was sory of your Graces absence, unto whom I had used like bouldnes, the rather upon[5] warrantize of your Graces letteres[6]. But I have writen truthe without any affection other then to the truthe, and would[7] answere the partycularities of your Graces letters[8] shortly, were it not that I will not contend with your Graces letters; unto whom I wrote simplie, for no suche purpose[9] as they bee[10] taken, not by your Grace, but by[11] others. For I trust your Grace will not require of me to beleefe that all the contentes of your Graces letters[12] proceed specially from your selfe. And in the meanetime I can flatter my selfe other wise then to take them so. Wherupon yf it shall [13]be further replied[13] unto me that I doe your Grace wronge, beinge in the place ye represent, not to take your Graces letters as thoughe every[14] sillable were of your Graces devise, beinge your hand sett to them, I will be sorie for it.

Thus I take the sume of your Graces writinge: that I shuld not for any respect withstand trewthe. And of that conformitie I am. And to agree ageynst the truthe can doe your Grace no pleasure. For truthe will continewe, and untruthe can not endure; in[15] discerninge wherof, yf I erre, and when all the rest were agreed (yf that were so) I onlye then

1–1 *F.*, especially in
3 *F.*, requireth
5 *B.N. adds* your, *not in F.*
7 *F.*, could
9 *F.*, purposes
11 *supplied by F.*
13–13 *F.*, further be applied
15 *F. adds* the

2 *supplied by F.*
4 *not in F.*
6 *F.*, letter
8 *F.*, letter
10 *B.N.*, by; *F.*, bee
12 *F.*, letter
14 *F.*, very

can not agree, yet I am out of the case of hatred. For I say as I thinke; and yf I thinke like a fole and can not say otherwise, then it shall be accompted as my punyshment and I to be rekened emongest[1] the indurate, who neverthelesse hertofore had used my selfe, when no man empeched me for religion, as frende to frendes. And although I were not (as it is of[2] some nowe thought) a goode Christen man, yet I was none[3] evill civill man. And your Grace, at our beinge with thEmperour, had ever experience of me that I was a good English man.

Nowe I perceve I am noted to have ij faultes: one, not to like Erasmus Paraphrasis; an other, not to like my Lord of Canturbyries homilie of salvation. Herin yf I mislike that all the realme likethe, and when I have benne harde speke in open audience what I can say, can shewe no good[4] cause of my so doinge, or els it can not [5]be so taken, it shuld yet[5] be taken for no wonder, seinge the like hathe benne seene heretofore. And thoughe your Grace will be sorie for it, I am[6] sure ye[7] will love me never the worse; for I adventure as muche as any man hathe donne to save my conscience. And I doe it, yf it may be so taken, in the best facion I can devise. For I accuse not the Counsell, whom I confesse ought to be honored. And yet[8] it is not always necessarie [9]that those[9] which be committed by the Counsell to prisonne [10]doe evermore[10] appeare giltie. For then shuld every prisoner yelde giltie for[11] avoydinge[12] contention with the Counsell.

And howe soever your Grace be enformed, I never gave advise, ne ever[13] knewe man commytted to prisonne for disagreinge to any doctrine onelesse the same doctrine [14]had benne[14] established by a lawe of the realme before. And yet nowe it myght be that the Counsell, in your Graces absence, fearinge all thinges as rulers doe in a common wealthe, myght, upon a cause to them suspected and without any blame, commytt me to prisonne; with whom I have not stryven in yt, but humbly declared the matter with myne innocency, as one who never had conference in this matter with any man but suche as came to me; and with them this[15]: to will them to say nothinge. Because I thought my selfe,

1 *F.*, emong 2 *supplied by F.* 3 *F.*, no
4 *not in F.* 5–5 *F.*, so be taken, yet shuld it
6 *end of B.N. and beginning of B.M.* 7 *F.*, you
8 *supplied by F.* 9–9 *F.*, for those; *B.M.*, that these
10–10 *F.*, ever more to 11 *F. adds* the
12 *F. adds of* 13 *F.*, never
14–14 *F.*, were 15 *F.*, thus

yf I spake, would speeke temperatly, and I mistrusted other; beinge verye lothe of any other[1] troble to ensewe in your Graces absence, and specially suche absence as I feared in vayne (thankes be to God!) as the successe hathe shewed; but not altogether without cause, seinge warre is daungerouse in the common sense of man, and the straunger ⟨*i.e.*, stronger⟩ hathe hadd evermore the victorie.

I alleage in my letteres to your Grace worldly respectes, to avoyde worldly reasons ageynst me. But I make not my fundacion of them. The world is mere vanytie, which I may learne in myne owen case, beinge nowe destitute of all suche helpe as frindshipp, [2]as service, as fameliaritie, as[2] gentlenese semed to have gotten me[3] in this worlde. And yf I had traveled my witte in considerations[4] of it since I came hither, as I thanke God I have not, it myghte have made me past reasoninge or this time.

I reserve to my selfe a good opinion of your Grace, beinge nothinge diminished by theis letteres; in remembraunce of whose avauncement to honoure, when[5] I spake of chaunce, yf I spake ethnycallie, as [6]it is[6] termed in your Graces letters, then is the Englishe Paraphrasis[7] to be condemned for that cause, besides al other, wherin that worde 'chaunce' is over commen in my judgment. And[8] yet, writinge to your Grace, I would not, beinge in this case, counterfayte an holynes in writynge otherwise then my speache hathe benne hertofore, to call all that comethe[9] to passe Goddes doinges; without whose worke and permission nothinge in deed is, and from whom is all vertue; and yet in common speache, wherin I have benne brought uppe, the name 'fortune' and 'chaunce' hathe benne used to be spoken in thadvauncement to nobilitie, and commended when vertue is joyned to[10] it. Wherin me thinkethe it is greater prayse and more rare, to adde vertue to fortune as your Grace hathe donne, then to have vertue goe before fortune; which I wrotte not to flatter your Grace, but to put you in remembraunce what a thinge it were, if[11] bearinge in hande of suche as myght have credite with you shuld cause you to enterprise that which indyrectly myght worke that your Grace mindethe not, and, by errour in a ver-

---

1 *not in F.*
3 *supplied by F.*
5 *B.M.*, whom; *F.*, when
7 *F.*, Paraphrase
9 *F.*, comes
11 *B.M.*, in; *F.*, with; if *would seem to be the necessary word*

2–2 *F.*, service, familiaritie, or
4 *F.*, consideration
6–6 *F.*, you
8 *B.M. adds* I, *not in F.*
10 *F.*, with

tuous pretense to the trewthe, avaunce that which is not trewthe; wherin I aske no further credite then that I cane shewe shall perswade; which is one of the matters I kept in store to shewe ageynst the Paraphrasis, entendinge onely to say truthe, withe sute to be hard, and instante request rather to be used to utter that I cane say then to be here wasted after this sorte.

I can tell[1] a great deale, and a great deale further then I have written to your Grace; and yet am so assured of that I have alreadye written as I knowe I can not [2]be therin convinced[2] of untruthe. As for Erasmus himselfe, I wrote unto your Grace what he writethe in his later dayes onely to shewe you the man throughly. And in speakinge of the state of the Churche in his old dayes, ⟨he⟩ dothe not so muche further the byshoppe of Romes mattere[3] as he did in his yonge daies, beinge wanton; which Paraphrasis[4], if I can, with spense of my life, lett from goinnge abroade, I shall[5] have donne as good a deed, in mine opinion, as ever was donne in this realme in the lett of an enterprise. In which booke I am nowe so well learned, and can shewe the matters I shall alleage so planelye, as I feare no reproche in my so doinge. And as for thEnglishe, eyther my Lorde of Cante⟨rbury⟩ shall say for hys defence that he hathe not read over thEnglishe, or confesse more of him selfe then I will charge him with. Therfore I call that the faulte of inferior ministers whom my Lorde trusteth. The matter it selfe is over farr out of the way, and the translatinge also. In a longe worke, as your Grace towchethe, a slumbre is pardonable, but this translator was a sleppe when he began, havinge suche faultes.

I can not nowe writte longe lettres thoughe I would. But, to conclud, I thinke ther was never man had more plane, evident matter to alleage then I have, without winches or argumentes or devises of witt. I meane planely, and am furnished with plane matter, entendinge onely planenesse; and, destitute of all maner[6] helpe, suche as the worlde in mans jud⟨g⟩ment shuld ministre, make my foundation onely upon the trewthe, which to here, servethe for your Graces purpose towardes God and the world also. And, beinge that I shall say treuthe in deede and apparaunte, I doubte not your Grace will regarde it accordinglye. For that will onely manteyne that your Grace hathe attayned. That will uphold all thinges and prosper all enterprises. Wherin, yf I may have libertie to

1 *not in F.*
3 *F.*, matters
5 *not in F.*

2–2 *F.*, therein be convicted
4 *F.*, Paraphrase
6 *F.*, mans

shewe that I knowe, I shall gladlye doe it, and otherwise abide that by
authoritie shalbe determined of me as patiently and quietly as ever did
man; continuinge your Graces bedman duringe my life unto Almyghtie
God; Who have your Grace in his tuicion. In the Fleet the[1]

Headed: A letter to the Lord Protector, out of the Fleete.

136. *To* SOMERSET

The Fleet, [*c*. 20 November, 1547]

Foxe, *1563*, 746–7; ed. Pratt, VI, 51.

Used to write merry tales to Henry VIII; cannot now play the pope-holy to
Somerset; faith and charity join in justification, as do Parliament and the King
in law making; ambassadors are commended for discovering faults in their
instructions; he is an ambassador sent to bring sound doctrine to his flock,
and should be praised for discovering faults in the *Paraphrase* and *Homilies*;
it is incredible that Somerset should authorize a book tending to subvert the
royal power; Erasmus might well have written to please Singleton the conspirator; has been here eight weeks, but let not Cranmer think he will wax
mad.

After my most humble commendations to your good Grace: Upon trust
that your Grace wold take my letters in good part and not otherwise
then I wrote them, I wrot to your Grace out of this prison as I was wont
to wryte to our late soveraign lord, whose soul God pardon, when I
was ambassador, refreshing my self somtime with a mery tale in a sad
mater; which his Highnes ever passed over without displesure, as I
trust your Grace wil do the semblable. For though some accompt me a
Papist, yet I cannot play the pope holy, as thold term was. I dare not use
that severity in wryting whyche my cause requireth: to speak of God
and his truth in ⟨e⟩very second sentence, and become sodenly a prophet
to your Grace, with a new phrase of spech, with whom I have ben
heretofore so familierly conversant.

As I think honor hath not altered your Graces nature, even so adversity hath not changed mine. Of your high place in the common
welth no man is more glad then I, nor no man shal doo his duety further
then I to acknowledge you, as your Grace is now, protector and
governor of the realme. But I have bene so traded to speak boldly that

1 *B.M. ends here; F. adds,* day of the moneth, etc.

I cannot chaunge my manor now, when percase it doth me no good. And althoughe here be an Italian in prisonne with me, in whom I se a like folly, who, living with a litle, miserably, wil not for his honour take almes, fansing to be stil in the state he was somtime; which maner I condempne in hym, yet I folow him thus far, rather to wryte after my old maner, which cometh plainly to minde, then to take almes and aid of eloquence, wherof I have, in this estate, nede. For your Graces letters returne every woorde of my letters in my neck, and take my flie as it wer a bee, whiche I thought shuld have stong no man; which matter, in mirth, declareth the necessity of thother matter as aptly as may be, nether to be necessarye. And when I wrote, I forgate, as my fellowe prisoner the Italien doothe, the state I am in now; and wrote as I had wrytten from Andwarp in the state of ambassade. The Italian my companion hath his follye of nature, and I have it of custome in bringing up, whiche hath theffect of nature and is called of learned men a nother nature. And then the proverbe of gentlenes hath place, when men say to him that is offended, 'You must bear with the mans nature'; and so I trust you wil do with me.

Two things ther be in your Graces letter whiche I trust I may touch with out contention. One is, that if your Grace will, in a playn similitude, se thissue of 'fayth only' and whether fayth may exclude charyty in the office of justifyeng or not, it may be wel resembled in the making of lawes in this Parliament, wher the actes be passed by three estates, which be al thre present and do somwhat to gether and concurre to the perfecting of the law; wherin we may not saie that any one estate only made the lawe, or that any one estate excludeth the other in the offyce of making the law. Thys maye be sayde, that these thre estates only, in respecte of the rest of the realme, make the law; and there nead no mo of the realme be present but they. But if we speake of these three estates wythin them selves, there is none estate only that maketh the lawe. But where the law hath as it were a body and a soul, the high house and the low house of the Parliament make, as it wer, the body of the law, which lieth, as it were, a dead matter, such as is not apte to take life til the Kings Majesty hath, by the breath of his mouth, saying, *le Roy le veult*, breathed a full life into it in the conclusion. Besides the life, the assemblye of the other estates hadde by his autority to assemble[1], whiche had els bene a dead assemblye[2], even as faith and hope be dead without

1 *1563*, assemblie   2 *1563*, assemble

charity. And as the Kings Majesty, in this similitude of making lawes, excludeth not in office of the whole the other two estates, no more doo the estates, because they devise and frame lawes, exclude the Kings Majesty in the office of making lawes. For withoute his autority they be nothing, as faith and hope be withoute charitye not effettuall. And looke, what absurdity and untruth this saying hathe in this realme, to saye the higher house and the lower house exclude the King in the office of making of lawes, the same absurdity is yet in religion to say that faithe excludeth charitye in the office of justification. And therfore it was never wrytten of auncient wryter. And therfore I desired my Lord of Canterbury to shewe me but one, and yet ⟨he⟩ cannot. In our time this dreame hath bene dreamed without Scripture, without autority, against Scripture, and against autorite, as I can shew; and further can shew how this imagination extendeth so farre by them that open their minde in it throughly, as your Grace woulde not at the firste beleve, if I did expresse it. But I can shew that I faine not evidently, as clearly for my discharge as I coulde wysh.

An other matter of your Graces leters is, wher your Grace reasoneth with me that I am over precise in finding of faultes in the Paraphrasis, seing every boke hathe some faultes. And then your Grace taketh not Erasmus for a Gospell, but as one in whome somwhat maye be reprehended or amended. After which maner of sort, if your Grace take the homelies (as, for like reason, in my judgemente they muste ⟨be taken⟩, for they be mennes compositions as the Paraphrasis is, and not the very Gospel it self), why should I be kept in prison, who offred to receive the homelies and Erasmus both, so far as they were not without fault either of Gods law or of the Kings?

Because I saw therrors before and spake of them, I have made more spede to prysonne then other have done, who percase, for troubling of their conscience, have received the bokes close, with such reverence as becometh men to receive that is sent from their prince; wherin I would have done as they did, if I had not sene the bokes before. But I did as I have seene divers noble men do (and among them, as I remember, your Grace), when they have bene[1] sente in service, to have used such diligence as to se their commission and instructions made or they went, and, finding somthing doubtful or amisse, after the commissyon was sealed and instructyons signed, worthy to be amended, have, upon de-

1 *1563*, beinge

claration of their minde therin, obtained amendmente with commendation. Nowe I have a charge in the bishopricke of Winchester, to se the people fed with wholesome doctrin; wherin if I be so diligent as to loke upon the commission, and, consydering what I shalbe charged wyth to do, take this or that for a fault in my judgement and labor to have it amended, wherin differ I from other mens diligence? And how can it be taken for a fault to say reverentlye to the Counsail, 'My Lords, me semeth this and this cannot stand togethers, ether instruct me in them, or amend them'? In what nature of crime shuld this humility be? Am I worthy for so saying to be condemned to a perpetual prison, and to be a close prisoner; to speke with no man, to here from no man, to talk with no man; for my houshold, which is a great nombre, ⟨to be⟩ wandring and lamenting for me? My case shuld be in the nature of praise, in the nature of commendation, in the nature of thancks, if none other have said that I can say. If one only man in a realme sayth he knoweth treason to subvert the whole realme and can shew evident profe of his so sayinge, shall he be prisoned because of good wil he offreth to saye and prove that no man els uttereth but he; and therwith offreth to prove that he sayeth to be true?

It is incredible that a king shuld set forth a boke tending to the subversion of hys owne estate, and therfore that I shal say cannot touch his Majesty, who knoweth not what is done, as reason judgeth, in his tender age. It is also incredible that your Grace, being uncle to him, shuld be content that any boke shuld be setforth that might tend to the subversion of his estate. And I dare say for your Grace, you wold not. If the boke be lyke the horse that the Troyans receyved into their citye, where in the Troyans knewe not what was in it, lette me be harde that knowe what is in it, and so know it as I can shew it as evidently as I can the sonne and the mone in bright daies and bright nightes, when both shine.

I do not trifle with my wit to undoo my selfe, but travel with mine honestye to preserve my country, to preserve my prince, to preserve religion. And this your Grace shal find to be true; which, knowing my letters to be construed to the extremity, I wold not wryte unles I were furnished with matter to discharge my wryting.

Your Grace, I doubte not, remembreth Singletons conspiracye. And Erasmus hathe framed his doctrin as though Singleton had required him therunto. I have such matter to shewe as though I had my self devised it for my justification. And yet I am reasoned with as thoughe one geven to let good doctrine, to finde a knot in a rushe, to trouble good enterprises; after whych sort your Grace is moved to wryte unto me; and therupon I remain here stil, wythoute hearing, having such matter to utter as shal confound them al; which I woulde not wryte, if I were not assured. For it were a smal plesure to me, wryting thus extremely, to be confounded when I had bene hard, and then worthely sent hether again for lying so manifestly; whyche I wold thinke a worthy punishment, as thys is unworthye—to be handled as I am for vertue, that I dare say the truth, can declare the abhomination of this Paraphrasis, and of the homely also; in both whiche matters, I have shewed al I can shew. I shal declare I am not worthy to be kept here, and yet here I have remayned this viij wekes, without speking with ani man saving my phisition, who, I thank your Grace, hath done me good. And yet when men se I am thus banished from the world, so as no manne may speake with me, it is not pleasant for any man to resort unto me, and that I perceive.

If my Lord of Canterbury think I wil wax mad, he is deceived; for I waxe every day better learned then other, and finde every day somewhat to impugne the Paraphrasis and homelies, not by wit or devise or other subtilty, but plain sensible matter, if I may be hard. And if I be not hard, my conscience telleth me I have done my duety, and therwith from travaile shall applye my self to prayer; wherin I shal remember the prosperous estate of your Grace, whom God preserve. In the Flete.

S. W.

Headed: To the Lord Protector.

NOTES TO NO. 136

Page 420. For Gardiner's embassy to the Imperial Court at Antwerp, 1545, *see* above, pp. 146 ff., 197 ff.

Page 422. Singleton's conspiracy. Foxe (iii, 367; v, 600) tells us that 'one Singleton, chaplain sometime to Queen Anne Bullen,' who was unjustly charged with the murder of Robert Packington, mercer of London (13 November, 1536—Wriothesley, *Chronicle*, i, 59), later in the reign of Henry VIII 'suffered as a traitor' for stirring up 'sedition and commotion,' although he 'did but preach the Gospel.' A Robert Singleton, priest, apparently one of Cromwell's agents in 1536, appears in *L.P.*, x, 612, 640, and the same or another of like name in *ib.* (1538),

XIII, i, 819; ii, 1192. In 1543 a Robert Syngleton recanted at Paul's Cross, along with Robert Wisdom and Thomas Becon (Foxe, v, App. XII), and a Shingulton is mentioned in connection with the heresy examinations of that year in Kent (*L.P.*, XVIII, ii, p. 359). Foxe (v, 696) names the Singleton who recanted in a list of those who 'recanted in King Henry's time, and yet good soldiers after in the Church of Christ.' Mr J. Gairdner takes Singleton the agent of Cromwell, Singleton the conspirator, and Singleton who recanted to be one and the same man (*Lollardy*, II, 382). He also suggests that perhaps he is to be identified with one Shengleton, arrested in the spring of 1553 (*ib.*, III, 372); but if Foxe is correct in saying that the conspirator suffered as a traitor under Henry VIII, this would be, obviously, impossible.

137. *To* SOMERSET

The Fleet, [after 20? November, 1547]

Foxe, *1563*, 748; ed. Pratt, VI, 53.

Why is he not heard? is it to keep him, and those he appoints to the lower house, from Parliament? Asks audience with Somerset; if Henry VIII was seduced, perhaps Somerset has been seduced too.

After my moost humble commendations to your good Grace; I cannot discusse by conjecture whye evidence is thus put of in my case, that hath bene wont commonly to be graunted to all men. If it should be of anye man through polecy to kepe me from the Parliament, it were good to be remembred whether mine absence from the upper house, with the absence of those I have used to name in the nether house, wil not engender more cause of objection, if oportunitye serve hereafter, then my[1] presence with such as I should appoynte were there; the signification wherof is the chefe cause of these letters, for as I am now encombred with being here, so might some be encombred therwith hereafter; which should doo me pleasure.

My matter that I have to saye toucheth the highest, and is worthye to be harde; wherunto my Lord of Canterbury can onlye answer that he wold never have thoughte it, or that he hathe bene otherwise enformed of them he put in trust. For it wold touch hym overmuch to graunt he had so much knowledge in the Paraphrasis as I nowe have, and knowing

1 *1563*, any

424

the same to have advised your Grace to set it forth to the people, I can say much whyche is expedient for your Grace to hear and consyder; desiring only this credit of your Grace, to thinke me worthy to be hard, and therupon geve me audience. I cannot enchaunt men, ne loke not to be beleved in the matter, unlesse it be so plain as no man can gainsay it, and therin the boke to be judge. The nature of my cause shuld move your Grace, my long imprisonment shuld move your Grace, the present assemblye of learned men shuld move your Grace to celebrate mine audience. And if your Grace knew what I could say of the long letters your Grace sent, good faith! your Grace wold make so much the more spede. For wheras the purpose of youre Grace in these letters is to alter my judgement, the handlinge of the matters is such as I am able to shewe good cause why they shoulde, as they do, work a contrary effect; as I am able to declare, if ever I com to your presence.

My lord of Caunterbury wil nedes maintain that our late sovereign lord was seduced; and then it is possible that your Grace may be seduced also; and therfore it is good for your Grace to heare and to hear in time. Whatsoever I have wrytten to your Grace is true, and I have not wrytten all the specialties I knowe in the greatest matters, which your Grace shal perceive to be true. I se evidently that unlesse my matter be very notable and also plain, it shal not bote ⟨*i.e.*, boot⟩ me to alledge it. Thus muche I am learned by your Graces letters, and therfore if I had any cause to mistrust it, I wold use a nother mean, wherof in your Graces letters I se some comfort; but my matter is so plain and so expedient to be understande, that I must neades desyre your Grace to be hard in it, wherin it mai like you to send me knowledge of your pleasure, and that my sute to your Grace may stand in some stead, for whose preservation in honor I shall dailye praye to Almightye God, Who preserve your Grace. In the Fleete.

Your Graces humble beadman,

S. W.

Headed: To the Lord Protector.

138. *To* SOMERSET

[The Fleet, *c.* 4 December, 1547]

Camb. Univ. Lib., Ee. 2. 12, 154 v.–155 v. Sixteenth- or early seventeenth-century copy.

> All who share his views are not in prison; cannot believe that Somerset either will not or cannot help him; Somerset needs no indirect means to maintain himself; it seems as if it were hoped he died in jail; has been here ten weeks though he has never willingly broken any law; why does Cranmer fear him? he must fear truth; asks to be heard in the presence of the bishops. (The reference to Cranmer tempting him is to the interview of 7 October—*see* Nos. 130–1.)

After my most humble comendacions to youer good Grace: I cannot tell what to wryte, nor howe to hold my peace in so just a cawse. Oft suyte implyeth contempt; suyte not received engendreth matter of dispayre. There is cawse whye I should be hard ⟨*i.e.*, heard⟩, and there can no policie counterveyle by usinge of me after this sorte. Many knowe my cawse, and I am not singler as I am borne in hand. Everye man is not in prison that is of my judgement; whiche will sone apere when I am harde speake. I beare all thinges pacientlye (thankes be to God), and yet sorye I am to suffre this under youer aucthoritie. Hit were harde to saye whiche were more lamentable, to thinke youer Grace would not helpe me, or, in such case as myne is, ye could not helpe me. The one I cannot thinke, that youer Grace would not helpe me, seinge that in one acte ye might satisfye both frendeship and justice; and the other excedeth the capacitie of myne understandinge, to thinke youer Grace so entangled with other, as that you should be enforced to beare with theim in the continuance of my punyshment. Yt were more expedient for me to remayne here quietlye then to be abrode in travayle; and dishonour is not in suffringe, what so ever I suffre. But in good faith, I wishe well to youer Grace, with whom I had familiaritie when this matter was not thought on; and am nowe sorye to se youer Grace troubled with other mens enterprices.

The realme hath of the Kynge⟨s⟩ Majesties person the greatest juell that ever had realme—a most certeyn undoubtid kinge as ever realme had, who nedeth for his mayntenaunce no by meanes. Youer Grace is his uncle, most certainlye knowen, a person thought mete for this estate you enjoye, without nede of any matier indirectlye to be compassed for youer assuraunce. God is all trueth, and of him selff able to advaunce that is trew, and to confounde that is untr[ew], without any such devise as is used to shut me up this secretlye, that I should not be hearde sp[eake]. Hit shalbe a discharge for youer Grace to let everye man beare his owne faulte, and to suffer the faulte to [be] found where the faulte is.

I remaine here as though it were said to me, 'Dye yf thou wilt, for thoug[h] who regardeth thee, or what becometh of thee, or who shalbe so bould to talke of thy case?' The ma[ner] of my handlynge signifieth this unto me; and the deedes speake without sound of wordes. For here [I] have continued x wekes without beinge herde, savinge when my Lorde of Canterburie tempted [me] without all learninge. If all other reasons faile, let tyme persuade whiche reapeth all thinges! And [x] wekes be thought a longe tyme to kepe such a one as I am in close prison without hearinge, how[e] so ever it hath ben required and suyde for on my behalff. And when I thus saye such one as I am, [I] bringe to youer remembraunce all the circumstances of me, who never offended any lawe of this r[ealme] willinglye, was never in suyte with anye, and at this tyme in enmitie with none. Other thinges I will no[t name], for what I am and have ben, it is well knowen; whiche is the greatest greef of my beinge here, where I [find] in my selff no privie displeasure nor torment of mynde with any of thes matiers, who ⟨*i.e.,* how⟩ so ever I write [unto] youer Grace; to whom I wishe all hono*u*r and prosperitie, who, as I may perceive by youer letter written unto [me], is not directlie handled where ye seme to trust. And I knowe myne owne conscience, howe well I mynde towardes you. Wherfore lett me be heard, my Lorde, and forget not in any cawse that ye were wont to say generallye, if he were a devill you wold have him harde.

Shall I be taken for an orato*u*r that can turne and tosse the trewith as I lust, and can not persuade to youer Grace that I should be herde? I cannot have a better matter then I have, wherein, if I can do no good, why should my Lorde of Canterburie so feare me, as he doth, that he may not suffer me to come abrode, as one that should hinder his enter-prices, when he saith my eloquence (if I have any) standeth me in no stede? There will no man be so mad to say as I saye, to do me pleasure, whom they se out of all aucthoritie, whiche in wordlye ⟨*i.e.,* worldly⟩ thinges is the ground of doinge pleasure. He that feareth me must feare onlye trewith. That is in dede lyke as the palme tree that beareth towardes the borden upwarde and from it dounward, as other woodes do.

Eftsones I require youer Grace to here me in the presens of the rest of the bisshopps, either to be there approved or disproved as matier shall enforce, whiche onelye must helpe me when all other thinges faile. I write ymportunelye, but without dispaire of youer Grace, what so ever have passed heitherto; for whose prosperitie I shall daylye pray to All-mightie God, Who send you encrease of honour.

Headed: A copie of a letter written by Stephene Gardener, Bisshope of Winchester, prisoner in the Tower of London to the Lorde Pro-tectors Grace. ⟨The letter is obviously from the Fleet.⟩

139. *To* SOMERSET

[The Fleet?]

B.M., Lansdowne 980, 154 v.–155 r., Bishop Kennet's (1660–1728) notes on Gardiner. A marginal note refers to the manuscript collections of Dr N[athaniel] Johnston (1627–1705), as, presumably, the source of these admonitions.

Advises restraint.

i. Take not all that you can, nor doe all that you maye, for there is no greater danger in a noble man then to let slip the raines of his lust, and not to be able to refraine them with the stronge bit of reason.

ii. Let not ambition entangle your minde, for her nature is to over-throwe herself, etc.

Headed: Admonitions written by Stephen Gardyner, Bishop of Winchester, prisoner in the Tower, to the Duke of Somerset, Pro-tector of K. Ed. VI and his Dominions. ⟨If authentic, they are more likely to have been written from the Fleet than the Tower.⟩

INTRODUCTORY NOTE TO NOS. 140–4

Gardiner was released from the Fleet by a general pardon, 7 January, 1548, two weeks after the end of the session of Parliament which had repealed the acts on which he had based his legal objections to the *Homilies.* He was asked by the Council to subscribe certain articles on justification (not extant), which he refused to do, on the ground that they had as yet no official sanction. He was, therefore, committed prisoner to his own house in Southwark in the Liberty of the Clink, 19 January, where he remained till 20 February, when his answer (not extant), involving a qualified agreement with the articles, was accepted, and he was permitted to retire to Winchester. Nos. 140–1, written while at Southwark, have to do with his answer to the articles on justification. No. 142 describes some of the difficulties he had to contend with at Winchester. (*See also* App. 3 for another matter which disturbed him at this time.)

On 1 April the Council summoned him to appear within a fortnight to answer to a report that his servants had been 'kindlinge upe of the peoples mindes againste thinges sette foreth by the Kinges Majestes authoritie' (Dasent, II, 550). He pleaded illness and was excused from appearing. Whereupon he thanked Somerset for accepting his excuse, and expressed his commendation of some of Somerset's statements concerning religious policy (No. 143).

Early in May he completed his third book against Bucer, which was not, however, published till 1554 (*see* No. 144).

140. *To* SOMERSET

[Southwark, between 19 January and 20 February, 1548]

B.M., Add. 28,571, 15 v.–16 v. Sixteenth-century copy, incomplete (?).

Cannot subscribe articles on justification since they attribute sayings to the Fathers which are not in the Fathers; tells what learned contemporaries he is acquainted with.

After my most humble commendacions to your good Grace: It hath pleased you, wherfore I most humbly thanke you, that I shuld to morrow repare unto[1] But I can heare of no bodie to common with me, which, as I understand, your Grace determined shuld be done before. And if I be now unlerned, as I am noted, how can I affirme so muche as lerned men have affirmed, unles I have that lerning shewed me that moved them? Tharticles in some pointes make report of doctors to say this and that, which I by my selfe can not fynd in the doctors. If they have found yt, let them shew it me; or if no man wil vouche sauf to come to me, let the places be signified unto me. But for me to affirme by my subscription to know eny thing which in dede I know not, but onelie by heare say, besydes the danger to God, me thinketh the world wold be sclandered in yt. If a number of men of reputacion affirme any thing for trew, I thinke yt not expedient to impugne their saing openlie; and eny one man to advaunt hym selfe as thogh he were Micheas and knew that all other knew not, I wold not allow yt, nor be my selfe occation of suche a sclander, but go to scole and lerne till I knowe as muche as they know, and have sene that they have sene, that I may affirme as they affirme. As Scripture sayth every man muste professe, and yet if I desyre to have yt showed me where and in what place the Scripture so saeth, yt hath bene ever used to tell the place. In these articles all myne ignorance is in doctors reportes, what they write, what they say; and wold se the places, and aske but to se one ancient doctor to say as tharticles say. And then is it an easy matter for me to affirme that one so to say, or, leaving the name of doctors owt, subscribe the saying.

Your Grace of your goodness willed me to remembre my selfe, and so I do, not wasting my tyme with grudge or melancholie, but, thinking quietlie of the matter, bicause no man cummeth to me, tosse and turne by my selfe suche bokes as I have, which be a good numbre, to see whether I can fynde alone that no man will tell me where I shall fynd. Which I beseche your Grace to consider, and to conceyve non other opinion of me then you have done, as I trust of your goodness ye will not. It pleased your Grace to ⟨hear me⟩ report my conformitie in wurdes to you, which your Grace then acceptyd, and my maner and behaviour shalbe suche as no man shall have justlie to say the contrarie. And therin can no wordly ⟨*i.e.*, worldly⟩ thing tempt me so muche as you to be noted a sclandre in your governament. Besydes my dewtie of allegiance, no man is more bound to desyre our soveragne lordes prosperous save-

<hr>

[1] *no blank in MS.*

gard then I, wherunto I know discord to be an enemy; and with your Grace and your familie have had speciall acquaintance, whose honour I do accompt myne owne commoditie.

And to make your Grace a planer reconing that I am not factiows, bicause your Grace asked me upon myne allegiance with how many I had conference, I will upon myne allegiance open the matter plainlie, how many lerned men I know, and how often to my remembra[nce] I have spoken with them my selfe. First I know in Cambridge but too by name, that is to say, Redman and Bill, and if there be any other that lurketh, I spake not with them theise xx yeres, and besides them, in all other lerninges, yonge and old, I know not six in all the towne. In Oxford I know Doctor Smyth, Doctor Weston, Doctor Coole, and Master Oglethorpe, and an other whose name I know not, but hard hym ones preache at Winchester. Withowt the universities I know Doctor Cockes, Doctor Robinson, Doctor Crome, the Deanes of Exiter, Westminster, and Powles, Layton thArchedeacon of London, with Edgeworth and Marshall, and these be all thacquaintance I have in England, which be in all but ⟨*blank*⟩ persons.

Headed: A letter from the Bishop of Winchester to the Lord Protector from the Clynke.

141. *To* SOMERSET

Southwark, [between 19 January and 20 February, 1548]

B.M., Add. 28,571, 9 v.–10 v. Sixteenth-century copy.

His chaplain (Thomas Watson—*see* Foxe, VI, 205–6) has heard from Thomas Smith (Clerk of the Council) that Somerset thinks he ought no longer be detained; has written to and conferred with Bishop Ridley; nine days ago sent Somerset his subscription (*i.e.*, a qualified acceptance of the articles on justification—*see* p. 429, above); desires to go to his house in Hampshire. (In B.M., Add. 28,571, 15 v. there is a copy of a note from Cecil to Gardiner, 20 February, 1548, expressing Somerset's thanks for Gardiner's 'conformitie in parte.')

After my most humble commendacions to your god Grace: For answere to my last letters to your Grace, Master Smyth by mowth shewed my chaplyn that your Grace thoght not reasonable to deteyne me thus, if nothing cold be shewed, as I had signified trewlie to your Grace ther can not. Which your Graces answere ⟨I⟩ estemed, as of reason I oght, very reasonable. Wherupon I sent my chaplyn againe to my Lord of

Rochester with more matter from me to shew the contrary of that my Lord of Canterbury wold have; and nether is ther falte found in any thing that I write, ne any thing shewed me in any ancient writers to the contrarie of that I say. So, with all myne humilitie to make my selfe a scholer, I remayne still in correction, as thogh I wold not lerne. And my scholemasters, bicause they can shew me nothing, give them selfe to other matters and let me alone. And now this is the ninth day sithens I sent your Grace my subscription. And my Lord of Canterbury is at Croydon, and my Lord of Rochester, as I told hym merlie had commission to treate with me, but not to conclude. He might grate of me and he cold with reasoning, but in no wise in any point yeild. Which maner of commission I have had in my dayes in other matters.

In the meane tyme, I want my libertie, which is the most preciowse thing that this life hathe; which, in effect, greveth more other men then me, suche as for their own commoditie wold speake with me and may not. And, as I heare say, your Grace removeth shortlie hence, and within a while after goeth into Hamshire, where, if I might se your Grace at my pore howse, yt wold comfort me more than all this turmoyle hath greved me. And yet this grefe the matter hath, to be noted contr[a]riows and contentiows, where in dede I am not. And yet the matter hath ben so sett forth to your Grace as thogh I were. Which is a good preservative to retaine suche opinion of your Grace and other of my Lordes as I am glad to continew.

And if your Grace will now give me licence to repare to my howse in Hampshire, being here now like a stranger withowt any provision, I shall take yt for a great benefite and remayne your Graces bedeman, entending to give almost as straite a commandement to my selfe, for medling with the world, as your Grace gave me at this tyme in thordre to kepe my howse. Herein I most humbly desire your Grace to know sumwhat of your pleasure, that I may facion my self accordinglie, sending herewith my chaplyn, who can instructe your Grace of all circumstances with my Lord of Rochester, if you shalle thinke good to heare hym. Thus leaving of to trowble your Grace with any lenger letter, I shall abyde your gracious and favorable answere, and continew your daly bedeman to Almighty God, Who have your Grace in His tuition. At my howse in Southwarke.

Headed: Another letter sent from the said Bishop of Winchester to the Lord Protector.

142. *To* Somerset

Wolvesey (at Winchester), [*c.* middle of] March, [1548]

B.M., Add. 28,571, 10 v.–12 r. Sixteenth-century copy.

> Somerset's brother (Thomas Seymour) can tell him of the troublesome be-
> haviour of John Philpot, which is described; never suffers his servants to
> brawl; a vicar in Winchester keeps a wife but Gardiner can do nothing about
> it. (The 'pulling down of the Banke' refers to the suppression of the stews
> on the Bankside in Southwark in 1546—*see L.P.*, XXI, i, 592; J. Stow, *Survey
> of London*, ed. C. L. Kingsford, Oxford, 1908, II, 54–5. The Bankside was
> within Winchester diocese and near the bishop's palace, hence, apparently,
> the phrase 'Winchester marriages.')

After my humble commendacions to your good Grace: For asmuche as
yt liked your brother at his repaire to London to offre hym selfe to deliver these letters to your Grace, as yt became not me to require yt of
hym, so cold I not refuse his gentlenes in this behalfe, who ⟨can speake⟩
of his owne knowlege, for that he hym selfe can declare to your Grace
the behavior of Philpot; with whom, knowing hym as I do, I am not yet
so infect by the contagion of speaking with hym as I shuld also be so
entred in madnes as to contend with hym upon any opinion in religion.
Your Grace, like my good Lord, semeth to feare to heare of my disordre.
But those fewe that wold be noted myne adversaries here be so few and
of suche sorte so vexed in them self, as I contend onely with them both
with good wurdes[1] and good dedes, to tame them that thay might heare
and do reasonably. And as none of them can charge me with any evill
word or any evill dede, so can I prove that I have used but gentle wurdes
towardes them, and preserved them, and delivered them by meane from
the trowble they had broght them selfes in, by their wurdes and disordre, not to me, but to other. Which mattier happined but one day
before, in the presence of your Graces brother, that some of them went
from some of them to your Grace to complayne of me.

Amonge my gentle wordes I told in dede Philpot that I wold ex-
comunicate hym, not for any opinion of his wherin I shuld contend
with hym, for that he wold wishe, but bicause withowt any occation
given of me, being called for other purpose by suche as had charge of
the musters, he untrewlie reported my sermond made a fortnight before, in suche matter as I thinke no man wold thinke to be my trade of

1 *MS.*, wurkes

433

teaching. One was, that if men had their eye upon God, all their wurkes were free; an other, that Christen men be bownd to obeye the Turkes lawes; which fondnes I never dreamed. And when he alleged an honest gentleman in the towne that day at diner to have taken my sermond so, the same gentleman, being sent for, before your brother incontinent and many other gentlemen mo then present, said in dede that at the diner that day Philpot so reported of my sermond to hym, but he knew that I taght not so, and rehersed my sermond very roundlie; whose saings your brother and other that hard my sermond affirmed. Wherupon they blamed Philpot of his untrewth, whereof he was ther convinced by the gentilman whose testimonie ⟨he⟩ alleged, and their awne knowlege also, who detested hym somuche the more, that he had made an untrew accusacion of an other preacher a lytill before, and perceyved he went abowt to inveigle men to say as he said, to the danger of trowble of all preachers.

In this communication, Master Cooke, in whose howse Philpot sojorneth, required Philpot to forbeare his howse from thenceforth, which was a more grevous excomunication then that I spoke of, as I declared yt. For when I had offered Philpot to forgive all gently, so he wold knowlege his fault, and yet cold get nothing of hym, I told hym in dede that if he came to my sermond the Sonday folowing, I wold tell hym his falte before all the audience. And if he did not there yeild, wheare all they cold be judges whether he misreported and sclandered my doctrine or no, he shuld not remaine there to heare me, but I wold, for his open fault, exclude hym that companye, which was thexcomunication I speake of. But he feared more thexcluding from his hostes howse then myne exclusion owt of the churche. The practize wherof on my partye towardes hym, I dare say he wold gladlie have sene, and therefor the Sunday folowing he presented hym selfe to me at my sermond before all men so galyandly as he may say he made me eate my worde, and that my excomunication toke no more effect then his hostes exclution; for he saw that nether wold do as we said. And I thinke in dede that Cooke had respectes that moved hym, as I had also that moved me. For I thinke not good for any purpose to contend with Philpot, but rather use hym in suffering hys contempt, and be put in remembrance therby of the state of this present lif, therin to have experience as well to be contemned somtyme of the lowest, as at other tymes to be honored of the best. But with Philpot I have none other matter nor will not. He will nedes call hym selfe heretique and therfore I blamed hym gentely, but no man will call hym so againe that I know. For my selfe, I call hym onelie unlerned and it angreth hym more then any other name I can call hym.

As for my servantes, ⟨they⟩ know so my condicions to detest quarelinge as they dare not aventure yt. For in them I punishe that fact without examination of the cause. For I take no cause sufficient to manteine a quarel. And let them brawle in the world that mislike their estate, wherby bye trowble they may percase thinke to wynne. All quiet serveth better my purpose, who do not mislike myne owne estate, the preservacion wher of I loke for at your Graces hand under the King, by quiet observacion of the lawes and peace, which my mennes troble or quarell can onely hynder. Upon which conclusion, I care for quiet onelie and wold passe all thing as quietly as I might. And yet here is a vicar in this towne, that bicause yt liked hym to call a woman his wife, he will kepe her as his wife, and therwith minister also. And I wold have hym bring me a testimonyall that she is a wife to hym, that is to say, in forme of the Churche maried, or els preistes shuld have more libertie in their mariage then any other have, and use Winchester mariages suche as were hindered in pulling down of the Banke at London; but herein I can do no good.

And thus these matters stand, like as your brother can declare to your Grace; as, for the good zele he hath to quiet, he offered hym selfe most gently to do. And thus forbearing to trowble your Grace any lenger with these matters, I shall pray Almighti God for preservation of your Grace in long felicitie. At Wolsey the ⟨*blank*⟩ of Marche.

Headed: Another letter sent to the Lord Protector from the said Bishop of Winchester.

143. *To* SOMERSET

[Winchester, early in April, 1548]

B.M., Add. 28,571, 9 r.–9 v. Sixteenth-century copy.

His illness is not feigned; Somerset may learn as much about him—as did Henry VIII—from his own mouth, as from any other; commends Somerset's saying that he would not favour novel interpretations of Scripture or condemn the religion of other countries; is no dissembler.

After my humble commendacions to your good Grace: These shalbe to give like thankes to the same, that it liked you so to consider myne

435

excuse, which is indede unfayned and the first that ever I maid these xvij yeres to delay to do as I was commanded, for any impediment in my body, which I wold now gladlie have wanted, to have purged my selfe, as myn have done, with your Graces favor. For your Grace may be assured no man can charge me with breach of any law, proclamation, or commandement, what so ever hath ben otherwise noysed.

I am at the point with your Grace now in the tyme of your autoritie that I was at with our late soveraigne lord, whose sowle God pardon, which was this: that he knew as muche by me hym selfe of myne owne declaration to hym as any other cold tell hym of me. Folowing which trade, I opened my selfe plainlie unto your Grace in your gallery at my departure, towching the Blessed Sacrament and the Masse, wherin it like[d] you very graciowslie to heare me, muche to my satisfaction. For I perceyved in you onely a generall determination to have the trewth prevaile. Too speciall sentences I have noted, uttered of your Grace; one of wisdome, an other of policie. Of wisdome, that how so ever the wordes of Scripture sounded to your eares, ye wold not take upon you to enterprete them, but rather conside[r] how they have bein ever understanded hither[to]. Thother sentence of policie was, that ye wold not condemne other contries; which clause, as your Grace shewed me, was by your meane put in to thact of Parliament for the Communion. Which ij pointes of wisdome and policie I shall pray God your Grace may follow, withowt further medling my selfe then to shew my conscience, and to shew it as I shuld shew yt, not like a mycher or with murmor, but quietlie and in place, withowt dissimulacion, when I shalbe required or necessitie enforce me.

And what so ever opinion I have given men occasion, by myne owtwarde life, to conceive of me, I trust to declare in effect that I esteme my conscience above any other thing, and shall as faithfully shew your Grace the trewth in these mattiers, as my lerning and conscience telleth me, as any other; wherin I have and do as muche travale also as any other, with lesse frute percace, but for the proportion of my capacitie. And as ther is no man that for many respectes wisheth your Grace better successe in all your enterprises then I do, so shall there no man in his manour and behaviour openlie and secretlie use hym selfe like a more humble, quiet subject in all pointes then I shall do, what so ever tailes shalbe fained or devised of me to the contrarie, only to inquiet and molest me, as in dede they do not for my selfe, but onely for other, who by occasion therof use me for a tale and speke they wot not what. No man is withowt faulte, but yt shall never be tried that I deceaved your expectacion. I wil have no suche maner of fault to be doble of wurd or in behavior a dissembler. Thus much I have thoght necessarie to signifie unto your Grace till I may come, which if I cold do, I wold not now write, as knoweth Almightie God, Who send your Grace long felicitie.

Headed: A letter from the Bishop of Winchester to the Lord Protector.

144. *To the* READER

[Winchester], 7 May, 1548

From *Exetasis testimoniorum, quae Martinus Bucerus ex Sanctis Patribus non sancte edidit, ut patrocinetur opinioni de caelibatus dono, quam sine dono spiritus, contra Ecclesiam defendit orthodoxam.* Louvain, 1554.

Has scrupulously used the Fathers, while Bucer has profanely misused them. (*Cf.* Nos. 67, 97, App. 2, p. 489. The volume to which this letter is a preface was sent to the printer in 1548, but, owing to Gardiner's imprisonment in the Tower shortly after, was withheld from publication till after his release, lest it cause him further trouble.)

Steph. VVinton. Episcopus Anglus, Candido Lectori S.

Quod a me factum iri Bucerus (opinor) non sperabat, et ut facerem tamen, rogavit obnixe, id si non plene praestiti, Lector, voluntatem certe et conatum videbis non defuisse. Etenim expendi, excussi, tractavi testimonia Patrum cum religione, quibus non est veritus Bucerus abuti prophane, hoc est, e veritatis penu, malo more deprompta, ad mendacii

Stephen of Winchester, English Bishop, to the Impartial Reader, Greeting

Reader, if I have not completely accomplished what I suspect Bucer was hoping I would not undertake, and yet demanded insistently that I should, surely you will see that I have neither lacked the will to do so nor failed to make the attempt. For I have pondered, I have searched, I have scrupulously handled the testimonies of the Fathers, which Bucer has not feared profanely to misuse; that is, to apply them, when taken wickedly from the storehouse of the truth, to the use of falsehood

usum et vanitatis pastum, accommodare. Ego quidem operam a Bucero rogatam adhibui cum fide, nullam hoc nomine ab eo initurus gratiam quam non promereor, sed officio satisfacturus meo, ne veritati per calumniam laboranti desim. Tu Lector, sine acceptione personarum, veritati fave, et Vale. Nonis Maiis Anno Domini MDXLVIII.

---

and the feeding of vanity. I, indeed, have conscientiously expended the effort demanded by Bucer, not, on this count, to gain favour from him, which I do not merit, but to fulfil my duty, lest I fail the truth, now in distress through calumny. Do you, Reader, befriend the truth without respect of persons, and farewell. The nones of May, in the year of our Lord, 1548.

INTRODUCTORY NOTE TO NOS. 145–54

Gardiner was again summoned by the Council in May 1548, and, on appearing before them (26 May), was told to tarry about London. Soon after he was asked to preach before the King, which he did on St Peter's Day, 29 June. The next day he was sent to the Tower. The single extant letter during the remainder of Somerset's rule is the fine, brief appeal for justice written early in November, 1548 (No. 145).

Almost a year later, on 12 October, 1549, Warwick seized the government and sent Somerset to the Tower two days later. He was aided in this *coup* by Wriothesley and other conservatives in the expectation of a Catholic revival; hence Gardiner wrote hopefully to Warwick (No. 146) and shortly thereafter sent three appeals to the Council (Nos. 147–9).

That much of his time in the Tower was spent in literary composition is evidenced by the six volumes of theological controversy he there produced. To four of them he wrote prefatory letters (Nos. 150–4). Perhaps the most interesting of these is that to his book against Cranmer, which appears in two totally different forms, one prefixed to a manuscript copy of the work, the other to the printed edition. This enables us to compare what he wrote when first stirred to answer the Archbishop, and what, on mature consideration, he thought wise to publish (Nos. 151–2).

145. *To* SOMERSET

[The Tower, *c.* 3 November, 1548]

In Gardiner's *Long Matter* (Article 43), presented by him in his defence at his trial, in Foxe, *1563*, 786; ed. Pratt, VI, 111.

> Demands justice; his imprisonment is without all form of law; can justify his St Peter's Day sermon. (Gardiner, in his *Long Matter*, prefaces this letter with these words: 'After xviij wekes imprisonment, the sayd Bishop, to provoke the sayd Duke to heare him speake, delivered to Maister Leiuetenant ⟨of the Tower⟩ the sayd folowinge, to be delyvered to the sayd Duke in thys forme conteined.')

The Bushop of Winchester maketh moste instant sute to have the benifyte of the lawes of the realme like an Englishman, and not to be cast in prison without baile or mayneprise, with out accusation or indictment, without calling to any presence to be charged with anye thinge; and so to remayne theise xviij wekes, and could have no reliefe to knowe what is ment with him.

As for his sermon, he made it by commaundement to prech there, wherein he sayd nothing but his conscience serveth him to justify his doings therein by Gods lawe and the lawes of the realme, the Kings proclamacions, the Kyngs commandement, my Lord Protectors open letters, and not agaynst his privy leters, the suerte of the Kings estate, the quietnes of this realm, the discharge of his duety to the Kinges Majesty, the rememberaunce of the kindnes of the Kinges Majesty that dead is—the declaracion truly to be made of him self, in eche of these points.

I doubt not to justify my doings if I maye be hard, and have the inheritaunce of an Englyshman, to be used by course of law.

Gardiner, in his *Long Matter*, adds, 'which nevertheles was not hard nor regarded.'

146. *To* WARWICK

The Tower, 18 October, [1549]

C.C.C.C., MS. 127, 117–8. Sixteenth-century copy, in Parker Collection.

Rejoices that Warwick has overthrown Somerset's tyranny; has been in the Tower over a year and a quarter; asks a hearing; is grateful to Warwick for the preservation of his life. (The reference to Warwick in Norfolk is to his suppression of the insurrection there in the summer of 1549.)

After my most harty commendacions to your good Lordship: I have gret cause to rejoyce and geve thankes tAmyghty God, that it hathe pleased Him to geve your Lordship the honnour to be such a meane for the relief of the captivitie and thrauldam[1] of this realme from the tyrannouse governement of the Duke of Somerset, the delyveraunce of the Kinges Majesties noble personne from gret daunger (which God longe preserve), and the socoure of suche as for want of justice have suffred moche wrong. Amonges whom I am oon of the most notable; who have remayned here miserably in prysonne above oon yere and a

1 *MS.*, thraudlam

440

quarter, without cause or colour of cause to be in this prysonne, and deteyned as injustely as they wer whom your Lordeship delyvered in Norfolk from the malice of certan of the commons.

And after that sorte entende I to sue for my delyveraunce, whenne, by your Lordships good meanes, I may be harde accordinge to justice; which is and hathe been myn oonly sute hitherto, and hitherto not regarded, but the secret destruction of my body oonly entended; in the withstandinge and lettinge wherof, howmoche I have been and am bounde to your Lordship, I knowe and wyll acknowlege whyles I lyve. And ther was never good lovinge sonne bare better affection to his naturall father, by whose meane, under God, he receyved life, thenne I shall be⟨re⟩ to your Lordship for the meane your Lordship hathe been, under God, for the preservacion of my life, and accompte youe in that place towardes me dueryng my lyfe; most hartely desyring your Lordship to have that opinion and estimacion of me, wherin you shall never be deceyved; by the grace of Almighty God, Who preserve and encreace your honour, with continual felicite. At the Tower, the xviij^th of Octobr.

Endorsed: A letter to my Lorde of Warwycke.

147. *To the* PRIVY COUNCIL

The Tower, [October, 1549]

C.C.C.C., MS. 127, 121. Sixteenth-century copy, in Parker Collection. Postscript only.

Complains of treatment by the Lieutenant of the Tower and asks an examination of it.

Post scripta: It maye like your Lordships tunderstande that I was not more extremely kepte when I was at the worst in the tyme of tyranne, whenne Master Lieutenaunt excused his doyng by commaundement of the chief ruler, thenne I am nowe in the tyme of justice, whenne I trust he doth thies extremites of his owne mynde, without your knowledge or any my deserte, as I saye. But I require not to be beleved but as the matter shal appere upon examinacion; which examinacion I doo require of youe by al the best wayes, wordes, and maner I maye obteyne the same.

And if I who pretende truely to have been kept thus miserably so longe, without any faulte in lawe, have committed nowe suche faulte in manners as to deserve to be thus used, or have not receyved and knowleged the mercy of God shewed to the hol realme generally, and specially to me, as I shulde, to the humblinge of my harte, but abused the joye thereof to waxe proude and vengeable—if I appere faulty in any of thies wayes, I am content my fault in maners be taken for a fault in lawe, and, by voluntarye submission in thies my letters, for punishement to be kept in pryson as vyely and abjectly as Master Lieutenant list; which he pretendeth he maye tyl he have asmoch of my substaunce as he list which he wolde. For I have offred him with harty good wyll asmoche as he shulde have, not as myne owne judge prescribinge howmoche shulde be due, which might make contention, but in a generalite, houmoch soever is dwe.

And if I appere not faulty, thenne I besech your Lordships, if ye mynd to have me kept any lenger here, that I maye be soo kept by your favorable order, as my kepinge maye be oonly a kepinge frohensforth and not a punnisshement at Master Lieutenauntes pleasour, byfore justice hath determyned I am worthy the same.

I wryte noo moo specialties, because I knowe ye shulde not credite my complaynte without hearinge thother partye; and a shorte examinacion shall make al thynge evydent unto yow; which I most instantly desyre, and that at the reverence of Christes Passion, and for the zele ye bere to justice and indifferent administracion of the same.

148. *To the* PRIVY COUNCIL

[The Tower, 30 October, 1549]

Stow, *Annales, 1592,* 1013.

have continued heere in this miserable prison now one yeere, one quarter, and one moneth, this same day that I write these my letters, with want of aire to releeve my bodie, want of books to releeve my minde, want of good company, the onely solace of this world, and finally, want of a just cause, why I should have come hither at all.

Stow says, 'More of this letter came not to my hands,' adding, 'the Lords tooke it in good part and laught very merily thereat, saying he had a pleasant head,' but made no reply.

149. *To the* PRIVY COUNCIL

The Tower, [November or early in December, 1549]

Stow, *Annales, 1592*, 1013–4. Mr J. P. Collier found among the Egerton Papers a manuscript copy or a draft (he does not say which) of this letter, without date, address, signature, or endorsement. He printed it in *The Egerton Papers*, Camden Soc., 1840, 25–7, unaware that it had appeared in Stow or that Gardiner was its author. I have been unable to find the manuscript at Bridgewater House from which Collier printed. Stow is here used as the basic text. Collier is cited in the footnotes as C.

> Is kept unjustly from attending Parliament; Somerset set a bad precedent in preventing a member of Parliament, without cause, from attending; decisions of a General Council, from which rightful members have been forcibly excluded, are not binding; urgently asks a hearing. (Parliament opened 4 November, 1549. Stow says this letter was written five or six weeks after No. 148. If so, it would bring the date of writing into December.)

After my due commendations to your good[1] Lordships: Howsoever the time is stolen from you with the multitude of businesses[2] and varietie of matters wherwith ye be travelled, wherby ye[3] rather want time, as I suppose, than be glutted with it, yet with me, being alone comfortles in this miserable prison, the time passeth more sensibly. And as the[4] grefe groweth in length, so it bringeth more encombry[5] and travell with it. And being now the time of Parliament, wherof I am a member in my degree, called unto it by writ, and not cut[6] from it by any fault, but only by power kept heere, it is a double calamitie to be detained in prison by so intolerable wrong, and excluded from [7]this assembly[7] so much against right.

I have suffered the like in the late Lord Protectors time, against all reason; which God hath given you power now to reforme. And among many other things which in his time were writhed amisse, no one thing, as I suppose, was of woorse example, ne more prejudicial to the good order of the high court of Parliament, ⟨in⟩ which is the direction of all mens lives, lands, and goods in this realme, than to allow for a president that any one[8] man, being a member thereof, might, without cause, be excluded, and so letted to parle there his mind in publike matters, for the welth of the realm, and such other private causes as do occur.

1 *not in* C.	2 C., busines	3 C., you
4 *not in* C.	5 C., incomberance	6 C., put
7–7 C., thassembly	8 *not in* C.	

If the strength of the Parliament be not empaired by wrong in one, bicause right consisteth not in number, it shall be at the pleasure of him that ruleth to do the same in moe[1]; wherby others may take more harm than I, as experience hath shewed in such examples. But I know it becommeth me not to reason the strength of that court, ne the order of it. The lawyers of this[2] realme know[3] that; and to their knowledge I submit my judgement, and take for good that they allow. But this I dare say, when religion is intreated[4] in a General Councel of Christendom, if the rulers of the Councel let any mans repaire thither that hath right to be there, what soever is there[5] concluded is, in the lawes of the world abroad, taken of no force, by excluding of one member wrongfully that shuld furnish the body. Which I write unto your Lordships[6], for the good opinion I have of you, trusting that ye intend not to uphold or follow the late Lord Protectors doings by wrong, but so fashion your proceedings as they may agree with justice at home, and seeme agreeable to reason to others abroad; being so[7] assured of mine innocencie that[8], when your Lordships shall hear what can be said against me and mine[9] answer thereunto, ther shal appeer cause why I shuld have had praise, thanks, and commendations of the late Lord Protector, if truth, honestie, and due obedience might looke therfore, and no cause of trouble or displeasure at al.

So wrongfully have I beene tormented in this[10] prison, so boldly dare I speake to you of my cause[11], with such an opinion and estimation of your wisedoms, which I know and reverence, as I ought not [12]ne would[12] not vainly hope to abuse you with words; but, upon certain confidence of your indifferences, verily I trust that ye[13] wil deem and take things in such sort as, being plainly and truly opened, shal appeere unto[14] you [15]by matter[15] indeed.

In consideration whereof I renew my sute unto your Lordships[16], instantly requiring you that I may be heard according to justice, and that with such speede as the delay of your audience give not occasion to such as be ignorant [17]abroad of my matter[17] to thinke that your Lordships allowed and approoved the detaining of me heere. Which, without

---

1 *Stow*, mew; *C.*, moe 2 *C.*, the 3 *C.*, knoweth
4 *C.*, treated of 5 *C.*, so 6 *C.*, Honors
7 *not in C.* 8 *C.*, as 9 *C.*, my
10 *C. adds* miserable 11 *C.*, case 12–12 *C.*, nor will
13 *C.*, you 14 *C.*, to
15–15 *Stow*, by-matter; *C.*, by matter 16 *C.*, Honors
17–17 *C.*, of my matter abroad

hearing my declaration, I trust ye[1] wil not, but have such consideration of me as mine estate in the commonwelth, the passing of[2] my former life amongst you, and other respects do require; wherin you shal bind me, and[3] do agreeably to your honors and [4]justice, the free[4] course whereof you have honorably taken upon you to make open to the realme without respect; which is the onely establishment of all commonwelths. And therefore the zeale of him was allowed that said, *Fiat iustitia, et[5] ruat mundus*, signifieng that by it the world is kept from falling indeed; although it might seem otherwise in some respect[6], and some trouble to arise in doing it.

And this I write bicause in the late Lord Protectors time there was an insinuation made unto me, as though I were kept heer by policie, which, with the violation of justice, tooke never good effect; as I doubt not of your wisdoms ye[7] can and will consider, and do therefore accordingly. For the effectual execution wherof I shal [8]not faile to[8] pray Almighty God, with the preservation [9]and increase[9] of your honors. [10]From the Tower.[10]

150. *To* Peter Martyr Vermigli

[The Tower, 1549 or 1550]

B.M., Arundel 100, 1. Prefatory letter from *In Petrum Martyrem Florentinum, malae tractacionis querela Sanctissimae Eucharistiae nomine edita, authore Stephano Winton.* Sixteenth-century copy.

Complains of Martyr's disingenuousness (in his *Tractatio*, 1549. Gardiner's reply is mentioned in his book against Hooper of 1550—*see* my *Gardiner*, 315).

Quod male, quod indigne Eucharistiam tractes, quam vafre et callide ad propositum tibi scopum, quaedam arte flectas, quaedam aperte violenter detorqueas, nihil ex fide et synceritate agas—haec sunt,

---

You discuss the Eucharist in a wicked and shameful way; with subtlety and shrewdness you cunningly twist certain considerations to your purpose, and openly and forcibly distort certain others; you treat nothing with honesty and integrity. These are the things, Peter, of

1 *C.,* you
4-4 *C.,* justice have a free
7 *C.,* you
10-10 *not in C.*

2 *C. supplies of*
5 *not in C.*
8-8 *not in C.*

3 *C.,* to
6 *C.,* respectes
9-9 *not in C.*

Petre, de quibus conqueror Eucharistiae nomine, recte ne an secus res ipsa iudicabit. Ego vero absque prohoemiis et minimo (quoad eius fieri poterit) affectu agam quod agitur; tua quum recitavero subiiciam mea, quo magis sint omnia conspicua Lectori.

---

which, in the name of the Eucharist, I complain; whether rightly or wrongly, the facts of the case shall be judge. But without further preface and with the utmost dispassionateness (as far as this is possible), I shall address myself to the subject. I shall subjoin my own arguments after first setting forth yours, that everything may be perfectly clear to the reader.

151. *To the* READER

[The Tower, 1550]

Trinity College, Oxford, MS. LXXXVII, 1–4. Prefatory letter from *An explicacion of the true Catholique faythe.* Sixteenth-century copy, once, belonging to Sir Thomas Pope.

> Cranmer's inconsistency; he denounced John Lambert (in 1538) as a heretic for holding the views which he now defends; he later agreed, with all the bishops, to the Catholic doctrine; yet he does not now repent of his former error, but speaks as if he always held his present views; he agreed with Gardiner on the Sacrament in January, 1548, and made no objection to Gardiner's views in May of the same year; he directs his book against Gardiner charging him with falsehood in the citation of certain Fathers and calling him Papist; hence Gardiner is compelled to reply. (*Cf.* the preface as actually printed, No. 152.)

To the Reder

God, who by his providence ruleth and governith this worlde by his infinite wisedom, soo ordreth and placeth mannes perverse and frowarde malice as, being nought in it self, it servith neverthelesse in the use of it in summe that be good to summe good effecte, according to the truth of Saincte Polles sentence, 'In them that love God, al thing workith to a good ende.' The cutting of of the Jewes, by their incredulite, was the receyving of the gentyles by their fayth. And, to my purpose, therrour of the chief Archebishop of this realme, against the true doctrine of the most Blessed Sacrament, shalbe, I trust, th[e] relief of a gret meany; bycause as the same is by malice very perniciously en-

446

tended, soo it is by Godes mercyful ordr[e], by fonde handlyng therof, more playne and evident thenne to the indifferent reader can doo any hurte; and to them that wel consider it, and to thauctour himself also, if he red[e] it over again, maye doo very moch good.

For if my Lorde of Cauntourbury doo but thinke with himself howe old he is, howe longe he hath been in the place of the chief teacher of relligion in this realme, what credite he had with our soverain lorde that ded is, and thenne shuld saye with himself thus: 'Howe vehemently did I reason openly in such a presence, as never was seen in Englande a more solemne, against oon Lambarde, thenne taken by me for an heretique, for defendinge the same doctrine which I nowe miself defende as Catholique! Was I not also the chief bishop in the place I am nowe in, whenne I and al the rest of the bishoppes, noon except, agreed that doctrine to be Catholique, which I nowe calle erroneous and fayned by the Papistes? Have I not said to many, secretly and openly, that I thought them madde that denyed the very presence of Christes body in the Sacrament? Have I not shewed myself angry with sum such as admonished me to take hede lest I wer not by other drawen to that errour? Did I not moch favour Luther, Hosiander, Justus Jonas, and Bucre, whom I knewe to detest the sacramentaryes?' If my Lorde of Cauntourburye did but oons accoumpte thiese matiers with himself and compare therwith what he hath nowe doon in wryting this booke after this sorte, he must nedes with thiese though[tes], fetching a syth from the botom of his brest, saye, 'What meane I? Who hath led me hereunto?' and soo yet with the grace of God recover himself.

But although he, being slypped into the depe botom of errour, cannot, for want of grace, recover; thoue, Reader, maiste see he might remember asmoch as I speake of, and esteme this a straunge matier to see that by him set forth for a Catholique doctrine nowe, that he himself, being in place of the chief teacher of the realme, and soo long, never taught bifore, but taught the contrary, and yet in this booke steppith sodenly aside and callith his felawes Papistes for that doctrine in which he bifore consented with them.

St Pol, after his conversion to the truth, did not dissemble his former errour, and said he had obteyne[d], for his ignoraunce, mercy, declaring therwith a tooke[n] from God of his calling; whose maner, nevertheles, if my Lorde of Cauntourbury had counterfeyted, his doing thenne had had a better colour. But God wold not suffre that kinde of hypocrise in him, for overmoch hinderaunce of the truth. And

447

therfor my Lorde of Cauntourbury, permitted to himself, speakith in this booke like oon that had been a straungier to the doctrine of England, and, as oon sodenly slypped out of the skyes, had never had noon other understanding in the matier he spekith of. And yet it is he, the very same man that soo vehemently reasoned against Lamberd. Howebeit, if he had lerned any thing synnes (as oon daye they saie is an others scoler), and thenne opened and told it his brethern and other, with a mylde evangelical spirite, shewing wherin he had erred, howe he had erred, by what occasion he had erred, what he had lerned synnes, what he had founde, what he had seen that he never sawe, whither any visions or revelations had been secretly made unto him to altre the doctrine he had so long continued in—if he had doo[n] thus, with tokens of repentaunce for the gret idolatrie he had soo long continued in, withe exhortations to other to repente ernestly withe hym, this maner of handeling had been more persuasible for suche an enterprise as he makith in this book, wherby to confounde the receyved truth.

If any shuld saye to me, What have youe to doo with the maner of handeling of it, if the matier be good? To this I saye, The matier is not good, and the maner towchith me thus: Whenne I was delyvered out of the Fleate, it chaunced, at my being withe the Counsaile at Hampton Courte, mention to be made of a booke I made in Englishe for the truthe of the Sacrament, at which tyme my Lorde of Cauntourbury, being present, sayde to me that summe founde faulte at certain wordes in my booke, in which I sayde the oonly substaunce of Christes body to be in the Sacrament, but yet he, for himself, could agree with those wordes and take them we[l]. I liked that spech wel, and toke him to agree with me in the Sacrament at the lest. At an other tyme, being bifore the Counsayl at Westmester a lytel bifore my committinge hither, and by occasion of the rehersal of a sermon by me made in the countrie, of the Sacrament, whenne I repeted my doctrine there, according to the true Catholique fayth in dede, even as I preached after, bifore the Kinges Majestie, therunto my Lorde of Cauntourbury thenne said nothing; wherby I thought him yet to remayne in his former fayth. Synnes which tyme I never spake with him or hard from him directly; and, bisides those two tymes, never spake with him of that matier, synnes the death of our late souverain lorde, whose soule God pardonne. And yet for al that, he directith this booke as it wer specially against me, charginge me with chrafte and falshode in thallegation of Hilarie and Theophilacte, and in an other place, spekinge of me by name, makith

448

me an exception in a pointe among the Papistes, bicause I am in prison, notinge me of the numbre of Papistes.

By whiche his wordes, he hath as it wer conjured me to saye for my-self, and the matier also, what I canne, and eyther, by adhering to his detestable errour, to adventure the daungier of my body and soule, or, by holdinge my peace, with disagrement from him, to make myself faulty to God (*quia tacui*) and suspecte to the worlde to be as he notith me, with sum lenger daungier and travayle of my body thenne I have yet susteyned. For which consideracion, beinge thus specially provoked and styrred to doo my duetie to God, and therwith purge myself to my soveraine lorde, have thought good, as I might in miserable pryson, to peruse his booke, and, for the more certain and compendious tryal of the truth, have used this newe facion of wrytinge, to reduce matier at large to certain issues, whiche for that purpose I joyne directly with hym, such as maye easely and without grete matier of lerninge be tryde; not meanyng other contention in this matier thenne my vocation, that placeth me to defende Christes truth, doth of necessite, for discharge of my duetie, require. Accordinge wherunto I shall desire my doing herin may be taken, and noo[n] other wise.

NOTES TO NO. 151

Page 446. Gardiner's *Explication* was written in refutation of Cranmer's *A Defence of the true & catholike Doctrine of the sacrament,* 1550. For an admirable discussion of Cranmer's views on the Sacrament *see* C. H. Smyth, *Cranmer and the Reformation under Edward VI,* Cambridge, 1926; for a brief exposition of Gardiner's views *see* my *Gardiner,* Chapter XXVI.

Page 447. For Lambert's trial *see ib.*, 353 n. 48.

Page 448. Gardiner's book on the Sacrament discussed at Hampton Court (8 January, 1548) must have been his *Detection of the Devils Sophistrie*, published 1546.

Page 448. Gardiner's 'sermon in the country' was probably that preached at Winchester, 15 April, 1548, after which he was summoned to appear before the Council. His sermon before the King was that of 29 June, 1548.

152. *To* [*the* READER]

[The Tower], 1551

From *An explication and assertion of the true Catholique fayth . . . Made by Steven, Byshop of Wynchester, and exhibited by his owne hande for his defence to the Kynges majesties Commissioners at Lambeth. Anno 1551.*

Marvels that the Archbishop should write such things, but will use him reverently because of his office.

The Preface

For asmuch as amonges other mine allegations for defence of my selfe in this matter, moved agaynst me by occasion of my sermon made before the Kynges Moost Excellent Majestye, touchyng partely the Catholique faith of the moost precious Sacrament of thAltare, which I see now impugned by a booke set furth under the name of my Lord of Cauntorburies Grace, I have thought expedient for the better opening of the matter, and consideryng I am by name touched in the sayde boke, the rather to utter partely that I have to say by confutation of that boke; wherein I thinke neverthlesse not requisite to directe any speache by speciall name to the person of him that is entitled autor, because it may possible ⟨*i.e.*, possibly⟩ be that his name is abused, wherwith to set furth the matter, beyng him selfe of such dignitie and auctorite in the commen welth as for that respect shuld be inviolable. For which consideracion I shal, in my speache of suche reproufe as the untruth of the matter necessariely requireth, omitting the speciall title of the auctor of the boke, speake onely of thauctor in generall; beyng a thing to me greatly to be merveiled at, that such matter shuld nowe be published out of my Lord of Cantorburies penne; but because he is a man I wil not wondre, and because he is such a man I will reverently use him, and, forbearyng further to name him, talke onely of the auctor by that generall name.

153. *To the* READER

[The Tower], before 20 July, 1552

From *Confutatio Cavillationum, Quibus Sacrosanctum Eucharistiae Sacramentum, ab impiis Capernaitis, impeti solet . . .* Paris, 1552. Dated at end, by printer, 20 July, 1552.

All the arguments against the Eucharist are of like folly; they will be demolished by the truth.

¹Marcus Antonius Constantius, Theologus Lovaniensis, Christiano Lectori S.¹

Si quaeras unde tam numerosa argumentorum cohors quae mysterii Eucharistici veritatem impetat, respondebo quod Calcidensis hospes, qui coenam splendidam et opiparam multis in speciem ferculis instructam quum exhiberet, interrogatus unde illa deliciarum copia, ingenue confessus est, ex suilla carne constare omnia, quae callida cocorum ars ita variarat. Et sane ut suilla caro omnium fere crassissima et maxime fatua sit; ita de iis ego responderim argumentis, nihil illis esse aut stolidius, aut magis insipidum, et una item stultitia, quasi dicas, suilla carne constare omnia; quaedam autem illorum speciosiora esse, prout alius alio ingeniosior et callidior inciderat artifex, qui maliciosa calliditate mutarit speciem, effeceritque ut fucus arte adhibitus aliquid veri coloris imitaretur. Qualia sunt cunque respondetur singulis, ex quibus interdum arripitur occasio veritatem etiam Catholicam illustrandi, quomodo loci

---

Marcus Antonius Constantius, Theologian of Louvain (*1554 ed.*, Stephen, Bishop of Winchester, Chancellor of England), to the Christian Reader, Greeting

If you ask whence comes so numerous a troop of arguments to assail the truth of the Eucharistic mystery, I shall answer as did the Chalcidian host, who was giving a splendid and sumptuous dinner, arranged ostentatiously in many courses. When he was asked whence this abundance of delicacies, he frankly admitted that they all consisted of pork, which the skilful ingenuity of the cooks had so varied ⟨Livy xxxv, 49⟩. And, indeed, as pig is well-nigh the grossest and most tasteless of meats, so, in regard to those arguments, I should reply that nothing is more stupid than they are, or more insipid, and that in the same way, by the same folly, they all consist, so to speak, of pork.

Certain of them are, however, more showy, according as one originator has happened to be more talented and more subtle than another, and has changed the appearance with malicious cleverness, bringing it about that the dye, artfully applied, imitated something of the true colour.

Reply is made to each of the arguments according to its nature, and now and then opportunity is taken of making clear the Catholic truth,

1–1 *Louvain ed., 1554*, Stephanus VVinton. Episcopus, Angliae Cancellarius, Christiano Lectori S.

451

quidam communes [1]proxima pagina annotati indicabunt[1]. Nam ut intelligas, Lector, diligentia in hoc maxima adhibita est, ut quod ex Patribus ad eorum cavilla diluenda commodum fuerit, huc tibi in medium proferatur. Et omnis noster labor eo incubuit, ut quicquid ab illis sectariis seu arguendo, seu confutando, seu denique regulas praescribendo dictum fuerit, id huc prolatum, et cum veritate collatum cerneres, eiusque vi confossum plane et iugulatum. Qua in re hunc ordinem secuti sumus. Primum respondetur eorum argumentis, sive ex arcanis, sive prophanis literis, aut etiam Patrum verbis undecunque petitis. Secundo excutiuntur confictae ab illis regulae. Tertio solutiones illae sectariorum, quibus argumenta quaedam Catholicorum (quae ex multis potissimum convellenda delegerant) conantur diluere, refutantur. Quarto quod in testimonia Patrum Catholicam fidem confitentium cavillantur, perpensis eorundem Patrum verbis et sententiis convellitur. Habes summam huius operis. Vale.

---

in the manner which certain topics, mentioned on the next page, will indicate (*1554 ed.*, certain topics, brought together in the index, will plainly show). For I would have you understand, Reader, that the greatest care has been taken to bring into the open for you here material from the Fathers suitable for refuting their captious arguments. And all our labour has been directed to this end, that whatever has been said by those sectaries, whether in arguing or in confuting or finally in laying down rules, you might see brought forth here and compared with the truth, and by the force of truth once for all pierced through and disposed of. In which matter we have followed this order: First, reply is made to their arguments, from whatever source they are brought, whether from the mysteries, or from profane literature, or also from the words of the Fathers. Secondly, the rules invented by them are examined. Thirdly, those solutions of the sectaries are rebutted by which they endeavour to refute certain arguments of the Catholics (which they had chosen from many as above all to be disproved). Fourthly, their frivolous objections to the testimony of the Fathers confessing the Catholic faith are confuted by the carefully weighed words and opinions of these same Fathers. You have the content of this work. Farewell.

1-1 *Louvain ed.*, indice compraehensi aperte commonstrabunt

154. *To* A PERSON UNNAMED

[The Tower?]

Lambeth, MS. 140, 225. Prefatory letter from *Annotaciones in Dialogum Iohannis Oecolampadii cum suo Nathanaele de mysterio Eucharistico disceptantis.* Sixteenth-century copy.

Has read Oecolampadius on the Eucharist (*Quid de Eucharistia...Dialogus* ...1530) with diligence; is careful to quote him accurately; will consider his treatment of passages cited from the Greek.

Quod me de Oecolampadii dialogo consulis, ecquid videatur ab ipsis fontibus, erudite ac fideliter repetere veritatem ut Eucharistie mysterium aperiret, sic accipe, magna me diligentia, et summa animi attentione legisse quae scribit, et pro ingenii mei captu perpendisse. Quam feliciter nihil dico, operam certe aliquam a me (quod volebas) in eo excutiendo navatam esse; ex schedis quas ad te mitto certo scies. Quod si tu pari attentione, nostras annotaciones cum illius scriptis contuleris, illis viz. quae nostris ea gratia, hic adiunximus me ne an illum error a vero distraxerit, facile aestimes. Illud a me maximopere curatum est, ut quae illius nomine edita sunt in quibus ego aliquid notandum putaverim, bona huc fide transferantur. Nam quem reprehendendum susceperis, eius dicta corrumpere, et aliter atque ille ediderit referre, a viro bono debet

---

Since you consult me about the dialogue of Oecolampadius, whether he seems to bring the truth at all learnedly and faithfully from the sources themselves in order to explain the mystery of the Eucharist, be assured that with great diligence and the utmost application of the mind I have read what he writes, and have weighed it according to the capacity of my intellect. How happily, I do not say; but I do say that certainly some labour has been performed by me, as you wished, in investigating it. From the pages which I send to you, you will assuredly know this. If, with like application, you will compare our observations with his writings, those, namely, which we have here added to ours for this purpose, you may easily judge whether error has drawn me or him from the truth. I have taken the utmost care that whatever has been published in his name, in which I thought something ought to be censured, should be set down here accurately. For to corrupt the words of him whom you have undertaken to censure, and to quote them otherwise than he published them, should be wholly foreign to a good man. Accordingly on this point I bid you be assured that all

esse alienissimum. Itaque in eo, te iubeo esse securum, quae a me ut ab Oecolampadio citata, dicta, allegata proferentur, ea omnia ad verbum ipsius Oecolampadii nomine, ab iis qui illius sectae faverent edita, et typis excusa esse. Quanti momenti mea censura fuerit, aliorum esto iudicium, et inprimis tuum. Non est mihi propositum, singula discutere, ea modo attingam quae proferuntur e Grecis, in quibus citandis et vertendis, Oecolampadii candor, si quis homini inesset, desideretur. Durius nihil dicam in hominem, quem e suis scriptis, potius quam verbis meis censeri cuperem. Ordo a me servabitur eiusmodi ut prolatis quae ab Oecolampadio dicuntur; subiiciam mea.

---

those things which will be brought forward by me as cited, said, or quoted by Oecolampadius, were issued, word for word under the name of Oecolampadius himself, by those who favoured his sect, and have been struck off in type. Of the weight of my censure let others and, in particular, yourself be the judge. It has not been my design to consider every point; those only will I touch on which are brought forward from the Greek, in citing and translating which, the sincerity of Oecolampadius, if any was in the man, is sadly lacking. I will say nothing more severe against him; for I would wish him to be judged rather by his own writings than by my words. This order will be followed: I shall first quote Oecolampadius, then add my own comment.

INTRODUCTORY NOTE TO NOS. 155–73

These letters were written in the reign of Queen Mary. Most of them are brief. As the Queen's chief minister of state Gardiner had little opportunity for prolonged correspondence on any topic. Ten are on academic affairs, one being a pointed admonition to the students of Christ Church, Oxford, to behave themselves (No. 166), the other nine dealing with matters at Cambridge (Nos. 155–7, 161, 163–5, 170, 172), to the Chancellorship of which Gardiner had been restored on his release from the Tower. Five letters have to do with political questions: Nos. 158–60 deal with matters connected with Wyatt's rebellion; No. 162 is a letter of advice to Cardinal Pole as to how to broach the matter of reunion with Rome to Parliament, and, in particular, to give assurances that possessors of erstwhile monastic property would not be disturbed in their possession; No. 167 is to Montmorency, concerning the peace of Europe. Of the remaining four letters two (Nos. 168–9) are characteristically vigorous rebukes, the first to the city fathers of Leicester who desire 'newfanglenes', and the second to an unnamed offender. No. 171 is a note on some legal business, and No. 173 a letter to Bonner instructing him to notify all the bishops to hold solemn obsequies for Pope Julius III. When the place of writing is given in brackets it is inferred from the records of the Privy Council.

155. *To the* VICE-CHANCELLOR AND SENATE OF CAMBRIDGE UNIVERSITY

Southwark, 25 August, 1553

C.C.C.C., MS. 106, 299. Sixteenth-century copy in Parker Collection. A copy of this, sent by Parker to Cecil, 1 March, 1559, is in R.O., S.P. 11, 1, 22. Another sixteenth-century copy is in Camb. Univ. Registry, Liber Rerum Memorabilium, 126 v. Eighteenth-century copies: Camb. Univ. Lib., Baker, xxxiv, 328; B.M., Add. 5843, 426; B.M., Sloane, 3562, 57. From C.C.C.C. in Lamb, 169; from Parker's copy in Parker, *Corresp.*, 56; Strype, *Parker*, 1, 85. C.C.C.C. is here followed.

Is prevented from coming in person; sends his chaplain (Thomas Watson).

Quam multae causae sint (viri doctissimi) quae animum meum, ut ad vos hoc potissimum tempore accederem, permoverent, totidem fere occurrunt impedimenta, quae, ⟨ne⟩ corpus in vobis adsit, iustissime prohibent. Interim autem, dum occasionem capto commodiorem, qua vos ipse inviserem; hunc sacellanum meum, vobis non omnino ignotum, et mihi notissimum, cuius fidem perspectam et exploratam habeo, mandare volui, eidemque demandare, ut meo nomine referat, quae vos ex me cuperem intelligere; cui ut credatis, oro, et bene valete. Londini ex aedibus meis, octavo calend. Septemb. 1553.

Vester Cancellarius,

STE. WINTON, Cancell.

Headed: Doctissimis Viris Vicecancellario et Senatui Cantabrigiensi.

As there are many circumstances which moved me in thought, learned friends, to visit you, especially at this time, so almost as many hindrances arise which prevent most justifiably my being with you in person. However, in the meantime, while I wait for a more convenient season for coming, I have decided to commission my chaplain—who is not altogether unknown to you, and is very well known to me, whose faithfulness I have thoroughly tested and proved—and to entrust to him the task of laying before you, in my name, the things which I desire you to know. I beg you to put confidence in him. Farewell. From my house in London, the eighth day before the Kalends of September, 1553.   Your Chancellor,

STE. WINTON, Cancell.

Headed: To the learned gentlemen, the Vice-Chancellor and Senate of Cambridge.

NOTES TO NO. 155

It is uncertain who was acting as Vice-Chancellor when this letter was written. Dr Sandys had been forced to give up the office on the collapse of Lady Jane Grey's government, and Dr Young did not, presumably, take office till Michaelmas of that year (*see* J. Venn, *Grace Book* Δ, Cambridge, 1910, xvi).

According to Parker's letter to Cecil, 1 March, 1559, Watson was sent by Gardiner 'with instructions to every college, and, as then I could gather, to report to him in what state every college stood in; and further, peradventure upon cause, to have the masters and others assured *de coram sistendo, et interim bene gerendo* until a further order' (Parker, *Corresp.*, 54).

156. *To the* VICE-CHANCELLOR [JOHN YOUNG] AND REGENTS OF CAMBRIDGE UNIVERSITY

Southwark, 18 October, 1553

Camb. Univ. Registry, Liber Rerum Memorabilium, 127. Sixteenth-century copy. Eighteenth-century copy from this in B.M., Add. 5843, 427–8. The former is here followed.

Gardiner decides a disputed election to the proctorship in favour of Henry Barleye.

After my ryght hartye commendacions: I have herde and considered the matier of appele towchynge thoffyce of the proctourship; and for as miche as in my jugemente the ryght of nomination shulde rather apperteyne to the new college, in the tytle of suche hostelles as be therunto united, then to the Hostell of Sainte Nicholas, so desolate as ther is noo commons kepte, and by reason therof, he that was by that Hostell of Sainte Nicholas nominate, by labouringe for the offyce, made hym selfe unhable therunto. Thellectyon passed in the person of Henrye Barleye, named by the newe college, all thowghe by the smaller number of regentes, shulde be demed good, and the voyces of the more number of regentes, geven to a person unhable and not eligyble, voyde and of none effecte. Wherfore I have thowght good by theise my letters to signifie unto you this my jugement and determinacion in this matyer of apele, and acordinge therunto to wyll and requyre you to accepte and admitt the seyde Henry Barleye to the seyde offyce of proctourshyppe[1], as one lawfullye electe and chosen to enjoye the same. And thus fare you hartelye well. From my howse in Southwerke the xviij^th of October, 1553.

Your lovinge frende,

STE. WINTON, Cancell.

Headed: To the Vicechauncelour and Regentes of thUniversitie of Cambryge.

1 *MS.*, protectourshyppe (? *a slip for* procutour- *or* procetourshyppe)

William Cole, on p. 428 of B.M., Add. 5843, after his copy of this letter adds the note: 'I suppose the new college here mentioned means Trinity College, then newly modelled out of 3 houses and united into one; especially as Mr Rymer in his 15th vol. of *Foedera*, p. 106, has given us a list of all the fellows then appointed to that college, among whom Henry Barkeley occurs as one, which I take to be a mistake for Henry Barleye.' On p. 400 Cole notes that 'Henry Barley was Proctor 1553, and was afterwards [1569–81 (Add. 5839, p. 350)] rector of Sherington near Newport-Pagnell, Bucks.'

On St Nicholas' Hostel *see* H. P. Stokes, *The Mediaeval Hostels of the University of Cambridge*, Camb. Antiq. Soc., 1924, 89–91, and *Outside the Barnwell Gate*, Camb. Antiq. Soc., 1915, 21–2.

The Liber Rerum Memorabilium or 'Black Paper Book,' in the Registry of Cambridge University, from which this letter and Nos. 161, 165, 170 are taken, is a volume of sixteenth-century copies of documents relating to the University, and was, according to a note on its second page, begun by John Mere, Registrary, 1543–58, who did little in it, and continued by his successor, Matthew Stokys, Registrary, 1558–91.

157. *To the* PRESIDENT AND FELLOWS OF ST CATHARINE'S HALL IN CAMBRIDGE

[Southwark], 13 January, 1554

St Catharine's College, Register, 41. Sixteenth-century copy. Another sixteenth-century copy, lacking heading, date, and address, in C.C.C.C., MS. 106, 299. G. F. Browne, *St Catharine's College*, London, 1902, 70; Lamb, 169.

> Since the mastership is vacant because the Master (Dr Edwin Sandys) is married, they are to choose the bearer, Edmund Cosyn.

After my hartye commendations: Wheras yt pleasyd the Quens Hyghnes to commytt unto me thorderyng of all matters appartaynyng to thUniversitie, and that nothyng ther ys more necessarie for the same than to have good and discrett heades in the colledges; therfor seyng that the maistershipe of your house[1], by reason[2] that the Maister ther of ys

1 *C.C.C.C.*, college   2 *C.C.C.C. adds* of

maryed contrary to thecclesisaticall lawes and your statuttes, ys nowe voyd, these shal be to desyer yow that ye[1] will chose the berare her of, Maister Cosyne, a man for his wysdome and honest behavor veray meett for that[2] rowme. And in so doyng ye[3] shall have me redye to do yow lyke pleasur whan tyme and occation shall serve, by Godes grace, Who prosper[4] yow in all godly studye and vertue.

Your loving frend,

STE. WINTON, Cancell.

Addressed: [5] To my lovyng frendes, the President and Fellowes in S. Katherins Hall in Cambridg[5].

Headed: [6] The copy of the letters wych my Lord Chancelor sent for thelectyone of Maister Cosyne, to be our Maister, Anno Domini 1554, Ianuarii 13, Principis Mariae primo[6].

158. *To* PETRE

Southwark, 28 January, 1554

R.O., S.P. 11, 2, 39–40.* *Chronicle of Queen Jane*, Camden Soc., 1850, 184.

> Has searched George Medley's lodging in the Minories, and arrested John Harington who has confessed to conferring with Master Wroth and Lord John Grey; has opened a packet of intercepted dispatches from the French ambassador (Noailles) in which he finds a copy of Elizabeth's letter to Queen Mary. (The date in the endorsement of this letter is 27 January, which at first sight appears to be that of the letter itself, and is that given by Lemon in his *Calendar*, by J. G. Nichols in *Chron. of Qu. Jane*, and myself in *Gardiner*, 247, 323. On more careful examination it appears that the date of the letter is 28 January, one i of the Roman numeral xxviij being written so close to v as to be almost merged with it.)

Master Secretary, after my most harty commendations: In the mornyng I thought good to serch the[7] Mynoresse and Medles lodging there for letters, and, among other, founde a letter lately wryten[8] by Harington,

1 *C.C.C.C.*, youe	2 *C.C.C.C.*, the
3 *C.C.C.C.*, youe	4 *C.C.C.C.*, preserve
5–5 *replaced in C.C.C.C. by marginal note,* To Katheryn Hall	
6–6 *not in C.C.C.C.*	7 *writ. over* in
8 t *in* wryten *writ. over something else*	

which Harington cam to me this night, and, after examiination, I have taken him tardy by occasion of that letter and kepe him with me as prisoner this night, entending in the mornyng to send him to the Towre; for he hath confessed howe upon Fridaye at night the Lord John Gray cam to Cheston, where Master Wroth and he was, and spake with Master Wroth and him to get a [1]gyde to leade him the waye to Saincte Albons, bicause he was commaunded by the Quene, he said, to levye men in his countrie in al the hast; and more I cannot get yet, but ye must in any wise send for thapprehension of Wroth, and this matier wyl cumme out and towche fully.

And as I was in hand with that matier, were delyvered such letters as in tymes past I durst not have opened, but nowe sumwhat hette with thiese treasons I waxed bolder. Wherein I trust I shalbe borne with; wherein happe helpith me, for they be worth the breking up, and ⟨*i.e.*, if⟩ I could holly disciphre them; wherein I wyl spende sumwhat of my laysour, if I canne have any; but this apperith, that the letter wryten from my Lady Elizabeth to the Quenes Highnes nowe late in her excuse is taken a matier worthy to be sent in to Fraunce, for I have the copy of it in the Frenche ambassadours pacquet. I wyl knowe what canne be doon in †the disciphring† it, and to morowe remitte that I cannot doo unto youe. And soo fare ye hartely wel. At my house in Sowthwerke, the xxviij of January.

Your assured loving frend,

STE. WINTON, Cancell.

Master[2] Wharton shall
tel youe the rest.

Addressed: To the Right Wourshipful Sir William[3] Peter, Knight, oon of the Quenes Highnes Principal Secretaryes.

Endorsed: My Lord Chancello[ur], xxvij° Januarii, 1553⟨54⟩.

NOTES TO NO. 158

This letter, written three days after the outbreak of Wyatt's rebellion, reflects the excitement caused by it as well as the suspicion that France was encouraging it, and that the Princess Elizabeth was a partisan of the rebels. *See* Gairdner, *Lollardy*, IV, 278 ff.

1 g *writ. over* l   2 *writ. over* Sir   3 *writ. over* Henry

The Minories (formerly the house of the Poor Clares outside Aldgate, surrendered 1538) was, in 1552, granted to Henry Grey, Duke of Suffolk, who sold it, 1553, to his brothers, Lord Thomas and Lord John Grey, his half-brother George Medley, Esq., and John Harington, Esq., as joint-owners (E. M. Tomlinson, *A History of the Minories*, London, 1907, 109–13).

159. *To* PETRE

Southwark, 31 January, 1554

R.O., S.P. 11, 2, 67–8.*

Suggestions concerning the safe departure of the Imperial ambassadors (Counts Egmont and Lalaing, Jean de Montmorency, and Philip Nigri who had arrived in London, 2 January, 1554, to conclude the marriage treaty of Queen Mary and Philip of Spain. Since popular mislike of this treaty, which was signed 12 January, was one of the chief causes of Wyatt's rebellion, the ambassadors had cause to fear for their safety as Wyatt advanced on London. They left London 1 February.)

Master Secretary, after my most harty commendations: Ye shal understand howe Monsieur dEgmont and the rest of thambassadours have sent this berer with an other his servauntes unto me, to knowe myn advise in ther suer going or taryng, and what waye. Wherin, after ther jugement, the waye by land to Harwich is over long, and ther passing thens semeth to them to be in the more daungier of the French men. There is offered an other opportunite to take shipping in the ryver here and soo to goo along the sees; for which purpose they have mete shippes of ther owne countrie, which they wold entre this night, if the imminent daungie[r] required the same. Or[1] elles if they taryed tomorowe they wold send ther stuf first to myn chambre or sum other place in the Quenes Courte, with ordre to convoye the same by barge, as it wer to the Towre, and thens to ther shippes; wherby al suspition of ther departure by water shuld be avoyded. Herin this berer wyl require your advise as he hath doon myn; and therewith to knowe of my Lord Admyral whither †two of† the Quenes shippes, which lye equipped in the streme, may be redy to departe with them for ther wafting or noo.

1 *writ. over* in (?)

Thus referring the further resolution to youe and them, I bydde youe hartely farewel. At my hous this evenyng.

Your assured loving frend,

STE. WINTON, Cancell.

Addressed: To the Right Wourshipful Sir William Peter, Knyght, oon of the Quenes Majesties Principal Secretaries.

Endorsed: My Lord Chancellour, Ultimo Ianuarii, 1553⟨54⟩.

160. *To* PETRE

Southwark, 11 February, 1554

R.O., S.P. 11, 3, 63–4.*

Sends information from Sir Robert Southwell concerning money in the hands of Nicholas Wotton, English ambassador in France, and French practices with the rebels; advises examination of 'one little Wyatt' in the Tower; sends report of one Parker. (Wyatt's rebellion had collapsed 7 February.)

Master Secretary, after my most harty commendations: I sende unto youe herwith such letters, with confessions and copies of letters, as I have receyved from Sir Robert Southwel, wherin is good matier [1]worthy knowledge, the summe of money in Wottons handes, if it be trewe, and evel matier worthy knowlege, towching the rumours of the French Kinges practises here, mentioned in a[2] letter from Parys.

Tomorowe at your going to the Towre it shalbe good ye be ernest with oon lytel Wyat there prysoner, who by al lightlywode canne tel al. He is but a bastarde and hath noo substaunce. And ⟨*i.e.*, if⟩ it might stande with the Quenes Highnes pleasour, there were noo gret accompte to be made whither ye pressed him to saye truth by sharp punishement or promise of life.

Ye shal also receyve herwith a[3] reaporte of Parkar, whose confession Sir Robert Southwel sent me, made by yong Darel that brought me thiese[4] letters which I send youe, subscribed with his hand; wherby it semeth this matier shalbe, by Goddes goodnes, throughly opened; Who

1 w *writ. over* t(?)   2 al *w.* l *c.o.*
3 saye *c.o.*   4 *alt. from* ther(?)

sende youe hartely wel to fare. At[1] my house this evenyng the xj[th] of February 1553⟨54⟩.

I pray youe send me worde what ye thinke good to be answered by me to Master Southwel, wherein I praye youe knowe the Quenes Highnes pleasour.

Your assured loving frend,

STE. WINTON, Cancell.

Addressed: To the Right Worshipful Sir [2]William Peter, Knight, oon of the Quenes Highnes Principal Secretaries.

Endorsed: My Lord Chancellour, xj° Februarii, 1553⟨54⟩.

161. *To the* MASTERS AND PRESIDENTS OF ALL THE COLLEGES AT CAMBRIDGE

Southwark, 4 April, 1554

Camb. Univ. Registry, Liber Rerum Memorabilium, 128. Sixteenth-century copy. Eighteenth-century copies from this in Camb. Univ. Lib., Baker, xxxiv, 328–9; B.M., Add. 5843, 428. Lib. Rer. Mem. is here followed.

> The Vice-Chancellor is to provide a processional cross, to which each college is to contribute; God is honoured by ceremonies; has also written about a solemn act to be done at Oxford (the disputation with Cranmer, Latimer, and Ridley, which began 14 April).

After my ryght hartie commendacions: I have willed Master Yonge, Vicechauncelour theire, to provyde a semely crosse of silver, for to be used in your processions, as hathe been amonge you in tymes past, and is through Chr⟨i⟩stendom at this day observed. And for asmyche as this charge redoundethe to the decent order which eche particuler man and every severall college of thUniversitie shuld desire, I thinke it meete that by a commen contribution ⟨of⟩ the colleges, in the name of all that inhabitt them, the saide charge shulde be borne, the revenues of the college consydered, and the summe to be proporcionably rated, acordinge to the same. Wherin I require you to shewe your selfe conformable, therbye

1 t *incomplete follows*   2 W *writ. over something else*

463

to declare your ernest goode will to the restitucion of Godes true honor, whiche, beinge grounded *in spiritu et veritate,* is utwardly testified by suche owtward godly rites and ceremonies as be receyved and alowed in the hole bodye of Christes Churche. I have further declared the Quenes pleasour to the saide Master Yonge, touchinge a solempne acte to be don at Oxforde, wherin I praye you to geve credite unto him. And so fare ye hartely well. Att my house in Southwarke, the iiij[th] of Aprill 1554.

Your lovinge frende,

STE. WINTON, Cancell.

Headed: To his lovinge frendes, the Masters and Presidentes of all the Colleges within the Universitie of Cambryge, and to everye of them.

Beside heading: Concerninge contribucion to the crosse.

NOTE TO NO. 161

In January, 1548, the University had sold its great cross of silver for £92. 18s., to defray expenses attendant upon royal confirmation of grants previously made to the University (Cooper, *Annals,* II, 9). The new cross cost £30. 0s. 8d. The amounts paid by each college may be found *ib.,* 85.

162. *To* CARDINAL POLE

Southwark, 5 April, 1554

B.M., Add. 25,425, 241. Seventeenth-century copy of translation into Italian.

> Acknowledges a letter from Pole (*see* App. 4); advises Pole to write to Parliament on unity in religion and to refer only vaguely to a future restoration of Papal power, while promising not to molest possessors of erstwhile monastic property.

Doppo le mie cordialissime raccomandazioni ringrazio humilmente Vostra Signoria Riverendissima delle sue lettere per le quali ella si è

After my most hearty commendations: I humbly thank your Most Reverend Lordship for your letters, in which you rejoice with me that

rallegrata con me, che io sia ritornato a quello stato, e condizione che longamente ho desiderato di ricuperare ed ottenere con speranza di vedere con l'aiuto di Dio il resto del regno, ridotto alla medesima unità per la quale potremo tutti uno ore glorificar Deum Patrem per Jesum Christum, per il quale effetto a voi è stata commessa un eminente⟨?⟩ legazione la quale non dubito che in tale maniera usarate, che condescendendo alle nostre infermità sicome fin que havete cominciato di fare vorrete con tali gradi procedere avanti, che schifando l'offesa d'alcuni, gl' altri potranno per buoni mezzi essere invitati et indotti a desiderare quello di che debbano essere desiderosi senza temer la perdita di quelle cose che essi così malvolentieri lasciarebbero, nel qual proposito saria ben che a Vostra Signoria Illustrissima piacesse di scrivere una lettera alli Signori del Parlamento che hora son ragunati la quale contenesse solamente in generale la materia dell' unità nella religione con tal temperamento che il dritto del pappa vi fosse più tosto insinuato che con chiare parole espresso ne anco così precisamente fatto⟨?⟩ che possano concludere essere in procinto. Una simile lettera saria un buon preparativo purche Vostra Signoria Riverendissima con quella occasione

---

I have returned to that state and condition which I have for a long time desired to recover and to achieve, in the hope of seeing, with the help of God, the rest of the realm restored to the same unity, through which we shall be able all with one voice to glorify God the Father through Jesus Christ. To which end an illustrious legation has been entrusted to you, which I do not doubt you will execute in such a manner that, condescending to our infirmities, as already you have begun to do, you will proceed with such steps that, by contemning, as beneath your notice, the offence of some, others may be encouraged and induced by good means to desire that of which they should be desirous, without fearing the loss of those things which they would so unwillingly abandon.

For this purpose it would be well that it should please your illustrious Lordship to write to the Parliament now in session a letter which should treat, in general only, the question of unity in religion, with such moderation that the right of the pope would be rather suggested than expressed in clear words, and even that not so precisely done that they could conclude it (*i.e.*, the restoration of Papal jurisdiction) to be imminent. Such a letter would be a good preparation, provided that your Most Reverend Lordship on this occasion declared and

dichiarasse e facesse intendere alli duci⟨?⟩ ⟨del⟩ popolo di questo regno
che nella riformazione che si desidera di fare nella nostra nativa patria
non s'intende di fare alterazione alcuna delle possessioni e beni tem-
porali hereditivi per il regno, ma che ognuno habbia a godere tutto
quello che tiene o per donazione o per haverle comprate secondo le leggi
e decreti del regno fatti per assicurare e confermare tale sorte di pos-
sessione. La quale materia così proposta e temperata con tali buone
parole co' quali la prudenza vostra la saprà proporre aggiungendo al
haver facoltà d'esseguire tal promessa havrà sicom' io penso tal forza
che basterà a rimovere della mente degli homini quel grande ostacolo il
quale solo come molti prudentemente temono potrebbe impedire appresso illo popolo il nostro santo proposito et intenzione in che io
m'estendo più diffusamente con Vostra Signoria Illustrissima che non
bisogna, potendo ella per se stessa facilmente conoscere ciò che gli con-
vien di fare e quali mezzi siano da usare per condurre la cosa al fine che
si desidera sopra questa materia et il stato di questo Regno. Ho rag-
giunto a lungo col vostro fedel servitore Enrico Piningo il quale son
certo che vi riferirà il tutto e così raccomandandomi a Vostra Signoria

---

made it known to the leaders of the people of this realm that in the
reformation which we desire to effect in our native land there is no
intention of making any alteration in the possessions and temporal
inheritances throughout the realm, but that each will be able to enjoy all
which he holds either by gift or by right of purchase, according to the
laws and decrees of the realm made to secure and confirm such possession. Which matter, so set forth and tempered with such good words
as your wisdom will know how to use, together with the knowledge
that you are able to perform such a promise, will have, as I think, such
weight as will suffice to remove from the minds of men that great
obstacle which alone, as many prudently fear, could hinder in the eyes
of the people our holy purpose and intention.

I am more diffuse with your illustrious Lordship than is necessary,
seeing that you can easily know of your own accord what is needful to
do, and what means should be employed to bring the affair to the end
we desire in this matter and the state of this kingdom. I have at length
met your faithful servant, Henry Pining, who, I am sure, will relate all
to you.

Illustrissima, con offerirle il mio servizio, prego Dio, etc. Dal mio palazzo di Sothwarck, li 5 Aprile, 1554.

Di Vostra Signoria Illustrissima
humile e quotidiano oratore,

STEFANO

Headed: Al Signor Cardinale Polo

With commendations to your illustrious Lordship and offers of my service, I pray God, etc. From my house in Southwark, 5 April, 1554.

Your Most Illustrious Lordship's
humble and daily orator,

STEPHEN

Headed: To Lord Cardinal Pole

163. *To the* PRESIDENT AND FELLOWS OF PETERHOUSE IN CAMBRIDGE

[St James, before 1 May, 1554]

Copies of this and the following letter are entered, one immediately after the other, in a probably contemporary hand, in the Old Register of Peterhouse, 302. Copies of both letters from this are to be found in the mimeograph (or letter press) long hand copy of the Old Register at Peterhouse, and in B.M., Add. 5843, 76–7. Both in J. Heywood, *Early Cambridge Statutes*, London, 1855, II, 79–80. Peterhouse Old Register is here followed.

Since the mastership is vacant because the Master (Ralph Ainsworth) is married, they are to choose Dr Thomas Segiswicke in his place.

After my hartye commendacions: Wheras it pleased the Quenes Highnes to commytte unto me the orderynge of all matters appertayninge to thUnyversytee; and that nothinge ther is more necessary for the same, than to have goode and discreete heades in the colleges; therfore, seyinge that the mastership of your colledge (by reason that the Master thereof is maryed contrary to the ecclessyasticall lawes and your statutes) is now voyed; these shalbe to desyer you that ye wyll chose the bearer herofe, Master Segiswicke, a man for his wisdome and honesty and behavyour very meate for that rowme. And in so doyng ye shall have me reddye to doe you the lyke pleasure, whan tyme and occasion shall serve, by Godes grace, Whoe prosper you in all godlye studye and vertewe.

Your loving frende,

STE. WINTON, Cancell.

Headed: To mie loving frendes the President and Felowes of Peter House in Cambridge.

164. *To the* FELLOWS AND COMPANY OF PETERHOUSE IN CAMBRIDGE

St James, 1 May, 1554

For source *see* under No. 163.

They are to choose Dr Andrew Perne as Master. (To explain the change in Gardiner's wishes which this and the preceding letter indicate, Dr T. A. Walker, historian of Peterhouse, suggests that Perne 'had evidently secured support in an influential quarter.' For Perne's remarkable mastership, 1554–89, *see* Walker, *Peterhouse*, London, 1906, 84 ff.)

After my hartye commendations: Forasmuch as I fynde this berer, Doctor Perne, a man of muche towardnes, and of so good conformytee in matters of religion, thies be therfor to requyre you aswell to accept and use hym as your Master of that house, as also, by your obedient behavyour towardes hym, to demeane your selves in the rest of your doynges accordinglye, and as best maye stande with good order and thauncient statutes of your sayde house. And thus fare ye well. At S. Jeames, the fyrst of Maye, 1554.

Your loving frende,

STE. WINTON, Cancell.

Headed: To my loving frendes the Felowes and Companie of Peter House in Cambridge.

165. *To* John Young, Vice-Chancellor of Cambridge University

The Court [at Oatlands], 17 June, 1554

Camb. Univ. Registry, Liber Rerum Memorabilium, 129 v. Sixteenth-century copy. Eighteenth-century copies from this in Camb. Univ. Lib., Baker, xxxiv, 330–1; B.M., Add. 5843, 429–30. Lib. Rer. Mem. is here followed.

> Young is to receive George Bullock (admitted Master of St John's, 12 May, 1554, succeeding Thomas Watson, resigned) as a member of the University, and favour his suit against John Mere (Registrary) for the recovery of the ornaments of St John's.

Master Vicechauncelour, after my ryght hartie commendacions: I have consulted the cause of Master Bullocke and Mere togyther with the privileges of the Universitie, the preservacion of whiche privileges I owght and doo favour; whyche by Master Bullokes sute be nothinge towched, *benigna interpretacione*, with respecte of my person, beinge Chauncelour ther, before whome is not exercysed *iudicium laicale*, which your statute forbyddethe. The cause of Master Bullokes sute owght so moche to be favored and Meres doinges, as I am informed of hym, so moche detested, as the maner of brynginge the matter to my knowlege may be excused. Wherfore theise shalbe to requyre you to receyve the seyde Master Bulloke as a member of that Universitie, and if you have pronownsed any sentens of excommunicacion agaynst hym, to absoyle hym from it. And because he hathe byn ever noted Catholike, regarde hym therafter, and so to tender his sute agaynst Mere as the recoverye of those ornamentes, wherof the college is shamfullye spoyled, shuld move all good men, and specyallye your selfe, beinge once a member of the same college; not doinge to Mere any wronge, but with dewe severytye to releve the college, so farre as justyce may permitt. And so finisshinge theise matters amonge your selfe, to agree in goodnes agaynst evell men, to ther discourage and comforthe of the good; which God graunte and send you well to doo. Att the Courte the xvij^th of June, 1554.

Your lovinge frende,

STE. WINTON, Cancell.

Headed: To Doctour Yonge, Vicechauncelour of Cambryge, concerninge the matter betwyxt S. Johns and Mere.

166. *To the* STUDENTS OF CHRIST CHURCH, OXFORD

The Court [at Hampton Court], 1 September, 1554

R.O., S.P. 11, 9, 29. A certified copy made by a notary in 1556. B.M., Harl. 7001, 233. A late sixteenth- or seventeenth-century copy. H. L. Thompson, *Christ Church*, London, 1900, 39. R.O. is here followed.

Rebukes their disobedience to their dean (Richard Marshall); they are to observe the decrees of the dean and chapter as statutes, until others are sent. (Copies of two letters of the same tenor from subsequent Lord Chancellors, 1556, 1581, are preserved in B.M., Harl. 7001, 233. The first is also in R.O., S.P. 11, 9, 29 v.)

I commend me to you: And being credeblie enformed of your willfull disobedience towards your deane and subdeane there, in refusing to observe their ¹lawfull and honest¹ injunctions, I marvaile not a little therof that you, being men of knowledge and learning, will practise such factious stubbornes, to the evill example of others and to the empayring of good and decent order in that² whole Universitie. Wherfore as your Visitor, in that I am Chauncellor of England, I require and charge you and every of you duly and forthwith to receyve and obey such lawfull and honest injunctions as your deane and, in his absence, the subdeane shall require you to observe. Assuring you that if further complaint of your misdemeanes³ hereafter be made and proved, the same shall be soe punished that all others, namely, the heads of such confederacies, shall have cause continually to abstaine from like presumption and disobedience. Also other decrees made by the deane and chapiter there, or hereafter to be made, yee shall duly keepe and observe as statutes, untill such time that⁴ it shall please the King and the Queenes Highnes to send you statutes indented according to the foundacion of that church. And these my letters shall remaine with the deane and canons there, you having a copye, if yee will. Fare yee well. From the Courte the first of Septembre, 1554.

STE. WINTON, Cancell.

Headed: To the Students of Christchurch in Oxford.

1-1 *B.M.*, honeste and lawfull	2 *B.M.*, the
3 *B.M.*, misdemeanour	4 *B.M.*, as

167. *To* MONTMORENCY, CONSTABLE OF FRANCE

London, 15 or 16 November, 1554

Noailles, *Ambassades en Angleterre*, Leyden, 1763, III, 321–2; and again, with slight variations, in the same, IV, 17–18 (cited as IV in the footnotes).

Hears of Montmorency's desire to maintain the friendship between England and France, and to make peace throughout Christendom; assures him of a like desire on his part. (This was an answer to a letter of credence from Montmorency, 24 September, 1554, brought to England by François de Noailles, approving Gardiner's desire to maintain peace between England and France—Noailles, III, 319.)

Monsieur le connestable, tant par la lettre qu'il vous a pleu m'escripre comme parce que [1]me a[1] monstré de vostre part, Monsieur le prothonotaire de Noailles, frere de Monsieur l'ambassadeur residant icy, j'ay entendu la bonne affection que portez devers la conservation de l'amytié d'entre[2] ces deulx royaulmes, avecques une saincte disposition à la paix pour le bien universel, chose certes qui correspond à l'opinion que j'ay tousjours eue de vostre seigneurie en cest endroict; car quant à moy je n'ay [3]oncques peu[3] apperceveoir que n'ayez tousjours monstré la mesme inclination, en quoy s'il[4] semblera bon à vostre seigneurie de persévérer, vous pouvez estre asseuré que aultant [5]qu'il sera en mon[5] possible, feray tout ce que je[6] verray estre non seullement à la conservation de ladicte amytié, mais aussy au bien et prouffict de toute la chrestienté, comme vous sçaura dire plus à plein ledict Monsieur le prothonotaire. Et ainsy en[7] me recommandant de bien bon cueur à la bonne grace de vostre seigneurie, je prie à Dieu vous voulloir donner, Monsieur le connestable, tres bonne vie et longue. [8]De Londres ce 16[8] jour de novembre, 1554.

Votre anciennement bon amy,

[9]STE. WINTON[9], Cancell.

Et au-dessus, à Monsieur, Monsieur le connestable de France.

1–1 *IV*, m'a	2 *IV*, entre
3–3 *IV*, peu oncques	4 *IV*, il
5–5 *IV*, que sera en moy	6 *not in IV*
7 *not in IV*	8–8 *IV*, Escript a Londres le 15
9–9 *IV*, Stermton	

168. *To the* MAYOR AND HIS BRETHREN
OF LEICESTER

Southwark, 8 January, [1555]

Leicester Book of Acts, p. 19. Sixteenth-century copy. M. Bateson, *Records of the Borough of Leicester*, Cambridge, 1905, III, 82; J. Nichols, *Hist. and Antiq. of Leicester*, London, 1815, I, ii, 395.

Hears they are desirous of newfangleness; bids them adhere to ancient customs.

After commendacions: I understand by advertysment from your towne that dyverse of you beynge rather desyerous of newfanglenes then contentyd to follow suche auncyent and laudable customes as have had, tyme out of mynde, ther contynaunce, whych yow have of late sowght meanes to breke and abolyshe suche therof wherby your common welthe ys most countenaunced and set forthe; wher uppon I thowght yt mete to requere so many of you as be thus fondly affectyd, that, levyng of suche vayne fances, ye woll henseforthe remayne quyet and contentyd to follow and allowe suche laudable customes and rewles as haue alwayes ben, tyme out of mynde, usyd amongest yow. Thus fare yow well. At my house in London, this viij^{th} of January.

Your loving frende.

Headed: A letter sent from my Lorde Chauncellour to Master Mayer and his brethren for the werynge of ther apparell in the tyme of meraltie of Master John Berredge with other letteres as followth ⟨'other letteres' appears to refer to a letter from Sir Robert Rochester, 19 January, 1555⟩.

169. NO ADDRESS

Southwark, 18 February, 1555

B.M., Add. 6668, 399. Original, probably in clerk's hand, signed by Gardiner.

The recipient had better reform himself.

After my harty commendacions: I sende youe herewith suche complaynte as is made agenste youe, the matter wherof, if it be true, you were better reforme your selfe for thavoydinge of further troble, then to be ordered at my handes as justyce shall require. I have a good hope thereof, and therfore rather send to youe then for youe, as the party desireth. So fare ye well. From my howse in Sowthwarke, the xviij^{th} of February, 1555.

Your lovinge frend,

STE. WINTON, Cancell.

170. *To the* VICE-CHANCELLOR AND COUNCIL OF CAMBRIDGE UNIVERSITY

Southwark, 19 February, 1555

Camb. Univ. Registry, Liber Rerum Memorabilium, 131 v. Sixteenth-century copy. Eighteenth-century copies from this in Camb. Univ. Lib., Baker, xxxiv, 334, and *ib.*, xxxi, 241. Lib. Rer. Mem. is here followed.

Requests the election of his old servant and scholar, William Muryell, as bedell (*see also* No. 172).

After my veray hartye commendacions: Where I am credyblye informed that the romme or place of one of the bedelles of your Universitie is voyde by the death of one Thomas Adams, nowe lately deceassed, and not yet geven to any man, ye shall understand that I, tenderynge the preferment of the berer hereof, William Muryell, my olde servaunte and scholer, and your neyghbour, desyre and requyre you, at the contemplacion of these my letters, that you wyll admitte and gyve unto my seyde servaunte, the seyde romme and place, and, in so doinge, I shall not fayle to consyder your towardnes to this my request, in other your sewtes here after; byddyinge you ryght hartelye farewell. From my howse by Sowthwerke, this xix^{th} of Februar⟨y⟩, 1554⟨55⟩.

Your lovinge freende,

STE. WINTON, Cancell.

Headed: To my lovinge fryndes the Vicechauncelour and other the Counsell of thUniversitie of Cambryge.

Beside heading: For thoffice of the bedleshippe.

473

Dr William Glyn, Vice-Chancellor, being appointed a member of the embassy to Rome led by Bishop Thirlby (February–August, 1555), was probably already away from Cambridge at this time. Dr Cuthbert Scott acted as deputy Vice-Chancellor during his absence, and succeeded to the office the following Michaelmas. But sometime during the academic year 1554–5 Dr Thomas Segiswicke acted as deputy in Scott's absence (J. Venn, *Grace Book* Δ, Cambridge, 1910, 108, 567).

For the office of bedell and information concerning all who have held it *see* H. P. Stokes, *The Esquire Bedells of the University of Cambridge*, Camb. Antiq. Soc., 1911.

171. *To* SIR JOHN SHELTON

Southwark, 22 March, 1555

B.M., Harl. 6989, 159–60. Original, in clerk's hand, signed by Gardiner.

Assures him that his servant has delivered certain examinations of felons, now mislaid.

After my hartie commendacions: For the better credite of this bearer your servaunte, of whome he saith, ye seeme to conceive some gelousye for not deliverirïg certaine examinacions of felons unto me according to your letters in that behalfe directed, thiese ben for troth to advertise you that the saide examinacions weare by hym delivered unto me accordinglie. Nevertheles, wheare the same at this present do remaine I do not now perfitlie remember. Thus fare you hartelie well. From my house in Southwerke, this xxij[th] of Marche, 1554⟨55⟩.

Your loving freende,

STE. WINTON, Cancell.

Addressed: To his veray loving freende, Sir John Shelton, Knight.

172. *To the* VICE-CHANCELLOR OF CAMBRIDGE UNIVERSITY

Southwark, 24 March, 1555

C.C.C.C., MS. 106, 299 v. Sixteenth-century copy in Parker Collection. Another sixteenth-century copy in Camb. Univ. Registry, Liber Rerum Memorabilium, 134 v. Eighteenth-century copy from the latter in Camb. Univ. Lib., Baker, xxxiv, 334–5. From C.C.C.C. in Lamb, 170; Cooper, *Annals*, ii, 94. C.C.C.C. is here followed. Lib. Rer. Mem. is cited in the footnotes as L.

Since Muryell (*see* No. 170) has not been elected to the bedellship, will appoint him to serve until he (Gardiner) can come and hold an election; no one hereafter shall vote or receive a degree who has not subscribed to Catholic doctrine.

Master Vic⟨echancellour⟩, after my hartye commendations: I have ben advertised from youe and other of the heedis of th[1]Universitie howe glad youe[2] be to gratefie me in such request as I have made for the preferment of my servant in[3] to the rome of a bedelship nowe voyd, wheronto such as be Catholique, as I am enformed, have also shewed themself wel wylling, and have gyven their voycis accordingly, wich I wil consider as oportunytie shal serve. And forasmoche as I perceyve these sondry elections engender contention, I have thought good to commawnd youe to forbere from eny furder scrutynie, and to differ this mater tyl I com myself to set such ordre as maye be a staye and quyet to the nombre ther[4]. And in the meane tyme, till such election maye pass as the statute req*ui*reth, consideryng the more part do already fynd themself content with the parson of my sayd[5] servant, commendyd unto youe by me, I entend by myn owne[6] authoritie, after these iij scrutynes passed, to appoynt hym to serve the[7] rome, lest, bi wilful contention of summe, the[8] place ther[9] shuld be disfurnyshed, and the honor of the Universitie therbi dymynished, as som wold have it. Wherfor I wil youe to admyt my sayd servant to occupie the[10] rome without prejudice of your[11] statut*e*s or such election as at my commyng shal, according[12] to the statut*e*s, be made in that behalf.

And furthermore, to thentent such slander as that Universytie hath fallen in to bi light and sedicious wytt*e*s maye be the better purged, I commawnd youe in all your[13] elections and gyving of voyces to eny gracys and admissions to all degrees, none shalbe admytted to gyve voyce or receyve degre but such only as have openly in the congregation house detested particularly and bi articles the heresies lately spred in this realme, and professed bi articles the Catholike doctryne nowe

1 *L.*, that	2 *L.*, they	3 *not in L.*
4 *space in C.C.C.C.; L. supplies* ther		5 *not in L.*
6 *not in L.*	7 *L.*, that	8 *L.*, that
9 *not in L.*	10 *L.*, that	11 *L.*, the
12 *L.*, acordinglye	13 *not in L.*	

receyved, and subscribed the same with their hond*e*s. Wherein I praye youe advertise me what youe have done, and see the premysses executed accordingly. And so fare youe well. At my house in Southwarke, the xxiiij of Marche, 1554⟨55⟩.

Your lovyng frend,

STE. WYNTON, Cancell.

Headed: For the bedelship.

To my lovyng frend the Vicechancellou*r* of Cambrige, and to hym that shal succede hym in that rome[1].

NOTES TO NO. 172

Dr Glyn, Vice-Chancellor, was certainly away from Cambridge at this time, and Dr Scott, or possibly Dr Segiswicke, acting in his place (*see* note, p. 474).

As a result of this letter the Senate chose four doctors who drew up fifteen articles for subscription (Cooper, *Annals*, II, 95).

On 20 November, 1555, eight days after Gardiner's death, his executors wrote to the Vice-Chancellor, Regents, and Non-regents requesting that Muryell 'be throwghlye stayed' in the office of bedell, since this was 'the last desyre of hym that was the fyrst autho*u*r of his preferment' (Lib. Rer. Mem., 135). Muryell lost the office 1 February, 1556 (H. P. Stokes, *The Esquire Bedells*, Camb. Antiq. Soc., 1911, 10, 83).

173. *To* BONNER

Esher, 10 April, 1555

Bonner Register, ccclviii. Contemporary copy. Another contemporary copy in the Register of Christ Church, Canterbury, *Sede vacante*, N va. A copy from this, made 1693, is in Camb. Univ. Lib., Add. 3, No. 45; another, made in the eighteenth century, is in B.M., Add. 5853, 439. Foxe, *1563*, 1118; ed. Pratt, VII, 37. Holinshed, IV, 77–8. Bonner is here followed.

Obsequies are to be said for the Pope (Julius III, d. 23 March, 1555) and the prayers enclosed used at Mass; Bonner is to notify the rest of the bishops.

After my hartye commendacyons to your good Lordship: The King and the Quenes Majestyes, having certayne knowledge of the death of

1 *L. heads the letter* (*it would seem erroneously*), To Master Doctou*r* Yonge, now Vicechauncelou*r* of Cambr. and to hym that shall succede hym in that rome; *adding, beside the heading*, for the bedleshippe and subscriptyons.

the Popes Holyness, thought good there shulde be aswell solemnpne obsequyes sayde for him thoroughoute the ralme, as also these prayers, which I sende you herin inclosed, used at Masse tymes in all places at this tyme of vacatyon; and therfore willed me to signyfye there pleasures unto you in this behalffe, that theruppon ye mighte proceade to the full accomplyshmente therof, by putting the same in dewe execucyon within your owne dioces, and sending woorde to the reste of the bysshopps to doo the lyke in theyrs. Thus doubting not but that your Lordship will use suche diligence in this matter at this tyme as shalbe necessary, I bidd your Lordship heartelye well to fare. From my house at Asshere, the tenth of Aprill, 1555.

Your Lordships assured frynde and brother,

STEPHANUS WINTON, Cancell.

Addressed: To my verey good Lorde the Bisshopp of London.

Apostolica sede vacante

⟨Oratio⟩

Supplici te, Domine, humilitate deposcimus, ut tua immensa pietas sacrosancte Romane ecclesie concedat pontificem illum, qui et pro in nos studio semper tibi gratus, et tuo populo pro salubri regimine sit assidue ad gloriam tui nominis venerandus, per Dominum nostrum.

Secreta

Tue nobis, Domine, pietatis abundantia indulgeat, ut gratum maiestati tue pontificem sancte matris ecclesie regimini preesse gaudeamus, per Dominum nostrum.

Post Communionem

Preciosi corporis et sanguinis tui, Domine, sacramento refectos mirifica tue maiestatis gratia de illius summi pontificis assumptione letificet, qui et plebem tuam virtutibus instruat, et fidelium mentes spiritualium aromatum odore perfundat, per Dominum nostrum.

APPENDIX

INTRODUCTORY NOTE

The first item in the Appendix is a hitherto unpublished and un-calendared copy of Gardiner's oath to Henry VIII for the temporalities of his bishopric, taken, presumably, at Hampton Court on 29 November, 1531, since the grant of the temporalities is thus dated (*L.P.*, v, 627 [8]). The oath is found in a collection of forms of oaths of homage and fealty at the end of a little volume of twenty-one folio pages, containing certain articles on the ordering of the King's Chamber and the duties of his servants, which appears to have belonged to Henry Fitzalan, Earl of Arundel, Lord Chamberlain, 1546–50. The oath is erroneously headed 'The renouncement of the popes power and jurisdiction.' For Gardiner's renunciation of the Papacy *see* Foxe, v, 71.

The second item is Gardiner's lost tract against William Turner, or at least as much of it as is to be found in Turner's reply to it. In 1543, Turner, under the pseudonym of William Wraghton, published *The huntyng and fyndyng out of the Romyshe foxe, which more then seven yeares hath bene hyd among the bisshoppes of Englonde*. This is dated 14 September, 1543; hence Gardiner's answer to it must have appeared after that date. No copy of Gardiner's book appears to be extant, but Turner wrote a reply to it, reprinting parts, perhaps the whole, of it, in sections throughout his own book. The volume is extremely rare. As far as I have been able to discover, only five copies of it are in existence. It is entitled *The Rescuynge of the romishe fox other vvyse called the ex-amination of the hunter devised by steven gardiner. The seconde course of the hunter at the romishe fox & his advocate & sworne patrone steven gardiner doctor & defender of the popis canon law and hys ungodly cere-monies*. It purports to be published at Winchester, and is dated 4 March, 1545. It is to William Turner, as the author of this volume, that Gardiner presumably refers as the 'jolly hunter' in Nos. 80–1.

When Gardiner's paragraphs are taken from this book and placed together they make a reasonably complete whole, affording an excellent and not too lengthy example of his manner as a popular controversialist in defence of the Henrician establishment. They also contain some interesting autobiographical references to his debate with Bucer and Alesius at Ratisbon in 1541.

The third item is a letter from Somerset concerning his plan to create a college of Civil Law at Cambridge by the union of Trinity and Clare Halls and the Hostel of St Nicholas. This involved the surrender of Trinity Hall by its Master, Gardiner. None of his correspondence on the subject exists; hence the value of Somerset's letter, not only as giving Somerset's side of the matter, but also as supplying some inkling of the reasons for Gardiner's refusal to surrender his college.

The fourth item is a letter from Cardinal Pole. We do not have Gardiner's to which it is a reply, nor do we have any other letter from Gardiner dealing with this topic; namely, his regret for his support of Henry VIII in the breach with Rome. If Pole's references to what Gardiner had written him be correct, and not merely Pole's own elaborations on the theme, the letter supplies important evidence of the way Gardiner, in 1554, looked back on his activities under Henry VIII. It may, however, be significant that in Gardiner's reply to this letter (No. 162, above) he touches very lightly on the subject.

The last item is the Heralds' account of Gardiner's obsequies and is of interest as a first-hand description of one of the lavish and vivid customs of the day.

1. GARDINER'S OATH TO THE KING
FOR HIS TEMPORALITIES

[Hampton Court, 29 November, 1531]

B.M., Add. 34,319, 21 v. Sixteenth-century copy.

I, Steven Gardener, Principall Secretarie to your Highnes, and clerk, Busshop of Winchester, renounce and clerely forsake all such clauses, wordes, sentences, and grauntes which I have or shall have herafter of the Popes Holines of the busshoprick off Winchester that in any wise is or may be prejudiciall to your Highnes, your heires, successours dignitie or estate roiall, knowleging my self to take and hold the said busshoprick immediately and only of your Highnes, most lowly beseching your Grace the same for restituicion of the temporalities of the said busshoprick, promising as afore that I shalbe faithfull, true, and obedient subject to your said Highnes, your heires and successours

479

during my life. And the service and other thinges due unto your High-nes for the restituicion of the said temporalities of the said busshoprick, I shall truly do and performe, so help me God and the holie Evangelistes.

2. GARDINER'S LOST TRACT AGAINST WILLIAM TURNER

[Probably 1544]

For source *see* Introductory Note to Appendix, p. 478. The emenda-tions listed in Turner's book under 'fautes' are here incorporated into the text.

A defence of Catholic practices in the English Church in the time of Henry VIII. Wraghton (pen-name of Turner), though pretending to hunt the Romish fox, is angry at the altar and the chalice; why the pope was expelled from England; things good in themselves not to be condemned because the pope uses them; discussion of Wraghton's attack on Church law, ceremonies, holy water, communion in one kind, Lent, use of Latin in services; what Gardiner heard in Brentius' church at Hall in Swabia; an account of Gardiner's discussion of clerical celibacy with Bucer and Alesius at Ratisbon, 1541 (*cf.* Nos. 67, 97, 144); Wraghton aims to drive all godliness from the Church of England.

The examination of a prowd praesumptuous hunter, who, under a crafty praetence of huntyng the Romishe fox, breakethe the pale of the enclosed park, and with hys rashe and knavishe houndes entendethe to destroy the dere of the same

Syth it hathe pleased Allmyghty God, autor of unite, to raduce thys realme to perfect accorde and agrement in the truthe, and, by good polytike lawes, hathe, under the only autorite of the Kyngis Majesti, enclosed and, as it were, imparked the derebeloved subjectes for theyr savegarde with in the forche and streynghe of the same, how mych is it to be lamented, to se arrogance in the eyes of the sayde subjectes, as with breache and violacion of the sayd lawes, to make a tumult and a clamor, under pretence of huntynge the fox that is all redy dryven out; therby to move and troble the hartes of the good peple, and to corrupt such other as be easy for theyr simplicite to be seduced.

But thus strangely the devel setteth furthe hys malice and hunteth, sumtyme roryng lyke a lyon to devoure the good, somtyme sleyghtly lyke the fox, whome he pretendeth to chace away. And seeing it hathe pleased the Kyngis Majesti thys hunter may be examined, and, for want of the presence of the man, to consydre the chefe poyntes and matters of the booke, I trust so in differently to handle the examination as, what so ever name the man hathe, he may appere to yow of such sorte as hys book, wel examined, dothe playnly declare. The man calleth hym self Wraghton, and, pretendyng in the begynnyng of hys booke to write suche matter as he wold have cum to the Kyngis Majesties knowledge, he can not be content to attributte[1] that stile to hys Majesti where withe the hole realme hathe trewly agreede hys Hygnes shuld be honored, to be Supreme Hede of the Chirche of Englond and Irelande. Thys can have no pretence of ignorance and simplicite, but it is a playn declaration of pryde and arroganci. In hys preface to the Kyngis Majesti he confessethe his ignorance of huntyng, whereby he belevethe to have the more learnyng; whiche of what sorte it is, shal after apere.

The man pretendeth to hunt the Romishe fox, and assigneth ij places specially, one under the aultare and an other under the chalice; where by he declarethe where at he shoteth. Albeit he wold gladly dissemble it, yit he cannot utterly hyde that[2] he is angrie withe the aultare and withe the chalice, and fareth as miners do that intend to throw down ther neyborres hows, pretendyng to fynde an othar. Ye may sown se wherfore he seketh that fyndeth fault in the altare and chalice. But let us heare the man speake, and examin hys resones whether ther be any reson in them.

Thus he begynneth hys huntyng: Ye lordly bisshoppes etc. He askethe whether the Kyngis Majesti bannisshed the popes name, hys purse, and hys doctrine. And by thys distribution the man, makyng hym self answere to eche membre and parte, devyseth hym self matter there upon to triumphe. But if an other shuld answer hym, he wold say that the Kyngis Majesti bannisshed not the bisshop of Rome ether for hys name alone, for hys purse alone, or for hys doctrine alone, but for all to gether. And not for all to gether so as all to gether were nought, but for all to gether so far as he misusethe them.

And as touchyng hys name, so far as it shuld signifi a superiorite above all princes and chalenge a dominion in thys realme, so far is the name of pope bannisshed. But els the good man Pope of Trumpyngton may in Englond lyve quietly; for the name was never abhorred but as it brought a wrong persuasione of the bisshop of Rome by that name;

---

1 *printed* attributto   2 *printed* it

where as els 'the bisshop of Rome' men call hym still withe out danger.

And as concernyng hys purse, as it was worthely expelled, so was it not because any mony myght ⟨not⟩ be taken of the spiritualti by theyr just superioures, but because it myght not be justly taken of hym that was nether superior nether yit did any thyng for it.

And as concernyng such doctrine as was under hym taught, it was never under stand of any good man that all that whiche was taught ether by the bisshop of Rome or under hys autorite was hys own doctrine and to be cast away; but only that whiche was worthely to manteyn hys auctorite to be reject with hym; and that[1] whiche was good to be reteyned and kept, not because it was hys, but because it is good. Shall not we confess Christe the Son of God because the devel sayd the same?

Finally, the bisshop of Rome was expelled nether for hys name only, hys purs only, ne hys doctrine only, but for all to gether, so far as eche of them exceded from the treuthe, whiche is only mynded. All noughty doctrine is expelled withe the bisshop of Rome, and not because it was hys, but because it was nought. It were pity that evel men shuld have suche a stroke in thynges of the world, and moche less of God, that what good thynge one medled withe shuld be called by and by nought. Kyng Richarde the thyrde, an usurper in thys realme, brak the trust committed unto hym by hys brother, concernyng the preservation of hys childer, and yit caused an act of the Parlement after to be made in hys tyme, that feoffes of trust shuld do acordyng to theyr trust. The autor we justly hate, and yit we make myche of the law, whiche is good and resonable. Wher fore the fundacion of thys mannis resonyng, to reprove or reject any ordinance becaus our enemy ether made it or used it, is very slender and folishe. God can be the auctor but of goodnes. Amongest men, that is nought is nought who soever hathe used it, and that that is good is good who soever hathe abused it. And therfore there cannot be more fond maner of provyng then to say, 'Thys is nought. And whi so? For such a man medled with it, suche a man used it, suche a man commanded it to be observed'—as myche agreyng to the fac⟨t⟩iones amongest the Florentines, whil they were in theyr comon welthe, when on, demanded what he sayd to suche a matter, beyng then in consultation, he loked about and, esspying out on of hys enemies,

---

1 *printed* it

sayd, what so ever suche a man wold say, poyntyng to hys enemy, he was of the contrari opinion.

The Kyngis Majesti, lyke a noble prince, hathe proceded in thys mater not upon faction, nor upon displeasure or enemite, but only truth; and therfore hathe rejected the bisshop of Rome so far as he swarveth from the truthe. And, so far as the truthe will beare, hys Majesti agreeth with all the world; intendyng by the expulsion of the bisshop of Rome not to confound the truthe, but to purge it from suche corruption as by the bisshop of Romis mantenance did infect it.

So as thys hunter chasethe far at large when, withe the only bisshop of Romis name, he wold hunt out all, and destroy withe the bad the good also. And so he myght have kept all hys ye hold still, with out ye can other wise disprove them, then because the bisshop of Rome used them or willed them to be used; for they remayne not be cause he wylled or used them, but becaus they be good. The man pleaseth hym self moche that he proveth by dyvers examples that lyke as Aristotellis doctrine is called Aristotel and Terences comedies Terence, so the popes doctrine shuld be called the pope. But herken agayn: if Terence spak that Plato had spoken, when Terence were bannisshed, myght we not use the speche still of Plato because it cam ones out of Terences pen?

Christe sayd, *Doctrina non est mea, sed eius qui misit me patris.* And miche more, what so ever is good, spoken or used by any man, is of God. And Hym ought we to make author of all goodnes, were it Balaames ass that uttered it. If Christ be preachede, sayeth Saynt Paule, be it *per contentionem* or *iudicium*, let it have place *modo Christus predicetur*. Looke upon the trewethe and goodnes of the thyng, settyng a parte the person that speakethe, precheth, uttereth, executethe, or commandethe the same. Ne ther was here to fore any man so mad as, expellyng a tyrant, wold cast away withe hym both that which was good and that whiche was evel also.

Wherefore, seynge in all hys ye hold still, he bringethe no other disprofe but only from the personage that hathe used them, I pas them over as of no force, and cum to hys cokkyng upon the clergie, when he saythe, 'What saye ye, gentle men of the clergie, concernyng the lawes of the Chirche?' I saye here your Mastership playeth bothe the partes, and, as he sayd at gamyng, ye wold win the game if ye played alone. And yit have ye spent a great meny wordes in vayn. Ye put no difference betwene dedes, lawes, and ordinances; and because it were in dede a great foly for any man by proclamation to cause an other mannis dedes

483

to be called hys, as ye put your example ryght lewedly in Sardanapalus, so by yow it shall be lyke foly to call and make an other mannis lawes and ordinances hys by proclamation. Vhere in how miche your foly is, ye evydently declare, that ether do not or will not speake the difference, but abuse the simplicite of the reder, as thoughe dedes and lawes were all one. Where as, in the one, it were madnes by proclamation to make an other mannis dedes hys, and the other of all wyse men used and observed. For in lawes and ordinances the Romanes, sendyng to the Grekes for them, made them by approbation thers. And there is no comon welthe but it hath taken in sum poynte example of an other concernyng the lawes whiche be worthely theyrs, where they have receyved them. And amongest the Athenienses lawes made of Solon were not Solones lawes, but the lawes of the city, as the text of the law sayeth; whiche sufficethe to reprove and confounde thys gentle mannis resonynge, where in he wold seme to excell. But the man concludethe that he wolde have no law but the Gospel in the Chirche; whiche is so far out of reson that I will not reson withe hym in it. And he semethe hym self to be ashamed of it, and therfore takethe upon hym to prove sum parte of suche cerimonies as we observe in the Chirche to be repugnant to the Scripture.

And first he beginnethe with the crepyng to the cros, which ceremonie he can in no wyse digest. Therin he laborethe stoutly from the beginnyng of gramner to the end of logik. For by hys resonyng to declare thys worde 'worship' (whiche he doth right worshipfully), it were idolatri for the servant to make curtesi to hys master, where in he shuld bow hys kne, or the good man to kiss his wyfe; but to knele and to kiss hys superiors hand, were by hym foul and filthy abominatione, for that were both to gether.

What an argument wold thys man set out of a worde in Greke or Latin, being general, to make thereby a speciall conclusion to hys purpose! Scripture usethe the worde *adoro*, as the worde worship is used in Englishe, to signifi godly honor; and Joseph suffered hym self to be worshipped of hys brethern withe reverent behavour; and there is on worde *adoro* in bothe. I may not worship the cros in the chirche with godly honor, for it is against Goddis commandement; but I may use before it reverent behavour, of whiche expressedly spak Saynt Jerom when he sayd, *Adhererem trunco crucis nec prius dimitterem quam veniam obtinuissem.* Thus they delude the simplicite of the peple with the ambiguite of the wordes, and as very enemies of the cros of Christe they labor to extinct all wayes and meanes whiche myght set out the glori of the cros, miche agreable to the Turkes procedynges, who forbiddeth open shewes or preching of Christis religion.

Thes men speak mich of prechyng, but note well thys, they wold we shuld se nothyng in remembrance of Christ, and therfore can they not abyde images. They wold we shuld smel nothyng in memori of Christe, and therfor speak they against anoyntyng and hallywather ⟨i.e., holy water⟩. They wold we shuld taste nothyng in memory of Christe, and therfore they cannot away with salt and holy brede. A supper they speak of, wich they wold handle lyke a dryngkyng. Finally they wold have all in talkyng, they speak so myche of prechynge, so as all the gates of our sences and wayes to mannis understandynge shuld be shit up, savyng the eare alone; as by talkyng the devel were so far onward of hys purpos to extinct Christe, which, with the subversion of the orders of the world, semeth to be the mark where at thys sect shoteth.

But to the purpos of the wordes 'worship' in English and 'adoro' in Latin may be the phrase in Scripture, admitt⟨yng⟩ both the significationes of godly service and reverent behavour. Shall I say that wher godly honor is forbidden reverent behavour is also forbidden, and, by alterynge the signification, juggle and mok with the peple? Of whiche sort be manny of theyr argumentes made, afterward as I shal sho in theyr places. Scripture sumtyme by the outer gesture express⟨es⟩ in speche the godly honor, as in kissyng and knelyng. And not because kissyng and knelyng is the godly honor, but because it was the expressyng of the inwarde affection, with whiche, when kissyng and knelyng is joyned directly to the thyng kissed or kneled unto, it is in dede idolatri. But if kissyng and knelyng be seperat from that opinion, then it is not idolatri; for as trew worship is only in sprete ⟨i.e., spirit⟩ and procedeth from the hart, so doth idolatri procede from the hart also. So that in only kissyng or knelyng can not be idolatri, as thys gentle man wold go about to persuade by such logical collation as he wolde seme clerkly to make upon the signification of the worde.

And yit to streyngthen hys argument he bringeth in the devellis sayng, as he doth in other places, to set furth hys madnes. But what shuld I resone with thys man of crepyng to the cross, that goeth about to prove ryght wisly that we may have no images at all? Which if he cold do, it shuld serve wel for hys purpos to prove that we ought not to worship the cross. If he could prove that antecedent hys consequent were insoluble.

And so is not hys last concludyng argument, whiche he calleth hym self not easy to assoyle, whiche is thys: We myght not worship the angel, Peter and Poul being the beter; ergo, not the cross, beinge of less estimation then Peter or Paul. I, to assoyl the matter easely, say the man useth sophistri in the worde worship; for if he take worship to signifi reverent behavour then I say that the antecedent is fals, and if he will it signifi godly honor it is trewly sayd, but nothing to the purpose. For nether Paule nether the cros can be worshipped with godly honor.

In speakyng agaynst holly water, whiche he entendeth to impugne, the mannis malice putrefieth for lak of salt, whiche he cannot abyde to be santified by the invocation of the name of God. With out learnyng he calleth it conjuryng, and with out wit he despiceth the good wordes.

If thys man had bene by Christe, when he anoynted the blynde mannis eyes with clay, he wold have asked hym whi he made clay an other god besyde him self; and when the woman was heled of hyr diseas, by touchyng of hys garment, why he made hys garment an other God. And when Christe answered to divers, theyr faythe made them hole, he made every mannis faythe a special saviour, after thys noble clerkis doctrine; whiche is so blynded with malice, to desprove al that he redeth that he fyndeth not in Scripture. Many and many tymes that instrumental or occasionative, concurrent or ministeriall cause hath attribute unto it in speche the hole effect, with out prejudice or blasphemi of many goddes or many savioures, as thys beste ⟨i.e., beast⟩, pretendynge to be learned, wold seme to be able to persuade. I shall only use thys one place of Scripture: Dothe Saynt Paule (answer to thys and ye wil) go a bout to make many savioures when he writeth to Timothe, 'Do thys and then thow shalt save thy self and other'? All that is good to man is wrought by God in Christe, for Christe, and by Christe; where he in all creatures may do suche ministeriall service as it shall please God, and that all may serve man to the helth of both body and soul. Good men by the grace purchased by Christe dare bo⟨l⟩dly pray God, and have don from the begynnyng, with prayer and callyng for help of God and expulsion of the devel in all thynge. The devel cannot abyde hally water.

From gestyng agaynst holy water ye descend to scolde with the hole realme, and go about to prove all thos to commit theft and sacriledge that suffer not lay men ⟨to⟩ communicate in ij kyndes. For your reformation there in, ther wanteth but on Ulisses with hys mace to knok yow be-twene the shulders, as he did Thersites for raylyng unsemely agaynst the governoures; by whose auctorite, according to Goddis treweth, the lay men ar there in ordered as hathe bene from the beginnyng, how so-ever it lyketh yow to talk in a mask unknowen. If ye take it (as it semeth ye do not) that in on kynde, of brede only, is hole Christis body and blode, then hathe the lay men nothyng taken from them, but reverently absteyn from other[1] kynde, the fruyt where of they receyve in form of brede. If ye understand not the mysteri of Christis supper as we do, then it is no great sklander for trew men to be called theves of an heretike, al thoghe the example were not to be unponisshed. We deny that the supper hath any halfe at all; then is not all your resonyng worth an half penny.

Ye make your self wrong principles and ther upon in gendre matter to talk on. Whether the prestis receyvyng may profit other is out of the mater, whiche mater ye reson as thoghe ye wold denye *communionem sanctorum* and the mutual help in prayer and oblation of on membre for an other. And then[2] ye make argument that no mannis receyving can profit him self to remission of syn; for, as ye say, ether he receyveth in sin to hys damnation, or out of sin, and then nedeth he no remission of sin, whose synnes be forgyven all redy. And here the man useth so-phistri in the worde 'sinnes,' only to delude and blynd the simple reder[3], which he desyreth to be of the unlearned sorte, that hys talk may be wondered at more then reproved.

When he speaketh of Lent which hath bene, as Origen testifieth, in the Greke Chirche ever from the beginnyng, the man speaketh not playnly whether he mislykethe the prohibition to eat fleshe, or the licens granted for money contrary to the prohibition. He sheweth no other fault here in but becaus the bishop of Rome dothe the lyke. And if the man wold ad to thys that because the bisshop of Rome in hys Chirche wold not suffer men to fast on the Sonday, that therfore we, to disagre with hym, shuld eat fish upon the Sonday and fast also, he spak even as wisely as he doth now.

But he hath made thys for a degre of foly to a grater that folowethe, where, for the hatred of the bisshop of Rome, he wold we shuld do away the use of the Latin tong in the Chirche. And alwayes he calleth the Latin tong the popis mother tong, denying that the Romanes spak Latine still, which whether they dyd or no, in the learned tong, sum have

1 *printed* ether   2 *printed* when   3 *text adds* with

bene that have probablely douted. But what so ever the Romanes have don, they do not so now, so litle cause hath he to call the Latin tong the popis mother tong, when in sum popis it hath happened, and in a great meany of cardinalles also, that nether father nor mother, ne they them selves, have knowen any whit of it.

The man speaketh wisely of the Grekes fallyng from the pope, that never was with hym! And they syng in suche Greke as the mother can no skil of unles she chanceth to be learned, nomore then the bisshop of Romis mother can skil of Latin.

After thys presumptuous ignorance there foloweth as shameful a lye, when he sayth in Germany suche as have left the bisshop of Rome have also left syngyng in Latin in theyr chirches. The contrari where of I have heard with in thes iij yeares in the chirche of Hala, where Brentius teacheth and is chefe preacher; where a servant of myne, in my hearyng, played at the organes at *Magnificat*, when the boys in the quere song *Magnificat* in Latin, as loud as they could crye, eche one utteryng his own breste to the loudest, with out regarde how he agreed with hys felowes. I dowt not but God understood them, but of the nombre that song I dare say a great meany understode not what they song; and we could mych less mark theyr wordes, other then began the verse and ended it. So that thys noble clerke shuld do wel to use all hys resones of Saynt Poule to them there, and ask them what edification the Chirche can have in the noyse of the organes; which, if the player have no other shift, may fortun ⟨to⟩ be furnisshed with the decant of *O lux* in the stede of *Te Deum*. Unto whome they wold answer that at the begynnyng they wer of Wraghtonis opinion, but sence, they have consydered that the learned parte of the Chirche singeth in a learned tong to prayse God in all thing. And upon the same reason they use also all semely wyses of instruments with *Laudate Deum in sono tubae* unto *Omnis spiritus laudet Dominum* ⟨Ps. CL⟩. Whiche solution at theyr handes I thynk Wraghton, if hys name be Wraghton, wold easely take, and I think he wold be ashamed of hys lye, it is so manifest and so apparent. But even as truth must perswade with truth, so lyes be mete to persuade ther with lies.

It appereth that the man is a frayed to be called heretike before he were answered, and he wolde have sum delay to know whether he wold stik in it. Who shal answer hym that thynketh no man hath wit but hym self, no man learned but hym self, as thys proud, arrogant, presumptuous foole doth in thys litle booke? Pryde maketh hym forgit what he sayeth in the begynnyng, the middes, and the endyng. When

488

he hath condemned our ignorance, then he wolde go to scool with us and abyde our answere. He may assoyle it thus, in thys part of hys book hys sprete ⟨*i.e.*, spirit⟩ speaketh mekely, in the other parte of hys book, where he is so vehement, the fleshe bresteth furthe; after which solution it shuld appere the man hath a great dele of fleshe and litle sprete in Goddis service. And in redyng of the Bible the man is all fleshe, and still very angri with the Latin tong; where in I remit hym to hys brethern Brentius and Oseander, that named holy man, which ij, becaus in dedes they disagre from thys mannis opinion, I thynk they can easely satisfice hym with wordes, where in I trust he will be content, and of them who hathe pleynty borow so myche of the sprete as where with to tempre hys gross carnalite to dissent there in both from us and them.

The rest of thys famous work is specially agaynst me, where in he calleth me the chefe setterfurth of the articles concluded in thys realm agaynst the mariage of priestes, where in he speaketh lyke hym self. Then[1] the man sayeth further that Martin Bucer asked me what Scripture I had to prove that prestes myght not mary; and thys reporteth he also lyke hym self. And because he wold seme to be pryvy unto the disputation betwene Martin Bucer and me, sum what he toucheth that was in our disputation spoken of, but fasshoneth it lyke hym self at the leste that I myght know the man lyeth even thorowly. Thus he reporteth my reson made to Bucer: The same autorite hath the kyng over all prestes of hys realme and hys other subjectes that a father hath over his childer, but a father may forbid the prestes of hys realme to mary, then if they mary when he forbiddeth them to mary, they break the commandment of God who sayeth, 'Childer obey your father and mother.'

I trust no man wold thynk I shuld have fasshoned the argument in thys wise, for it hath no sequence in it. And the father that hath but childer in the major, I have gyven hym a realm and hys childer prestes in the minor. And then in the conclusion I have forgoten the kyng that I spak of, and speke only of the father. Whos mater is mych what, in lyke perplexite, ⟨was⟩ rehersed as an honest simple mannes example[2], of Johan that maried Alice and Robert that maryed An, ⟨and⟩ in process of the mater called An Johannis wyfe and joyned to Robert; which the audience heard merely ⟨*i.e.*, merrily⟩ and called it playn adulteri. And after thys sorte Wraghton hathe wranglyngly rehersed my argument. And then he gathered thes conclusiones: first, that a kyng may forbid

1 *printed* when   2 *text adds* was

all mariage; second, that ones mariage of prestes was lawful befor the kyng forbad it; thyrdly, that the prince maketh sin that before was no syn with God.

To which conclusiones I will answer when I have trewly rehersed my communication with Bucer; with whome, upon the desyre he had to confer with me, I told hym I was glad to speak. Who, when he cam to me, after the maner of Germany made along oration unto me, conteynyng only the zeale he had to the truthe, for trying out where of he sayd he was desyrous to talk with me. I told hym I was glad to hear hym speak so indifferently; but for as myche ⟨as⟩ all autorite wher by to press one an other was clerely taken away by dissention, I told hym that Scripture was out of autorite to any one parte, becaus both partes wolde apply to theyr partye theyr own interpretation and there in stand obstinatly. The spret is diffamed by the Anabaptistes; miracles theyr be none wroght; eche parte be sinners; and the doctores of the Chirche, when they made agaynst them, they called them men and estemed them not. And therfore I sayde, for want of autorite to prove, I wold use Socrates[1] maner of disputyng with hym, and pres hym, which he shuld hymself grant. He sayd he was content. Then I asked hym where in, and he sayd he cared not, but he thought that the mariage of prestes was very cruelly handled to forbid it *sub poena mortis*. I told ⟨hym⟩ he was a sore adversari in thys becaus the mater touched hym self. How be it, the Kyngis Majesti myght forbid it. Of the payn, I wold reson with hym afterwarde, and dowted not but the extremite of payne was, in respect of the multitude, mercifully to kepe them by feare from danger, rather then cruel as he calleth it.

'Why,' quod Bucer, 'how can the Kyng forbid it?' I told hym then, ere I entred the mater with hym *de iure divino*, I wold ask hym thys question: what he ment by thys precept, *Honora patrem et matrem*; whether the son, brekyng hys fathers commandment in suche a thyng as the father myght command, brak the commandment of God or no. Bucer answered, 'Yis.' I asked hym then whether *pater* was under-stande only of father in nature or father in goverment also. He sayd of the father in goverment also. Then quod I, 'By yow, the prince hathe the same autorite to command over hys subjectes that the father hath toward hys childer.' He granted that also. Then upon it that he had granted I fasshoned my argument: The prince hathe the same

---

1 *printed* Sacrates

poure of commandment and order of his subjectes that the father hath over hys childer. But by Saynt Poule the father may order sum of hys childer not to mary; ergo, the prince may order sum of hys subjectes not to mary. Bucere by and by denyed the minor. We turned to the place of Saynt Poul. We red the text, which is playn that the father may so do. At the which text Bucer so stumbled and stayed, miche contrari to my expectation, as thoghe he had never red it before. And becaus Alisius the Scot was by and hyther to spak nothyng, Bucer took the book to Alisius and bad hym speak hys mynde; wher unto Alisius went to the first parte of the chapter, out of owr purpose, which the sayd Alisius understood so folishly that there upon rose a new communication in whiche were interlaced many maters which Bucer and I afterwardes intreated by writyng, where in thys argument of the father was not yit answered, and therein on my parte the mariage of prestes to be forbidden *de iure divino* so defended (how so ever it liketh Master Wraghton to have me acompted unlearned and so perversly to set furth the argument) that nether he ne Bucer can yit assoyle. And I se no cause to yelde to Bucere there in.

And now to Master Wraghtonis conclusiones. Becaus I made thys argument, shal he say that I admit princes may destroy mariage as thought ⟨*i.e.*, though⟩ that which upon consyderation may be good in sum shal be absolutely allowed in all? They that commanded virginite moste wold not have all virgines, ne Saynt Paul, that wissheth all to be as he hym self, intended not therby the destruction of mariage, althoghe him self were not maried. But suche frantike conclusions thys unlearned arrogancie gathereth.

The seconde conclusion is as wise: that I grant by thys argument that prestes myght have maried, if the prince had not forbiden it. If I prove that prestes may not mary becaus of theyr vow, do I therfore grant that, the vow falyng, they myght mary? If I took upon me to prove that one oweth me monie for my labor becaus he promised me, doth thys infer thys conclusione, that if he had not promised me, he had ought me nothyng for my labor?

The thyrd conclusione is the self same with the seconde, in other termes, that by me mariage of prestes was no sin before God til the Kyngis Majesti made it sin before God. Bucer was of an other mynde: that if the prince myght commande, it was before a sin a fore God to do the contrari; for he sayd princes myght only commande that God had ordened to be commanded, where in he swarved from that he had first granted me, where upon I resoned. I have hys writyng to show, where in shall apere I had more Scripture to show for the purpos I spak of then such as I communed with could well resolve[1], when they were touched with them.

I will reson nomore with thys hunter that wanteth all reson. He rangeth in a licencious liberti, and bresteth in to thys Chirche of Englond under colour to hunt the fox, and ranchseth and halloweth at every dere, with a purpose to dryve all godlynes, all semelynes, all religious and devout behavour out of the parke. He begynneth with the Kynges Majesti in alteracion of hys style, and then at lerge callethe the hole realme theves. Hys chace is agaynst the cross and all images; he cannot abyde Lent and Fridayes; he lyketh no lawes and ceremonies in the Chirche, allthoghe they be good; for prestes wyves he maketh a busy suite; he can not away with divine service in the Latin tong, which he utterly abhorreth.

He hath, be lyke, a mervelous plat form in hys hede to buylde, that he wold rid Christis religion of all thes ornamentes. Calleth he thys the huntyng of the fox and Romish fox? Rather goeth the fox a huntynge. The best is, the man hunteth by day, and declareth for so miche what he is, only hydyng who he is, for Wraghton, me semeth, shuld not be hys name. But what so ever the kynred name of the man is, he may have plenyty of other names; for whether a man call hym fool, proud, arrogant, glorious, disdaynful, spitful, haytful, unlearned, untaught, busy, partly lyer, wrangler, seditious, malicious, or many other of that sort, he can not speake amiss.

No man can speake here in farther then the man in hys booke will make god and a vow ⟨*i.e.*, make good and avow⟩. I wold have spoken of heretike, but he may not so be called till the book be ansuered; therfore he hath made a speciall request, as I have before noted.

But now, Master Hunter, your houndes have ron at ryot, and, levyng the fox, yerned only at the dere, whiche, in the Kyngis Majestes clos ground, with your maskery, is felony, all thoghe ye speake so playnly as it may be acompted day. Thys is your fault, so manifest and apparant as it excedeth your pour to close or hyde it. God gyve yow grace to make a more fruit ful suit to Hys goodnes, and to the Kingis Majestie, for your reconciliation to bothe theyr favoures, then your undiscrete suit in thys huntyng hath deserved.

1 *printed* recolve

3. Somerset *to* Gardiner

[London ?, before 25] March, 1548

B.M., Add. 28,571, 4 v.–5 v., 15 r. Sixteenth-century copy.

An answer to Gardiner's refusal (not extant) to surrender Trinity Hall, Cambridge (of which he had been Master since 1525). Marvels at Gardiner's objection to the proposed college of Civil Law (to be formed by the union of Trinity and Clare Halls and the Hostel of St Nicholas); more Civil Lawyers are needed; intends also to establish a house for them at London; Gardiner need not fear for the existence of his college; Parliament would have put all colleges at the disposal of the crown had not Somerset objected; arrangements may be made for the preferment of Gardiner's countrymen; since distance prevents Gardiner's presence in both his diocese and his college he should choose which he will give up.

After our right hartie commendacions to your good Lordship: We have receyved your answere to our letters of the erection of the College of Civill ⟨Law⟩, at the which we do not a litill marvaill. For, where we have thoght you wold have bene one of the most ernest setters forward of that learning and rather to have labored for thincrease of the number of the students in that facultie, and to have helped therunto with some giftes, as your predecessors in other places hath done, we perceave by your letters almost the cleane contrarie and a precise answere to the stopp therof. And, where you reason to have a few ⟨students⟩[1], we can not agre unto you in that. For, if many be incorporate to that studie, as you terme yt, amonges the moo peradventure some shall rise well lerned and fyt for the comen wealth; where as now, as they be but few, yt is hard to fynd one, and rather, as we are informed, in dede there is none, whom for excellencie we can have commended unto us. For further hope also, the Kings Highnes doth intend to provide and establishe in London a howse of Civill Lawyers, of suche as be most excellent and best lerned to be taken owt of Cambridge and Oxford, and have there a more larger interteinment, and to be redie then to shew ther advise, when they shall be required, and so to practise in the Admirall Court, or others, as they may. All the whiche encoraging to that study, earnestlie minded of us, we would be sory if yt shuld be interruptyd by you having no profitt by yt, as you say, nor as yet these dosen yeres or more coming thither, and, of all this space, not being hable to fynd one

1 *blank in MS.*

493

that wold or were hable to be maister there and to se lerninge preferred and the college to go forward.

You do very muche mistrust our doings and are in to great a feare of the surrender; betwixt the which and thestablishing of a new college, we had thoght to have had no meane tyme, in the which the college shuld be put in aventure, as you write, except it be by your meanes. Where you write that the Parliament hath graciouslie preserved them, I am sure you are not ignorant that the Parliament, wherat you were your selfe, did put them all in the late Kings Majesties handes, and wold have done the same at this tyme, but that yt was thus our expresse motion and mynd, for the good will we beare to lerning, that they shuld in no case be discoraged, as not thoght upon. And yet, for so muche as the feloships be chauntries for the more parte, lerned men in the law hath opinion that they be yet in the Kings Majesties disposition, to alter by this new acte.

For the preferment of your countrymen, it is, as we understand, a thing reproved in Cambridge and Oxford and cald parcialitie, that, for the countrye sake, the better lerned shuld be rejecte, the wurse and more unapt preferred. How be yt, in that point also, yf yt be thoght convenient, an ordre may be taken.

We eftesones require you to send us your consent hereunto, and do trust so to ordre the mattier that you shall therwith be content and your college increased and adorned, not hindered. Thogh nothing els shuld move you hereto, nor the Kings Majesties pleasure, by our advice, minding to honour that science, can styrre you, yet we thinke you shuld the rather be inclyned for your conscience sake, having your dioces so farre of and your absence so long tyme and the college alredie in so great a skarcitie of lerned men. To the which, bicause you have not loked as we wold have wished ye hadd, eyther the Kings Highnes and we muste spedelie loke, or, as we are informed, shortelie his Highnes shall have want, by the decay of that lerning and studentes in the same. Your bishopriche and the college, eche of them being cures requiring presens of their head, and suche attendance as perteineth muche to the wealth of the Kings Majesties realme that they shuld be with great care loked unto, the which, we perceve, in that distaunce, you can not do; wherfor, in so muche as you declare thestimation of oon to be reputed in you almost as moche as the other, and in dede almost they require, consydering the necessitie of the universities, eche as great care and furtheraunce, we pray you declare unto us, whether you had rather

494

leave. For we do not thinke mete that bishops, havinge suche charge of their flocke as in dede they have, and require suche presence, shuld have also cure and charge owt of their dioces.

And as for ordring of the same with so litil cost to the Kings Majestie, as may be and must for thonor and profet of the realme, do you not feare but we will take especiall care, withowt any danger to lerning, and for thavancement of the godlie mind of the founders. Thus we byd you right hartelie farewell, and require of you a resolute answer of your minde, with spede. From ⟨*blank*⟩ the ⟨*blank*⟩ day of Marche, 1547 ⟨48⟩.

Your lordships loving frend,

E. SOMERSETT

Addressed: To our very good Lord, the Bishop of Winchester.
Headed: Another letter sent from the said Lord Protector to the Bishop of Winchester

NOTES TO APPENDIX 3

Gardiner at his trial spoke of 'divers letters' from Somerset on this topic, 'wherein I might perceive the secretary ⟨Cecil⟩, with his pen, took occasion to prick me more than, I trusted, my Lord's Grace himself would have done' (Foxe, ed. Pratt, VI, 65).

Thomas Fuller, who may have seen some of Gardiner's replies, says, 'Most politic Gardiner, not without cause, suspecting some design or casualty might surprise the interval between the dissolution of the old and erection of this new foundation, civilly declined his consent to the motion. He informed his Grace that the way to advance the study of the laws was by promoting the present professors of that faculty (now so generally discouraged) and not by founding a new college for future students thereof, seeing Trinity Hall could alone breed more civilians than all England did prefer according to their deserts' (*History of the University of Cambridge*, ed. M. Prickett and T. Wright, Cambridge and London, 1840, 242).

Somerset's plan was not carried out (*see* G. Peacock, *Observations on the Statutes of the University of Cambridge*, London, 1841, App. A, p. L; Lamb, 140; my *Gardiner*, 171–2, 369 n. 32).

4. CARDINAL POLE *to* GARDINER

St Denis, 22 March, 1554

B.M., Add. 25,425, 204 v.–206 v. Seventeenth-century copy of translation into Italian.

> Has received Gardiner's letter expressing repentance for separation from the Church; God has preserved Gardiner from falling into heresy, despite his fall into schism; he fell through frailty, not choice; rejoices that there were martyrs for the faith in England; hopes for speedy restoration of the Church there; the preservation of the Queen is an augury of this; his book, sent previously, was to give Gardiner a picture of the Pope.

Monsignore. Doppo le mie cordialissime raccomandazioni nel nostro Salvator Christo Giesù, la presente sarà per dirvi che io hò ricevuta, e con mio gran piacere letta la lettera vostra del 12 del presente, la quale mi havete mandato confermando nell' opinione che già lungo tempo io haveva conceputa dei gran doni e gratie concessevi largamente dal Signore Dio, le quali et allora più fruttuosamente cominciorno a manifastarsi, quando alla divina Bontà piacque darvi occasione e fortezza di patir per causa sua persecuzione et incarcerazione et al presente ancora si dimostrano in questa vostra lettera, nella quale riconoscendo voi la propria colpa in esservi lasciato separare dall' unità della Chiesa, con segni di vero pentimento della fragilità che a ciò v' indusse, rendete infinite gratie alla misericordia di Dio, che in tal modo, e con si patern' ammonizione vi habbia fatto ravvedere dall' errore vostro, dandovi

---

My Lord. After my most hearty commendations in our Saviour Christ Jesus: This present is to inform you that I have received and, with great pleasure, read your letter of the 12th of the present month, confirming me in the opinion which long time I had conceived of the great gifts and graces freely granted you of the Lord God; which did more fruitfully begin to manifest themselves at that time when it pleased the divine Goodness to give you occasion and fortitude to suffer persecution and imprisonment for His cause, and at present show themselves in your letter, in which, acknowledging your own sin in having permitted yourself to be separated from the Church, with marks of true repentance for the frailty which did lead you to that, you give infinite thanks to the mercy of God, which, in such a manner and with such fatherly admonition, hath made you to repent of your error, giving you

496

fermo proposito non solo di lasciarlo voi, mà con le parole e con l'essempio, e con ogni altro mezzo possibile incittar gl' altri, che sono incorsi nel medesmo errore a fare il simile et essere partecipi della medesma misericordia concess' a voi. Il che mi fà vedere in voi similitudine di quella gratia che fù data a quel gran Rè e Profeta eletto secundum cor Dei, il quale essendo anch' esso per fragilità gravemente caduto e dimandandone perdono fece simile promessa a Dio con dire 'Docebo iniquos vias tuas, et impii ad te convertentur.'

Ch' è quello che hora da voi tanto più si aspetta, quanto maggiormente sete a ciò obligato, oltre il rispetto del grado che tenete nella Chiesa di Dio per speciale favore della divina Bontà verso di voi in non lasciarvi cadere nel modo che altri han' fatto in simile caso con tanta pernicie e ruina dello spirito con quanta del corpo cascante uno da un' alta torre sopra duri sassi, che in tutto viene a frangersi. Il che suole avvenire in spirito a quelli che si dividono e separano dall' unità et obedienza della Chiesa, i quali ogn' ora più ostinatamente perseverando nel loro errore vengono a partecipare in altre false opinioni, et heresie con estinguere al fine in se ogni lume di verità. Il che non essendo

---

firm purpose not only to depart from it yourself, but with words, with example, and in every other way possible to provoke others, who have stumbled into the same error, to do the like, and to be partakers of the same mercy which is granted you. The which causeth me to see in you a similitude of that grace, which was given to that great King and Prophet, elected after God's heart, who, likewise having gravely fallen through frailty and asking pardon therefor, made like promise to God, saying, 'I will teach Thy ways unto the wicked, and sinners shall be converted unto Thee.'

Now this is so much the more expected of you as you are the more bound to do so, apart from the consideration of the rank which you hold in the Church of God, because of the special favour of the divine Goodness toward you, in not leaving you to fall, as others have done in like case, with as great injury and destruction of the spirit, as is that of the body of one who falls from a high tower upon hard stones and is broken in pieces. This is wont to happen to the spirit of those who withdraw and separate themselves from the unity and obedience of the Church, who, standing each hour more stubbornly in this error, come to partake of other false opinions and heresies, and at last put out in themselves every

avvenuto a voi, in ciò si vede il favore speciale che Dio vi ha fatto supponens manum suam, ne collideret a gravitie casus, e si conferma quello, che voi scriveste, che non per malitia, mà per fragilità sete caduto, e che non di vostra elettione, e volontà per persuasione di Satana vi precipitaste tanquam a pinnaculo templi, mà per la vehemenza della tentazione, quasi turbine e tempestate foste spinto e gittato a terra, la quale tentazione fu invero molto grande così a dextris, come a sinistris, essendovi da un canto offerto tutto quello che si può sperare dal favor del suo principe e dall' altro minacciato tutto quello che si può temere dalla disgratia del medesmo tanquam a rugitu leonis.

E veramente quanto più mi si rappresenta la memoria della perturbazione e miseria di quelli tempi con tanta confusione della religione e d'ogni buon ordine, tanto più io riconosco l'amore e particolare gratia, che la bontà di Dio hà mostrato verso la nostra patria, donando in essa a molti tal fortezza di spirito che ne da offerte ne da minaccie alcune si siano lasciat' indurre a separarsi dall' unità della Chiesa rendendo a questa verità testimonio col proprio sangue, il che non si è veduto in

---

gleam of truth. That this hath not befallen you, is evidence of the special favour of God who laid His hand upon you, lest you be overcome by the heaviness of the happening. And that which you wrote is confirmed, that not through malice but through frailty did you fall, and not of your own will and choice through the persuasion of Satan did you cast yourself, as it were, from the pinnacle of the temple, but by the vehemence of the temptation you were swept away and hurled down as by whirlwind and tempest; which temptation was in sooth very great upon the right hand and upon the left, in that you were on the one hand offered all that a man might hope from the favour of his prince, and on the other threatened with all that a man might fear from the ill-will of the same, as from the roaring of a lion.

And truly the more there cometh to my mind the memory of the turmoil and misery of those times, with so great confusion of religion and of all good order, so much the more do I recognize the love and particular grace which the goodness of God hath showed toward our country, in giving to many in her such fortitude of spirit that by neither offers nor threats have they permitted themselves to be brought to separate from the unity of the Church, bearing witness to this truth with their own blood; which hath not been seen in other lands which

altre provincie incorse nel medesmo errore: e fù questo il primo favor di Dio verso la patria nostra in darle per difesa della sua causa tali e così forti campioni. Il secondo s' è mostrato in coloro, i quali, benche siano caduti nel primo grav' errore, sono po' stati dalla divina Bontà non solo preservati e sostentati a non cadere in heresia, ma hanno havuto gratia della medesma, costanza e fortezza in diffendere contro gli heretici la vera e sacra dottrina, ch' ebbero i primi a diffendere l' unità et obedienza della Chiesa contro i scismatici, essendo al fine con paterna correzione in cotal[1] tempo, e modo ridotti alla pristina unità, che non minor servizio si può sperare da loro ad honor di Dio in mantenerla insieme con le altre verità cattoliche, che dalli primi, i quali si gloriosamente morirno per essa.

Dalla considerazione dei quali favori io vengo ogn' ora più a confermarmi in speranza che la infinita misericordia di Dio non vorrà patir più lunga dilazione in far restituire alla sposa sua in quel Regno la pristina bellezza et ornamenti dei quali n' è stata così miserabilmente spogliata di che niun più certo pegno ne maggior principio si può havere che la preservazione di quella bona santa la Regina pulchra ut

---

have fallen into the like error. And this was the first favour of God toward our country in giving her for the defence of His cause such and so valiant champions. The second is showed forth in those, who, though they fell into the first grave error, have since been, by the divine Goodness, not only preserved and sustained that they fell not into heresy, but have had the grace of the same constancy and fortitude in defending the true and holy doctrine against the heretics, that the first had in defending the unity and obedience of the Church against the schismatics; being at last with fatherly correction in such time and manner brought back to the former truth, that no less service may be expected of them to the honour of God in maintaining it, together with the other Catholic truths, than from the first, who so gloriously died for it.

From the consideration of these favours I come more and more every hour to confirm me in the hope that the infinite mercy of God will not suffer longer tarrying in making restitution in that realm to his bride, whose former beauty and adornments have been so miserably despoiled. Of this, no more certain pledge nor greater beginning could be had than the preservation of that good saint, the Queen, fair as the moon, whom

1 *word blurred in MS. It appears to be* c, *an abbreviation mark*, al

luna, la quale Dio non ha lasciata contaminare con alcuna macula ne di scisma ne d'heresia, mantenendo sopra il spirito di essa il pieno splendore del Sole di Giustizia per diffonderlo e communicarlo poi per mezzo di lei a tutto il regno, sicome sua Altezza hora più che mai ha mostrato di fare nell' atto per il quale ricerca al presente il servizio e l'opera mia, nel che la conclusione che io ho presa a consolazione e sodisfazione della pia e casta mente di Vostra Signoria, potrà intendere dal presente messo, al quale sarà contenta in ciò dar quella fede ch' ella daria alla persona mia propria.

Quanto a quello che voi dite del libro, che io vi mandai, che sicome era stato scritto da me, così io ero espresso in esso; l'intento mio invero quando io lo scrissi non fu altro che d'esprimer con quei colori, che come semplice pastore io habbi l'imagine di quel Pastore, all' elettione del quale io interveniva non senza qualche timore di dover havere tal carico, nel qual caso il desiderio mio saria stato di rappresentarla con l'aiuto della gratia di Dio più vivamente che io havessi potuto. Ne ad altro fine io vi mandai il detto libro se non per darvi anco questa occasione di poter meglio esprimere e rappresentare con parole e con fatti

---

God hath not suffered to be tainted with any spot, either of schism or of heresy, maintaining over her spirit the full splendour of the Sun of Righteousness, to diffuse and communicate it afterward by means of her throughout the entire realm; as her Highness hath appeared now more than ever to do in the act whereby she seeketh at present my work and service. The conclusion concerning this which I have made to the consolation and satisfaction of your Lordship's pious and chaste mind may be heard from the present messenger, to whom you will be pleased in this matter to give that faith which you would give to my own proper person.

As to that which you say of the book I sent you, which, as it was written by me, so I was precise in it; my intent indeed, when I wrote it, was no other than to express with those colours, as a simple shepherd, the image I had of that shepherd at whose election I was present, not without some fear that I would be constrained to undertake such a task, in which case my desire would have been to represent it, with the help of the grace of God, in more lively fashion than I could have done. Nor did I send the book to you to any other end than to give you also this occasion of being able the better to express and represent with words

tal persona non solo a beneficio particolare del gregge commesso e ricevuto alla cura vostra, ma ad universale consolazione ancora di tutto il Regno per l'autorità che havete appresso quella virtuosa Signora così dedicata e pronta al servizio et honor del gran Pastore. E così piaccia alla divina sua Bontà darvi gratia di poter fare. Di S. Dionigi, li 22 Marzo, 1554.

Vostro assicurato amico,

REGINALDO CARDINALE POLO
Legato

Headed: Al Vescovo Wintoniense

---

and deeds such a person, not only for the particular benefit of the flock committed and received into your care, but to the universal consolation even of the whole realm, through the authority which you have in the sight of that virtuous Lady, so devoted and ready in the service and honour of the great Shepherd. So may it please His divine Goodness to give grace to enable you to do it. From St Denis, 22 March, 1554.

Your assured friend,

REGINALD CARDINAL POLE
Legate

Headed: To the Bishop of Winchester

NOTE TO APPENDIX 4

The collection of copies of Pole's correspondence, for the most part translated into Italian, from which this letter is taken, also contains Gardiner's reply (No. 162), as well as a previous wordy letter from Pole to Gardiner, dated from the Monastery of St Francis on the island in Lake Garda, 9 September, 1553, in which Pole rejoices at Gardiner's release from the Tower, and expresses the hope that he will use his influence to bring the realm back to the Roman obedience. A translation of the latter into English from another Italian copy in St Mark's Library is given in R. Brown's *Venetian Calendar*, v, No. 777, where, however, it is dated from Maguzzano, 28 August, 1553.

College of Arms, I, II, Burials, 121–4 and 127–33. In the Bodleian, MS. Ashmole 818, 10–11 (here cited as A.), there are the first and last leaves of a four-leaf contemporary account of the obsequies, which agrees with the College of Arms MS. in essentials, but presents many verbal variants and some condensation of statement. Except for a few which may be of some significance, these differences are not indicated here. The portions preserved in A. correspond to pages 502–505, l. 24 and 512, l. 21–517, below.

Gardiner's executors; his death at Whitehall, 12 November, 1555; removal to Southwark; temporary burial there, 22 November; removal to Winchester 23–7 February, 1556; obsequies en route, at Kingston, Farnham, and Alresford; burial beside the high altar at Winchester, 28 February, until his chantry be built. ('The Place,' frequently referred to, is Winchester Place or Winchester House, the palace of the bishops of Winchester in Southwark; 'the Deanes Place,' is the Dean's House, Winchester; 'Wolsey' or 'Wolvesey' is the bishop's palace there. Gardiner's arms, frequently mentioned, were argent a cross sable between four griffins' heads razed azure with a garden lily argent upon the cross. For sixteenth-century funerals see J. G. Nichols, *Machyn's Diary*, Camden Soc., 1848, xx ff.)

121 r.

The enterement of the[1] Reverent Father in God, Steven Gardner, late Bushop of Wynchester, Lord Chauncelor of England, Prelate of the moste noble Order of the Garter, and late Councelour unto the King and Quenes Moste Excellent Majeste, who lefte to be his executors as foloeth, viz.:

The Viscount Mountagew,
The Bushope of Ely,
The Bushop of Lyncolne,
Sir Robert Rochester, Comptroller of the Quenes Howsse,
Sir Fraunces Ingelfylde,
Master Basset, of the Quenes Prevey Chamber,
Master Twates, the defunctes comptroller,
Docter Harding[2], one of his chaplens.

1 *A. adds* Ryght *here, but not subsequently in the same formula*
2 *A. adds* his kynesman

The said defunct departed owt of this transitory worlde on Tewsday, the xijth day of November, betwene xj and xijth of the cloke, in the night, in the yere of Our Lord God, M^{l}v^c LV ⟨1555⟩, and in the second and thryd yeres of our soverayne lord and lady, King Phelip and Quene Mary, at theire Highnes Pallayse of Westmester, in the gallary there, on the right hand the gate going into the cowrt, his bardg lying in a redynes under the Quenes prevey steres, at the breke of day was conveyd therein and, from thence, brought to his Place at St Mary Overyes, where, in the grete chamber, he was layde and opened, his interelles taken fourth and closed up in ij pottes of a gallen and a halff a pece, and the water within his body reserved in a grete ketell; the quantety of the water was vij gallens. And after that, had into a lytell closse howsse at the further end of the same chamber on the left hand, where he was dryed and put into his wyndyng shete and, upon that, sered. And after that, his awbe and other vestmentes put upon hym, 121 v. which he was invested withall when he was fyrst consecrate bushope. And after, chested and wraped in lede, wherin was cast epytathes graven on copper, towching the prayse of the said defunct; and so set in his chapell, with lightes abowt hym burning day and night, and contynuall servyce tyll his remove.

The Thersday foloing, the xiiijth day of the said mounth, was prepared for solempne Dyrge at St Mary Overyes Cherche:

In primis, the quere honge rownd abowt with cotton and the high aulter with velvet, bothe above and benethe, enbrodered on ether end iiij scochins, one benethe the other, of his armes and see in pale. And in the mydest of the quere was made doble rayles the one within the other, hanged with blacke cotton. And within the inner rayles was set iiij grete candelstyckes, gylt, which belong to the Company of the Chaundlers, at ether corner one, and in every candelstycke a high percher of wood, and at the toppe of ether vij morter lightes, and, from the lightes downeward, covered thicke with bolles of wax and garneshed with scochyns, for the setyng owt of the same. And within the inner rayle was set ij tresselles; thereon a coffynne, covered with a pall of cloth of golde, and at ether end on^1 the same a whyt braunche. Betwene, within the mydst, was set the crusyfyx; ^{2}behynd that^2, his myter, and, on the left syde, layde his crosyers staffe; and stowles and

1 *writ.* one   2–2 *A.*, on the ryght syde

503

cushyns, covered with blacke cotton, set within the utter rayles, on eyther syde iij and at hed one.

Thus, all thinges being in aredynes in the cherche, betwene iij and iiij of the cloke, the mynisters for the servyce being in a redynes, Garter Principall King of Armes gave knoledge to the morners, who ymmediatly proceded to the cherche; as to say:

> Garter Principall King of Armes, before the chef morner, wering the Quenes cote of armes,
> The Viscount Mountagew, alone;
> Other iiij morners foloing:
> Sir Robert Rochester,
> Sir Fraunces Ingelfylde,
> Master Basset,
> Master Twates.

There were no more morners, nether gentelmen nor other offycers to proced before them, according to thorder; for that there morning aparell was not redy. Therefore, so they proceded, accompanied with certene bushops that folowed them, the nomber of xij. A gaynst there comyng into the cherche, all the lightes were light, and of the defunctes owne servantes, in there lyvery cotes, for that there black were not made, stode on ether syde the corps, viij, with torches in there handes, brenyng. The morners being plased, Rugecrosse Pursuyvant bad the bedes:

'Of your charytie, pray for the sowle of the Reverent Father in God, Steven Gardner, late Bushop of Wynchester, Lord Chauncelour of England, prelate of the moste honorable Order of the Garter, and late Counselour to the King and Quenes Moste Exellent Majeste. *Pater Noster.*'

Then the Bushop of London *in pontificalibus*, beganne *Placebo*, and so proceded with the other bushopps and mynisters of the cherche there, very solempnely, with soche seremonyes as apertened, unto thend. Which done, the morners were conducted agayne to the Place by Garter, and after, every man toke his leve and departed for that night.

The Morow Masse:

On Fryday, the xv[th] day of the said mounth, in the morning, abowt ix of the cloke, the morners assembled at the Place and, after that all thinges was in a redynes in the cherche, understanding was geven unto

504

the morners, who were conducted thether, as on the eve before, [1]saving that the bushopps had plased them selves in the quere, and Mas of the Holy Gost and of Our Lady was said before there comynge[1]. And, after that the morners were playced, the bedes was bydde by Rugecrosse.

Then ymmedyately beganne the Masse of Requiem, selebrated by the Bushop of London, with his assystaunce, pysteler and gospeler, using soche seremonyes as thereunto belonged. And at the tyme of thoffetory Garter fett up the chef morner to offer, accompanied with the other morners, and after brought hym to his place agayne; and then offered them selffes the one after the other. Then offered all the bushoppes and, after them, all others that wolde.

The offering being done, begonne the sermond, preched by the Bushop of Lyncolne, which lasted an owre and a halff, and then the Mas proceded to thend.

And at *Verbum caro factum est*, Garter Principall King of Armes brought the morners to the Place, and, after they were gonne, came 123 r. downe the Bushop *in pontificalibus* and sensed abowt the corps iij tymes and said soche seremonyes, standing at the hed, as apertened. And after that all was done, all soche thinges as was upon the corps, as his myter and crosyers staff, was had to the Place.

And after that the Bushop of London had unvested hym, he departed to the Place, with all the rest of the bushoppes foloing, to dynner, where was grete fare and, after dynner, a grete dole, bothe of meate and money, geven to the power ⟨*i.e.*, poor⟩.

The bryngyng of the body to the Cherche of St Mary Overyes:

On Thersday, the xxj[th] day of the foresaid mounth of November, the executers, with the morners and all other gentellmen and yemen apoynted to atend, assembled at the defunctes howsse, all at ij of the cloke in the after none, where every man prepared hym selff to serve, accordyng as he was apoynted. Where, betwene iij and iiij of the cloke, after that all thinges was as apertened in the cherche, and the mynisters redy, word was brought to the chef morner. And then the⟨y⟩ proceded as foloeth.

1–1 *A.*, save that the busshopps were there readye afore theyre comyng and had donn the Trynyte Masse and Oure Ladye Masse

505

In primis, ij porters, with there staves in there handes;

Then the ✠ before which was borne, by ij yomen in blacke cotes, ij whyt braunches;

Then the prestes and clerkes in there order;

123 v. Then all gentelmen, in blacke gownes, there hoodes on ther shoulders, ij and ij, to the nomber of L;

Then the bushoppes, ij and ij;

Then the Bushop of London *in pontificalibus*, alone, and, on ether syde of hym, a prebendary of Powles, and his crosyers staff borne before hym;

Then the defunctes chaplens;

a Then the executors, which morned not;

b Then thoffycers of the howsholde, as steward and comptroller[1], with ther staves in there handes;

Then the banner of his armes, borne by Master Somerset; ꝗ

Then Garter, in the Quenes cote, and, on ether hand of hym, a gentel-man husher, his hood on his hed;

Then the corps, covered with a pall of blacke velvet, on which was pynned vj scochyns of bokeram, ij on ether syde and one at ether end, borne by viij tall yomen in blacke cotes;

Torches borne by yemen in blacke cotes;

The banner of St Steven, borne by Master Harry Dycam;	*The corps*	The banner of St Gorge, by Thomas Greneacres;
The banner of the Trenety, by Master Harry Stafford;		The banner of Our Lady, by Master John Temple;

Then the chief morner, the Viscount Mountagew, alone;

1 *in this and all subsequent instances of* steward *and* comptroller, treasurer, *c.o., follows* steward

Then after hym foloing, the other vj morners:

Sir Robert Rochester,	Master Thomas Wyngfelde,
Master Basset,	Master Kempe,
Master Jakes Wyngfelde,	Master Whyt;

Then all yemen of me Lordes howsse and others, in blacke cotes, ij and ij.

And so proceded in goodly order to the cherche, where, at the cherche dore, the corps was sensed and so brought up into the quere and plased upon ij tresselles within the inner rayles. And thereone was set the crusyfyx, betwene the ij whyt braunches, and his myter and crosyers staff plased as aforsaid. The morners placed within the utter rayles, every man accordyng to his degrey; the gentelmen hushers standyng at the hed, withowt the rayles; Master Somerset with the banner of his armes at the fete, and the iiij gentelmen with the iiij banners of sayntes at the iiij corners, in order as the⟨y⟩ proceded; and, on ether syde the rayles, yemen with torches brening.

Thus, every man placed, Rugecrosse bad the bedes, and then the Bushop of London begane *Placebo*, and so proceded with thother mynisters to thend, which was solempnely done, as apertened to soche an estate. And after, the morners were conveyd home agayne in the same order they came, and every man departed his way for that night.

The Morowe Mas:

In the morning, after the Masses of the Trenety and of Our Lady was done, betwene ix and x of the cloke, the morners being in a redynes proceded to the cherche, in order as on the day before, saving the procedyng of the bushoppes. And, every man placed accordyngly, Rugecrosse bad the bedes.

Then ymmedyatly beganne the Masse of Requiem, selebrated by the Bushop of London *in pontificalibus*, with his assystans, pystler and gospeler. And at the tyme of the offretory, after that the people were avoyded on bothe sydes the rayles, that the morners might have lyberte to passe to and from, Garter fet the chef morner up to the offering, the rest foloing hym, and, after that he was conveyd agayne to his place, the other morners were conducted to offering.

Then offered the executors;
Then offered the bushopes;
Then thoffycers of the howsholde;
Then all gentelmen that wolde.

After which offering was done, beganne the sermond, preched by the Bushop of Lyncolne. After which, the Masse proceded to thend. And after *Verbum caroo factum est*, was offered the banner of his armes. Then Garter brought the chef morner and the rest of the morners, with a nomber of gentelmen before them, home to the Place. Then came downe the Bushop *in pontificalibus*; standing at the hed, sensed the corps and red soche collettes as apertened. In the meane tyme, was taken a way all soche thinges as was upon the body; which body was caryed by the yemen that brought hym to cherche, and leyd above on the left hand by the high aulter, and the gentelmen with there banners of sayntes standing abowt hym. Then proceded the⟨y⟩ in the servyce of the beryall, as apertened; the offycers of the howsholde, as steward and comptroller, ij gentelmen hushers standyng by, put there staves holle into the vaulte, and in lyke casse dyd the ij porters.

Then, after *De profundys* said, the vault was covered with the pall of blacke velvet, with a crosse of whyt saten; ij candelstickes with tapers set thereon, and the crusyfyx betwene. Then every man departed into the Place to dynner, where was grete chere and, after dynner, order taken for the poore people, which had bothe meate, drynke, and money.

And thus ended the funerall of this noble bushop, fully accompleshed and ended, tyll the tyme he shoulde be taken up agayne, his body to be buryed at Wynchester (which was prolonged by reason of his executors, sundry causes them movinge), on whose solle Jesu have mercy.

The same day, after dynner, the chaundelers worke was defased and Garter toke the rayles and the clothe abowt the same, the stowles and coshins, with the coverynges, for his fee. The morow after, the⟨y⟩ brake up howsholde and payd bothe gentelmen and yemen there yeres wages, that is to say, to every gentelman twenty nobles and to every yoman fowre marke.

127 v.

The tyme of the removing of the corps
from St Mary Overyes to Wynchester ward:

On Sonday, the xxiij[th] day of February, abowt iiij of the cloke, after that all thinges was prepared in the cherche as apertened, the morners proceded in there order, conducted by Garter Principall King of Armes, and Rugecrosse attendant, from me Lord Mountage⟨v⟩s howsse to the cherch, and ther had solempne Dyrge; after which was done, were conducted home agayne. Then every man departed to his logyng for that night.

On the next morow, the xxiiij[th] day, betwene viij and ix in the mornyng, proceded they in lyke manner, after the Lawdes was done and certene other Masses, to the Mas of Requiem, solempnely song, with soche seremonyes as there unto apertened. And after the tyme of the offretory, beganne the sermond, preched by the Bushop of Lyncolne. After which was done, proceded the Mas to thend, and the morners conducted to me Lord of Mountagews howsse, who was the chef morner.

Then ymmedyatly was the charet brought to the cherche dore, whether the body was brought and leyde in the bulke thereof, and after drawen unto me Lord of Mountagews howsse, the coffyn covered with a pall of black cloth, with a crosse of whyt saten. Then ymmedyatly was brought fourth the presentacion *in pontificalibus*, invested accordingly, and so layd on the coffyn upon coshyns of sylke, fast bound to the charet for removing, holding in his left hand his crosyers staff, his gloves on[1] his handes, and on[2] his medell fynger on the right hand a ryng of golde, wherein was a[3] safewre[4]. 128 r.

There was also a carte laden with torches and scochins of the defunctes armes delivered to the almoner to dystrybute them, with certene money, to every parishe cherche a long the way. Which cart went fourth a nowre before the removing, with the almoners deputey, and delivered the same to the curates and clerkes of the cherches, hereafter enshewing:

a	b	c
Saint Towles,	Saint Gorges,	Newington,
Wensworth,	Kingston,	Temps Dytton,
Long Dytton,	Asher,	Cobham,
Rypple,	Gylford,	Trenety Cherche,
St Mary,	St Nicolas,	Stoke,
Putnam,	Wanborough,	Zele,
Fernam,	Bentley,	Froyle,
Newton Valence,	Alton,	Selborne,
Hartley,	Holyborne,	Alford,
Maytestede,	Wynchester.	

1 on *writ. over* in *or perhaps* in *writ. over* on
2 *writ.* one   3 ryche *c.o.*
4 counterfet *c.o.*

All thesse curates and clerkes of the cherches, when the corps was comyng, the⟨y⟩ stod in the way, in there best ornamentes, and honerably received the same, byddyng there oraysons and prayers, as apertened, and devoutly sensed the corps as yt proceded; which order was kept all a long the way betwene St Mary Overyes and Wynchester, ever as the corps removed. Every parishe cherch had iij *s.* iiij *d.*, and money geven in every place to the powre, where the⟨y⟩ came.

128 v.   Thesse and all other thinges requisyte to the removing, in manner aforesaid, ordered and provyded, betwene xj and xij of the cloke proceded the⟨y⟩ with the corps.

The order of proceding:

In primis, twoo porters conducters, ryding in there blacke cotes, with there staves in ther handes, before the corps;

Then foloing, the prestes and clerkes, in there order;

Then gentelmen, ij and ij, on horsebacke, ryding in there blacke cotes and hoodes on there shoulders;

Then the defunctes chapplens, in there short gownes and typpettes;

Then the executors that morned not, ij and ij;

Rugecrosse Pursuivant of Armes, his horsse traped and garneshed with scochyns;

Then thoffycers of the howsholde, as steward and comptroller, ethere of them, there horsse traped;

Then the ⊐ banner of the defunctes armes, borne by Master Somerset, his horsse traped and garneshed with scochins of armes and a shafron in the forhed;

Then Garter Pryncipall King of Armes, in the Quenes cote, his horsse traped and garneshed with scochyns;

Then foloing, the charyot with the corps, covered over with a pall of black cloth, with a crosse of whyt saten, frynged abowt with sylke frynge and lyned within with blacke velvet, garneshed with scochins of his armes and the see in pale; so that the presentacyon
129 r.   of his corps might be seene, all the way, *in pontificalibus*, drawen with v horses, traped with blacke clothe, garneshed with scochyns, and ether horsse a shafron in his forhed, and at the iiij corners of the chere, the iiij banners of sayntes, borne by iiij gentelmen, whosse horsse were traped and garneshed with scochyns, and a shafron in ether forhed;

510

Then was borne by yomen, ryding in black cotes, xxiiij staffe torches, on ether syde porsion lyke from the hether part of the chariot forward;

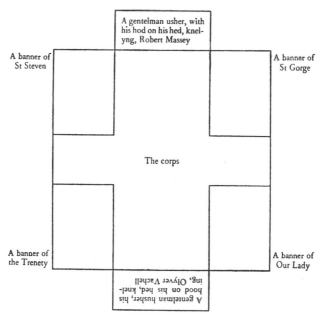

Then foloing, the chef morner alone, the Viscount Mountagew;
Then all other morners foloing, ij and ij:

Master Whyt,	Sir Fraunces Ingelfylde,
Master Basset,	Master Harvey,
Docter Marten,	Master Jakes Wyngfelde;

Then foloing, all the defunctes yemen and others, in ther blacke cotes.

Thus the⟨y⟩ marched forward in goodly order, and in tyme the⟨y⟩ came to Kyngstone, abowt iiij of the cloke in the after none; where the charet was rested before the west dore of the cherche of Kyngston.

Where ymmedyatly was the presentacion unlosed, sensed, and holy water cast on hym, with oraisons, as apertened, and after brought by iiij gentlemen into the quere; and there leyd upon a coffyn that was covered with the pall of the cherche, and on every syde the coffyn, iij stowles with coshyns, and one at the hed for the chef morner; who being placed, Rugecrosse bad the bedes. Then beganne the Dyrge by the defunctes chaplens and others, the mynisters of the cherche, very devoutly, with soche seremonyes as apertened, to thend. Then the chef morner was conducted unto his logyng, with a nomber of gentelmen before, and the other morners foloinge. And then every man departed unto his owne lodging, where the⟨y⟩ toke there rest for that night.

Tewsday, the xxv[th] of February:

Abowte vj of the cloke in the morning the bell range and the mynisters of the cherche assembled and ymmedyately went to Lawdes. After

130 r. which was done, certene gentelmen there, being in a redynes, according as they were commaunded overnight, put on there hoodes and placed them selffes in the liew of the principall morners. Rugecrosse there, geving his attendaunce, bad the bedes. Then ymmedyatly beganne the Masse of Requiem and many other Masses said at by aulters. After which was done and the sermond, in lyke casse, preched by Docter Harding, one of the defunctes chaplens, a kynsman, the said presentacion was bestowed in the said chariot, with lyke reverence as aforesaid, and then ymmedyatly the morners and every man mounted on horsse backe and plased them selffes in the same order as they were the day before, and so marched fourth from towne to towne, tyll the⟨y⟩ came to Fernam, where they had Dyrge and other seremonyes as aforesaid.

Wensday, the xxvj[th] day of February:

A bowt viij of the cloke in the morninge, after Mas of Requyem was done and the sermonde ended, preched by the Bushop of Lyncolne, the⟨y⟩ proceded from Fernam to Alsford, in manner abovesaid, where they contynued that night and had Dyrge in manner as aforesaid.

The preparacion in the cherche of Wynchester
in manner foloing, agaynst ther comynge:

In the cherche of Wynchester was prepared a goodly herce of v principalles, garneshed with scochins and pencelles, with majeste and vallence for the same, the utter and inner rayles covered with borde clothe, blacke, as also was the postes. And within the utter rayle was set on

130 v. ether syde iij stowles and one at hed, all covered with blacke cotton, and to every stowle ij coshyns, in lyke case covered with blacke cotton, for the morners to knele and layne upon. And withowt the rayles, v stowles more, at every corner of the herce one, and at the foote an other, all covered with blacke. And to every stowle, a quyshion, which were for

512

the iiij banner berers of sayntes and the banner berer of his armes. And in lyke manner was the high aulter hong with blacke, and rownd abowt the chauncell, from the steppes upward, garneshed with scochins.

Thersday, the xxvij[th] day of February:

In the morning, a bowt vij of the cloke, after servyce was done and sermond ended, preched by Master Boxall, Warden of the New Colledg at Wynchester, the morners wer conducted to there logyng, where the⟨y⟩ brake there fast. And abowt xj of the cloke, after all thinges was in a redyness, as aforesaid, every man mounted on horsebacke, and so, in order, proceded from that towne of Alford to Wynchester.

And at the townes end the Mayre and all his bretherne stode on the one syde and the prestes and clerkes on the other syde, which proceded in there order through the towne of Wynchester, with vij crosses of sundry parishe cherches that went before, tyll they came before the west dore of St Swythens, where the charyot rested; the prestes and clerkes standing on ether syde, from the cherche dore upward. Then came the Bushope of Lyncolne *in pontyficalibus,* and sensed the corps and cast holy water, saing soche oraysons as belonged. Then was the presentacion take⟨n⟩ up by vj spyrituall persons; that is to say, Sir Rychard Edon, Sir William Medow, Sir John Seton, Sir Leonard Vynsent, Sir Steven Cheston, and Sir Peter Langryge. Then the corps 131 r. was taken owt and borne by viij tall yomen. Over the same was cast a ryche pall, and at every corner of the same, a gentelman assystant[1].

And so proceded with the same and the presentasion in ther order, with the prestes and clerkes before them[2], in to the quere, where the body was set within the herce, covered with the ryche pall, and there on leyde the presentacion and, on the pall, pynned vj scochyns of sarsenet.

Where, after certene prayers said, every man departed in dew order, to conduct the morners to[3] the Deanes Place, and then every man departed and shyfted hym of his ryding aparell in to there gownes and hoodes on there shoulders, and retorned within half a nower and gave there attendaunce tyll the chef morner was redy. Then went they in there[4] order to the cherche, as foloeth:

Fyrst, gentellmen, ij and ij, the nomber of L[5];
Then the executours;

1 *A. adds* and the banners of seyntes
2 *A. adds* and the morners and other aftre them   3 there loggyng in *c.o.*
4 *writ.* they   5 *A. adds* then the chapleyns

Rugecrosse, in the Quenes cote;

Then the steward and comptroller;

Garter Principall King of Armes, in the Quenes cote of armes, and on ether hand of hym, a gentelman usher, there hoodes on there hedes and roddes in there hondes;

Then foloing, the chef morner alone, Viscount Mountagew;

Then foloing, other vj morners:

Sir Fraunces Ingelfylde,

Master Whyt, Master of Request,

Master Basset,

Master Harvy,

Master Norrys, gentelman husher,

and Docter Marten.

And after them foloing, all the yomen in there blacke cotes, ij and ij.

131 v. And so proceded in goodly order, every man placed according to his degrey; within the herce, the morners; the ij gentelmen hushers standyng at the hed withowt; the iiij banner berers of saingtes at the corners, holdyng in there handes every man his banner, and the banner berer of his armes at the feete.

Then Rugecrosse, at the quere doore, bad the bedes:

'Of your charytie, pray for the sowle of the Reverent Father in God, Steven Gardner, late Bushop of Wynchester, Lord Chauncelour of England, prelate of the most noble Order of the Garter, and late Counselour to the King and Quenes Moste Exellent Majeste. *Pater Noster.*'

Then ymmedyatly the Bushop of Lyncolne *in pontificalibus* beganne *Placebo,* and so solempnely proceded in Dyrge. And after the last Lesson, the corps was sensed by the Bushop of Lyncolne *in pontificalibus,* with his assystaunce, iiij tymes abowt the herce, and in lyke manner, after the last Respond. So, after that Dyrge with all other servyce and solempnetyes were done, the chef morner with the rest were conducted by Garter to the New Colledge, where they soped, and other gentelmen and yemen to Wolsey to soper, where was grete chere; and after, every man departed to his lodgyng for that night.

132 r. Fryday, the xxviij day of February:

In the morning, abowt vj of the cloke, after the Lawdes were said, gentelmen being in a redynes in the cherche, according as it was over-night apoynted it shoulde be, to execute the rowme of the chef morner and others that wanted, for the Mas of the Holy Gost and Our Lady, the⟨y⟩ being placed, Rugecrosse bad the bedes: 'Of your charytie, etc.'

Then proceded the Mas of the Holly Gost, executed by Docter Seton, with pysteler and gospeler, Master Woodlocke and Master Carcas; the iiij recters:

Sir John Tredegolde } prestes,
Sir John Symnell

John Denyng and } vycars.
Robert Mortymer

Which Mas was solempnely song and, at the tyme of the offretory, the chef morner, conducted by Rugecrosse, assysted with thother morners, offered the Masse peny, and after departed into there places agayne. And so that Mas fyneshed.

Then ymmedyatly beganne the Mas of Our Lady, by Docter Steward, Deane of Wynchester, with his assystant, Master Fygge; gospeler and pysteler, Master Lebourne and Master Carcus; the iiij rectors:

Sir William Alen } peticanons,
Sir Symon Palmer

Richard Houghton and } vycars.
Robert Mortymer

Which was very solempnely songe and all soche seremonyes had as at the Mas before, to thend.

Be that tyme yt was fast upon ix of the cloke. The morners were conducted to the Deanes Place, where all other gentelmen were there 132 v. attendant, that after the chef morner [1]and morners had broke there fast[1], to procede with them to the Mas of Requyem. Who, being in a redynes, dyd procede as on the eve before, and ther every man placed hym selff accordyngly; and, after certene prayers, retorned agayne downe into the body of the cherche to here the sermond, preched by the Bushop of Lyncolne, for that yt was the coustome there, the sermond to be preched before the Masse of Requiem begynne.

After which sermond was done, the morners proceded agayne up into the quere and there placed them selves, every man according to his degrey, as aforesaid. Then ymmedyatly Rugecrosse bad the bedes: 'Of your charytie, pray for the sowle of the Reverent Father in God, Steven Gardner, etc.'

[1]–[1] c.o., *but evidently intended to remain; A.*, and other had broken theyre faste

Then proceded the Mas of Requiem, executed by the Bushop of Lyncolne *in pontificalibus*, with his assystans, Master Boxall, Sir Peter Langryge, Sir William Medowes, Docter Seton; gospeler and pysteler, Sir Edmond Carcas, Sir John Lobourne; the iiij rectors:

Master Bylson ⎫ prestes,
Master Marvyn ⎭

John Erle and ⎫ vycars.
Symond Palmer ⎭

And somewhat before the offretory, after *Gloria in excelsis*, the Bushop came downe *in pontificalibus*, with his assistans, making his obesans at the hed, and sensed thre tymes abowte the body.

And at the tyme of the offretory, the chef morner proceded to the offeryng, with all the other morners foloing hym, and, after that he was conducted agayn into his place, then offered the other morners.

133 r. After them offered the executors;
Then thoffycers of howsholde;
Then the Deane and the rectors;
Then the Mayre, conducted up by Rugecrosse to offer;
Then all gentelmen that wolde;
Then the quere.

Then the Mas, after that the offering was done, proceded to thend.

And at *Verbum caro factum est*, Master Somerset offered up the banner, conducted up by Rugecrosse, and Garter conveyd the morners to Wolsey to dynner.

Then came downe the Bushop of Lyncolne *in pontificalibus*, with his assystans and the Deane, and sensed the corps thryse abowte, saing soche seremonyes as there unto belonged.

Then was the presentacion taken a way by the vj petycanons, which received yt at the cherche dore, and caryed yt up to a chapell, behynd the high aulter.

Then was taken up the body by viij tall yomen, assysted with gentelmen at every corner, and brought up on the left hand the high aulter and there set above the grownd, betwene ij walles, made of brycke, a yerd of height. The Bushop of Lyncolne *in pontificalibus*, with his assystans, standing at the hed, and abowt the same the gentelmen, holding the banners of sayntes, proceded in the servyce of the beryall, the offycers of the howsholde, the ij gentelmen hushers, and the ij

516

porters standyng by, with there staves and roddes in there handes. And when the mowlde was cast upon the coffyn, by the prelate executing, at the wordes of *pulverem pulveri et synerem sineri*, they brake there staves and roddes on there heddes and cast them into the place where the body lay; which was all done with exceding sorow and hevynes, not only of them but of many other standers by.

Then, after *De profundis* said, was layed over a borde, covered with a ryche pall, so that there was no grownde broke for hym, but ley there in manner as he dyd at St Mary Overyes, tyll soche tyme as a chapell sholde be made for hym, as was apoynted by his executors. After which seremonyes was done, every man avoyded the cherche and went to Wolsey to dynner, where was great chere.

After dynner, the executors departed from Wolsey to the New Colledge, and there sat all the day, determening of matters, and the next day, being Saterday, the last day of February, every man departed his way.

Garter Principall King of Armes had for his dyet, by the day, x *s*., and Rugecrosse, attendant with hym, by the day, ij *s*. vj *d*., [1]and all blackes abowt the rayles, as well within the inner rayle and thoter, stowles, coverynges of stowles, and coveryngs of coshyns, with majeste and vallence, as also the tymber, with all other thinges, except only the wax, the which retorned agayne to the chaundler. Howbeyyt, yt was agreyed that the herce showlde remeane hole, without demynishing a way any thing from the same before Whytson tyde next comyng[1].

And thus ended the funerall of this holy Bushope, on whose sowle God have mercy.
                                   Amen.

NOTES TO APPENDIX 5

Pages 502, 512. Dr Thomas Harding, mentioned in here as Gardiner's kinsman, is probably the kinsman of whom Gardiner speaks on p. 398.

Pages 506 ff. The name of Gardiner's steward at this time is given in his will as Master Raynes.

1–1 *A*., with the stoles, cuyssheons, and coverynges thereof. And the rest, the hersse and baryers, by thexecutors ordre stodde whole unto Whytsontyd; at which tyme Garter toke yt downe and had all the same, aswell majeste and vallence as tymbyre and clothe, the waxe onlye excepte, which was returnyd to the waxe chaundeler agayne

Pages 506 ff. Thomas Somerset was one of Gardiner's proctors at his trial and was remembered in his will, hence was, presumably, in his service from 1550 or before till 1555. He is probably the same person as Thomas Somerset, Gentleman, who, with John Davy and John Lloyde, was a patron of Hannyngton rectory, Hants, in 1550 (*Reg. Gardiner,* 132), and doubtless also the same as Thomas Somerset, Gentleman, whose name appears in a list of evil disposed persons, prisoners in the Fleet in 1561 (?) (*Cal. St. P., Dom., Addenda* 1547–65, p. 524), and who, on 27 June, 1562, was returned thither after an appearance before the Council, because he justified himself rather than humbly submitted for translating an oration by the Cardinal of Lorraine (Dasent, VII, 108).

Pages 507, 511, 514. Master Whyt, Master of Requests, was Sir Thomas White, who became a Master in the Court of Requests in 1553 (I. S. Leadam, *Select Cases in the Court of Requests,* London, 1898, cviii, cxvii, 197). He is so referred to in the records of the Privy Council, 1553 and 1556. How much longer he held the office is uncertain. He is identified, with probable accuracy, by Leadam with the Thomas White who was co-grantee, in 1538, with Thomas Wriothesley, of the reversion of the offices of Coroner and King's Attorney in the King's Bench (*L.P.,* XIII, i, 646 [23]). This Thomas White appears in 1543 as Clerk of the Crown and King's Attorney in the King's Bench, when, with Agnes his wife, he purchased the manors of Crowdale and Anstye in Hampshire. Two years later he acquired the manor of Haddyngton in the same shire, and, early in 1547, a house and garden in Winchester (*ib.,* XVIII, ii, 107 [39]; XX, ii, p. 547; XXI, ii, 771 [37]). This connection with Hampshire and Winchester makes it probable that he was the Thomas White whose name appears among the three submitted for sheriff of Hampshire in 1545, 1546, 1547, 1552, as well as on various commissions for Hampshire and the city of Winchester, 1546–53 (*ib.,* XX, ii, 910 [52]; XXI, i, 970 [32]; XXI, ii, 472; *Pat. Rolls,* I, 84; IV, 142, 396; V, 316, 358, 361, 387, 416). It is also probable that he is the Thomas White, Esquire, who testified at Gardiner's trial (Foxe, VI, 130), and the Thomas White who is referred to as Gardiner's treasurer in 1541, 1546, 1551 (*L.P.,* XVII, p. 137; XVIII, ii, p. 125; XXI, i, 267; *Pat. Rolls,* IV, 179). Thomas White, Master of Requests, was knighted 1553 (W. C. Metcalfe, *A Book of Knights,* London, 1855, 220). He is a different person from Sir Thomas White, Lord Mayor, knighted the same year (*ib.,* 110), from Thomas White, M.A., prebendary of Winchester, 1541–51, and, presumably, from Thomas White, D.C.L., prebendary of Winchester, 1554–74, d. 1588 (*Reg. Gardiner*, 134, 140; Le Neve, III, 36–7).

Page 508. The delay in taking Gardiner's body to Winchester. *Cf.* Wriothesley's *Chronicle*, II, 132: 'His bodie...was caried by water to his place at St Marie Overies, where it was closed in leade, and x dayes after layde in a vaute of brick made for it, tyll the springe of the yeare. For his will was to be buried in Winchestre. But because of the great waters that have fallen this winter it could not convenientlie be carried.'

Page 509. The presentacion. *Cf.* Wriothesley's *Chronicle*, II, 133: 'His corps were sett in a chariott covered with blacke, and a picture made lyke unto him lyeing on his coffin, with a miter on the heade, and a cope of golde on the bodye of the picture, with gloves and ringes on his fingers.' *See also* Machyn's *Diary*, 101.

Page 509. In the journey from Froyle the parishes were probably traversed in an order different from that given; namely, Froyle, Holybourne, Alton, Hartley, Selborne, Newton Valence, Meadstead (Maytestede), Alresford (Alford).

NOTE ON GARDINER'S PUNCTUATION, CAPITALIZATION AND ENGLISH SPELLING

These observations are based not only upon the holograph letters here printed, but also upon all the letters in Gardiner's hand written in the names of himself and his colleagues on diplomatic missions.

Punctuation. Gardiner frequently uses the slanting dash or virgula (/), sometimes the period or punctum, sometimes punctum and virgula together (./), and occasionally the comma and question mark. The virgula is used indiscriminately where we use comma, semi-colon, colon, or period, and often where we use no mark at all; the punctum with virgula, where we use the period; the punctum, comma, and question mark, when used, are used about as with us. Frequently, however, whole pages occur with little or no punctuation. The caret is sometimes used with interlineations, and parentheses are sometimes used as we use them, sometimes as quotation marks. Modern use is here followed.

Capitals. He always begins paragraphs and usually sentences with capitals. He frequently capitalizes the names of days, months, places, countries, persons, and titles. He tends to capitalize nouns beginning with i (j). But he is not consistent in any of these uses except the first. He almost always capitalizes the word *realm*, which may have some significance as to his thought. Modern use is here followed.

Use of i, j, u, v. He uses the same letter for i and j. He uses v initially for v and u; he shows a marked tendency to use v and u medially in the modern fashion, but he is not consistent in this. In some words he uses u medially where we use v, but in many he uses v and u interchangeably, e.g., *advertise, aduertise; convey, conuey; devise, diuise; ever, euer; have, haue; prove, proue; serve, serue,* etc. I have counted over sixty such words, spelled in both ways, sometimes the same word appearing in both forms within a few lines. Modern use as to i, j, u, v is here followed.

Elision. He usually elides *e* in *the* before a word beginning with a vowel; *e.g.*, *thacte*. When, however, *the* comes at the end of one line and the vowel at the beginning of the next, or when he capitalizes the vowel, *e* is not elided. But his use of capitals is not consistent, and we may find *the Admyral* on one line and *thadmyral* on the next, and frequently he writes *the* in full although the vowel following is neither separated from it by the end of the line nor capitalized; *e.g.*, *the admyral*. His elisions are reproduced here, but capitalization is made uniform, so that, *e.g.*, *thadmyral* is printed *thAdmyral*.

Suspension. He frequently makes a flourish, which may be taken as a mark of suspension, over final *ll, m, n, ch, gh, ght, th, sh*. In some cases the mark seems to be meaningless, for when he omits it, he makes no change in spelling; in others it appears that he was himself uncertain whether an *e* should be added or not. Occasionally he spells some of these words with final *e* (doubling the preceding *m* or *n*) and no mark of suspension; sometimes without either final *e* or mark of suspension. Thus many words in this class appear in at least three spellings, *e.g.* (the mark of suspension is here indicated by an apostrophe): *cam, cam', camme*, and, rarely, *came; man, man', manne; oon, oon', oone*, and, rarely, *one; French, French', Frenche; such, such', suche; which, which', whiche; wish, wish', wishe; hath, hath', hathe*; etc. In the foregoing pages the mark of suspension is not indicated.

Superior r. He seems usually to have intended this to represent *ur*, for he often spells out words sometimes so written, but that there was some uncertainty in his mind as to their spelling is evidenced by his writing *docto^r, doctor, doctour; fo^{r}me, forme, fourme; jo^{r}nay, jornay, journay;* etc. I have, therefore, italicized the *u* in extending superior *r* to *ur*, except in five frequently recurring words: *our, your, ambassadour, oratour, emperour*. Gardiner often so spells the first four of these words; the fifth he usually spells *emp'o^r* and, very rarely, *empero^r*. I have not met with it spelled out in full. The word *furnite^r* is printed *furniter*.

Plural and possessive. He makes frequent use of the sign ę. He also frequently spells out plural and possessive. In his early letters, however, he appears, in the case of a few words, to have hesitated between *ys* and *es*. Although in 1528 he regularly spells out many words in *es*, and uses ę and *es* interchangeably for several others, he spells out four in *ys: bullys, gracys, mannys, perillys*. But before the year is over we find him writing *mannes*, and in the next year *graces* and *bulles* (*perillys* does not recur). From this time on whenever he spells out any plural or possessive it is *es*. I have noted eighty words, many of them of frequent occurrence, which he sometimes spells with *ę*, sometimes *es*. Not infrequently both forms of the same word appear within a line or two of each other. Hence in letters written after 1528 I have simply extended the sign to *es*; in those of 1528 I have used the same extension with *e* italicized.

Other abbreviations. Superior *a* is extended to *au* in such words as *servaunt, convenaunt,* that being Gardiner's way of spelling them in full. He uses the same sign occasionally before final *m* in names, where it seems to represent simply *a*, and is here so printed; *i.e., Durham, Farneham, Notingham, Vaugham, Waltham.*

The ending *c'on* is extended to *cion*, which is often so spelled.

D is extended to *Doctor*, that spelling being used by Gardiner more frequently than *Doctour*.

Ihu' is extended to *Jesus*.

L're (plural *l'res*, usually with singular meaning) is used with great frequency. Among the half-dozen instances in which the word is spelled out, *letter, latter, lettre, letters,* and *lettres* appear. *Letter* and *letters* is the extension here used.

M is extended to *Master*, which is frequently so spelled, *Maister* appearing only occasionally.

Ma^{te} is extended to *Majestie*, which is Gardiner's invariable and often used full spelling.

M'chaunt and *m'velous* are extended to *merchaunt* and *marvelous,* with the vowel italicized. Gardiner sometimes writes *merchaunt, marvelous,* sometimes *marchaunt, mervelous.*

The signs for *pro, pr(a)e, per(par)* are frequently used. Most of the words so abbreviated are also spelled out, hence there is no difficulty about their extension. Some words, however, appear in two forms: *apparel, apperel; parson, person; pardonne, perdonne.* Hence in abbreviated words beginning *per* or *par* which do not appear spelled in full, or which appear in different spellings, the *a* or *e* is italicized in the extension.

ꝗ is extended to *quod*, but I do not recall having seen it ever spelled out in the English letters.

The *ser* sign is used not only in such words as *serve, preserve,* and

522

servaunt, which are so extended, but also usually for *Sir*, invariably for the last syllable of *Monsieur*, and occasionally for the last syllable of *pleasure* and *leisure*. When used for *Sir* and *Monsieur* it is so extended. The former is occasionally so spelled; the latter never spelled out. For the other two words I follow Gardiner's usual, though not invariable spelling, *pleasour*, *leysour*, italicizing the whole of the last syllable.

Secr is extended to *secretary*, which is Gardiner's usual spelling, although *secretarye* also appears.

*W*ᵗ is extended to *with*.

The infrequently used *et* sign is extended to *and*.

From some of the examples here given, it is obvious that Gardiner's spelling, like that of his contemporaries, was not always consistent. I cannot, however, refrain from noting what, as far as I recall, is the crowning example of inconsistency; namely, the spelling of the word *dead* in five different ways within thirteen lines of manuscript: *ded*, *dede*, *dead*, *deade*, and *deed*! *See* pp. 309–10, above.

NOTE ON ENGLISH SPELLING AND ABBREVIATIONS IN THE CHIEF MANUSCRIPTS, OTHER THAN GARDINER HOLO-GRAPHS, AND IN THE EARLY-PRINTED BOOKS USED

In all these manuscripts, except that of the eighteenth century (Harbin), the same letter is used for *i* and *j*; *v* is used initially for *v* and *u*; *u* and *v* are used medially without consistency, although in the letters taken from B.M., Add. 28,571 and Vesp. D, and in App. 5 the medial use of *u* and *v* approximates that of to-day.

No. 60, from Petyt MS. 538, 47. Abbreviations are thus extended: *Ihu'*, *Jesus; l're, letter; Ma*ᵗᵉ*, Majestie; M*ʳ*, Master; y*ʳ*, your;* e, es. Superior *r* is, in other cases, extended to *ur*, with *u* italicized; the *ser* sign is treated as in Gardiner's hand, being similarly used; *yo*ᵘ (superior *u* being written with a flourish) is extended to *youe*, that being the usual, but not invariable, spelling of the writer. The ending *c'on* and the words *w*ᶜʰ, *w*ᵗ, *w*ᵗʰ, are extended to *cion*, *which*, *with*, although the writer uses *y* perhaps more frequently than *i* in these words when spelled out. Marks of suspension over *ch*, *gh*, *th*, *pp*, and final *n*, used frequently but not quite uniformly, are not here reproduced.

Part of No. 124, from Harbin MS., eighteenth century. Abbreviations are thus extended: acc^t, *account;* ag^t, *against;* *althô*, *although;* *bp*, *bishop;* c^d, *could;* sh^d, *should;* *thô*, *though;* w^{ch}, *which;* w^d, *would;* w^m, *whom;* w^n, *when;* w^t, *what;* w^{th}, *with;* y^e, *the;* y^m, *them;* y^n, *then;* y^r, *your;* y^s, *this;* y^t, *that;* y^u, *you;* &, *and.* The endings *'d* and *'on* are extended to *ed,* and *tion.*

No. 125, from B.N., Latin 6051. Abbreviations are thus extended: *L, Lord;* *l're, letter;* *p'che, preache;* *sp'iall, speciall;* w^{ch}, *which;* w^{th}, *with;* y^e, *the;* y^t, *that;* the *et* sign, *and;* the endings *c'on, cion;* ℮, *es;* all of which are also so spelled in the manuscript. Others are extended thus: M^r, *Master;* o^r, *our;* *p'te, parte;* *p'tie, partie;* yor, *your.* *R℮* and *rec℮* are extended to *receave, reac℮* to *reaceave,* although when spelled out this word appears variously as *receave, reaceve, reaceyve.* An upward flourish occasionally over final *n* is not here reproduced.

Nos. 126–7, 140–3, App. 3, and passages on pp. 285–6, from B.M., Add. 28,571. Abbreviations are thus extended: *D, Doctor;* *l're, letter;* M^r, *Master;* o^r, *our;* *p'liament, parliament;* *p'te, parte;* *p'tie, partie;* w^{ch}, *which;* w^{th}, *with;* y^e, *the;* yor, *your;* y^t, *that;* the *et* sign, *and;* the endings *c'on, cion;* ℮, *es.*

No. 129, from C.C.C.C. 127. Abbreviations are thus extended: *Ihu', Jesus;* o^r, *our;* w^t, *with;* yor, *your;* y^t, *that;* the endings *c'on, cion;* ℮, *es.* Marks of suspension over final *ll, gh* are not here reproduced.

Part of No. 130, from Vesp. D. Abbreviations are thus extended: w^{ch}, *which;* w^{th}, *with;* y^e, *the;* yor, *your;* y^t, *that;* the *et* sign, *and;* all of which are occasionally so spelled in the manuscript.

No. 135, from B.N., Latin 6051, and B.M., Add. 28,571 (a different hand from No. 125 and from Nos. 126–7, 140–3). W^{ch}, w^t, ℮ (the last being seldom used) are extended to *which, with, es.*

No. 138, from Camb. Univ. Lib. Ee–2–12. Abbreviations are thus extended: Ma^{te}, *majestie;* w^{che}, *whiche;* w^{th}, *with;* you^r, *youer;* ℮, *es;* the *et* sign, *and.* Final *d* is written with a downward flourish; final *m, n, u* with an upward flourish, which may be meant for a mark of suspension, not here reproduced.

Nos. 146–7 from C.C.C.C. 127. Abbreviations are thus extended: *l're, letter;* Ma^{tes}, *Majesties;* M^r, *Master;* w^{ch}, *which;* w^t, w^{th}, *with;* yor, *your;* the *et* sign, *and;* the endings *c'on, cion;* ℮, *es.* Marks of suspension over final *ch, gh, l, m, n, p* are not here reproduced.

No. 151, from Trin. Col. Ox. LXXXVII. Abbreviations are thus extended: Ma^{te}, *Majestie*; o^r, *our*; w^{ch}, *which*; w^t, *with* (sometimes spelled out *withe*); y^e, *the*; y^t, *that*; $ę$, *es*; the *et* sign, *and*. Marks of suspension over final *ch*, *ght*, *m*, *n*, *p*, *pt*, *th*, are not here reproduced.

Nos. 156, 161, 165, 170, from Liber Rerum Mem., Cambridge. Abbreviations are thus extended: *l'res*, *letters*; w^c, *which*; $w^r of$, *wherof*; w^t, *with*; y^e, *the*; y^{is}, *this*; yor, *your*; y^t, *that*; the *et* sign, *and*; the endings *c'on*, *cion*; *ę*, *es*.

No. 157, from St Catharine's Register. Abbreviations are thus extended: *l'res*, *letters*; o^r, *our*; y^e, *the*; y^{or}, *your*; y^{ow}, *yow*; y^r, *ther*; y^t, *that*; the *et* sign, *and*; *ę*, *es*.

Nos. 163–4, from Peterhouse Register. Abbreviations are thus extended: w^{th}, *with*; yor, *your* (also so spelled); yo^u, *you*; the *et* sign, *and*; the endings *c'on*, *cion*; *ę*, *es*.

No. 169, from B.M., Add. 6668. Abbreviations are thus extended: $p'ty$, *party*; w^t, *with*; yor, *your*.

No. 172, from C.C.C.C. 106. Abbreviations are thus extended: M^r, *Master*; w^{th}, *with*; y^e, *the*; y^{or}, *your*; y^t, *that*; the *et* sign, *and*.

No. 173, from Bonner's Register. Abbreviations are thus extended: *L*, *Lordship*; w^{ch}, *which*; w^{th}, *with*; yor, *your*.

App. 1, from B.M., Add. 34,319. Abbreviations are thus extended: w^c, *which*; y^e, *the*; yor, *your*; y^t, *that*; *ę*, *es*.

App. 5, from Coll. of Arms. Abbreviations are thus extended: *gent'*, *gentelman*; ma^{te}, *majeste*; y^e, *the*; y^{er}, *ther*; all of which are also so spelled in the manuscript. Others are extended thus: *dd*, *delivered*; M^r, *Master*; o^r, *our*; re, *received*; S^r, *Sir*; w^{ch}, *which*; w^t, *with*; yor, *your*; y^t, *that*; the *et* sign, *and*; the endings *c'on*, *cion*; *ę*, *es*. Marks of suspension over final *ch*, *gh*, *ght*, *n*, *th* are not here reproduced.

In the early-printed books from which letters are here taken the same letter is used for *i* and *j*. In Gardiner's *Declaration* (Nos. 80–1) *v* is used initially, *u* medially; a printer's sign is used for *and*; *q̨* for *quod*; w^t, ye occasionally for *with*, *the*. In Turner's *Rescuynge of the romishe fox* (App. 2) *v* and *u* are used indiscriminately as initials, *u* is used medially, and *&* for *and*. In Stow, ed. 1592, *v* is used initially, *u* medially; a printer's sign is used for *and*; all of which is also true of Foxe, ed. 1563, where sometimes the abbreviations y^e, y^t are used for *the*, *that*, and *B.*, *L.*, and *M.* for *Bishop*, *Lord*, and *Master*, which are here so extended.

PRINTED BOOKS CITED

This list contains only those books cited in abbreviation or by name of author or editor. Those cited with sufficiently full title for ready identification are not here listed.

ALLEN, P. S. *Opus Epistolarum Des. Erasmi.* Oxford, 1906 ff.

ATTERBURY, F. *The Rights, Powers, and Privileges of an English Convocation.* London, 1701.

BROWN, R. *Calendar of State Papers...in the Archives of Venice.* London, 1864 ff.

BURNET, G. *The History of the Reformation of the Church of England.* Ed. N. Pocock, 7 vols. Oxford, 1865.

Calendar of State Papers, Domestic...with Addenda 1547–1565. Ed. M. A. E. Green. London, 1870.

Chronicle of Calais, The. Ed. J. G. Nichols. Camden Soc. London, 1846.

COLLIER, J. *An Ecclesiastical History of Great Britain.* 2 vols. London, 1704–14.

COOPER, C. H. *Annals of Cambridge.* 5 vols. Cambridge, 1842–1908.

DASENT, J. R. *Acts of the Privy Council.* London, 1890 ff.

EHSES, S. *Römische Dokumente zur Geschichte der Ehescheidung Heinrichs VIII.* Görres Gesellschaft. Paderborn, 1893.

ELLIS, H. *Original Letters.* 3 series. 11 vols. London, 1825–46.

ENTHOVEN, L. K. *Briefe an Des. Erasmus.* Strasbourg, 1906.

FOXE, J. *Actes and Monuments.* (The early editions are always cited with date, 1563, 1570, 1576, 1583. When no date is given the edition by J. Pratt is referred to. *See* p. xxi.)

GAIRDNER, J. *Lollardy and the Reformation in England.* 4 vols. London, 1908–13.

GARDINER, STEPHEN. *Register.* See *Reg. Gardiner.* His will is printed in *Wills from Doctors' Commons.* Ed. J. G. Nichols and J. Bruce. Camden Soc. London, 1863.

HAVERCAMP, S. *Sylloge Altera. Lugduni Batavorum,* 1740.

HOLINSHED, R. *Chronicles of England, Scotland, and Ireland.* 6 vols. London, 1807–8.

JANELLE. *See* p. xxxv.

LAMB, J. *A Collection of Letters, Statutes, and Other Documents from the Manuscript Library of Corpus Christi College.* London, 1838.

LEMON, R. *Calendar of State Papers, Domestic...1547–1580.* London, 1856.

LE NEVE, J. *Fasti Ecclesiae Anglicanae.* Ed. T. D. Hardy. 3 vols. Oxford, 1854.

L.P. See p. xxxviii.

MAITLAND, S. R. *Essays on the Reformation.* London, 1849.

MIGNE, J. P. *Patrologiae Cursus Completus. Series Latina* (cited as *P.L.*). Paris, 1844 ff. *Series Graeca* (cited as *P.G.*). Paris, 1857 ff.

MULLER, J. A. *Gardiner. See* p. xvi.

N. and P.N.F. = *Nicene and Post-Nicene Fathers.* 1st series. Ed. P. Schaff. New York, 1886–94; 2nd series. Ed. P. Schaff and H. Wace. New York, 1890–5.

NOAILLES, A. DE and F. DE. *Ambassades de Messieurs De Noailles en Angleterre.* Ed. l'Abbé de Vertot. 5 vols. Leyden, 1763.

PARKER, M. *Correspondence.* Ed. J. Bruce and T. T. Perowne. Parker Soc. Cambridge, 1853.

Pat. Rolls = *Calendar of Patent Rolls, Edward VI.* Ed. R. H. Brodie. 6 vols. London, 1924–9.

P.G. See MIGNE.

P.L. See MIGNE.

POCOCK, N. *Records of the Reformation.* 2 vols. Oxford, 1870.

POLLARD, A. F. *Wolsey.* London, 1929.

PRATT. *See* FOXE.

Reg. Gardiner = *Registra Stephani Gardiner et Johannes Poynet.* Ed. H. Chitty and H. E. Malden. Canterbury and York Soc. Oxford, 1930.

STOW, J. *The Annales of England.* London, 1592.

St. P. See p. xxxviii.

St. P. For. Mary = *Calendar of State Papers, Foreign Series, Mary.* Ed. W. B. Turnbull. London, 1861.

STRYPE, J. *Ecclesiastical Memorials* (cited as *Mem.*). 3 vols. in 6. Oxford, 1822. *The Life and Acts of Matthew Parker.* 3 vols. Oxford, 1821. *Memorials of… Thomas Cranmer.* 2 vols. Ed. P. E. Barnes. London, 1853.

RYMER, T. *Foedera.* 20 vols. London, 1726–35.

TYTLER, P. F. *England under the Reigns of Edward VI and Mary.* 2 vols. London, 1839.

VENN, J. and J. A. *Alumni Cantabrigienses.* Part I. 4 vols. Cambridge, 1922–7.

WILKINS, D. *Concilia Magnae Brittaniae.* 4 vols. London, 1737.

WRIOTHESLEY, C. *A Chronicle of England.* Ed. W. D. Hamilton. 2 vols. Camden Soc. London, 1875–7.

GLOSSARY

For readers not conversant with mid-sixteenth century uses the following, of frequent though not uniform occurrence in this volume, are noted: *cold* is often used for *could*; *college* for *colleague*; *hard* for *heard*; *hast* for *haste*; *lest* for *least*; *letters* for *letter*; *mary* for *marry* (interjection); *merely* for *merrily*; *on, oon* for *one*; *other* for *others*; *party* for *part*; *peace* for *piece*; *that* for *that which*; *then* for *than*; *thing* for *things*; final *e* for *y*, e.g., *gentle* for *gently, smalle* for *smally*.

Only the more unusual obsolete words and words used in the more unusual obsolete senses are given below. Those with which the reader is likely to be familiar from Shakespere and the Bible or whose meaning is clear from the context are not entered. Where no page references appear the word is of frequent occurrence.

abuse, deceive, 99, 144, 291, 444

acception, meaning, 337

adhibite, used, 4

advaunt, avaunte, boast, 259, 430

advocate, advoke, summon (a cause from an inferiour court), 18, 37

advotrie, adultery, 385

afterdel, afterdeal, disadvantage, 180

allightlywode, all likelihood, 39

almesse, alms, 65

apertened, as, as was proper, 41, 504–5, 507–12

appere, apere, be equal, accord with, 375

appeyre, appair, decay, 14

apply, hearken, 275

arrecte, aret, impute, 16

assembre, assembly, 213 (? misspelling)

attemptate, outrage, 84, 161; attempt, 265

avaunte. See advaunt

awbe, alb, 503

balowing, bellowing, 271

bear in hand, pretend, 156; accuse, 181, 426; delude, 167, 202, 417; maintain (a false interpretation of), 365

bobbed, buffeted, 281

bogge, bugbear, 177

bolles of wax, ? bowls with floating wicks *or* ? bulls, *i.e.* seals, 503

borde cloth, table cloth *or a slip for* brode cloth, 512

borden, ? meaning, 427

braunche, candlestick, 503, 506–7

bulke, the part of a vehicle which holds the load, 509

busher, bushel, 142 (? misspelling)

campe, ? champ, field for a judicial duel, 195, 226

capitulate, stipulated, 25

charet, carriage, 509, 511

checke, revile, 384

chere, char, carriage, 510

civil man, citizen, 416

civilitie, citizenship, 275

cokkyng, fighting (as a cock), 483

comfort, aid, 4, 142; upon comfort of, on the strength of, 80, 265

comfortative, cordial, 286

command, commend, 483, 491 l. 22

commen, confer, converse

commodite, suitability, advantage, opportunity

compendius, expeditious, 449

compone, settle, 122

comprobacion, proof, 10, 356

compromise, entrust for decision, 46

conciliable, illegal church council, 237

conduct, engage, 14

continue, content, 27, 37

convince, confute, 171, 261; convict, 418, 434

528

coursye, cursye, courtesy, 158; curtsy, 152, 214, 217
custumer, collector of customs, 56

decerne, decide, 372
declare, expound, 484 l. 24
delyvere, deliberate, 32
demore, stay, 222
depech, dispatch
derive, turn, 231; impart, 289
deul, duel, grief, 179, 216
digest, dissipate, 223
discusse, remove, 313
distresse, plundering, 227; *v.* plunder, 228
divise upon, conjecture concerning, 71
doubteful, apprehensive, 221
dromslade, drumslade, drummer, 153
duel. *See* deul
dulce(ly), agreeable, 18; soothingly, 194
duty, payment due, 353, 381, 384

eclarishement, a clearing up, 235
eclarsye, clear up, 187
empech, hinder, 41, 194
engreve, aggravate, represent as grievous, 221, 282
entend, attend, 66
entering, interring, 254
entertayne, keep a person in a certain frame of mind, 18; have communication with, 74
equipolleth, equals, 332
ethnycallie, as a heathen, 417
expende, consider, 49

fashious, causing anxiety, 178
fech, fet(t), fetch(ed), 59, 505, 507
finde to scole, maintain at school, 64
flebyting, flea-biting, 307
foranempst, opposite, 52
forme, course of exercises for a degree, 315; in forme, formally, 177
for though, ? *meaning*, 427
furror, courier, 91

galyandly, gallantly, 434
gistes, list of stopping places in a royal progress, 23, 27

good morowes, trivialities, 173
grate of me and he cold, harass me if he could, 432

havour, estate, 176, 196
herce, herse, frame, bearing candles, set up in church to receive a coffin, 512–7 *passim*; hearse-cloth or pall, 215
hindre, injure, 18, 174, 180, 270 l. 7, 287, 406, 494
hucke, bargain, 50
hucsters handeling, in, beyond likelihood of recovery, 239

impech, impair, 277
impetrable, obtainable, 16
impetrate, obtain by request, 13, 17, 41
importable, unbearable, 282
indict, convoke, 73
insoluble, irrefutable, 486

jobbe, *probably* gob, mass, 143
justitiaries, those who hold that a man can of himself attain righteousness, 344

kneling, knelling, ringing, 511

legier, nimble, 359
legitime, legitimate, 87
levye, raise (a siege), 143
lewedly, ignorantly, 484
liberall, unrestrained, 391
lightely, likely, 84, 88–9
lightlywode, likelihood
lowe, bellow, 153
lust, choose, 291, 427

majeste, majesty, canopy for a hearse, 512, 517
malicolyke, melancholic, 403
manchet, finest wheat bread, 142
matter: by matter indeed, as a matter of fact, 444
mayne, manage, 90–1, 195, 201
meane(s), by, ? by this (that, some) means, 373, 405, 433
merlie, *possibly* merely, *probably* merrily, 432
miscontentation, dissatisfaction, 267

morow masse, first Mass of the day, 504, 507

morter light, bowl of wax with floating wick *or* thick candle, 503

mycher, secret grumbler, 436 ·

named, famous, 489

nede, for a, at a pinch, 351

nugation, trifling, 332

numbre, the multitude, 356

obeisaunce, jurisdiction, 28

obsequie, dutiful service, 10

onward, as an 'earnest', 66, 195; onward of, advanced towards, 485

oter, outer, 517

ought, owght, owed, 236, 384, 491

overthwarte, adverse, 190

pagauntes, tricks, 153

peace, piece, stronghold, 192, 200

peason, peas, 144

pencelle, small pennon, 512

percase, perhaps

percher of wood, pole or imitation candle inserted in candlestick and bearing lights at the top, 503

permixt churche, *presumably* visible church in which saints and sinners are mingled, 262

plat form, design, 265, 372, 492

point, at a, agreed, 50; at the, in the emergency, 184

pope holy, hypocrite, 419

porsion like, ? portion like, properly apportioned, 511

presentacion, image, 509–16 *passim*

presidie, garrison, 11

prested, hired, 123

pret(t)y, pretilye, ingenious(ly), 233, 305, 315, 349, 386

pricke, acme, 386

princippalles, upright pillars with branches to bear tapers, used on a hearse, 512

proces, discourse, 174

pullery, poultry, 205

raduce, reduce, bring back, 480 (? *misprint*)

ranchseth, ? *misprint for* rangeth, 492

raye, array, rank, 153

rebellyon, traitor, 84

recesse, agreement, 225

reciproque, equivalent, 74, 87

redubbe, make up for, 179

refaicte, restored, 228

remayne, remainder, 143

repelled, repealed, 369–70

repugne, be contradictory, opposed, 249, 261, 377

reverence: at the reverence of, for the sake of, 366, 442

rome, romme, roome, rowme, room, post, 85, 151, 459, 468, 473, 475–6, 514

rowe, rough, 162

sacramentary, one who denies the doctrine of the real presence, 277, 305, 332, 447

safewre, sapphire, 509

said and sworn, examined and sworn, 26

salve, save, 397, 408

scochin, skochen, scutcheon, 503–13 *passim*

seding, ? settling, 187

sentence, sense, 85, 312 l. 12, 351, 371

set in fote, enter on an undertaking, 239

shafron, frontlet of an armed horse, 510

shamefast, shameless, 228 (? *a misuse*)

signifie, intimation, 41

sithens, since, 369, 391, 432

skase, skasete, scarce, 153; scarcity, 15

skil, can, have knowledge of, 80, 170, 180, 270, 274, 488

slaunderous, disgraceful, 288, 291

sleyghtly, cunningly, 480

sparkel, disseminate, 296

sponyng, spooning, running before the wind, 347

square from, deviate from, 373

squorge, scourge, 180

staffe torches, tall thick candles for ceremonial purposes, 511

standing, in view of, 187

stauld, stalled, fixed before *or* stayed, 294

stole, stowle, stool, 503–17 *passim*

story, history, 240, 259–60, 266, 312–4

stowrely, stourly, fiercely, 153
supersede, not to proceed, 40
supersticious, extremely careful, 177
supersticiously, punctiliously, 196
surmyse, allegation, 59

take tardy, take by surprise, 460
tender, favour, 469, 473; cherish, 35
tent, tempt, 181, 290, 302
thinke long, be impatient, 194
tormoyling, moving unremittingly, 219
tosse, turn the leaves of, 430
towche fully, ? explain (things) fully *or*
? fully indicate (the guilty), 460
tractation, treatise, 293
trade, way, course, 95, 433, 436; ? sort,
kind, 310; *v.* practice, 419
traverse, opposed, 309
tromperye, fraud, 169
tuition, safe-keeping, 411, 419, 432

utter, outer, 504, 507, 512

violente, strain the meaning of, 386;
coerce, 25
voyage, military expedition, 388; enterprise, 176

wafting, convoying or transporting by
sea, 461
warrantize, warranty, 415
waye, for the, because of the road, 203
welth, welfare
what we had talked, ? *a slip for* when
etc., 239
while(s), until, 150, 153, 174, 386, 388
wight money, white money, silver, 152
winches, twists in argument, 418
wittie, crafty, 260; ingenious, 280
wrydeth, writheth, 384

ye, yee, yie, eye, 142, 213, 307; at the ye,
at sight, 142
yern, bark at prey, 492

NOTE ON EARLY USES OF WORDS

While preparing the glossary almost three hundred instances came to my attention of words which, in the senses, phrases, or constructions in which they are used in this volume, seem to me to be of earlier date than the earliest examples given in the *New English Dictionary* (ed. J. A. H. Murray and others, Oxford, 1888–1928). Considerations of space make it impossible to give more than a bare list of such words with a single page reference for each. Where two or more page references áre given they indicate what appear to me to be two or more different uses earlier than the corresponding examples in the *New English Dictionary*.

Accounpte, 14; 77; acquiete, 61; acquital, 18; adhere, 186; adjuration, 204; Admirall Court, 493; admonysh, 356; advocate, 18; affected, 239; allegacion, 369; allow, 65 l. 13; 260; allowaunce, 342; allure, 98; alott, 49; altre, 41; amendmente, 422; anathemization, 256; apposite, 182; apprehension, 460; arbitrement, 46; asseveration, 58; assurednes, 364; assystaunce, 505; astate, 97; avoid, 370; avower, 350; barbary, 230; bill of exchaunge, 47; bowelles, 340; brave, 213; by aulter, 512; bye thing, 290; by matter, 297; calumniate, 176; capitulacion, 25; 225 l. 10; celebrate, 282; charge, 152; 398; chargeably, 15; charging, 353; cively, 244; 269; civile, 161; 243; 377; civil man, 416; clemencie, 247; clerkly, 234; close upp, 89; cloth, 213 l. 6; commission, 393; commodite, 74 l. 8; 74 l. 2 from bottom; common sense, 417; communicate, 186; compasse, 5; 300; complement, 141; compromise, 46; concurre, 72; 279; 341; 420; constante, 408; contaminate, 313; conteyn, 12; contracte, 258; convince, 339; countenaunce, 472; coursye, 152; 158; cowch, 7; credit, 188; 224; 291; 354; deflect, 325; delicate, 61; desperate, 201; desperatly, 411; determinacion, 388; deyntye, 151; digest, 390; 484; digress, 83; disagrement, 262; disapoint, 176; discharge, 221; discontentement, 156; discourse, 203; 235; 259; disfavor, 287; disordre, 433; disprove, 167; disproving, 273; disquiet, 265; dissemble, 132; dissipation, 279; dissolutely, 121; distribution, 481; doubteful, 221; dysordered, 340; dystemperyd, 325; eclarishement, 235; eclarsye, 187; ? either, 383; either of both, 172; elegancy, 203; eligyble, 457; elucidacion, 277; encoraging, 493; entertenement, 29; ? 192; ? 288; enterteyne, 37; 74; entisement, 168; entre, 180; envey, 292; establishment, 278; estimate, 412; ether, 503; ethnycallie, 417; exasperate, 18; exclude, 434; excogitate, 34; expedite, 13; expenses, 141; explication, 164; expunge, 11; extynguishe, 296; face out, 59; ? feate, 349; fill uppe, 384; flatt, 338; flebyting, 307; forme, 177; frame, 95, 161; ? 344; furnish, 291; furniter, 144; 216; 343 l. 16; fytly, 340; galyandly, 434; garboyle, 163; gaye, 226; ? gayly, 200; grave, 407; gravely, 135; grosse, 225; handsomely, 288; 305; 314; 337; where to have hym, 237; hucsters handeling, 239; impech, 277; impetrable, 16; impetrate, 13; implecation, 385; incompatible, 72; inculcation, 367; indict, 73; inducement, 245; infest, 97; innovation, 25; insinuate, 89; instaunte, 63; interception, 41; ? interrupt, 344; intitule, 353; invest, 503; send (goo) to Jherico, 159; labyrinth, 190; at large, 449; 483; lokyng on, 97; loosenes, 354; lowe, 134; maskery, 492; ? matche, 188; mean, 312 l. 28; medle, 168; meere, 337; ? merely, 353; ministeriall, 486; miscontentement, 64; misdemeanes, 470; mixtly, 351; munificence, 132; for a nede, 351; nugation, 332; numbre, 356; occasionative, 486; odde ende, 200; opinion, 179; ordre, 66; 122; take ordre, 130; out of ordre, 211; outbrage, 179; pacquette, 39; parte, 10; 269; in good parte, 16; passe, 82; passeporte, 80; penultime, 33; perished, 123; perniciously, 446; perplex, 74; perswaded, 311; perverted, 325; platform, 492; polyte, 68; popularite, 230; poster, 80; precisenes, 177; presentacion, 509; preter, 26; prosecute, 121; prosecution, 173; prostrate, 179; provocation, 94; pryenge, 340; qualification, 31; questionyng, 340; quondam, 305; rablement, 333; rake up, 261; range, 492; ranke, 214; reciprocation, 233; reciproque, 74; recommende, 53; recommendation, 224 l. 20; reduce, 340; reliefe, 411; remitte, 315; remove, 503; rencontre, 184; reprobation, 13; repugne, 377; resemblaunce, 153; resolution, 27; 30; 60; 194; resolve, 195; 269; 290; 363; respecte, 6; 97 l. 18; retractation, 293; retyre, 79; say, 290; scrupulous, 177; ? 223; 283; seducyng, 300; sequence, 489; set forth, 33; set out, 228; ? setyng owt, 503; severaltie, 340; shift, ? 234; 257; siftinge, 408; sithens, 432; slip, 297; 303; in this, that, such sorte, 16; after this, that, such, sorte, 41; speche, 331; sponyng, 347; spoore, 170; staye, 78; 158; staying, 58; strayte after, 354; sumptuously, 15; supremite, 72; symbole, 385; terme, 170; 204; 412; tolleration, 122; tosse, 430; towards, 281; tractation, 293; trade, 419; travayl, 189; 331; triumphantlye, 167; untowarde, 100; unvest, 505; uttre, 373; variete, 10; varlat, 404; vehement, 160; 394; violente, 25; 386; visitacion, 158; wafting, 461; winches, 418; wonderment, 278; worthy, 423 l. 7; wrangle, 357; wranglyngly, 489; wrappe up, 59.

The following, in the senses or constructions in which they appear on the pages indicated, do not seem to be in the *New English Dictionary*: ? benefite, 219; capacite, 31; cariers out, 391; putt by case, 350; charge, 132; conduce, 41; diffamacion, 173; distresse, 227; ? enquire, 415; ? entre, 392; equipolle, 332; excede from, 482; ? furnish, 444; Germany, 275; herafter, 238; lyghtely, 84; ? by meanes, 373; morter light, 503; ? move, 24; mycher, 436; offension, 96; ? owt of, 312; lower parte, 203; partie, 186; percher of wood, 503; procure out, 169; put over, 38; ? quiet, 221, *cf.* 475; ? refaicte, 228; ? seding, 187; shamefast, 228; signifie, 41; stike upon, 36; teaching, 355; ? trade, 310; traverse, 309; victualment, 228.

INDEX

Considerations of space have made it inexpedient to cite sources of information here given concerning persons. Where dates or other statements differ from those in the standard works of biographical reference, they are based on information found chiefly in the calendars and collections of state papers, collections of contemporary letters, contemporary chronicles, and episcopal registers. The same sources have normally furnished the information concerning persons who do not appear in the biographical dictionaries.

Where two or more dates are given, the latest, unless otherwise indicated, is the death date.

Almayn. *See* Germany

Almoner, The King's, *see* Lee, Edward, *c.* 1523–31; Fox, Edward, 1531–8; at Gardiner's funeral, 509

Alms, 64–5

Alresford (Alford, Alsford), Hants, 502, 509, 512–3, 519; deanery of, 65

Altar, 480–1; Sacrament of, *see* Sacraments

Alterations in religion. *See* Religion

Alton, Hants, 509, 519

Amatrice (Matrice), in Abruzzo, 11

Ambassadors, behaviour of, 86, 88–91; advice of an old, 397; instructions of, 373, 419, 421–2; should support each other, 220; at Imperial Court, 227–8; from all Germany, 236–7; English and Imperial, 401; of Saxe and Lansgrave in England, 1538, *see* Saxe and Lansgrave. *See also* Emperor's ambassador; Pope's ambassador; France; Venice

Amica Exegesis, Zwingli's, 316

Amiens (Amyas), Treaty of. *See* Treaties

Anabaptists, 166–7, 317, 319

Anatomy, 340

Andria, of Terence, 115, 188, 338

Andwarp, Andwerp(e). *See* Antwerp

Angelus. *See* Quiñones, Francis

Anglo-American Historians, Committee of Conference of, on editing historical documents, xx

Anglo-Saxon invasion of England, Gardiner's account of, xxxv

Angus (Anguish), Earl of. *See* Douglas, Archibald

Anne Boleyn, Queen of England, 1533–6, xxvi, 22, 286, 375, 377, 423

Anne of Cleves, married to and divorced from Henry VIII, 1540, d. 1557, xxiii, xxix

Anne, daughter of Ladislas, King of Hungary, first wife, 1521–47, of Ferdinand I, 268

Anne de Pisseleu, Duchesse d'Étampes, mistress of Francis I, *c.* 1523–47, d. *c.* 1576, 176, 188

Annebaut, Claude d', Admiral of France, 1544–52, ambassador at Imperial Court, 1545, 146–7, 149, 155–6, 176, 180–2, 188, 191–3, 197, 201, 203, 222

Annotaciones in Dialogum J. Oecolampadii, Gardiner's, 453

Anointing, 485

Anstye Manor, in Alton, Hants, 518

Answer of the Ordinaries to the *Supplication of the Commons*, 1532, 48–9

Antwerp, xxiv, 124, 146, 160, 180, 194, 196–205, 237–42, 401, 420, 423

Apostles, The, 332

Archbishops. *See* Canterbury; York

Archdeacons, 269

Archebolde. *See* Douglas, Sir Archibald, of Kilspindie

Ardres (Ardre), in the Boulonnais, 98

Argo, a ship made of pines from Pelion, 110

Aristotle, 104, 138, 351, 361, 483

Arms, Gardiner's, 502–3, 506–14 *passim*; the King's and nobles', 274–5; the Emperor's coat of, 215; the Queen's coat of, 504, 506, 510, 514

Arras, Bishop of. *See* Perrenot, Antoine

Arthur, King, 312

Arundel, Earl of. *See* Fitzalan, Henry

Arundel, Sir Thomas, in Wolsey's service, *c.* 1522–30, knighted, 1533, executed 1552, 7

Ascham, Roger, d. 1568, xxxiv

Ascot. *See* Aerschot

Asher, Asshere. *See* Esher

Ashes (on Ash Wednesday), 260

Askew, Anne, burned for views on Sacrament, 1546, 251, 277–8, 284, 293

Assertion and defence of the sacramente, Richard Smith's, 295

Athenians, 484

Aucher (Ager), Sir Anthony, in Cromwell's service *c.* 1534–6, Paymaster, 1537–44, and Controller, 1544–? of the works at Dover, Master of the Jewels, 1545–52, surveyor of victuals at Boulogne, 1545 (replaced by Vincent Mondye, Dec. 1545), chief victualler at Boulogne, Sept. 1546, knighted, 1547, Knight Marshal of Calais, 1552–3 (and later?), d. 1558?, 150–1

Audley (Audelay, Audeley, Audely, Awdly), Thomas, Baron Audley of Walden, 1538, Lord Keeper of the Great Seal, 1532–3, Lord Chancellor, 1533–44, 52, 58, 369–70, 380, 391–2. Lord Audeley, 56, is probably John Tuchet, Lord Audley, *q.v.*

Augmentations, Court of, 380, 393

Augsburg Confession, 1530, 71

Augustine, Austen, Austin(e), St. *See* St Augustine

Austin Friars, 165, 167. *See also* Barnes, Robert; Stanforde

Avery, Thomas, Cromwell's servant, *c.* 1529–40, in army in France, 1544, Commissary with Reiffenberg, 1545, living in 1548, 146–7, 158 195, 226

534

Awdly(e), Lord. *See* Audley, Thomas

Ayre (Aire), Dr Giles, Vice-Provost of King's College, Cambridge, 1534–8, canon of Ely, 1541–9, prebendary of Winchester, 1548–51, Dean of Chichester, 1549–51, 397

Balaam's ass, 483

Bale, John, one-time Carmelite friar, Protestant controversialist and playwright, Bishop of Ossory, 1553, d. 1563, 251, 276–9, 283–4, 293, 295, 299, 305, 307, 334

Ballads, about Lent, 280, 283, 285; about Bonner and Gardiner, 271, 280

Baly of Troys. *See* Dinteville, Jean de

Bangor, Bishop of. *See* Capon, John, 1534–9; Glyn, William, 1555–8

Baptism, 261, 343–4, 346, 348, 402, 407–9

Barbançois, Lion de, Sieur de Sarzay, wounds François St Julien in judicial duel, 1538, d. 1544?, 81

Barcelona, Treaty of. *See* Treaties

Barletta (Barlet), in Kingdom of Naples, 11

Barleye, Henry, Proctor at Cambridge, 1553–4, rector of Sherington, Bucks, 1569–81, 457–8

Barlow, William, Bishop of St Asaph, 1536, of St David's, 1536–48, of Bath and Wells, 1548–53, of Chichester, 1559–69, 251, 265–6, 285–6, 295

Barnaby (Barnabe), Thomas, London merchant, mentioned in *L.P.*, 1515–42, carried letters abroad for Henry VIII, 1523–42, d. ?, 80

Barnes, Robert, one-time Austin friar, recanted heretical views, 1526, in Germany, c. 1528–31, subsequently employed by Cromwell on missions to Germany, burned at stake, 1540, xxiii, xxviii, 149, 165–75, 317, 339

Barnet, Middlesex, 27, 29–30

Bartlet. *See* Berthelet, Thomas

Barwick. *See* Berwick

Basill. *See* St Basil

Basset, James, son of Honor Grenville, *q.v.*, and Sir John Basset, in Gardiner's service, c. 1538–55, proctor at his trial, gentleman of Queen Mary's privy chamber, 1555 ff., brought news of her pregnancy to Philip, 1558, d. ?, 502, 504, 507, 511, 514

Bath and Wells, Bishop of. *See* Foxe, Richard, 1492–4; Wolsey, Thomas, 1518–23; Clerk, John, 1523–41; Knight, William, 1541–7; Barlow, William, 1548–53

Baumbach, Ludwig von, Marshal of Philip, Landgrave of Hesse, 1540–8, Councillor of the same, 1536–40, '48–52, ambassador to England, 1539, '40, '45, to Calais, to mediate peace between France and England, 1545, 230

Bayard, Gilbert, Sieur de la Font, Francis I's Secretary of State and General of Finances, ambassador at Imperial Court, 1545, d. 1547, 147, 176, 181–4, 188, 191–3, 197, 203, 222

Becket, Thomas, Archbishop of Canterbury, 1162–70, 385

Becon, Thomas, chaplain to Somerset, d. 1567, 424

Bedford, Shire of, 43; Earl of, *see* Russell, John

Bell (Bel), Dr John, Archdeacon of Gloucester, 1518–39, Bishop of Worcester, 1539–43, d. 1556, 9, 16

Bellawey, a name used in a pen trial, 218

Bellay, Guillaume du, brother of Jean, Sieur de Langey, on missions to England, 1529, '30, '32, '33, d. 1543, 30–1, 34, 38–9

Bellay, Jean du, Bishop of Bayonne, 1524–32, of Paris, 1532–51, of Limoges, 1541–4, of Le Mans, 1542–56, Cardinal, 1535–60, ambassador to England, 1527–30, '33, 26, 31, 34, 38–9, 181

Bellaye, Cardinal of. *See* Bellay, Jean du

Bellerophon (Belerophon), mythical hero, slayer of the Chimera, 289

Benefit of Clergy, 359, 361

Benet, Dr William, Archdeacon of Dorset, 1530–3, on embassies to Rome, 1529–33, 8, 44–8; his colleges (*i.e.* colleagues at Rome, 1532, Bonner and Carne), 46; his chaplain, 48

Benson or Boston, William, Abbot, 1533–40, and Dean, 1540–9, of Westminster, 431

Bentley, Hants, 509

Bernardino (Bernardin), Giovanni, of Ferrara or Pavia, secretary to Sir Gregory Casale at Rome, newsgatherer for English ambassadors at French and Imperial Courts, c. 1538–55, English agent at Venice, 1557–8, d. ?, 196

Berredge, John, Mayor of Leicester, 1554–5, d. ?, 472

Berthelet (Bartlet), Thomas, royal printer, 1530–47, d. 1555, 68

Berwick, Captain of. *See* Clifford, Sir Thomas

Bethell, Robert, Mayor of Winchester, 1552-3, '55-6, d. ?, 513, 516

Bible, 332, 489; burnt, 285; reading of, restrained, 289; Matthew's, 361; Tyndale and Coverdale's, xxix, 361; proposed translation, 1542, xxix, 252, 299, 313-4, 317, 353; faults in Cranmer's edition of the Great Bible, 313-4, 317, 358-61. See also Scripture; Word of God

Biez (Bies, Buyes), Oudart du, Captain or Seneschal of Boulogne, 1524-44, Marshal of France, 1541-9, d. 1553, 4, 228

Bill, Dr William, Master of St John's College, Cambridge, 1547-51; Vice-Chancellor, 1548-9, Master of Trinity College, 1551-3, '58-61, Dean of Westminster, 1560-1, 431

Bishops, agreed to make homilies, 1542, 296; had better preach than make homilies, 314; their names put to Bishops' Book, 350; approved Henry VIII's religious policy, 294; were not deceived by King's Book, 372; those responsible for doctrine of justification in King's Book, 317, 323, 325, 360, 365; agreed to Catholic doctrine of the Sacrament, 447; cannot make laws without royal permission, 293, 303, 315; should agree to no alteration in religion in Edward VI's minority, 291, 312-3; should not hold cures outside their dioceses, 495; called kings by Erasmus, 385; Gardiner seeks retention of their power, xxviii; he asks to be heard in their presence, 426, 428; to hold obsequies for the Pope, 1555, 455, 476-7; at Gardiner's obsequies, 504-7; various references indicating their unpopularity, 257, 260, 268, 270-1, 291, 315, 321, 334, 353, 356, 384, 392, 478, 481; what becomes a Christian bishop, 365, 372, 375-6, 403-4, 422

Bishops' Book, The, or The Institution of a Christian Man, 1537, xxix, 252, 305, 317, 345, 350-2, 361

Bishop's Waltham. See Waltham

Black Paper Book, at Cambridge, 458

Bocholt (Bochold, Buckholt), Godfroi de, a captain of German mercenaries in Henry VIII's employ, 1544-5, d. ?, 235, 237; his wife, 237

Body, William, in Cromwell's service, c. 1532-40, bought rights of archdeaconry of Cornwall, 1537, killed by mob while destroying images in Cornwall, 1548, 391, 401

Bois-le-Duc, in Brabant, 233

Bolen, Boleyn, see Boulogne; Captain of, see Biez, Oudart du

Boleyn, Anne. See Anne Boleyn

Boleyn, George, brother of Anne, Viscount Rochford, Dec. 1529, executed 1536, 83-4

Boleyn, Thomas, father of Anne, Viscount Rochford, 1525, Earl of Wiltshire, Dec. 1529, Lord Privy Seal, 1530-6, d. 1539, 22-3, 34, 286-7

Bollen. See Boulogne

Bologna (Bononye), 11

Bonela or Bulla, Thade (Thadeus), courier of Henry VIII, 1527-33, '38-44, d. ?, 4

Bonner (Boner), Edmund, chaplain to Wolsey, 1529-30, Bishop of Hereford, 1538-40, of London, 1540-9, '53-9, d. 1569, 25, 33-5, 40, 45, 46 (colleague of Benet), 70, 81-91, 268, 270-1, 387-8, 455, 476-7, 504-7; his Commissary, 218

Bononye. See Bologna

Book of Common Prayer, xxxii, 368

Books, not one hundredth of the realm can read, 274; of the unlearned (i.e. images), ib., see also Images; in Latin and Greek, 289; proposal to suppress religious, 303; Bale's, see Bale; Gardiner's, see Gardiner, works

Borbrough. See Bourbourg

Borgoionons. See Burgundians

Borough towns, 28

Boston, William. See Benson

Boulogne, Henry VIII's conquest of, 1544, and discussion concerning his retention of, 92-3, 98, 127-8, 147, 156, 177-201 passim, 230, 307, 366; estimate of provisions for army at, 141-4; repulse of the French near 227-8; other references, xxiv, 124, 148, 150; Captain of, see Biez, Oudart du

Boulonnais (Bulloignois), 187

Bourbon, François de, second son of Charles, Duke of Vendôme, Duke of Enghien, killed, 1546, 240

Bourbourg (Borbrough, Burborowe), Diet at, 1545, 194, 220-1, 225

Bourchier, Henry, Earl of Essex, 1483, d. 1540, 148, 161-2

Bourchier, Margaret, daughter of Humphrey, Lord Berners, wife of Sir Thomas Brian, mother of Sir Francis, Lady Mistress to Henry VIII's children, Mary, Elizabeth, Edward, d. 1552, 161

Bourg, Antoine du, Baron de Saillans, Chancellor of France, 1535-8, 89, 90

Bowser. *See* Bourchier, Henry

Boxall, John, Warden of Winchester College, 1554–6, Archdeacon of Ely, 1556–9, joint Principal Secretary, 1557–8, Dean of Norwich, Peterborough, and Windsor, 1557–9, d. 1571, 513, 516

Boyneburg, Georg von, one of the ambassadors of 'Saxe and Lansgrave' to England, 1538, 161

Bradford, John, prebendary of St Paul's, 1551–4, martyred, 1555, xxxiv

Brandon, Charles, Duke of Suffolk, 1514, commanded army in France, 1523, '44, Lord Great Master, 1540–5, 38, 45, 92, 123–4

Braye, Anne, daughter of Edmund, Lord Braye, married George Brooke, later Lord Cobham, before 1526, d. 1558, 205

Brazen serpent, the, 286, 289–90

Brentius, Johannes, Lutheran preacher at Hall in Swabia, 1522–48, Provost of Stuttgart, 1554–70, 480, 488–9

Brerewood, Thomas, Chancellor of Bishop Voysey, Archdeacon of Barnstaple, 1528–44, 391, 401

Breton, Claude le, Sieur de Villandry, secretary to Francis I, d. 1542, 90

Brevia consectaria, 339

Brian, Lady. *See* Bourchier, Margaret

Brian, Sir Francis, knighted, 1522, Lord Marshal of Ireland, 1548–50, 1, 8–10, 13 (colleague of Gardiner)

Bridgewater House, London, xviii, 443

Briefe treatyse, A, Richard Smith's, 285

Brinklow, Henry, one-time Greyfriar, mercer, of London, author of social and religious satires under pseudonym of Roderigo Mors, d. 1546, 148, 159–60, 163

Bristol, Bishop of. *See* Holbeach, Henry, 1538–44

Bromley, Sir Thomas, Lord Chancellor, 1579–87, 470

Bronswicke. *See* Henry II, Duke of Brunswick-Wolfenbüttel

Brooke, George, Lord Cobham, 1529–58, Deputy of Calais, 1544–50, 205, 227–8; his wife, *see* Braye, Anne

Browne, Sir Anthony, knighted, 1523, Master of the Horse, 1539–48, 96, 100, 171

Browne, Sir Anthony, the younger, son of the foregoing, knighted, 1547, Viscount Montague, 1554–92, 380, 393, 502–16 *passim*

Brucel(les). *See* Brussels

Bruges, xxiv, 146, 149, 155, 157–9, 163–4, 175, 178–9, 181, 183, 185, 190–1, 193–6, 234

Bruneswike, Brunneswike, Brunswike. *See* Henry II, Duke of Brunswick-Wolfenbüttel

Brussels, xxiv, xxx, 93, 125, 196, 203, 220, 239

Bryan. *See* Brian, Sir Francis

Bucer, Martin, leader of the Reformation at Strasbourg, 1523–49, professor at Cambridge, 1549–51, xxiv, xxx, xxxi, xxxv, 93, 124–5, 149, 168, 205–9, 299, 306, 333, 429, 437–8, 447, 479–80, 489–91

Buckholt. *See* Bocholt, Godfroi de

Buckingham, Shire of, 43

Budaeus, Gulielmus, French humanist, d. 1540, 361

Bullen, Anne. *See* Anne Boleyn

Bullock, Dr George, Master of St John's College, Cambridge, 1554–9, Lady Margaret Professor of Divinity, 1556–9, d. *c.* 1580, 469

Bulloignois. *See* Boulonnais

Burborowe. *See* Bourbourg

Burchart, Franz, Vice-Chancellor of Saxony, 1536–60, ambassador to England, 1538, '39, '40, '47, '59, 161 (one of the ambassadors of Saxe and Lansgrave)

Bure, Bures, Burez, M. de. *See* Egmont, Maximilien d'

Burgundians (Burgoignons, Borgoionons), 77

Burnet, Gilbert, historian, Bishop of Salisbury, 1689–1715, xviii, 253

Bury St Edmunds, xxiii, xxv

Butts (Buttes), Dr William, physician to Henry VIII, d. 1545, 351

Buyes, M. de. *See* Biez, Oudart du

Byckeley, Henry. *See* Portsmouth, Mayor of

Bylson, Leonard, rector of Havant, Hants, 1548, of King's Worthy, Hants, 1558, prebendary of Winchester, 1551, held all benefices at least till 1559, d. ?, 516

Caesar, 272, 275, 384

Calais, xxvii, 4, 8, 30, 42, 54, 70–1, 76, 87, 92–3, 123, 147, 150, 156, 176, 196–7, 199, 202, 205, 211, 227, 240–1, 402; Council of, 76; Deputy of, *see* Wingfield, Robert, 1526–31; Plantagenet, Arthur, 1533–40; Fitzalan, Henry, 1540–4; Brooke, George, 1544–

Cassia phistola, *i.e.* cassia fistula, 47

Cassiodorus, Roman statesman and historian, d. *c.* 580, 264

Castelnau, Antoine de, Bishop of Tarbes, 1534–9, French ambassador in England, 1535–7, on special mission to England, 1538, 78

Castillon (Chastilion). *See* Perreau, Louis de

Cathedrals, 14, 289, 353. *See also* Canterbury; Southwark; Winchester

Catherine of Aragon, Queen of England, 1509–33, princess-dowager, 1533–6, d. 8 Jan. 1536, xxv–xxvii, 12, 15–8, 25, 40–1, 75; her Council, 37, 40–1. *See also* Henry VIII, divorce

Catherine Howard, Queen of England, 1540–2, xxix

Catherine de' Medici, niece of Clement VII, married, 1533, Henry (later Henry II) of France, d. 1589, 83

Catherine Parr, Queen of England, 1543–7, d. 1548, xxix, 150

Catholicism, xxxii; Gardiner's, xv, 168; Catholic doctrine, xxviii, 253, 446–52, 475–6; Catholic practices in England defended, 480–92; Catholic revival expected at Somerset's fall, 439; movement toward reunion of Catholics and Protestants, 209

Catullus, 332

Cecil, William, secretary to Somerset, 1547–9, Principal Secretary, 1550–3, '58–72, Chancellor of Cambridge, 1559–98, Baron of Burghley, 1571, Lord Treasurer, 1572–98, xxxii, 431, 455–6, 495

Celibacy of the clergy, 380, 385–6, 433, 435, 437, 458–9, 467–8, 480, 489–92

Ceremonies, in English Church, 371, 480, 484–5, 492; attacked by Ridley, 255; defended by Gardiner, 255 ff.; testify to God's honor, 464; at French Court, 90; at meeting of Order of the Golden Fleece, 149, 212–7; Gardiner's delight in, *ib.*; at his funeral, 503 ff. *See also* Cross; Procession

Certain sermons or homilies, etc., 1547, 368. *See also* Homilies

Chalcidian host, 451

Chaldeans (Chaldeyes), 233

Chalice, 480–1

Châlon, Philibert de, Prince of Orange, 1502–30, 11

Chamber, the Emperor's, 223; the King's, 478

Chamberlain, Lord (not to be confused with Lord Great Chamberlain). *See* Sandys, William, 1526–40; Paulet, William, 1543–5; Fitzalan, Henry, 25 July, 1546–50; Howard, William, 1558–72

Chamberlain, Lord Great. *See* Great Chamberlain

Chamberlain (Chamberlayn, Chamberleyne), Sir Thomas, Governor of the English Merchants at Antwerp, 1544–8, commissary with Reiffenberg, 1545, knighted, *c.* 1547, ambassador in Flanders, 1550–3, in Spain, 1560–2, still living, 1576, 146–7, 158, 195, 224, 226, 237, 240, 242

Chancellor, of Cambridge, *see* Cambridge University; of the Duchy, *see* More, Sir Thomas; of England, *see* Lord Chancellor; of France, *see* Prat, Antoine du, 1515–35; Bourg, Antoine du, 1535–8; Olivier, François, 1545–60; of Ireland, *see* Tiptoft, John; of the Order of the Golden Fleece, *see* Nigri, Philip; Gardiner's, *see* Steward, Edmund, 1531–51; Martin, Thomas, 1553–5

Chancery hand, 275–6

Chandlers, Company of, 503

Chantries, xxxiv, 65, 218, 494

Chapuys (Chapuce, Chapuis), Eustace, Imperial ambassador in England, 1529–39, '40–5, still living, 1555, xxix, 69, 92, 94–100, 155–6, 354, 375, 392; his secretary, 94

Charity, 385; in justification, 309–10, 343–7, 363–4, 375, 381–2, 403–7, 419–21

Charles III, Duke of Savoy, 1504–53, 98, 235; his ambassador at Imperial Court, 1546, 235

Charles V, King of Spain (as Charles I), 1516–56, Emperor, 1519–56, d. 1558, relation to Henry VIII's divorce, xxvi, 1, 12–3, 16–8; his forces in Italy, 10–1; alliance with Clement VII, 2, 25–6, 37; said by Clement to have destroyed the temporalities of the Church, 17; peace with England, 30; head of Church in Germany, 70, 72–5, 161; at war with France, 75–9; interview with Francis I, 82, 87; alliance with England, xxix, xxx, xxxiii, 92–100, 125–8, 146–8, 157, 176, 187, 191–3, 233, 253, 266; Treaty of Crespy, 93; regards Henry VIII as his father, 97; and as a true Christian prince, 374; at meeting of Order of Golden Fleece, 211, 213–7, 223; in good

Cromwell—*continued*
notable negligence, 174; his opinion of his own learning, 399; his attempt to persuade Henry VIII to make his will law, 378, 380, 399; other references, xxiii, xxvi–xxix, 20, 54, 58–9, 69, 71, 88, 217, 350, 401, 423–4
Crosier staff, 166, 503, 505–6, 509
Cross, the adoration of, creeping to, reverent use of, 255, 257–8, 274, 290, 484–6, 492; the sexton's handling of, and churchwarden's use of, 257; sign of, 262; in procession, 366, 463–4; Wolsey's, 166; Christ's death on, 281; the thief on, 363
Crowdale, Manor of, Hants, 518
Croy, Philip de, General of Charles V, Marquis of Aerschot, 1521–33, Duke of Aerschot, 1533–49, 202–3
Croydon, Surrey, 432
Crucifix, 255, 257, 288. *See also* Cross
Cryto, a character in Terence, *Andria*, 338
Curson, John, Groom of the Chamber, 1516–42 or later, employed in carrying diplomatic dispatches, 1524–5, '29, d. 1547, perhaps the same as John Curson, captain in the army, 1513, paymaster at Guisnes, 1528, 41–2
Curson, Margery, Book of Generation of, 153

Dacre (Dacres), William, Lord Dacre of Gilsland or of the North, 1525, Warden of the West Marches, 1527–34, '49–51, '54–63, 28, 55
Damon and Phintias, 102
Damsel, or Dansell, Sir William, English agent at Antwerp, 1544–*c.* '52, Receiver of the Court of Wards, *c.* 1551–78 or after, knighted, *c.* 1553, d. 1582, 240–1
D'Annebaut. *See* Annebaut
Darel, Young, possibly William, son and heir of Sir Edward Darrel (d. 1551), 462
Das dise wort, etc., Zwingli's, 316
David, King of Israel, 174–5, 367, 497
Davus, a character in Terence, *Andria*, 115
Davy(e), John, in Gardiner's service, 1545 or before –'55, witness at his trial, remembered in his will, d. ?, 218–20, 518
Day, George, Bishop of Chichester, 1543–51, '53–6, 317, 323, 325, 360, 365
Dean, The (168), probably of the Chapel Royal, *see* Thirlby, Thomas; of Paul's, *see* May, William

Declaration of such true articles..., *A*, Gardiner's, 164
Defence of the blessed masse..., *A*, Richard Smith's, 296
Defence of the sacrifice..., *A*, Richard Smith's, 296
Defence of the true & catholike..., *A*, Cranmer's, 449
Delburgo, Nicholas, Italian Minorite, at Oxford, 1517–35, worked for Henry VIII's divorce, prebendary of Timsbury (as result of letter 21), 1530–7 or after, in Italy, 1535 ff., d. ?, 31
De Lege et Fide (erroneously ascribed to Chrysostom), 363, 368
De Mendacio, St Augustine's, 294, 296
Denmark, 28, 98–9; King of, *see* Frederick I
Denyng, John, cleric at Winchester, 1556, 515
De profundis, 508, 517
Derbyshire, 43
De recta & emendata Linguae Graecae Pronunciatione, Thomas Smith's, 100–1
Detection of the Devils Sophistrie, *A*, Gardiner's, xxx, 249, 448–9
Dethicke, Sir Gilbert, Hammes pursuivant, 1536, Rougecroix pursuivant, 1540, Richmond Herald, 1541, Norroy King of Arms, 1547, Garter Principal King of Arms, 1549–84, knighted, 1551, 504–17 *passim*
De Vera Obedientia, Gardiner's, xxiii, xxvii, xxxv, 54, 67–9
Devil, the, 161, 169–70, 259, 263, 275, 305, 480, 482, 485–6
Devils, 255, 260–2, 309
Devonshire, Earl of. *See* Courtenay, Edward
Diet at Bourbourg, 1545, 194, 220–1, 225
Diet of the Empire, at Ratisbon, 1541, 209; Mar.–June, 1546, 236
Dinteville, Jean de, Bailly of Troyes, *c.* 1527–55, Sieur de Polisy, 1531–55, on missions to England, 1531, '33, '35, '36, '37, 68, 70
Dionysius, tyrant of Syracuse, 102
Diphthongs in Greek pronunciation, 101, 114–5, 118
Dirge, Dirige, 215, 253, 503, 508, 511–2, 514; Dirige Mass, 215
Doctors, three in part responsible for doctrine of justification in *King's Book* (Cox, Redman, Robinson), 325, 360, 365; of the Church, *see* Fathers
Doctrine, not to be rejected because held by Pope, 482–3; established by Parlia-

544

Exorcism, 259–63

Explicacion of the true Catholique faythe, An, Gardiner's (also entitled *An explication and assertion of*, etc.), 446, 449–50

Eyre, Dr Giles. *See* Ayre

Faith, 262–3, 309–10, 486; justification by, *see* Justification

Falaix, François de, Toison or chief herald of the Order of the Golden Fleece, 1541–6, d. ?, 213–6

Falier, Lodovico, Venetian ambassador in England, 1528–31, d. ?, 26

Falling evil (epilepsy), 261

Fane, Sir Ralph, knighted, 1544, commissary with Landenberg, 1544, with Reiffenberg, 1545, executed, 1552, 146–7, 158, 195, 226

Farnese, Alessandro. *See* Paul III

Farnese, Alessandro, grandson of Paul III, Cardinal, 1534–89, 196

Farnese, Ottavio, Duke of Camerino, 1540–5, of Parma, 1547–86, 'nephew', *i.e.* grandson, of Paul III, married Margaret, natural daughter of Charles V, 1538, 78

Farnham (Farneham, Fernam, Fernham), Surrey, 55, 60–1, 141, 145, 502, 509, 512

Fasting, 169, 280. *See also* Lent

Fathers, the (*also referred to as* Doctors *and* ancient writers), 293, 363, 404, 406, 408–9, 421, 429–30, 432, 437, 446, 452, 490. *See also* Sts Augustine, Gregory Nazianzen, Hilary, Jerome, John Chrysostom

Feldwig, Gerhard. *See* Veltwick

Ferdinand I, brother of Charles V, Archduke of Austria, 1521, King of Bohemia and Hungary, 1526, of the Romans, 1531, Emperor, 1556–64, 46, 98, 229–30, 268; his daughters, 267–8; his first wife, *see* Anne, daughter of Ladislas

Fernam, Fernham. *See* Farnham

Ferrara (Ferrare), ambassador of, in England, 26; Cardinal of, *see* Este, Ippolito d'; Duke of, *see* Este, Ercole II d'; House of, 182

Festival, The, or *Liber Festivalis*, sermons and tales for festival days by John Mirk, *c.* 1400, printed by Caxton, 1483, and frequently thereafter to 1532 (and from MS. in Early Eng. Text Soc., 1905), 299, 311–2, 314

First examinacyon of A. Askewe, Bale's, 284

Firstfruits, 63

Fish, economic reasons for use of, in Lent, 280

Fisher, John, Bishop of Rochester, 1504–35, xxvii, xxxv, 54, 67

Fitzalan, Henry, Earl of Arundel, 1544, Deputy of Calais, 1540–4, Lord Chamberlain, 25 July, 1546–50, Lord Steward, 1553–64, d. 1580, 245, 478

Fitzroy, Henry, natural son of Henry VIII, Duke of Richmond and Somerset, 1525, Lord Admiral, 1525–36, 54, 58–60

Fitzwater, Lord. *See* Radcliffe, Thomas

Fitzwilliam, William, Earl of Southampton, 1537, Lord Admiral, 1536–40, Lord Privy Seal, 1540–2, 95, 171

Flanders, xxviii, 40, 81, 146–7; Regent of, *see* Mary, sister of Charles V; President of the Council of, *see* Schore, Louis van

Flandre, Louis de, Sieur de Praet, member of Privy Council of Charles V, 1517 ff., grand bailli of Gand, 1515–22, of Bruges, 1523–49, Governor of Holland, 1544–7, d. 1555, 147, 157, 162, 179, 184, 195–6, 220, 222–4, 227–8

Flea, Merry tale of a, 407–8

Fleet, the, London prison, xv, xxiv, xxxi, 218, 375, 378–80, 395, 400, 402–5, 410–1, 413–4, 419, 423–6, 428–9, 448, 518; Warden of, 411

Florence, 11; Duchess of, *see* Margaret, daughter of Charles V

Florentines, 482

Fontainebleau (Founten de Blewe), in France, 77

Forest, Wolsey's servant, 1519–29, possibly Miles Forest, of the King's Chamber, 1516–46, d. ?, 40, 42

Fox, Edward, Provost of King's College, Cambridge, 1528–38, King's Almoner, 1531–8, Bishop of Hereford, 1535–8, xxvi, 1, 2, 4, 5, 48, 69, 71, 317, 351

Foxe, John, martyrologist, d. 1587, xxxiv, 284–5, 299, 378–80, 423–4; his *Actes and Monuments*, xviii, xxi, 285

Foxe, Richard, Bishop of Exeter, 1487–92, of Bath and Wells, 1492–4, of Durham, 1494–1501, of Winchester, 1501–28, 50

France, King of, *see* Francis I, 1515–47; Henry II, 1547–59; Queen of, *see* Eleanor; Admiral of, *see* Admiral; Chancellor of, *see* Chancellor; Constable and Great Master of, *see* Montmorency, Anne de; Court of, *see* Court; Dolphin, *i.e.* Dauphin, of, *see* Henry II; ventures of, in Italy, 1, 2, 68;

France—*continued*

possible brides for Henry VIII from, 87; Chapuys' opinion of, 99; Gardiner's dislike and distrust of, 94, 180, 265, 267, 271; scholars of, on Greek pronunciation, 110; soldiers of, not paid, 179; hates England, 180; French customs and character, 94, 229, 267, 277, 280; a French libel on England, 240; relations of, with England, xxvi–xxx, 12, 20, 26, 30–9, 42, 51, 68, 70, 78–90, 92–100, 123–8, 144, 146–7, 155–6, 175–7, 179–202, 214, 221, 226–9, 235, 240, 243–4, 307, 364, 366, 371, 460, 462, 471; with the Empire, xxvi, xxix, xxxiv, 33, 75–9, 82, 87, 92–9, 125–8, 146–7, 155–6, 179–203 *passim*, 214–5, 229, 366, 461; with Scotland, 83–4, 98–9, 147, 184, 192; with the Papacy, 83; *see also* Treaties; ambassadors of, at Rome, 1529, *see* Passano; in England, 1529, *see* Bellay, Jean and Guillaume du; in England, 1538, *see* Perreau; at Imperial Court, 1545, *see* Annebaut; Bayard; Olivier; at Imperial Court, 1546, *see* Menage; in England, 1554, *see* Noailles. *See also* Castelnau; Dinteville; Marillac; Pommeraye; Selve

Francis I, King of France, 1515–47, his children, Francis and Henry, hostages with Charles V, 33; his daughter, Madeleine, 83; his daughter, Margaret, 192; his son, Henry, *see* Henry II; his Queen, Eleanor, 46, 192; his mistress, *see* Anne de Pisseleu; his Council, 83, 85–6; his character, 211, 222; his illness, 75; his ruptures, 227–8; his opinion of the Protestants, 229–30; his refusal to deliver Cardinal Pole, 180; his definition of justification, 364; his relations with Henry VIII and Charles V, *see* France, relations of, with England, with the Empire; his relations with the Turks, 97–8

Francis, first son of Francis I, hostage with Charles V, 1526–9, d. 1536, 33

Francisco, Franciscus, Courier. *See* Picher, Francisco

Fraunces, Henry, son of Gardiner's sister, in Gardiner's service, 1532 or before–'38 or after, bailiff of the Clink, farmer of the rectory of Overton, Hants, 1546, lessee of the same, 1547 (possibly = Francis, Gardiner's secretary, 1547—Foxe, vi, 205), d. ?, 80

Frederick I, King of Denmark, 1523–33, 27–8

Frederick II, Count Palatine, Elector, 1544–56, 245–6

French, John, Mayor of Canterbury, Sept. 1545–Sept. 1546, d. ?, 152–3

Friars, 56, 63, 165, 167, 170, 219, 252, 299, 305, 315, 333–4, 337, 366, 368. *See also* Bale; Barnes; Brinklow; Delburgo; Guzman; Joseph; Pecock; Quiñones; Stanforde

Fridays, observance of, 492

Froyle, Hants, 509, 519

Fründlich verglimpfung, Zwingli's, 316

Fuller, Thomas, divine and historian, d. 1661, 495

Fygge, Thomas, one-time monk of St Swithun's Priory, minor canon of Winchester, 1551 or before, rector of Bishopstoke, Hants, 1553–6, became a monk again, 1556, d. ?, 515

Gairdner, James, historian, d. 1912, xxxvi, 44, 68, 150, 218, 424

Gambara, Uberto de, Bishop of Tortona, 1528–48, Cardinal, 1539–49, nuncio to England, 1526, '27, '28, 4 (Pope's ambassador)

Garda, Lake, 501

Gardiner, Agnes, mother of Stephen, xxv

Gardiner, Germain, secretary and probable kinsman of Stephen, executed, 1544, xxix

Gardiner, John, father of Stephen, d. 1507, xxv

Gardiner, Stephen:

Dates in his life, xxiii–xxiv; sketch of his life, xxv ff.; aims and policies, xxviii, xxxii–xxxiv; recent literature concerning, xxxv–xxxvi; register, xxxv; works, xvi–xvii, xxvii, xxx–xxxii, xxxv, 54, 67–9, 93, 124, 149, 159, 163–4, 205, 249, 429, 437, 439, 445–6, 448–50, 453, 478, 480; method of composition, 378; 'new fashion of writing', 449; spelling, 520 ff.; handwriting, 276; postscripts, xxii; signature, 44; called Dr Stephens, *see* Stephens; pseudonym, 451, cf. 217; arms, 502–3, 506–14; motto, 168, 175, 380, 394; country (Suffolk), 269; MSS. of letters, xvii–xix; kept no copy of letters, 88, 196; letters written jointly by him and others, not here printed, referred to, xvi, 1, 70, 93, 148–50; letters to, 493–501; letters to, not here printed, referred to, xvi, 2, 5, 12, 20, 31, 36, 44, 71, 92, 94, 129, 131, 149, 157–8, 195, 231, 243, 248, 251–2, 272, 471, 495, 501, *see also* Cranmer; Seymour, Edward

Gardiner, Stephen—*continued*

Boyhood, 2–3; studies law, 200, 272, 312; acts in *Miles Gloriosus*, 149, 186; in Wolsey's service, 1–19, 166; Master of Trinity Hall, 493; embassies to Clement VII, 1, 2, 4–18; colleagues at Rome, 1529, *see* Brian; Casale, Gregory; Vannes; anticipates breach with Rome and fall of Wolsey, 18; further relations with Wolsey, 20–43; at divorce trial, 2; secretary to Henry VIII, 2, 20–1, 54, 479; devotion to Henry, 5–6, 10, 16, 48, 60, 80, 189, 247–9; advises Henry not to follow Cromwell's advice, 399

Bishop of Winchester, 44, 287, 375, 422, 478–80; Prelate of the Order of the Garter, 312, 502, 504, 514; vestments, 503; crosier, 503, 505, 509; household and servants, 62–3, 70, 79–80, 218–20, 376, 422, 429, 433, 435, 473, 475–6, 504 ff.; chaplains, 131, 168–9, 398, 413–4, 506, 510–1, *see also* Harding; Medowe; Runcorn; Seton; Watson; Chancellor, *see* Steward; Martin; registrar, *see* Cooke; controller, *see* Thwaites; steward, *see* Muryell; Raynes; treasurer, *see* White, Thomas; gentlemen-ushers, *see* Massey; Vachell; kinsman, 398 (probably Harding, *q.v.*); study, 376; education of youth, 376; cathedral, *see* Winchester; Southwark church, *see* Southwark, St Mary Overies; houses, *see* Esher; Farneham; Southwark; Waltham; Winchester, Wolvesey; horses and mules, 70–1, 76, 78–80, 182; revenues, 50

Mission to France, 1532, 20, 44–7; opposes policy of King and Cromwell, 20, 48–9, 54; renounces Papacy, 478, 498; Pole's explanation of this, 498; retires to diocese, 54 ff.; in royal displeasure, 54, 60–1; administers oath to Act of Succession, 56; refutes charges of Cooke, 58–61; evaluates ecclesiastical revenue, 63–5; teaches Royal Supremacy, translates Luke and John, 66; *De Vera Obedientia* and reply to Paul III, xxxv, 54, 67–9; mission to Clement VII at Marseilles, referred to, 62, 84

Ambassador in France, 1535–8, 68–91, 94, 182, 260, 350; opposes league with Germans, 70–5; comments on death of Catherine of Aragon, 75; and on Continental situation, 77–80; asks Francis I to surrender Pole, 82, 179–80; objects to *Bishops' Book*, 350–2;

advises Bonner on English relations with France and on conduct as ambassador, 70, 82–91; not in Privy Council for a year or more preceding Cromwell's fall, 174; sermons at Court and Paul's Cross, 1540, 165, 168–70, 175; relations with Robert Barnes, *see* Barnes; mission to Imperial Court, 1540–1, 92, 236; debates with Bucer and Alesius at Ratisbon, 479–80, 489–91; visits Brentius' church in Swabia, 480, 488; hears William Gardiner preach at Canterbury, 1541, 328, 360

Henry VIII's chief minister, 1542, 252, 326, 354; collects Loan, 354; negotiates with Chapuys, 92, 94–100, 354, 361; part in proposed Bible translation, 252, 313; as Chancellor of Cambridge treats of Greek pronunciation, xvi, 92, 100–22, 133–8; deals with regents who eat flesh in Lent, 121–2; objects to the play *Pammachius*, 129–35, 139–40; refers humorously to his office, 152; part in *King's Book*, 259, 264, 302, 361, 364–5; plot against Cranmer, 252, 317, 325–8, 360; defends Henrician establishment against Turner, 478, 480–92; controversy with Bucer, *see* Bucer; at Boulogne, 92, 124, 303; Purveyor to the forces, 93, 129, 280, 284, 303, 318, 354; at Imperial Court with Hertford, 1544, 93, 125–8, 146, 267, 303, 416; examines accounts of provisions for Boulogne, 141–4

Embassy to Imperial Court, 1545–6, 146–50, 268, 303, 420, 423; importance of letters then written, 148–9; colleagues, *see* Carne; Thirlby; mirth at behaviour of soldiers at Canterbury, 148, 151–4; receives Brinklow's *Lamentacion*, attributes it to Joye, 148, 159–60; reply to Joye, 149, 159, 163–4; account of relations with Barnes, 149, 165–75; never wrote so much in a month as in that preceding 5 Nov. 1545, 163; negotiations with French ambassadors at Imperial Court, 147, 175–203 *passim*; advises making peace, 178–80, 188–9; negotiations for revision of treaty with Empire, 147–8, 191–235 *passim*; would grant demands of Imperial merchants, 221; will not exceed instructions, 177; how he would write his own instructions, 178; is perplexed at the international situation, 176–8, 183–90; is concerned at advance of Protestantism in England and at German Protestants

Gardiner, Stephen—*continued*
meddling in international affairs, *see*
Protestantism; describes meeting of
Order of Golden Fleece, 149, 212–7;
commends Henry VIII's speech in
Commons, 211–2; asks to have hospitals of St Cross and Mary Magdalene
stand, 149, 218–9; issues statement
concerning an English victory, 227–9;
brings money to England, 239–42

Mission to Boulogne to confer with
Hertford on its defence, **1546**, 303;
confers with Philip of Bavaria, 245–6;
checks reform, 265, 267; reluctance to
exchange lands with Henry VIII not
well taken, 246–8; *Detection of the
Devils Sophistrie*, 249; officiant at
Henry VIII's funeral, 371

Fall, **1547**, 251, 271; secretary
robbed, 286; protests against a play in
Southwark, 251, 253–4; and against
Ridley's attack on images and holy
water, 251, 255–63; tells Somerset quiet
is England's need, 265–7; hears that
some desire to kill him, 265, 267;
objects to wording of commissions
renewing ecclesiastical jurisdiction,
268–72; advises Paget as to conduct,
270; protests against destruction of
images, circulation of Bale's books, and
rhymes depraving Lent, 251, 272–83;
likes Somerset's proclamation of **24
May**, **1547**, 287, 292, 298, 366; investigates iconoclasm at Portsmouth,
288; objects to restraint of episcopal
preaching, 286, 289, 299, 306, 353; how
he hears of innovations, 292–3; urges
retention of Henrician religious settlement, 294–5, *see also King's Book*; is
said to be little concerned at burning
of Scripture, 285; objects to issuing
homilies, 296 ff., *see also* Homilies

Writes at length to Cranmer opposing homilies, upholding *King's Book*,
and discussing justification, saints'
legends, Bible translation, religious
habits of Englishmen, royal authority,
and other matters, 299–360 (for analyses
of contents of these letters *see* 299,
317); summarizes his activities, **1542**–
7, 303–4, 354; protests to Council and
others against *First Book of Homilies*,
indicating its possible political consequences, and against injunctions of
1547 as unconstitutional, 253, 361–77;
fears no hurt from Somerset and Council, 377; interview with Council, 25

Sept. **1547**, ending in imprisonment,
378, 380, 394–6

Prisoner in Fleet, 218, 375, 378–9,
395–8, 400, 403; hardships there, 402,
404–5, 409–14, 422–3, 427; writes to
Somerset explaining opposition to
injunctions and *Homilies*, chiefly on
constitutional grounds, and to Erasmus'
Paraphrase (*q.v.*), for political, social,
and religious reasons, 378–428 (for
analyses of contents of the longer of
these letters *see* 380, 402); how these
letters reveal his character, 378–9; interview with Cranmer at Deanery of St
Paul's, 380, 397–8, 402–4, 406, 426–7;
disclaims enmity with Cranmer, 406;
excluded from Parliament, 378, 410,
424; is used to name certain members
of Commons, 424; complains of illegal
imprisonment, sues to be heard, 410,
414–6, 423–8; deserted by friends, 378,
417; would give life to prevent circulation of *Paraphrase*, 414, 418

Released from Fleet, 7 Jan. **1548**,
429, 448; at Hampton Court before
Council next day, 448–9; prisoner in
own house, confers with Ridley, gives
qualified assent to articles on justification, 429–32; what learned men he
knows, 431, cf. 166; retires to Winchester, 429; is troubled by John Philpot and a married cleric, 433–5;
refuses to surrender Trinity Hall, 479,
493–5; is unable to obey summons of
Council, 429, 435–6; sermon at Winchester, 448–9; third book against
Bucer, 429, 437; before Council, 439,
448–9; St Peter's Day sermon, 439–40,
448–50

Prisoner in Tower, 218, 375, 437,
439; books written there, 439, 445–6,
449–53; asks for justice, 439–41, 444–5;
ill treated by Lieutenant of Tower, 441–
2; is kept from Parliament, 443–4; twofold preface against Cranmer, 439,
446–50; expects release, 375; trial, 439,
450, 495, 518; *Long Matter*, 439

Released from Tower, 437, 455, 501;
letters written as Lord Chancellor, 455–
77; restored to Chancellorship of
Cambridge, 455; activities in this office,
455–9, 463–4, 467–9, 473–6; activities
in connection with Wyatt's rebellion,
459–63; regret for breach with Rome,
479, 496; return to Roman obedience,
465; advises Pole on reunion with
Rome, 455, 464–7; writes to Mont-

Gardiner, Stephen—*continued*
morency on peace, 455, 471; rebukes
students of Christ Church, Oxford,
Mayor and aldermen of Leicester, and
an unknown offender, 455, 470, 472–3;
account of invasions of England for
Philip II, xxxv; instructs Bonner about
obsequies of Julius III, 476–7; will,
517–8; death, 476, 502–3; executors,
476, 502–17 *passim*; obsequies, 479,
502–17, 519; chief mourner, *see* Browne,
Sir Anthony, the younger; chantry, 502

Qualities of character indicated in
his letters or claimed by him: does not
pretend to be a saint, yet is no devil,
163; is a good Englishman, 416; is
reported to be stubborn, 287; is no
dissembler or hypocrite, 66, 163, 437;
cannot play the pope-holy, 419; is said
to be eloquent, 280; is called the
Sophister, 397–8; is charged with
cavillation, 359; abhors lies, is a plain
speaker, prefers truth to possessions,
288–9, 365, 372, 376–7, 404; is not
Wily Winchester, 372; never willingly
broke a law, 427, 436; is not factious,
296, 405, 431; never kept scholars at
the universities to be brought up in
his opinion, 168; never thought of
returning evil for evil, 327; cannot be
bribed to change his opinion, 403–4,
406, 416, 422, 436; cannot be indifferent,
372; denies that he likes nothing unless
he does it himself, 398; disclaims author-
ship of anything new, *ib.*; can admit no
innovations, 298; has never disdained
the world, 402–3; but finds it vanity,
417; never complains of what he dislikes to the people, but only to those
in authority, 357, 372; his importunity,
367; his concept of his duty as an
ambassador, 86, 88–9, 158; as a bishop,
365, 372, 375–6, 403–4, 422, 449; and as
Chancellor of Cambridge, 129 ff.; was
never a persecutor, 270; how he deals
with heretical preachers, 304–5; his character in adversity, 378–9; dejection and
resilience of spirit, 149, 191; writes to
quiet his mind, 149, 184–5; delights in
ceremonies, 149, 212–7; dislikes fish,
280; resents imputation of ignorance,
102–3; has a merry head, 318, *see also*
Merry tales; his philosophy, 270

His comment on: licence and iniquity
of the times, 89, 102, 111, 136–9, 160–1,
178, 211, 249; the world troubled by
words, 210, 332; disadvantages of

wealth, 198; infelicity of preeminence,
266; uncertainty of fortune, 270;
display and judgment in scholarship, 119; danger of precedents, 399;
function of usage in language and law,
104–7; shortcomings of the nations,
280; English character, *see* Englishmen;
for his comment on legal and constitutional matters *see* Justice; Law; Acts of
Parliament; Royal supremacy; Praemunire; Injunctions; for comment on
religious practices and beliefs *see*
Religion; Christ; Sacraments; Justification; Lent; Holy water; Images;
Saints; Celibacy; Ceremonies; Preaching; Friars; Protestantism; for comment on Reformation measures *see*
Henry VIII, ecclesiastical policy; Edward VI, religious changes; Pope;
Bishops' Book; *King's Book*; Bible;
Homilies; Erasmus' *Paraphrase*

His characterizations of persons: Anne
Askew, 277; Bale, 277–8, 305; Barnes,
165 ff.; Bayard, 181–2, 188; Bourchier,
162; Brinklow, 160; Bucer, 206;
Charles V, 223, 229; Clement VII, 12–3,
17; Cranmer, 447–8; Cromwell, 174,
399; Erasmus, 118, 383, 403; Francis I,
180, 211, 222, 228; Henry VIII, 287; the
Imperial councillors, Granvelle, Nicolas
de, de Praet, Scepperus, Schore, 222, 234;
Joseph, 305; Joye, 160, 305; Luther,
166, 277, 335; Olivier, 181; Paget, 269–
71; Philip of Hesse, 161–2, 192; Thomas
Smith, 120; Turner, 488, 492; for
further reference to these and other
persons *see* names of persons concerned

Gardiner, William, *alias* Sandwich, monk
of Canterbury, warden of Canterbury
College, Oxford, 1537 or before -'41,
prebendary of Canterbury, 1541–4,
317, 328, 360

Garret, Thomas. *See* Gerard, Thomas

Garter, Order of the, 213, 258, 312, 502,
504, 514; Prelate of, *see* Gardiner,
Stephen

Garter Principal King of Arms. *See*
Dethicke, Sir Gilbert

General Council, 443–4; a future, 71, 73,
84, 86–7, 185–6. *See also* Constance;
Trent

Geometry, 226

George Joye confuteth, etc., 149

Gerard or Garret (Jerarde, Jherard),
Thomas, rector of All Saints, Honey
Lane, 1537–40, burned with Barnes
and Jerome, 1540, 165, 173–4

Gerard(e) (Gerardus), in Nos. 97, 103. *See* Veltwick, Gerhard

Gerardus, bookseller, in No. 1. *See* Godfrey, Garrat

Germans (Almaignes, Almaynes), characteristics of, 230, 280, 490; mercenaries in English employ, 146–7, 183–4, 203, 235, 237. *See also* Bocholt; Landenberg; Pennink; Reiffenberg

Germanus, a name used in a pen trial, 75, 218

Germany (Almayn), 94, 203, 234–6, 275, 325, 351; Protestant princes of, 12, 69, 197; proposed leagues with England, 70–5, 245–6; Protestants of, try to make peace between England and France, 146–7, 155–6, 162, 176–7, 182, 190, 192, 194, 199, 201–2, 210, 227, 229–30; civil wars in, xxviii, 155–6, 277, 279, 284, 308; fear of the Turk in, 98; Church of, 72; churches in, 256, 274, 488; images in, 256, 273–4; preaching in, 314; Vice-Chancellor of, *see* Naves. *See also* Protestantism

Ghinucci, Girolamo; Bishop of Ascoli, 1512–8, of Worcester, 1522–34, Cardinal, 1535–41, 28, 30, 32; his servant, 32

Giberti, Gian Matteo, Datary to Clement VII, Bishop of Verona, 1524–43, 10

Gloria in excelsis, 516

Gloucester, Bishop of. *See* Hooper, John, 1550–4

Glyn, William, Lady Margaret Professor of Divinity, 1544–9, President of Queens' College, Cambridge, 1553–7, Vice-Chancellor, 1554–5, Bishop of Bangor, 1555–8, 474, 476

Godfrey, Garrat (Gerrat), of Limburg, stationer, at Cambridge, 1503–39, University printer, 1534–9, 3

Godly and faythfull retractation, A, Richard Smith's, 284

Godsalve, Sir John, clerk of the Signet, *c.* 1531–47, knighted, 1547, Visitor of dioceses of London, Norwich, and Ely, 1547, Controller of the Mint, 1548–52, d. 1556, 44, 51, 375–7

God's Word. *See* Word

Golden Fleece, Order of (Toyson d'Or), 147, 149, 211–7, 220, 223, 238–9; Chancellor of, *see* Nigri, Philip; chief herald of (*or* Toison), *see* Falaix, François de; treasurer of, 213 (probably Henri Sterck, ?–1549); registrar of, 213, 216, 239

Golden Legend. See *Legenda Aurea*

Good Friday, 255, 257

Gospel, the, 159, 161, 202, 259, 330, 333, 381, 384–6, 395, 421, 423, 484; in the Mass, 169–70, 355

Governour, Master (of the English Merchants at Antwerp). *See* Chamberlain, Thomas

Grace, 343, 346–7, 364, 486

Grammar, 170, 172, 484

Grant, M. de la, in the Emperor's service, 1544–6, d. ?, 223

Granvelle (Grandevela, Grandevilla, Grandvela, Grandvele). *See* Perrenot, Nicolas

Granvelle, Antoine Perrenot de. *See* Perrenot, Antoine

Gravelines (Graveling), 205, 220, 245

Great Bible. *See* Bible

Great Chamberlain, Lord (not to be confused with Lord Chamberlain). *See* Vere, John de, 1526–20 Mar. 1540; Cromwell, Thomas, 1540; Radcliffe, Robert, 1540–2; Seymour, Edward, 1543–7; Dudley, John, 1547–50

Great Master, Lord. *See* Brandon, Charles, 1540–5; Paulet, William, 1545–50; Dudley, John, 1550–3

Great Master of France. *See* Montmorency, Anne de

Great Seal of England, 177, 274

Great sickness, the, 1535, 70

Greek Church, 280, 289, 363, 487

Greek language, 264, 286, 289, 358–9, 399, 453–4, 484, 488; pronunciation of, xvi, xxiii, xxix, 92, 100–22, 129, 133–8

Greeks, 484, 488

Greenwich, 21–6, 44–5, 52

Gregory I, Pope, 590–604, 256–7, 263–4

Gregory, Master, Sir. *See* Casale, Sir Gregory da

Gregory Nazianzen. *See* St Gregory Nazianzen

Greneacres, Thomas, remembered in Gardiner's will, presumably in his service, 506

Grenville, Honor, widow of Sir John Basset (d. 1528), mother of James Basset, second wife, 1528, of Arthur Plantagenet, Viscount Lisle, *q.v.*, d. ?, 54, 57, 62, 76, 79, 81

Grey, Henry, father of Lady Jane Grey, Marquis of Dorset, 1530, Duke of Suffolk, 1551, executed, 1554, 461

Grey, Lady Jane, executed, 1554, 456

Grey, Lord John, brother of Henry, condemned to death for part in Wyatt's rebellion, pardoned, d. 1569, 459–61

Grey, Lord Thomas, brother of Henry, executed, 1554, 461

Greyhounds, 150, 158, 199

Grimsby, Lincs, 218

Gropper, Johann, jurist and theologian, in service of Hermann von Wied, 1526-43, Provost of Bonn, 1547, refused Cardinalate, 1556, d. 1559, 208-9

Guildford (Gylford), Surrey, 54, 60-1, 509; Churches of the Holy Trinity, St Mary, St Nicholas at, 509

Guildford, Sir Henry, Controller of the Household, 1522-32, 29

Guisnes, 93

Guzman, Gabriel, Spanish Dominican, used by Francis I to induce Charles V to desert Henry VIII, 1545, 366, 368

Haddyngton, Manor of, Hants, 518

Hagenau, Colloquy at, 1540, 209

Hall (Hala), in Swabia, 480, 488

Hall (Hal), Francis, nephew of Sir Robert Wingfield, spear of Calais, c. 1539 ff., commissary to muster wagons for English army in France, 1544, commissary with Reiffenberg (but not detained by him), 1545, Controller of Calais, 1545-52, 123

Hampshire, 43, 56, 63, 142, 273, 431-2, 518; church revenue in, 63-5; churches in, 509; Gardiner's house in, 431-2 (probably at Winchester, possibly at Waltham)

Hampton. See Southampton

Hampton Court, 12, 44, 121, 165, 167, 243-4, 301, 399, 448-9, 470, 478-9

Handwriting, 275-6

Hannibal, 321

Hannyngton rectory, Hants, 518

Harbin, Rev. George, non-juror, d. 1744, 299, 316

Harding, Dr Thomas, kinsman of Gardiner, chaplain to Henry Grey, c. 1542-53, chaplain to Gardiner, 1553-5, prebendary of Winchester, 1554-9, abroad, 1559-72, 402, 502, 512, 517

Hare, Sir Nicholas, knighted, 1539, justice of Chester and Flint, 1540-5, Master of the Rolls, 1553-7, 220

Harington, John, imprisoned for complicity in Wyatt's rebellion, 1554, father of Sir John Harington, d. after 1577, 459-61

Hartley, Hants, 509, 519

Harvey, Master, probably William, servant to Thomas Wriothesley, 1539, Hammes

pursuivant, 1541, Bluemantle pursuivant, 1544, Somerset Herald, 1545, Norroy King of Arms, 1550, Clarenceux King of Arms, 1557-67, 511, 514

Harwich, 461

Havering atte Bower, Essex, 100-1

Hawks, 199

Haynes, Simon. See Heynes

Heath, Nicholas, Bishop of Rochester, 1540-3, of Worcester, 1543-51, '53-5, Archbishop of York and Lord Chancellor, 1555-8, 317, 323, 325, 360, 365, 470

Heaven, 278, 307-8, 310, 359

Heding. See Hesdin

Heidelberg, 245

Helizeus. See Elisha

Hellyer, John, rector of Warblington, Hants, 1533-8, Vicar of East Meon, Hants, fled abroad, 1535, attainted for adherence to the Pope, 1539, Master of the English Hospital, Rome, c. 1540-1, 67

Henry II, Duke of Brunswick-Wolfenbüttel, 1514-68; prisoner of the Protestant princes, 1545-7, 156, 195-6

Henry II, King of England, 1154-89, 385

Henry II, King of France, second son of Francis I, married Catherine de' Medici, 1533, Dauphin, 1536, King, 1547-59, 33, 83, 240, 462

Henry VII, King of England, 1485-1509, 184, 240

Henry VIII, King of England, 1509-47, letters to, 5-7, 9-17, 48-9, 94-6, 123, 204-5, 246-8; divorce, xxiii, xxv-xxvii, 1, 2, 5-18, 20-1, 25-6, 36-42, 46, 49, 75; communicates with Wolsey through Gardiner, 21-43; prevents Wolsey from seeking support in Parliament, 43; denounced by Paul III, 54, 67-8; fears sweating sickness, 27; hunts late, 33; book against Luther, 49; wants to see possible French brides in person, 87; Chapuys' opinion of, 94-100; crosses Channel, 124; munificence to Cambridge, 132; sends greyhounds to Regent of Flanders, 150, 158, 199; attitude toward Protestantism, 149, 159, 162; relations with German Protestants, 70-5, 245-6, 319; relations with Barnes, 165, 170-1, 174, 339; speech in Commons, 1545, 211-2; his palace, New Hall, 290; his chamber, 478; blesses cramp rings, 255, 260; approves phrase *Our Lord*, 259, 264; regard for Lent,

Henry VIII—*continued*
121, 277, 283; reverence for the Sacrament, 165, 171; discusses images, 286, 290; appoints Gardiner his chief minister, xxix, 252, 317, 326, 354; Gardiner's relations with, xxvi–xxix, 5–7, 16, 22, 48–50, 60–1, 243, 246–8, 251, 286–7, 307, 349, 375, 399, 419, 436, 478–80; ecclesiastical policy and settlement, xxiii, 20, 48–9, 72, 122, 131, 148, 252, 268, 278, 286, 290, 294–7, 299, 301, 306, 308, 320, 357–8, 361–70, 373–4, 478, 480–92, *see also King's Book*; Royal supremacy; his religious settlement divinely inspired, 122, 301; his knowledge of theology, 290, 362, 364, 369; his death in Edward's minority would be a calamity, 187; speaks of himself as the old man, 252, 308; slandered by Bale, 277–8, and by the homilies, 361–2, 369, 371, 374; objects to homilies, 303; not seduced in *King's Book*, 299–302, 317, 321–5, 331–2, 345; abhorred justification by faith, 305, 345–6, 364; persuaded Cranmer to give up that doctrine, 317, 329, 336, 338; encouraged Bible translation, 1542, 313–4; annotated *Bishops' Book*, 305, 317, 345, 351; inflamed against Cranmer, 326; made no religious changes without a convocation, 361, 367; permitted free speech on a matter before it was made law, 380, 398, 402, 405–6; advised by Cromwell to make his will law, 378, 380, 399; his virtue and wisdom, 16, 162, 287; character, 287; was a noble and a true Christian prince, 365, 374; death, burial, executors, xxiv, xxxi, 187, 251, 253–4, 301, 304, 307, 324, 371, 375, 448; has gone to heaven, 307–8, 310; relations with France, *see* France; relations with the Empire, *see* Empire; conquest of Boulogne, *see* Boulogne; wives, *see* Catherine of Aragon, Anne Boleyn, Anne of Cleves, Catherine Howard, Catherine Parr; Council, *see* Council; mentioned, xv, xvii, xxx, xxxii–xxxiii, 44–6, 50, 54–66 *passim*, 71, 76–7, 80, 131–2, 142, 148, 158, 160, 218–9, 238, 261, 265, 267, 269, 278, 280, 291–2, 294, 320–2, 352, 372, 377, 389–90, 400–1, 403, 423–5, 435, 440, 479
Heralds' account of Gardiner's obsequies, 479, 502–17
Hereford (Herford), Bishop of. *See* Fox, Edward, 1535–8; Bonner, Edmund, 1538–40

Heresy, xxix, xxxiv, 168, 252, 258, 277, 299, 304–5, 308, 310, 312, 369–70, 424, 475, 496, 499–500; laws against, xxiv, xxxiv
Heretical books, xxix, 159–65, 251, 277–9, 284, 293, 296
Heretics, xxviii, 305, 370, 434, 446–7, 487–8, 492, 499. *See also* Anabaptists
Hermann von Wied, Elector and Archbishop of Cologne, 1515–47, attempted unsuccessfully to introduce the Reformation in Cologne, excommunicated, 1546, retired, 1547, d. 1552, 209, 236–7
Hertford (Herford), Earl of. *See* Seymour, Edward
Hertford-Lisle group in Privy Council, 1546–7, xxx, 243
Hesdin (Heding), in Artois, 79, 203
Hesse, Landgrave of. *See* Philip, Landgrave
Heussenstamm, Sebastian von, Archbishop of Mainz, Jan. 1546–55, 178
Heynes, Dr Simon, President of Queens' College, Cambridge, 1528–37, Vice-Chancellor, 1532–4, Dean of Exeter, 1537–52, 431
Hezekiah (Hezekias), King of Judah, 313
Hilarie. *See* St Hilary
Hippinus. *See* Aepinus
History Tripartite, 259, 264
Hocstrate, M. de. *See* Lalaing, Philip de
Holbeach, Henry, Bishop of Bristol, 1538–44; of Rochester, 1544–7, of Lincoln, Aug. 1547–51, 397
Holles, Sir William, merchant, knighted, 1533, Lord Mayor of London, 1539–40, d. 1542, 173–4
Holybourne (Holyborne), Hants, 509, 519
Holy bread, 263, 382, 385, 485
Holy Ghost, 122; chapel of, in Isle of Wight, 65; Mass of, 505, 515
Holy Land, 3
Holy League (between France and Italian powers, led by Pope), 1525–9, 11–2
Holy water, 251, 255, 259–64, 480, 485–6, 513
Homer, 289, 351, 385
Homilies (proposed, 1542, proposal revived by Cranmer, opposed by Gardiner, 1547, First Book of, issued, 1547), xxxi, 252–3, 296–9, 302–4, 309–11, 314–5, 317, 353–4, 356, 361–74, 376–8, 380–3, 386, 388–9, 394–8, 403, 406, 408, 411, 413, 416, 419, 421, 423, 429; Homily of Salvation, 253, 361–2, 367, 371, 374, 382, 397, 403, 406, 408, 413,

Homilies—*continued*
416; of Works, 367, misquotes Chrysostom, 361, 365, 368, 374, 380, 382-3
Hooper, John, Bishop of Gloucester, 1550-4, of Worcester, 1552-3, martyred, 1555, xxxiv
Hope, in justification, 344, 363-4, 382, 420-1
Horace, 117
Horawitz, A., 2
Hosiander. *See* Osiander, Andreas
Hospitals, 149, 218-9
Houghton, Richard, probably Richard Hutton, rector of Alderbury, Surrey, in 1536, of Stoke d'Abernon, Surrey, 1545-56, 515
Howard, Catherine. *See* Catherine Howard
Howard, Henry, poet, son of Thomas, Earl of Surrey (by courtesy), 1524, executed, 1547, xxx
Howard, Thomas, Earl of Surrey, 1514, Duke of Norfolk, 1524, Lord Treasurer, 1522-47, in Tower, 1546-53, d. 1554, xxx, 28-30, 43, 45, 61, 77-8, 92, 176
Howard, William, son of Thomas, Baron Howard of Effingham, 1554, Lord Admiral, 1554-73, Lord Chamberlain, 1558-72, Lord Privy Seal, 1572-3, 461
Humber barrels, 141-2
Hungary, Queen of. *See* Mary, sister of Charles V
Hunsdon (Hundesdon), Herts, 28-9
Hunter, The jolly. *See* Turner, William
Huntyng...of the Romyshe foxe, Gardiner's reply to Turner's, 478-92
Hutton, John, English agent at Antwerp and Governor of the English Merchants there, 1536-8, 81
Hutton, Richard. *See* Houghton

Idolatry, 257, 275, 484-5
Idols, 255-6, 275. *See also* Images
Images, destruction and defence of, 153, 251, 255-9, 262, 264, 272-6, 285-6, 288-90, 485, 492
Imperial ambassadors, Council, Court. *See* Charles V
Incent, Dr John, Vicar-General of Bishops of Winchester, 1523-30, Master of Holy Cross Hospital, Winchester, 1524-45, Dean of St Paul's, 1540-5, 62-3
Indulgences. *See* Pardons
Ingelfylde, Sir Fraunces. *See* Englefield
Injunctions of 1547, xxiv, 252-3, 361, 366-74, 378, 380-2, 387-8, 394, 400, 412
In Petrum Martyrem, etc., Gardiner's, 445

Institutes, The, 315
Institution of a Christian Man, The. See *Bishops' Book*
Ipswich, Wolsey's college at, 19
Isaiah, 168, 175
Isle of Wight, 56, 65
Italian hand, 276
Italians, 77-8, 179-80, 184, 224, 228, 420; characteristics of, 252, 280, 355, 372
Italy, 1, 2, 10-1, 26, 68, 77, 228, 277, 280, 283

Jack of Lent's Testament, 293
Jackson, Rev. J. C., d. 1895, xviii
James V, King of Scotland, 1513-42, married Madeleine, daughter of Francis I, 1537, 83-4, 215
Janelle, P., xix, xxxv-xxxvi, 68-9, 124
Jerarde, Jherard. *See* Gerard, Thomas
Jericho (Jherico), 148, 159
Jerome (Jherome), William, vicar of Stepney, 1537-40, burned with Barnes and Gerard, 1540, 165, 173-4
Jewels, case at law concerning, 380, 392-3, 401-2
Jews, 262, 275, 290, 348, 446
John III, King of Portugal, 1521-57, 90
John Albert of Brandenburg, Archbishop of Magdeburg, 1545-50, 178
John Frederick I, Elector of Saxony, 1532-47, captured by Charles V, 1547, d. 1554, 73, 276, 279, 284, 293, 317, 319; his ambassadors, *see* Saxe and Lansgrave, ambassadors of
Johnston, Nathaniel, physician and antiquarian, d. 1705, 428
Jonas, Justus, German humanist and reformer, d. 1555, 447
Joseph and his brethren, 484
Joseph, husband of Mary, 407
Joseph, Dr John, Cranmer's chaplain, onetime Minorite, rector of Chiddingstone, Kent, 1545-53, of St Mary-le-Bow, London, 1546-53, prebendary of Canterbury, 1550-3, 281, 299, 300, 302, 304-5, 307, 317, 324, 333-4, 337-8, 354-5
Joye, George, Protestant controversialist, author of two books against Gardiner, d. 1553, xxiv, xxx, 148-9, 159-60, 163-75, 277, 299, 305, 307
Judges, 105, 108, 271, 390-1, 415
Julius II (Giuliano della Rovere), Pope, 1503-13, his brief, xxvi, 1, 12-4
Julius III (Giovanni Maria del Monte), Pope, 1550-5, xxxiii, 455, 476-7, 496, 500

Law(s)—*continued*
of Edward VI, 291; of Moses, 344, 348, 363; of Solon, 484; suits at, 166; profession of, 119, 200; some principles of, 162, 269, 352–3; functions of King and Parliament in making, 378, 419–21; relation of royal power to, xv, 253, 369–70, 373–8, 380, 389–93, 399; benefit of, due to all Englishmen, 375–7, 439–40. *See also* Acts of Parliament; Canon Law; Civil Law; Common Law; Judges; Justice; Lawyers

Lawyers, 200, 268–9, 312, 349, 353, 369–70, 390, 393, 444, 493

Laymen, in Parliament, 372; their interest in all laws, 373–4; protected by praemunire, 392; abstain from cup, 486–7

Layton, Archdeacon of London, perhaps a slip for William Layton, prebendary of London, 1544–51, 431

Leadam, I. S., d. 1913, 518

Lebourne (Lobourne), John, cleric at Winchester, 1556, 515–6

Leclerc, Jean, editor of Erasmus, d. 1736, 2

Lee, Edward, King's Almoner, *c.* 1523–31, Archbishop of York, 1531–44, 24, 372

Lee, Rowland, Bishop of Coventry and Lichfield, and Lord President of Wales, 1534–43, 51

Legate, Lord. *See* Wolsey

Legates, Lords. *See* Wolsey *and* Campeggio

Legatine Court, for trial of Henry VIII's divorce, xxiii, 2, 20

Legenda Aurea or *Golden Legend*, a collection of legendary lives of the saints by Jacobus de Voragine, Archbishop of Genoa (d. *c.* 1298), translated into English and printed by Caxton, 1483, 299, 311–2, 314

Leicester, xxvi, 455, 472; Mayor of, *see* Berredge, John

Lent, 92, 121–2, 131, 168, 251, 254, 277, 280–5, 480, 487, 492

Lesbian measuring-stick, 118

Liars, All men are (text of Richard Smith's sermon, 1547), 278, 283–4, 293–4, 296

Liber Festivalis. See *Festival*

Liber Rerum Memorabilium or Black Paper Book at Cambridge, 458

Liege, the (11–2). *See* Holy League

Lincoln, 218; Bishop of, *see* Wolsey, Thomas, 1514; Holbeach, Henry, Aug. 1547–51; White, John, 1554–6; Watson, Thomas, 1557–9

Lisle, Lady, *see* Grenville, Honor; Viscount, *see* Plantagenet, Arthur, 1523–42; Dudley, John, 1542–7

Litany, 368. *See also* Procession

Literacy in England, not one per cent., 272, 274

Livy, 136, 451

Lloyde, John, joint patron of Hannyngton rectory, Hants, 1550, 518

Lobourne, John. *See* Lebourne

Lockwood, Henry, Master of Christ's College, Cambridge, 1531–48, rector of Navenby, Lincs, 1529–55, 129–30

Logic, 484

Lollards, 272–3, 275

London, 2, 30, 47, 57, 70, 129–35, 140, 148, 150–1, 159–60, 173, 241, 243, 245–7, 293, 352, 354, 388, 433, 439, 461, 471, 493; Aldgate, 461; Bridge, 304, 316; Bridgewater House, xviii, 443; Cheapside, 338; Gardiner's house at, *see* Southwark; Old Jewry, 259, 264; St James, 467–8; St Martin's, Ironmonger Lane, 264; St Stephen's, Coleman St, 264; Spital, 173, 304; Tower Hill, 390; *see also* Fleet; Southwark; Tower; Westminster; aldermen of, 160; diocese of, 388, 477; Archdeacon of, *see* Layton; Bishop of, *see* Warham, William, 1502–4; Tunstall, Cuthbert, 1522–30; Stokesley, John, 1530–9; Bonner, Edmund, 1540–9, '53–9; Ridley, Nicholas, 1550–3; Sandys, Edwin, 1570–7; Lord Mayor of, *see* Holles, Sir William, 1539–40; White, Sir Thomas, 1553–4

Long Ditton, Surrey, 509

Lorayne (Loreyn), Cardinal of. *See* Lorraine, Jean de

Lord Chancellor. *See* Wolsey, Thomas, 1515–29; More, Thomas, 1529–32; Audley, Thomas, 1533–44; Wriothesley, Thomas, 1544–7; Gardiner, Stephen, 1553–5; Heath, Nicholas, 1555–8; Bromley, Thomas, 1579–87

Lord's Prayer. *See* Pater Noster

Lords (of the Council), 393–5. *See also* Council; Privy Council

Lorraine, Charles de, son of Claude, first Duke of Guise, Archbishop of Rheims, 1538–74, Cardinal, 1547, 518

Lorraine, Jean de, brother of Claude, first Duke of Guise, Bishop of Metz, 1505–50, Archbishop of Narbonne, 1524–50, of Rheims, 1532–8, Cardinal, 1518, 89–90, 211, 222

Louis, Don, Infant of Portugal, brother of John III, d. 1545, 78

556

Louvain, 437, 451
Luther, Martin, d. 1546, 39, 49, 166, 255–6, 274, 276–7, 284, 293, 317, 335, 402–3, 447
Lutherans, 71–5, 181, 256, 274, 488. *See also* Protestantism in Germany
Lymden *or* Lyonden, Robert. *See* Portsmouth, Mayor of
Lyons, 8, 9, 71, 79, 351

Maastricht (Mastryke), 235–6, 238
Madeleine, daughter of Francis I, married James V of Scotland, 1537, d. 1537, 83
Madrel, Madryl (*i.e.* Madrid), Treaty of. *See* Treaties
Magdeburg, Archbishop of. *See* John Albert
Magna Carta, 391
Magnificat, 488
Magunce. *See* Mainz
Maguzzano, 501
Mainz, Archbishop of. *See* Heussenstamm, Sebastian von
Malet, Francis, Vice-Chancellor of Cambridge, 1536–7, '40, chaplain to Princess Mary, *c.* 1544, Dean of Lincoln, 1554–70, 401
Marcellus, Bishop of Apamea, in Syria, 4th c., 259, 262, 264
Marcus Antonius Constantius, pseudonym of Gardiner, 451
Margaret, daughter of Francis I, married Emmanuel Philibert of Savoy, 1559, d. 1574, 192
Margaret, daughter of Maximilian I, married (1) Infant John, 1497 (d. 1497), (2) Philibert II of Savoy, 1501 (d. 1504), Regent of the Netherlands, 1507–30, 42
Margaret, Lady (42). *See* Margaret, daughter of Maximilian I
Margaret, natural daughter of Charles V, married (1) Alexander de' Medici, 1536 (d. 1537), (2) Ottavio Farnese, 1559–67, Regent of the Netherlands, 1559–67, d. 1586, 78 (Duchess of Florence)
Margaret, sister of Francis I, married (1) Charles, Duke of Alençon, 1509 (d. 1525), (2) Henry II of Navarre, 1527, d. 1549, 87
Marillac (Maryliake), Charles de, French ambassador in England, 1539–43, Bishop of Vannes, 1550–7, Archbishop of Vienne, 1557–60, 200
Markham, Sir John, Lieutenant of the Tower, 1548–51, d. after 1557, 439, 441–2

Marriages proposed for Henry VIII, Mary, Elizabeth, Edward VI, xxxiii, 78, 87, 155–6, 198–9, 204, 245, 268
Marseilles, xxiii, xxvii, 83–4; Bishop of, *see* Serenus
Marshall, Dr Richard, Dean of Christ Church, Oxford, 1553–9, prebendary of Winchester, 1554–9; d. 1563, 431, 470
Marshalsea, the, 405
Martha, sister of Lazarus, 371
Martin (Marten), Dr Thomas, fellow of New College, Oxford, 1538–53, Gardiner's Chancellor, 1553–5, royal proctor at examination of Cranmer, d. 1584 ?, 511, 514
Martyr, Peter. *See* Vermigli
Martyrs, xxxiv, 277, 293, 496, 498
Marvyn, Edmund, rector of Bramshott, Hants, 1549–55, of Sutton, Surrey, 1554, prebendary of Winchester, 1554–9, Archdeacon of Surrey, 1556–9, d. ?, 516
Marwel, Hants, 63, 65
Mary I, Queen of England, 1553–8, marriages proposed for, xxxiii, 78, 87, 155–6, 204, 245; coronation of, xxiv, xxxii; marriage to Philip, xxxiii, 461; her religious policy, xxxii; began translation of Erasmus' Paraphrase on St John, 401; letter of Elizabeth to, 459–60; Pole's praise of, 499–501; mentioned, xv, xvii, 129, 218, 455, 458, 462–4, 467, 470, 476, 496, 502–14 *passim*
Mary, sister of Charles V, married Louis II of Hungary, 1522 (d. 1526), Regent of the Netherlands, 1530–55, d. 1558, 147, 150, 158, 179, 191, 194–5, 199, 235, 239–40
Mary, the Virgin. *See* Our Lady
Maryliake. *See* Marillac, Charles de
Mason, Sir John, French secretary to Henry VIII and Edward VI, 1542 ff., knighted, 1547, Visitor of Canterbury, Chichester, Rochester, Winchester, 1547, Dean of Winchester, 1549–54, Chancellor of Oxford, 1552–6, '59–64, d. 1566, 245–6, 369–70, 373–5; his colleagues in the visitation, 1547, *see* Visitation
Mass, 131, 215, 258, 296, 436, 476–7; High, 213, 368; Morrow, 504, 507; of Our Lady, 216, 505, 507, 515; of the Holy Ghost, 505, 515; of the Trinity, 505, 507; of Requiem, 505–16 *passim*; behaviour of the people at, 252, 317, 355–6; Mass penny, 515. *See also* Sacraments

Massey, Robert, in Gardiner's service, c. 1533–55, remembered in his will, one of two gentlemen-ushers at his funeral, Burgess in Parliament, 1548–9, d. ?, 80, 286–7, 507–8, 511, 514, 516

Massilia. *See* Marseilles

Master of the Horse. *See* Browne, Sir Anthony

Mastres (*i.e.* Mistress), Lady. *See* Bourchier, Margaret

Mastryke. *See* Maastricht

Matins, behaviour of the people at, 317, 355–6

Matrice. *See* Amatrice

Matthew's Bible, 361

Maurice, Duke of Saxony, 1541, Elector, 1547–53, 238

Maverlie, a gentleman in the train of the French ambassadors at Imperial Court, 1545, 201

May, William, President of Queens' College, Cambridge, 1537–53, '59–60, Dean of St Paul's, 1546–53, '59–60, Archbishop-nominate of York, 1560, 431; his house, 397

Mayor, Lord, of London. *See* Holles, Sir William, 1539–40; White, Sir Thomas, 1553–4

Meadstead (Maytestede), Hants, 509, 519

Medici, Catherine de', *see* Catherine de' Medici; Giulio de', *see* Clement VII

Medley (Medle), George, half-brother of Henry Grey, implicated in Wyatt's rebellion and imprisoned, d. 1562, 459, 461

Medowe (Medow, Medowes), William, chaplain to Gardiner, 1531–51 or after, witness at his trial, rector of Calbourne, Isle of Wight, 1536, of Meonstoke, Hants, 1551 or before –'57, of Wetheringset, Suffolk, 1554–7, prebendary of Winchester, 1541–57, Master of St Cross Hospital, 1545–57, 218–9, 513, 516

Melanchthon, Philip, d. 1560, 101, 118, 209

Menage, Jacques, French ambassador with Charles V, 1546–7, with the Swiss, 1549, d. ?, 214

Mercenaries, 220, 224. *See also* Germans

Merchants, complain of hostilities between England and France, 1545, 185; treatment of, discussed, 202, 220–1, 225

Mere, John, Esquire Bedell, 1530–58, and Registrary, 1543–58, at Cambridge, 458, 469

Merry tales, 230, 252, 311, 317, 337–8, 352, 402, 407–8, 419

Michael, Dominus, counsel employed for Henry VIII at Rome, 1529, 14

Micheas (*i.e.* the Prophet Micah), 430

Milan, 77–8, 87, 188

Miles Gloriosus, Plautus', 149, 185–6

Milphidippa (Miliphidippa), a female character in *Miles Gloriosus*, 186

Minories (Mynoresse), the, 459, 461

Miracles. *See* Christ, his miracles

Molines, Molyns. *See* Moulins

Monastic property in lay hands, xxxiii, 455, 464, 466

Mondey, Vincent, servant of Norfolk, a collector of the subsidy of 1534, surveyor of victuals at Calais, Sept.–Dec. 1545, and at Boulogne (replacing Anthony Aucher), Dec. 1545–6, d. ?, 150

Money, 50, 63, 73–4, 77, 147, 152, 183–4, 199–200, 211, 237–42, 267, 280, 356, 412, 462, 510

Monks, 219. *See also* Friars

Montague, Viscount. *See* Browne, Anthony, the younger

Montmorency, Anne de, Grand Master of France, 1526–59, Constable, 1538–67, 77, 81, 85, 89, 90, 455, 471

Montmorency, Jean de, Sieur de Courrières, Imperial ambassador in England, 1552, '53, '54, Governor of Lille, 1559–63, 461

Montreuil (Muttrel), in Picardy, 92, 98

More, The, Herts, Wolsey's house at, 24, 27

More, Sir Thomas, Chancellor of the Duchy of Lancaster, 1525–9, Lord Chancellor, 1529–32, executed, 1535, xxvii, 36

Moria (Praise of Folly), Erasmus', 2, 3

Mors, Roderigo. *See* Brinklow, Henry

Mortymer, Robert, cleric at Winchester, 1556, 515

Moses, 290, 344, 348, 363

Moulins (Molines, Molyns), 77, 81

Mountagew, Mountagu, Viscount. *See* Montague

Mühlberg, 284

Muryell, William, Gardiner's steward in 1538, Esquire Bedell at Cambridge, 1555–6, d.?, 473, 475–6

Music, in church services, 488

Musica, Antonio de, a Spaniard in the Netherlands, 1544–6, employed by Henry VIII as newsgatherer but found to be indiscreet, d. ?, 238–9

Musters, Commissions for, 66, 433

Muttrel. *See* Montreuil

558

Orsini, Lorenzo, Sieur de Ceri, called Renzo da Ceri, Italian mercenary general, d. 1536, 11
Orvieto, xxiii, xxvi
Oseney, Oxon, 218
Osiander (Oseander, Hosiander), Andreas, reformer, preacher at Nürnberg, 1522–48, professor at Königsberg, 1549–52, 447, 489
Ouercentanus, Dr Eustathius, ambassador from Frederick II, Elector Palatine, 1546, 245
Our Lady, banner of, 506, 511; day of, 22; Evensong of, 216; Mass of, 216, 505, 507, 515; merry tale of, 402, 407–8
'Our Lord', the phrase preferred to 'the Lord', 259, 264
Oxford, 31, 303, 395, 404, 431, 463–4; University, 132, 135, 140, 168, 493–4; Christ Church, 455, 470; Wolsey's college at, 19; Manor of, 385; Earl of, see Vere, John de, 1526–40; Vere, John de, 1540–62

Packington, Robert, mercer, of London, murdered, 1536, 423
Paget, William, joint Principal Secretary, 1543–8, Controller of the Household, 1547–9, Lord Privy Seal, 1556–8, Baron de Baudesert, 1549–63, letters to, 124, 141–5, 150–63, 175–204, 210–31, 233–46, 248–9, 253–4, 268–72; pupil and friend of Gardiner, 148; acts in Miles Gloriosus, 149, 185–6; ambassador to treat with German Protestants for peace with France, 147, 199; loves no extremes, 151; his 'recess', 220, 225; deserts Gardiner to support Hertford, xxx, 243, 251; offended at Bonner, 271; his character, 269–71; mentioned by Bale, 293
Pagetto, M. See Paget, William
Palestrio, a character in Miles Gloriosus, 186
Palmer, Symon, petty canon at Winchester, 1556, 515–6
Palmer, Sir Thomas, knighted, 1532, Knight Porter of Calais, 1534–41, prisoner in Tower, 1541–2, captain under Sir John Wallop in Flanders, 1543, muster master to Count de Buren, 1544, 76
Palmer, William, gentleman pensioner to Edward VI, author of a poem on Gardiner, 1547, xxxv
Palms, hallowing of, 382
Palm Sunday, 281

Palm tree, 427
Pammachius, anti-papal drama by Thomas Kirchmeyer, 1538, 129–35, 139–40
Pamphilus, a character in Terence, Andria, 338
Papacy, 285, 478; English relations with, xxiii–xxviii, xxxii–xxxiv, 1–2, 5–6, 8–20, 25–6, 36–42, 44–6, 54, 67–8, 83, 185, 374, 390, 455, 464–6, 474, 479, 481–3, 498–501; relations of, with France, 83, 99; with the Empire, 78; Papal Court, xxvi, 1, 14, 48; Papal methods, 402, 409. See also Pope; Rome; Treaties; Holy League
Papists, 419, 447, 449; papistry, 310; papistical superstitions, 382
Paraphrase upon the New Testament, Erasmus', and its translators. See Erasmus
Pardons, 169–70, 255
Paris, xxiii, xxv, 2–4, 8, 75–6, 93, 407–8, 462
Parkar, a person presumably implicated in Wyatt's rebellion, 462
Parker, Matthew, Master of Corpus Christi, Cambridge, 1544–53, Vice-Chancellor, 1545–6, '48, Archbishop of Canterbury, 1559–75, xvii, 129–40, 455–6
Parliament, 1529, 43, 401; 1532, xxvii, 48; 1534, xxiii, xxvii, 54, 63; 1536, 377; 1543, 289, 300, 364, 370–2 (see also King's Book, legalized by this Parliament); 1545, 211, 218, 493–4; 1547, xxxi, 378, 410, 424–5, 429; 1549, 443; 1553, xxxiii; 1554, 464–5; 1555, xxiv, xxxiv; censured by Brinklow, 160; Paget's 'Parliament answers', 233; clerk of, 350; free speech in, 282, 392; its functions in law making, 378, 419–21; how Pole should broach reunion with Rome to, 455, 464–5; members named by Gardiner, 424; House of Lords, 350, 420–1, 424; House of Commons, 48–9, 211, 282, 393, 420–1, 424. See also Acts of Parliament
Parr, Catherine. See Catherine Parr
Pasquillus, Pasquil, or Pasquin, a name popularly given to an ancient statue dug up in Rome, 1501, upon which anonymous lampoons were posted, and to the writers of these lampoons, 179
Passano, Giovanni Gioachino (John Joachim) di, Sieur de Vaux, French ambassador in England, 1524–5, '26–7, '30–2, to the Pope, 1529, aged and living in Padua, 1545, 11
Pater Noster, 169, 234, 504, 514

560

Paul III (Alessandro Farnese), Pope, 1534–49, 72–3, 78, 185; his brief condemning Henry VIII, xxiii, xxvii, xxxv, 54, 67–8; his nephew (*i.e.* grandson), *see* Farnese, Ottavio

Paulet, William, Lord St John, 1539, Earl of Wiltshire, 1550, Marquis of Winchester, 1551, Controller of the Household, 1532–7, Lord Chamberlain, 1543–5, Lord Great Master, 1545–50, Lord Treasurer, 1550–72, 50, 124, 245, 380, 393

Paul's Cross, 168–70, 304

Paulus, possibly Julius Paulus, Roman jurist, *fl.* A.D. 220, 111

Pawles. *See* St Paul's

Peace, any, better than war, 189, 266; England's chief need, 265–7; of Europe, 455, 471. *See also* Treaties

Pearls before swine, 272–3

Peasants' Revolt, in Germany, 308

Pecock, Gabriel, Warden of the Observants at Southampton in 1534, 56

Pelagians (Pellagians), followers of Pelagius, d. *c.* 420, whose assertion of the freedom of the will and denial of inherited original sin was held to be heretical, 346

Pelion, forests of, 110

Pelle or Plee, Nicholas de, courier in service of Henry VIII and Edward VI, 1538–52, in Tower, Nov. 1552, released, Feb. 1553 and told to avoid the realm, d.?, 158, 191, 242

Pembroke Hall, Cambridge, 263

Penance, 348, 364, 408

Penne, Sybil, daughter of Sir Hugh Pagenham, wife of John Penne, barbersurgeon to Henry VIII (d. 1557), drynurse to Prince Edward, Oct. 1538 ff., d. after 1562, 161

Penning (Pining), Henry, servant of John Hellyer, *q.v.*, fled abroad with him, 1535, in Pole's service, presumably after Hellyer's d., 1541–58, called Pole's chamberlain and receiver-general in Pole's will, d. after 1569, 466, 500 (messenger)

Pennink, Cord or Conrad (Courtpenyng), German mercenary captain in service of Christian III of Denmark, *c.* 1535–45, in English service at Boulogne, 1546, and on Scottish border, 1548–9, knighted, 1546, d. in Hamburg, 1555, 235

Percy, Henry, Earl of Northumberland, 1527–37, 52

Perfect life, Gardiner's hypothetical homily on the, 299, 309–10

Peripatetics, 127

Periplectomenus, a character in *Miles Gloriosus*, 186

Perne, Dr Andrew, Master of Peterhouse, 1554–89, Dean of Ely, 1557–89, Vice-Chancellor of Cambridge, 1551–2, '56–7, '59–60, '74–5, '80–1, 468

Perreau, Louis de, Sieur de Castillon, on missions to England thrice in 1527–8, ambassador in England, 1533–4, '37–9, d. 1553, 78, 83

Perrenot, Antoine, son of Nicolas, Bishop of Arras, 1538–61, Archbishop of Mechlin, 1561–83, of Besançon, 1584–6, Cardinal, 1561, 93, 125–8

Perrenot, Nicolas, Sieur de Granvelle, chief minister of Charles V, 1530–50, 125–8, 147–8, 156, 179, 191, 196–7, 203, 220–2, 225, 228, 231–5, 354, 366

Persecution, 270, 288

Peter, Master. *See* Vannes, Peter

Peterhouse, Cambridge, 467–8

Petre (Peter), Sir William, knighted, 1544, joint Principal Secretary, 1544–57, d. 1572, 243, 459–63

Petty canons, six, at Winchester in 1556, 516. *See also* Alen, William; Erle, John; Fygge, Thomas; Palmer, Symon; Tredegolde, John

Pety Roy, possibly the same as Petie Roy, a groom of the Chamber in 1509, 184

Pexsal, Ralph, clerk of the crown in Chancery, 1522–37, 28

Philip II, son of Charles V, King of Spain, 1556–98, xxiv, xxxiii, xxxv, 204, 470, 476, 502–4, 514

Philip, Duke of Bavaria, nephew of Frederick II, the Elector, in England thrice as suitor for Princess Mary, 1539–47, d. 1548, 245–6

Philip, Landgrave of Hesse, 1509–67, bigamous marriage, 1540, prisoner of Charles V, 1547–52, 146–7, 156, 159, 161–2, 183, 185, 187, 190, 192, 195; his ambassadors, *see* Saxe and Lansgrave, ambassadors of; his Marshal, *see* Baumbach, Ludwig von

Philip Francis, Rhinegrave, ambassador from Frederick II, the Elector, 1546, d. 1561, 245

Philosophers, 127, 283, 339, 359, 412. *See also* Aristotle, Plato

Philpot, John, Archdeacon of Winchester, 1552–4, burned at stake, 1555, 433–5

Philpot, William. *See* Compton

Phintias, friend of Damon, 102

Phonasci, 119

Phratry, 351, 361

Physicians, 270, 320, 405, 411–2, 414–5, 423. *See also* Surgeons; Butts, William; Turner, William

Picher or Pitcher, Francisco, a Piedmontese, courier in service of England, 1530–55, d.?, 46, 80, 159, 236

Piedmont (Piemont, Pyemont), 76–7, 155, 197; Prince of, *see* Emmanuel Philibert

Pierrelatte (Pierelate), in Dauphiné, 79–80

Pilate, 162

Pindar, 347

Pining, Henry. *See* Penning

Pinkie, Battle of, 1547, 401

Place, The (in App. 5). *See* Southwark, Winchester House

Placebo, 504, 507, 514

Plantagenet, Arthur, Viscount Lisle, 1523, Deputy of Calais, 1533–40, d. 1542, 54, 57; letters to, 62, 75–6, 79, 81; his wife, *see* Grenville, Honor

Plato, 104, 114, 307, 483

Plautus, 187 (? 'the poete'), 195, 332; his *Miles Gloriosus*, 149, 185–6

Players, 251, 253–4, 276, 278

Plays, xxix, 384. *See also Miles Gloriosus; Pammachius*

Pliny, 346

Plutarch, 138, 270, 347

Pocock, Nicholas, his *Records of the Reformation*, xvi

Poggio (Pogge) Bracciolini, Gian Francesco, Italian scholar, d. 1459, 281, 284

Poland (Pole), King of. *See* Sigismund I

Pole (Poole), Reginald, lived abroad, 1532–54, Cardinal, 1536, Archbishop of Canterbury, 1556–8, xxiv, xxxiii, '82, 179–80, 455, 479, 501; letter to, 464–7; letter from, 496–501; his messenger (500), *see* Penning, Henry

Poley, Arture, Gardiner's poster, 1538, 80

Pollard, A. F., 43, 401

Pollard, Sir George, joint captain of the crew at Guisnes, 1544, killed at Boulogne, 1546, 227

Polles. *See* St Paul's

Pommeraye (Pomeraye), Giles de la, French ambassador in England, 1531–2, special envoy to England, 1534, '36, d.?, 82–5

Ponynges, Lord, *see* Poynings, Thomas; Master, *see* Poynings, Edward

Poole. *See* Pole, Reginald

Poor Clares, 461

Pope (Bishop of Rome), his dispensing power, 12, 14; Pammachius, an imaginary, 129; ridiculed at Cambridge, 133, 139; England at enmity with, 185; Protestants play his part, 201–2; his pretended authority, 255; nations have existed without him, 279; favoured by frequent change in religion, 291–2; hated, 321; has seduced men in religion, *ib.*; how reverence to his person is enforced, 409; how Pole is to broach reunion with him, 465–6; why expelled from England, 480–3; mentioned, 72, 335, 399, 418, 478–9, 487. *See also* Gregory I, 590–604; Julius II, 1503–13; Clement VII, 1523–34; Paul III, 1534–49; Julius III, 1550–5; Papacy

Pope, Sir Thomas, founder of Trinity College, Oxford, 1555, d. 1559, 446

Pope, the good man, of Trumpyngton, 481

Pope's ambassador (4), *see* Gambara, Uberto de; (46), *see* Trivulcis, Caesar de

Portents in the sun, 279, 306

Porter, Master. *See* Palmer, Sir Thomas

Portsmouth, 152, 272–3, 286, 288; Captain of, *see* Vaughan, Edward; Mayor of, 1547, either Henry Byckeley, M.P. for Portsmouth, 1553, and, according to R. East, *Portsmouth Records*, 1891, 312, Mayor, 1539–40, '46–7, '51–2, d. 1570, or Robert Lymden or Lyonden, mentioned as Mayor in Privy Council minutes, 26 Jan. 1547, but appearing in East's list as Mayor, 1544–5, 273, 275, 288

Portugal (Portingale), Infant of, *see* Louis, Don; King of, *see* John III; place of his ambassador at the French Court, 90

Postscripts, their position in 16th c., xxii

Powles. *See* St Paul's

Poynings, Edward, English captain killed at Boulogne, 1546, 227–8

Poynings, Thomas, Baron Poynings, 1545, d. 1545, 144, 228

Praemunire, 370, 380, 390–2, 401

Praet (Prate), Louis, Sieur de. *See* Flandre, Louis de

Prat, Antoine du, Archbishop of Sens, 1525–35, Cardinal, 1527, Chancellor of France, 1515–35, 36

Prayer(s), 169, 261, 263, 355, 476–7

Preachers and preaching, xxix, 168–74, 252, 272–3, 275–6, 278, 284, 286, 289, 293, 296, 299, 304–6, 311, 314–5, 317, 334, 336, 353–6, 368, 370–1, 373, 433–4, 485

Predestination, 345

President, Lord, of Wales. *See* Wales

Preston, Dr, probably Walter, D.D. (Cambridge, 1522), fellow of Christ's till 1526, prebendary of St Paul's, 1528–33, 166

Priests, 161, 271, 281, 355, 368, 371, 487, 489–90, 506, 510, 513, 515–6; not respected, 252, 258, 315. *See also* Clergy; Celibacy of the Clergy

Prince, Lord. *See* Edward VI

Princes, Erasmus on, 384–6

Principal Secretary (usually joint Principal Secretary after 1540). *See* Knight, William, 1526–9; Gardiner, Stephen, 1529–34; Cromwell, Thomas, 1534–40; Wriothesley, Thomas, 1540–4; Sadler, Ralph, 1540–3; Paget, William, 1543–8; Petre, William, 1544–57; Smith, Thomas, 1548–9, '72–7; Wotton, Nicholas, 1549–50; Cecil, William, 1550–3, '58–72; Cheke, John, 1553; Boxall, John, 1557–8

Printers and printing, 218, 258, 276, 278, 362, 369, 372–4, 382, 388, 437

Privy Chamber of Mary, 502

Privy Council, of Henry VIII, xix, 51, 101, 121, 133, 165, 174, 243; of Edward VI, 264, letters to, 361–73, 441–5; of Mary, xix, xxxii, 518. *See also* Council

Privy Seal, Lord. *See* Tunstall, Cuthbert, 1523–30; Boleyn, Thomas, 1530–6; Cromwell, Thomas, 1536–40; Fitzwilliam, William, 1540–2; Russell, John, Oct. 1542–55; Paget, William, 1556–8; Howard, William, 1572–3

Procession, 153, 286, 291, 361, 366, 368, 463

Proclamations, 440; Act of, 380, 391, 401; against exporting corn, 391, 401; against rumours of innovations in religion, 286–7, 295, 298, 366

Protector, Lord. *See* Seymour, Edward

Protestantism, Erasmus on, 333; in Germany, its character and effects, xxviii, 129, 147, 149, 161–2, 185, 187–8, 201–2, 205–9, 279–80, 299, 305–8, 335, 364, 371, 407; in England, xxix, xxx, xxxiv, 148–9, 159–63, 169–70, 249, 251, 253, 276–83, 292–3, 307, 334, 485; Henry VIII's attitude toward, 149, 159, 162. *See also* Germany; Justification; Reformers; Sectaries

Provence, 62

Proverbs, 89, 264, 293, 420

Pseudolus, a character in Plautus, *Pseudolus*, 332

Pucci, Lorenzo, Bishop of Pistoja, 1509–18, Cardinal, 1513–31, 14, 17 (Sanctorum Quatuor)

Punctuation, in manuscript, printed sources, and in this edition, xx, xxi, 520

Purgatory, 383

Pursuivant, 274. *See also* Rugecrosse

Puttenham (Putnam), Surrey, 509

Queen, the (158, 179, 195, 199, 235, 239–40), *see* Mary, sister of Charles V, Queen of Hungary; this (46), *see* Eleanor; of England, *see* England; of France, *see* Eleanor; of Hungary, *see* Mary, sister of Charles V

Queen's Council. *See* Catherine of Aragon, her Council

Quiñones, Francis (also called Angelo, his monastic name being Francis of the Angels), General of the Franciscans (Observants), 1523–7, Cardinal, 1528, revised Breviary, 1535, d. 1540, 8, 9

Radcliffe, Robert, Baron Fitzwalter, 1506, Viscount Fitzwalter, 1525, Earl of Sussex, 1529, Lord Great Chamberlain, 1540–2, married, as second wife, Lady Margaret Stanley, 1532, 47

Radcliffe, Thomas, known as Lord Fitzwalter (Fitzwater) from 1542, Earl of Sussex, 1557–82, 211

Rainsford, George, translator into Italian of Gardiner's account of the invasions of England, xxxv

Ratclyf, Roger, agent in Scotland, 1524, gentleman-usher of the Chamber (at first to Queen Catherine, then to the King), 1509–38, 29

Ratisbon (Regensburg), xxiii, xxix, xxx, 236, 479–80; Diet at, 1541, 209; 1546, 236; Colloquy at, 1546, 299, 306, 316

Raynes, Master, Gardiner's steward, at time of his death, 506, 508, 510, 514, 517

Reader, the, letters to, 124–5, 164, 205–9, 249–50, 437–8, 446–52

Reading, Prior of, 38–9

Real presence. *See* Sacrament of the Altar

Reatus, 346

Rede, Peter, servant to Richard Pate (ambassador to Charles V), 1535–6, carried letters from England to Sir Thomas Wyatt in Spain, 1537, '38, d. ?, 80 *bis* (Rede *and* This berer)

Redemption, 340, 343

Redman, Dr John, Master of Trinity College, Cambridge, 1546–51, Lady Margaret Professor of Divinity, 1538–42, '49–51, 325, 360, 365, 431

Reformers, xxiv, xxxi, xxxiv, 205–8, 265. *See also* Alesius; Bale; Barlow; Barnes; Bucer; Cranmer; Joseph; Joye; Luther; Melanchthon; Ridley; Turner; Zwingli; Protestantism

Regensburg. *See* Ratisbon

Regensburg Book, 209

Regent, Lady. *See* Mary, sister of Charles V

Reiffenberg (Riffen-, Riffem-, Ryffenberge), Friedrich von, German mercenary captain, in Henry VIII's employ, 1545, d. 1595, 146, 159, 162, 180, 192, 195, 220, 224, 226; English commissaries with, *see* Commissaries

Religion, innovations in, 286, 291–2, 298, 308, 367, 371; books of, 303; in Erasmus' *Paraphrase*, 385; Wriothesley's measures touching, 405; Somerset entangled in matters of, *ib.*; close religions, 414. *See also* Edward VI, religious changes; Henry VIII, ecclesiastical policy; Englishmen, their religious habits; Homilies; Images; Justification; *King's Book*; Sacraments

Remuchius, Dr, a Dane in England, 1529, 28

Renzius. *See* Orsini, Lorenzo

Repentance, in justification, 382

Requiem. *See* Mass

Rescuynge of the romishe fox, The, Turner's, 478

Richard III, King of England, 1483–5, 322, 482

Riches, increase of, makes a man poor, 198

Richmond, Duke of. *See* Fitzroy, Henry

Rickmansworth (Rikemansworth), Herts, 27

Ridley, Nicholas, Bishop of Rochester, 1547–50, of London, 1550–3, martyred, 1555, 251, 255–63, 265, 267, 286, 356, 397, 431–2, 463

Riffenberge, Riffemberge. *See* Reiffenberg, Friedrich von

Rikemansworth. *See* Rickmansworth

Rings, given by serjeants-at-law, 369, 371; blessed by English kings, *see* Cramp rings

Ripley (Rypple), Surrey, 509

Rither, John, cofferer to Prince Edward, 1541–7, cofferer of the Household, 1547–52, d.?, 150–1

Robertet, Bayly, presumably a member of the family of Florimond Robertet, Treasurer of France (d. 1527), 8

Robinson or Robertson, Dr Thomas, Archdeacon of Leicester, 1541–60, Dean of Durham, 1557–9, d. 1561, 171–2, 325, 360, 365, 431

Rochester, Bishop of. *See* Fisher, John, 1504–35; Heath, Nicholas, 1540–3; Holbeach, Henry, 1544–Aug. 1547; Ridley, Nicholas, Sept. 1547–50

Rochester, Sir Robert, Controller of the Household of Mary, as Princess, from 1551 or before, as Queen, 1553–7, knighted, 1553, Privy Councillor, 1553–7, 472, 502, 504, 507

Rochford (Rocheford), Viscount. *See* Boleyn, Thomas, 1525–Dec. 1529; Boleyn, George, Dec. 1529–36

Rogers, John, *alias* Thomas Matthew, editor of Matthew's Bible, 1537, prebendary of St Paul's, 1551–3, martyred, 1555, xxxiv, 361

Rokwod or Rokewood, John, undermarshal or under-steward of Calais, c. 1527–9, bailiff of Mark and Oye, 1529–41, 42

Romans, 484, 487–8; Epistle to the, 344, 381; King of, *see* Ferdinand I

Rome, xxiii, xxvi, xxxiv, 2, 8–12, 15, 17–8, 25, 37, 39, 41, 44–8, 99, 129, 374, 381, 390, 409, 455, 474, 479; Church of, 255–6, 487; Bishop of, *see* Pope. *See also* Papacy

Romish fox, 478, 480–1, 492

Rouen (Roone), 45–7

Rowse, Sir Anthony, Norfolk's treasurer, c. 1536–9, Treasurer of Guisnes, 1541–2, Controller of Calais, 1543–4, Master of the Jewels, 1544–5, Treasurer of the Chamber, 1545–6, 141–2

Royal arms and seal. *See* King

Royal authority, power, prerogative. *See* King

Royal supremacy, xv, xxvii, xxix, 54, 66, 68, 70, 72, 75, 303, 315, 481; limited by Common and Statute Law, 253, 369–70, 373–8, 389–92

Rugecrosse pursuyvant. *See* Cotgrave, Hugh

Ruler, duty of a, 320

Runcorn, Thomas, Archdeacon of Bangor, 1525–54?, chaplain to Gardiner, 1534 or before –'39 or after, Provost of St Elizabeth's College, Winchester, 1536–44, prebendary of Winchester, 1541–54, d. 1556, 55

Russell, John, Lord Russell, **1539,** Earl of Bedford, **1550,** Lord Admiral, **1540–2,** Lord Privy Seal, Oct. **1542–55,** 96, 100, 391
Russell, Rev. John Fuller, d. **1884,** xviii
Ryffenberge. *See* Reiffenberg, Friedrich von
Rymer, Thomas, editor of *Foedera,* d. **1713,** 458
Ryngeley, Sir Edward, Marshal, **1530–5,** and Controller, **1539–43,** of Calais, d. **1544,** 57
Rypple. *See* Ripley
Ryther, Master. *See* Rither, John

Sacramentaries, 277, 305, 332, 447
Sacraments, 278–9, 348, 408; Sacrament of the Altar, xxiv, 131, 171, 214, 277, 293, 295–6, 299, 305, 316, 335, 369, 380, 385, 436, 445–54, 487. *See also* Baptism; Communion; Penance
Sacring, 355
Sadler, Sir Ralph, knighted, **1540,** ambassador to Scotland under Henry VIII (**1537** ff.) and Elizabeth, joint Principal Secretary, **1540–3,** d. **1587,** 95–6, 100
St Albans, Herts, 27, 460
St Ambrose, d. **397,** 363
St Andrew, Evensong of, 213
St Asaph, Bishop of. *See* Barlow, William, **1536**
St Augustine (Austen, Austin), d. **430,** 166–7, 294, 296, 314, 349, 363, 368
St Barnard. *See* St Bernard
St Basil, d. **379,** 363
St Bernard of Clairvaux, d. **1153,** 363
St Catharine's Hall, Cambridge, 458–9
St Chrisostome (Crissostom). *See* St John Chrysostom
Saintclere, Gardiner's poster, **1538,** 80
St Cross Hospital, Winchester, 149, 218–9
St David's (Davies), Bishop of. *See* Barlow, William, **1536–48**
St Denis, suburb of Paris, 496, 501
St Francis, Monastery of, in Lake Garda, 501
St George (Gorge), Patron of England, 260–1, 274, 289–90, 312, 506, 511; Order of, *see* Garter
St George's (Gorges) Church, Southwark, 509
St Gregory Nazianzen, d. *c.* **389,** 282, 284, 289–90, 295, 314, 317, 331–2, 341–3, 358–61, 363
St Hierome. *See* St Jerome
St Hilary of Poictiers, d. **368,** 448

St James, 250, 309–10, 343, 362; Epistle of, 331
St James (Jeames), London, 467–8
St Jerome (Jherome, Hierome), d. **420,** 349, 363, 484
St John Baptist, 153
St John Chrysostom, d. **407,** 282, 361, 363, 365, 368, 374, 380, 382–3
St John the Evangelist, 288, 309, 341; Gospel of, 66; Paraphrase on, 401
St John's College, Cambridge, 469
St Joseph, 407
St Julien, François de, Sieur de Veniers, d. **1538** of wound received in a judicial duel with Lion de Barbançois, 81
St Luke, Gospel of, 66; Paraphrase on, 401
St Mark, Paraphrase on, 401
St Mark's Library, Venice, 501
St Martin's, Ironmonger Lane, 264
St Mary, Church of, Guildford, 509
St Mary Magdalene Hospital, Winchester, 149, 218–9
St Mary Overies Church. *See* Southwark
St Mary Spital, 173, 304
St Mary, the Virgin. *See* Our Lady
St Matthew, Paraphrase on, 401
St Nicholas (Nicolas), Church of, Guildford, 509
St Nicholas' Hostel, Cambridge, 457–8, 479, 493
St Olave's (St Towles) Church, Southwark, 509
St Paul (Paule, Pawle, Pol, Poule), 129, 164, 166, 189, 259, 290, 322, 328, 337, 339–42, 344, 346, 349, 360, 367, 381, 383, 385–6, 396, 446–7, 483, 486, 488, 491
St Paul's, Dean of, *see* May, William; prebendaries of, 506
St Peter, 259, 262, 386, 486
St Peter's Day, Gardiner's sermon on, xxiv, xxxi–xxxii, 439–40, 449–50
St Pol, in Artois, 77
St Pol, Poul(e). *See* St Paul
St Stephen, banner of, 506, 511
St Stephen's, Coleman Street, 264
St Swythens. *See* Winchester, Cathedral
St Timothy, 486
St Towles. *See* St Olave's
Saints, Bale's, 277–8; banners of, 506–16 *passim*; images of, *see* Images; invocation of, 261, 383; legends of, 299, 311–2, 314
Salcot, John. *See* Capon
Salisbury, Bishop of. *See* Campeggio, Lorenzo, **1524–34;** Capon, John, **1539–57**

Salt, blessing of, 485–6
Salvation, 343. *See also* Homilies
Sampson, Richard, Bishop of Chichester, 1536–43, of Coventry and Lichfield, 1543–54, Lord President of Wales, 1543–8, 219–20
Sanctorum Quatuor, Cardinal. *See* Pucci, Lorenzo
Sandwich, William. *See* Gardiner, William
Sandys, Edwin, Master of St Catharine's Hall, Cambridge, 1549–53, Vice-Chancellor, 1552–3, Bishop of Worcester, 1559–70, of London, 1570–7, Archbishop of York, 1577–88, 456, 458–9
Sandys, William, Baron Sandys, 1523, Lord Chamberlain, 1526–40, 56
Sara, wife of Abraham, 175
Sardanapalus (Assurbanipal), King of Assyria, 668–26 B.C., 484
Sarysbury (*i.e.* Salisbury), Lord of. *See* Capon, John
Sarzay, Sieur de. *See* Barbançois, Lion de
Satan, 129. *See also* Devil
Saul, King of Israel, 174
Saunders, Lawrence, rector of All Hallows, Bread Street, 1553–4, martyred, 1555, xxxiv
Savoy, 77; Duke of, *see* Charles III
Saxe, Saxon, Duke of. *See* John Frederick I
Saxe and Lansgrave (*i.e.* John Frederick I, Elector of Saxony, and Philip, Landgrave of Hesse), ambassadors of, in England, 1538 (Franz Burchart, Georg von Boyneburg, Friedrich Myconius), 161
Scepperus or Schepper, Cornelius Duplicius, Sieur d'Eecke, member of Privy Council and Council of State of the Netherlands, 1535–55, on missions to England, 1545, '46, 147–8, 150, 155, 157, 177, 189, 191, 194–9, 203, 220–2, 224–8, 231–2, 234–5; his fellow in England, *see* Vander Delft, François
Schism, 496, 499–500
Schmalkald, Protestant princes at, propose league with England, 70–5
Scholastic theology, 118
Schoolmen, New, 282
Schore (Score, Scory, Skore), Louis van, member, 1535–40, President, 1540–8, of Council of State and Privy Council of the Netherlands, 147, 157, 179, 194, 203, 220, 222, 234, 238–9
Scotland and the Scots, relations with England, chiefly hostile, xxiii, xxix, xxx, 29–30, 52, 55, 83–4, 92–3, 98–9, 146–7,

184–6, 189, 192, 253, 354, 364, 371, 378, 401; relations with France, *see* France; Gardiner's advice concerning, 265, 267, 271; King of, *see* James V
Scott, Cuthbert, Master of Christ's College, Cambridge, 1553–6, Vice-Chancellor, 1555–6, Bishop of Chester, 1556–9, d. 1564, 129, 131, 135, 474, 476
Scotus, Duns, d. 1308, 118
Scripta duo adversaria, Bucer's, 209
Scripture, abused, 169, 175, 275, 277, 332, 362, 381, 384–6, 408; authority of, 293–4, 331; the Church the interpreter of, 250; discussion of, requires learning, 164; Somerset on interpretation of, 435–6; Gardiner's motto from, 168, 175; quotations from, xx, 22, 162, 168, 175, 180, 182, 212, 256, 258–9, 262–3, 273, 275, 281, 284, 290–1, 293, 300, 304, 309–10, 312, 322, 331, 338, 340–5, 347, 349, 354, 357, 362, 384–5, 394–6, 446, 483–4, 486, 488, 490, 497–8, 505, 508, 516; other references, 72, 166, 170, 172, 255, 259, 261, 264, 272, 275, 291–2, 304, 313, 317, 340, 344, 346, 358–9, 361–2, 382, 397–8, 404, 406, 409, 421, 430, 484–6, 489–91, 492. *See also* Bible; Commandments; Gospel; New Testament; Old Testament; Word of God
Seal (Zele), Surrey, 509
Seconde course of the hunter, etc., Turner's, 164
Secretary hand, 275–6
Secretary, Master. *See* Principal Secretary
Sectaries, 452, 454, 485
Segiswicke, Dr Thomas, Lady Margaret Professor of Divinity, Cambridge, 1554–6, Regius Professor of Divinity, 1557–9, d. after 1567, 467–8, 474, 476
Selborne, Hants, 509, 519
Selve, Odet de, French ambassador to England, 1546–9, d. 1563, 290
Seneca, 101
Serenus, Bishop of Marseilles, 596–601, 256
Serjeants-at-law, 369, 371
Serpent, in Eden, 301; brazen, 289–90
Seton, Dr John, chaplain to Gardiner, *c.* 1543–51 or after, rector of Hinton, Hants, 1545–58, of Alresford, Hants, 1558–9, Master of St Mary Magdalene Hospital, Winchester, 1554–9, prebendary of Winchester and York, 1554–9, d. at Rome, 1567, 513, 515–6
Sewers, Commissions of, 66

Southwark—*continued*
 chester House or Place (the bishop's house), xxiv, xxvi, xxix, 173, 244, 254, 267, 272, 376, 395, 429, 432–3, 456–7, 460, 462–4, 467, 472–4, 476, 502–5, 508, 519; St Mary Overies Church (now Southwark Cathedral), xxvi, xxxiv, 503–5, 507–10, 517, 519; St George's Church, 509; St Olave's (St Towles) Church, *ib.*; Clink, 429, 431; Marshalsea, 405
Southwell, Sir Richard, knighted, 1540, one of the three General Surveyors, 1542–7, under-treasurer of the 'battle' in France, 1544, Master of the Ordnance, 1553–9, d. 1564, 151
Southwell, Sir Robert, brother of Sir Richard, knighted, 1541, Master of the Rolls, 1541–50, Sheriff of Kent, 1554, d. 1559, 462–3
Sozomen, Church historian, d. *c.* 450, 264
Spain, 16, 24, 28, 32, 78, 80, 98, 202, 204, 461; Prince of, *see* Philip II; bearer of Gardiner's letter who desires to go to (80), *see* Rede, Peter
Spelling, in this volume and in sources, xx, xxi, 520 ff.
Speyer (Spyre), 238
Spittle, The. *See* St Mary Spital
Stafford, Harry, remembered in Gardiner's will, presumably in his service, possibly Henry, son of Henry, first Baron Stafford, succeeded as Baron 1563, d. 1566, 506
Stamp, A. E., 217
Stanforde, friars beside (Austin Friars without St Peter's Gate, Stanford or Stamford, Lincs), 167
Stanhope (Stannop), Sir Michael, brother-in-law of Protector Somerset, Lieutenant, 1542–7, and Governor, 1547–9, '51–2, of Hull, 142
Stanley, Lady Margaret, daughter of Thomas, second Earl of Derby, second wife of Robert Radcliffe, Earl of Sussex (d. 1542), d. 1584, 47
Stannop, Master. *See* Stanhope, Sir Michael
Star Chamber, 269
Statute Law. *See* Acts of Parliament
Steken (Stekon), in Flanders, 241
Stephens, Stephyns, Stevens, Stevins, Stevyns, Master or Doctor (familiar designation of Gardiner, being the Anglicization of *Stephanus*), 4, 8, 10, 22–43 *passim*, 167, 276
Stepney, 92, 94, 96, 100, 354, 361

Steven Stockfish, 283
Steward, Dr Edmund, Gardiner's Vicar-General, Chancellor, and Principal Official, 1531–51, prebendary of Winchester, 1541–54, Dean of Winchester, 1554–9, xviii, 515–6
Steward, Gardiner's. *See* Muryell; Raynes
Stews, 433
Stoics, 127, 339, 412
Stoke, Surrey, 509
Stokesley, John, Bishop of London, 1530–9, 66, 317, 351
Stokys, Matthew, Esquire Bedell, 1557–85, Registrary, 1558–91, at Cambridge, 458
Story, Gardiner's poster, 1538, possibly Leonard, 'rider', in the King's pay, 1539, 1546, officer of the King's stable, 1544, d.?, 80
Stow, John, chronicler, d. 1605, xvii–xviii, xxi, 442–3
Strangwish, Master, probably either Dr William Strangeways, Wolsey's surveyor of Durham (? prebendary of York, 1533–41), or his kinsman Thomas, controller of Wolsey's house, *c.* 1523–7, Marshal of Berwick, 1527–9 (?d. as steward of Lord Darcy, 1537), 27
Sturmius, Johannes, rector of Strasbourg Gymnasium, 1538–81, ambassador of Protestant princes to Calais to mediate peace between England and France, 1545, d. 1589, 230
Subsidy, 1535, 66
Suffolk, 269; speech, *ib.*; Duke of, *see* Brandon, Charles, 1514–45; Grey, Henry, 1551–4
Superstition, 233, 261–2, 382
Supper, Lord's, 485. *See also* Sacrament of the Altar
Supplication of the Commons against the Ordinaries, 48
Surgeons, 314. *See also* Physicians
Surrey, churches in, 509; Earl of, *see* Howard, Thomas, 1514–24; Howard, Henry, 1524–47
Sussex, Earl of. *See* Radcliffe, Robert, 1529–42; Radcliffe, Thomas, 1557–82
Sutton, Henry, partner of John Kingston in printing service books, 1553–7, continued printing till 1563, d.?, 218
Sweating sickness, 27, 92
Sybald, David. *See* Compton
Symnell, John, stipendiary priest at chapel of St Elizabeth, Winchester, in 1541, at Gardiner's funeral, 1556, d.?, 515

Symo, a character in Terence, *Andria*, 339

Syngleton. *See* Singleton

Syrus, a character in Terence, *Heauton Timorumenos*, 157, 332

Tamps, Madame de. *See* Anne de Pisseleu

Tarbes, Bishop of. *See* Castelnau, Antoine de

Tares and wheat, 312

Tartars, 279

Taunton, Soms., xxv

Taylor, Rowland, rector of Hadleigh in Suffolk, 1544–54, Archdeacon of Exeter, 1551–4, martyred, 1555, xxxiv

Te Deum, 488

Temple, John, in Gardiner's service from 1538 or before, witness of his will, possibly the founder of the Temple family of Stowe, d. ?, 506

Temps Dytton. *See* Thames Ditton

Terence, 102, 115, 127, 157, 188, 264, 332, 338, 483

Terouenne (Turwyn), in Artois, 98

Terra Nova, Marquis of, probably Don Giovanni d'Aragona e Tagliavia, Marquis of Terra Nova, 1537–?, President of Sicily, 1539, '40, '44, 179

Tetney, Lincs, 218

Thadeus, courier. *See* Bonela, Thade

Thames Ditton (Temps Dytton), Surrey, 509

Thames River, 461

Theobald (Tibald), Thomas, godson of Thomas Boleyn, student in Germany, c. 1534–7, in Cromwell's service, 1538–40, with Gardiner at Imperial Court, 1540–1, d. ? (a Thomas Tebold of Wrentham is mentioned in Privy Council minutes, 1566), 317, 327–8

Theodoret, Bishop of Cyrus, d. 457, 264

Theological controversy, 439. *See also* Homilies; Justification; Sacraments; Erasmus' *Paraphrase*; *King's Book*

Theophylact, Archbishop of Achrida in Bulgaria, c. 1078, 448

Thersites, 487

Thirlby (Thyrleby), Thomas, Gardiner's colleague in France, 1538, and at the Imperial Court, 1545–6, Dean of the Chapel Royal, 1540 or before –'47 or after, Bishop of Westminster, 1540–50, of Norwich, 1550–4, of Ely, 1554–9, d. 1570, 89, 146, 154, 157, 168 (the Deane,? of the Chapel Royal), 195–6, 200, 210, 238–9, 317, 323, 325, 360, 365–6, 474, 502

Thwaites (Twates), Thomas, in Gardiner's service, 1535 or before –'55, his controller, 1555 or before, d. ?, 502, 504, 506, 508, 510, 514

Tibald. *See* Theobald, Thomas

Tichborne (Ticheborn), Hants, 65

Tiptoft, John, Earl of Worcester, Constable of England, 1462–7, '70, Chancellor, Deputy, and Lieutenant of Ireland, 1464, '67, '70, executed, 1470, 390

Tithes (Tenths), 63, 269, 387

Tittenhanger (Titenhanger), Herts, 27–8

Toison d'or. *See* Golden Fleece

Tonge (Tongue), Dr Roger, chaplain to Edward VI, prebendary of Winchester, 1548–9, Dean of Winchester, Mar.–Sept. 1549, 281

Tower, the, xxiv, xxx–xxxii, 218, 375, 428, 437, 439–46, 449–50, 453, 455, 460–2, 501; Lieutenant of, *see* Markham, Sir John

Tower Hill, 390

Toyson (Toson) or chief herald of the Order of the Golden Fleece. *See* Falaix, François de

Tractatio, Peter Martyr's, 445

Trani (Trane), in Apulia, 11

Translators of Erasmus' *Paraphrase*. *See* Erasmus

Trauth, Thome. *See* Trouth, Tom

Treason, 319–20, 377, 422–4

Treasurer, Lord. *See* Howard, Thomas, 1522–47; Seymour, Edward, 1547–9; Paulet, William, 1550–72; Cecil, William, 1572–98

Treasurer, Master (*i.e.* of the Chamber). *See* Tuke, Brian

Treaties, 268; Treaty of Madrid (France and Empire), 1526, 31, 34–6; of Amiens (England and France), 1527, 32–4, 82; of Barcelona (Empire and Papacy), 1529, 2, 25–6, 37; of Cambrai (England, Empire, and France), 1529, 20, 30, 32–4, 36; between England and France, 1532, xxvi, 51, 82–5; between England and Empire, 1543, revised, 1546, xxviii–xxx, 146–8, 177, 191–2, 231–3, 253, 265; of Crespy (France and Empire), 1544, 93; between England and France, 1546, xxx, 243–4. *See also* Holy League; Paget's Recess; Truce

Tredegolde, John, one-time monk of St Swithun's Priory, minor canon of Winchester, 1554 or before, rector of Colemore, Hants, 1545, d. ?, 515

Tregonwell (Tregonel, Tregonnel), Sir John, judge of the Admiralty Court, 1524-42, Master in Chancery, 1533, knighted, 1553, d. 1565, 147, 199-203, 211-2

Trent, Council of, 1545 ff., 237

Trinity, the, 290, 311, 506, 511

Trinity (Trenety) Church, Guildford, 509

Trinity College, Cambridge, 458

Trinity Hall, Cambridge, xxiii-xxv, xxxii, 479, 493-5

Trivulcis, Caesar de, Bishop of Como, 1519-48, nuncio in France, 1529-33, 46

Trojans, 422

Trouth (Trauth), Tom, fictitious printer of Brinklow's *Lamentacion*, 148, 159

Troy, 422; horse of, *ib.*

Troyes, Bailly of. *See* Dinteville, Jean de

Truce, between France and Empire, 1538, 79, 82

True hystorie of...Martyne Luther, Bale's, 284

Trumpyngton, the good man Pope of, 481

Truth, Time's daughter, 50; God's, 313

Tuchet, John, Lord Audley, 1512-58, 56

Tuke, Sir Brian, knighted, 1529, French secretary to Henry VIII, 1522-42?, Treasurer of the Chamber, 1528-45, 5, 7, 24, 32

Tunstall, Cuthbert, Lord Privy Seal, 1523-30, Bishop of London, 1522-30, of Durham, 1530-52, '53-9, 30, 33, 147, 199-203, 205, 211-2, 286, 292

Turks (invade Austria, 1529, 1532, ally with France, 1535, make Hungary a Turkish province, 1541), 46, 75, 78-9, 94, 96-8, 188, 229-30, 279, 334, 434, 485

Turner, William, reformer, botanist, lived abroad, c. 1542-7, '53-9, chaplain and physician to Somerset, Dean of Wells, 1550-3, '60-8 (suspended for nonconformity, 1564), xxiv, xxx, 164-5, 478, 480-92

Turwyn. *See* Terouenne

Twates, Master. *See* Thwaites, Thomas

Tyndale, William, Bible translator, martyred at Antwerp, 1536, xxix, 361

Tytenhanger. *See* Tittenhanger

Udal, Nicholas, dramatist, d. 1556, 401

Uiber doctor Martin Luthers buch, etc., Zwingli's, 316

Ulysses, 487

Universities, the, 131-2, 402, 408, 431, 494. *See also* Cambridge; Oxford

Utrecht (Utrek, Utrik, Utryk), 180, 203, 205, 210-2, 217-8, 220, 223, 226-7, 231

Vachell, Oliver, in Gardiner's service, c. 1535-55, witness at his trial, remembered in his will, one of two gentlemen-ushers at his funeral, d.?, 80, 159, 195, 507-8, 511, 514, 516

Vana salus hominis, Gardiner's motto, 168, 175, 380, 394

Vander or Vander Ee, M., Charles V's commissary with Reiffenberg, 1545, 195

Vander Delft, François, Imperial ambassador in England, 1544-50, 157 (fellow of Scepperus), 226, 235

Vannes, Peter, an Italian, Latin secretary to Wolsey, Henry VIII, Edward VI, Archdeacon of Worcester, 1534-63, Dean of Salisbury, 1540-63, 1, 8-9, 13 (colleague of Gardiner), 18-9, 21

Vaughan (Vaghan, Vaughin), Edward, a captain at Guisnes, 1541-3, commissary with German mercenaries, 1544, Captain of Portsmouth, 1545-9, retired with pension because of sickness, living in 1553, 272-6, 284-5, 288

Vaughan (Vauhand, Vaugham), Stephen, employee of Cromwell, 1526 ff., ambassador in Flanders, 1538-41, Governor of the English Merchants at Antwerp, 1538-44, Henry VIII's financial agent there, 1544-6, Under-Treasurer of the Mint, 1544-9, 124, 237, 239, 241-2

Vayuoda. *See* Zapolya, John

Vecman, Gerard, importer of jewellery, 401

Veltwick or Feldwig, Gerhard (Gerardus), von Rabenstein, Hebrew scholar, Imperial secretary and ambassador (twice to Constantinople), 1540 ff., President of the Council of the Netherlands, 1554-5, 208-9, 229-30

Venice, 14; ambassador of, to Pope, 1529, *see* Contarini, Gasparo; to England, 1529, *see* Falier, Lodovico; league against the Turk headed by, 1538, 79

Veniers, Sieur de. *See* St Julien, François de

Verbum caro factum est, 343, 505, 508, 516

Vere, John De, fifteenth Earl of Oxford, 1526, Lord Great Chamberlain, 1526-20 Mar. 1540, 168?, 175

Vere, John de, sixteenth Earl of Oxford 1540-62, his players, 253-4

Vergerio, Pietro Paolo, nuncio in Germany, 1533–6, Bishop of Modrus, 1536, of Capodistria, 1536–49, became Protestant, 1549, d. 1565, 71, 73

Vermigli, Pietro Martire, Augustinian prior, adopted Protestant views and fled from Italy, 1542, professor at Strasbourg, 1542–7, '54–6, at Oxford, 1548–53, at Zurich, 1556–62, 445–6

Verona (Verone), Bishop of. *See* Giberti, Gian Matteo

Vestments, 503; alb (awbe), 503; copes, 213, 519; mitres, 166–7, 213, 503, 505, 519; tippets, 510. *See also* Ornaments

Veysey, John. *See* Voysey

Vice-Chancellor, of Cambridge, *see* Cambridge University (in 1529, 166, *see* Natares, Edmund); of the Empire, *see* Naves, Jean de

Victuals, 141–4, 158, 227–8, 235, 238–9, 303

Vierzon (Vieronne), in France, 81, 91

Villandre. *See* Breton, Claude le

Villeneuve St Georges, in France, 77–8

Vincentius, Master. *See* Casale, Vincenzo da

Virgil, *Aeneid*, 160, 188, 323; *Eclogues*, 190

Virginity, 491. *See also* Celibacy

Visitation, 1547, xviii, 366, 370, 373–4, 380–1, 388, 395–6 (the visitors for Winchester were John Mason, *q.v.*, James Hales, Anthony Cope, Francis Cave, Simon Briggs)

Viterbo (Viterbe), 5, 7

Voysey or Veysey, John, Bishop of Exeter, 1519–51, '53–4, 380, 391, 401; his Chancellor, *see* Brerewood, Thomas

Vraye Reaporte, Gardiner's, 228–9

Vynsent, Leonard, cleric at Winchester, 1556, 513

Wales, 218–9; Lord President of, *see* Lee, Rowland, 1534–43; Sampson, Richard, 1543–8

Walker, T. A., 468

Wallop, Sir John, knighted, 1514, ambassador in France, 1532–7, '40–1, Captain of Guisnes, 1541–51, 70, 76, 83, 88, 205, 397

Waltham, Essex, 27

Waltham or Bishop's Waltham, Hants, 60–1, 66–7, 316–7, 356, 361, 368, 373, 375

Wanborough, Surrey, 509

Wandsworth (Wensworth), Surrey, now part of London, 509

War, nature of, 266; any peace better than, 189, 266; in Italy, 11; between France and Empire, 75, 77–9; between England and France, 125, 185–90, 303; between England and Scotland, *see* Scotland

Warblington, Hants, parish priest of, 1535, perhaps Thomas Harryson, mentioned as curate there, 1538 and 1541, 67

Warham, William, Bishop of London, 1502–4, Archbishop of Canterbury, 1504–32, xxvii

Wartburg, the, 276

Warwick, Earl of. *See* Dudley, John

Watson, Thomas, Gardiner's chaplain, 1545–53, rector of Overton, Hants, 1549–57, Master of St John's College, Cambridge, 1553–4, Dean of Durham, 1553–7, Bishop of Lincoln, 1557–9, d. 1584, 252, 431–2, 455–6, 469

Wensworth. *See* Wandsworth

Weple. *See* Whelpeley, George

West, Nicolas, Bishop of Ely, 1515–33, his executors, 52–3

Westminster (Westmester), 7, 18–9, 243, 263, 353, 448, 503; Bishop of, *see* Thirlby, Thomas, 1540–50; Dean of, *see* Benson, William, 1540–9; Weston, Hugh, 1553–6; Bill, William, 1560–1; Palace at, *see* Whitehall

Weston, Dr Hugh, Rector of Lincoln College, Oxford, 1538–55, Lady Margaret Professor of Divinity, 1540–9, Dean of Westminster, 1553–6, d. 1558, 431

Wharton, Master, possibly Sir Thomas, Privy Councillor, 1553–9, Baron Wharton, 1568–72, 460

Wheat, 141, 241; exporters of, 380, 391, 401

Whelpeley (Weple), George, silkman and haberdasher of London, employed by Henry VIII, 1535 ff., presumably to detect corruption among customs officials (for his 'informations' against them *see* *L.P. Addenda*, 1, 1490; xvi, index), 188

White, Agnes, wife of Thomas, King's Attorney in the King's Bench, 518

White, John, Master, 1535–42, and Warden, 1542–54, of Winchester College, prebendary of Winchester, 1541–54, Bishop of Lincoln, 1554–6, of Winchester, 1556–9, d. 1560, 502–17 *passim*

White, Thomas, Gardiner's treasurer, 518 (probably = Sir Thomas, Master of Requests, *q.v.*)

White, Thomas, D.C.L., Warden of New College, Oxford, 1553–73, prebendary of Winchester, 1554–74, Archdeacon of Berks, 1557–88, Chancellor of Salisbury Cathedral, 1571–88, 518

White, Thomas, M.A., rector of Chale, Isle of Wight, 1537–51, of Bishopstoke, Hants, 1545–51, prebendary of Winchester, 1541–51, 518

White, Sir Thomas, Lord Mayor, 1553–4, d. 1567, 518

White, Sir Thomas, Master of Requests, 1553–6 or after, d.?, 507, 511, 514, 518

Whitehall, xxiv, xxxiv, 502–3

Whyt, Master. See White, Sir Thomas, Master of Requests

Wicliefe. See Wyclif, John

Wider die himmlischen Propheten, Luther's, 276

Wied, Hermann von. See Hermann

Wiltshire, Earl of. See Boleyn, Thomas, 1529–39; Paulet, William, 1550–1

Winchester, xxiv, xxxiv, 56–8, 60, 67–8, 219, 276, 284, 286, 295, 316, 429, 431, 433, 435, 437, 449, 478, 502, 508–10, 513, 518–9; diocese of, xxiii–xxiv, xxvi–xxvii, xxxi–xxxii, 50, 54, 56, 60, 64, 66–7, 287, 294, 304, 316, 369, 372–3, 375–7, 398, 422, 433, 478–80, 493–4; Bishop of, see Foxe, Richard, 1501–28; Wolsey, Thomas, 1529–30; Gardiner, Stephen, 1531–51, '53–5; White, John, 1556–9; bishops of, 219; castle, 56; Cathedral (St Swithun's), xxxiii, 512–9; clergy of, 369, 373; Dean of, see Tonge, Roger, 1549; Mason, John, 1549–54; Steward, Edmund, 1554–9; Dean's house, 502, 513, 515; Gardiner's chantry, 502; Hospitals of St Cross and Mary Magdalene, 149, 218–9; New College, 65, 513–4, 517; market, 293; Marquis of, see Paulet, William; Mayor of, see Bethell, Robert; petty canons of, see Petty canons; Registrar of, see Cooke, John; scholars of, 66; Wolvesey (the bishop's house), 62–3, 272, 276, 433, 435, 502, 514, 516–7; Winchester House or Place (the bishop's house in Southwark), see Southwark; 'Winchester marriages', 433, 435

Windsor, xxix, 43, 51; Windsor College, 222

Wine, 94, 143, 280

Wingfield, Sir Anthony, Captain of the Guard, 1539–50, Controller of the Household, 1550–2, 395

Wingfield (Wingfeld, Wyngfelde), Jacques (Jakes), in Gardiner's service, c. 1530–55, a proctor and witness at his trial, remembered in his will, Constable of Dublin Castle, 1562 or before –'86, Master of the Ordnance in Ireland, 1558–87, 227–8, 507, 511

Wingfield (Wingfeld), Master, probably Sir Richard (nephew of Sir Richard, d. 1525), knighted at Boulogne, 1544, prisoner of the French, 1544–6, captain of a ship of war, 1546, Paymaster, 1548–51, and Captain, 1551–3 or 4, of Portsmouth, d.?, 151

Wingfield, Sir Robert, Deputy of Calais, 1526–31, d. 1539, 4

Wingfield (Wyngfelde), Thomas, possibly Thomas, son of Charles, of Kimbolton, Hunts, a minor at Charles' death, 1544, living in 1580, 507

Winter, Thomas, son of Thomas Wolsey, Dean of Wells, 1526–8, Archdeacon of Cornwall, 1537–43, d. c. 1543, 401

Wisdom, Robert, Archdeacon of Ely, 1560–8, 424

Wittenberg, 276

Wodal, Gardiner's servant, d. 1535, 70

Wolman, Dr Richard, Archdeacon of Sudbury, 1522–37, Dean of Wells, 1529–37, 9, 16, 45

Wolsey (Wolvesey), the bishop's house at Winchester. See Winchester

Wolsey, Thomas, Cardinal, 1515, Bishop of Lincoln, 1514, Archbishop of York, 1514–30, Bishop of Bath and Wells, 1518–23, of Durham, 1523–9, of Winchester, 1529–30, Lord Chancellor, 1515–29, letters to, 4, 8–9, 21–43; dealings with Barnes, 165–7; his praemunire, 380, 390–1, 401; his colleges, xxvi, 19; other references, xv, xxiii, xxv–xxvi, xxviii, 1, 2, 7, 10–6, 18–20, 54, 218, 269, 276; his son, see Winter, Thomas

Wolvesey. See Winchester

Woman who touched hem of Christ's garment, 341, 486

Woodlocke, Master, possibly Richard, one-time monk of Hyde Abbey, vicar of Holy Rood, Southampton, 1554, d.?, 515

Woodstock (Wodstok), Oxon, 30–43

Worcester (Worceter, Worcetour), Bishop of, see Ghinucci, Girolamo, 1522–34; Latimer, Hugh, 1535–9; Bell, John, 1539–43; Heath, Nicholas, 1543–51, '53–5; Hooper, John, 1552–3; Sandys, Edwin, 1559–70; Archdeacon of, xxv

Word of God, 72–4, 161, 271, 292, 313–4; what the Protestants call, 267, 272, 307. *See also* Bible; Scripture

Words, change their meaning, 105–6; trouble the world, 210, 332; ambiguity of, 268; Christ's, *see* Christ

Works, in justification, 345, 347, 360, 363–4, 383, 406; Homily of, *see* Homilies

Worms, Colloquy at, 1540, 209

Worship of the cross and of images. *See* Cross; Images

Wotton, Sir Edward, brother of Nicholas, Treasurer of Calais, 1540–51, 241–2

Wotton, Dr Nicholas, Dean of Canterbury, 1542–67, of York, 1544–67, joint Principal Secretary, 1549–50, 220, 462

Wraghton, William, pseudonym of William Turner, *q.v.*

Wriothesley, Thomas, Baron Wriothesley, 1544, Earl of Southampton, 1547, joint Principal Secretary, 1540–4, Lord Chancellor, 1544–7, d. 1550, 149, 185–7, 211, 218, 245, 317, 325–6, 380, 393, 402, 405, 439, 518

Wroth, Sir Thomas, of Edward VI's Privy Chamber, implicated in Wyatt's rebellion, fled abroad, 1554–8, d. 1573, 459–60

Wyat, one little, probably Edward, whose release from the Tower was ordered by the Privy Council, 24 Apr. 1554, 462

Wyatt, Sir Thomas, poet, knighted, 1537, ambassador to Charles V, 1537–9, '39–40, d. 1542, 79, 81

Wyatt, Sir Thomas, son of the preceding, knighted, 1545, executed for rebellion, 1554, xxiv, xxxiii, 455, 460–1

Wyclif, John, d. 1384, 49, 279

Wyngfelde. *See* Wingfield

York, Archbishop of, *see* Wolsey, Thomas, 1514–30; Lee, Edward, 1531–44; Heath, Nicholas, 1555–8; Sandys, Edwin, 1577–88; House of, 240

Yorkshire, East and West Riding, 52

Young (Yonge), Dr John, Vice-Chancellor of Cambridge, 1553–4, Master of Pembroke Hall, 1554–9, d. 1580, 456–7, 463–4, 469, 476

Zapolya, John, Voivode of Transylvania, 1511, elected King of Hungary, 1526, as rival to Ferdinand, d. 1540, 46

Zebedee, sons of, 252, 317, 338

Zele. *See* Seal

Zwingli (Zuinglius), Ulrich, Swiss reformer, d. 1531, 299, 305, 316–7, 335, 360